Lonely Planet Publications
Melbourne | Oakland | London | Paris

Beth Greenfield &
Robert Reid

New York City

The Top Five

1 East Village
Cornucopia of cheap ethnic eats,
boutiques and pierced freaks (p90)

2 Hudson River Park
Best waterfront path for working
up a sweat (p97)

3 Brooklyn Bridge
A gorgeous span to gaze at or to
stroll across, and the gateway to
the borough of Brooklyn (p79)

4 Central Park
An oasis in the middle of the best
city in the world (p118)

5 Empire State Building
Best bird's-eye view in town (p109)

Contents

Published by Lonely Planet Publications Pty Ltd
ABN 36 005 607 983

Australia Head Office, Locked Bag 1, Footscray,
Victoria 3011, ☎ 03 8379 8000, fax 03 8379 8111,
talk2us@lonelyplanet.com.au

USA 150 Linden St, Oakland, CA 94607,
☎ 510 893 8555, toll free 800 275 8555,
fax 510 893 8572, info@lonelyplanet.com

UK 72–82 Rosebery Ave, Clerkenwell, London,
EC1R 4RW, ☎ 020 7841 9000, fax 020 7841 9001,
go@lonelyplanet.co.uk

France 1 rue du Dahomey, 75011 Paris,
☎ 01 55 25 33 00, fax 01 55 25 33 01,
bip@lonelyplanet.fr, www.lonelyplanet.fr

Printed by SNP SPrint Pte Ltd Singapore

The Authors

BETH GREENFIELD

Beth grew up longing to be a New Yorker, making as many trips as possible as a teenager from her hometown across the Hudson in Eatontown, NJ. She moved into her first big-city pad, in Chelsea, after college, and attended the graduate journalism program at New York University before real life began: writing and editing for local newspapers and magazines (including *Time Out New York*, where she is currently still an editor), teaching travel writing classes at NYU, writing the New York & the Mid-Atlantic States chapter for Lonely Planet's latest *USA* book, and moving every few years in search of the perfect apartment. After stints in the East Village and Brooklyn, she's settled on the Upper West Side – near Central Park, Hudson River Park, some amazing Jewish delis, and the express train, which whisks her to any one of her favorite spots.

ROBERT REID

In 1992, fueled by a surprise ticket for a Keith Richards show, Robert moved from Oklahoma to New York, where he settled in the East Village. He filled his 'evening space,' after a day job at *House Beautiful* magazine, co-producing a Manhattan public-access show (about his actual rock band, a fictional lacrosse league from Saskatchewan, and theories about Roosevelt Island). In 1997 Robert moved to San Francisco to work for Lonely Planet as commissioning editor and publishing manager of shoestring guides. In 2003, after a year in London, he returned to New York (no parade), where he writes full time from his home in Brooklyn.

CONTRIBUTING AUTHORS

KATHLEEN HULSER

Kathleen is the public historian at the New-York Historical Society. She specializes in New York City history, and teaches urban studies and gender history at New York University. She has curated exhibitions including German New York and lectured on topics such as Before the World Trade Center: Terror in the City. Kathleen wrote the History chapter (p57) for this book.

GLENN KENNY

Glenn's writing has appeared in the *Village Voice*, *New York Times* and *Playboy*, and for a good chunk of the 90s he was the Pop Scene columnist for the *New York Daily News*. He's also the film critic for *Premiere* magazine. Glenn wrote the NYC Music in the 21st Century boxed text (p33).

KATY MCCOLL

Katy moved to New York City after graduating from Smith College in 1999 to join Style.com, the online home of *Vogue* and *W* magazines. Katy writes and edits monthly feature stories for *JANE Magazine*, many of which require her to wear unusual outfits. Katy wrote the Fashionable NYC boxed text (p17).

JOYCE MENDELSOHN

Joyce teaches New York's architectural history at New School University and writes books about her favorite neighborhoods and articles on offbeat urban topics. A preservationist, she fights to protect significant buildings and historic districts that make New York special for locals and visitors. Joyce wrote the Architecture chapter (p43).

Introducing New York City

Hop a New York City subway and take a look around. Notice the myriad shoes – smooth loafers, shiny thigh-high boots, ratty Nike high-top sneakers, corporate pumps? Now see the types – a dread-locked hipster plugged into his iPod, an unfazed commuter paging through the *New York Times*, a fed up young mom anxiously shushing her baby. Finally, look at the faces: Chinese, Jamaican, Indian, Irish, Dominican, Polish and Mexican visages, scattered about the car. Beneath all the jaded exteriors, you may or may not detect a sense of oneness, but it's there.

Lying dormant, but ready to awaken beneath every New Yorker's mask is a sense that were in this together. We're all waiting for the next train rerouting or tap-dancing homeless man – even a random act of kindness. Oh, we don't acknowledge this, of course, as doing otherwise would lay us too bare. So it remains a muted, almost imperceptible subtlety and this collective unconscious proves that the city's most poignant overview exists several stories underground.

Not much else about New York City is subtle. Everything is audacious and wonderfully unrestrained, from the dense, bustling subway platform you step onto when you exit the car to the series of neighborhoods and subcultures you encounter up at street level. That in-your-face quality is a reflection of all the city's elements: vibrant architecture, snarling traffic, world-class culture, spirited politics, and a rich and radical history, infused with the tradition of immigration that endures today. It's this constant influx of newcomers that keeps the city fresh and bawdy – how else for a place to incorporate such an indefatigable stream of newness than to embrace it full on? New York is an expert in welcoming and accepting newcomers. And that, of course, is one of the best attributes for visitors.

Exploration here can can go as deep as you let it. The international influences, for starters, give you the world in just a single city. You can experience this on purpose – have a Mexican tamale breakfast, catch a Bollywood flick in an all-Hindi theater, for example. Or simply visit the Statue of Liberty or grab a slice of pizza – two of the many, beloved foreign imports of this cobbled-together global city. You can also get worldly by accident: listen for foreign tongues on any street corner, order a feta-cheese omelette in a Greek diner, or drop your clothes off at a Chinese laundry. Or discover the myriad subcultures based on shared interests, manifested in endless microcosms of urban living: yoga fanatics posing at gyms, Wiccans praying in Central Park, pug owners bonding in dog runs, wheat-free vegans clamoring to Whole Foods, Chelsea boys downing protein shakes as they shop.

But whom you passively encounter is only part of the equation in NYC, where choices of how to be active are just as abundant, and greatly varied based on the season. Parks come alive in spring, as bikers, runners and lawn lubbers can finally bust out of their closet-sized apartments to bask in longer days and warmer air; rent some blades and join the locals in their worship of the great urban outdoors. Spring's also the start of new ballet, opera and baseball seasons, blooming cherry blossoms, various flower shows and the ever-popular Fleet Week. Fall's crisp mornings and crimson leaves bring the US Open, the New York Film Festival and the raucously unique Halloween Parade that snakes ostentatiously through the West Village. But New York is certainly not a city to avoid at other times. With winter comes the chance for brisk walks, the thorough scouring of museums, repeat theater visits and lingering stops in shops and cafés. The chance fierce snowstorm guarantees you'll see locals giddy with excitement as the gritty city gets a white facelift. And summer rewards you with more space to yourself wherever you go – restaurants, parks, museums, bars and nightclubs – as many residents flee to Long Island, the Catskills or the Jersey Shore for long weekends, leaving Manhattan blissfully calm.

Don't confuse the reliable changing of the seasons with predictability. This is a city where people constantly need to adjust. And the fallout of September 11 – tighter security and a rawer sense of vulnerability – taught everyone to be adaptable for good. It was a valuable lesson for folks who get bored easily – moving on from yoga to Gyrotonics, Pan-Asian to Mexican-fusion, mojitos to sake-tinis – without batting an eye or mourning what they've left behind. And it was ultimate proof that New Yorkers are in this together, even – or especially – when we're jammed together in that subway car, looking distant and cynical, and ever so falsely disconnected.

Essential New York City

- **Empire State Building** (p109) The best bird's eye view in town.
- **Central Park** (p118) An oasis in the city, bursting with greenery and colorful characters.
- **Barney's** (p283) The annual warehouse sale, where you can tussle for half-priced Armani or Oscar de la Renta.
- **East Village** (p90) A cornucopia of cheap ethnic eats, boutiques and pierced freaks.
- **Florent** (p182) A 4am steak-frites feast with all the other night owls.

BETH'S TOP NEW YORK CITY DAY

Please, just let me sleep late! And then feed me, pronto. I love a good veggie brunch of scrambled tofu at my neighborhood veggie place, the unsung **Mana** (p199), to prepare for an afternoon steeped in culture. I'll head to an ethnic neighborhood – preferably **Little India** (p144) in Jackson Heights, Queens, **Little Italy** (p147) in Belmont, the Bronx – where I can stroll through food markets as if they were museums, be awash in foreign languages and basically pretend I'm traveling the world. If it's a beautiful day I will have a sunset run around the sparkling **Jacqueline Onassis Reservoir** (p119) or a bike ride along the **Hudson River Park** (p97) path. Evening should start with a martini somewhere fabulous – the sidewalk café of **Esperanto** (p213) or the sleek lounge of **xl** (p217), for example – and continue with a feast, perhaps delectable Indian fusion at **Tabla** (p185). The perfect ending comes 102 stories above street level, with a late-night visit to the top of the **Empire State Building** (p109), and marveling at my beloved, glittering city below.

Lowdown

Population 8 million
Time zone Eastern Standard
Three-star room $250
Coffee $1
Subway ride $2
Slice of pizza $1.75
Essential drink Cosmopolitan $6 to $12
No-no Moving slowly

City Life

City Life

NEW YORK CITY TODAY

Many, many out-of-towners still expect to visit here and find the New York of the '70s. They are shocked – pleasantly so – by the absence of graffiti-covered subway cars, menacing muggers or tranny hookers plying their wares. The major city cleanup of the former mayor, Rudy Giuliani, has been widely publicized, but sometimes you just have to see something to believe it. And, though a bit of the debauchery has inevitably returned since Mayor Bloomberg took the torch, evidence of the extreme makeover is everywhere: the overall crime rate has continued its 10-year decline, with the murder rate down a startling 69% since the early '90s. Times Square and the famous 42nd Street thoroughfare continue to evolve into a bright-lights, family-friendly circus, with memories of its seedy porn days becoming more and more difficult to recall. Even the least savvy, most wide-eyed tourists ride the subways at night, encouraged by primped signage and immaculate new subway cars. These days, it's nearly impossible to even find a Manhattan neighborhood that's off-limits after dark. There was perhaps no better proof of New York's drastic change than during the August 2003 blackout. Instead of looting and rioting and letting all of our ugliness out (like in 1977), folks of the new NYC threw mellow candlelight parties on stoops. And that calm, almost celebratory air showed that we did learn something from September 11 after all.

That's all not to say, of course, that this is a city without problems. The homeless situation, for starters, is out of control. Between 2003 and 2004, the homeless-shelter population reached the highest number in New York City history – 38,400 – and that's not even counting those who sleep on the street or in subway stations, or on the floors of city offices; overtaxed housing workers cannot place families fast enough in the overcrowded system.

The economy, meanwhile, is still far from healthy, as the city went into a recession following the attacks of September 11. Things are definitely improving, according to the city comptroller, who reports that the final quarter of 2003 added more than 4000 jobs to the local economy – but not without difficulty. Despite the new building initiatives touted by developers, the city lost more than 206,500 jobs between 2001 and 2003.

Health-wise, New York City has seen better days – especially with regards to the AIDS crisis, which far too many people think is over. New York City ranks number one in the country when it comes to its rate of AIDS cases per population – and has more cases than the four runner-up cities combined. According to the most recent statistics (from 2002), HIV infection rates among gay men have continued to rise. And a fierce problem with the drug crystal meth within the local gay-male community here has only added to the infection problem.

Another big issue sure to provoke cocktail-party debate is that dreaded yet inevitable shift toward gentrification. Some New Yorkers point accusingly to the Giuliani makeover as having created this grim problem, with rising housing costs boxing-out poor people. But the folks who moan about it, interestingly, are practically always the ones who are causing the problem – the middle-class, upwardly mobile, trend-obsessed folks who fled

Hot Conversation Topics

- Bloomberg is such a bore-ass!
- Chain stores are ruining the city.
- Do you think the West Side development project will really happen?
- Have you been to the **Time Warner Center** (p111) yet? It's just a big mall.
- Having the Olympics here would be an absolute nightmare.
- How long do you think it'll be before gay marriage is legal in New York?
- I'll be trapped in my rent-stabilized apartment forever.
- Too bad A-Rod can't play for the Knicks, too.
- We're thinking of buying in Brooklyn. What's more affordable – Prospect Heights or Kensington?
- Will the Second Avenue subway ever be completed?

the suburbs to live life on the urban edge. Starbucks and Barnes & Noble and Target superstores are sapping the soul out of the city, they say. Rapid gentrification of outer-borough neighborhoods is snuffing out the city's multi-ethnic blend, they complain. And overdevelopment – including the frenetic construction of high-rise condos and a sweeping, Olympic-minded vision to construct a massive sports stadium in Hell's Kitchen – will be the death of our city as we know it, they cry. But someone's drinking those tall decaf soy lattés – and shopping for armloads of discounted books, and moving into Bedford-Stuyvesant, and buying waterfront condos and cheering silently for the new sporting zone. It all makes for a contentious, adventurous, incredibly exciting time in this town. New Yorkers, of course, can't get enough of it. And you won't be able to, either – promise.

CITY CALENDAR

It seems as though there's always some sort of festivities planned in New York. National holidays, religious observances and just plain ol' weekends are perfect times for parades or parties or street fairs. Highlights include the annual Lesbian & Gay Pride March, the Caribbean Day Parade in Brooklyn, and Halloween, which sends mobs of creatively dressed revelers into the West Village streets for an evening parade.

Public holidays may affect business hours and transit schedules. So while they won't affect your ability to eat out, explore or be entertained, they may not be the best days to head to the passport office or local embassy. For additional information of special events in the city, visit www.nycvisit.com.

JANUARY

Each year kicks off with late sleeping after New Year's Eve and fireworks in Central Park. Martin Luther King day is celebrated on the third Monday. It's cold and often snowy as folks trudge back from Christmas holidays, hit the gym with a vengeance and spend lots of time in movie theaters and stores.

LUNAR NEW YEAR FESTIVAL
☎ 212-966-0100
One of the biggest Chinese New Year celebrations in the country. Head down to Chinatown to see fireworks, parades of dancing dragons and extravagant floats, and mobs of thrill-seekers crowding into the streets. The date of Chinese New Year fluctuates from year to year, often falling in late January but sometimes early February.

THREE KINGS PARADE
☎ 212-831-7272
Every year on January 5, the streets of Spanish Harlem, up Fifth Ave to 116th St, are filled with parading schoolchildren, donkeys and sheep in honor of that one and only holy birth.

WINTER RESTAURANT WEEK
☎ 212-484-1222; www.nycvisit.com
Usually held only for a week in June, the city has added a second Restaurant Week to its calendar, this one beginning near the very end of January. It's a wonderful opportunity to try the expensive, high-profile restaurant of your dreams, as those participating (nearly 200) offer three-course lunches for $20 and three-course dinners for $30.

FEBRUARY

It may be dreary outside – 30°F most days, and often snowy and blustery – but inside, all around town, there's plenty to do. Presidents' Day, which closes down federal and most city businesses, is celebrated on the third Monday.

FASHION WEEK
The second week of February is when the couture world descends upon Manhattan to strut and gawk over new looks. A second fashion week is held in the second week of September.

VALENTINE'S DAY
Yes it's a silly Hallmark holiday. But New York couples take it seriously, jamming into trendy restaurants on the 14th for the special evening menu, usually a five-course meal for at least $65 per couple. Join in the madness or grab a slice of pizza and take a free moonlight stroll instead.

MARCH

The weather during this month is said to be 'in like a lion and out like a lamb,' steadily getting milder and sunnier, climbing from about 30°F to 50°F or higher as the days pass. The first trickles of spring bring locals to parks in droves, as well as into the streets, where they watch a couple of big parades.

ST PATRICK'S DAY PARADE
☎ 718-793-1600

A massive audience, most with green-painted faces and clutching plastic cups of beer, lines Fifth Ave for this massive, celebratory parade on the 17th, made up of bagpipe blowers, sparkly green floats and clusters of Irish-lovin' politicians. A small but feisty group of gay protesters can be found each year near the beginning of the route, at 42nd St, as the march organizers specifically ban any gay groups from joining in the festive march.

APRIL

Flowers bloom, light rains fall and temps finally warm up once and for all, hovering around the 60°F mark most afternoons. It's finally spring, and truly a lovely time to visit the city.

ORCHID SHOW
☎ 212-632-3975; www.rockefellercenter.com

Quickly becoming one of the largest orchid shows in the world, this massive display of the rare flowers, now in its 25th year, includes competitions in both orchid-art and fragrance categories. Held around the middle of the month.

MAY

This is perhaps the most perfect month in the city: it's balmy, people have full-on spring fever, and the pre-summer excitement puts additional electricity in the air, which features average temps of 65°F to 70°F. May is also Bike Month here, which brings weekly bike-oriented tours, parties and other events to pedal-pushing New Yorkers. Visit www.bikemonthnyc.org for more information. The official start of the summer is Memorial Day, which generally falls at the end of the month (and sometimes at the beginning of June).

CHERRY BLOSSOM FESTIVAL
☎ 718-623-7200; www.bbg.org

Known in Japanese as Sakura Matsuri, this annual tradition, held the first weekend in May, celebrates the pink, puffy flowering of the Kwanzan cherry trees along the Garden's famous esplanade. It's complete with entertainment, refreshments and awe-inspiring beauty.

TRIBECA FILM FESTIVAL
☎ 846-941-3378; www.tribecafilmfestival.com

Robert DeNiro co-organizes this annual Downtown film fest, held in the first week of May. Quickly rising in prestige and held at various locations around the neighborhood, the week of screenings features several world and US premieres.

BIKE NEW YORK
☎ 212-932-2453; www.bikemonthnyc.org

The main event of Bike Month. Thousands of bicyclists hit the pavement for this 42-mile ride, much of it on roads closed to traffic or on waterfront paths, that takes you through each of the city's five boroughs.

NINTH AVENUE INTERNATIONAL FOOD FESTIVAL
☎ 212-541-8880

One of the oldest and largest food fests in the city, this row of stalls dishing out tastes of the world lines Ninth Ave between 42nd and 57th Sts in mid-May.

Only In New York
The city's flamboyant populace gets into full swing at these festive events:
- Annual Village Halloween Parade (p12)
- Howl! Festival (p12)
- Lesbian, Gay, Bisexual & Transgender Pride (opposite)
- Mermaid Parade (opposite)
- West Indian American Day Carnival Parade (p12)

FLEET WEEK
☎ 212-245-0072; www.intrepidmuseum.com

Manhattan resembles a 1940s movie set this week, as clusters of fresh-faced, uniformed sailors traipse around, leaving the docked ships that arrive from around the world for this annual end-of-the-month celebration.

JUNE

The first full summer month brings a slew of parades, street festivals and outdoor concerts – featuring SummerStage shows in Central Park (p118), which bring an amazing lineup of pop, rock and world musicians to the outdoor stage – plus temperatures that head into the 70s.

PUERTO RICAN DAY PARADE
☎ 718-401-0404

The second weekend in June attracts thousands of revelers for the annual Puerto Rican pride parade, now in its 45th year, up Fifth Ave from 44th to 86th Sts.

RESTAURANT WEEK
☎ 212-484-1222; www.nycvisit.com

The second week of the year for big-time discounts at top-notch eateries falls in the last week of June, with three-course lunches for $20 and three-course dinners for $30.

LESBIAN, GAY, BISEXUAL & TRANSGENDER PRIDE
☎ 212-807-7433; www.heritageofpride.org

Gay Pride month lasts throughout June, and it culminates in a major march down Fifth Ave (held on the last Sunday of the month) that is a five-hour spectacle of dancers, drag queens, gay police officers, leathermen, parents and representatives of just about every other queer scene under the rainbow. Other weekend events include a Dyke March, which kicks off at 5pm from the **New York Public Library** (p113) the night before the main event, and a street fair that happens along **Christopher Street Pier** (p92), as well as countless parties held at various bars and nightclubs. Pride marches are held in **Brooklyn** (☎ 718-670-3337) and **Queens** (☎ 718-429-5648) prior to this weekend, and many adherents to these marches believe them to be more fun and less corporate than the march in Manhattan.

MERMAID PARADE
☎ 718-372-5159; www.coneyisland.com

One of the most wonderfully quirky events of the year. This afternoon parade, held on the last Saturday of the month, is a flash of glitter and glamour, as elaborately costumed folks display their mermaid finery along the Coney Island boardwalk. It's not uncommon to see girls in their mermaid suits at the Dyke March, which starts directly afterwards in Manhattan.

JVC JAZZ FESTIVAL
☎ 212-501-1390; www.festivalproductions.net /jvcjazz.htm

More than 40 jazz shows go on in clubs around the city for this mid-June fest, with big names such as Abbey Lincoln, João Gilberto and Ornette Coleman.

SHAKESPEARE IN THE PARK
☎ 212-539-8500; www.publictheater.org

Each year the Public Theater sponsors a star-studded Shakespeare production in the Delacorte Theater of Central Park. Tickets are free, although waiting in line to receive yours may take a while, with queues forming early on the morning of the show, and sales beginning at 1pm.

JULY

Along with oft-oppressive heat (temperatures can climb into the 90s, but usually hover in the 70s or 80s) comes the explosion of July 4th fireworks and weekend treks to nearby beaches, which often leaves the city feeling blissfully deserted to those who remain behind to take advantage of uncrowded bars and restaurants.

JULY FOURTH FIREWORKS
☎ 212-494-4495

The Independence Day tradition of fireworks over the East River begins at 9pm. Good viewing spots include the Lower East Side waterfront park, waterfront pubs over in Williamsburg, Brooklyn, and any high-up rooftop. The pyrotechnic display, with explosives from the renowned Grucci fireworks company, will be one of the best you've ever seen.

PHILHARMONIC IN THE PARK
☎ 212-875-5656; www.newyorkphilharmonic.org

Free night-time concerts in the park from the country's premier orchestra are among the most wonderful treats of summer in the city. Grab a blanket and pack a picnic and choose from Central Park, Prospect Park in Brooklyn, or parks in Queens, Bronx or Staten Island; the symphony visits each one, beginning in early July, bringing a different music program to each.

AUGUST

It's hot – in the 80s – but tourists flock here while locals escape to the beaches and the mountains as frequently as possible. Wear sunblock and enjoy; there are plenty of street fairs and other events to keep you busy.

WEST INDIAN AMERICAN DAY CARNIVAL PARADE

To most New Yorkers, Labor Day is a wistful day that signals the official end of summer. But to two million Caribbean-Americans and other fun-loving onlookers, it's time to head on over to Eastern Parkway in Brooklyn for the annual Carnival parade – a colorful, daylong march and party featuring over-the-top costumes, delicious Caribbean eats and non-stop music.

FRINGE FESTIVAL

☎ 212-279-4488; www.fringenyc.org

This annual mid-August theater festival is the best way to catch the edgiest, wackiest, most creative stage talents in New York.

HOWL! FESTIVAL

☎ 212-505-2225; www.howlfestival.com

A relatively new fest on the scene, this weeklong celebration focuses on arts in the East Village, with highlights including the Charlie Parker Jazz Festival in Tompkins Square Park, the Avenue A Processional, Art Around the Park, the Allen Ginsberg Poetry Festival and a slew of scheduled readings and performances.

US OPEN TENNIS TOURNAMENT

☎ 914-696-7000; www.usopen.org

One of four Grand Slam tournaments of professional tennis, where top-ranked men and women compete in singles and doubles matches at the **US Tennis Center** (p247) in Queens.

SEPTEMBER

September is official back-to-school month, as well as the return of cool evenings and bearable warmth. It's an ideal time to visit.

FASHION WEEK

Round two for designers, fashionistas, jetsetters and assorted others clamoring for advance peeks at the outfits soon to be all the rage come spring.

SAN GENNARO FESTIVAL

www.sangennaro.org

Rowdy, loyal crowds descend on Little Italy for carnival games, sausage-and-pepper sandwiches, deep-fried Oreos and more Italian treats than you can stomach in one evening. For more than 75 years, it's been a sight to behold.

SEPTEMBER 11

This somber anniversary brings a mood of plaintive mourning over the city, as well as city-sponsored memorial services at the actual World Trade Center site.

NEW YORK FILM FESTIVAL

www.filmlinc.com

The Film Society of Lincoln Center has been bringing amazing cinematic premieres to New Yorkers, in a plush theater setting, for more than 40 years.

OCTOBER

Though the last day of the month, Halloween and all its fanfare – bright orange pumpkins at every Korean deli, decorations and masquerade theme parties at bars and clubs – dominate. Cooling temperatures, hovering in the 40s and 50s, usher in the beautiful changing leaves of autumn in New York. If all is well in the baseball universe, October signals play-off season for the Yankees.

D.U.M.B.O. ART UNDER THE BRIDGE FESTIVAL

www.dumboartscenter.org

Celebrating and promoting Dumbo's local artist community, with open studios and galleries, performances and street displays.

HALLOWEEN PARADE

www.halloween-nyc.com

All sorts of freaks and geeks gather in the streets for a wild night of prancing about in costume. The outfits range from extremely clever to over-the-top raunchy, and the audience lining the streets loves one and all.

NOVEMBER

This month segues from autumn into winter with colder days, bare trees and big Thanksgiving dinners with family at the end of the month. Holiday madness begins the next day, when Black Friday is traditionally the biggest shopping day of the year.

NEW YORK CITY MARATHON
www.nycmarathon.org
Held in the first week of November, this annual 26-mile run through the streets of the city's five boroughs draws thousands of athletes from around the world – and just as many excited viewers, who line the streets to cheer folks on.

THANKSGIVING DAY PARADE
www.macys.com
This famous cold-weather event, for hardy viewers only, parades its famous floats and balloons along Broadway, from 72nd St to Herald Square. For an even better view, join the throngs who gather at the southwest corner of Central Park to watch the balloons being inflated the night before.

DECEMBER
It's all about Christmas (December 25) for the entire month, when holiday lights appear in the streets and on buildings, and Christmas music seeps into absolutely every store in the city. Temperatures are cold, usually in the 30s, and snow is always a possibility.

ROCKEFELLER CENTER CHRISTMAS TREE LIGHTING
☎ 212-632-3975
Join the hundreds who encircle Rockefeller Center in Midtown and watch as the world's tallest Christmas tree is alighted to a chorus of 'ooohs' and 'aaahs.'

NEW YEAR'S EVE
☎ 212-883-2476; www.visitnyc.com
In addition to the world-famous countdown to midnight in Times Square – which is a raucous, freezing, alcohol-fueled spectacle that you're better off missing – the city has plenty of other celebratory events, namely the **Midnight Run in Central Park** (☎ 212-860-4455) and midnight fireworks in Central Park, Prospect Park and the South Street Seaport.

CULTURE
IDENTITY
New Yorkers have attitude, and they're not afraid to use it. But it's a lot more complicated than simple rudeness, which has long been how outsiders have mischaracterized the folks of this fair metropolis. Instead, it's a mixture of being tough, brave, on your toes, jaded, overworked and intensely focused. Hang out on a subway, for example, and you'll quickly notice that no-one's making eye contact, but rather studiously avoiding it. The thought is, 'who needs to be pulled into a conversation or potential conflict with a crazy person?' Or, 'why would I want to be waylaid with small talk when this 15-minute commute is the only time I have to myself all day?' Ask one of those blank-faced people for directions, however, and they'll respond with explicit instructions and a nurturing smile, and perhaps even escort you themselves if it's on the way to where they're headed. Or, step onto that train as an elderly person (very elderly only) or pregnant woman (very pregnant only) and see several of these same closed-off folk jumping up to offer you a seat. New Yorkers are friendlier than ever, actually. It's as if September 11 let some warm, oozy center be exposed in all of us; we feel more vulnerable, and we're more empathetic to the vulnerability of others, and that has manifested itself in countless ways – from smiling at strangers on the street to dropping a dollar into that subway busker's basket, even though he drives you crazy with his off-key serenading at 8am.

Still, we're a street-smart, jaded bunch, and we don't like being played. But the tough outer shell that New Yorkers adopt is simply out of necessity. How else to keep your sanity intact in a city that's rife with homeless people starving before your eyes, the financial pressure of keeping yourself afloat in this expensive town, sneaking suspicions that a tragedy – whether it's construction debris raining down from a not-yet-finished high rise or another terrorist attack – is just around the corner? The locals must balance all that skittish energy with a constant feeling of being stressed out. Sure, some of it's drama; certainly all those people barking into cell phones as they march down the street can't be the VIP they fancy themselves to be. In fact, being swamped with work becomes a point of pride with most New Yorkers, who frequently try to one-up each other with tales of endless responsibilities and deadlines, as if it were all just one big contest on reality TV. But it's true that they are most likely busy, overworked, highly focused and goal-oriented. 'If I can make it there I'll make it anywhere' is more than just a clever line from a song. This is a tough place to succeed, and that's because it's also the place to succeed. If San Francisco is a laid-back paradise, then New York is utopia for the workaholic, forcing you to constantly shape up or ship out. All that can lead to lots of real pressures, and the feeling that you're running after something with a vengeance while you're actually chasing your own tail. Still, you keep rushing to that point on the horizon, because living here is really, really worth it.

And all that is enough to make you a bit bonkers, or at least neurotic, which explains yet another New York obsession: psychotherapy. While Woody Allen and his onscreen characters – usually in therapy for 20 years or more – may be a bit of an exaggeration, the sentiment is right on. There are no official counts of how many locals go to a therapist, but anecdotal evidence suggests it's high. New Yorkers want to get everything, including themselves, figured out, and not necessarily in the spiritual, earthy-crunchy way the West Coast is known for (although the spiritual movement is growing here). We want answers and solutions, and we're open about that quest, not thinking twice about explaining to someone that Tuesday night for dinner doesn't work because 'that's therapy night.'

We're also trend-obsessed, tiring of the next big thing before it peaks. Not long ago, for example, it seemed like a fleet of Razor scooters popped up onto the streets overnight. Everyone could be seen using them to glide along the sidewalks in the morning – Wall Street traders, publishing types, Midtown secretaries, schoolchildren. And then poof, just like that, they were gone. We were over it. It's happened with countless other must-haves – Vespas, *mojitos* (a Cuban cocktail), Pilates, Uggs, trucker caps, Seven jeans, Rollerblades, tribal armband tattoos, pierced septums, hits of Ecstasy – and it'll happen again and again, to be sure.

There's at least one trend, though, that looks like it's here to stay, and that's the growth of delivery services. Because New Yorkers are stressed out and always in a hurry (and extremely impatient), a good many find they've got absolutely no time to tend to the normal daily tasks of life – things like shopping for groceries, cooking dinner, washing clothes. So the constant additions to the widespread service industry, which includes supermarkets and health-food stores that deliver groceries, and laundromats that pick up, wash, and then return your bundle of perfectly folded laundry to your doorstep, are quite well-loved by overtaxed locals.

When In New York, Do As New Yorkers Do

- Only hail a taxi if its middle roof light is on. If the lights on either side of that are on, it's off duty; if no lights are on, there's already a passenger inside. Hailing a taxi with no light is the number-one tourist blunder.
- Don't stand on corners waiting for the 'walk' sign. Rather, cross against the light as soon as there's a big enough lull in the traffic.
- It's How-sten Street. Not Hew-sten. Got it? Good.
- Be politely aggressive when boarding a crowded subway. Do not stand and wait for your turn to board, or you'll most likely miss your chance.
- Think of yourself on the sidewalk as a car on the street: don't stop short; pay attention to the speed limit; and pull to the side if you need to look at a map or dig through your bag for an umbrella.

But not every one of these wacky characteristics applies to all New Yorkers, of course. This city is, after all, known for its extreme diversity more than anything else. This is a melting pot more than any other place in the country, and while everyone might not always get along perfectly, we're pretty well behaved, considering. This is a city of eight million people, and the economic, racial and religious differences are extreme, so just about any generalization is sweeping. For starters, New York is a city for the young; the median age of residents is 34. Sixty-two percent of the population is white, while 16% is black (compared with 12% nationally), 15% is Latino (compared with 12% nationally) and 5.5% Asian. The median household income in all of NYC is $42,000 (slightly higher in Manhattan), and 19% of New Yorkers are living below the poverty line. A whopping 32% of the population is foreign-born (46% in Queens), speaking one of hundreds of languages. An average of 73% of the population has graduated from high school, while 27% of these have completed some form of higher education.

Professional dog-walking service

Religiously, New York is much more Semitic than the rest of the country: about 2% of the national population is Jewish, while about 12% of New Yorkers are Jewish; though that's high, recent studies show that the Jewish population here has dipped below one million (972,000) for the first time in a century, due to Jewish families leaving NYC for the suburbs. Around 70% of locals are Christian, many Catholic, with the remainder adhering to Eastern religions, mostly Islam and Hinduism; but about 14% of New Yorkers claim no religious affiliation whatsoever – a figure that is twice what it was about a decade ago. And while outsiders could see that as a signal of defeat, it's more likely a sign of strength. We're looking inward now for answers, and that self-reflection is only adding to the new warmth of today's eclectic but grounded breed of New Yorker.

LIFESTYLE

It doesn't take long to figure out how New Yorkers live while in public – they're harried, hurried and constantly moving – but what about how locals live behind closed doors?

First of all, know that New Yorkers are absolutely obsessed with housing issues, and it's largely due to the simple scarcity of places to live: the housing vacancy rate has never gone above 4%, and rents here are among the highest in the country. The rental market is also governed by a wacky, myriad set of laws. These laws affect the average New Yorker, who lives in a rental apartment, spending about three-quarters of his or her income on those monthly bills. The majority of these folk live in rent-stabilized prewar (1947) buildings, meaning the units are covered by city laws that regulate how much rent can go up each year (usually between 3% and 6%). These units can become destabilized, though, when a tenant moves out and a landlord decides to do major upgrade work in the unit; the landlord can then raise the price to what's known as 'fair-market rent,' usually an extremely unfair amount that can triple what the price was before. So folks lucky enough to be in stabilized apartments often talk about how they're 'stuck'; if they were to move, they most likely won't land another stabilized home – unless they know someone who needs to transfer a lease, moves into a family member's apartment or has some other sort of lucky break. Most other renters live in rent-controlled units – an endangered protection left over from the '30s – or public housing, which offers government-subsidized units to those living below the poverty line. Those who don't rent their home own one – a luxury reserved for the high-income bracket, as an average one-bedroom apartment in Manhattan is about $500,000 these days.

New Yorkers lucky enough to have jobs (the unemployment rate stands at about 7%) do any number of things for their income, but most work for one of the city's top-four industries: healthcare, professional services (such as accounting, advertising, finance, public relations), media and entertainment (which includes broadcasting, publishing, film and recording), and tourism (which employs 400,000 people alone). While the average income is $42,000, figures range wildly, depending on your job. A top editor at a magazine, for example, makes about $100,000, while a government employee in the service sector is more likely to pull in about $30,000 – though working for the city government brings an excellent health-benefit package. People work hard, averaging at least 40 hours a week in many cases; and while the majority still live nine-to-five lives like those in the rest of the country, workers in creative fields are likely to be freelancers who make their own hours and often toil from home – which explains the fact that nightclubs pull in crowds nightly and adults can be found doing anything from laundry to café-lounging smack dab in the middle of what many would define as a 'work day.'

> **Top Five New York Lifestyle Books**
>
> - *Back Where I Came From* (1938) by AJ Leibling
> - *The Colossus of New York: A City In 13 Parts* (2003) by Colson Whitehead
> - *Here Is New York* (1948) by EB White
> - *Radical Chic and Mau-Mauing the Flak Catchers* (1970) by Tom Wolfe
> - *Up In the Old Hotel* (1993) by Joseph Mitchell

Blame it on advertising, or the city's reputation as the center of so many worlds – from fashion to dining out – but New Yorkers are extremely status-conscious. Folks complain about feeling strapped for money no matter how high their income, feeling constantly on edge about whether they have the right clothing, haircuts, apartment decor, laptops, restaurant reservations, summer-home locations, gym memberships, baby strollers, PDAs, cell phones, briefcases – even dogs (and you'd better believe that there is a right and wrong dog; purebreds, of course, are best, and mini-dachshunds and pugs are among the trendiest of breeds). This is a city in which most residents do not have access to a car, thanks to a combination of at-capacity street parking, exorbitant parking-garage rates (averaging about $300 monthly) and remarkably good regional mass transit options. But that doesn't stop many from owning vehicles, and from getting caught up in the nation's current SUV obsession; it's amazing how many New Yorkers drive those massive gas- and space-guzzling boats, just so they can keep up with the Joneses.

Often, the items we desire are handed to us on a silver platter – for a price, of course. Want fresh, gourmet groceries delivered to your door? Log onto the new food-delivery service, Fresh Direct, load the virtual shopping basket, and get actual boxes of groceries within a couple of hours. Caught out on the street in an unexpected rainstorm? Hold tight: vendors hawking $5 umbrellas will appear on practically every corner before you can say, 'I'm wet.' Need to get somewhere quickly? Stick your hand in the air, and a taxi will come to your rescue within minutes.

For New Yorkers with kids, the status thing doesn't end with the stroller (although it's extremely important to have a late-model Maclaren – especially if you're on the Upper West Side). Getting your child into a good private school – as well as some good outfits and shoes and the hands of a top-notch nanny – are also top concerns.

At the same time that local urbanites are stressing over which brand of jeans to buy, however, they're also desperately searching for the best ways to get rid of their stress. New Yorkers are into yoga and fitness in growing numbers, as well as spa services, such as facials and massages. But it's often an exercise in irony, as many find themselves feeling competitive in yoga class ('Is my downward dog as good as that skinny, pretty lady's in the corner of the studio?'), or running breathlessly to their massage appointment, which is sandwiched into a hectic workday and an alcohol-tinged dinner date. There is also demand for organic produce and health-food items, judging from the Whole Foods superstores that have opened or are slated to open; and that in itself seems ironic – buying foods to save your body and the earth in a hyper-consumerist atmosphere.

But being at odds is central to residing in New York – a place where multitudinous types share space, but also clash over lifestyle ideas. Bicycle enthusiasts dislike the motorists in this city, lobbying for more bike lanes and closed-to-traffic park roads and cursing the drivers among us every time one of them gets doored. Dog owners will go to the ends of the earth for pets' rights in apartments and the creation of more dog runs in parks, while the dogless often hate the massive dog population, pointing to public-health concerns such as the amount of faeces that gets generated (and often left on the street). Some people hate the idea of all the chain stores moving into the city, saying it spoils the character of New York; others embrace the change, relieved to finally have as much opportunity for discounts as suburbanites.

Fashionable NYC *Katy McColl*

Contrary to the love-affair-with-fashion image conjured by Carrie Bradshaw & Co on the New York City–based program *Sex and the City*, it is possible to live an entire life in Manhattan without ever owning a pair of Manolo Blahniks. While an improbably high number of women and men in the city do own $500 shoes, there is truth – and comfort – to be found in the fact that most paparazzi shots of Greenwich Village resident and *Sex* star Sarah Jessica Parker show her pushing a stroller, wearing simple overalls (albeit carrying a very fancy bag). Considering that the US taught the rest of the world about blue jeans and that the most famous American designers – Calvin Klein, Ralph Lauren, Michael Kors and Donna Karan – have built their empires on their sportswear, it's not surprising that in New York City, chic equals sleekly casual. The worst fashion sin to commit is to overdress or try too hard.

Though the punk kids hanging out on St Mark's Place or the Broadway hoofers living six to an apartment might opt out of a fashion discussion by rolling their eyes, truth is almost everyone in New York is interested in looking stylish. The definition is different, however, depending on the neighborhood. What works on the classic and conservative Upper East Side (eg Diane Sawyer) doesn't gel with Tribeca's nuanced industrial chic (Robert DeNiro). Fashionable work duds on Wall St won't equate with those from Williamsburg, and vice versa.

While in much of NYC denim and sneakers rule the day, choice accessories are de rigueur; it's definitely a very studied look. It's about the right jeans (Seven, Habitual) paired with the right sneakers (Puma, Adidas) and a white or candy-coated iPod in your pocket. But not all gadgets and looks are created equal, as Blackberries are viewed as the professional choke-chains preferred by sadomasochistic bosses. And don't expect to throw on high-waisted Levis and ratty high-tops and pass.

This cult of casual wear might seem strange to someone accustomed to London, where residents are far more experimental and susceptible to fads, or Paris, where haute couture is a more serious affair. But one of the draws of this city life is anonymity, which is why New Yorkers prefer to mix their designer items back in with their regular clothes so that what they're wearing doesn't scream Prada or look like a glorified ad.

What New Yorkers aren't nonchalant about is their grooming. A real metrosexual expresses himself not by the foppishness of his ties but a slavish devotion to scrubs, cuticles, and perfectly coiffed just-rolled-out-of-bed hair. It takes hard work to make that impression of effortlessness. On the other hand, the city will always have plenty of high-maintenance types who have their roots touched up every two weeks or apply leg makeup so they can remain bare-kneed in the dead of winter. Most Manhattan women, though, after a decade of thrice-weekly blowouts and even a foray into the $1000 Japanese thermal reconditioning process that leaves hair inalterably limp, have finally learned the value of a good haircut that is 'wash and go.'

Studied casualness aside, there are those, in addition to various thermometer-thin starlets and magazine editors, who you'll find in the front rows of the shows during Fashion Week, held every February and September in tents erected in Bryant Park. With almost all of America's major designers and magazines based in New York, it's no surprise the city is the nexus of the latest inspirations and trends. In recent years, Fashion Week shows have become more diverse, embracing hip-hop's influence and musicians like Sean 'Puffy' Combs and Beyoncé Knowles as both designers and muses. While some clamor for entrance tickets, most New Yorkers will never attend a runway show during Fashion Week and are content to peruse the highlights on Style.com.

When they need designer goods, New Yorkers check the sample sales, which bring out the worst in everyone but are a great way to acquire famous labels for 30% to 90% off. Find out where they're happening at www.nysale.com or www.dailycandy.com. Other delicious bargains are waiting at **Century 21** (p257), a designer discount department store which can be crowded with aggressive stylists but is worth a visit. If the end of the season seems too long to wait for a must-have bag, zip down to Canal St where all manner of knockoff bags can be found. Just make sure your Louis Vuitton wannabe isn't plastered with the words Looey Vitawn.

A word of caution: it would be a mistake to bring anything trendy when visiting New York, because New York's attention span for fads – like Capri pants and trucker hats – is short and unforgiving to latecomers. When in doubt, the cliché about New York fashion is true: you'll always look chic clad in black.

SPORTS

Wall St banks, high-brow arts, global publications, off-the-runway fashion design, punk rock, subway rats – sure, it's all here. But down deep, New York is a sports town for the ages. New Yorkers love their teams, and they love to play.

Urban reality – ie limited green space – has prompted creative liberties of traditional games played in the street, like stickball's take on baseball, with sewer-lid bases and broom-handle bats. All year Central Park is flooded with the active – runners, ice-skaters, cyclists, cross-country skiers and soccer players. Little league groups freckle the metropolis – soccer, hockey, softball, flag football, basketball – with other league rosters extending way, way beyond the teens. In summer, crusty old-timer (fully uniformed) softball vets bark at calls in Central Park, and dunk-a-thons at outside b-ball courts attract boisterous crowds. Sports are so big here, that when a historic pier – one built by Grand Central Station architects – faces closure, New York transforms it into a super-sized sports facility (see p97).

When New Yorkers don't play, they watch – at stadiums, rinks and courts, or on sports bars' TVs. Seasons overlap, so it's a ceaseless passion. Before and after the game, subway commuters pass the stops reading pull-no-punches accounts by sports media (such as the back pages of the *New York Daily*) – all seemingly bent on throwing coaches into tantrums. Anything but winning is unacceptable.

2012 or Bust

Despite years of trying, NYC is one of the few great international cities that has never hosted the Olympic Games. But this time, the administration is determined to land the 2012 summer games. New York won the nod in 2001 as the nation's bid city, beating out San Francisco and Washington, DC, and now must wait until 2005 to see if the International Olympic Committee will choose it over rivals such as London, Paris, and Moscow. The fight to make this happen has morphed into a fight to get approval for a $2.8 billion development project on Manhattan's West Side, which would expand the Jacob Javits Convention Center and construct a 75,000-seat football stadium for the Jets – the pièce de résistance of an NYC Olympic Village (see West Side [Redevelopment] Story, p110). Other major elements of the Olympics-inspired development plan include building another sports stadium in downtown Brooklyn, creating a complex mass-transit system for Games-goers and athletes that would expand the city's No 7 subway line, and shoring up more than 35 other athletic sites around the five boroughs.

Leading the charge for the development – and the chance to finally host the 16-day Games – is deputy mayor for economic development Daniel Doctoroff, who founded the nonprofit NYC 2012 lobbying group (www.nyc2012.com) before entering politics, and was the force that pulled together the original Olympic bid. He and other supporters of the project (and of the larger Olympic vision), which include New York State Governor George Pataki, say that hosting the Games would give a big financial boost to the city, generating an estimated $3.1 billion from TV ads, corporate sponsorship and ticket sales; minus the $2.2 billion to operate the Games, that would leave $1.2 billion for capital investments. Plus, supporters say, the stadiums and other new business would bring an influx of jobs, not to mention raise the tourism profile of New York and provide a much-needed emotional boost to a city that's still hurting from post–September 11 trauma. But the development plan – which supporters want to go ahead with regardless of whether New York gets to host the Games – has countless hurdles to cross before it becomes a reality. It has yet to gain approval from the state legislature, where there is much resistance over the plan to put $350 million of the Battery Park City Authority's funds toward the financing of the construction (other funding will come courtesy of combined city and state funds, and from corporate sponsors that include Verizon and Time Warner). The city council must also approve many aspects of the plan, and several members have expressed outrage over the expense, considering that the city's school system and many social programs are financially hurting.

And then there are the folks who live in the proposed development areas, many of whom are staunchly opposed to stadiums and anything else that would bring the logistical nightmare of the Olympics. Anti-plan alliances have formed in Hell's Kitchen and downtown Brooklyn, with angry folks saying the stadiums and their crowds would bring nothing but traffic congestion and pollution to town. Joining that camp is at least one potentially powerful ally – Cablevision, which owns Madison Square Garden, the Knicks and the Rangers. It opposes the stadium plan because of the potential future competition for events including concerts, circuses and sporting events. All opponents have vowed to fight it to the end, taking the battle into the courts if necessary, making the road to gold look quite long indeed.

New York has helped establish and popularize many of the country's pro sports. The first recorded baseball game took place in Hoboken, across the Hudson River, in 1846. A Brooklyn team nationalized the sport by introducing it to Union troops during the Civil War. First curve ball, you ask? That was in Brooklyn. Look up any season, and chances are that a New York team played in the finals. Then look around, and see more New York Yankee hats in use than 'I love NY' shirts.

On the gridiron, the Giants made a dent in football from the moment they laced their cleats. In their second year (1926), when the NFL struggled for life, the Giants shut out a rival league champ – and knocked the league into bankruptcy. In 1930, the Giants helped give the sport cred by playing (and winning) a charity game during the Depression. In the 1990s, the Giants and their younger cousin, the Jets, did what no other pro team in the country has done: returned to retro uniforms from the '60s, for good. It's all about tradition.

Nowadays, many would argue, basketball is becoming the new king of New York sports (in and out of Madison Square Garden). The Knicks, despite a three-decade dry spell of late, are loved by many more than Spike Lee, their most visible fan. If the Nets, over in Jersey, move into Brooklyn (as the new owner plans), they'll be the borough's first major-league team since the Dodgers betrayed the borough by leaving for Los Angeles in 1957. Anyone up for a Brooklyn Nets/LA Lakers championship series?

See the Sports, Fitness & Health chapter (p243) for information on where to partake.

MEDIA

With all of its magazines, broadcast stations and publishing companies, New York City can stake a claim as the media capital of the world. And the history of this rise is particularly long and strong. It was here, in fact, that the notion of 'freedom of the press' was first truly challenged and upheld. Though the first newspaper here was William Bradford's *New York Gazette*, it was the city's second paper, John Peter Zenger's *New York Weekly Journal*, founded in 1733, that had such a profound effect on the future of journalism. Zenger reported some controversial truths about the colony's governor – a bold move during a time when the country's newspapers had been mostly seen as puppets of the government. The governor had Zenger arrested and jailed for seditious libel (his wife continued publishing the paper in his absence), but the journalist's lawyer, one Alexander Hamilton, passionately defended the idea of liberty through the writing of the truth. The jury found Zenger innocent, and it was a major step for the scruples of journalists everywhere.

While journalistic standards – both of quality and integrity – have fluctuated markedly since then, the city has only gained in importance as the home of numerous and influential publications. While today's newspaper offerings are not quite as multitudinous as they were in, say, the late 1800s, when there were no less than 20 dailies published in New York – or even in 1940, when there were eight – there's certainly no newspaper shortage. The mainstream dailies are the *Daily News* and *New York Post* tabloids, known for screaming headlines and sensationalist takes on grisly crimes or tragic downfalls; and the definitive *New York Times*, a hefty, many-sectioned paper that's cited daily by all sorts of professionals and intellectuals. Also, recently reinstated after a long hiatus is *New York Newsday*, sister paper to the successful *Long Island Newsday*. Though the *Times* has long been known by its nickname of 'the gray lady' because of its straightforward, oft-boring approach to news, it's received a major facelift in recent years, as publishers and editors have sought to keep hold of readers who may be more drawn to getting their news in quick, snappy doses delivered either on TV or via the internet. And though the new reason to poke fun at the paper is its sometimes ridiculous number of modern sections (they change daily) – as well as its problems in upholding its high journalistic standards in the face of the recent Jayson Blair scandal (the guy who made up stories, had them printed and praised, got fired and is now getting rich by telling his deceitful tale thought his best-selling book *Burning Down My Master's House: My Life At The New York Times*), it's the most widely read news source in the city. Many still say it's the best, although its closest rival is the more financially geared (but extremely well-written) *Wall Street Journal*.

The alternative and ethnic press is jumping, bringing the latest count of local newspapers to about 275 and leaving little room to complain that there are not enough perspectives accounted for. *The New York Press* and the *Village Voice*, both weeklies, battle it out for liberal, anti-establishment types who like colorful, investigative journalism doled out of newspaper street boxes for free. The salmon-colored *New York Observer* weekly focuses on the political and social escapades of the upper class. And a slew of ethnic papers – the *Haitian Times, Polish Times, Jewish Forward, Korea Times, Pakistan Post, Irish Echo, El Diario* and the *Amsterdam News* among them – offer more focused news reports from all sorts of angles.

Newspapers (p348)

In addition to all the publishing houses for trade paperback and hardcover books, New York is home to many magazine publishers. Condé Nast, one of the largest, publishes titles including *Gourmet, Vogue, Vanity Fair* and the *New Yorker* out of its Times Square headquarters. Other empires include Hearst (*Cosmopolitan, Marie Claire, Esquire, Town and Country*), which also owns a dozen national newspapers including the *Seattle-Post Intelligencer* and the *San Francisco Chronicle*; and Hachette Filipacchi (*Premiere, Elle, Woman's Day, Metropolitan Home*). Major regional magazines focusing on entertainment and dining include *New York Magazine, Paper* and *Time Out New York* (for more newspaper and magazine details, see p348).

For all the publications in this town, though, there are really just a few players in the muddled media world – conglomerations that each own way too many news channels and newspapers, making it all too easy to fall into a lull of getting all your news from just one or two powerful sources if you don't seek out alternatives. News Corporation, for example, owns the Fox News network, Fox Sports Net, National Geographic Channel, the Madison Square Garden Network, the *New York Post*, the 20th Century Fox film company and 35 radio stations across the nation – and that's not even all of it. Time Warner, the world's largest media conglomerate, has endless properties, including biggies like CNN, HBO, Warner Books, *Time* magazine, *Life* magazine, *In Style, Entertainment Weekly*, Time Warner Cable, AOL, the Warner Music Group (with labels including Maverick, Elektra and Rhino), Fine Line Features, and so much more it's scary. It even owns the beloved local TV news station New York 1, which has an unpolished, local style that New Yorkers just love.

The conglomerates provide no real diversity of opinion or analysis, even in this media-saturated city, and news-follower are all the more grateful for publications like the *Village Voice* and the *Jewish Forward*. How grateful New Yorkers are, though, is unclear. Check back in a few years and see which indies have gotten enough support to survive.

LANGUAGE

To get a sense of the many languages spoken in New York, check out these census figures: of the city's population aged over five and over, a whopping 48% speak a language other than English at home – up 7% from 1990. The foreign-born population here reached a new all-time high as it hit 2.9 million, and a full 1.7 million residents are not proficient in English. Of those, 52% speak Spanish, 27% speak an Indo-European language (French, German, Swedish etc) and 18% converse in an Asian or Pacific language (mainly Korean, Japanese or Hindi). Another hint at the range of tongues lies in the city's newsstands: there are hundreds of foreign-language papers published in New York, for those speaking everything from Hebrew and Arabic and German to Russian, Croatian, Italian, Polish, Greek and Hungarian. Or step up to an ATM or Metrocard machine; the first question you'll be asked is what language you'd like to continue in and, depending on the neighborhood, you could find not only Spanish, but Chinese, Russian and French among your options.

Of course just going about your day is an adventure in dialects. Listen carefully on the street or the subway, and you're bound to overhear a minimum of five different languages in an hour. Many times you'll hear a blend of English with foreign languages – Jamaican patois peppered with New York turns of phrase, a fast-moving concoction of Puerto Rican Spanish and New Yorkese known locally as 'Spanglish,' young hip adults of Indian ancestry bringing Hindi words into their 'Desi' American English. Hail a cab and chat up the driver, hearing inflections of Pakistani, Sri Lankan, Russian, Arabic. Take one of those taxis to one of the many ethnic 'hoods around the five boroughs and you'll find closed communities where no English is spoken at all: Dominican neighborhoods in the south Bronx, Korean pockets of Flushing, Queens, Chinese neighborhoods in Sunnyside, Brooklyn, some of the Russian areas in Brighton Beach.

Many American English words, of course, have been adapted by the successive waves of immigrants who arrived in New York. From the Germans came words including 'hoodlums,' from Yiddish-speaking Jews terms like 'schmuck' (fool), and from Irish words like 'galore.' And then there are all the long-time locals, speaking with that old-school Noo Yawk dialect that many natives – though they love it – still struggle to understand (see Local Passwords below).

Local Passwords

Knowing the following New Yorkisms can help you make yourself clear – or at least understand what others are talking about:

- **Bridge-and-Tunnel** A disdainful term for folks who come to party in NYC from New Jersey, Long Island or other suburbs that are found across the city's bridges and tunnels; as in 'Yuk, that club's crowd is so bridge-and-tunnel now!'
- **Hizzoner** A slang term for the mayor, most often used by the *New York Post*.
- **Regular** A coffee with one sugar and one splash of milk; used when ordering.
- **Schmear** A small amount of cream cheese; used when ordering at a bagel counter, as in, 'I'll have a sesame bagel with a schmear.'
- **Slice** A serving of pizza, as in 'Let's get a slice.'
- **Straphangers** Subway riders.

ECONOMY & COSTS

In the spring of 2004, Mayor Bloomberg declared that New York's recession had ended, simultaneously unveiling his $46.9 billion budget plan for 2005. Through it, he promised tax breaks for homeowners and wage increases for all city workers. It was a break from the doom and gloom that usually surrounds his budget announcements; since he took office in 2002, he has been behind the cutting of 18,000 city employees, swiping $3 billion from agencies, and increasing property taxes by 18.5%. It was a testament to the strength of a city that has struggled to bounce back economically following the events of September 11. In 2001, New York faced a $6.7 billion budget deficit. Estimates for lost revenue following the attacks were $750 million for the 2002 fiscal year and $1.3 billion for 2003.

But, while the city does appear to have weathered the storm, the recovery is fragile. Prosperity has returned to many sectors – mainly Wall Street and tourism – but many other areas have not recovered, such as manufacturing and information, and many individuals are still suffering financially. New York City's high cost of living is accelerating rapidly. And many big-name corporations are gone, having relocated offices from lower Manhattan and moved across the Hudson River to New Jersey or up north to Westchester after September 11.

So what does all this mean for visitors? The short of it is that a trip to New York will not be a cheap one. The long of it is that there are many ways to travel in this city, with something for just about every style and budget, and finding deals just takes some forethought and creativity.

Basic costs for a NYC trip start with accommodations, unless you're lucky enough to have a friend or relative who's willing to put you up in their sure-to-be-cramped apartment. The average night in a city hotel is $200, though beds in hostels can be had for as low as $25, while a room at a budget hotel can go as low as $75. On the high end, those willing and able could easily shell out more like $300 a night or higher, as the sky's the limit when it comes to tricked-out luxury rooms with views and techie bonuses. Bargain rates aplenty can be found through various online booking resources, though, and the sheer number of them keeps prices competitive (see Brave New Rooms, p292).

Next comes food. The absolute cheapest way to go is to forgo the foodies' paradise of eateries and stick to making your own meals (if you have access to a kitchen) or subsist on packaged and prepared foods bought at the city's many markets. Basic nongourmet delis, found on practically every corner, make egg-and-cheese sandwiches for breakfast ($2 average), and a range of other basic sandwiches throughout the day, whether it's egg salad on rye for $4 or roast beef on a roll for $5. Street food, while not too healthy, is also way-cheap, with everything from hot dogs for $1.50 to gyros for $2.50. Or you can try to be wholesome by trolling the city's vast array of **Greenmarket Farmers Markets** (www.cenyc .org) for fresh fruits, breads and cheeses for

How Much?

- 8oz bottle of water: $1
- Bagel with cream cheese: $1.50
- Chicken and broccoli at a Chinese takeout: $7
- Cup of coffee: $1
- Hot dog: $1.75
- 'I Love New York' T-shirt: $10
- Movie ticket: $10
- Pair of Levi's 501 jeans: $45
- Pint of Brooklyn Lager: $4
- Taxi ride from Midtown to the East Village: $10
- Yankees Field Box ticket: $50

in-room backpacker meals. Eating at restaurants is gonna cost ya – but the prices range tremendously. Cheap Eats options (provided throughout the Eating chapter, p169) can get you hearty, usually ethnic, meals for under $10. Mid-range restaurants with table service can be about $10 to $15 per person for dinner, with the numbers going up from there. Head to a five-star dining establishment, order three courses and throw in a bottle of wine, and you could easily drop $100 per person – even $200 at pricier places. Families should head to diners and other low-key spots with kids menus, with prices (and portions) that are less than half that for adults.

If you want to shop while you're here – and who doesn't? – then you'll also find extreme price ranges in just about every category. For clothing, there are bargain spots aplenty, with stores like Daffy's, Century 21, Loehmann's and H&M high on the radar screens of local bargain shoppers for knockoffs and discounted labels that can go for less than half of what they cost in high-price stores (see p255). Downtown is loaded with great thrift and vintage shops, perfect for folks who love to dig for their gold. Fifth Ave shops are among the priciest, and folks who want to spend should set their sights on places like Bergdorf Goodman, Barney's, Saks Fifth Avenue, Bloomingdale's and one-name designer shops, such as Marc Jacobs and Giorgio Armani. If you're looking for affordable electronics, you'll no doubt feel overwhelmed by the 'discount' electronics shops that line the avenues in Midtown; many prices are good, but the shops may be fly-by-night. For excellent, reliable bargains, try **J&R Music & Computer World** (p257), on Park Row, across from City Hall in Lower Manhattan.

Entertainment is no bargain either – but it can be if you want it to be. Museums often charge up to $12 for entrance, but many have 'pay-what-you-wish' days or hours, plus discounts for students and seniors. Broadway tickets, which go for an average of $100 these days, can be bought for half price at one of two TKTS booths in Manhattan (p228). And plenty of venues all over the city – music, comedy, cabaret, dance and theater – offer frequent free performances; check local arts listings in publications including *Time Out New York* and the *Village Voice* for daily free and cheap activities. Or peruse a copy of the wonderful *Cheap Bastard's Guide to New York City: A Native New Yorker's Secrets of Living the Good Life – For Free!* by Rob Grader (Globe Pequot Press, 2002).

GOVERNMENT & POLITICS

New York City's government is older than that of the USA. Its political history has been spirited, strange and contentious, highlighted by such characters as William 'Boss' Tweed, Fiorello LaGuardia, Nelson Rockefeller and Edward Koch. New Yorkers have had a long record of voting for the Democratic Party, though there are conservative pockets in the blue-collar sections of Queens and Brooklyn, and suburban Staten Island is almost exclusively Republican. Despite the Democratic tradition, socially liberal Republican reformers can be elected mayor, as proven by two-term mayor Rudy Giuliani – remembered as a hero only based on his post–September 11 performance, and mostly as a control freak who 'cleaned up' the city, making it more safe and, say many opponents, less fun and even less tolerant to those in need.

The latest in the long line of characters (though he's a bit flatter than most) is Mayor Michael Bloomberg, elected in 2001 in an atmosphere of turmoil and grief. He's come under fire for his severe fiscal policies and draconian moves at the head of the beleaguered public school system; he was most recently criticized for setting 'no-social-promotion' standards for third-graders, which make them repeat the grade if they cannot pass specific standardized tests.

Besides the mayor, the city's political structure includes five borough presidents, who have their own local staffs and smaller budgets for community-level works and patronage. Historically, these positions are held by career political hacks and/or mayoral candidates-in-waiting. The administration also includes a citywide comptroller (who serves as budget administrator and auditor), a public advocate (who largely is concerned with consumer affairs) and a 51-member city council. These elected officials, who are paid over $70,000 a year, are meant to represent individual neighborhoods and serve as a check on mayoral power, though many spend little time on their four-year jobs, instead focusing on full-time legal practices. In addition to being divided into council districts, each borough is made up of community boards – 59 in total, led by unsalaried members appointed by the borough president, and meant to play an advisory role in zoning and land-use issues, community planning, municipal services and in the city's budget process. Monthly community board meetings, open to all but frequented by the biggest activists (or gadflies) in each neighborhood, can be fascinating or boring, depending on what the contention (and there's always contention) is based upon – dog runs, homelessness problems, broken streetlights or a new Trump condo.

The city has plenty of foreign governmental elements as well, namely through its many consulates. The first consulates in the city were set up by the governments of France, Spain and the Netherlands shortly after the American Revolution to promote their interests

Five Great NYC Politics Books

- *Eyes on City Hall: A Young Man's Education in New York Political Warfare* (2001) by Evan Mandery and Fran Reiter
- *The Great Mayor: Fiorello LaGuardia and the Making of the City of New York* (2003) by Alyn Brodsky
- *The Power Broker: Robert Moses and the Fall of New York* (1975) by Robert Caro
- *Power Failure: New York City Politics and Policy Since 1960* (1993) by Charles Brecher
- *Rudy Giuliani: Emperor of the City* (2001) by Andrew Kirtzman

abroad; there are now 85 in New York, mostly on the Upper East Side. The city strives to maintain good relations with diplomats – who are given many privileges here, such as taxation and prosecution exemptions – as the consulates enhance the city's reputation as an international center and contribute an estimated $1 billion annually to the local economy. The United Nations headquarters is also here, on Manhattan's east side, put here in part because the Soviet Union threatened a boycott if it were located on the West Coast. Although the grounds are not counted as part of the US, its physical fact draws about 500,000 tourists each year, contributing heartily to the city's economy.

Though in the past a visitor may not have had any need to deal with any arm of the government while in New York – except for US customs, as you enter or exit the country, and your own embassy or consulate, should you run into a major problem – that's all been in constant flux since September 11. And, as of September 2004, your contact with officials is sure to grow, as new security measures require foreigners to be fingerprinted and photographed before entering the country, and, by default, the city. The move affects citizens of 27 countries, including Britain, Japan and Australia.

ENVIRONMENT

The Land

Though it's now a concrete jungle, New York City has a geological history that provides an accurate picture of the entire Earth's evolutionary process. Manhattan's formation dates from over 1000 million years ago, from a combination of glaciers and the erosion of rocks including quartz, feldspar and mica; the land is marked by a series of faults and underwent its most important topographical changes during the Ice Age. But the movement of the ocean, in a constant cycle of erosion and land shifting, continually alters the miles of shoreline in the city.

It was the waterways of the city that inspired the city's founding, as they have served as a major asset in its growth and development. New York Harbor has 65 square miles of inland waterways and 772 miles of direct shoreline. The rich marine life provided food to Native Americans and early colonists, and the strategic importance of the New York Harbor did not go unnoticed by the British. Through the years, its waters have become ferry routes and host to some of the busiest ports in the world. It's because of all that use – as well as now-prohibited practices such as dumping raw sewage directly into the water and toxic runoff from manufacturing plants – that the waters inevitably became polluted, with most traces of marine life disappearing (the city's drinking water, more than 1½ billion gallons daily, luckily, comes from upstate reservoirs). Efforts to control the dumping of raw sewage in the 1970s and '80s helped a bit, as did more recent plans, which also targeted the city's air quality.

Top Five Nature Breaks Beyond Central Park

- Bird-watching in the marshes of the **Jamaica Bay National Wildlife Refuge** (p146) in Queens.
- Hiking the miles of trails through **Inwood Hill Park** (p134), at Manhattan's northern tip.
- Meditating at the **New York Chinese Scholar's Garden** (p150) in the Staten Island Botanical Garden.
- Strolling the **New York Botanical Garden Forest** (p148) – 40 pristine acres of hemlock, oak and hickory trees, right in the Bronx.
- Wandering along the shoreline in the Bronx's **City Island** (p147).

The air quality in Lower Manhattan has been a topic of much heated debate since September 11, with the Environmental Protection Agency (EPA), City Hall, business interests and community groups all conducting independent tests in an effort to evaluate what exactly is floating around in the air down there. Interpreting the tests is especially difficult since there are no guidelines for certain airborne particles, though one Department of Labor report stated that all the dust that has settled since the collapse 'must be assumed to contain asbestos.' Indeed, an inordinate amount of emergency personnel have been diagnosed with what has been dubbed the 'World Trade Center cough' and residents are receiving 100% reimbursements from the Federal Emergency Management Agency (FEMA) for in-home industrial-strength air purifiers. Additionally, in March 2002, Senator Clinton and Mayor Bloomberg established the Lower Manhattan Air Quality Task Force, replete with lofty rhetoric and an air-quality hotline (☎ 212-221-8635).

Green New York

Today, thanks to environmental reforms, it's actually possible to catch striped bass, blueback herring, yellow perch and blue crab in the Hudson and East Rivers, and health officials say they're safe to eat if you're so inclined. Even more incredible is Brooklyn's Gowanus Canal, a formerly filthy, stinking, lifeless cesspool of rust-colored water that stood stagnant for 30 years following an accident that broke its freshwater propeller.

Grand Central Terminal (p112)

Following its reopening a few years ago and subsequent cleanup project, the waterway is now full of life in the form of blue crabs, minnows, jellyfish and frequent canoeists (see Gowanus Canal, p137). Another fantastic success story has been the return of bald eagles to Inwood Hill Park in far Northern Manhattan (see Bald Eagles Have Landed – in Manhattan, p134).

And, although the environmental awareness here is nowhere near what it is in greener cities, such as those on the West Coast, the tides are definitely changing. When Mayor Bloomberg temporarily suspended the city's comprehensive recycling program as one of his earliest money-saving efforts, there was much outcry; it was reinstated as of April 2004, though New Yorkers, finally accustomed to throwing all their glass and plastic in the trash, are having a hard time getting used to recycling once again. Green spaces tend to unite folks over the land more than any other environmental concern. The city's Community Gardens program grew during the Depression, when city-owned land was made available; they were uprooted after WWII and then reappeared in the 1970s, when communities transformed abandoned and garbage-strewn lots, led by activist groups such as the Green Guerrillas. The city's Operation Green Program also made municipal lots available to gardeners for just $1 a year, though various refuges have often found themselves destroyed or at least endangered by sweeping development projects, especially in the rapidly gentrifying East Village. The desire to eat organically has risen in recent years, as evidenced by the construction of more health markets (most notably, the massive new Whole Foods store at the Time Warner Center and another on its way to Brooklyn), and folks who have weekly produce packs delivered by one of the area's CSAs (Community Supported Agriculture groups) or are members of the **Park Slope Food Coop** (www.foodcoop.com), a member-owned-and-operated natural-food store that's been thriving and growing since its founding in 1969.

One group that has a hand in practically all green issues in the city is the **Council on the Environment of New York City** (www.cenyc.org), a privately funded citizens' organization in the Office of the Mayor. Its programs include Open Space Greening (community gardens), Greenmarket & New Farmer Development Project (supporting 42 greenmarket sites citywide), Environmental Education (for outreach) and Waste Prevention & Recycling, which encourages sustainable practices in schools and other institutions.

Arts

Arts

Spend just a few days enjoying cultural pursuits in New York and you'll realize that diversity is a term that applies to much more than just the population here. It's quite easy to find yourself gazing at Impressionist masterpieces one hour and checking out an edgy installation made of discarded toothpaste tubes the next. You can be sitting, transfixed, as the Philharmonic delivers a dose of Beethoven, and then bopping before a screeching band at Luna Lounge, getting mocked by a drag-queen cabaret star or dancing until breakfast at a massive club to one of the world's foremost DJs. When it comes to culture fixes, nothing is implausible here – not even a comeback from disaster.

The arts, similar to every other aspect of life here, have had trouble recovering economically since September 11 – perhaps more than other parts of city life, since in tough economic times, some view the arts as not vital. Fiscal casualties have included the recent dissolution of the New York Chamber Orchestra, the scaling back of concerts from the Brooklyn Philharmonic, low box-office sales in dance and theater, and a decrease in private funding to groups including those as esteemed as the Metropolitan Opera.

Metropolitan Museum of Art (p123)

Still, the future looks quite bright, especially for the big guys. Plenty of institutions have expanded or renovated or are planning on it – the Metropolitan Museum of Art (the Met), the Guggenheim, Carnegie Hall, the Brooklyn Museum, the Brooklyn Academy of Music and the Museum of Modern Art. Even Lincoln Center's getting a facelift, as it has just unveiled a $325 million transformation plan – a glass-walled restaurant with a grass roof, scrolling electronic billboards, spiffed-up buildings – set to begin in 2006. In addition, though they've been priced out of Manhattan, the city remains fertile ground for young, burgeoning artists of multiple media, who are drawn to New York by its kinetic energy (and all-important patrons of the arts). They've just lit out for warehouse spaces in the boroughs and built vibrant arts community in places such as Long Island City, Queens, Williamsburg, Dumbo and Brooklyn.

Citywide, concerts still sell out, clubs get mobbed, new theater productions lure folks in from all over the tristate area. So hopefully, the financial crisis is in the past. Because the truth is that many New Yorkers *do* see the arts as vital. They are, after all, living in this, one of the cultural capitals of the world.

Top Five Not to Overlook

The Met and MoMA are world-class art repositories, and the Guggenheim's got the architectural pedigree. But some of New York City's premier art moments – and fewer crowds – can be found at these local faves:

- **Brooklyn Museum** (p138) With its new look, family-friendly theme and moniker (it's dropped 'Art' from the name), this is a joyous place to spend an afternoon.
- **Cloisters** (p132) The Met's charming outdoor cousin in northern Manhattan.
- **Frick Collection** (p123) Skip the crowds, not the classics.
- **Isamu Noguchi Garden Museum** (p143) This precious sculpture castle makes Long Island City worth the travel time.
- **Neue Galerie** (p124) It's a Viennese waltz, all over the walls.

LITERATURE

Greenwich Village has perhaps the most glorified literary history in New York, and deservedly so. Literary figures including Henry James, Herman Melville and Mark Twain lived in the Washington Square area at the turn of the 19th century. And by 1912, the tight-knit, storied clan of John Reed, Mabel Dodge Luhan, Hutchins Hapgood, Max Eastman and other playwrights and poets wrote about bohemian life and gathered at cafés in these parts for literary salons and liquor-fueled tête-à-têtes. But when Prohibition sent too many uptowners searching for hooch downtown and the party broke up, things remained quiet for a time, until Eugene O'Neill and his cohorts came along, followed by such luminaries as novelists Willa Cather, Malcolm Cowley, Ralph Ellison and poets ee cummings, Edna St Vincent Millay, Frank O'Hara and Dylan Thomas, who is said to have died in this 'hood after downing one too many drinks at the local White Horse Tavern in 1953.

The area is still most closely associated with the late 1950s and '60s, when the wild and wonderful Beat movement was led by William Burroughs, Allen Ginsberg, Jack Kerouac and their gang. These poets and novelists rejected traditional writing forms and instead adopted rhythms of basic American speech and jazz music for their literary musings. Ginsberg is best known for *Howl*, which he wrote in 1956 as an attack on American values. Kerouac's prose, as seen in novels including *On the Road, The Subterraneans* and *The Dharma Bums*, similar to that of Burroughs (*Naked Lunch*), reflect a disdain for convention and a thirst for adventure.

In 1966, Ginsberg helped found the Poetry Project at St Mark's Church-in-the-Bowery (131 E 10th St) in the East Village, still an active, poet-staffed literary forum and resource – and sort of all-around community center – for New York writers. Ginsberg gave an historic, joint reading here with Robert Lowell, and some of the many other literary legends to read here have included Adrienne Rich, Patti Smith and Frank O'Hara.

That this center took root in the East Village is one of the best proofs that intellectual, writerly activities and inspirations have never been confined to the fabled Greenwich Village. Harlem, for example, has a long literary history. James Baldwin, born in this uptown 'hood, was a black, gay, preacher's son who wrote about conflicts of race, poverty and identity in novels including *Go Tell It on the Mountain* and *Giovanni's Room*, published in the 1950s. Audre Lorde, a Caribbean-American lesbian, activist and writer, was raised in Harlem and attended Columbia University. Her poetry, written mostly in the '70s, and memoir, *Zami: A New Spelling of My Name* (1982), dealt with class, race and gay and lesbian issues. Much earlier, in the 1920s, Dorothy Parker held court at the famous Algonquin Round Table – a private clique of writers who hung out and drank and talked endlessly about American culture, politics and literature. Soon, the regular

NYC in Literature

- *The Age of Innocence* by Edith Wharton (1920) Peek into upper-class, old New York brownstones through this tale of one family and its constricting high-society rules.
- *The Alienist* by Caleb Carr (1994) Crime fiction set in sordid Lower East Side of the late 19th century.
- *Bonfire of the Vanities* by Tom Wolfe (1987) A long career of literary journalism already on his list of accomplishments, the man who recorded the world of 1960s Acid Tests and high-class society's love affair with Black Power delved into the status-obsessed '80s with this gripping novel of an investment banker's entanglement with the world of the black South Bronx.
- *Breakfast at Tiffany's* by Truman Capote (1958) Before Audrey Hepburn made the tale of Holly Golightly an American classic on the screen, Capote did so on the page, with his wonderful story of an endearing, eccentric free spirit in the big city.
- *Bright Lights, Big City* by Jay McInerney (1984) A Manhattan yuppie with everything on his side has a big downward spiral when he's forced to deal with his mother's death and the seduction of drugs.
- *The Catcher In the Rye* by JD Salinger (1951) This tale of adolescent angst follows narrator Holden Caulfield on a search for himself in Manhattan after he's expelled from prep school. It's a classic, and with very good reason.
- *Go Tell It on the Mountain* by James Baldwin (1953) This emotional, lyrical, tight novel shares the details of just one day in the life of 14-year-old John Grimes, a Harlem preacher's son, and his despaired, moral awakening during the Depression.
- *The Great Gatsby* by F Scott Fitzgerald (1925) Jazz Age classic of the 1920s highlife-lovers and assorted hangers-on.
- *Jazz* by Toni Morrison (1992) Pulitzer Prize–winner Morrison explores the Harlem Jazz Age through the tales of three tragic, intersecting lives.
- *Marjorie Morningstar* by Herman Wouk (1955) Set in Depression-era New York, the classic tells the story of a woman who makes grand attempts at rebelling against the middle-class values of her Jewish-American family by attempting to become an actress.
- *Martin Dressler* by Stephen Millhauser (1997) Pulitzer Prize–winning rise and fall of an ambitious NYC hotelier, captures in elaborate details NYC's gilded age at the turn of the 20th century.
- *Motherless Brooklyn* by Jonathan Lethem (1999) This genius novel had a quick rise to cult status among north-Brooklyn residents, as its oddly compelling tale – of grown-up orphan Lionel Essrog, a detective with Tourette's syndrome who is investigating the death of his boss – explores crevices and histories of Brooklyn neighborhoods that recent transplants never knew existed.
- *The Nanny Diaries: A Novel* by Emma McLaughlin and Nicola Kraus (2002) The authors, both former nannies, take readers inside the odd world of privileged, Park Avenue mothering in this hilarious tome. The patronizing Mrs X wields her power over the NYU student/nanny narrator, who's in charge of one very sophisticated four year old.
- *The New York Trilogy: City of Ghosts, Glass, The Locked Room* by Paul Auster (1985) This troika of novellas – spooky, noirish detective tales that delve into the psyche of both the characters and the writer – broke new ground with its unusual blend of fiction and mystery genres.
- *Push* by Sapphire (1996) Brooklyn writer Sapphire's wrenching story about an abused young Harlem woman, 16-year-old Precious Jones, is almost too much to bear. But her gorgeous, honest prose pulls you through it all – including the girl's sexual abuses, HIV status and pregnancy by her father.
- *Rubyfruit Jungle* by Rita Mae Brown (1973) This lesbian cult classic follows Molly Bolt who, after charming the high-school cheerleader and getting kicked out of college for being immoral, arrives in Greenwich Village for a classic, whirlwind coming-out adventure.
- *Slaves of New York* by Tama Janowitz (1986) This real-estate–obsessed collection of deadpan, quirky stories about folks living Downtown in the '80s is a nostalgic glance at a time when real-life starving artists could scrape by and find their own little nests, whether in illegal lofts or dilapidated studios.
- *The Story of Junk* by Linda Yablonsky (1997) Years after her grim existence as a heroin junkie living in the down-and-out artists' Lower East Side, Yablonsky recalls all the shocking, seedy details – with startling clarity – through the point of view of an unnamed narrator.
- *A Tree Grows In Brooklyn* by Betty Smith (1943) This poignant classic is the tale of Francie Nolan, a young girl living in Williamsburg squalor as she observes the adult complexities of her dysfunctional family.
- *Underworld* by Don DeLillo (1997) Elegiac epic about the Bronx, rooftop parties, historic home runs and the end of the 20th century.

gatherings – which included *New Yorker* founder Harold Ross, author Robert Benchley, playwrights George S Kaufman, Edna Ferber, Noel Coward and Marc Connelly and various critics – turned into a national amusement, as stories were written about the gatherings and tourists often came to gawk at the intellectual bunch.

In the 1980s, literary journalist Tom Wolfe entered the fiction realm, publishing his massive novel *Bonfire of the Vanities*, about narcissistic, consumerist life on the Upper East Side on Manhattan. Other novelists illuminating the greedy, coke-fueled '80s era included Bret Easton Ellis (*American Psycho*), Jay McInerney (*Bright Lights, Big City*) and Tama Janowitz (*Slaves of New York*), who wrote about mainly uptown antics. During the same era, notable poets and writers of the East Village (where Allen Ginsberg actually lived) included Eileen Myles, whose poetry and unconventional novel *Chelsea Girls* took readers into the rebellious Downtown art world, as well as poets Gregory Masters and Michael Scholnick; Linda Yablonsky wrote about this scene long after she had survived it, with *The Story of Junk*, published in 1997.

And way before any of this, of course, came Long Island native Walt Whitman, who wrote from his home in the borough of Brooklyn, publishing *Leaves of Grass* in 1855, paving an early way for more contemporary Brooklyn authors, including Betty Smith, who wrote *A Tree Grows In Brooklyn* in 1943, and modern darling Jonathan Lethem, whose *Motherless Brooklyn* (1999) sparked new interest in the area around Cobble Hill and Brooklyn Heights. Other breakout Brooklynites of this century and the late '90s include Rick Moody (*Purple America, The Ice Storm*), who mixes suburban and urban adventure; Sapphire (*Push*), whose heartbreaking novel tells the tale of a young girl's abuse; Paul Auster (*New York Trilogy, Mr Vertigo, Timbuktu*), who writes about current-day New York; Meera Nair (*Video*), whose focus is on Indian culture and its clashes with Western ideologies; and Jonathan Safran Foer (*Everything Is Illuminated*), who traced his Ukrainian roots in his breakout novel.

DANCE

All dance roads lead to New York City, where the dance world is really comprised of two separate halves – the classical and the modern – and its split personality is what makes it one of the most renowned dance capitals of the globe. You can see this two-spirited self by browsing dance listings, whether you're a fan or not – or you can experience it firsthand, by taking a dance class while you're in town. Most any dance school in the city, whether it's Steps on the Upper West Side or Dance Space in Soho or anything in between, offers a wild blend of classes – modern or jazz or some blend, or ballet, whose students are known as 'bunheads' by the modern folks. And most amateurs pick one side of the line and stick with it, similar to pros and their fans. The Entertainment chapter has details of dance companies, studios and arts centers (p229).

It all started in the 1930s, when American classic ballet took off here and laid the foundation for what would soon become the world-class American Ballet Theatre and New York City Ballet. Lincoln Kirstein envisioned a US ballet for native dancers, and wanted them trained by the ballet masters of the world so they could create a repertory that had a built-in cast. Kirstein met the Russian-trained George Balanchine in 1933 in London, and the two started their now legendary American school, the New York City Ballet, together in New York that year, later performing with Jerome Robbins as assistant artistic director. In 1964 they opened the New York State Theater and have been its resident ballet company ever since. Since then, ballet bigwigs, including Balanchine, Robbins and Peter Martins, have choreographed dances for the troupe, which has boasted stars such as Maria Tallchief, Suzanne Farrell and Jacques D'Amboise.

Meanwhile, the American Ballet Theatre (ABT) was making its own inroads, founded in New York in 1937 by Lucia Chase and Rich Pleasant and made famous through works by Balanchine, Antony Tudor, Jerome Robbins (*Fancy Free*), Alvin Ailey, and Twyla Tharp (*When Push Comes to Shove*). After defecting from the Soviet Union, Mikhail Baryshnikov found fame with ABT as a principal dancer in the '70s, and remained as its artistic director from 1980 to 1989 before founding his own White Oak Dance Project.

At the same time, Martha Graham, Charles Wiedman and Doris Humphrey sowed the seeds of the modern movement in NYC, which was continued here after WWII by masters including Merce Cunningham, Paul Taylor, Alvin Ailey and Twyla Tharp. Today both scenes continue to be global forces, with the more experimental, avant-garde dance world constantly growing as well – enabling you to see pretty much anything from muscle-bound women mixing circus-type trapeze acts into their performance to naked troupes rolling around on a bare stage.

Today's up-and-coming dancers continue to move in new directions, bringing their own interpretations to small, Downtown theaters including the **Kitchen**, the **Joyce Theater** and **Danspace Project** (see p229 for all venue information). Modern companies great and small continue to build new homes around the city, whether its Mark Morris and his new base near the **Brooklyn Academy of Music** (BAM; p136) in Brooklyn or the **Alvin Ailey American Dance Theater's** (p229) brand-new, state-of-the-art home, which just opened its doors in the Theater District. And the dancers themselves, often forced to work other jobs to support themselves and their craft in such an expensive city, are remarkably supportive of each other. Dancers can apply for financial grants, studio space and other creative assistance through organizations such as the Field, Movement Research, Pentacle, New York Foundation for the Arts and Dance Theater Workshop – which hosts the Bessies, a prestigious, annual awards-ceremony for dancers (named after Bessie Schönberg, a highly regarded dance teacher who died in 1997).

The best way to tap into what's going on in dance is to read – especially the words of the dance critics at the *Village Voice* and the *New York Times*. Or, for a complete list of dance venues, organizations and news updates, visit www.dancenyc.org. Then pick a side in the modern-classical dichotomy – or don't. You can enjoy it all here, the most influential dance capital you'll find.

CLASSICAL ARTS

If Downtown Manhattan is home to all things contemporary – indie rock bands, clever drag shows, cutting-edge art installations and experimental dance theater – then Uptown is the refuge for more classical, timely pursuits. A visit to the Upper West Side, a neighborhood for old-school artists, reveals this quickly enough, as musicians who make their living as cellists, bassists or tuba players for orchestras and ensembles can almost always be spotted lugging their instruments, secured in bulky, odd-shaped cases, home from the 96th St stop on the 1, 9, 2, or 3 trains. For a good number of them, work has probably included gigs at either the **Lincoln Center** (p121) complex or **Carnegie Hall** (p239) at one point or another, just as a fair amount have most likely studied – or at least taken a class – at one of the premier schools for classical music and opera in the country: the **Juilliard School** or the **Manhattan School of Music**, which are also host to top-notch concerts.

Lincoln Center was built in the 1960s as part of an urban renewal plan under development commissioner Robert Moses, controversially clearing out a slew of slums (the ones used as the basis for *West Side Story*, actually) in the process. And what started as a questionable project for many preservationists and arts fans has largely won over much of New York with its incomparable offerings. Housed in the massive mini-world – complete with fountains and reflecting pools and wide-open spaces – are the main halls of Alice Tully, Avery Fisher, Metropolitan Opera House (the most opulent of all the venues here) and the New York State Theater, as well as the Juilliard School, the Fiorello La Guardia High School for the Performing Arts, and the Vivian Beaumont and Mitzi Newhouse theaters. Resident companies include the Metropolitan Opera and the New York City Opera, the New York Philharmonic, the New York City Ballet and the Chamber Music Society of Lincoln Center, among others. Its programs are far reaching, with some free offerings – such as the popular summer Concerts in the Parks series of the Philharmonic, itself founded in 1842 and America's premier orchestra, currently directed by Lorin Maazel. The Metropolitan Opera is the grand, more classic company, while the New York City Opera is the more unique, imaginative and down-to-earth sibling.

The smaller, more contained and limited Carnegie Hall, meanwhile, is just as beloved a venue – especially since opening Zankel Hall, offering eclectic world-music and jazz sounds,

NYC Music in the 21st Century *Glenn Kenny*

Tin Pan Alley. Carnegie Hall. The Great White Way. Birdland. The Village Vanguard. The Apollo. Fillmore East. CBGB. Studio 54. All these place-names and place nicknames say two things with equal force: New York City and music. And if the New York live music scene hasn't produced a legendary name since Studio 54 – which opened in the late 1970s – that doesn't mean the town's music scene isn't still a vital part of its culture.

True, nightlife these days is different. The ban on smoking in public places, including nightclubs, put into effect by NYC Mayor Michael Bloomberg in 2003, has made New York after dark feel different, even for nonsmokers. While it's certainly refreshing for many to come home from a night of rocking and rolling (or related activity) without having their clothes smell like stale tobacco, it's never been said that the experience of rocking and rolling (or related activity) is supposed to be sanitary. So the health benefit is accompanied in many cases by a slight cognitive disconnect. And then there's the fact that while New York is a music industry center, the music industry itself is in a bit of a state these days, with profits plummeting as increasingly impotent execs take both defensive and offensive postures against music downloading. Still, the city is blessed with a ton of great venues, and fans will have live music options any night of the week. The fact that skyrocketing rents (contrary to some speculation, September 11 did not wind up rendering Manhattan real estate any less expensive) have led to a blossoming of music venues outside of the city 'proper', means that travelers to New York looking for a new music fix will as often as not find themselves making a trek over the Williamsburg or Brooklyn bridges, or through some tunnel or other.

Rock

New York has seen a sort of mini-renaissance in this genre in recent years, what with bands such as The Strokes, Yeah Yeah Yeahs, The Rapture, Radio 4, The Fever, The Stills, Stellastarr, The Furnaces and TV on the Radio to name but a few capturing international attention, or 'buzz' if you will. Grousers will grouse as to how most of these bands are, if not out-and-out retreads, at the very least highly derivative of forebears from NYC and elsewhere; admittedly, out of this crew, only The Furnaces and TV on the Radio boast truly distinctive (and hard to pin down) sounds. Still, they've all made decent-to-excellent records and some do in fact kick ass live.

CBGB, once at the forefront of breaking great new bands, is now by and large a showcase for any combo wanting to show off how young, loud and snotty they are. Mind you, most of the bands listed above have trekked down its narrow front corridor to its small stage – built, legend has it, by the members of Television in preparation for their first gig there – but the gig has become more of a rite of passage than a defining event. They – and the scores following in their wake – are likely to be more in their natural element at a Lower East Side venue such as **Pianos** (p239), or Brooklyn clubs such as **North Six** (p239) or **Southpaw** (p239), the audience a veritable fall harvest of trucker hats. The success trajectory for an up-and-coming local or out-of-town rock combo as measured by venue goes something like this: first go-round at **Pianos** or the **Mercury Lounge** (p239) or as an opener at the **Knitting Factory** (p241), second go-round a sold-out weekend at the **Bowery Ballroom** (p238), third go-round at **Irving Plaza** (p238), or, if you're really good, really lucky, or your record company has a really expert promo department (or some combination of all three) the relatively cavernous climes of the **Hammerstein Ballroom** or **Roseland**. Then on to arenas, headlining Coachella, acrimonious breakup followed by decade layoff followed by triumphant reunion headlining Coachella . . . or if you really screw up, back to the Mercury Lounge, and no drink allowance. And that's why we love the rock!

Jazz & 'Free' Music

It's kind of awful to see this city – once the home of Minton's and Birdland, clubs where modern jazz evolved and countless legends were forged – take such hits in the jazz department. In recent years, the sensitively-programmed Sweet Basil and the jamming hotbed Smalls both shut their doors, and since co-founder Michael Dorf parted ways with the Knitting Factory, forward-thinking jazz is scarcer than ever there. Strangely, the Times Square club **Iridium** (p241) is picking up some of the slack in that department – the venue recently hosted the shamanistic pianist Cecil Taylor and his big band (we wonder if any of his thunder leaked into next door's Winter Garden Theater, which hosts the ABBA musical *Mamma Mia!*). Thank God also for Downtown's **Tonic** (p241), now the home ground for John Zorn and a home away from home for the likes of Derek Bailey, Peter Brotzman and other blowers. Thank God too for the **Village Vanguard** (p242), presided over by the indefatigable Lorraine Gordon and offering the town's most intimate (and, when you think about it, reasonably priced) jazz experiences. The **Blue Note** (p240), with its take-out-a-second-mortgage cover and contemptuous minimum, remains the Blue Note – sometimes they'll bring someone (you've just got to see, so you suck it up and take the abuse. And it's too soon to tell whether jazz at **Lincoln Center** (p240), the brainchild of musician/entrepreneur Wynton 'I'll Tell You What Jazz Is or Isn't and You'll Like It' Marsalis, will be a godsend or a tourist trap in its new Columbus Circle location.

Classical

The classical music world was set abuzz a little while ago at the news that the fabled New York Philharmonic would be moving from the acoustically, um, appalling Avery Fisher Hall into the acoustically, well, stunning **Carnegie Hall** (p239), the beneficiary of a sound-sensitive mid-1990s restoration/renovation. But it was only a dream – the deal fell through. Lincoln Center announced in 2004 that they would be giving Avery Fisher Hall a tune-up instead. Well, we've sent a spacecraft to Mars so anything's possible. Dates haven't been announced yet, but the remodeling will require the Philharmonic to spend at least one season away from home. Hopefully, they'll choose Carnegie Hall! Carnegie itself recently opened Zankel Hall in its basement, such as it is; despite sometimes distracting subway rumblings, it's a great space adventurously programmed, offering tasty treats of so-called world music and contemporary classical. Lincoln Center remains true to its roots, while the nearby Merkin Hall (no jokes about the name, please) offers eclectic and daring classical fare.

Hip-Hop

Back in the good, or maybe it was the bad, old days, certain venues had particular racial connotations...not so much anymore. In spring 2004, Morrissey, one of the most Caucasian rock musicians of this century and the last, was concluding a wildly successful run at the Apollo, and it's not unusual to find a Wu-Tang Clanner or two entertaining the blunted-out hipsters of Williamsburg at North Six. Hip-hop, now the dominant form of mainstream popular music, has come a long way from its late-'70s South Bronx origins, the days of Grandmaster Flash, 'Rapper's Delight' and scratched-up LPs. Today you're most likely to catch stars such as Jay-Z at big-billed arena shows.

Miscellany

If you want old-school rock and blues and reggae and whatnot, you could do worse than **BB King's Joint** (p240) on 42nd St itself, where you can see Toots and the Maytals one night, John Mayall the next, Blue Oyster Cult the next, Al Stewart the next – it's like an edgier, urban version of Branson, Missouri, in one building! Cabaret is still alive and well despite the impending retirement of defining saloon singer Bobby Short; a couple of venues offering new twists on a venerable New York style are **Joe's Pub** (p238) in the Village's Public Theater and the Westbeth Theater.

New York's 10 Greatest Music Names (Not Counting Sinatra, Who Really Belongs To Hoboken)

- **Irving Berlin** The Great White Way is forever aglow with the names of the song scribes who penned *The Great American Songbook* – George M Cohan, Rodgers and Hart, the Gershwin brothers, and tons more. Russian-born Berlin gets pride of place for being preternaturally prolific and for penning an astonishing range of tunes. *What'll I Do, There's No Business Like Show Business, Blue Skies, Puttin' on the Ritz*, and *Always* are just the tip of a monumental iceberg.
- **Miles Davis** While Charlie Parker and other architects of bebop honed their styles in juke joints in towns such as Kansas City, Miles' real development began when he moved up from St Louis to NYC as a teen trumpet prodigy, to study at Julliard, where his love of jazz was supplemented by a fascination with Stravinsky and such. From there, it was into the ranks of Parker's band, and then on to invent 'cool' jazz, hard bop, orchestral jazz, fusion etc.
- **Philip Glass** This composer crafted his own brand of minimalism – loud, full of vertigo-inducing shifts and repetitions, and extremely difficult to play – in the lofts of Soho way back when the fashion-victim *Sex and the City*-wannabes currently trolling that nabe weren't even gleams in their accursed parents' eyes. He then softened and popularized that sound and became a much-in-demand film scorer in the bargain. And up until recently he was still living in an East Village townhouse.
- **Thelonious Monk** Another architect of bebop, he never had to change styles or invent new genres, because his way of playing the piano – initially klutzy sounding, but in fact brimming over with humor, attitude, understated anxiety and acute musical intelligence – made him a law unto himself. And anyone who's ever sported a beret or grown a goatee owes him big time.
- **The New York Dolls** & **The Ramones** *Invasion of the Outer Boroughs, Volumes One and Two*. In the first, some boys from Astoria and Staten Island decide to take over St Mark's Place by being trashier than anything that trashy block had ever seen. And louder. Glam rock at its hardest and smartest. In the even better sequel, a motley crew of Queens misfits adopt the same surname and invent punk (for all intents and purposes).
- **Run-DMC** *Invasion of the Outer Boroughs, Volume Three*. All the way from Hollis, Queens. Hip-hop has had its innovators before and after this trio. But nobody put it together like these guys, 'rocking without a band' and creating a hip-hop paradigm that's still impossible to top.

- **Beverly Sills** The Brooklyn-born diva had a 25-year career with the New York City Opera. Her soprano is only one of her talents – as both a performer and administrator, she's one of the greatest ambassadors of opera in the world.
- **Sonic Youth** Fusing punk attitude and volume with voluminous knowledge of the avant-garde, and keeping it together after so many of their compatriots either exploded or imploded, this band's going to pass its quarter-century mark soon, and they're still making music that's as challenging as it is immediate and emotionally involving.
- **Sarah Vaughan** The greatest vocal virtuoso jazz will ever produce was born in Newark, New Jersey, and got her first break at an amateur night at Harlem's legendary Apollo Theater. Nobody could sing *Lullaby of Birdland* the way she did. In fact, nobody could sing anything the way she did.
- **The Velvet Underground** These Downtown experimentalists were fusing folk and drone rock at dangerous volumes when they were adopted by Andy Warhol, who foisted a German model 'chanteuse' on them. As such, they came to epitomize NYC cool even if they didn't sell many records – and as Brian Eno pointed out, it seems that everyone who bought their first album went out and formed a band of his or her own, so influential have they proven.

beneath the main Issac Stern Hall, whose stage has been graced by all the big names. This is the place to catch visiting orchestras from all over the world, acclaimed soloists such as violinist Midori and pianist Nelson Freire, and big concerts including the New York Pops series.

Outside of these biggie venues, there's plenty more. But one of the main attractions is the **Brooklyn Academy of Music** (p136), the country's oldest academy for the performing arts, where you'll find opera seasons and concerts from its resident Brooklyn Philharmonic, which also plays for free in the summer, in nearby Prospect Park. (For other classical performance venues, see p223.) To catch quality classical sounds anytime without paying a penny, tune in to one of the local radio stations that serve as community center for lovers of the genre: the 75-year-old 96.3-FM WQXR, which is all classical all the time; and 93.9-FM WNYC, the city's local NPR affiliate, which goes classical weekdays at 2pm and 7pm and weekend evenings at 8pm.

COMEDY, CABARET & PERFORMANCE ART

If you visit New York City, and especially if you live here, you had better be able to laugh – at yourself, at others, and at exceptionally trying or tragic situations. New Yorkers grappled with this fact in the months and years following September 11 – what's inappropriate? When will it have been long enough to laugh again? Is irony dead? The answers were, luckily, not much, about a year, and absolutely not. Life can be hard here, and laughing makes it easier, and there are plenty of funny folks around who are willing to lend a hand. Mayor Bloomberg even joined forces with **Carolines on Broadway** (p233) comedy club, announcing the first-ever New York Comedy Festival, a five-day event to be held November 9 to 14, 2004, that was to feature performances throughout the city from some of the nation's top comedy talents (visit www.nyc.gov/film for details).

New York has a great history of discovering great comedians – it's the town that brought us Jerry Seinfeld, after all, as well as Eddie Murphy and Chris Rock, who began their careers at Carolines on Broadway, and Jim Belushi, Dennis Miller, Joe Piscopo, Kevin Nealon and Dana Carvey (along with many others) all had their careers launched on the hit New York series *Saturday Night Live* (p42).

Similar to many other entertainment forms here, the comedy scene is sharply divided between the big-name, big-ticket clubs and the more experimental and obscure places – which often host the best shows in town, sometimes bending the typical stand-up style to include music, burlesque or comedy sketches. For that kind of anything-goes format, check out the **Upright Citizens Brigade Theater** (p233), which specializes in improv and often sees comedy celebs in its audience. Luna Lounge's **Eating It** series (171 Ludlow St), on Mondays on the Lower East Side, as well as **Automatic Vaudeville,** on Thursdays at Ars Nova Theater (511 W 54th St), also deliver unexpected goods. But to be made fun of, and to hear wisecracks about the state of the country or the city or the $12 drinks you're sipping, stick with the standard stand-up shows. Besides Carolines, perhaps the most well-known such place in the city, there's the

Boston Comedy Club, Comedy Cellar, Stand-Up NY and the **Gotham Comedy Club** (see p233 for all venue information). The Gotham is home to a monthly queer-comedy series, Homocomicus.

Cabaret, meanwhile, often has plenty of comedic overtones – but they're much more subtle. Usually consisting of a performer at a piano or a microphone who holds court in an intimate venue, the clever riffs or anecdotes are just highlights to the real purpose: live music. Jazz and standards are the most popular fare, although at Theater District venues – **Danny's Skylight Room, Don't Tell Mama** – you'll get a big dose of Broadway show tunes. Styles also differ depending on the pricing, and if the venue is considered 'classic' – such as at the **Oak Room** or **Feinstein's** or the **Carlyle** – where cabaret stars including Bobby Short, Woody Allen, Betty Buckley, Karen Akers and Ann Hampton Callaway grace the stage. Though all cabaret has a gay bent by its very (campy) nature, the queer feel is more evident at the **Duplex**, on Christopher St, where performers will often be in drag; gay bars and lounges often become ad hoc cabaret venues – **Barracuda Lounge** (Map pp382-5), **Bar d'O** (p215) and **xl** (p217), among others.

Some of the gay nightspot shows verge on performance art, although there are plenty of other places to go to find that murky genre, as well. The hottest style right now is burlesque, which has been seized by dancers and exhibitionists all over town to be updated and sexed up for fans of kitschy nostalgia. The Va Va Voom Room, one of the longest running burlesque shows of this new wave, can be seen at the **Fez** (p238), a reliable showcase for all things eccentric, such as its Cause Celeb series, which has local stars doing dramatic readings from the autobiographies of some of the campiest celebs in history. The new **Marquee** (356 Bowery) theater, upstairs from the Slide gay bar in the East Village, churns out all sorts of wacky, clever shows, usually involving at least one drag queen; **Galapagos Art and Performance Space** (70 N 6th St) in Williamsburg , a **La MaMa ETC** (74A E 4th St) and the all-women's **WOW Café Theater** (59 E 4th St), both in the East Village, are also excellent places to find burlesque, strange music revues, live soap-opera series and all-around cleverness.

THEATER

The biggest, splashiest dramas and musicals are probably what's best associated with New York's entertainment world – mainly because of that term known round the world: Broadway. But Broadway shows, while they do make up a significant portion of the local theater scene, refer strictly to productions staged in the 38 official Broadway theaters – lavish, early-20th-century jewels surrounding Times Square. Public opinion about the state of the Great White Way changes drastically every couple of years, with some folks constantly moaning that, with the constant revivals, there's just no good, original theater anymore. But the very latest wave of innovative, musical works – *Avenue Q*, *The Boy From Oz* and *Wicked* – has changed many minds. And repackaged movie hits such as *The Producers* and *Hairspray* have even taken the town by storm.

New York has a rich history of taking folks by storm when it comes to the development of the theater world. The Theater District as we see it today was begun in 1893 by Charles Frohman, who opened the Empire Theater on 40th St, beginning the shift of the district from the 30s to what would later become Times Square. That same year, the first-ever industry trade union – the National Alliance of Theatrical Stage Employees, for stagehands – was formed. By 1901, the flood of lights coming from theater facades in the area was so great that designer OJ Gude deemed the Broadway district the Great White Way. Soon after, the Theater Guild began its long and distinguished history of producing big hits, from Eugene O'Neill, George Bernard Shaw and others, and musicals begin to soar in quality and popularity. The first Tony Awards took place in 1947, the Theater Development Fund was established 20 years after and, by the late '80s, nearly every Broadway theater was designated as a historic landmark.

Broadway, though, doesn't tell nearly the whole story. Off Broadway – more adventurous, less costly theater shown in houses that seat 200 to 500 people – or off Broadway – even edgier, more affordable performances housed in theaters for crowds of less than 100 – are both big businesses here. They often provide venues for more established actors to let their hair down a bit, and sometimes produce shows that wind up either on Broadway (*Rent*, for example, premiered at the Downtown New York Theater Workshop, just as *Angels in America* started at the Public Theater and *The Vagina Monologues* took off at the tiny HERE in Soho. To see a lot of experimental theater in a short amount of time, watch for the **Fringe Festival** (p12; www.fringenyc.org), held in various Downtown venues every August. Also in the summer, usually beginning in June, is the acclaimed Shakespeare in the Park festival, produced by the Public Theater and taking place at the Delacorte Theater in Central Park. Tickets are free, but you do need to line up on certain days at specific times to claim yours.

To purchase tickets for any other show in town, you can either head to the box office, or use one of several ticket-service agencies to order by phone or Internet. **Broadway Line** (☎ 212-302-4111; www.broadway.org) provides descriptions of plays and musicals both on and off the Great White Way, and lets you charge tickets. **Telecharge** (☎ 212-239-6200; www.telecharge.com) sells tickets for most Broadway and off-Broadway shows (though there's a per-ticket surcharge); for strictly off Broadway, try **SmartTix.com, Theatermania.com, Ticketcentral.com** or **Ticketmaster.com.**

Bargain-hunters can try to score same-day standing-room tickets for sold-out shows for about $15. You'll get great views and sore feet, but you can always scope out vacant seats at intermission. In Times Square, **TKTS booth** (Map pp226-7; ☎ 212-768-1818; Broadway & W 47th St), run by the Theater Development Fund, sells same-day tickets to Broadway and off-Broadway musicals and dramas. (There's also a smaller, less crowded **TKTS outlet**, Map pp380-1, at South Street Seaport, with the same rates, plus a $3 service charge per ticket.) The booth's electric marquee lists available shows; availability depends on the popularity of the show you're looking to see, so be prepared to be flexible. On Wednesday and Saturday, matinee tickets go on sale at 10am, and on Sunday the windows open at 11am for afternoon performances. Evening tickets go on sale at 3pm daily, and a line begins to form up to an hour before the booth opens. Note that TKTS accepts cash or travelers checks only.

VISUAL ARTS

Though there may not be much of a place for the so-called starving artist these days – high rents took care of that, thank you very much – artists (and the people who love them) are in grand supply. That's clear in the number of major art museums (25), independent art galleries (about 600), public-art installations and less formal displays of creative talents, from ad hoc art shows hung in bars and restaurants to all-out graffiti murals scrawled on building facades and walls within the subway's underground labyrinth. The absolute center of the gallery world lies in Chelsea, which has close to 200 art spaces in its neighborhood alone – big names such as Matthew Marks and Barbara Gladstone among them (see p158). Parts of the Lower East Side and Williamsburg, Brooklyn, are also gaining notoriety as more galleries open doors there. But it hasn't always been this way, and it probably won't be for long.

The history of shifting art scenes is a fickle one, with the earliest galleries opening on and around 57th St because it was the vicinity of the immensely popular **Museum of Modern Art** (MoMA, p115). Opened in 1929 as a challenge to the conservative policies of traditional museums (such as those of the Met), MoMA spawned a slew of smaller spaces, such as the galleries owned by Julien Levy and Peggy Guggenheim, which showed the progressive work of artists including Mark Rothko and Jackson Pollock. The scene moved uptown for a while during the pop-art movement of the '50s, and then shifted down to the East Village, when showcases for the second generation of abstract expressionism opened along East 10th St. Andy Warhol gained notoriety for his Marilyn Monroe and Campbell's Soup can images during this period, displaying much of his work in the early '60s before opening his infamous Factory.

An entrepreneur by the name of Paula Cooper moved all the fun into Soho, though, when she opened the first commercial gallery there, on Wooster St, in 1969. It launched a neighborhood revolution, as artists flocked to Soho lofts that worked as both living and work spaces, and galleries opened here en masse. The year 1980 brought the scene back to the East Village for a while, as the Fun Gallery anchored the district and about 50 other spaces popped up, too, all brandishing a highly ironic set of works that actually helped to bring about the swift gentrification of the 'hood. It ended just as suddenly as it began, jumpstarting a brief Soho revival which ended in 1993, when high rents forced the art crowd into West Chelsea, a barren area that was ripe for taking over.

And it's where the pulsing gallery heart remains today. Chelsea is where the trendy masses roam from opening to opening on Thursday and Friday nights. It's where the hottest artists are bought and sold, where collectors clamor to be and where some of the most innovative yet high-profile pieces are displayed. But all the former hot spots – Soho (especially with its popular **New Museum of Contemporary Art**, p84), the high 50s and, to a lesser degree, the East Village – still have plenty to show off. New galleries on the Lower East Side such as **Rivington Arms** and **Maccarone Inc** are flexing muscle, similar to Pierogi and similarly edgy spaces out in Williamsburg. Another great spot geared toward fans of more wild, off-kilter creations is **White Columns**, a much-admired, unique gallery space in the West Village that's been showing daring works since it opened in 1969. Its openings, held on Fridays, get jam-packed with tuned-in hipsters. The best way to ensure you've hit all the spaces that might interest you is to pick up the *Gallery Guide*, a small, magazine-like booklet available at any city gallery.

Another couple of areas worth checking out are western Queens, mainly Astoria and Long Island City, and Dumbo in Brooklyn. For years now, Queens has been on the radar of art fans because of places such as **PS 1 Contemporary Art Center** (p143), a massive contemporary-art space which became affiliated with MoMA in 2000; the **Socrates Sculpture Park** (p143), an outdoor, waterfront patch of land (and former abandoned landfill) with large-scale works by Mark di Suvero and others; and the **Isamu Noguchi Garden Museum** (p143), with his sculptures presented in a peaceful garden setting (undergoing renovations until late 2004). But whoever didn't know about this corner of the city before 2002 certainly became aware of it then, when **MoMA** moved here (becoming MoMA Queens) so it could continue to operate until its permanent Midtown home had gone through its massive, $850 million expansion project, which will double that space in size.

Dumbo, meanwhile, is where artists flocked in the 1970s and '80s, drawn by the abandoned, industrial feel of the area. But by the end of the '90s, every artistic type – whether they were an artist or not – had discovered the area, falling in love with its couple of eateries, tiny waterfront park and cobblestone streets. Needless to say, it's rapidly gentrified since then, bringing in big restaurants, shops and upscale residences. But the artists remained. The **Dumbo Arts Center** (30 Washington St btwn Plymouth & Water Sts) shows local artists and sponsors an annual d.u.m.b.o. Art Under the Bridge festival (p12) in October.

Of course the city's museum classics are still worth visiting – more than ever, in fact. The **Metropolitan Museum of Art** (p123), which houses extensive collections of American, European, Asian, African, Egyptian and Greco-Roman art, plus galleries devoted to fashion, furniture, medieval armor, stained glass, jewelry, written arts and more, is in the process of adding massively to its halls. The Met began a $155 million remodeling project in early 2004 that will put every inch of space to use; it will allow loads of works (including an Etruscan chariot) to come out from storage, renovate galleries of 19th-century and modern art, and add a new Roman Court (scheduled to open in 2007) that will increase the number of Hellenistic and Roman art works from 2500 to 7500.

Other classic museums, including the **Brooklyn Museum** (p138), the **Frick Collection** (p123), the **Solomon R Guggenheim Museum** (p125), the **American Folk Art Museum** (p114) and the **Whitney Museum of Art** (p125), are impressive places to spend afternoons, as they are gorgeous structures filled with awe-inspiring works of art that reflect classical, modern or both sensibilities. The Whitney enjoys an explosion of notoriety – from both fans and critics – every two years when it pulls out all the stops for its Biennial, a sprawling showcase of the latest, most cutting-edge rising stars of the art world. It's sometimes derided, often controversially, and occasionally lauded, as was the case with the 2004 show. It was particularly commended because of the sparkling mix of artists – 108 in total – pulled together by the group of three relative-newcomer curators, all young women. New museums continue to open, as well, such as the brilliant **Neue Gallerie** (p124), near the Met, which showcases German and Austrian works of the late 19th and early 20th centuries. Fans of Gustav Klimt and Egon Schiele shouldn't miss it.

But for art fans more interested in buying than browsing, the most fun and efficient option is to attend art fairs, usually held in the spring and swiftly becoming one of the most high-profile, trendy games in town. Among the hottest is the **Armory Show** (www.thearmoryshow .com), an international modern-art show held every March in pier spaces that jut out over the Hudson. The show staged in 2004 featured booths with fine works from more than 200 galleries, brought together from cities all over the world, from Antwerp to Zurich.

PUBLIC ART

Public art – artwork that graces public spaces, that is – has a rich history in New York. Just a couple of days here and you'll see it for yourself, whether it's through the colorful tile mosaics that grace the walls of many subway stations or one of the myriad sculptures dotting the urban landscape.

Two wonderful public-art programs are behind much of the works – the Public Art Fund and the Department of Cultural Affairs' Percent for Art plan. Percent for

Top Five Public Art Pieces

- *Alamo* by Tony Rosenthal (Astor Place)
- *Reclining Figure* by Henry Moore (Lincoln Center)
- *Romeo and Juliet* by Milton Hebald (Delacorte Theater in Central Park)
- *The Sphere* by Fritz Koenig (Battery Park City at Bowling Green)
- Untitled series by Tom Otterness (A, C, E 14th St subway station)

Art, initiated by the then-mayor Edward Koch in 1982, requires that 1% of the city's budget for construction projects be spent on integrating art into the design or archi-tecture of new facilities. Since its inception there have been about 200 such projects at public schools, libraries, parks and police stations – even a Marine Transfer Station for garbage, located at 59th St and the Hudson River, got the artist's touch when Stephen Antanakos souped it up in 1990 with a neon-light installation that glows pink and green and blue when the sun sets each evening. Other Percent for Art projects include Valerie Jaudon's brick and granite mosaic at Manhattan's police headquarters, Kit-Yin Snyder's wire mesh *Judgment* piece at the White St Detention Center, and Jorge Luis Rodriguez bright orange steel flower in the East Harlem Artpark at Sylvan Place and E 120th St.

The Public Art Fund, meanwhile, is a nonprofit organization dedicated to working with both established and emerging artists to present large-scale works to the public. The fund commissions new projects, works with museums to help expand outside of its gallery space (such as when it collaborates with the Whitney to place sculptures in Central Park as part of its Biennial), has open calls for innovative new works every year, and organizes a 'Tuesday Night Talks' lecture series about public art. To find up-to-date locations of commissioned works, visit www.publicart fund.org.

A failed program that has left many beautiful impressions on the city was the 'Creative Stations' project of the Metropolitan Transit Authority (MTA), which runs the subway system. Today you'll find remnants at a slew of stations – including a glass-wall and mural installation at the 28th St stop on the 6 line; colorful tile mosaics at the Bowling Green 4, 5 station; and the sonic, synthesized-music piece hanging overhead at the 34th St N, R platform.

Come February 2005, the city will be treated to one of the most large-scale public art shows yet: *The Gates* by Christo and Jeanne-Claude, known for wrapping Berlin's Reichstag in silvery plastic and planting 3100 umbrellas across California and Japan. The duo will be draping the pathways of Central Park with one million feet of saffron cloth, creating 7500 billowy gateways for pedestrians and joggers to pass beneath. The privately funded project, set to last some 10 weeks, has been controversial, both for commercializing the park and for the basic disturbance it will create. But the artists, who have been trying to secure permission for the display since 1979, finally gained approval from the current administration – mainly because of the $3 million er, donation, to the Central Park Conservancy.

For some excellent, permanent examples of public artwork, check out the whimsical bronze sculptures of Tom Otterness, whose *Real World* exhibit in Battery Park and untitled installation in the 14th St subway station on the A, C, E line features lovable, cartoonish characters that have gotten chuckles out of the most jaded New Yorkers. Also in Battery Park is *The Sphere*, by Fritz Koenig, moved here from the World Trade Center as a memorial piece after it sustained damage during the September 11 attacks (see p80).

In other parts of town, be sure to check out Tony Rosenthal's legendary cube sculpture, *Alamo,* on Astor Place (which spins if you turn it with some muscle), Henry Moore's *Reclining Figure* and reflecting pool at Lincoln Center, and Milton Hebald's dramatic *The Tempest* and *Romeo and Juliet* pieces at the Delacorte Theater in Central

Art gallery, Soho

Park. The Socrates Sculpture Park in Long Island City, Queens, with permanent, massive sculptures by Mark di Suvero and a constant rotation of works by visiting artists, is quite a find for fans of outdoor art. Spend an afternoon climbing on pieces, picnicking in their shadows and gazing out over the East River and the east side of Manhattan just across it.

CINEMA & TV

As both a subject and venue, New York has a long and storied life in television and the movies. At least a dozen films are in production here at any given time, while 20 primetime TV shows (*Law & Order, Without a Trace, Queer Eye for the Straight Guy*) are regularly produced here, along with 40 daytime and late-night shows (*All My Children, The Today Show, Saturday Night Live*) and about 30 cable shows (*The Sopranos, Chapelle's Show, Inside the Actors Studio*). And while some are set here only in theory and filmed in LA studios (*Seinfeld, Friends* and *Mad About You*, for example, all in reruns), they've definitely added to the city's allure. And, nestled in with the endless array of TV stations with homes here – NBC, ABC, CNN, the local NY1 news network, and the Food Network and Oxygen Media, both housed in the Chelsea Market – are now a couple of major film companies, including New Line Cinema (a division of Time Warner), New Yorker Films, and Miramax and Tribeca Productions (owned by Robert DeNiro), both housed in the 14-year-old Tribeca Film Center, proving that the entire industry, at least, is not confined to Hollywood. Local cable shows (there are two cable carriers, Time Warner and Cablevision) are popular forms of entertainment, with the public-access Manhattan Neighborhood Network (MNN) channel providing constant cultural programming and just plain weird shows, as the station grants airtime to just about any local resident who wants it. The New York Metro channel (Cablevision 60, Time Warner 70), part of *New York* magazine, features slick NYC-centric programming, including fashion, entertainment, reality and talk shows.

The Mayor's Office of Film, Theater & Broadcasting (MOFTB) has definitely been a driving force behind the success of the local industry – worth more than $5 billion and 75,000 city jobs. As a result of MOFTB's efforts – through strong incentives which

NYC on Film

- *Angels in America* (2003) Directed by Mike Nichols. Starring Al Pacino, Meryl Streep, Jeffrey Wright. This exquisite, HBO-movie version of Tony Kushner's Broadway play recalls 1985 Manhattan: relationships are on the brink, AIDS is out of control and a closeted Roy Cohn does nothing about it – but fall ill himself – as part of the Reagan administration.
- *Annie Hall* (1977) Directed by Woody Allen. Starring Woody Allen and Diane Keaton. It's what many fans would call *the* New York film of all time – as well as Allen's best. He plays neurotic Jewish New York comedian Alvy Singer, who falls for Keaton's ditzy, WASP-y Annie Hall.
- *Basketball Diaries* (1995) Directed by Scot Kalvert. Starring Leonardo DiCaprio and Lorraine Bracco. A baby-faced DiCaprio plays writer Jim Carroll in this mesmerizing, autobiographical tale of heroin addiction that's set in the East Village.
- *Big* (1988) Directed by Penny Marshall. Starring Tom Hanks and Elizabeth Perkins. A seriously heartwarming tale of a little boy who gets his wish to be big, Hanks plays the bogus grown-up who becomes an executive at a toy company, creating wonderful scenes in loft apartments, FAO Schwartz, glitzy restaurants and other hallmarks of 1980s NYC.
- *Chasing Amy* (1997) Directed by Kevin Smith. Starring Ben Affleck and Joey Lauren Adams. Affleck's breakout film, though far from a cinematic masterpiece, put Meow Mix and other aspects of Manhattan lesbian life on the map.
- *Crossing Delancey* (1988) Directed by Joan Micklin Silver. Starring Amy Irving and Peter Riegert. Isabelle is set up with Sam the pickle man by her grandmother in a romantic comedy showing the Lower East Side before the trendies moved in.
- *Do the Right Thing* (1989) Directed by Spike Lee. Starring Ossie Davis, Danny Aiello and Ruby Dee. Spike Lee's breakout film, this quintessential New York story of racial tensions that reach the boiling point in an Italian and black neighborhood of Brooklyn should be required viewing.
- *Fatal Attraction* (1987) Directed by Adrian Lyne. Starring Michael Douglas, Glenn Close and Anne Archer. This psycho thriller is about a happily married man whose one-night stand turns into a series of run-ins with his trick-turned-stalker. Catch great glimpses of the pregentrification Meatpacking District (and that famous lift scene).
- *The French Connection* (1971) Directed by William Friedkin. Starring Gene Hackman. This crime thriller about an on-the-edge cop tracking the leaders of an elusive heroin syndicate features one of the greatest filmed car chases ever, under the elevated subway tracks in Queens. Look out for that baby carriage.
- *Kids* (1995) Directed by Larry Clark. Starring Leo Fitzpatrick, Chloë Sevigny and Rosario Dawson. Shot in documentary style and starring a bunch of then-unknowns, this chilling tale of privileged Manhattan kids growing up with no rules tackles sexual promiscuity, drugs and AIDS.
- *Manhattan* (1979) Directed by Woody Allen. Starring Woody Allen, Diane Keaton and Mariel Hemingway. A divorced New Yorker dating a high-school student (the adorable, baby-voiced Hemingway) falls for his best friend's mistress in what is essentially a love letter to NYC.
- *Midnight Cowboy* (1969) Directed by John Schlesinger. Starring Dustin Hoffman and Jon Voight. A Best Picture Oscar-winner despite an X-rating for its provocative (for then) content on the sordid life of big-city hustlers, this drama now stands as a time capsule for a bygone Times Square.
- *Moscow on the Hudson* (1984) Directed by Paul Mazursky. Starring Robin Williams and Maria Conchita Alonso. When a Russian musician defects in Bloomingdale's, he finds adjusting to life in the big city more difficult than he could have imagined. It's a great look at local immigration, despite its Hollywood style.
- *On the Town* (1949) Directed by Stanley Donen and Gene Kelly. Starring Gene Kelly, Frank Sinatra and Ann Miller. 'The Bronx is up and the Battery down. New York, New York: it's a wonderful town!' This campy, classic musical follows the romantic adventures of three sailors let loose in the Big Apple on a 24-hour pass.
- *Paris Is Burning* (1990) Directed by Jennie Livingston. This stunning documentary captures the subculture of drag balls, and of the families that are formed among many underclass drag queens of color. Madonna may have sung 'Vogue,' but she learned what it meant from these divas.
- *Party Girl* (1995) Directed by Daisy von Scherler Mayer. Starring Parker Posey, Anthony DeSando and Guillermo Diaz. Mary is a fabulous fag-hag and club kid who gets some down-to-earth lessons when she gets a job as a librarian.
- *Saturday Night Fever* (1977) Directed by John Badham. Starring John Travolta and Karen Lynn Gorney. Travolta is the hottest thing in bell-bottoms in this tale of a streetwise Brooklyn kid who becomes king of the dance floor.
- *Summer of Sam* (1999) Directed by Spike Lee. Starring John Leguizamo, Mira Sorvino and Jennifer Esposito. One of Spike Lee's best, the sordid tale puts the city's summer of 1977 in historical context by weaving together the Son of Sam murders, the blackout, racial tensions and the misadventures of one disco-dancing Brooklyn couple.
- *Taxi Driver* (1976) Directed by Martin Scorsese. Starring Robert DeNiro, Cybill Shepherd and Jodie Foster. DeNiro is a mentally unstable Vietnam war vet whose urges to lash out are heightened by the high tensions of the city. It's a funny, depressing, brilliant classic that's a potent reminder of how much grittier this place used to be.
- *You've Got Mail* (1998) Directed by Nora Ephron. Starring Tom Hanks and Meg Ryan. A peek into life on the Upper West Side, this romantic comedy follows the online love of two people who don't realize they are business enemies, as one runs an indie bookstore and the other runs the big bad chain store that will drive it out of business.

Live From New York...

Since 1977, *Saturday Night Live* (*SNL*) has been the highest rated late-night show in America. The incredibly popular variety show – a pastiche of comedy sketches, commercial parodies, fake news, live-music performances and a different special guest star each week – first went on the air in 1975, when Johnny Carson asked NBC to stop airing reruns of his *Tonight Show* on Saturday nights. Producers created *SNL* to fill the gap and, as its 30th anniversary nears, it's clear that no-one's tiring of its surefire formula.

Not long after the show began, *SNL* gained a reputation as being the launching pad for the funniest comedians in the country. Indeed, countless comedic stars got their start on the series, and longtime fans of the show still long for its first decade – widely agreed to have been the glory years – when now-legends Gilda Radner, Dan Akroyd, John Belushi, Chevy Chase, Jane Curtin and Steve Martin ruled. The '80s ushered in some ups and downs for the series, when writing was weak but stars such as Eddie Murphy and Joe Piscopo carried it. Murphy was seen as the savior, but got famous quickly and left; celebrities began to join the cast at this point, namely Billy Crystal and Martin Short, but critics complained that it still wasn't funny enough. Finally, by about 1985, *SNL*'s original producer Lorne Michaels returned, making changes that resurrected the comedy: he hired new writers and a new cast, replacing Robert Downey Jr and Anthony Quaid with Dana Carvey, Phil Hartman, Kevin Nealon, Chris Farley, Chris Rock and Mike Myers, and it rose to heights not seen since the beginning. It did, of course, falter again, getting low ratings in the mid-'90s, despite the presence of Janeane Garafalo and Adam Sandler; some of this was because of new competition from Fox's *Mad TV*.

In addition to its frequent ups and downs from critics and viewers, the show has suffered through plenty of its own stars' tragic deaths: Gilda Radner of cancer, John Belushi and Chris Farley of ODs, Phil Hartman of murder by his own wife, who committed suicide after shooting him. And if a show can survive such human traumas, it can survive anything. Today it's still immensely popular, anchored by the comedic skills of Tina Fey, Fred Armisen, Jimmy Fallon, Rachel Dratch and Will Forte.

include free permits, free locations, free police assistance, and zero sales tax on production consumables – New York City is currently ranked as the second-largest production center in the country, according to a recent study by the US Department of Commerce. Spend just a little time in this city and you will most likely see the evidence of this for yourself, as it's not uncommon to happen upon on-location shoots, which often close down city blocks, blast them with floodlights at night and surround them with massive trucks and bossy assistants who'll stop you in your tracks if you try to walk through the filming area – much to the dismay of the locals, who are often barred from even going home to make dinner after a long day of work until the scene-in-session has ended!

As a showcase for film, New York is a star as well. There have been quite a few new movie theaters built over the past several years, most with stadium seating, wide screens and other glamorous amenities, such as gourmet snack stands. And the number of annual film festivals held here throughout the year just keeps rising: the number currently stands at around 30, including Dance on Camera (January), Jewish Film Festival (January), New York Film Festival (January), African-American Women in Film Festival (March), Williamsburg Film Festival (March), Tribeca Film Festival (May), Lesbian & Gay Film Festival (June) and the Human Rights Watch Film Festival (June).

New York is home to some of the top film schools in the country – NYU's Tisch Film School, the New York Film Academy, the School of Visual Arts, Columbia University and the New School – and the students get great support from MOFTB, which offers free film permits to students for use of any public property. But you don't have to be a student to learn, as plenty of museums – namely the **American Museum of the Moving Image** (p143) in Astoria, Queens, and the **Museum of Television & Radio** (p114) – serve as major showcases for screenings and seminars about productions both past and present.

Finally, you can always go and get a glimpse of locations made famous from appearances in TV shows and movies, from the Dakota building (Central Park West and 72nd St), the apartment building used in the classic thriller *Rosemary's Baby*, to Tom's Diner (Broadway and 112th St), the facade of which was used regularly in *Seinfeld*. The best way to find all the spots you want to see is to take a movie- or TV-location guided tour; try **Kenny Kramer**, the real-life inspiration for the *Seinfeld* character, who offers fun three-hour tours past major sites from the TV, or **On Location Tours**, which takes you to spots where your favorite TV shows were filmed, including *Sex and the City, Sopranos, Friends* and more. (See p72 for tour information.)

Architecture

Architecture Joyce Mendelsohn

Architecturally speaking, there's never been a more exciting time to be in New York. Buildings are going up like crazy, many by well-known international architects, such as France's Christian Portzamparc and Britain's Sir Norman Foster. Boring glass-box office buildings are old news, overpowered by new crystalline towers with experimental geometric forms and fragmented facades. Stylish apartment buildings up by American architects Philip Johnson and Michael Graves are sprouting. A competition for the proposed Olympic Village in Queens (see 2012 or Bust, p18) brought submissions from architects worldwide. Redevelopment for the **World Trade Center site** (p81) envisions dramatic office towers and a new 24-hour neighborhood with housing, shops, parks and cultural facilities.

New York's neighborhoods are rejuvenating as older, deteriorating areas across the city such as Harlem, Carroll Gardens in Brooklyn and Mott Haven in the Bronx are sparking interest, and their historic housing is being restored to earlier glory days. Ever since New York City enacted the Landmarks Law in 1965, grass-roots preservationists have been battling big-time developers with some success, as city planners try to keep a balance between preservation and progress and ordinary New Yorkers keep a watchful eye on their own turf.

DUTCH DOMESTICITY
None of the 17th-century stepped-gable buildings from New Amsterdam are left but a few Dutch Colonial farmhouses survive and are open to view. The Pieter Claesen **Wyckoff House** (☎ 718-629-5400; 5816 Clarendon Rd; admission free; ☺ 10am-4pm Tue-Sun), in Brooklyn, is the oldest house in the city. Its first section, constructed in 1652, is easily recognized by the shingled exterior and peaked roof with flaring eaves. Built later, but in a similar style, the **Dyckman House** (p133), 1785, is Manhattan's last surviving farmhouse.

GEORGIAN GENTILITY
British rule brought buildings popular during the reign of the four English Hanoverian kings, Georges I–IV, 1714–1830. They were rectangular and symmetrical with hipped roofs, tall end chimneys and, sometimes, topped with a cupola. English originals were made of fine stone; the transplants built of brick or wood. A model of the British City Hall, erected in 1703 but later demolished, is displayed at **Federal Hall National Memorial** (p76). **Fraunces Tavern** (p76), 1907, imitates the original pub where George Washington said goodbye to his officers.

Morris-Jumel Mansion (p133), 1765, the oldest house in Manhattan, is one of the best built in Colonial America. The white-painted, clapboard and shingled mansion boasts a two-story colonnade and exquisite entrance. **St Paul's Chapel** (p81), 1766–94, is a copy of St Martin-in-the-Fields in London, but built of Manhattan fieldstone and brownstone. French architect Pierre L'Enfant designed the high altar, crowned by a golden sunburst, in the sanctuary.

Top Five New Additions
- **American Folk Art Museum** (p114) An eight-story fragmented facade of alloyed bronze panels of different sizes and shapes, playing on textures and light, by the husband-and-wife architectural team of Tod Williams and Billie Tsien.
- **Maritime Hotel** (p297) A gleaming white, former Maritime Union headquarters with 120 porthole windows, decked out as a chic hotel, passing for a cruise ship.
- **Prada Soho** (p85) Dutch architect Rem Koolhaas reinventing the shopping experience in a high-tech space with stunning visual effects and a round lift.
- **Rose Center** (p120) Replacing the old Planetarium at the American Museum of Natural History is this seven-story-tall glass cube that its architect, James Stewart Polshek, calls 'the cosmic cathedral.' It encloses a giant aluminum-clad sphere.
- **Time Warner Center** (p111) Two huge crystalline glass towers, rising from a six-story curved base, by David Childs/Skidmore, Owings & Merrill, incorporating the world's largest cable-net glass wall.

FEDERAL FINERY

After the Revolutionary War, heavy solid forms of the Georgian period were replaced by refined Federal architecture of the new republic, based on designs popularized by the Adam brothers, Scottish architects inspired by the delicate details of ancient Roman architecture.

Diminutive **City Hall** (p78), 1812, owes its French form to émigré architect Joseph Francois Mangin and its Federal detailing to American-born John McComb Jr. Originally faced with white marble, the rear was covered in brownstone to cut costs. The interior contains an airy rotunda and curved cantilevered stairway. **Gracie Mansion** (p123), 1799, the official residence of the mayor since 1942, was built as a country villa. The cream-colored frame house features Chinese Chippendale railings, a fanlight doorway with leaded glass sidelights and a porch that runs along the length of its river-view facade. The James Watson House, converted to the **Shrine of the Blessed Elizabeth Seton** (p80), 1792 and 1806, is the sole survivor of a row of elegant redbrick houses. The newer section has a two-story colonnade of slender Ionic columns and Adam touches.

You can recognize Federal row houses by their small size, distinctive Flemish bond (alternating long and short bricks), peaked roofs with dormer windows, and decorative doorways. **Harrison Houses** (p83), 1796–1820, a row of nine modest dwellings, were restored and grouped together. The **Merchant's House** (p93), 1832, combines a late Federal exterior with Greek Revival ironwork and interior ornament. It's the only home in the city preserved intact from the 19th century and containing original furnishings.

Who to Know?

- **Frederick Law Olmsted & Calvert Vaux** Creators of Central Park in the 1870s, they took 843 acres of wasteland and transformed them into an oasis of natural beauty.
- **McKim Mead & White** Pre-eminent 19th-century architects, their designs of mansions, private clubs, churches and monuments brought European splendor to New York.
- **The Rockefellers** Their big bucks funded Rockefeller Center, Lincoln Center, the Museum of Modern Art and the site of the United Nations.
- **Skidmore, Owings & Merrill** A leading architectural firm, specializing in office towers, their know-how in building technology and design has changed the skyline of the city.
- **Donald Trump** New Yorkers roll their eyes at his glitzy buildings while foreign investors outbid each other to buy into his empire.

GREEK-REVIVAL RELICS

Greek fever spread through the US in the 1820s as Americans linked the populist presidency of Andrew Jackson with ancient Greek democracy. Architects and builders who had never stepped foot in Greece cribbed designs from pattern books. Churches and public buildings dressed up like Greek temples with tall columns supporting a horizontal entablature and a Classical pediment. Two of the best are still standing. The gray granite **St Peter's Church** (Map pp380-1), 1838, replaces the first Roman Catholic church in the city, erected in 1785 and destroyed by fire. The white marble **Federal Hall National Memorial** (p76), 1842, originally the US Custom House, is now a museum. Narrow redbrick row houses sported takeoffs of ancient Greek architectural elements and ornament. The **Row** (Map pp382-5) of 13 Greek Revival homes on the north side of Washington Square in Greenwich Village, built in 1833 for New York's most fashionable families, is considered the city's finest 19th-century block front.

GOTHIC GLORIES

In the 1840s, pagan Greek Revival was abandoned for the spiritual Gothic, uplifting toward the heavens, echoing English and French church architecture of the late Middle Ages. Churches were built with advanced vaulting techniques supported by buttresses, filled with colored light shining through stained-glass windows, punctuated by pointed-arch windows and doors, spouting gargoyles and topped by ornamented towers and spires.

Richard Upjohn jump-started the Gothic Revival in New York with his **Church of the Ascension** (Map pp382-5), 1841, a square-towered English country church faced in brownstone. Architect Stanford White gathered a group of artists in 1888 to redecorate the interior with paintings, sculptures and stained-glass windows. Upjohn's next project, **Trinity Church** (p77), 1842, also brownstone, used Gothic forms and ornament but 'modern' building techniques, adding fake buttresses and a plaster ceiling. James Renwick Jr designed two of the city's stunning churches. **Grace Church** (p93), 1846, features a pointed French Gothic spire, splendid stained-glass rose window and lacy stonework. **St Patrick's Cathedral** (p116), 1878, inspired by Cologne Cathedral, has a central gable flanked by identical spires, and plenty of ornament. An enduring icon of the city, the **Brooklyn Bridge** (p79), 1883, with its great stone Gothic towers and webbing of steel cables, was designed by Prussian engineer John Roebling.

ITALIANATE IMPERIALISTS

In the middle of the 19th century, a new style invaded New York, evoking connections with great wealth and power, based on imposing palazzi of the Italian Renaissance. McKim Mead & White designed private hangouts fit for the Medici, such as the **Metropolitan Club** (Map pp389-91), 1894, and the **University Club** (Map pp386-8), 1899.

AT Stewart Store (Map pp380-1), 1846 with additions to 1884, now a municipal building, was the first department store in America and the first Italianate commercial building in the city. It's faced in white marble with cast-iron columns. New York County Courthouse, known as **Tweed Courthouse** (p154), 1881, was inspired by the US Capitol in Washington, DC. A grand staircase leads to a dazzling interior, occupied by the Department of Education and closed to the public.

Villard Houses (Map pp386-8), 1884, by McKim Mead & White and modeled after the Cancelleria in Rome, were six splendid brownstone mansions for the super-rich, grouped around a courtyard, appearing as a unified palazzo. They are now part of the Palace Hotel; some of the exquisite rooms, designed by Stanford White and his artist friends, are intact in Le Cirque 2000 restaurant. Ordinary families moved into rows of Italianate brownstones, forming chocolate-coated streetscapes in neighborhoods such as Chelsea and Murray Hill.

BEAUX-ARTS BEAUTIES

By the start of the 20th century, somber brownstone was out. Gleaming white was the newest fashion, reflecting the impact of the 1893 Chicago World's Fair, a make-believe city created by top American architects trained at Paris' Ecole des Beaux-Arts. Public buildings across America were disguised as palaces loaded down with rich materials, lush ornament and sculpture. **Grand Central Terminal** (p112), 1913, engineering by Reed & Stem, facade and interior by Warren and Wetmore, showcases a giant clock and sculptural grouping by Jules Coutan. The breathtaking concourse is topped by a high vaulted ceiling covered with a zodiac mural by Paul Helleu. Allegorical sculptural figures decorate the facade of the **New York Public Library** (p113), 1911, by Carrere & Hastings. Two marble lions guarding the steps, nicknamed Patience and Fortitude, added in 1920 are by Edward Clark Potter. The monumental **US Custom House** (p77), 1907, now the Museum of the American Indian, by Cass Gilbert is a homage to trade. Figures on the massive attic portray mercantile nations. Sculptural groups on ground level by Daniel Chester French represent the Four Continents. The **Metropolitan Museum of Art** (p123) was built in several stages, the Fifth Ave facade in 1902 by Richard Morris Hunt and 1926 side wings by McKim Mead & White. Three giant Roman arches alternate with paired Corinthian columns, topped with uncut blocks of stone, originally planned as massive sculptures.

SOARING SKYSCRAPERS
Cast-Iron Buildings

Before steel-frame skyscrapers there were cast-iron buildings, pioneering advances in building technology, but with facades chosen from stock books. At first, iron fronts were attached to conventional brick load-bearing outer walls. Later, buildings evolved as primitive cages with interior iron framing and columns. The Venetian-style, cast-iron **Haughwout Building** (p85), 1856, holds the first passenger elevator installed in the US. Soho, once manufacturing, now million-dollar loft apartments and must-have shopping, flaunts the largest concentration of cast-iron buildings in the world.

Eclectic Office Buildings

After the elevator was perfected by Elisha Otis in 1853 and steel-frame construction invented in Chicago in 1885 by William Le Baron Jenney, skyscrapers shot up. The problem for architects was how to cover those steel skeletons; the answer was to suit them up in historic clothing. The 21-story **Flatiron Building** (p107), 1902, by Daniel Burnham, owes its distinctive shape to the triangular site. A wavy midsection is clad in white terra-cotta, decorated with Renaissance ornament. Cass Gilbert, architect of the **Woolworth Building** (Map pp380-1), 1913, modeled his designs on the 1830s Houses of Parliament in London and emphasized the upward thrust of his office tower with continuous vertical rows of windows. The building is covered with cream-colored terra-cotta and Gothic ornament. Its ornate lobby is now off-limits to visitors.

Art Deco

In the 1930s, architects turned away from history, creating unique buildings, configured with setbacks, required by new zoning laws, and decorated with original ornament. The **Chanin Building** (Map pp386-8), 1929, by Sloan & Robertson, took the lead with its wedding-cake silhouette, exterior decoration of exotic plant forms and sea life, and singular lobby. The **Chrysler Building** (p111), 1930, by William Van Alen, a corporate headquarters for an auto maker, rises with setbacks to a tower with a radiant stainless steel crown of sunbursts. Silver radiator hood caps jut out like gargoyles and cars race in the brickwork. The lobby glows with colorful marble and inlaid wood, its ceiling covered with a mural celebrating technological progress. The **Empire State Building** (p109), 1931, by Shreve, Lamb & Harmon, was conceived as the world's tallest and planned for maximum amount of rental space. The clean lines of the building need little ornament. Soaring from a series of setbacks, the tower pierces the sky with a silver mast.

International Style

Architects Mies van der Rohe, Walter Gropius and Marcel Breuer, who left Europe in the early 1930s, brought the vision and know-how of the avant-garde German Bauhaus to America. Architecture that rejected the past, it imagined future cities of functional glass towers. **United Nations** (p113), 1947–52, was the combined effort of many architects: Swiss-born Le Corbusier, Brazil's Oscar Niemeyer, Sweden's Sven Markelius and reps from 10 other countries, co-ordinated by America's Wallace K Harrison. The angular slab of the Secretariat, New York's first building with all glass walls, looms over the ski-slope curve of the General Assembly. **Lever House** (Map pp386-8), 1953, by Gordon Bunshaft/Skidmore, Owings & Merrill, composed

Architecture – Soaring Skyscrapers

Top Five in the Outer Boroughs

- **Brooklyn Bridge** (p79), 1883. A masterpiece of engineering and art with massive granite towers linked by a web of supporting steel cables. The supreme achievement of the Roebling family: John, son Washington and his wife, Emily. The pedestrian promenade offers the city's best photo-op.
- **Enid A Haupt Conservatory** (p148), 1902. In the New York Botanical Garden is this, the largest Victorian glass house in America. By William R Cobb, it is modeled after Palm House in Kew Gardens, outside of London.
- **Green-Wood Cemetery Gate** (p138), 1865. Don't let the location spook you. The work of Richard Upjohn, this is a spectacular Gothic Revival brownstone entranceway, with elaborately ornamented gables and towers and carvings of scenes of death and resurrection.
- **Sailor's Snug Harbor** (p150) An outstanding collection of Greek Revival buildings, constructed in the mid-19th century as a housing complex for poor, elderly seaman and now a cultural center.
- **TWA Flight Center** at JFK International Airport (p337), 1962. The great Finnish modernist architect Eero Saarinen designed this soaring concrete and glass terminal with curvilinear forms that suggest flight.

Rebuilding Lower Manhattan

After the initial shock of September 11, planning began to turn the horrific rubble-strewn 16-acre World Trade Center (WTC) site into a place to honor the victims and restore 10 million square feet of office space. Major players are the New York and New Jersey Port Authority, who built the WTC, and developer Larry Silverstein, who leased the twin towers for 99 years, just six weeks before the terrorist attacks. Adding to the mix are groups representing families of the dead and rescue workers, and anyone with opinions about skyscraper design, air quality and transportation. The Lower Manhattan Development Corporation (LMDC), coordinating the rebuilding, sponsored forums, opening the planning process to public debate.

After the public turned thumbs down in the summer of 2002 to six boring plans commissioned by LMDC, a worldwide competition was held for a master plan that would preserve the footprints of the towers, include a memorial, create a bold new skyline and replace lost office space. The winning proposal, chosen from 406 entries, was by Daniel Libeskind, an internationally acclaimed architect known for the spiritual qualities of his buildings, who was born in Poland to Holocaust survivors and grew up in the Bronx. His plan created a memorial space for meditation 70ft into the bedrock, retaining the concrete walls, designed to hold back the Hudson River, that withstood the attacks. A 1776ft-high spire, topped by gardens, would rise ringed by four high towers and two cultural centers with adjacent parks. As soon as the applause died down, the makeovers began. The Port Authority nixed 70ft because it interfered with plans for parking, but did allow 30ft below ground. The developer brought in superstar skyscraper architect David Childs to redesign the spire, dubbed Freedom Tower, and then lost an insurance claim that left him with prospects of low-rise retail stores instead of surrounding towers.

The winner of the memorial competition, which attracted 5201 entries worldwide, was 34-year-old architect Michael Arad, who worked for the New York City Housing Authority. His minimalist concept was based entirely on street level with two voids of pools with cascading waters, marking the footprints of the twin towers, and a few trees. That plan was altered with lusher plantings, designed by landscape architect Peter Walker, and the addition of an underground memorial center, approached down a ramp, exposing the concrete walls. The space will be filled with artifacts recovered from the site and a stone container holding the unidentified remains of victims of the attacks.

Work is moving along at the site and trains are running again on new tracks. A temporary station is to be replaced by a spectacular glass and steel transportation hub, designed by Spanish architect Santiago Calatrava, with glass wings and a retractable cathedral-like roof. Planners estimate rebuilding the entire WTC site by 2011 with a price tag of $9 billion.

of a green glass tower rising from a horizontal slab on freestanding columns above an open courtyard, appears to float over Park Avenue. The **Seagram Building** (Map pp386-8), 1958, designed by Mies van der Rohe, a stunning amber glass and bronze slab, is set on an open plaza. Van der Rohe, given an unlimited budget, produced a masterpiece of the International Style. Cheaper glass towers that followed didn't measure up.

Postmodern

Rebelling against glass boxes, architects in the 1980s had a brief fling with vintage styles. Philip Johnson, who designed the pink granite AT&T Headquarters, now **Sony** (Map pp386-8), 1984, borrowed from three eras, producing a giant Romanesque Revival base and Chicago-skyscraper–style midsection, crowned by a neo-Georgian pediment. Most people shrugged off this phase and architecture continued to move forward with hardly a backward glance.

THE ARCHITECTURAL SCENE TODAY

Shaking off its notorious reputation for resisting architectural innovation, New York's new buildings are cutting edge and computer generated, catching the beat of the 21st century. Architects are global winners; their latest creations are top notch, such as Japan's Yoshio Taniguchi's expansion of the **Museum of Modern Art** (p115) and Fumihiko Maki's in-the-works addition to the **United Nations** (p113). Coming soon will be the dramatic New York Times Tower by Italy's Renzo Piano, and in the dream stage is Frank Gehry's stadium (see New Brooklyn?, p135) for downtown Brooklyn. The City Planning Department's proposals for rezoning dying manufacturing districts for mixed use, outside of the city's overbuilt core, will open timeworn neighborhoods for new housing and commercial development. Understandably, some New Yorkers are not happy about losing their old way of life and the struggle continues between holding on to the past and making way for the future.

Food

Food

HISTORY

Eating out in New York City is an event that rivals going to the opera, theater or symphony in its magnitude. It's a serious situation, an evening in itself, and a complete form of entertainment. And while it hasn't always been this way, it's a tradition that began more than 175 years ago.

Delmonico's, America's very first restaurant, was a lavish eatery that opened in Lower Manhattan in 1827, starting out as a confectioner's shop and quickly evolving into a gathering spot for high society. It's where a 100-page menu listed items such as Lobster Newburg and Baked Alaska (both created here) in both French and English, and featured a massive wine cellar that held 16,000 bottles. Delmonico's moved locations several times, once after being destroyed in the Great Fire of 1835, and wound up on the corner of Fifth Ave and 44th St. But in 1923 it eventually closed its doors – a victim of the Prohibition – and was not reopened again until 1999, as a Lower Manhattan steakhouse. But, in its early era, Delmonico's was the inspiration for other high-class restaurants – places such as Café Martin, Sherry's and the **Waldorf-Astoria** (p302), where the European foods of the wealthy set, such as boiled salmon, soufflés, mutton chops and charlotte russe, appeared on menus.

Everyday New Yorkers, meanwhile, got their eating-out fixes at either cheap restaurants or pushcarts (25,000 of them by 1900), which, by the turn of the century, proffered foods from all over the world – not surprising for a city that served as a major port for both immigrants and global commodities. Oyster houses, cafeterias, kosher delis, the first hot-dog vendors and pizzerias (the first, **Lombardi's**, opened in 1905; p181) were everywhere, as were Chinese and German restaurants, all reflecting the ethnic makeup of the time. Lobster houses were also popular – a beloved blend of high-class and down-to-earth dining, as they were cheaper, more democratic and big with folks who could afford a fancier scene but were lured by the idea of 'slumming.'

While the foreign cuisines served mostly the immigrant communities who were used to such strange foods, this was the beginning of today's thriving global foodie obsession, in which New Yorkers cannot wait to try the latest *dosas* (thin rice crepes rolled around various masala-spiced fillings, such as potatoes with peas) from India or *arepas* (thick corn cakes topped with melted cheese) from Colombia. And, while the talked-about 'scene' might have revolved around the high-class diners, a simultaneous trend was beginning with the proliferation of affordable dining spots. Today it's the cheap eats of Chinatown and the East Village which draw low-income food aficionados; then it was the Automats, dropping sandwiches out of vending machines (the last, on 42nd St, closed in 1991), cafeterias including the Child's chain, German spots offering 45¢ lunches, Irish pubs in Manhattan and 'penny restaurants' in Brooklyn – especially along the seashore of Coney Island.

Another major influence in the globalization of New York cuisine was the World's Fair of 1939. While it wasn't meant to be a food festival, nearly every country present took it as a chance to show off its national specialties and introduce locals to a world of flavors. And many of the foreign-food purveyors at the fair stayed behind to run restaurants, including the French Le Pavillon, which started the ongoing legacy of French food as a standard here. Also introduced were treats from Japan, Turkey and Belgium. After this period and until the '60s, Greek and Middle Eastern restaurants sprang up all over Greenwich Village, bringing even more tastes to the middle and working classes. French food dominated the upscale scene, with new spots including La Cote Basque and La Grenouille, as well as a new wave of American eateries, such as the Four Seasons and '21' Club, which served luscious cuts of beef.

It was during this time that one man, James Beard, revolutionized the idea of cuisine in America – and he did it from his home base, New York City. Starting out by running a small food shop here, Hors d'Oeuvre Inc, in 1937, Beard eventually wrote a slew of cookbooks, including *Paris Cuisine* and *Fowl and Game Cookery*, appeared on TV's first cooking show, and established the James Beard Cooking School, through which he taught the gospel of good food prepared with fresh and wholesome American ingredients. After his death in 1985, Julia Child had the idea to preserve his Greenwich Village brownstone as the James Beard Foundation – North America's only historical culinary center, offering educational programs, meals from great chefs, and annual awards to the biggest players in the industry.

CULTURE

Unlike California or the South or even the Southwest, New York never really gets referred to as having one defining cuisine. Try asking for some 'New York food,' for example, and you could wind up getting anything from a hot dog or a slice of pizza to a Chinese banquet or some snapper with chestnuts and juniper berries from local celebrity chef Wylie Dufresne. Cuisine here is global by definition, constantly evolving by its very nature. This is a town with room for every taste and budget, every whim and every diet. But, while the healthy, organic and veggie landscape has been expanded and revolutionized in recent years (see p51), the dining-out world (at least on the high end of the scale) is skewed much more toward exotic excess – with the new wave of celebrity chefs churning out all manner of duck, pork belly, beef cheek, foie gras, lamb loin, venison and rabbit-sausage concoctions.

Five-star chefs of note – either local, national or both – abound. The most prominent include Mario Batali (of the Babbo empire), David Bouley (of the French Danube, and **Bouley** p173), Daniel Boulud (of DB Bistro Moderne, Café Boulud, and **Daniel**, p200), Tom Colicchio (eclectic Craft, and **Gramercy Tavern**, p184), Wylie Dufresne (of the eclectic 71 Clinton Fresh Food and **WD 50**, p178, both on the Lower East Side) and Thomas Keller (of the new French-influenced American **Per Se**, p195, in the Time Warner Center). In the past several years they have all had a major part in transforming the New York dining scene into a high-profile whirlwind of steep prices, celebrities, excruciatingly long waits for reservations and, of course, awe-inspiring food. In 2004 the James Beard Awards team duly noted their accomplishments, as chefs from New York City dominated the year's list of nominees – including those in the top three categories of Best New Restaurant, Most Outstanding Restaurant and Best Chef.

The frenzy has made eating out about much more than just the grub. It must be presented as a complete experience now – complete with sweeping designs, tantalizing lighting aesthetics and even physically cool menus – all adding up to a totally transporting ambience for diners. It's a necessity now, in a dining-out climate in which customers will clamor with fever pitch to get into the hottest new place (**Nobu**, p173, which hit its peak in the mid-'90s, was a perfect example), only to grow tired of it and yearn for the next new eatery in a matter of months. It all fuels the constant grand openings and neighborhood shifts; witness, for example, the recent blossoming of the Upper West Side as a dining destination, thanks to restaurateurs such as Tom Valenti, whose 'Cesca (p198) and Ouest (p199) transformed the 'hood into a place foodies could finally be proud of. The easily bored pattern, of course, also leads to monumental closures, which cause nostalgic pangs – but not for long. Recent casualties of changing tastes and rising rents have included: 12-year-old Grange Hall, a former speakeasy that served hearty fare on a quiet street in the West Village and became an instant classic; Lutece, a renowned French standby that served Manhattan's East Side for 43 years; and Gage and Tollner in Brooklyn, an old-school steakhouse with gaslight fixtures that had been in business since 1879. The local press all ran high-profile stories about the monumental closures, and long-time regulars moaned. But no-one swooped in to save the day at the last minute, and everyone has since moved on.

ETIQUETTE

Please don't use your cell phone at the table. Some restaurants have signs up about this rule, some don't. But as soon as you answer that annoying ring and start jabbering away, every single patron will wish the signs were there, and that's a promise. Also, have some respect for the wait staff; speaking politely, making unusual or last-minute requests with a 'please,' and signaling for a server silently, with a finger in the air (without hisses or whistles or 'hey, you!'), all work wonders. And be sure to leave a fair tip – 15% of the bill for average service, at least 20% for anything above that, and just a little bit less if it sucked. If there is a major slight or mistake on the part of the waiter or chef, a good restaurant will often comp a small part of your meal – a glass of wine, dessert, appetizers. Complaining politely, of course, ups these chances.

Making Reservations

To avoid disappointment, always assume that a reservation is necessary – especially on weekends, when it's almost certainly going to be the case. Cheap-eats places are the exception, as people move in and out quickly (not to mention the fact that there is probably a no-reservations policy). The hottest eateries in town require reservations, and many times you'll be told that there's nothing available for weeks; if you know way ahead of time that you want to be able to experience **WD 50** (p178) before you leave town, for example, reserve your table before you even get to town – or at least the second you arrive. However, as much as New Yorkers like to talk about how you'll *never* get into certain places, there's almost always a way to do it. One trick is to accept a reservation at a less-than-popular dining time – before 7pm or after 10:30pm – which is almost always available. Also, many hot spots have bars, and many of these bars have food service. Sure, it's not the same as getting lavish table service, but it's considered a cool way to experience a place. And getting a seat is rarely a problem.

HOW NEW YORKERS EAT

Table manners of locals here are pretty much the same as in the rest of the country: put the napkin on your lap and do the 'fork-shift' thing, using the fork in your left hand to anchor what you are cutting with the knife in your right, then shift the fork into the right to pick up what you've just cut (or visa versa if you're a leftie). It's cumbersome, it's colonial, it's American. But one way New Yorkers tend to distinguish themselves is by being a bit chopstick-obsessed; in Chinese, Japanese, Thai or any other sort of Asian restaurant – even in an eclectic restaurant in which you are eating an Asian dish – locals ask for chopsticks. It's part respect, part showing off, and it's pretty much the norm.

STAPLES & SPECIALTIES

Cuisines with the longest histories here include a range of tastes. Specialties from Italians and East European Jews, because these groups were among the earliest wave of immigrants, are integral parts of the city's food history; a good pastrami on rye (Jewish) and slice of pizza (Italian) are just a couple of the uncontested staples of New York eats. The Reuben, a grilled sandwich consisting of corned beef, sauerkraut, Swiss cheese and mustard on rye was invented in NYC in 1914, by Arnold Reuben at his now-defunct Reuben's sandwich shop; you can find the concoction on most deli menus today. Steakhouses, a tradition begun back before the World Fair's global influences, are the best places to go if you want to feel like you're eating in a long-passed era; **Peter Luger Steakhouse** (p204), in Williamsburg is among the best, most classic such institution in New York. But while 'New York steak' might mean something in every other part of the country (prime shell steak, rare), the term loses meaning here, where steakhouses specialize in forms from aged porterhouse to garlic-rubbed tenderloin. And then there's Chinese. Since the late 1800s, when chop suey is said to have been invented here to suit American tastes by the cooks of Chinese ambassador Li Chung Hang, who was visiting New York at the time, locals – especially Jews, who have a storied love affair with the food because it was available on Sunday, the Christian Sabbath – have embraced the cuisine. Though you can barely find chop suey on any New York menu these days, you can find more evolved versions of the country's food – usually Hunan or Szechuan versions – on practically every corner in Manhattan. 'Chinese' has become practically synonymous with 'takeout.'

HOT DOG

The history of the hot dog is long and storied, with many different versions. A derivative of sausage, one of the oldest forms of processed food, goes back thousands of years, and made its way to New York via various European butchers in the 1800s. German butcher Charles Feltman was apparently the first to sell hot dogs (the origin of that term is a contested history in itself) from pushcarts along the Coney Island seashore. But it was Nathan Handwerker, a German immigrant, who made the food famous. Originally an employee of Feltman's, the shrewd entrepreneur saved up enough money to open his own hot-dog shop across the street. Nathan put up huge signs advertising his dogs, which were half the price of those at Feltman's. His business grew, and when the Stilwell Avenue subway station opened right across the street in the 1920s, Nathan's benefited from its location, exploding in popularity and finally putting Feltman's out of business in the '50s. Today the original Nathan's (p204) still stands in Coney Island, at the corner of Stilwell and Surf Avenues (while its empire has expanded on a national scale), where it hosts an annual July 4th hot-dog eating contest – a disturbingly amusing display of gluttony. Nathan's also inspired hot-dog sellers all over NYC, and today there is barely a neighborhood in existence that does not have at least a few hot-dog vendors on its street corners. Some locals would never touch one of these 'dirty-water dogs,' preferring the new wave of chi-chi hot-dog shops such as F&B (p185) or Dawgs on Park (p180); still, others swear by them. Enjoy yours with 'the works': plenty of spicy brown mustard, relish, sauerkraut and onions.

PIZZA

Pizza's certainly not indigenous to the Big Apple. But New York–style pizza is a very particular thing – and the first pizzeria in America, Lombardi's (p181), opened in 1905, is here. While Chicago-style is 'deep dish' and Californian tends to be light and doughy, New York prides itself on having pizza with thin crust and an even thinner layer of sauce – and slices that are triangular (unless they're Sicilian-style, in which case they're square). Pizza made its way over to New York in the 1900s through Italian immigrants, and its regional style soon developed, its thin crust allowing for faster cooking time in a city where everyone's always in a hurry. Today there are pizza parlors about every ten blocks, especially in Manhattan and most of Brooklyn, where you'll find standard slices for about $1.50. The style at each place varies slightly – some places touting cracker-thin crust, others offering slightly thicker and chewier versions, and plenty of nouveau styles throwing everything from shrimp to cherries on top. Some of the most popular local chains include La Famiglia, Grimaldi's (p203) and Ray's (and the various Ray's options, most unrelated, are the source of constant confusion – as you'll see Ray's Famous, Famous Ray's, Original Ray's and Famous Original Ray's all over town; don't sweat it, they're all good). No matter where you get your slice, though, you should learn how to properly eat it and walk at the same time: fold in half lengthwise, hold in one hand and chomp away.

New York Egg Creams

This frothy, old-fashioned beverage contains no eggs – just milk, seltzer water and plenty of chocolate syrup (preferably the classic Fox's U-Bet brand, made in Brooklyn). But when Louis Auster of Brooklyn, who owned soda fountains on the Lower East Side, invented the treat back in 1890, the syrup he used was made with eggs, and he added cream to thicken the concoction. The name stuck, even though the ingredients were modified, and soon they were a staple of every soda fountain in New York. While Mr Auster sold them for three cents a piece, today they'll cost you anywhere from $1.50 to $3, depending on where you find one – which could be anywhere from one of the few remaining old-fashioned soda shops, such as Lexington Candy Shop (p200) on the Upper East Side, or at a trendy, kitschy diner such as Empire Diner (p184). They were hard to find for a while, but a wave of nostalgia for the beverage has brought them back.

BAGEL

Bagels may have been invented in Europe, but they were perfected during the turn of the 19th century in New York City – and once you've had one here, you'll have a hard time enjoying one anywhere else. Basically, it's a ring of plain-yeast dough that's first boiled and then baked, either left plain or topped with various finishing touches, such as sesame seeds or dried onion flakes. 'Bagels' made in other parts of the country are often just baked and not boiled, which makes them nothing more than a roll with a hole. And even if they do get boiled elsewhere, bagel-makers here claim that it's New York water that adds an elusive sweetness never to be found anywhere else. You can find 50¢ bagels from street vendors in the morning, though they're not great. Which baker creates the 'best' bagel in New York is a matter of (hotly contested) opinion, but most agree that **H&H Bagels** (locations around Manhattan) rank pretty high up there. The most traditionally New York way to order one is by asking for a 'bagel and a schmear,' which will yield you said bagel with a small but thick swipe of cream cheese. Or splurge and add some lox – thinly sliced smoked salmon as was originally sold from pushcarts on the Lower East Side by Jewish immigrants back in the early 1900s. Bialys, by the way, are a cousin of the bagel, but more like a crusted roll; they're not nearly as popular as bagels, but just as New York. Find the undisputed best in the Lower East Side at **Kossar's** (p179).

NEW YORK–STYLE CHEESECAKE

Sure, cheesecakes, in one form or another, have been baked and eaten in Europe since the 1400s. But New Yorkers, as they do with many things, have appropriated its history in the form of the New York–style cheesecake. Immortalized by **Lindy's** (Broadway at 50th St) restaurant in Midtown, which was opened by Leo Lindemann in 1921, the particular type of confection served there – made of cream cheese, heavy cream, a dash of vanilla and a cookie crush – became wildly popular in the '40s. **Junior's** (p204), which opened on Flatbush Ave in Brooklyn in 1929, serves its own famous version of the creamy cake, but with a graham-cracker crust. Today, you'll find this local favorite on more dessert menus than most, whether you're at a Greek diner or haute-cuisine hot spot.

DRINKS

WINE

While wine-making in New York State has a history that stretches back to the 1800s, it wasn't until 1976 that the industry began to explode. That was when the NY State Legislature passed a bill that approved the establishment of small-farm based wineries, allowing entrepreneurs to sprout vineyards wherever the soil and climate would allow. Among the state's biggest producers is the Finger Lakes region, upstate, which is home to more than 60 wineries. Closer to the city are the wineries of eastern Long Island, located mainly on its North Fork but also on the South Fork (otherwise known as the Hamptons; see p313). **Vintage New York**, with a flagship store in **Soho** (482 Broome St) and another on the **Upper West Side** (2492 Broadway), sells strictly New York wines, offering free tastings and knowledgeable advice. Perhaps its best quality, however, is that, because it's affiliated with an upstate winery and technically considered such, it's open on Sunday, when all other wine and liquor stores are closed. New Yorkers' appreciation of wine, local or otherwise, seems to only keep getting hotter: just a few years ago there were about a dozen wine bars in the city; now there are more than 50. Among the excellent options are **Rhône** (p216) and **Il Posto Accanto** (p213).

BEER

NYC lags far behind most major US cities when it comes to brewing its own suds – but there is one star on the scene. The **Brooklyn Brewery** (p222), located in Williamsburg (79 N 11th St), is the city's first successful commercial brewery since Schaefer and Rheingold both closed their doors in 1976. Founded in 1987, it opened its 70,000-sq-ft warehouse and brewery in 1996; it has since developed a cultish following, producing more than a dozen award-winning brews, with its most popular, Brooklyn Lager, widely available at bars and shops around the city. Head on over to its factory for tours and a popular Friday happy hour, held from 6pm to 10pm. Two other local breweries, operating on a much smaller scale, are the **Heartland Brewery** (p219) and **Chelsea Brewing Company** (p216). And the appreciation of the stuff can be found far and wide, with many bars now offering a slew of on-tap and bottled selections. **D.B.A.** (p213) has a ton of options.

Shaken or Stirred – Specialty Martinis

Classic martinis are certainly loved here. But it's all the creative variations of the elixir that are the trendiest sips in town. The cosmopolitan – chilled vodka, cranberry and grapefruit juice served straight-up with lime – was the first wave of the craze. And though it's still a popular drink, club and lounge fans, it seems, are on a never-ending quest for the newest, wackiest mix in the triangle glass. You'll find lycheetinis and chocolatinis, even saketinis (with sake replacing the vodka) and Tablatinis (at **Tabla**, p217), infused with a tangy blend of fresh pineapple and lemongrass.

COFFEE

It wasn't so long ago that nary a good cup of joe could be found in this city – you had to hit the West Coast for that. But something happened about five years ago (namely the hijacking of the city by Starbucks), and now gourmet coffee purveyors are a cinch to find. Among the excellent local latte sources are **Dean & DeLuca** (Map pp382-5; University Pl), **Jack's** (Map pp382-5; 136 W 10th St) and **Porto Rico Importing Co** (three Downtown locations). But old-school diehards are sticking with the $1 version – served in a to-go cup festooned with a blue-and-gold Roman column design and often ordered 'regular,' which is New York speak for 'with milk and one sugar.' Teahouses are also in the midst of a takeoff, with spots such as **Teany** (p179) and **Franchia** (p186) offering book-thick menus of various brews.

CELEBRATING WITH FOOD

New Yorkers, like most people, enjoy a good dinner party now and then. But alas, urbanites' always-busy nature coupled with cramped living quarters makes such occasions few and far between – if they happen at all. It's why dining out has become the solution for any holiday you can think of, even traditionally home-style ones, such as Thanksgiving and Christmas dinners, where gathering around someone's dining room table is thought to be the most important aspect of the holiday in the rest of the country. And restaurants in NYC are only too happy to comply. Recently, menus offered Passover menus (in lieu of in-house seders) with items that ranged from an appetizer of mixed-vegetable soup with chipotle matzo balls (at a Mexican restaurant owned by a Lithuanian Jew born in Mexico City) to a dessert of chocolate-covered matzo-and-marshmallow brulée with chocolate-dipped gooseberries (at an Upper West Side hot spot). Even on July 4th, most New Yorkers are restaurant-bound for their ribs and chicken – unless you live in one of the outer boroughs, in which case you might just fire up your own barbecue right on your front sidewalk or stoop.

WHERE TO EAT & DRINK

Restaurants come in myriad forms, but the most common are the upscale dining room, replete with tablecloths, some sort of subtle dress code that's not so much enforced as understood (such as no dirty cut-offs or bras worn as shirts, for example), and high prices; the casual restaurant, with medium prices, absolutely no dress code and not such fawning service; the Greek diner, ultra-casual spots with booths, old-school waitresses, revolving dessert display cases, and massive menus that always feature moussaka as an option; delis, sort of like diners but more harried and hurried and offering traditionally Jewish foods such as pastrami on rye or matzo-ball soup; and cafés, small places with limited menus and affordable prices.

For imbibing, you'll find several different types of spots to belly up to. The general categories are as follows: dive bars, which are dark and filled with a mix of hardcore alcoholics and hipster slummers who despise pretentious watering holes; pubs, usually Irish, with the requisite on-tap Guinness and jolly bartenders; sports bars, filled with rowdy men, lots of beer and multitudinous TV screens; wine bars, stylized spots featuring a large selection of wines by the glass; and lounges, the trendiest spots around, often sleek in design and always featuring couches, cool music and low lighting.

Katz's Deli (p178)

VEGETARIANS & VEGANS

The herbivore scene here has long lagged behind that of California and other areas of the West Coast – and it's still mocked by serious foodies. Still, though NYC doesn't really have a local version of Alice Waters to call its own, there's been a major shift towards healthfulness and vegetarianism in recent years, and places catering to those who believe in it have exploded. The East Village is where you'll find most of them – at least a dozen – with groovy takes on earthy-crunchy including **Sanctuary** (p180), **Angelica Kitchen** (p179) and **Counter** (p179). Chinatown has long been a good place to find vegan options because of the Buddhist vegetarian tradition of cooking with faux-meat products; **Vegetarian Dim Sum House** (p176) is a perfect example. But no matter where you are these days – Chelsea, the West Village, even Harlem or the Upper East Side – there are options, and they're good to boot. Also, while health-food stores have always existed here, the demand for them seems to only be rising, according to the evidence: **Whole Foods** (Map pp386-8), a national natural-foods superstore chain, opened a flagship shop in Chelsea just a couple of years ago; it was a success, and a massive new one just opened with great fanfare in the **Time Warner Center** (Map pp386-8). Yet another one is slated to open in Park Slope, Brooklyn.

CHILDREN

Where children are and are not welcome is not so clear at first. But just use common sense and it should be OK. For example, will your one-year-old begin to scream when she wakes from her nap in the stroller? Then don't bring her to Babbo. And don't bring her there – or any other high-profile haven – anyway. Folks who are serious about their adult eating experience are not keen on having child energy around. Diners, in all their noisy activities, are perfect for kids, as are most delis. And many places court children with elaborate under-12 menus, crayons and other activities; try **Bubby's** (p173) and the East Village location of **Two Boots Pizzerias** (p181).

QUICK EATS

For good on-the-go grub, NYC's got it goin' on. From street vendors hawking everything from hot dogs and tacos to homemade soups and falafel sandwiches, to Korean delis offering massive salad bars and sandwich counters, you'll never go hungry. Plus, the entire city, especially in Downtown areas such as the East and West Village, is awash with teensy little specialty storefronts and parlors, where you'll find quality crepes, Thai food, curries, gyros, pizza, sushi, pomme frites – anything, really – for under $5 and in under five minutes. That's New York for you.

History

History *Kathleen Hulser*

THE RECENT PAST
THE ROARING NINETIES

A *Time* magazine cover in 1990 sported a feature story on 'New York: The Rotting Apple.' Still convalescing from the real estate crash at the end of the 1980s, the city faced crumbling bridges, tunnels and roads, jobs leaking south, and Fortune 500 companies sniffing the green, green air of suburbia. And then in roared the dot.com market, turning geeks into millionaires and the New York Stock Exchange into a speculator's fun park. Buoyed by tax receipts from IPO (initial public offering) profits, the city launched a frenzy of building, boutiquing and partying unparalleled since the 1920s.

With pro-business, law-and-order Rudy Giuliani at the helm, the dingy and destitute were swept from Manhattan's yuppified streets to the outer boroughs, leaving room for Generation X to score digs and live the high life. Abrasive, aggressive and relentless, Mayor Giuliani grabbed headlines with his campaign to stamp out crime, even kicking the sex shops off 42nd St. The energetic mayor succeeded in making New York America's safest large city, by targeting high crime areas, using statistics to focus police presence, and arresting subway gate-crashers, people committing a minor infringement of city law but who often had other charges pending. So, in the 1990s crime dropped, powering a huge appetite for nightlife in the city that never sleeps. Restaurants boomed in the spruced-up metropolis, Fashion Week gained global fame and *Sex and the City* beamed a vision of sophisticated singles in Manolos around the world.

Meanwhile, to the delight of unionized plumbers, electricians and carpenters, real estate prices sizzled, setting off a construction spree of new high-rises, converted warehouses and rejuvenated tenements. Throwing off the uncertainty of the era of David Dinkins, a cautious politician who was New York's first African-American mayor, New Yorkers flaunted the new wealth. Areas of the Lower East Side that housed artist storefront galleries in the 1970s and '80s morphed overnight into blocks of gentrified dwellings with double-door security and maintenance charges equal to normal humans' entire take-home pay. Bars switched from pitchers of beer to $9 microbrews and designer vodka cosmopolitans.

Those left behind seldom seemed to bother the mayor. No new housing for ordinary people was built, but plenty of solid apartment stock disappeared from the rent rolls, as landlords converted rentals into pricey cooperative buildings. And yet, the city's population grew and grew, as ambitious young graduates flocked to the financial center. At the new Ellis Island, JFK airport, customs officials greeted wave after wave of South Asians, South Americans and other immigrants willing to double up in cramped quarters in the boroughs. So many Dominicans came to Washington Heights that politicians back in the Dominican Republic launched New York campaigns for their local elections. For refugees from super-slick Manhattan, ethnic enclaves in Brooklyn and Queens beckoned as intriguing places to nosh on exotic foods and sample goods without labels.

DAY OF INFAMY

Good times were already faltering as the electronic-stock bubble burst, but the terrorist attack on the World Trade Center on September 11, 2001, ushered in a period of high unemployment and tightened belts. Downtown Manhattan took months to recover from the ghastly fumes

TIMELINE

c. 1500 AD	1625–26
About 15,000 Indians live in 80 different sites around the island	Dutch West India Company imports 11 slaves to New Amsterdam

wafting from the ruins of the World Trade Center, as forlorn missing-person posters grew ragged on brick walls. While recovery crews coughed their way through the debris, the city gamely braved constant terrorist alerts and an anthrax scare to mourn the estimated 1749 dead. Shock and grief drew people together, and united the often fractious citizenry in a determined effort not to succumb to despair. Before the year was out, community groups were already gathering in 'Imagine New York' workshops, to develop together ideas for renewal and a memorial at the World Trade Center site.

FROM THE BEGINNING
NATIVE INHABITANTS

The signature shoreline of New York was sculpted by glaciers between 75,000 and 17,000 years ago. The end of the Ice Age left New York with hills of glacial debris now called Hamilton Heights and Bay Ridge, and the numerous inlets and drowned valleys known as Long Island Sound, the East River and Arthur Kill. Glaciers scoured off soft rock leaving behind Manhattan's stark rock foundations of gneiss and schist. Around 11,000 years before the first Europeans sailed through the Narrows, the Lenape people foraged, hunted and fished the regional bounty. Spear points, arrowheads, bone heaps and shell mounds testify to their presence. Some of their pathways still lie beneath such streets as Broadway, originally part of a trail linking Manhattan with the beaver-trading post, Albany. In Munsee, the Lenape language, the term Manhattan may have translated as hilly island, or more descriptively, 'place of general inebriation.'

The bands of Lenape did not think of themselves as a nation, but rather functioned in small groups whose evocative names still linger as the names of rivers, towns and bays. Hackensacks lived on the Jersey side of the Hudson, Raritans there and on Staten Island, Massepequas, Rockaways and Matinecocks along Long Island Sound. On Manhattan Island dwelled Wiechquaesgecks, Rechgawanches and Siwanoys, whose campsites still sometimes yield archaeological riches when bulldozers dig.

Top Five History Books

Check out the ubiquitous street sellers for cheap copies of these books, old and new.

- *Gotham. A History of New York City to 1898* by Edwin G Burrows and Mike Wallace. A hugely entertaining, 1000-page tome that lends itself to chapter-by-chapter sampling. Chock-full of evildoers, absurdity and contention – just what you would expect from an NYC history. Won a Pulitzer Prize.
- *Lowlife* by Luc Sante. Rollicking look at 19th-century criminality, drawing heavily on Herbert Asbury's *Gangs of New York*. Be sure to read about characters such as the fat fence Marm Mandelbaum, who gave dinner parties on chairs her clients stole.
- *Invisible Frontier: Exploring the Tunnels, Ruins and Rooftops of Hidden New York* by LB Deyo and 'Lefty' Leibowitz. Idiosyncratic chronicle of how this team of urban explorers penetrated forbidden spaces in NYC to see the actual bricks, mortar and steel bones of the city's history. After September 11, of course, security concerns have barred entry to many of these places, but their trip diaries are a unique way of experiencing city history.
- *Gay New York* by George Chauncey. The hidden history of dandies, the docks, drag balls and brief encounters, demonstrating how gay urban habits evolved within surprisingly variable sexual cultures and practices.
- *American Ground: The Unbuilding of the World Trade Center* by William Langewiesche. Thought-provoking look at issues surrounding the nine-month recovery efforts at the World Trade Center site, based on long hours with engineers and construction workers underground. Controversial because the firefighters have hotly denied that any looted Gap jeans from the underground Mall were ever found in a fire truck.

1690s	1788–90
Governor Benjamin Fletcher passes out huge estates to his friends; welcomes pirates to port of New York	New York is capital of the USA

EXPLORERS

In 1524 the Florentine Giovanni da Verrazzano explored the Upper Bay, which he termed a 'very beautiful lake.' Today's seaborne visitors enter that 'lake' under the magnificent Verrazano Bridge (seen from helicopters every fall at the opening of the New York Marathon). Only a year later the black Portuguese Estaban Gomez, a former helmsman with Magellan, sailed further up the Hudson. However brief his New World sojourn, he did pause long enough to seize 57 Native American captives to sell as slaves in Lisbon. By the time the Dutch West India Company employee Henry Hudson arrived in 1609, encounters with Native Americans were already beginning to be dichotomized into two crude stories, alternating between 'delightful primitives' and 'brutal savages.'

COLONIAL ARRIVALS

Like the other foreign outposts of European empires bursting at the seams, the tiny port of New Amsterdam attracted the best and worst of the international flotsam and jetsam of the 17th century. Marked by its sailor-friendly abundance of taverns and endless supply of languages, the trading town was owned by the Dutch West India Company. Common currencies included Indian wampum, Spanish pieces of eight, gold doubloons, silver, furs and tobacco. One early administrator may have sealed the real estate transaction of the millennium by 'purchasing' Manhattan for 60 guilders, or $24. More likely, the Native American side of the deal thought the exchange was about rent, and permission to hunt, fish and trade, rather than a permanent transfer of property – an unfamiliar custom in the New World.

From the beginning New Amsterdam's governors displayed more talent for self-enrichment than for administration. As colonists grumbled about the Dutch West India Company's stingy provisions and primitive wood huts, the walls and ramparts of the 'fort' crumbled under the assault of free-roaming pigs, cattle and sheep. Meanwhile, Governor Willem Kieft stirred up so much trouble with the surrounding Native Americans that they formed an alliance to subdue the aggressive Europeans. By the time Peter Stuyvesant stumped off a ship to clean up the mess in 1647, the population had dwindled to around 700, and Kieft had retreated to count his gains in various corrupt transactions.

PEG LEG PROSPERITY

Peter Stuyvesant busily set about remaking the demoralized colony, establishing markets and a night watch, repairing the fort, digging a canal (under the current Canal St) and authorizing a municipal wharf. His vision of an orderly and prosperous trading port was partially derived from his previous experience as governor of Curaçao. Indeed, the burgeoning sugar economy in the Caribbean helped to inspire an investment in slave trading that soon boosted New Amsterdam's slave workforce to 20% of the population. After long service some of them were partially freed and given the 'Negroe Lots' areas near today's Greenwich Village, the Lower East Side and City Hall. (You can see the remnants of their **African burial ground**, p76, recently unearthed on Reade St.) The Dutch West India Company encouraged the fruitful connection to plantation economies on the islands, and issued advertisements and offered privileges to attract merchants to the growing port. Although these 'liberties' did not encompass religious freedom for Jews and Quakers, settlers did come. By the 1650s, warehouses, workshops, and gabled houses were spreading back from the dense establishments at the river's edge on Pearl St.

A brisk trade in furs, tobacco and timber supplied residents and Native Americans with liquor, guns, kettles and cloth. The memory of this trade lingers in the city's seal, visible on municipal buildings and documents. Although the city on the tip of the island commanded a strategic position to monitor the fur trade flowing down the Hudson River and over from

1795	1864
Yellow Fever epidemic; wealthy flee to country	Confederate rebels plot to burn New York

the Connecticut River, its very success made it vulnerable. The 'wall' along Wall St was meant to keep both English and Indian raiders out of town.

In the long run, prosperity counted for more than nationality, and when the English showed up in 1664 in battleships, Governor Stuyvesant surrendered without a shot. King Charles II promptly renamed the colony after his brother the Duke of York. Nevertheless, Dutch laws and customs coexisted with English ways, which included large land grants to royal favorites in the regions surrounding New York.

TURMOIL

Local forces were prone to squabbling, and one such contretemps called Leisler's Rebellion terminated with its leader being hanged and beheaded in what is now City Hall Park in 1691. Sharp-tongued colonials did not hesitate to publish their complaints in the colonial press. Peter Zenger's *Weekly Journal* flayed king and royal governor so regularly the authorities tried – unsuccessfully – to convict Zenger for libel. His acquittal signaled that juries would no longer help the ruling powers squash criticism. Some 2000 enslaved New Yorkers continued to resist their involuntary servitude. In the Great Negro Plot of 1741, black slaves and white accomplices were accused of plotting arson and rebellion in a tavern not far from today's World Trade Center site. The facts have remained forever unclear, but the city fathers executed as many as 64 people, burning 17 of them at the stake. Remains of two of them may be among the bodies found at the African Burial Ground.

Trade with the Caribbean accelerated, and wharves lined the East River to accommodate the bulging merchant men. By the 18th century, the economy was so robust the locals were improvising ways to avoid sharing the wealth with London. Smuggling to dodge various port taxes was commonplace, and the jagged coastline, full of coves and inlets,

Apollo Theater (p128)

1882	1883
Oriental Exclusion Act bans Chinese immigration and limits rights	Brooklyn Bridge debuts on May 24 and 150,000 walk across

hid illegal activity well (as 20th-century drug smugglers also discovered). New York, that hotbed of hotheads and tax dodgers, provided a stage for the fatal confrontation with King George III.

WAR

From dodging port taxes to formally declaring 'independence' and the right to bear arms, the colonists soon found themselves well along the road to revolution by the 1760s. The Boston Tea Party was echoed by a similar episode of tea-tax defiance in New York Harbor.

Patriots and the Tories loyal to the king clashed in public spaces – the patriots erected Liberty Poles and the royalists ripped them down. General George Washington's performance in New York consisted mostly of unimpressive battles and a stealthy escape across the East River at night. After winning the Battle of Long Island and chasing Washington's ragtag forces up to Washington Heights in 1776, the British occupied the town for the rest of the American Revolution. Patriots fled, and royal rule was aided by a policy of liberating slaves who fought for the king. When the British fleet sailed out of New York Harbor in 1783, it took as many as 3000 ex-slaves along to Canada and the colonies. After a series of celebrations, banquets and fireworks at Bowling Green, General Washington bade farewell to his officers at **Fraunces Tavern** (p76), and retired as commander-in-chief.

But in 1789 to his surprise, the retired general found himself addressing crowds at **Federal Hall** (still standing at Wall St, p76) gathered to witness the inauguration of President Washington. Signaling simplicity and patriotism, he wore a suit of American-made broadcloth, and walked to prayers afterwards in a pew still visible in nearby **St Paul's Chapel** (p81). Characteristically, people distrusted a capitol located adjacent to the financial power of the merchants of Wall St, and New Yorkers lost the seat of the presidency to Philadelphia shortly thereafter.

BIGGER, BETTER, FASTER

After setbacks at the start of the 19th century, the prospering city found mighty resources to build mighty public works. Irish immigrants helped dig a 363-mile 'ditch' from the Hudson to Buffalo, known as the Erie Canal. The canal's chief backer, Governor Clinton, celebrated the waterway by ceremonially pouring a barrel of Erie water into the sea (Clinton's cask is on view at the **New-York Historical Society**, p122). A great aqueduct system brought Croton Water, relieving thirst and dirt. No longer would cholera sweep the town, as new water meant ordinary folks needn't drink from the brackish river and the polluted ground water.

Another project to boost the health of the people crammed into tiny tenement apartments was a grand park of 843 acres. Begun in 1855 in an area so far uptown some immigrants kept pigs, sheep and goats there, **Central Park** (p118) was both a vision of green reform and a boon to real estate speculation. As much as Central Park promised a playground for the masses, the park project also offered work relief for the city when the Panic of 1857 (one of the city's periodic financial debacles) shattered the nation's finance system. Further down, after several winter freezes had underlined the weakness of the ferry system connecting Brooklyn and Downtown Manhattan, John Roebling, an inventive German-born engineer, designed a soaring symphony of spun wire and gothic arches to span the East River. The **Brooklyn Bridge** (p79) accelerated the fusion of the neighboring cities. The proudly independent city of Brooklyn, already nearing a million residents, bowed to the inevitable in 1898 when the five boroughs were consolidated in one big, powerful unit.

1904	1907
Luna Park in Coney Island opens, followed by Dreamland amusement park; IRT subway carries first passengers	Times Square's first New Year's ball drops

Five Turning Points

In history as in physics, every action has a reaction:

- **The Torching of NYC** (Sep 21, 1776) Who burned down New York City during the American Revolution? The triumphant British, who had only captured the port town a fortnight earlier, blamed rebel arsonists. The patriots denied it, saying the vengeful British had torched it. Surveying the smoking ruins of 500 dwellings from his headquarters in Harlem Heights, General George Washington observed: 'Providence or some good honest fellow, has done more for us than we were disposed to do for ourselves.' It was a low point for the patriots in the revolutionary war, but it did send them scurrying to territory where their guerrilla tactics could later defeat the colonial power.

- **Commissioners Plan of 1811** Orderly but bland, squashing the motley heights and valleys of hilly Manhattan into a flat checkerboard, the plan imposed a grid on a city that had yet to develop above Houston St. It did make city navigation a cinch for strangers. But the plan also forestalled agreeable variety, in the name of creating tidier and more marketable real estate bundles – each rectangle equal to another.

- **Triangle Shirt Waist Fire** (Mar 25, 1911) A tossed cigarette probably ignited the raging inferno in the top stories of a sweatshop full of young immigrant women. The terrified garment makers collapsed at a locked door to the staircase; the owners had fastened it to prevent employee pilfering. Within minutes, dozens of workers had jumped from the 9th floor. The death toll of 146 spurred public sympathy for workers, and new safety codes to prevent a repetition. But to this day firemen avoid sleeping on high floors because they know the limits of ladders and hoses.

- **Dodgers Leave Brooklyn** (1957) The borough's favorite baseball team got its name from fans dodging trolleys that turned around near its playing field. When owner Walter O'Malley moved the team to Los Angeles, cries of pain and rage echoed across the east. Did this mean the end of great cities and their valiant athletic teams? Only two years earlier the Dodgers had finally won the World Series against hated rivals, the Yankees. Since the Dodgers (and Manhattan's Giants) moved to California, many sports-team owners have yanked their teams out to suburban stadiums with big parking lots. And many more threaten to do so, in an intricate game of blackmail to force cities to build new facilities. Right now New York is debating a new football stadium on the Far West Side as part of New York's bid for the 2012 Olympics (see also p18).

- **Demolition of Pennsylvania Station** (1963) Despite public outcry, the magnificent McKim Mead and White Pennsylvania Station, built in 1910, was demolished. The grand structure modeled on the Roman baths of Caracalla was replaced by the current underground maze. Architectural historian Vincent Scully summed up the difference saying, 'one entered the city like a god...now one scuttles in like a rat.' The infamous preservation defeat led directly to New York City's Landmarks Law in 1965. Jacqueline Kennedy Onassis was a member of the Landmarks Commission when it prevented a repeat demolition of **Grand Central Terminal** (p112).

BUSINESS & BOODLE

Construction fueled great expectations among New York City's political fixers. Boss Tweed, a ward politician from the heavily Irish immigrant neighborhoods, forever known through Thomas Nast's biting caricatures in the 1870s, created a powerful ring of corrupt officials and fee-splitting contractors to build a courthouse that cost nearly $12 million and took 20 years to complete. (See it now elegantly restored in **City Hall Park**, p78, now home to Mayor Bloomberg's revamped Department of Education.) Running the famous Tammany Hall political machine, the clubhouse bosses passed out patronage jobs, holiday turkeys and free firewood in neighborhoods such as Five Points and Little Germany. The Tweed political style, portrayed in the Martin Scorsese film *Gangs of New York* (2002) included graft, corruption, vote tampering, ballot stealing, cronyism and lots of municipal pork. Then and now, the gargantuan scale of public works has attracted financial geniuses equipped to capture some of the booty – on both sides of the law.

1918	1931
Yankees acquire slugger Babe Ruth, to the agony of Red Sox fans everywhere	Empire State Building (1454ft tall) built in 410 days

Other big boodlers included the private rapid-transit companies that fought for city franchises. By the turn of the 20th century elevated trains carried a million people a day in and out of the city. Rapid transit opened up areas of the Bronx and Upper Manhattan, spurring mini-building booms in areas near the lines. At this point, the city was simply overflowing with the masses of immigrants from southern Italy and Eastern Europe, who had boosted the metropolis to around three million. The journey from immigrant landing stations at Castle Garden and Ellis Island led straight to the Lower East Side. There, streets reflected these myriad origins with shop signs in Yiddish, Italian, German and Chinese. Ethnic enclaves allowed newcomers to feel comfortable in home languages, buy familiar and New World staples from pushcart peddlers, and worship in varied versions of the Christian and Jewish faiths. Experience their extremely tight living quarters today at the Lower East Side **Tenement Museum** (p89).

CIVIL STRIFE

In the 19th century New York also became famous for its radical politics and militant workers, who challenged the system that created both huge fortunes and impoverished workers. Over and over again labor movements went on strike for the eight-hour day and a living wage. In the roller-coaster economies of the time, workers confronted unspeakable hardships when bubbles burst and factories closed. Some winters in the city found 100,000 working men laid off, shivering in soup lines, and shoveling snow for nickels. Children collected rags and bottles, boys hawked newspapers, and girls sold flowers to contribute to family income. In already crowded apartments, a kitchen table or two chairs jammed together could earn rent as beds for boarders. Then, during the day whole families assembled paper flowers or sewed sleeves in shirts for precious pennies. Family budgets were so meager it was common to pawn the sheets to raise food money before a payday.

Harsh conditions and competition for scarce jobs produced regular outbreaks of violence. New York finally abolished slavery in 1827, and many working-class jobs excluded African Americans. Gangs of young men regularly broke windows in black churches and harassed the worshippers. Writers and community activists responded by publishing appeals for justice, and heartening news of progress in *Freedom's Journal,* the first black-owned and operated newspaper in the US, produced on Church St and later Lispenard St. Mobs sometimes took out their rage on the city's black neighborhoods, or caricatured African Americans in minstrel shows and popular entertainment. The most dramatic clash between the races occurred in 1863, when President Lincoln instituted a draft to replenish his dwindling Civil War army. Grumbling that wealthy men could buy an exemption from service for $300, the working classes also feared that black men would take their jobs while they were sent to war. Many Irish immigrants resented fighting for the emancipation of people who, as they saw it, stood ready to steal their jobs and drive down wages. So during the first days of the draft, mobs burnt conscription offices, pulled down the houses of abolitionists, attacked police and chased and lynched African Americans in the street. The mob even surged uptown to 42nd St to burn down the Colored Orphan Asylum. Troops had to be yanked from the front to quell the violence in the Union's largest city.

FABULOUS WEALTH

After the Civil War, the old aristocratic elements retreated uptown, far from the sons and daughters of Europe. The newly wealthy began to build increasingly splendid mansions on Fifth Ave. Modeled on European chateaux, palaces such as the Vanderbilt home, on the corner of 52nd St and Fifth Ave, reached for new summits of opulence. Tapestries adorned marble halls, mirrored ballrooms accommodated hundreds of bejeweled revelers, liveried footmen handed grand ladies from their gilded carriages. Mrs Astor and her friends in old New York tried to resist the onslaught of robber-baron wives eager to break into society. Mrs Astor's

1939	1961
RCA previews television at World's Fair in Flushing, Queens	Young folk singer Bob Dylan arrives in NYC, plays Cafe Wha? on his first night in town

idea of the right people encompassed only 400, which, she sniffed, sufficed for all the people one would want to know socially, in any case. Her snobbery could not withstand the tidal wave of fortunes being made by Rockefeller in oil, Gould in railroads, and Carnegie in steel. The latecomers included a substantial group of German Jews such as Jacob Schiff, Otto Kahn, Solomon Guggenheim, and Felix and Paul Warburg, who formed their own elite society known as 'our crowd.'

WOMEN TAKE TO THE STREETS

With the start of the 20th century, piquant accounts of the foibles of the rich competed with rabble-rousing crusades for the masses in the flamboyant press of New York. Joseph Pulitzer and William Randolph Hearst vied for public affection with racy stories, lavish illustrations and the new fad for comic strips. Even women began to penetrate the Fourth Estate. Nellie Bly, a girl stunt reporter, committed herself to an insane asylum to pen an exposé, before she traveled 'Round the World in 80 Days,' filing telegraphed dispatches all the way.

Woman power was evident on the streets of Manhattan too, as female garment workers 20,000-strong marched on City Hall. Suffragists held street-corner rallies to obtain the vote for women, and Margaret Sanger opened the first birth-control clinic in Brooklyn, where purity police promptly arrested her. Women New Yorkers definitely had a lot to complain about, given their abysmal pay and wretched working conditions in sweatshops and factories.

JAZZ AGE

But manufacturing jobs did put change in people's pockets, and they began to spend it on such new entertainments as movies and jolly outings to Coney Island **amusement parks** (p140). By the 1920s the Great Migration from the South made Harlem the center of African-American culture and society, turning out poetry, music, painting and innovative attitude that continues to influence and inspire to this day. The **Apollo Theater** (p128), still humming on 125th St, began its famous Amateur Night in 1934 – it's a venue that has boosted the careers of unknowns such as Ella Fitzgerald, James Brown and the Jackson Five. Harlem's daring nightlife in the 1920s and '30s attracted the flappers and gin-soaked revelers that marked the complete failure of Prohibition. Indeed, the Jazz Age seems to have taught women to smoke, drink and dance at speakeasies, a foretaste of the liberated nightlife that New Yorkers still enjoy today (although they are forced to smoke their coffin nails outside bars these days.) Broadway seemed to thrive in good times and bad, supplying leggy chorines for Busby Berkeley spectacles such as the cynically titled *Gold Diggers of 1933* and oodles of sporty slang that still permeates American speech today.

HARD TIMES & WAR TIMES

New York made it through the Great Depression of the 1930s with a combination of grit, endurance, rent parties, militancy and a slew of public works projects. The once-grand Central Park blossomed with shacks, derisively called Hoovervilles, after the president who refused to help the needy. But Mayor Fiorello LaGuardia found a friend in President Franklin Roosevelt, and worked his Washington connections to great effect to bring relief money home. **Riverside Park** (p122) and the **Triborough Bridge** (Map p396) are just two of the still functioning monuments to New Deal projects, brought to New York by the Texas-born, Yiddish-speaking son of an Italian bandmaster.

WWII brought troops galore to the city, ready to party down to their last dollar in Times Square, before being shipped off to Europe. Converted to war industries, the local factories hummed, staffed by women and African-American workers who had rarely before had

1976–77	1977
David Berkowitz says a demon in a dog told him to commit Son of Sam murders	Studio 54 opens at the height of disco fever; John Travolta struts his stuff in *Saturday Night Fever*

access to these good union jobs. The explosion of wartime activity led to a huge housing crunch, which brought New York its much-imitated Rent Control Law.

But there were few evident controls on business, as Midtown bulked up with skyscrapers after the war. The financial center marched north, even while the banker David Rockefeller and his brother Governor Nelson Rockefeller dreamed up the twin towers to revitalize Downtown.

Wise Guy New York

Romanticized by Hollywood and fanned by popular culture, New York's organized crime underground made its greatest marks in the 20th century. Fleeing economic disasters in southern Italy and Sicily, Italian immigrants faced discrimination and dislocation in their new home. But being marginalized can have the unintended side effect of stimulating new underground business. Its economy in New York began before WWI, when the Society of the Black Hand, a band of smalltime grafters, tossed Molotov cocktails in storefronts if the owner failed to pay protection money.

The New York Mafia took off during Prohibition, when the Volstead Act banning liquor sales offered a golden opportunity to unofficial business. Running rum down Lake Champlain from Canada, hijacking each other's trucks, hosting backroom gambling, loan-sharking, pimping, the big names – Lucchese, Genovese, Anastasia, Costello, Bonanno, Gambino and Castellano – muscled in on the various branches of entertainment that had long made New York City a mecca for the sporting man. Raw competition unfettered by above-ground rules meant that the families inflicted more damage on each other than law enforcement ever managed.

Lucky Luciano got his nickname after he survived having his throat slashed, ear to ear, in 1929 when he challenged mob leadership with his pals Meyer Lansky and Bugsy Siegel. Crazy Joe Gallo whacked Albert Anastasia as he sat in a barber's chair in 1952, but he himself was shot full of holes less than 20 years later in Umberto's Clam House (still on Mulberry St a few doors up from the original location). Joe Colombo was killed in front of thousands at a 1971 rally, undermining his public statements about the non-existence of the Mafia. In a successful challenge to the Gambino family control, John Gotti ordered Paul Castellano gunned down in front of Sparks Steakhouse in 1985. Before he finally received a prison term, Vincent Gigante was famous for wandering the village in his bathrobe in the 1970s and '80s to demonstrate his mental incompetence, thus preventing a successful prosecution until 2002.

Sometimes it seems hard to distinguish the movies from the facts. Marlon Brando from *On the Waterfront* to *The Godfather* offers a mythical compendium of society's affection for rule-breakers, outsiders and hoods, which persists through *GoodFellas* and on to Tony Soprano.

Like all big businesses, the Mafia diversified as it grew, moving from petty extortion to large-scale drug trade by the 1960s. By the time of the Pizza Connection, a cocaine and heroin smuggling operation that used pizzerias as fronts to distribute drugs in the 1970s, Mafia entrepreneurship had reached new levels of sophistication. Then in 1986 US Attorney General Rudolph Guiliani successfully prosecuted Gaetano Badalamenti, who was sentenced to 45 years in the pen. The phrase 'Pizza Connection' went on to become the name of a popular video game.

FROM HEARTBREAKING DODGERS TO POT-SMOKING POETS

A mere decade after Jackie Robinson joined the Brooklyn Dodgers, breaking the color barrier, owner Walter O'Malley moved the team to Los Angeles, breaking Brooklyn hearts. The population of the gutsy borough had peaked at 2.7 million at just about the time that its famous breweries began to close. (The classic Rheingold is back in the 1990s.) But under the Manhattan approaches to the Brooklyn Bridge, an art movement was brewing that wrested the crown from the previously reigning French. Abstract expressionism, a homegrown, large-scale outbreak of American painters, offended with its incomprehensible squiggles and blotches, but charmed with its color and energy. Artists such as Willem de Kooning, Mark Rothko and Helen Frankenthaler exhibited as much flair in their personal lives as in their canvases. Jackson Pollack, the great dripper, and his friends often quenched their

1980	1982
Deranged gunman Mark David Chapman kills John Lennon on steps of The Dakota at 1 West 72nd St	One million people protest nuclear arms race in Central Park

thirst at the **Cedar Tavern** (Map pp382–5) still there on University Place, then known as the home of alcoholic expressionism.

These cultural high jinks soon broadened into the broader social movements of the 1960s, which parlayed artistic defiance into maverick urban lifestyles. Beat poets such as Allen Ginsberg made the Village the Downtown capital of the word, while gay revelers found their political strength in fighting a police raid at the **Stonewall Bar** (p216). The lesbian and gay community flourished in the tolerant atmosphere of a neighborhood that did not even bother to open its shops till 10am or 11am. And then bearded merchants sold sex toys, drag queen accessories and roach clips.

TAILSPIN/RENEWAL

The fiscal crisis of the mid-1970s demoted the elected Mayor Abraham Beame to a figure-head, turning over the city's real financial power to Governor Carey and his appointees. The president's message to the beleaguered town – Ford to City, Drop Dead! – marked the nadir of relationships between the US and the city it loved to hate. As massive layoffs decimated the city's working class, untended bridges, roads and parks reeked of hard times. Even the bond raters turned thumbs down on New York's mountain of debt.

But the traumatic '70s actually drove down rents for once, and helped to nourish an exciting alternative culture that staged performances in abandoned schools, opened galleries in unused storefronts and breathed new life into the hair-dye industry. For example, the fees from shooting the movie *Fame* at PS 122 at 10th St and Second Ave, helped pay for the renovation of the still popular performance space. Blue-haired punks turned former warehouses into pulsing meccas of nightlife, transforming the former

The Good, the Bad & the Abrasive Mayor Guiliani

In a city ravaged by the crack-cocaine epidemic, tortured with unbalanced budgets, dilapidated from deferred maintenance, newly elected Mayor Rudolph Guiliani stepped into a troubled post in a troubled city in 1994. He had stockpiled a glorious list of convictions as a US prosecuting attorney, sending '80s junk-bond traders Ivan Boesky and Michael Milkin to jail, bringing the ruling Mafia families to heel, wreaking the people's justice on old-line corrupt politicians such as Bronx Borough President Stanley Friedman and Congressman Mario Biaggi. But acting as avenging angel was not a possible mayoral policy, so what could the novice politician do with the ungovernable city?

Nephew of four policemen and elected in a law-and-order campaign, the mayor immediately launched a war on crime. He succeeded by targeting high crime areas, using statistics to focus police presence and mopping up low-level 'quality of life' crimes to create a safer civic atmosphere. Lucky for him, the birth statistics cooperated: since young men 16 to 18 years old commit most violent crime, the drop in the number of teens made crime plummet across the US too.

But aggressive policing can fan fears of police brutality and evaporating civil rights. The NYPD 'spot-checked' cars with minority drivers so often, that the mayor's own African-American deputy mayor (Rudy Washington) was issued a special ID to ward off harassment stops of his official NYC car. The citizenry watched in amazement as Guiliani assigned officers to arrest Bowery squeegee men, who washed windshields at stoplights for a quarter.

Had New York really become a place where swaggering bullies in uniform could send cowering citizens running for cover? 'Guiliani Time' incidents began to confirm these anxieties, such as the fatal police shooting of Amadou Diallo, an African immigrant who did not instantly understand a police order. Or the time cops visited a nightclub, and took Haitian immigrant Abner Louima back to the station house for a torture session. These polarizing events reduced Guiliani's popularity in the African-American community, already resentful of its exclusion from city governance. Guiliani did little to counteract bad publicity, when he banned what seemed like permanent demonstrations from the City Hall steps – long a home for protestors exercising the city's late lamented free speech.

But these negative moments faded when Guiliani braved the smoke and chaos to act decisively at the World Trade Center. Much was forgiven on September 11, 2001, when he responded to a reporter's question about the number of victims, saying 'the losses will be more than we can bear.'

1988	1990
East Village squatters and cops clash in the Tompkins Square riots	Ellis Island Immigration Museum opens

industrial precincts of Soho and Tribeca. Immortalized in Nan Goldin's famous performance piece *The Ballad of Sexual Dependency*, this lowlife renaissance bent gender roles into pretzels and turned the East Village into America's center of tattooing and independent filmmaking.

B-BOYS, BREAKING & BASQUIAT

Meanwhile, in the South Bronx, a wave of arson reduced blocks of apartment houses to cinders. But amid the smoke of arson, an influential hip-hop culture was born in the Bronx and Brooklyn, fueled by the percussive rhythms of Puerto Rican salsa. Rock Steady Crew, led by 'Crazy Legs' Richie Colon, pioneered athletic, competitive break-dancing. DJ Kool Herc spun vinyl for break beat all-night dance parties, drawing on his Jamaican apprenticeship in appropriated rhythms. Afrika Bambaataa, another founding DJ of hip-hop, formed Zulu Nation, to bring DJs, break-dancers and graffiti writers together to end violence. Daring examples of the latter dazzled the public with their train-long graphics. Perhaps the best-known 'masterpiece' belied the graf writer's reputation as vandals: Lee 163, with the Fab 5 crew, painted a whole car of trains with the message 'Merry Christmas, New York.' Some of these maestros of the spray can penetrated the art world. Jean-Michel Basquiat, once known by his tag 'Samo,' began to hang with Andy Warhol and sell with the big boys in the go-go art world of the 1980s.

Some of the easy money snagged in the booming stock markets of the 1980s was spent on art, but even more was blown up the nose of young traders. While Manhattan neighborhoods struggled with an epidemic of crack cocaine, the city reeled from the impact of addiction, citywide crime, and an AIDS epidemic that cut a swath through communities. Mayor Ed Koch could barely keep the lid on the city. Homelessness burgeoned as landlords converted the cheap old single-room hotels into luxury apartments. Squatters in the East Village fought back when police tried to clear a big homeless encampment, leading to the Tompkins Square Park Riots of 1988. Hard to imagine that just a few years later, Manhattan would yet again become the shiny apple of prosperity's eye.

1997–99	2003
Abner Louima assault and Amadou Diallo shooting cases focus attention on aggressive NYPD tactics	Last of NY subway tokens phased out for Metrocards

Neighborhoods

Neighborhoods

New Yorkers are rather neighborhood-obsessed, and 'Where do you live?' is bound to be one of the first questions you're asked (after 'What do you do?') when meeting someone new at a party. Your answer will sketch an immediate character type in the asker's mind: Lower East Side? Hipster. Upper West? Yuppie. Chelsea? Gay party boy. Of course, urbanites do understand the subtleties of each 'hood, too – and know that just having one to call your own is a vital, complex, and comforting need. Once you know your nabe, and your neighbors – from the guy across the hall to the cashier at your corner deli – it's like you live in a little village.

Someone once said, 'New York is just a series of small towns.' Of course, the methodology for what separates one neighborhood from the next varies greatly, depending on who's interpreting. A realtor, for example, would say that the West Village is comprised only of that area west of Sixth Ave, while the eastern stretch, to the East Village border of Third Ave, is Greenwich Village. To regular Joes, though, the whole swatch east of Third is the West Village, and 'Greenwich' is a term of the past. Same arguments go for the borders of almost every other area, with newfangled monikers – Soha (South of Harlem) and Bococa (Boerum Hill, Cobble Hill and Carroll Gardens in Brooklyn) – popping up daily. Don't worry so much about the names and the dividing lines; just enjoy the various atmospheres.

One important detail about the main borough: to most visitors and residents alike, Manhattan (population 1.5 million) *is* New York City. Even residents of the outer boroughs refer to it as 'the city,' and if you mention you're going to Queens you might get astonished looks, or comments about needing a visa. (One exception here is Brooklyn, much of which has surpassed Manhattan in its coolness factor, especially among its many cool young residents.) But the outer boroughs – the Bronx, Brooklyn, Queens and Staten Island – each have their special something, whether bars or parks, beaches or stadiums, well-revered restaurants or world-class museums. Take advantage of these 'foreign locales' and you'll be treated to secret delights that even many locals aren't hip to yet.

City Hall (p78)

ITINERARIES
One Day
Splurge on breakfast at **Balthazar** (p174), then pick one of the diverse neighborhoods of downtown – the meandering old city streets of the **West Village** (p92) or the hip and happening **Lower East Side** (p88) – and wander for an hour or so, checking out boutiques and parks and local characters. Make a compulsory stop at the **World Trade Center viewing platform** (p81), then zoom up to **Chelsea** (p158) for a couple of quick gallery hops. Have early-evening cocktails at **Campbell Apartment** (p218) in the impressive Grand Central Terminal, dine expensively at **Tabla** (p185) or reasonably at **Cho Dang Goi** (p186) and then have the best nightcap of all time: a late-night trip to the top of the **Empire State Building** (p109), which keeps its viewing tower open till midnight.

Three Days
Get a small dose of all the major tourist spots, plus the lay of the land, by taking a guided tour on your first morning, either on the **Circle Line ferry** (p72) or a double-decker bus. Go for a late-afternoon hot chocolate and snack at **City Bakery** (p183), grab treats for later at the **Greenmarket Farmers' Market** (p107) and hit a gallery opening or two in nearby **Chelsea** (p158). Get a late-night feast at **Florent** (p182) or **Paradou** (p182) followed by some sophisticated drinking at **Rhône** (p216) or another nearby watering hole. On day two, stick to the itinerary of day one, minus the gallery visits, and tack on a live-music venue of your favorite genre (New York's got 'em all). On your third day, venture to an outer borough. Relax in Brooklyn's **Prospect Park** (p138) before visiting the nearby **Brooklyn Botanic Garden** (p138) and just-renovated **Brooklyn Museum** (p138), followed with dinner at a (Park Slope) Fifth Ave hotspot like **Blue Ribbon Brooklyn** (p203); or take the No 7 train to **Astoria** (p143), Queens, where art and film museums and Greek food galore await.

One Week
Spread the three-day guideline out over four days, spending more time at each venue. Then plan an excursion out of the city – a day trip to **Jones Beach** (p315) in summer, or an overnight jaunt to the **Hamptons** (p310) whatever the season. Pick a quirky **walking tour** (p151) for the day you return, and explore a downtown 'hood more completely – take time to observe East Village action at the **Tompkins Square Park** (p91) dog run, for example, or spend hours in a **Chelsea café** (p183), watching the beautiful boys go by. Have dinner at an eatery that tickles your fancy. On day six, hit a major museum like the **Met** (p123), or **Guggenheim** (p125), or score half-price tickets to a Broadway show at the **TKTS booth** (p117). Have early cocktails somewhere fabulous like the bar of the **Church Lounge** (p209) at the Tribeca Grand, then go clubbing late into the night.

ORGANIZED TOURS
Adventure
BIKE THE BIG APPLE
☎ 212-201-837-1133; www.bikethebigapple.com; around $65
The emphasis is on bike tours at night, through Central Park and around the outer boroughs; most average three hours.

BITE OF THE APPLE TOURS
☎ 212-541-8759; www.centralparkbiketour.com; adult/child from $35/20
This company provides several clever options for bicyclists – the two-hour Central Park Bike Tour or Movie Scenes Bike Tour (adult/child $35/20);

three-hour Manhattan Island Bike Tour ($45, 10am, weekends only).

MANHATTAN KAYAK COMPANY
Map pp386-8
☎ 212-924-1788; tours $25-65
Tour the skyline from New York Harbor or the East River as you paddle your own way around, running trips of varying lengths and prices for folks of all abilities.

NEWROTIC NEW YORK CITY TOURS
☎ 718-575-8451; www.newroticnewyorkcitytours.com; adult/child $199/99
This company offers unique, 'untouristy' excursions with themes ranging from ethnic eating to architecture.

Air
LIBERTY HELICOPTER TOURS
Map pp380-1

☎ 212-967-6464; www.libertyhelicopters.com; 12th Ave at W 30th St; per person 5min/30min $56/$275, per couple private 15min Romance Over Manhattan $849; ☽ 9am-7pm

Enjoy a bird's-eye view of the city, whisking you high above the skyscrapers – for a price.

Boat
BEAST Map pp386-8
☎ 212-630-8855; per person $16

For a 30-minute rush, the *Beast* will take you around the Statue of Liberty at 45mph. For a cheaper, slower ride, take the free **Staten Island Ferry** (☎ 718-815-2628; www.siferry.com).

CIRCLE LINE TOURS Map pp386-8
☎ 212-563-3200; per person $24; ☽ Mar-Dec

The three-hour, 35-mile boat cruise around Manhattan leaves from Pier 83, at W 42nd St on the Hudson River. This is a very popular and informative tour, especially attractive when the weather is good, though it's still OK if it's not – boats are covered and heated. Shorter tours are offered, but go the whole way if you can.

NEW YORK WATERWAY Map pp380-1
☎ 800-533-3779; www.nywaterway.com; adult/senior/child $11/10/6

Offers 50-minute cruises from Pier 17.

PIONEER SAIL Map pp380-1
☎ 212-748-8786; adult/senior/child $25/20/15; ☽ Tue-Sat

Offers summer sailing trips on the East River, as well as lunch, sunset and late-night trips.

Bus
Though bus tours may offer a quick introduction to the city, many have non-native guides who aren't well informed. This is especially true of some foreign-language tours.

GRAY LINE Map pp226-7
☎ 212-397-2620; per person $35-71

A reliable option, Gray Line has nearly 30 different tours from its main terminal at the Port Authority, including a hop-on, hop-off loop of Manhattan. Short loop tours on the red, double-decker bus cost from $35, while the comprehensive 'Essential New York' tour is $71.

For Children
- **Bronx Zoo** (p147) Lions and tigers and bears, oh my!
- **New York Aquarium** (p141) Peer in on fish, dolphins and manatees.
- **Brooklyn Children's Museum** (p138) More discoveries, for little ones only.
- **Central Park** (p118) Get your ya-yas out for miles.
- **Children's Museum of Manhattan** (p121) A place all your own.
- **Coney Island** (p141) Ride the Ferris wheel and win Skee Ball games.
- **Firehouse Museum** (p84) Slide down the pole and climb aboard an engine.
- **Museum of Natural History** (p120) See bones, stars and butterflies.
- **New York Unearthed** (p80) Dig through unburied treasures.

Theme
FOODS OF NEW YORK
☎ 212-239-1124; per person $36

Eat your way through Chelsea and the West Village on three-hour tours.

KENNY KRAMER Map pp386-8
☎ 212-268-5525, 800-572-6377; 358 W 44th St; per person $38; ☽ noon Sat & Sun; reservation required

The real-life inspiration for the *Seinfeld* character, Kenny Kramer offers fun three-hour tours past major sites from the TV series.

MUNICIPAL ART SOCIETY
☎ 212-935-3960; per person $10

Has various scheduled tours focusing on architecture and history. Tour-start locations vary tremendously based on the area of exploration, from uptown subway platforms to Grand Central Terminal.

ON LOCATION TOURS
☎ 212-209-3370; per person $15-35

Offers two- and three-hour tours to spots where your favorite TV shows were filmed (*Sex and the City*, *Sopranos*, *Friends* and more).

WILDMAN STEVE BRILL
☎ 914-835-2153; www.wildmanstevebrill.com; per person $10

Steve is an urban naturalist and takes folks on foraging journeys through Central Park and outer-borough parks, helping you collect edible berries, herbs and mushrooms (check the website for schedules).

Walking

ADVENTURE ON A SHOESTRING
☎ 212-265-2663; per person from $5
This company gives excellent bargain tours of Chinatown, Gramercy, Little Italy and the Lower East Side.

ALFRED POMMER'S CULTURAL WALKING TOURS
☎ 212-979-2388; per person $10
Focuses on a neighborhood's architecture, history and quirky stories.

BIG APPLE GREETERS PROGRAM
☎ 212-669-8198
Conducts volunteer-led tours of lesser-known neighborhoods, featuring greeters who are multilingual and in particular, help the disabled. Tours are free; book at least two days ahead.

BIG ONION WALKING TOURS
☎ 212-439-1090; per person $12
Has popular and somewhat quirky tours specializing in ethnic New York. Tours operate year-round.

RADICAL WALKING TOURS
☎ 718-492-0069; per person $10
Conducts radical-history (encompassing anarchists, protestors, suffragists etc) tours of a number of neighborhoods, including the Lower East Side, West Village and the Upper West Side.

LOWER MANHATTAN

Walking Tour pp152–4, Eating p172, Drinking p209, Shopping p257, Sleeping pp292–3

Before September 11, images of Lower Manhattan ran the gamut: frantic stock traders, suit-clad Wall Streeters, political rallies on the steps of City Hall, majestic views of New York Harbor framed by the Statue of Liberty on one side and the World Trade Center (WTC) on the other. Now it's more apt to make folks think of trauma – especially visitors, who have not had time to get used to the new tenor down here, and to

slowly let the painful visions fade away. While both memorials and construction activity still overshadow much of this area, plenty of Lower Manhattan's old spry self is back, too. On any given weekday, you'll see hopeful (and frustrated) immigrants lined up outside of the INS building, powerful lawyers and frightened families rushing into court buildings, financial traders chatting wildly into cell phones, and curious, sensitive tourists strolling from one landmark to the next.

Security remains heightened, though, and that means bag checks – sometimes with x-ray machines – and the closure of some sites to the public. At the time of writing, this included the New York Stock Exchange, which will remain closed indefinitely.

The **Alliance for Downtown New York** (Map pp380-1; ☎ 212-566-6700; www.down townny.com; 120 Broadway, Ste 3340) publishes maps and brochures and staffs the area from City Hall to Battery Park City, providing information crews who are armed with neighborhood factoids; look for the friendly folks wearing red vests.

> ## Transportation
> **Subway** 1, 9, E, N, R, W, J, M, Z and 4, 5, 6.
> **Bus** M1, M6, M15, M9, M22 or M103.
> **Ferry** New York Water Taxi (☎ 212-742-1969) zips to and from Midtown, Brooklyn, Chelsea and the Upper East Side.

Orientation

Lower Manhattan encompasses the area below Canal St (where you'll also find a section of Chinatown) down to Battery Park, including the Financial District and Tribeca, the 'Triangle Below Canal St,' bordered by Canal St in the north, West St in the west, Chambers St in the south and Broadway in the east. Waterfront areas include South Street Seaport and the New York Harbor, home to the world-renowned icon, Lady Liberty, and to Ellis Island.

Top Five Lower Manhattan

- **African Burial Ground** (p76) Seeing justice for those long gone.
- **Ellis Island** (opposite) Trace your ancestors.
- **Federal Hall** (p76) Feel a sense of history with some help from GW.
- **Fraunces Tavern Museum** (p76) Restaurant-museum combo, both a step back in time.
- **National Museum of the American Indian** (p77) Gorgeous architecture and fascinating exhibits.

NEW YORK HARBOR

Just like the city's first immigrants, foreigners – whether from as close as New Jersey or as far as Australia – often make a beeline down here to recapture that initial feeling of excitement. And it's a fine way to do it – not only because of the Statue of Liberty and Ellis Island, but because of the gorgeous waterfront lawns and bike paths of Battery Park, festive outdoor concerts at Castle Clinton and overall big-sky feeling you get just from lazing on benches or grassy patches along the shoreline.

STATUE OF LIBERTY Map p378

☎ 212-363-3200; www.nps.gov/stli; ⏰ ferries leave every 30 min 9:30am-3:30pm; incl Ellis I adult/senior/child $10/8/4; subway 4, 5 to Bowling Green

This landmark is the most enduring symbol of New York City and, indeed, the New World. Modeled after the Colossus of Rhodes, the statue was the brainchild of political activist Edouard René Lefebvre de Laboulaye and sculptor Frédéric-Auguste Bartholdi. In 1865, the pair decided something monumental should be created to promote French republicanism, and Bartholdi dedicated most of the next 20 years to turning that dream into reality.

Once New York was chosen as the site for Lady Liberty and $250,000 was raised to cover costs, Bartholdi got busy creating his most famous sculpture, which included a metal skeleton by railway engineer Alexandre Gustave Eiffel. In 1883, poet Emma Lazarus published a poem called *The New Colossus* as part of a fund-raising campaign for a statue pedestal. Her words have long since been associated with the monument: 'Give me your tired, your poor. Your huddled masses yearning to breathe free. The wretched refuse of your teeming shore. Send these, the homeless, tempest-tost to me. I lift my lamp beside the golden door!' Ironically, these famous words were added to the base only in 1901, 17 years after the poet's death. On October 28, 1886, the 151ft Liberty Enlightening the World was finally unveiled in New York harbor.

Badly in need of restoration by the 1980s, more than $100 million was spent to shore up Lady Liberty for her centennial. The rotting copper skin required substantial work, and workers installed a new gold-plated torch, the

third in the statue's history. The older stained-glass torch is now on display just inside the entrance to the staircase. The exhibition also shows how the statue has been exploited for commercial purposes.

Speaking of which, the **Statue of Liberty ferry** (Map pp380-1; ☎ 212-269-5755; www.statue-oflibertyferry.com), run by the Circle Line, has made more than a few dollars shuttling visitors to the statue and back. Well over four million people a year ride the boats to the Statue of Liberty and Ellis Island, while millions more take the 1½-hour boat ride just for the view of Manhattan, which surpasses the view from the statue itself. If the crowds are too much, try the nearby **Staten Island ferry** (☎ 718-815-2628; www.siferry.com). It doesn't take you to the statue but provides a great view of it and Downtown Manhattan – best of all, it's free! (For details, see Staten Island Ferry, p149.)

Give Me Liberty!

The Statue of Liberty's interior, crown and museum remained closed for almost two years after September 11, but reopened with much fanfare in July 2004 following a multimillion-dollar renovation. Although you still cannot enter the statue itself, you can visit its museum and peer into its intricate interior through a glass ceiling at the Lady's base. The 16-story observation deck reopened as well. Expect tighter security than ever before, with officials discouraging visitors from bringing backpacks or other bulky bags. Although the ferry ride lasts only 15 minutes, a trip to both the Statue of Liberty and Ellis Island is an all-day affair. In summer, you may wait up to an hour to embark on an 800-person ferry.

ELLIS ISLAND Map p378

☎ 212-363-3200; www.nps.gov/elis; ferries leave every 30 min 9:30am-3:30pm; adult/senior/child $10/8/4 incl Statue of Liberty; subway 4, 5 to Bowling Green

Ferries to the Statue of Liberty make a second stop at Ellis Island, New York's main immigration station from 1892 until 1954. More than 12 million people passed through here before the island was abandoned; the record number of immigrants processed in one day was just under 12,000.

A $160-million restoration has turned the impressive red brick main building into an **Immigration Museum**, where you can explore the history of the island through a series of galleries. The exhibition begins at the baggage room and continues on to the 2nd-story rooms where medical inspections took place and foreign currency was exchanged.

The exhibits emphasize that, contrary to popular myth, most of the ship-borne immigrants were processed within eight hours and that conditions were generally clean and safe (especially for 1st- and 2nd-class passengers, who were processed on board; only immigrants from the steerage class were subjected to whatever conditions prevailed on Ellis Island). The 338ft-long registry room, with its beautiful vaulted tile ceiling, is where the polygamists, paupers, criminals and anarchists were turned around and sent back from where they came. Walking though the registry today – described as 'light and airy' in the museum literature – surely can't compare with the days when this room held 5000 confused and tired people waiting to be interviewed by immigration officers and inspected by doctors. The latter had literally seconds to diagnose a list of diseases; anyone with a contagious illness was rejected.

You can take a 50-minute audio tour of the facility for $6. But for an even more affecting take on history, pick up one of the phones in each display area and listen to the recorded memories of real Ellis Island immigrants, taped in the 1980s.

If you want still more, see **Embracing Freedom** (☎ 212-883-1986, ext 742; adult/senior & child over 14 yrs $3/2.50), a 30-minute play about the Ellis Island experience which shows five times a day on the half-hour from 10:30am to 3:30pm. A free 30-minute film on the immigrant experience, *Island of Hope, Island of Tears*, is also worth checking out, as is the exhibition on the influx of immigrants just before WWI.

Give Me Governor's!

After two centuries of restricted military use, the 172-acre **Governor's Island** (Map p378; ☎ 212-514 -8285; www.nps.gov/gois; admission free; tours twice daily Tue-Sat; subway 4, 5 to Bowling Green) was returned to the public from the federal government in 2003. For decades, New Yorkers knew the swath of land only as an untouchable, mysterious patch of green in the harbor, but now the Governor's Island National Monument (encompassing 22 acres) has changed all that by offering 1½-hour guided tours. Highlights of the haven, just a five-minute boat ride from Manhattan, include two 19th-century fortifications – Fort Jay and the three-tiered, sandstone Castle Williams – plus open lawns, massive shade trees and unsurpassed city views. Its historic significance is far reaching: besides serving as a success story in the Revolutionary War, the central army recruiting station during the Civil War and the take-off point for Wilbur Wright's historic 1909 first-ever flight, it's where the 1998 Reagan-Gorbachev summit signaled the beginning of the end of the Cold War. As far as the future of the island goes, it's yet to be determined, because a general management plan for the entire island – which open-space advocates hope will include plenty of parkland and public activities – won't be completed until 2006.

FINANCIAL DISTRICT

Anchored by the mile-long Wall St, which was named for a defensive wall the Dutch built in 1653 to mark the northern line of New Amsterdam, this history-steeped area is where the US Congress first convened and where America's first president, George Washington, was inaugurated. The concentrated feel of the area is distinguished by cramped, circuitous and sometimes confusing side streets flanked by Federal homes, Greek Revival temples, Gothic churches, Renaissance palazzos and one of the finest collections of early-20th-century skyscrapers. And then there's the New York Stock Exchange (currently closed to visitors) and Federal Reserve Bank, reminding anyone who passes by the hushed, guarded exteriors that they have most definitely stumbled into the seat of capitalism.

AFRICAN BURIAL GROUND Map pp380-1

☎ 337-2001; 290 Broadway btwn Duane & Elk Sts;
🕐 9am-4pm Mon-Fri; subway TK

Builders were shocked when, during preliminary construction of a Downtown office building in 1991, more than 400 stacked wooden caskets were discovered only 16 to 28 feet below street level. When it became clear that the boxes held the remains of enslaved Africans (the nearby Trinity Church graveyard had banned burial of Africans at the time), construction was halted, an investigation was launched and all hell broke loose – Mayor David Dinkins rallied and citizens held protests and vigils, demanding that no building be erected on such sacred ground. The rally cries worked; today the site is permanently protected as a National Historic Landmark.

BOWLING GREEN Map pp380-1

Cnr Broadway & State St; subway 4, 5 to Bowling Green

New York's oldest – and possibly tiniest – park is believed to have been the spot where Dutch settler Peter Minuit paid Native Americans $24 to purchase Manhattan Island. The verdant triangle was leased by the people of New York from the English crown beginning in 1733, for the token amount of one peppercorn each. But an angry mob, inspired by George Washington's nearby reading of the Declaration of Independence, descended upon the site in 1776 and tore down a large statue of King George III; a fountain now stands in its place. The big charging bull at the northern edge of the park, incidentally, was placed here permanently after it appeared mysteriously in front of the New York Stock Exchange in 1989, two years after a market crash. *Charging Bull*, a 7000lb bronze sculpture by Arturo Di Modica, is now the un-witting subject of constant tourist photos.

FEDERAL HALL Map pp380-1

☎ 212-825-6888; www.nps.gov/feha; 26 Wall St;
🕐 9am-5pm Mon-Fri; admission free; subway 2, 3, 4,
5 to Wall St, J, M, Z to Broad St

Distinguished by a huge statue of George Washington, Federal Hall stands on the site of New York's original City Hall, where the first US Congress convened and Washington took the oath of office on April 30, 1789, as the first US chief executive. After that structure's demolition in the early 19th century, this Greek Revival building gradually rose in its place between 1834 and 1842. Considered to be one of the country's premier examples of classical architecture, it served as the US customs house until 1862. Today, the building contains a small museum dedicated to postcolonial New York.

Federal Hall serves as the starting point for four self-guided Heritage Trail walking tours that explore the area's history in greater detail. Look for the wrought-iron, free-standing maps and site descriptions sprinkled all over Lower Manhattan's sidewalks. Maps and an accompanying Junior Ranger Guide are available from the **Alliance for Downtown New York** (Map pp380-1; ☎ 212-566-6700).

FEDERAL RESERVE BANK Map pp380-1

☎ 212-720-6130; 33 Liberty St at Nassau St; admission
free; subway J, Z to Fulton St–Broadway Nassau

The only reason to visit the Federal Reserve Bank is to ogle the facility's high-security vault. Located 80ft below ground, more than 10,000 tons of gold reserves reside here. You'll only see a small part of that fortune, but you'll learn a lot about the US Federal Reserve System on the informative tour. You can also browse through an exhibition of coins and counterfeit currency. Reservations are required for the tour, which is held every hour from 9:30am to 2:30pm Monday to Friday.

FRAUNCES TAVERN MUSEUM

Map pp380-1

☎ 212-425-1778; www.frauncestavernmuseum
.org; 54 Pearl St; adult/senior, student & child $3/2;
🕐 10am-5pm Tue, Wed & Fri, 10am-7pm Thu, 11am-
5pm Sat; subway 4, 5 to Bowling Green, 2, 3 to Wall St

This museum-restaurant sits in a block of historic structures that, along with nearby Stone St and the South St Seaport, comprise the best-preserved examples of early-18th-century New York.

Originally built as a tony residence for merchant Stephan Delancey's family, barkeep Samuel Fraunces purchased it in 1762, turning it into the Queen's Head Tavern in honor of the US victory in the Revolutionary War. It was in the 2nd-floor dining room on December 4, 1783, that George Washington bade farewell to the officers of the Continental Army after the British relinquished control of New York City. In the 19th century, the tavern was closed and the building fell into disuse. It was also damaged during several massive fires that swept through old downtown areas, destroying most colonial buildings and nearly all Dutch-built structures. In 1904, the Sons of the Revolution historical society bought the building and returned it to an approximation of its colonial-era look – an act believed to be the first major attempt at historical preservation in the USA. In 1975, the Fuerzas Armadas de Liberación Nacional, a radical group from Puerto Rico, detonated a bomb here, killing five people. The museum hosts a Lunchtime Lecture series on occasional weekdays at 12:30pm, covering topics from American cuisine to local archaeology; call for the schedule.

Just across the street from the tavern are the excavated remains of the old Dutch Stadt Huys, which served as New Amsterdam's administrative center, courthouse and jail from 1641 until the British takeover in 1664. This building, destroyed in 1699, was originally on the city's waterfront until landfill added a few more blocks to southern Manhattan. The excavation here between 1979 and 1980 was the city's first large-scale archaeological investigation, and it reaped many artifacts (including the privy and cistern remains displayed under Plexiglas).

NATIONAL MUSEUM OF THE AMERICAN INDIAN Map pp380-1
☎ 212-514-3700; www.si.edu/nmai; 1 Bowling Green; admission free; ⏰ 10am-5pm Fri-Wed, 10am-8pm Thu; subway 4, 5 to Bowling Green

This museum, an affiliate of the Smithsonian Institution, moved to the spectacular former US Customs House on Bowling Green in 1994. This is an ironically grand space for the USA's leading museum on Native American art, established by oil heir George Gustav Heye in 1916. The facility's information center is in the former duties collection office, with computer banks located next to old wrought-iron teller booths.

The galleries are on the 2nd floor, beyond a vast rotunda featuring statues of famous navigators and murals celebrating shipping history. This museum does little to explain the history of Native Americans but instead concentrates on Native American culture, boasting a million-item collection of crafts and everyday objects. Computer touch-screens feature insights into Native American life and beliefs, and working artists often offer explanations of their techniques.

NEW YORK STOCK EXCHANGE
Map pp380-1
☎ 212-656-5168; www.nyse.com; 8 Broad St, ticket booth 20 Broad St; subway 1, 2, 4, 5 to Wall St, J, M, Z to Broad St

Though Wall St is the widely recognized symbol for US capitalism, the world's best-known stock exchange is actually right here on Broad St. Before its closing to the public due to stepped-up security measures, more than 700,000 visitors a year passed behind the

portentous Romanesque facade to see where about a billion shares valued at around $44 billion change hands daily.

Feel free to gawk outside the exchange, though, where you'll see dozens of brokers dressed in color-coordinated trading jackets popping out for a quick cigarette or hot dog; lucky for you, the street scene outside is often more entertaining than the money swapping within.

Truly frantic buying and selling by red-faced traders screaming 'Sell! Sell!' goes on at the **New York Mercantile Exchange** (☎ 212-299-2499; www.nymex.com; 1 North End Ave; subway A, C, 4, 5 to Fulton St–Broadway Nassau), near Vesey St. This exchange deals in gold, gas and oil commodities, but not tourists anymore; like NYSE, it's closed to visitors, but encourages you to check back periodically to see if the policy has changed.

Trinity Church

TRINITY CHURCH Map pp380-1
☎ 212-602-0800; www.trinitywallstreet.org; cnr Broadway & Wall St; ⏰ 8am-6pm Mon-Fri, 8am-4pm Sat, 7am-4pm Sun; subway 2, 3 4, 5 to Wall St, N, R to Rector St

This former Anglican parish church was founded by King William III in 1697 and once presided over several constituent chapels, including St Paul's Chapel, on the corner of Fulton St and Broadway. Its huge landholdings in Lower Manhattan made it the country's wealthiest and most influential church throughout the 18th century. The current Trinity Church is the third structure on the site. Designed by English architect Richard Upjohn, this 1846 building helped to launch the picturesque neo-Gothic movement in America. At the time of its construction, its 280ft bell tower made it the tallest building in New York City.

The long, dark interior of the church includes a beautiful stained-glass window over the altar, while the small, fenced-in cemetery out back,

filled with ancient headstones smoothed by the centuries is a fascinating, serene place to wander. Trinity, like other Anglican churches in America, became part of the Episcopal faith following US independence from Britain. One of the best times to visit Trinity is during lunchtime, weekday services or for its excellent Concerts at One midday music series (also held at **St Paul's Chapel**, see p81) for just a $2 suggested donation. Call the concert hotline at ☎ 212-602-0747 for a schedule.

CIVIC CENTER & CITY HALL AREA

Government business is stationed in this downtown region, where the infectious buzz of change and progress and pro-action (no matter how delusional it is) will jazz you with its earnestness. City council members dash from public hearings to constituent brunches at nearby diners, and reporters clamor to City Hall Park for press conferences, TV satellite vans camp out across from the majestic row of courthouses – New York County and US Supreme among them – where resentful locals drag themselves to jury duty each afternoon. Towering over it all is the massive **Municipal Building** (100 Centre St), which houses everything from the city's Marriage Bureau to local NPR affiliate radio station, WNYC, as well as the floating span of the Brooklyn Bridge, an ever-present reminder that Manhattan is not the island it often purports to be. South of City Hall is Park Row, known as Newspaper Row when it was the center of the newspaper publishing business from the 1840s to the 1920s (now, incidentally, it's the spot of a veritable strip mall, including the excellent computer and electronics purveyor, **J&R Music World**, p257); to the west is the Cass Gilbert's magnificent Woolworth Building, the city's tallest skyscraper at 792ft when it was completed in 1913.

CITY HALL Map pp380-1

☎ 212-788-6865; Park Row; admission free, tours by appointment only; subway 4, 5, 6 to Brooklyn Bridge–City Hall, J, M, Z to Chambers St

The hall, in placid City Hall Park facing the entrance to the Brooklyn Bridge, has been home to New York's government since 1812. In keeping with the half-baked civic planning that has often plagued large-scale New York projects, officials neglected to finish the building's northern side in marble, gambling that the city would not expand uptown. The mistake was finally rectified in 1954, completing a structure that architectural critic Ada Louise Huxtable called a 'symbol of taste, excellence and quality not always matched by the policies inside.'

One highlight inside includes the spot where Abraham Lincoln's coffin sat for a brief time in 1865. (Walk to the top of the staircase on the 2nd floor to view the historic site.) The Governor's Room, a reception area where the mayor entertains important guests, contains 12 portraits of the founding fathers by John Trumbull, George Washington's old writing table and other examples of Federal

furniture, and the remnants of a flag flown at the first president's 1789 inaugural ceremony. If you take a quick peek into the City Council chambers, you might see lawmakers deliberating over the renaming of a city street in someone's honor – an activity that accounts for approximately 40% of all the bills passed by the 51-member body.

For generations, City Hall's steps had been a popular and visible site for political protests, but exercising free speech in this way was considered inappropriate – like so much other behavior – by former mayor Giuliani who banned the practice. Citing security concerns, Mayor Bloomberg allows demonstrations here, as long as you get a permit first. The entire complex was closed to visitors following the September 11 attacks but was reopened for tours by appointment only; call for details.

City Hall Park received a multimillion-dollar facelift and its gas lamps, fountains, pretty landscaping, chess tables and benches make it a nice place to kick back for a spell, especially in summer, when a Summerfest concert series brings live R&B and jazz here on weekends.

Brooklyn Bridge

A New York icon, the **Brooklyn Bridge** (Map pp380-1; subway 4, 5, 6 to City Hall) has seen many protests, joys and tragedies. It was the span that held angry, plunger-wielding marchers who were outraged by the sodomy-based police torture of Haitian immigrant Abner Louima in 1997. In spring 2004 it hosted a crowd of gays and lesbians who marched in support of legalizing same-sex marriage. It's been part of countless marathons and group bike rides, the backdrop for annual July 4 fireworks, and the path to refuge for hundreds of traumatized downtown workers, who walked or ran over it, soot-covered, after fleeing their work days following the tragic events of September 11, 2001. But its long, long history has many more stories to tell.

When the world's first steel suspension bridge opened in 1883, the 1596ft span between its two support towers was the longest in history. Although its construction was fraught with disaster, the bridge became a magnificent example of urban design, which inspired poets, writers and painters. Today, the Brooklyn Bridge continues to dazzle and many regard it as the most beautiful bridge in the world.

This East River suspension bridge was designed by the Prussian-born engineer John Roebling, who was knocked off a pier in Fulton Landing in June 1869; he died of tetanus poisoning before construction of the bridge even began. His son Washington Roebling supervised construction of the bridge, which lasted 14 years and managed to survive budget overruns and the deaths of 20 workers. The younger Roebling himself suffered from the bends while helping to excavate the riverbed for the bridge's western tower and remained bedridden for much of the project (his wife oversaw construction). There was one final tragedy to come in June 1883, when the bridge opened to pedestrian traffic. Someone in the crowd shouted, perhaps as a joke, that the bridge was collapsing into the river, setting off a mad rush in which 12 people were trampled to death.

The bridge entered its second century as strong and beautiful as ever, following an extensive renovation in the early 1980s. The pedestrian walkway that begins just east of City Hall affords a wonderful view of Lower Manhattan, and you can stop at observation points under the support towers to view brass 'panorama' histories of the waterfront. Just take care to stay on the side of the walkway marked for folks on foot – one half is designated for cyclists, who use it en masse for commuting and pleasure rides, and frustrated peddlers have been known to get nasty with oblivious tourists who wander, camera pressed to an eye, into the bike lane! Barring any such run-ins, you should reach Brooklyn after about a 20-minute trek. Bear left to Empire Fulton Ferry State Park or Cadman Plaza West, which runs alongside Middagh St in the heart of Brooklyn Heights, which brings you to Brooklyn's downtown area, including the ornate Brooklyn Borough Hall and the Brooklyn Heights Promenade (see p166).

BATTERY PARK CITY

Try the following experiment if you're lucky enough to be down in BPC on a balmy afternoon: Lay yourself right in the tickly green carpet of North Lawn at the water's-edge park. That's right, don't even bother with a blanket. Now close your eyes and float. We'll bet you can't even tell you're in NYC. Of course, you're not visiting the city to shelter yourself from the urban storm, but snuggling into the grass will at least give you a first-person taste of why this park is so loved by New Yorkers. The 30-acre waterfront swath stretches along the Hudson River from Chambers St to Pier 1 on the southern tip of the island, encompassing Rockefeller Park, the Battery Park City Esplanade, Robert F Wagner Park and Battery Park. It's a fantastic getaway from Manhattan's madness, with glorious sunsets and Statue of Liberty views, outdoor concerts and films in the summer, playgrounds and soccer games, and smooth paths for cycling, running, strolling or blading.

CASTLE CLINTON

Map pp380-1

☎ 212-344-7220; www.nps.gov/cacl; Battery Park; ⏱ 8:30am-5pm; subway J, M, Z to Broad St, 1, 9 to South Ferry

Built as a fort to defend the New York Harbor during the War of 1812, the circular wall got its current moniker in 1817 to honor then-mayor DeWitt Clinton. It has been restored as a national monument – after turns as an opera house, entertainment complex, immigration center and aquarium – and now serves as a visitor center, with historical displays, as well as a massive performance space, where musicians from Natalie Merchant to Rosanne Cash have taken the roofless stage within the wall for weeknight summer shows under the stars.

IRISH HUNGER MEMORIAL Map pp380-1

290 Vesey St at North End Ave, Battery Park; admission free; subway 1, 9, N, R to Cortlandt St

This small and poignant maze of low limestone walls and patches of green grass is the creation of artist Brian Tolle. It's here to raise awareness of the Great Irish Famine and Migration (1845–52) which led so many immigrants to leave the Republic for the chance of a better life in the Big Apple; today almost 800,000 city residents trace their ancestry to Ireland.

Recharge at the Battery

At the Park House near Rockefeller Park you can borrow pogo sticks, basketballs, jump ropes, board games or billiard balls and a cue (for use on the outdoor tables gazing on Lady Liberty), free with identification. Kids will love romping in the playgrounds and climbing on the whimsical bronze sculptures by Tom Otterness. Plus the Battery Park Conservancy offers a range of free or low-fee walking tours, group swims, children's programming and classes in these parks; for information you can contact the **Conservancy** (☎ 212-267-9700; www.bpcparks.org).

MUSEUM OF JEWISH HERITAGE

Map pp380-1

☎ 646-437-4200; www.mjhnyc.org; 36 Battery Pl, Battery Park City; adult/senior/student $10/7/5, free 4-8pm Wed; ⏰ 10am-5:45pm Sun-Tue & Thu, 10am-8pm Wed, 10am-5pm Fri; subway 4, 5 to Bowling Green

This 30,000 sq ft waterfront memorial museum, with a six-sided shape and three tiers to symbolize the Star of David and the six million Jews who perished in the Holocaust, explores all aspects of what it means to Jewish in 20th-century New York. Displays include personal artifacts, photographs, a serene memorial stone garden, documentary films about Holocaust survivors and ongoing lectures and other programs. An onsite kosher café, **Abigael's at the Museum**, serves light food during museum hours.

NEW YORK UNEARTHED Map pp380-1

☎ 212-748-8628; www.southstseaport.org /archaeology/nyunearthed.html; 17 State St btwn Pearl & Whitehall Sts; admission free; ⏰ noon-5pm Mon-Fri; subway N, R to Whitehall St, 4, 5 to Bowling Green, 1, 9 to South Ferry

Who knows what you may find here? Shards of dinnerware, pieces of a pipe, old shoes – they help you piece together more than 6000 years of NYC history. This archaeologist-staffed outpost of the South St Seaport, just across the street from Battery Park, is filled with artifacts mined from city sites; it also hosts frequent rotating shows – a recent show featured remnants of the 19th-century Five Points neighborhood (depicted in the film *Gangs of New York*).

SHRINE TO ST ELIZABETH ANN SETON Map pp380-1

☎ 212-269-6865; Our Lady of the Rosary, 7 State St; admission free; ⏰ 6:30am-5pm Mon-Fri, before & after 12:15pm Mass Sat & 9am & noon Masses Sun; subway N, R, W to Whitehall St

This mystical, silent escape from the city is a tiny church and shrine to Mother Seton, housed in the red brick Federal style where America's first saint lived in 1801. Born in NYC, Elizabeth Ann married and had five children but was eventually widowed, which inspired her to become a nun and found the Sisters of Charity. Today, devotees can often be found on their knees, praying inside this spiritual space at all hours of the day.

SKYSCRAPER MUSEUM Map pp380-1

☎ 212-968-1961; www.skyscraper.org; 39 Battery Pl; adult/senior & student $5/2.50; subway 4, 5 to Bowling Green

Sent to a temporary home following September 11, this ode to tall buildings moved into its new permanent space in March 2004, occupying the ground-floor space of the Ritz-Carlton Hotel. It features two galleries, one to focus on rotating exhibits – past shows have looked at the Empire State Building, Times Square and the World Trade Center – the other dedicated to a permanent study of high-rise history, including a size chart of the world's biggest buildings (Kuala Lumpur's Petronas Towers are currently in the lead – built in 1998, they are a whopping 1483ft high!).

SPHERE Map pp380-1

Battery Park, Bowling Green Entrance; subway 4, 5 to Bowling Green

Partially damaged in the World Trade Center attacks, this 45,000lb, 15ft-wide orb used to stand atop a granite fountain in a plaza between the WTC towers. Now it stands here as an indestructible reminder of its past home. Fritz Koenig's massive steel and bronze sculpture, created in 1971 as a symbol of peace through world trade, was partially damaged in the tragedy; it was moved here as a tribute to the dead shortly after, and a hearty gash across its center is a potent reminder of what it has seen. The piece is now fronted by an eternal flame, and has a simple plaque at its base: 'In honor of all those who were lost,' it reads. 'The Sphere endures as an icon of hope and the indestructible spirit of this country.'

ST PAUL'S CHAPEL Map pp380-1
☎ 212-602-0800; www.saintpaulschapel.org; Broadway at Fulton St; subway 2, 3 to Fulton St

George Washington worshipped here after his inauguration in 1789, and that was the biggest claim to fame for this colonial-era church (part of Trinity Church, which sits farther down Broadway) prior to September 11. After that fateful day, when the World Trade Center destruction occurred just a block behind this Classic Revival brownstone, the mighty structure became a spiritual support center for all who needed it when volunteers worked round the clock, serving meals, setting up beds, doling out massages and counseling rescue workers. Today a moving shrine of posters, tapestries, photographs and writings remains beneath the cut-glass chandeliers.

WORLD FINANCIAL CENTER
Map pp380-1
☎ 212-945-2600; www.worldfinancialcenter.com; 200 Liberty St; subway A, C, 4, 5 to Fulton St–Broadway–Nasau St

This mall-like complex, behind the former WTC site in Battery Park City, stands on the landfill created by the excavation for the WTC's foundation. A group of four office towers surrounds the Winter Garden, a palm-filled, glass atrium that hosts free concerts and dance performances year-round. This is a good place to head if the weather turns nasty as you can pass an hour or so by shopping at the various chain stores (Ann Taylor, Banana Republic, Gap) or eating at the large food-court area.

WORLD TRADE CENTER SITE VIEWING PLATFORM Map pp380-1
Church St at Fulton St; admission free; subway N, R, W to Rector St, 4, 5 to Wall St

Tourists snapping photos, locals meditating during a lunch break, shoppers headed to Century 21 across the street stopping to remember – all mill about before this high metal gate that wraps around the ever-changing construction site of the former twin towers. Photos along the fence-like wall show the WTC before, during and after the September 11 attacks, with facts about both the buildings and the rescue efforts. Floodlights give it all an eerily comforting glow once the sun goes down.

SOUTH STREET SEAPORT
SOUTH STREET SEAPORT ATTRACTIONS Map pp380-1
☎ 212-732-7678; www.southstseaport.org; subway 2, 3, 4, 5, J, Z to Fulton St–Broadway–Nassau St

This 11-block enclave of shops, piers and sights combines the best and worst in historic preservation. Pier 17, beyond the elevated FDR Dr, is a waterfront development project that is home to a number of shops and one recommended restaurant, **Cabana** (p172); there's also a rare public bathroom here. Clustered around the piers is a number of genuinely significant 18th- and 19th-century buildings dating from the heyday of this old East River ferry port, which fell into disuse with the building of Brooklyn Bridge and the establishment of deep-water jetties on the Hudson River. The many pedestrian malls, historic tall ships and riverside locale make the seaport a picturesque destination or detour. Schermerhorn Row, a block of old warehouses bordered by Fulton, Front and South Sts, contains novelty shops, upscale boutiques and the **New York Yankees Clubhouse** at 8 Fulton St (where you can purchase fee-free tickets for the Bronx Bombers). Across the street, the **Fulton Market Building**, built in 1983 to reflect the red-brick style of its older neighbors, is a glorified fast-food court and shopping arcade. In the summertime, though, the outdoor courtyard becomes home to an oft-worthy series of performers from local blues, jazz and rock bands.

SOUTH STREET SEAPORT MUSEUM

Map pp380-1

☎ 212-748-8600; 207 Front St; adult/senior & student/child $8/6/4; ⏱ 10am-5pm; subway 2, 3, 4, 5, J, Z to Fulton St, A, C to Broadway–Nassau

Opened in 1967, this museum offers a glimpse of the seaport's history and a survey of the world's great ocean liners in its permanent exhibits and interesting sites around the 11-block area, including three galleries, an antique printing shop, a children's center, a maritime crafts center and historic ships.

Just south of Pier 17 stands a group of tall-masted sailing vessels, including the *Peking*, *Wavertree*, *Pioneer*, *Ambrose* and *Helen McAllister*. The admission price to the museum includes access to these ships. You can join sails aboard the gorgeous, iron-hulled *Pioneer*, built in 1885 to carry mined sand. The two-hour journeys ($25/20/15 per adult/senior/child) run from Memorial Day through mid-September from Tuesday to Friday evenings and Saturday and Sunday beginning at 1pm; passengers are encouraged to bring snacks and even a bottle of wine for this relaxing, view-rich sail. Reserve a spot by calling ☎ 212-748-8786.

For more than 130 years, Pier 17 had been home to the Fulton Fish Market, where most of the city's restaurants got their fresh seafood. But the bustling, gritty and historic open-air moved up to Hunt's Point in the South Bronx in 2003, following months of labor unrest, a suspicious 1995 fire and a crackdown on corruption by Giuliani. The new Hunt's Point Fish Market, eagerly anticipated for Bronx economic revitalization, was set to be up and running by fall of 2004. Besides the welcome absence of fishy smells, the market and its characters have really been missed in Downtown Manhattan.

TRIBECA

Eating pp173–4, Drinking pp209–10, Sleeping pp293–4

Prior to September 11, Tribeca (which stands for 'TRIangle BElow CAnal St,' with Broadway on the eastern side and Chambers St to the south) was the hottest neighborhood most visitors had never heard of. For those in the know, Tribeca meant huge lofts and relatively tolerable rents, world-class restaurants, historic bars, quaint cobblestone side streets and a strong shopping and art scene, all with a neighborhood feel.

In addition, Tribeca has amazing public transportation connections, few tourists (despite the presence of Robert De Niro's Tribeca Films production company and the home of the late John F Kennedy Jr) and even fewer of those ubiquitous chain stores that are overtaking the city. Thanks to community preservation efforts, there are four separate historic districts within Tribeca's boundaries.

As it borders the WTC site, Tribeca was rocked by the terrorist attacks and reeled for years. But now the regrouped residents and business owners – after filing for emergency aid and salvaging belongings and benefiting from massive incentives (mainly from the Lower Manhattan Development Corporation) to keep folks in the neighborhood, the remarkable rebirth here is strikingly apparent.

Although it will never be the same, there is a hopefulness pervading the restaurants and boutiques and the streets; and it's more important than ever to come and lend your support to this resilient little village.

> ## Transportation
> **Subway** 1, 9, 2, 3, A, C, E, N, R, W, 6.
> **Bus** M6, M9.

Orientation

Tribeca is bordered by Canal St in the north, West St in the west, Chambers St in the south and Broadway in the east. Its waterfront areas include South St Seaport and the New York Harbor, home to Lady Liberty and Ellis Island. A good way to get acquainted with the neighborhood is through the **Tribeca Organization** (www.tribeca.org). Trains including the 1, 9 to Franklin St and the 2, 3 to Chambers St are your best bets for traveling to the 'hood.

CLOCKTOWER GALLERY Map pp380-1

☎ 212-233-1096; www.ps1.org; 108 Leonard St btwn Broadway & Lafayette St; ☽ noon-6pm Wed-Sat; subway 1, 9 to Franklin St

The PS1 Contemporary Art Center runs a free gallery space and studios known as the Clocktower Gallery. It's at the top of the ornate old headquarters of the New York Life Insurance Company (currently the headquarters of the New York City Probation Department and the Public Health & Hospitals Corporation). The Institute for Contemporary Art, which funds the gallery, also sponsors the artists working in the studios. You can see their works in progress during the gallery's opening hours. Take the elevator to the 12th floor – as far as it goes – and climb the stairs to the tower on the 13th floor.

HARRISON ST HOUSES Map pp380-1

Subway 1, 2 to Franklin St

Built between 1804 and 1828, the eight townhouses on the block of Harrison St immediately west of Greenwich St constitute the largest collection of Federal architecture left in the city. But they were not always neighbors: six of them once stood two blocks away, on a stretch of Washington St that no longer exists. In the early 1970s, that area was the site of Washington Market, a wholesale fruit and vegetable shopping area. But development of the waterfront (which resulted in the construction of Manhattan Community College and the Soviet-type concrete apartment complex that now looms over the townhouses) meant the market had to move uptown and the historic row of houses had to be relocated. Only the buildings at 31 and 33 Harrison St remain where they were originally constructed.

Tribeca Film Festival

Just past its third year, the Tribeca Film Festival – founded by Robert DeNiro and Jane Rosenthal as a way to boost downtown economy and provide NYC with a competitive film event – has become a beloved, successful cinematic soiree. The part-showcase, part-contest fest is a weeklong event in April that featured more than 150 movies in 2004 (along with simultaneous outdoor concerts and other festive events), many screened at the Tribeca Film Center (see below). And while the relatively new event is still finding its focus in many ways, this year screenings were mainly narrative and documentary features from new filmmakers, many from around the globe. Highlights from 2004 included a doco on the war in Iraq, a portrait of a Brazilian prison, a film adaptation of Dorothy Allison's *Cavedweller* novel, and a film of improvised vignettes from director Jim Jarmusch. And one of the much sought-after prizes is in the newest category, 'New York, New York,' which awards outstanding locally produced indies.

TRIBECA FILM CENTER Map pp380-1

☎ 212-941-2000; www.tribecafilm.com; 375 Greenwich St btwn North Moore & Franklin Sts; subway 1, 9 to Franklin St

Though this nexus of downtown filmmaking, a labor of love from movie legend Robert DeNiro, is mainly an office complex and screening room for film professionals, the public is encouraged to attend the various special projects here. In May 2004, DeNiro teamed up with Jane Rosenthal for the Tribeca Film Festival (see above), which includes various screenings and educational panels. Check the website for upcoming events and screening schedules.

SOHO

Eating pp174–5, Drinking p210, Sleeping pp293–4

This hip and trendy neighborhood has nothing to do with its London counterpart but instead takes its name from its geographical placement: South of Houston St. The rectangular area, graced by many cobblestone streets and grand buildings, extends as far south as Canal St and runs west from Broadway to West St.

Soho's filled with block upon block of cast-iron industrial buildings (hence its nickname Cast-Iron District) that date to the period just after the Civil War, when this was the city's leading commercial district. These multistory buildings housed linen, ribbon and clothing factories, which

Top Five Tribeca & Soho

- Apple Soho Store (p84) Hands-on approach to technology.
- Balthazar (p174) Brilliant bistro brunch.
- Clocktower Gallery (above) Discover new artists.
- Hoomoos Asli (p175) *Hoomoos,* not hummus.
- Prince St vendors (p85) Have a shopping spree.

often featured showcase galleries at street level. But the area fell out of favor as retail businesses relocated uptown and manufacturing concerns moved out of the city. By the 1950s, the huge lofts and cheap rents attracted artists, misfits and other avant-garde types. Their political lobbying not only saved the neighborhood from destruction but assured that a 26-block area was declared a legally protected historic district in 1973. Unfortunately, the pioneers who were responsible for preserving the attractive district were pushed out by sky-high rents when Soho became gentrified and attained hyper-fashionable status.

While many of the top galleries have hightailed it to Chelsea, today Soho is a shopping mecca, with designer-clothing stores and shoe boutiques falling over each other for the same clientele. Still, there are several museums and some good galleries keeping the flame lit.

Soho is mobbed with tourists shopping and gawking on weekends, when it can be annoyingly crowded. Weekdays are more real, when 'gallerinas' and other assorted office and gallery workers dominate the traffic flow. True to the clichés, you'll see a lot of black-on-black fashions worn by all the outrageously beautiful people here.

Orientation

Houston St marks the northern boundary for Soho, hence 'South of Houston Street.' Its edges mingle with Little Italy around Lafayette St to the east and Chinatown and Tribeca around the west end of Canal St. Train stations to put you where the action is include the C, E, 6 to Spring St; N, R to Prince St; F, V to Broadway-Lafayette St and 1, 9 to Houston St.

APPLE STORE SOHO Map pp382-5

☎ 212-226-3126; www.apple.com/retail/soho; 103 Prince St at Mercer St; ☽ 10am-8pm Mon-Sat, 11am-7pm Sun; subway B, D, F, V to Broadway –Lafayette St, N, R to Prince St

The massive retail shop – a sparse and modern space with cement floors, high ceilings and incredibly knowledgeable salespeople who roam around with bemused smiles on their faces – has become much more than a place to buy computers. Sure, you can do that here – after spending as many hours as you want test-driving the various desktop and laptop models that sit out as nonchalantly as cheese samples on sprawling display tables. But you can also feed your techie mind with information through a constantly rotating syllabus of lectures, classes and films on Mac-based topics such as digital photo and music making. Programs are held in the upstairs theatre, an impressive space with cushy chairs and a wide movie screen. For more details, see p258.

NEW MUSEUM OF
CONTEMPORARY ART Map pp382-5

☎ 212-219-1222; www.newmuseum.org; 583 Broadway btwn Lafayette & Prince Sts; adult/artist, senior & student/child under 18 yrs $6/3/free; ☽ noon-6pm Tue & Wed, Fri-Sun, noon-8pm Thu; subway B, D, F, V to Broadway–Lafayette St, N, R to Prince St

This museum is at the vanguard of the contemporary Soho scene. Its mission is to give space to works created in the last decade, meaning you'll probably encounter artists you don't already know. Check out the new Media Z Lounge, with its digital, video and audio installations. There's also a fine bookstore here with an impressive selection of art reference titles and monographs.

NEW YORK CITY FIRE MUSEUM
Map pp382-5

☎ 212-219-1222; www.nycfiremuseum.org; 556 W 22nd St at Eleventh Ave; suggested donation $3; ☽ 10am-5pm Tue-Sat, 10am-4pm Sun; subway C, E to Spring St

Occupying a grand old firehouse dating to 1904, this museum houses a well-maintained collection of gold horse-drawn fire-fighting carriages along with modern-day red fire engines. Exhibits explain the development of the New York City fire-fighting system, which began with the 'bucket brigades.' All the heavy equipment and the museum's particularly friendly staff make this a great place to bring children. The tone was somber here after September 11 – not surprising since the New York

---

It's *How*-ston!

No one can satisfactorily explain why the street is pronounced 'how-ston,' though it's presumed that this is the way a man named William Houstoun, who lived in the area, pronounced his surname. (Somewhere along the line the second 'u' in the spelling of the street was dropped.) No matter really, except out-of-towners are instantly pegged if they make this pronunciation gaffe.

Fire Department lost half of its members in the attacks; memorials and exhibits are now a permanent part of the collection. An excellent gift shop sells official FDNY clothing, patches and books about fire-fighting history. As of spring 2006, the museum will move to 235 Bowery at Prince St.

PRADA SOHO Map pp382-5
☎ 212-334-8888; 575 Broadway at Prince St;
🕙 11am-7pm Mon-Sat, noon-6pm Sun; subway B, D, F, V to Broadway–Lafayette St, N, R to Prince St

This 28,000 sq ft building formerly housed the Guggenheim Soho museum, but don't let the consumer angle here fool you – it's still a veritable art house. In a $40 million 2001 project, architect Rem Koolhaus blended retail with theater, and now you'll find flat-screen televisions beaming messages about merchandise, limited quantities of vintage wear, movable overhead display cages, mannequins imported from Italy, 'magic mirrors' in dressing rooms that let customers see their backs and fronts simultaneously, and even a revolving stage that's host to occasional performances. So don't worry if you can't afford any of the signature shoes or fashions inside – respectful gawkers are most definitely welcome. For more details, see p260.

PRINCE ST Map pp382-5
Subway N, R to Prince St

Strolling this strip on a sunny day is a great way to get infused with all aspects of Soho. In warm months especially, the wide sidewalks are lined with local artists hawking quality jewelry, knitwear, paintings, clothing and other sorts of arts

and crafts between Broadway and Sixth Ave. Checking out the shops could eat up hours, as you've got everything from high-quality journals from **Kate's Paperie** (p260), to chic shoes from **Sigerson Morrison** and **John Fleuvog** (east of Broadway), matte foundation at **Face** cosmetics, and an amazing gift selection at the Met Store, an outpost of the gift shop at the **Metropolitan Museum of Art** (p123). Quick gourmet noshes can be had at **Dean & DeLuca** (p171) on Broadway, a feast for the eyes as well as the stomach.

CHINATOWN & LITTLE ITALY

Walking Tour pp154–6, Eating pp175–7, Drinking p211, Shopping pp261–2

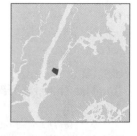

More than 150,000 Chinese-speaking residents live in cramped tenements and crowded apartments in Chinatown, a community with its own unique rhythms and traditions. For example, some banks along Canal St keep Sunday hours, newsstands sell no fewer than six Chinese newspapers and plenty of illegal fireworks (the highlight of many a Chinese New Year's parade) are peddled openly. Stroll the streets for dinner fixings and you'll find fresh tofu as well as live frogs a-swirl in barrels, shark fins and exotic fruits and elixirs. In the 1990s, Chinatown attracted a growing number of Vietnamese immigrants, who set up their own shops and opened inexpensive restaurants here; depending on what street you're on, you'll often notice more of a Vietnamese than Chinese presence. The latest immigrants have been coming from Fuzhou, a Fujian province.

In contrast to Chinatown, Little Italy's ethnic character has been largely diluted in the last 50 years. The area began as a strong Italian neighborhood (film director Martin Scorsese grew up on Elizabeth St), but in the mid-20th century, Little Italy suffered a large exodus, as many residents moved to the Cobble Hill section of Brooklyn and the city's suburbs. For that reason, few cultural sites and traditions remain. One exception is the raucous **San Gennaro Festival** (p12) honoring the patron saint of Naples, which is held for 10 days starting in the second week of September. At this time, Mulberry St from Canal to Houston Sts is closed off to make room for the festival's games of chance, kiddie rides and enough food and wine to sate the Bacchus in all of us.

Transportation

Subway J, M, N, Q, R, W, Z, 6 to Canal St.

Orientation

Two of Manhattan's most dynamic ethnic enclaves, Chinatown and Little Italy are just north of the Civic Center and the Financial District. Chinatown sprawls largely south of Canal St and east of Centre St to the Manhattan Bridge; over the years, however, it has steadily crept further east into the Lower East Side and north into Little Italy, which is a narrowing sliver extending north of Canal St.

CHINATOWN

CANAL ST Map pp380-1
Subway J, M, Z, N, Q, R, W, 6 to Canal St

While the hidden treasures of Chinatown are found on its tiny side streets, this wide avenue is the pulsing artery of Chinatown, and a walk along it will not only be an exercise in frustration (the crowds are relentless) but in pure thrills. You'll pass open, stinky seafood markets hawking bloodied, slippery fish; mysterious little herb shops displaying all manner of roots and potions; storefront bakeries with steamed-up windows and the most tasty 50¢ pork buns you've ever had in your life; restaurants with whole roasted ducks and pigs hanging by their skinny necks in the windows; produce markets piled high with fresh lychee nuts and bok choy and Asian pears; and street vendors selling endless forms of tchotchkes, from knock-off Gucci sunglasses and Rolex watches to whimsical windup toys and three-for-$1 panties. Don't miss it.

Top Five Chinatown & Little Italy

- **Canal St** (above) Hustle and bustle.
- **Ferrara's Pasticceria** (p177) Espresso and a cannoli.
- **Mare Chiaro** (p211) With a crusty old bartender and cheapo drinks.
- **Mulberry St** (opposite) Clinging onto Little Italy.
- **Museum of Chinese in the Americas** (right) Unexpected exhibits.

COLUMBUS PARK Map pp380-1
Mulberry & Bayard Sts

This is where outdoor mah-jongg and dominoes games take place at bridge tables while tai chi practitioners move through lyrical, slow-motion poses under shady trees. Judo sparring and family relaxing are also not uncommon sights here – an active, communal space that's property of the warm locals. Visitors are welcome, though – or at least ignored. Plus, there's a rare public bathroom here.

MUSEUM OF CHINESE IN THE AMERICAS Map pp380-1
☎ 212-619-4785; www.moca-nyc.org; 70 Mulberry St at Bayard St; suggested donation $3; ☽ noon-5pm Tue-Sun; subway J, M, Z, N, Q, R, W, 6 to Canal St

This small, 2nd-floor homage to Chinese Americans grew out of a community-based organization founded in 1980. Today it features ongoing exhibits about the history of Chinatown as well as oral histories of residents, shown through artifacts, written stories and photos. Special exhibits have covered topics from gay Chinese visibility to General Lee's LA banquet room.

WING FAT SHOPPING Map pp380-1
☎ 8-9 Bowery btwn Pell & Doyers St; subway J, M, Z, N, Q, R, W, 6 to Canal St

The strangest mall you've ever seen lies underground, and has businesses offering reflexology, collectible stamps and feng shui services. But the most fascinating aspect is its history, as the tunnel served as a stop on the Underground Railroad, as well as an escape route in the early 20th century for members of rival Tong gangs who waged battle up on the street and then disappeared down into the darkness before police could even begin to search.

LITTLE ITALY

MULBERRY ST Map pp380-1

Although it feels more like a theme park than an authentic Italian strip, Mulberry St is still the heart of the 'hood, as well as being the home of landmarks such as the Old St Patrick's Church and eateries **Umberto's Clam House** (☎ 212-431-7545; 386 Broome St at Mulberry St), **Da Nico** (☎ 212-343-1212; 164 Mulberry St btwn Broome & Grand Sts) and **Casa Bella** (☎ 212-431-4080; 127 Mulberry St at Hester St), as well as the old-time bar **Mare Chiaro** (p211), which was one of the favorite haunts of the late Frank Sinatra. You'll see lots of red, white and green Italian flags sold

in souvenir shops, and you'll also enjoy the lovely aroma of fresh-baked pastries and pizzas wafting out of doorways. Make sure you don't miss the **Ravenite Social Club** (247 Mulberry St). Now, somewhat predictably, it's a gift shop. But it's still a reminder of the not-so-long-ago days when mobsters ran the neighborhood. Originally known as the Alto

Fish stall, Chinatown

Knights Social Club, and a place where big hitters such as Lucky Luciano spent some time, the Ravenite was a favorite hangout of John Gotti (and the FBI) before he was arrested and sentenced to life imprisonment in 1992.

LOWER EAST SIDE

Walking Tour pp154–6, Eating pp177–9, Drinking pp211–2,
Shopping pp262–3, Sleeping pp294–5

In the early 20th century, half a million Jews from Eastern Europe streamed into the Lower East Side (LES), and today it remains one of New York's most desirable entry-level neighborhoods (read: it's relatively cheap). Lately, it's become a magnet for the hyper-trendies of Manhattan – fabulous folk either from the neighborhood or from slick uptown digs (they're the ones who are 'slumming it') – who flood the area, cramming into the latest low-lit lounges or four-star eateries, shopping at new art galleries or clothing boutiques, and generally just wanting to see and be seen.

Architecturally, this storied old tenement area still retains its hardscrabble character, with block after block of crumbling buildings. You can see why the early residents lamented that 'the sun was embarrassed to shine' on their benighted neighborhood.

Like Little Italy, the LES has lost much of its historic ethnic flavor, and only a small Jewish community and a handful of traditional businesses remain – take what remains by sampling pickles out of a barrel at **Gus's Pickles** (Map pp382–5; 85–87 Orchard St), or smoked fish and other treats at **Russ & Daughters Appetizing** (Map pp382–5; 179 E Houston St btwn Orchard & Allen Sts).

But it's far from homogenous. Today, the LES is populated by youngsters experiencing city living for the first time; some holdout punks, painters, squatters and sculptors; and a good many 'lifers' holding onto rent-controlled apartments. Also, the Latino community has spilled over from the lower East Village (known by old-timers as Alphabet City, so-named for its Avenues A, B, C and D), and Chinatown continues to colonize adjacent neighborhoods, making for a flavorful mix that is unique to the LES.

With its array of restaurants and nightlife, the LES ranks as one of New York City's hottest neighborhoods. In New York, to remain hot, high and mighty means to adapt, and in this sense the LES is mercurial, with cafés, shops, bars and lounges turning over constantly. Poke around and find what you like down here among the old classics and the New Wave.

Orientation

The Lower East Side extends east of the Bowery to the East River. Houston St and 14th St to the north. Visit the **Lower East Side Visitors Center** (Map pp382–5; 261 Broome St btwn Allan & Orchard Sts) to orient yourself in the neighborhood.

EAST RIVER PARK Map p394

Flanked by a looming housing project and the clogged FDR Drive on one side and the less-than-pure East River on the other, you might wonder what the draw is here. But one visit – especially if it's during the spring or summer – and you'll understand. In addition to the spanking-new ballparks, running and biking paths, 5000-seat amphitheater for concerts and lovely patches of green thanks to a recent $4 million face-lift, it's got cool, natural breezes and stunning views of the Williamsburg, Manhattan and Brooklyn bridges. Though much of the park is still in various stages of construction, it's an urban-nature experience at its best.

ORCHARD ST BARGAIN DISTRICT

Map pp382–5
Orchard, Ludlow & Essex Sts btwn Houston & Delancey Sts; Sun-Fri; F to Delancey St, subway J, M, Z to Essex St

When the LES was still a largely Jewish neighborhood, Eastern European merchants set up pushcarts to sell their wares here. While it's no longer as quaint as that, bargain hunters comb the 300-odd shops in this modern-day bazaar for sporting goods, leather belts, hats and a wide array of 'designer fashions' (which are quite often rather cheesy, truth be told). Rather than searching high and low for label-whore knockoffs – better grabbed at the new, pricier boutiques in the area – know that it's more the type of place for scoring cheap basics like

---

Transportation

Subway F, V to Second Ave–Lower East Side, F to Delancey St & J, M, Z to Delancey–Essex Sts.
Bus The crosstown Houston St and Delancey St lines are best.

Top Five Lower East Side

- **East River Park** (opposite) Strolling among nature near the projects.
- **Teany** (p179) Tea and vegan treats.
- **Tenement Museum** (right) Revisit old New York.
- **Toys in Babeland** (p262) Check out the array of dildos and vibrators.
- **WD 50** (p178) Wining and dining.

bras, shoes, army-navy bags and leather jackets. While the businesses are not exclusively owned by Orthodox Jews, they still close early on Friday afternoon and remain closed on Saturday in observance of the Sabbath. Serious shoppers should try bargaining to save some cash, although you're up against the world's best here, so don't get your hopes up.

ELDRIDGE ST SYNAGOGUE Map pp380-1

☎ 212-219-0888; 12 Eldridge St btwn Canal & Division Sts; adult/senior $5/3; subway F to East Broadway

The landmark Eldridge St Synagogue, built in 1887, attracted as many as 1000 worshippers on the High Holidays at the turn of the 20th century. Membership dwindled in the 1920s with restricted immigration laws, and by the 1950s the temple closed altogether. It fell into major disrepair due to water damage and neglect, but became the focus of a massive restoration effort – the Eldrige Street Project – in the late '80s, which is still underway. While the project is far from complete, the synagogue is stable, holding Friday evening and Saturday morning worship services, as well as frequent concerts, art exhibitions and educational lectures. **Tours** (adult/senior & student $5/3; ☺ 11am-4pm Sun, 11:30am-2:30pm Tue-Thu or by appointment) of the building are available.

ESSEX ST MARKET Map pp382-5

☎ 212-312-3603; www.essexstreetmarket.com; 120 Essex St btwn Delancey & Rivington Sts; ☺ 8am-6pm Mon-Sat; subway F, V to Delancey St, J, M, Z to Delancey–Essex St

This 60-year-old historic shopping destination is the local place for produce, seafood, butcher-cut meats, cheeses, Latino grocery items, even a barber. The **Schapiro Wines** stall is popular. The Schapiro family's kosher winery was founded on the Lower East Side in 1899. NYC's first winery, it gave tours of its dank cellar and its 50,000-gallon tanks, but moved to upstate New York in the mid-1990s. Taste or purchase the wine and catch the vibe of the place at its new shop.

LOWER EAST SIDE TENEMENT MUSEUM Map pp382-5

☎ 212-431-0233; www.tenement.org; 90 Orchard St at Broome St; adult/senior & child $10/8; visitor center ☺ 11am-5:30pm; subway F, V to Delancey St, J, M, Z to Delancey–Essex St

This museum puts the neighborhood's heart-breaking heritage on full display in several reconstructed tenements. The visitor center shows a video detailing the difficult life endured by the people who once lived in the surrounding buildings, which were more often than not without any running water or electricity. Museum visits are available only as part of scheduled tours (the price of which is included in the admission), which typically operate every 40 or 50 minutes. But call ahead for the schedules, which change frequently.

The museum has re-created three turn-of-the-20th-century tenements, including the late-19th-century home and garment shop of the Levine family from Poland, and two immigrant dwellings from the Great Depressions of 1873 and 1929. On weekends the museum has an interactive tour where kids can dress up in period clothes and touch anything in the restored apartment (from around 1916) of a Sephardic Jewish family. Walking tours of the neighborhood are held from April to December.

STREIT'S MATZO COMPANY Map pp382-5

☎ 212-475-7000; www.streitsmatzos.com; 148-154 Rivington St

Like the Schapiros, the Streits opened their business, a matzo factory, in the 1890s. The bakery and shop still survive, doling outfresh samples of whole-wheat cracker-thin creations amid the modern-day bustle of the trendy LES.

TOYS IN BABELAND Map pp382-5

☎ 212-375-1701; www.babeland.com; 94 Rivington St; ☺ noon-10pm Mon-Sat, noon-7pm Sun; subway F, V to Lower East Side–Second Ave

This women-run sex-toy shop takes a warm, hands-on-museum approach to selling potentially embarrassing items: All the dildos are out on display, along with candy-colored anal beads, dildo harnesses, flavored lubes, slings, porn videos and erotica books and magazines. The staff are educated and gentle, knowing just when to step in with some advice and when to butt out. A newer location in **Soho** (Map pp382-5; ☎ 212-966-2120; 43 Mercer St btwn Broome & Grand Sts) is just as fun and welcoming, and both places host occasional readings and sex workshops. For more information, see p262.

EAST VILLAGE

Eating pp179–81, Drinking pp212–15, Shopping pp263–5,
Sleeping p295

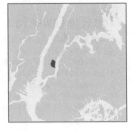

It's hard to encapsulate life in the East Village, an area that has swung between drugged-out and dirty to slick and hip.

While the neighborhood takes its name from Greenwich Village, the two areas don't have much in common historically. Large farmland estates once stretched over this area, but as New York became more industrial and extended northward from Lower Manhattan in the late 19th century, urban development devoured the acreage. By the early 20th century, this region was considered the northern section of the Lower East Side, a poorer cousin to Greenwich Village. But it has come fully into its own over the last decade. The East Village is now completely gentrified, and the trend continues creeping east, to the once dangerous Aves A, B, C and D (see Learn Your ABCs, below).

Good exploration grounds in the East Village include First and Second Aves and Aves A and B between 14th and Houston Sts. Among the vintage clothing stores, used-record shops, herbal apothecaries and gin joints, you can find virtually every type of cuisine here, including Italian, Polish, vegetarian, Indian, Lebanese, Japanese and Thai. Steer clear of St Mark's Place between Third and Second Aves, inundated with cheesy-jewelry hawkers, not-great cuisine and lost weekend warriors from New Jersey.

Orientation

The East Village is generally considered the swath of Village that's east of Third Ave to the river and north of Houston St to 14th St, with Tompkins Square Park functioning as its pulsing nexus. Trains don't really go far enough east to carry you to most locations in the nabe, but mostly it's a quick walk (and even quicker cab or bus ride) from the 6 to Astor Pl, F, V to Lower East Side–Second Ave or L to First or Third Aves.

AVE A Map pp382-5

Ave A btwn 14th & Houston Sts

The first of the East Village's alphabet avenues to become completely gentrified, Ave A has long been a symbol of change here. It was a dividing line in the early '90s, as it was the strip separating the 'OK' part of the neighborhood from the part still too dicey for most slumming hipsters. Today the edgiest locals find that it's practically too far west to even bother with, but it's still fun, quirky and bustling. It's chock-full of cafés, bars, bistros, nightclubs and tiny cheap-eats spots, and is *the* place to find a cheap slice, a newsstand that serves egg creams, a peaceful park, trendy houseware items, the best Friday-night '80s party (1984 at **Pyramid**, p237) and a DJ-equipped sushi spot – all on one strip.

ST MARK'S-IN-THE-BOWERY

Map pp382-5

☎ 212-674-6377; 131 E 10th St at Second Ave; ⊙ 10am-6pm Mon-Fri; subway 6 to Astor Pl, L to Third Ave

Though it's most popular with locals for its cultural-center offerings – poetry readings hosted by the **Poetry Project** (☎ 212-674-0910) or cutting-edge dance performances from

Danspace (☎ 212-674-8194) – it's also a historic site. This Episcopal church stands on the site of the farm, or *bouwerie*, owned by Dutch Governor Peter Stuyvesant, whose crypt lies under the grounds. The 1799 church, damaged by fire in 1978, has been restored, and you can enjoy an interior view of its abstract stained-glass windows during opening hours.

Learn Your ABCs

Not long ago, 'Assault, Battery, Crime and Drugs' could have easily been what Aves A, B, C and D stood for; going to them, except for the most daring and cutting-edge New Yorkers, was unthinkable. But now those streets are home to some of the edgiest, hippest hangs, and a new acronym might mean 'Attitude, Beautiful people, Costly, and Dining Destination.' Rents have soared, old-timers have either been made bitter or pushed out altogether, late-night taxis are plentiful, and folks who wear suits to work now practically outnumber those who don't go to work at all. It's either all good or all bad, depending on who you are. For lovers of cool dining and drinking, though, it's all good.

Transportation

Subway N, R, W, 6, L or F, V.
Bus The crosstown Houston St and M14 Ave A, B and C lines.

RUSSIAN & TURKISH BATHS

Map pp382-5

☎ 212-473-8806; www.russianturkishbaths.com; 268 E 10th St btwn First Ave & Ave A; daily/10 visits $25/175; ☉ 11am-10pm Mon, Tue, Thu & Fri, 9am-10pm Wed, 7:30am-10pm Sat & Sun; subway L to First Ave, 6 to Astor Pl

The waning of Eastern European traditions on the Lower East Side led to the closure of many old bathhouses in Manhattan, and the AIDS crisis ensured that most of these popular gay romping spots were shuttered as well. But the historic old Russian and Turkish steam baths still remain. Since 1892, this spa for the lumpen proletariat has offered steam baths, an ice-cold plunge pool, sauna and sun deck. All-day access includes the use of lockers, locks, robes, towels and slippers. Extras such as Dead Sea salt scrubs ($30) and black-mud treatments ($38) are also available, and an onsite Russian café boosts your blitzed-out spirit with fresh juices, potato-olive salad, blintzes and borscht.

You must wear shorts, unfortunately, when the baths are open to both men and women – which is the case most hours except between 9am and 2pm Wednesday (women only) and between 7:30am and 2pm Saturday (men only). These are widely considered the best times to visit, as the vibe is more open, relaxed and communal.

TOMPKINS SQUARE PARK Map pp382-5

Btwn 7th & 10th Sts & Aves A & B; subway F, V to Lower East Side–Second Ave, L to First Ave

Long gone are this park's glory days, when the band shell on the southern edge hosted impromptu concerts, protests and the annual Wigstock dragfest (which moved to the west side piers and turned corporate before dissolving altogether), and where genuine hardcore punks and anarchists gathered. But also long gone are this park's upsetting days, when it was a dirty, needle-strewn homeless encampment and unusable for folks wanting a place to stroll or read or picnic. The turning point for this park was sparked by the razing of the band shell and highly publicized eviction of the squatters living in the 'tent city' within the park in 1991. That protest turned violent and the Tompkins Square Riot, as it came to be known, ushered in the new era of yuppies in the dog run, fashionistas lolling in the grass and undercover narcotics agents trying to pass as hippies or home boys and bust the same.

Today, 16-acre Tompkins Square Park is still a good spot for a game of hoops, a chess challenge at one of the concrete tables, a picnic with some ethnic take-out or a guitar jam on a sunny day. In warm weather, it's often the site of a joyous special event, whether it's the annual May Day art and culture fest, the Howl! Festival or summer's yearly jazz marathon. On any day, come here to mingle and play with a good cross section of locals.

East of Tompkins Square Park is Alphabet City, which technically includes all the avenues with letter designations. Traditionally a Puerto Rican barrio, young gringos and trendy international types started colonizing the area in the 1990s. Walk around and you'll find stretches of vintage-clothes shops and French bistros among the murals, graffiti and bodegas. The area is also dotted with Green Thumb Gardens (with several on 8th St between Aves B and D), interesting urban artifacts, where small gardens (some with on-site shanties) serve as social clubs for neighborhood men.

Community Gardens

After a stretch of arboreal celibacy in New York City, the community gardens of Alphabet City are breathtaking. A network of gardens were carved out of abandoned lots to provide low-income neighborhoods with a communal backyard. Trees and flowers were planted, sandboxes were built, found-art sculptures erected, domino games ensued – all within green spaces wedged between buildings or claiming entire blocks. On Saturdays and Sundays, most gardens are open to the public to admire the plantings or chat with gardeners; many gardeners are activists within the community and are a good source of imformation about local politics. The **6 & B Garden** (Map pp382-5; E 6th St at Ave B) is a well-organized space that hosts free music events, workshops and yoga sessions; check the website for details (www.6bgarden .org). Three dramatic weeping willows, an odd sight in the city, grace the twin plots of **9th St Garden** and **La Plaza Cultural** (Map pp382-5; E 9th St at Ave C). After a three-year lawsuit, the 9th St gardens were recently spared from the city's plans to build affordable housing in its place.

WEST (GREENWICH) VILLAGE

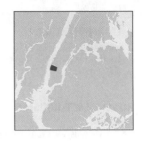

Walking Tour pp157–8, Eating pp181–3, Drinking pp215–16, Shopping pp266–9, Sleeping pp295–6

Once a symbol for all things artistic, outlandish and Bohemian (see Bohemian Greenwich Village, opposite), this storied and popular neighborhood – known by most visitors as 'Greenwich Village,' although that term is not used by locals – can look downright somnolent these days. That's especially true since privileged residents of high-rent townhouses inspired Giuliani-era crackdowns on noisy clubs, public drinking and other facts of city life. But the student culture at New York University (NYU) – which owns most of the village, especially around Washington Square Park – keeps things fresh and inspired. South of Washington Square Park (including Bleecker St, all the way west to Seventh Ave), you'll find an eclectic and crowded collection of cafés, shops and restaurants; beyond Seventh Ave is the West Village proper (although anything west of the East Village is called such these days), a leafy, upscale neighborhood of winding streets and townhouses.

Orientation

Roughly bordered by 14th St in the north and Houston St in the south, 'the Village' runs from Lafayette St all the way west to the Hudson River.

ASTOR PLACE Map pp382–5

8th St btwn Third & Fourth Aves; subway R, W to 8th St–NYU, 6 to Astor Pl

This square is named after the Astor family, who built an early New York fortune on beaver trading and lived on **Colonnade Row** (429–434 Lafayette St), just south of the square. Four of the original nine marble-faced Greek Revival residences on Lafayette St still exist, but have seen better days. Across the street, in the public library built by John Jacob Astor, is the **Joseph Papp Public Theater** (425 Lafayette St), built in 1848 for the enormous sum of $500,000. It's now one of the city's most important cultural centers and presents the famous Shakespeare in the Park every summer (for more details, see p228).

Astor Place itself is dominated by the large brownstone Cooper Union, the public college founded by glue millionaire Peter Cooper in 1859. Just after its completion, Abraham Lincoln gave his 'Right Makes Might' speech condemning slavery in the Union's Great Hall. The fringed lectern he used still exists, but the auditorium is only open to the public for special events.

Right across the square, you'll see a symbol of the change that was once shocking to this now-gentrified neighborhood – the city's first Kmart, which opened in 1996. The following year, Irish rock band U2 kicked off its Rock Mart tour here and, despite initial protests from the neighborhood, the megastore seems to have won over lazy residents who enjoy the its multi-tiered convenience.

The cube sculpture entitled *Alamo*, in the middle of the square, is a popular spot for skate punks and the occasional guerrilla art act. Get a group together and give it a whirl; with some powerful backs and legs you can set it spinning. The uptown subway entrance here is an exact replica of one of the first subway kiosks in the early 20th century.

CHRISTOPHER STREET PIER

Map pp382–5
Christopher St at Hudson River; subway 1, 9 to Christopher St–Sheridan Sq

Once strictly the domain of young gay hustlers and sassy 'pier queens' – the effeminate gay boys and trannies who were depicted in the 1990 film *Paris is Burning* – this just-renovated concrete finger is now a magnet for downtowners of all stripes (including young gay holdouts). The Hudson River Park Project paid special attention to this spot, adding a grass lawn, flower bed, wooden deck, tented shade shelters, benches and a grand fountain at its entrance. It offers sweeping views of the Hudson and relieving breezes in the thick of summer.

Transportation

Subway 1, 2, 3, 9 to Christopher St–Sheridan Sq; A, C, E, F, V, S to W 4 St; R to 8 St–NYU; 6 to Astor Pl.
Bus M8, M14, M1, M6.

Bohemian Greenwich Village

The Village's reputation as a creative enclave can be traced back to at least the early 20th century, when artists and writers moved in, and by the '40s the neighborhood became known as a gathering place for gay folk. In the '50s, the Village's coffeehouses, bars and jazz clubs attracted scores of bohemians, including the Beat poets, who adopted the neighborhood as their east coast headquarters and listened to bebop and poetry throughout the 'hood. The area became an important incubator of American literature. Poet Allen Ginsberg lived here most of his life, and novelist Norman Mailer helped to found the influential *Village Voice* newspaper.

In the '60s, the area's rebellious spirit led to the birth of today's gay rights movement (see If It's Queer, It's Here, p345). Today, many still think of Christopher St as the center of queer culture in New York, although its move to hipper gay Chelsea, just north of here, has left mostly rainbow-flag stores and old-school bars in its wake. Crowds of gay men and lesbians continue to make pilgrimages to the Village on the last weekend in June, though, for the annual **Lesbian, Gay, Bisexual & Transgender Pride March** (p11).

FORBES COLLECTION Map pp382-5
☎ 212-206-5548; www.forbescollection.com; 62 Fifth Ave at 12th St; admission free; ☯ 10am-4pm Tue, Wed, Fri & Sat; subway L, N, Q, R, W, 4, 5, 6 to 14 St–Union Sq

These galleries house curios from the personal collection of the late publishing magnate Malcolm Forbes. The eclectic mix of objects on display include Fabergé eggs, models of ships, autographs and tin soldiers.

GRACE CHURCH Map pp382-5
800-804 Broadway at 10th St; R, subway W to 8th St–NYU, 6 to Astor Pl

This Gothic Revival Episcopal church was made of marble quarried by prisoners at Sing Sing, the state penitentiary in the town of Ossining 30 miles up the Hudson River (which, legend has it, is the origin of the expression 'being sent upriver'). After years of neglect, Grace Church has recently been cleaned up, and its floodlit white marble is an elegant night-time sight. The Broadway and 4th Ave views are completely different and it's worth checking it out from both vantage points.

James Renwick Jr designed the church, and many also credit him with creating nearby **Renwick Triangle** (112–128 E 10th St), a stately cluster of brownstone Italianate houses one block to the east. This is one of New York's most pleasant residential pockets, especially considering its hectic East Village location. This same designer is responsible for the **Renwick Apartments** (808 Broadway) just north of Grace Church, which figured prominently in Claeb Carr's *The Alienist*.

MERCHANT'S HOUSE MUSEUM
Map pp382-5
☎ 212-777-1089; www.merchantshouse.com; 29 E 4th St; adult/senior & student $6/4; ☯ 1-5pm Thu-Mon; subway 6 to Bleecker St

Little remains of the neighborhood that existed here before the tenement boom, but this museum between Lafayette St and the Bowery is a remarkably well-preserved example of how the business class lived. The house, dating from 1831, once belonged to drug importer Seabury Tredwell. His youngest daughter Gertrude lived here until her death in 1933, so its original furnishings were intact when it began life as a museum three years later. Period clothing and the fully equipped kitchen add to the historical allure.

NEW YORK UNIVERSITY Map pp382-5
☎ 212-998-4636; www.nyu.edu; Information Center at 50 W 4th St

In 1831 Albert Gallatin, secretary of treasury under President Thomas Jefferson, founded an intimate center of higher learning open to all students, regardless of race or class background. He'd scarcely recognize the place today, as it's swelled to a student population of 48,000, with high school grads attending 14 schools and colleges at six Manhattan locations. It just keeps growing, too – to the dismay of landmark fans and business owners, who have seen buildings (including the legendary Palladium nightclub on 14th St) rapidly bought out by the

Top Five West (Greenwich) Village

- **Christopher Street Pier** (opposite) Soak up the sun.
- **Cielo** (p236) Discover a stellar DJ.
- **LGBT Community Center** (p345) Tap into all things queer.
- **Marc Jacobs** (p267) Give your credit card a workout.
- **Washington Square Park** (p94) Watch street buskers and drug dealers.

No Cover: Music Landmarks

Why is the Rock & Roll Hall of Fame in Cleveland, when everyone knows New York is the 'Big Apple'? This is the top of the heap, king of the hill. If you make it here, never mind making it anywhere else, you've arrived. (Incidentally, jazz musicians are often credited for the term, 'Big Apple,' but it dates back even further to the 1920s when it was used by stable hands in a New Orleans racetrack to refer to races in New York City).

Before and during many great musicians' careers, Greenwich Village and East Village were their sleeping and performing grounds. To impress out-of-towners or annoy loved ones, these are vital pieces of trivia to add to your expansive New York file.

- Bob Dylan once lived here and was inspired to write *Positively 4th St* at 161 W 4th St.
- One of rock's most romantic album covers, the 1963 *Freewheelin' Bob Dylan,* was shot on Jones St between Bleecker and W 4th St; big shaggy trees now obscure the apartment buildings' facades.
- Jimi Hendrix lived and recorded at the **Electric Lady Studios** (55 W 8th St at Sixth Ave). The brown-brick building is now a shoe store.
- The cover shot for Led Zeppelin's *Physical Graffiti* album was taken at 96–98 St Mark's Place between First Ave and Ave A.
- Charlie Parker lived in the ground-floor apartment at 151 Ave B and Tompkins Square Park from 1950 to 1954, the height of his career as bebop cofounder.

the 'Hangman's Elm,' though no one is sure if it was actually used for executions. Note that the streets bounding the park are called Washington Square North, Washington Square South etc.

Though a welcoming and historically important oasis, Washington Square Park suffers from the usual urban ills: drug dealing, vandalism and rat infestation. Neighborhood activists have been trying to drum up support for a conservancy and $7 million restoration but as yet to no avail.

The community was able to raise $3 million, though, for the much-needed renovation of the **Stanford White Arch**, colloquially known as Washington Square Arch, which dominates the park. The project is nearing an end but still ongoing, which explains the pesky chain-link fence that surrounds the base of the towering figure. Originally designed in wood to celebrate the centennial of George Washington's inauguration in 1889, the arch proved so popular that it was replaced in stone six years later and adorned with statues of the general in war and peace (the latter work is by A Stirling Calder, the father of artist Alexander Calder). Although string quartets played atop the arch as recently as 1991, the entire structure has been off-limits since that year because of its disrepair.

In 1916, artist Marcel Duchamp climbed to the top of the arch by its internal stairway and declared the park the 'Free and Independent Republic of Washington Square.' These days, the anarchy takes place on the ground level,

academic giant and replaced with dormitories or administrative offices. Still, the offerings are highly regarded and wide ranging, especially its film-studies, writing, medical and law programs. For a unique experience that'll put you on the fast track to meeting locals, sign up for a weekend or one-day class – from American history to photography – offered by the School of Professional Studies and Continuing Education and open to all.

WASHINGTON SQUARE PARK

Map pp382–5
Subway A, C, E, B, D, F, V to W 4th St, R, W to 8th St–NYU, 6 to Astor Pl

This park, like many public spaces in the city, began as a potter's field – a burial ground for the penniless. It also served as the site of public executions, meaning ne'er-do-wells were dead and buried in one fell swoop. The magnificent old tree near the northwestern corner of the park bears a plaque memorializing it as

Court & Spark

Otherwise known as 'the Cage,' the small basketball court that stands enclosed within four walls of chain-link fence on West 4th St and Sixth Ave is home to some of the best streetball in the country. Though it's more touristy than its counterpart, Rucker Park in Harlem, that's also part of its charm, as games, held right here in the center of the Village, draw massive, excitable crowds, who grasp at the fence and often stand 10 deep to hoot and holler for the skilled, competitive guys who play here. Prime time is summer, when the West Fourth Street Summer Pro-Classic League, now in its 26th year, hits the scene. While the height of this court's popularity was back in 2001 – the year Nike capitalized on the raw energy of the place by shooting a commercial here – b'ball lovin' throngs still storm the place on weekends. You'll need to be aggressive if you want to get close enough to get a good view.

Brownstone building, Greenwich Village

as comedians and buskers use the park's permanently dry fountain as a performance space. Every May 1, the **Marijuana March** takes over the park. The Judson Memorial Church graces the park's south border.

At 245 Greene St, on the park's eastern border, sits the building where the Triangle Shirtwaist Fire broke out on March 25, 1911. This sweatshop had locked its doors to prevent the young seamstresses from taking unauthorized breaks. The inferno killed 146 young women, many of whom jumped to their deaths from the upper floors (the fire department's ladders only extended to the 6th floor of the 10-floor building). Every year on March 25, the New York Fire Department holds a solemn ceremony in memory of the city's most deadly factory fire. Near here is **Grey Art Gallery** (☎ 212-998-6780; 100 Washington Sq East; suggested donation $2.50; 🕙 11am-6pm Tue, Thu & Fri), showing a wide spectrum of works, from classic watercolors to Cuban photographic retrospectives.

The row of townhouses at Washington Square North (now home to NYU offices) inspired *Washington Square*, Henry James' novel about late-19th-century social mores. James did not live here, as is popularly assumed, but he was born on the northeast corner of Washington Place and Greene St in 1843.

Has the Meatpacking District Lost its Beef?

Less than 10 years ago, the West Village's Meatpacking District – home to 250 slaughterhouses in 1900 but only 35 today, as most have been squeezed out by high rents – was best known for its groups of tranny hookers, racy S/M sex clubs and, of course, its sides of beef, which often left a bloody, smelly detritus for clubgoers to wade through at the end of the meat packing work day. Now it's one of the hottest new 'hoods in town, with sleek new eateries, nightclubs, clothing boutiques and hotels popping up weekly. The general response was what it always is when a neighborhood begins to rapidly gentrify – a mix of annoyance, disdain and secret excitement. But when developers proposed a 420ft luxury apartment building a few years ago, a group of fed-up citizens, politicians and activists banded together to make sure the gentrification wouldn't go too far. Though the apartment complex could still come to fruition (it was blocked at a major level by the city's zoning board), the group, led by the Greenwich Village Society for Historical Preservation and calling itself 'Save Gansevoort Market,' in honor of the neighborhood's old name, won a major victory in 2004, when it convinced the city to designate a 12-block area of the Meatpacking District as a historic landmark area. The ruling will ensure that historically significant details of the area's architecture – from cobblestone streets to old stables and brick facades – will be protected in that area. As far as the character of what goes on inside new hotspots? That's up for grabs.

CHELSEA

*Walking Tour pp158–60, Eating pp183–6, Drinking pp216–17,
Shopping pp269–71, Sleeping pp296–7*

During the city's Gilded Age in the late 19th century, this was
the dry goods and retail center, drawing well-heeled shoppers
to its varied emporia. Closer to the Hudson River, you can still
find plenty of old warehouses, and many of the townhouses,
especially those in the historic district, are beautifully restored.
At the heart of the neighborhood, on Eighth Ave – known by
locals as the 'runway' – you'll find a parade of eye-poppingly
beautiful gay men, making beelines to gyms and trendy happy hours. You'll also be drawn
into scads of cafés, shops and restaurants, which have exploded in the past couple of years.
Further west, around 10th and 11th Aves, is the hub of the city's art-gallery scene, which has
long since stolen Soho's thunder (see p158). The area's absolutely crawling with jaded reviewers
and buyers on Thursday and Friday evenings, as simultaneous openings lure out even those
who seem like they have already seen it all.

Orientation

North of Greenwich Village, Chelsea extends from 14th St north to 26th St and west from
Broadway to the Hudson River.

ANNEX ANTIQUES FAIR & FLEA MARKET (CHELSEA FLEA MARKET)

Map pp386–8

Sixth Ave btwn 24th & 26th Sts; ☽ **sunrise-sunset Sat & Sun; subway 1, 2, C, E to 23rd St**

Expert trollers of second-hand treasures won't miss a morning at this parking-lot market, stocked with an ever-changing rotation of vintage furniture, antique clothing and all manner of funky accessories and brilliant tchotchkes. Get there before 9am to score the best offerings.

CHELSEA HOTEL Map pp382–5

☎ **212-243-3700; 222 W 23rd St btwn Seventh & Eighth Aves; subway 1, 2, C, E to 23rd St**

The prime sight on noisy 23rd St is a red-brick hotel with ornate iron balconies and no fewer than seven plaques declaring its literary landmark status. Even before the Sex Pistols' Sid murdered heroin girlfriend Nancy here, the hotel was famous as a hangout for the likes of Mark Twain, Thomas Wolfe, Dylan Thomas and

---

Transportation

Subway A, C, E, 1, 9, F, V to 14 St; L to Eighth Ave; C, E, 1, 9 to 23 St.
Bus M14, M23, M11, M20.
Ferry New York Water Taxi (☎ 212-742-1969) zips to and from Midtown, Brooklyn, South Street Seaport and the Upper East Side.

Top Five Chelsea

- **Annex Antiques Fair & Flea Market** (left)
  Find the perfect vintage mirror.
- **Chelsea Market** (below) An array of wine, cheese and flowers.
- **Chelsea Piers** (opposite) Climb, swim or play golf.
- **Gallery hopping** (p158) Any day of the week.
- **Roxy** (p237) The only way to spend a Saturday night.

Arthur Miller. Jack Kerouac allegedly crafted *On the Road* during one marathon session at the Chelsea. Musicians have long favored the Chelsea, and it counts Leonard Cohen and Bob Dylan among its former guests. This is also where the fabulous Jean Reno and then little-known Natalie Portman got busy in *The Professional*. For more information, see p296.

CHELSEA MARKET Map pp382–5

www.chelseamarket.com; 75 Ninth Ave btwn 15th & 16th St; subway A, C, E to 14 St, L to Eighth Ave

Culinary fans will think they've entered the pearly gates once they've stepped into this 800ft-long shopping concourse, bursting with some of the freshest eats in town. But it's part of a larger, million-sq-ft space that occupies a full city block, home to the Nabisco cookie factory in the 1930s (which created the Oreo cookie), and current home to the Food Network, Oxygen Network and the local NY1 news channel. Its prime draw for locals, of course, are the 25 market shops, including the **Amy's Bread** bakery, **Fat Witch Brownies**, **Fromagerie** cheese seller, **Hale & Hearty Soups**, the **Green Market** organic-food café, **Chelsea Wholesale Flowers** and the expert-staffed **Chelsea Wine Vault**.

Chelsea's Historic Charms

The Chelsea Historic District, from W 20th to W 22nd Sts, between Eighth and Tenth Aves, is an urban gem. Leafy streets, refurbished Greek Revival and Italianate townhouses and set-back buildings help create a spacious, welcoming atmosphere – something of an anachronism in crowded, chaotic New York City.

CHELSEA PIERS Map pp382-5
☎ 212-336-6000; www.chelseapiers.com; Hudson River at end of 23rd St; subway C, E to 23rd St
This massive waterfront sports center caters to the athlete in everyone. You can set out to hit a bucket of golf balls at the four-level driving range, ice skate in the complex's indoor rink or rent in-line skates to cruise along the new Hudson Park waterfront bike path down to the Battery. There's a jazzy bowling alley, Hoop City for basketball, a sailing school for kids, batting cages, a huge gym facility with an indoor pool (day passes for nonmembers are $50), indoor rock-climbing walls – the works. Kayaks are let out free at the Downtown Boathouse just north of Pier 64. There's even waterfront dining and drinking at the **Chelsea Brewing Company** (Map pp382-5; ☎ 212-366-6440; Pier 61), which serves great pub fare and delicious home brews. Though the Piers are somewhat cut off by the busy West Side Hwy, the wide array of attractions here brings in the crowds; the M23 crosstown bus, which goes right to its main entrance, saves you the long, four-avenue trek from the subway. For more information see Chelsea Piers (p248).

CUBAN ART SPACE Map pp382-5
☎ 212-242-0559; www.cubanartspace.net; 124 W 23rd St; donations welcome; ☽ 11am-7pm Tue-Fri, noon-5pm Sat; subway F, V, 1, 2 to 23rd St
This art gallery, which boasts the largest collection of Cuban art outside the island (collectors should inquire about holdings on the 3rd floor), was launched as an educational project of the Center for Cuban Studies in 1999. Openings are exciting affairs, and often feature live music, delicious nosh and the artists in the house.

DIA CENTER FOR THE ARTS
Map pp382-5
☎ 212-989-5566; www.diacenter.org; 535 W 22nd St btwn Tenth & Eleventh Aves; closed for renovations until 2006; subway C, E to 23rd St
Thought it's not currently open for gallery viewing, the lecture series will continue from this important member of the Chelsea arts community. It's known for its innovative large-scale, single-artist projects, with past shown artists including Pierre Huyghe (whose homage to social space was exhibited on the center's rooftop), Jorge Pardo and his full-scale plywood structures, and Romemarie Trockel, who displayed her feminist bent through video projections aimed at cantilevered aluminum walls.

GENERAL THEOLOGICAL SEMINARY
Map pp382-5
☎ 212-243-5150; www.gts.edu; 175 Ninth Ave btwn 20th & 21st Sts; ☽ noon-3pm Mon-Fri, 11am-3pm Sat; subway C, E to 23rd St
This campus-cum-garden is a peaceful haven that's open to the public – both pious and not so – and is accessible through the Ninth Ave entrance.

Hudson River Park

Yes, there really is a waterfront in Manhattan! While for years the west side was known more for snarling highway traffic, unseemly pastimes and smoggy New Jersey vistas, it's now followed the lead of most other cities that sit on bodies of water – Chicago, San Francisco, Miami – and turned the shoreline into something spectacular. The five-mile, 150-acre water-front Hudson River Park, overseen by the state-city partnership known as the **Hudson River Park Trust** (www.hudsonriver-park.org), runs from Battery Park to 59th St along the West Side, with a bike/run/skate path snaking along its entire length. It's dotted with community gardens, basketball courts, playgrounds and dog runs, and has renovated piers (some with facelifts still in progress) jutting out into the water and serving as riverfront esplanades, miniature golf courses and al fresco movie theaters and concert venues come summer. The tree-lined **Christopher Street Pier** (p92) and Pier 25, equipped with a sand-filled volleyball court, are particularly excellent, and the massive **Chelsea Piers** (left) fitness complex draws the crowds. For a detailed map of the entire park, visit the Trust's website.

UNION SQUARE, FLATIRON DISTRICT & GRAMERCY PARK

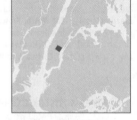

Eating pp183–6, Drinking pp217–18, Shopping pp269–71, Sleeping pp297–9

While these three areas are distinct in character – Union Square young and bustling, Flatiron hip but mature and Gramercy Park quiet and stately – all three share similar qualities of nonpretension, lovely architecture and a good blend of residences and businesses. Their boundaries are often blurred, too, as all sit nestled together east of Fifth Ave and between 14th and 34th Sts.

Originally one of New York City's first Uptown business districts, Union Square offered a convenient site for many workers' rallies and political protests throughout the mid-19th century. In fact its name has more prosaic origins: this was simply the 'union' of the old Bowery and Bloomingdale (now Broadway) roads. By the 1960s, this area was overrun by junkies and gigolos. But the '90s heralded a big revival, helped along by the arrival of the **Greenmarket Farmers' Market** (p107). Today, **Union Square Park**, which underwent restoration work in 2002, hops with activity; its plethora of bars, and restaurants and the new **Virgin Megastore** (p269) make it a popular place to hang out night or day, while its southern end has become the new 'in' place for antiwar, anti-Bush and other liberal-leaning demonstrators.

For a 10-block radius, the Flatiron District, loaded with loft buildings and boutiques, does a good imitation of Soho without the pretensions, prices or crowds. There are some fine restaurants and a dance club or three hiding out up here, too. The neighborhood takes its name from the **Flatiron Building** (opposite), a thin and gorgeous work of architecture that sits just south of Madison Square Park. Madison Ave at 26th St was the site of the first and second Madison Square Garden arenas (1879 and 1890, respectively). The second, designed by Stanford White, was awe-inspiring: Moorish in design with several turrets and a tower, it held 8000 and was crowned by a gilded Diana. It was razed in 1925, a year after it hosted the Democratic National Convention.

Gramercy Park, loosely comprising the 20s east of Madison Ave, is named after one of New York's loveliest parks – the kind of public garden area found in Paris and other European cities. But while the botanical sentiment did translate across the Atlantic, the socialist sense did not: when developers transformed the surrounding marsh into a city neighborhood in 1830, admission to the park was restricted to residents, and still, to this day, you need a key to get in. If you're strolling the area, though, peer through the gates and get a good look at what you're missing.

Orientation

Union Square, the area that juts a few blocks in each direction from the actual Union Square Park at 14th St and Broadway, runs seamlessly into the newly energized Flatiron District, which is generally the area that juts a few blocks in each direction out of Madison Park, at 23rd St and Broadway.

Ladies' Mile

In the late 19th century, the area encompassing Sixth Ave between 9th and 23rd Sts was known as the Ladies' Mile district – so named because of the original department stores, such as B Altman's, Lord & Taylor and the original Macy's (located at Sixth Ave and 14th St), and the opening of the Sixth Ave elevated train line, which brought scores of ladylike shoppers who strolled from one store to the next done up in dresses, feathered hats and parasols. Present-day zoning laws have welcomed retail stores back to the strip, and a complex featuring Bed, Bath & Beyond and Filene's Basement paved the way for all the other chains to move in, including Staples, Old Navy, TJ Maxx and **Barnes & Noble** (p269). Now this stretch, along with a smattering of chains along the parallel stretch of Fifth Ave, has made the area a shopping destination once again – for gentlemen *and* ladies – sans the parasols.

(Continued on page 107)

1 Bryant Park (p111) *2* Street-stall photographs (p256) *3* Buskers, Union Square (p107) *4* Traffic police, Times Square (p116)

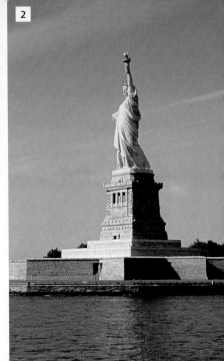

1 Great Hall, Immigration Museum (p75) *2* Statue of Liberty (p74) *3* Financial district, Wall St (p153) *4* Battery Park (p79)

1 *Radio City Music Hall (p115)*
2 *Atlas statue (p115),*
Rockefeller Center 3 *Fifth Ave*
(p114) 4 *Flatiron Building (p107)*

1 Durians, Chinatown (p85)
2 Street signs, Union Square (p107) 3 Slippers, Pearl River Mart (p260)

Tour guide, Harlem (p127)
2 *Prayer flags, Jacques Marchais Center of Tibetan Art (p150)* **3** *Kick boxing*

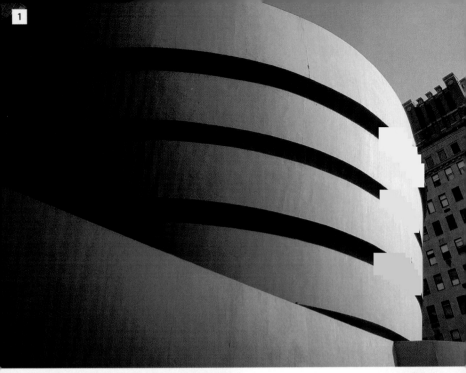

1 *Solomon R Guggenheim Museum (p125)* 2 *Window, the Cloisters (p132)* 3 *Frick Collection museum (p123)* 4 *Metropolitan Museum of Art (p123)*

1 Children's Museum of Manhattan (p121) 2 Stone Buddha, Jacques Marchais Center of Tibetan Art (p150) 3 PS1 Contemporary Art Center (p143) 4 Cooper-Hewitt National Design Museum (p122)

1 Clock, Grand Central Terminal (p112) 2 Chrysler Building (p111) 3 New York Public Library (p113) 4 Stanford White Arch (p94), Washington Square Park

(Continued from page 98)

Transportation

Subway L, N, Q, R, W, 4, 5, 6 to 14 St–Union Sq; 6 to 23, 28, 23 Sts.
Bus M23, M34, M22, M103.

UNION SQUARE
ABC CARPET & HOME
Map pp382-5

☎ 212-473-3000; www.abchome.com; 888 Broadway at 18th St; ☽ 10am-8pm Mon-Thu, 10am-6:30pm Fri & Sat, noon-6pm Sun; subway L, N, Q, R, W, 4, 5, 6 to 14 St–Union Sq, W Mon-Fri only

This incredibly popular home store is a mind-numbing example of NYC excess. The seven-floor retail center has entire departments dedicated to luxury textiles, antique furniture reproductions, fashion bedding, Oriental rugs, global accessories, and its high-end lines include collections from Ann Gish (silk bedding), Gabrielle Sanchez (jewelry), Keith Skeel (antiques), Ralph Lauren (furniture) and French Heritage (antiques). You can even take a shopping break with a full-on sit-down meal at **Lucy's Mexican Barbecue**, or with a haircut and dye job at **Mudhoney Salon**. Even those not in the market for an Indian throw pillow or English country headboard flock here, simply to stroll and soak in the offerings – especially around Christmas, when the place goes all-out with decorative lights and sparkly baubles. For more information see p269.

GREENMARKET FARMERS' MARKET
Map pp382-5

☎ 212-477-3220; www.cenyc.org; 17th St btwn Broadway & Park Ave S; ☽ 8am-4pm Mon, Wed, Fri & Sat; subway L, N, Q, R, W, 4, 5, 6 to 14 St–Union Sq, W Mon-Fri only

Of the 42 greenmarkets scattered throughout the five boroughs, the cornucopia at Union Square remains one of the most popular. This is where celebrity chefs come for just-picked rarities like fiddlehead ferns and fresh curry leaves, and where all sorts of food aficionados head for anything fresh and seasonal. Regional farmers tote all manner of edibles – such as homemade cheeses and hand-milked creams, organic fruits and vegetables, bundled herbs, maple syrup and honey, and baked goods – to this stretch of pavement across from, ironically, a massive Barnes & Noble.

FLATIRON DISTRICT
FLATIRON BUILDING
Map pp382-5

Broadway, btwn Fifth Ave & 23rd St; subway R, W, 6 to 23rd St

Built in 1902, the Flatiron Building, best viewed from the island on 23rd St between Broadway and Fifth Ave, dominated this plaza when the district contained the city's prime stretch of retail and entertainment establishments. The 20-story Flatiron, designed by Daniel Burnham, has a traditional beaux arts facade and a uniquely narrow triangular footprint.

MADISON SQUARE PARK
Map pp386-8

Btwn 23rd & 26th Sts & Fifth & Madison Aves

This park defined the northern reaches of Manhattan until the city's population exploded just after the Civil War. It has enjoyed a rejuvenation within the past few years due to a renovation project and rededication in 2001, and now neighborhood residents head here to unleash their dogs in the popular dog-run area, as workers enjoy lunches while perched on the new, shaded benches, perfect points from which to gaze up at the landmarks that surround the park, including the **Flatiron** (above), art deco **Metropolitan Life Tower**, and the **New York Life Insurance Company Building** (topped with a gilded spire). The space also sports 19th-century statues of folks including Senator Rosco Conkling (who froze to death in a brutal 1888 blizzard) and Civil War admiral David Farragut. Between 1876 and 1882 the torch-bearing arm of the Statue of Liberty was on display here, and in 1879 the first Madison Square Garden was constructed here (at Madison Ave and 26th St).

Neighborhoods – Union Square, Flatiron District & Gramercy Park

Top Five Union Square, Flatiron District & Gramercy Park

- **Flatiron Building** (above) Gaze up in wonder.
- **Gramercy Tavern** (p184) Sip on early-evening cocktails.
- **Greenmarket Farmers' Market** (above) Stock up on fresh produce.
- **Museum of Sex** (p108) Slink through all those exhibits.
- **Tabla** (p185) Grab a parkside table.

MUSEUM OF SEX Map pp386-8

☎ 212-689-6337; www.museumofsex.org; 233 Fifth Ave at 27th St; adult/senior & student $14.50/13.50; ☽ 11am-6:30pm Sun-Fri,11am-8pm Sat; subway N, R, W to 23 St, W Mon-Fri only

Not as racy as you might imagine, this house of culture, which opened in 2002, intellectually traces the interwoven history of NYC and sex, from tittie bars and porn to street hustling and burlesque shows. But don't expect any sex parties or naked go-go dancers here; the collection consists of films, magazines and odd artifacts from vintage blow-up dolls to sex-house coins. Frequently changing exhibitions tackle subjects such as how New York has affected sex around the world and ideas of Chinese erotic obsession, while events include erotica readings, one-person shows and sex-ed seminars.

GRAMERCY PARK

NATIONAL ARTS CLUB Map pp382-5

☎ 212-475-3424; 15 Gramercy Park South; subway 6 to 23 St

Also quite exclusive, this club boasts a beautiful, vaulted, stained-glass ceiling above its wooden bar. Calvert Vaux, who was one of the creators of Central Park, designed the building. But the space does hold art exhibitions, ranging from sculpture to photography, that sometimes open to the public from 1pm to 5pm.

THEODORE ROOSEVELT'S BIRTHPLACE Map pp382-5

☎ 212-260-1616; www.nps.gov/thrb; 28 E 20th St btwn Park Ave & Broadway; adult/child $3/free; ☽ 10am-4pm Tue-Sat; subway N, R, 6 to 23rd St

This National Historic Site is a bit of a cheat, since the house where the 26th president was born was demolished in his lifetime. This building is simply a re-creation by his relatives, who joined it with another family residence next door. If you're interested in Roosevelt's extraordinary life, which has been somewhat overshadowed by the enduring legacy of his younger cousin Franklin, visit here, especially if you don't have the time to see his summer home in Long Island's Oyster Bay. Included in the admission price are house tours, offered on the hour from 10am to 4pm.

MIDTOWN

Eating pp186–96, Drinking pp218–19, Shopping pp271–84, Sleeping pp299–303

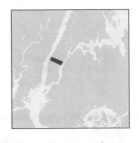

Home to many of the city's most popular attractions, New York's teeming Midtown area is where you'll probably wind up spending plenty of time; which you might find to be a mixed blessing. It can be cold in both temperature – little sunlight reaches the shadowy streets below the skyscrapers – and temperament, as most people are attending to the business of work rather than life, making it overwhelmingly crowded on weekdays (especially at lunchtime!). Very few people live in the center of Manhattan, and most apartment houses are located east of Third Ave and west of Eighth Ave.

Orientation

While this section has broken down all the more specific areas of Midtown for organization purposes, the actual borders are not so cleanly defined. Loosely speaking, Midtown West is the area west of Sixth Ave and north of 34th St to about 50th St, while Midtown East is between the same north–south borders but from Sixth Ave to the East River. Hell's Kitchen is the way-western portion of Midtown West, from about Eighth Ave to the river. The Rockefeller Center and Fifth Ave areas generally refer to regions north of

Transportation

Subway All lines pass through here; major stops are 42 St–Port Authority, 34 St–Penn Stn, Times Sq–42 St, 34 St–Herald Sq, Grand Central–42 St, 59 St–Columbus Circle, 47-50 Sts–Rockefeller Ctr.

Bus M23, M34, M22, M103.

Ferry New York Water Taxi (☎ 212-742-1969) zips to and from Brooklyn, South St Seaport and the Upper East Side.

Hell's Kitchen = Clinton?

For years, the far west side of Midtown was a working-class district of tenements and food warehouses known as Hell's Kitchen, a neighborhood that predominantly attracted Italian and Irish immigrants, who drifted into gangs after arriving. Hollywood films have often romanticized the district's gritty, criminal character (*West Side Story* was set here), but by the 1960s, the population of junkies and prostitutes had made it a forbidding place that few cared to enter, including many movie directors.

In 1989, the construction of the **Worldwide Plaza** (Map p226-7; W 50th St & Eighth Ave) building was supposed to juice the area's revival, as it took over the site of the 1930s-era Madison Square Garden, which had been a parking lot in the interim. Yet until the mid-1990s, Hell's Kitchen was largely unchanged. Eighth and Ninth Aves between 35th and 50th Sts was still the domain of wholesale food stores, and few buildings rose more than eight stories above the street.

But the economic boom of the late '90s seriously changed Hell's Kitchen and developers reverted to using the cleaned-up name Clinton, a moniker originating from the 1950s; locals are split on usage. A perfect link between the Upper West Side and Chelsea, the neighborhood (especially on Ninth Ave) exploded with nightspots and restaurants, as chefs eyed the large quantities of fresh food from nearby wholesalers and the large-ish spaces at cheap(er) rents. Moreover, many tourists began to filter into the neighborhood after glimpsing it on David Letterman's *Late Show*, taped at the Ed Sullivan Theater at Broadway between 53rd and 54th Sts. Culturally, there's not much here but it's a great place to grab a meal away from the congested streets around Rockefeller Center or to start your day with a hearty plate of pancakes at a typical New York City diner.

50th and up to 59th St, while the Theater District and Times Square are a small swath within Midtown West and defined more by the businesses and theaters and a state of mind rather than actual boundaries. Confused yet?

MIDTOWN WEST

EMPIRE STATE BUILDING Map pp386-8

☎ 212-736-3100; www.esbnyc.com; 350 Fifth Ave at 34th St; admission $11; ⏱ 9:30am-midnight; subway B, D, F, N, Q, R, V, W to 34 St–Herald Sq

Here's the real deal: New York's original symbol in the sky is a limestone classic built in just 410 days, or seven million man-hours, during the depths of the Depression at a cost of $41 million. Located on the site of the original Waldorf-Astoria Hotel, the 102-story, 1472ft (to the top of the antenna) Empire State Building opened in 1931 after the laying of 10 million bricks, installation of 6400 windows and setting of 328,000 sq ft of marble. The famous antenna was originally meant to be a mooring mast for zeppelins, but the *Hindenberg* disaster slammed the brakes on that plan. One airship accidentally met up with the building: a B25 crashed into the 79th floor on a foggy day in July 1945, killing 14 people.

Since 1976, the building's top 30 floors have been floodlit in seasonal and holiday colors (eg green for St Patrick's Day in March, black for World AIDS Day on December 1, red and green for Christmas, lavender for Gay Pride weekend in June; visit the website for each day's lighting scheme and meaning). This tradition has been copied by many other skyscrapers, notably the Metropolitan Life Tower at Madison Square Park and the Con Edison Tower near Union Square, lending elegance to the night sky.

The view from the Empire State Building is a dandy, but be prepared – the lines to get to the observation decks, on the 86th and 102nd floors, are notorious. And the basement area where you must buy tickets and queue up for the elevator ride is a shabby, poorly ventilated waiting pen, especially in the summer, when big old fans do little but blow hot air in your face. Though getting there very early or very late will help you avoid delays, sunset is one of the most magical times to be up there because you can see the city don its night-time cloak in dusk's afterglow. Once up there, you can stay as long as you like. Coin-operated telescopes offer an up-close glimpse of the city, and diagrams map out the major sights. You can even smoke up top, to either the joy of dismay of just about everyone there.

Neighborhoods – Midtown

Top Five Midtown Manhattan

- **Bryant Park** (p230) Take in a Monday-night summer film.
- **Empire State Building** (p109) Join the queues and look down from the top.
- **Grand Central Terminal** (p112) Admire the star-filled ceiling.
- **International Center of Photography** (p110) Catch a show from a top shutterbug.
- **Little Korea** (p110) Eat, stroll or experience karaoke.

West Side (Redevelopment) Story

Just when you thought there were no more frontiers left to explore in this over-saturated city, others appear. City and private planners have been brewing some of the largest redevelopment plans in New York's history, with schemes for new residential and commercial districts in areas including Fresh Kills Park in Staten Island, western Queens on the site of a former Pepsi plant and Downtown Brooklyn. But the one receiving all the attention seems to be the plan for Manhattan's West Side – probably because the impetus for the plan is the possibility of NYC getting the 2012 Olympic bid (see p18). But the development plan for this spot, also known as Hudson Yards and comprising 28th to 43rd Sts west of Eighth Ave, goes far beyond a sports complex (including a proposed football stadium to lure the wayward New York Jets back from New Jersey). It would rezone the entire area to allow for more hotels, offices and residences, and could create more than 12,600 apartments over the next 20 years – the vast majority of them high-end. But area residents are getting their hackles up over the sweeping nature of the plan, and have proposed an alternative, less extreme proposal that's backed by many area officials. What the outcome will be is anyone's guess, but the struggle is sure to heat up before anything is decided.

GARMENT DISTRICT Map p226-7

Seventh Ave btwn 34th St & Times Sq; subway B, D, F, N, Q, R, V, W to 34th St–Herald Sq

This is the district where many New York fashion firms have their design offices and where, on weekdays, the side streets are packed with delivery trucks. Broadway between 23rd St and Herald Square is called the Accessories District because of the many ribbon and button shops that serve the city's fashion industry. These are trippy places with thousands of snaps, cinches and closures displayed among feathers, lace, sequins, rhinestones and hand-carved, painted and woven buttons.

HERALD SQUARE Map pp386-8

Subway B, D, F, N, Q, R, V, W to 34 St–Herald Sq

This crowded convergence of Broadway, Sixth Ave and 34th St is best known as the home of Macy's department store, where you can still ride some of the remaining original wooden elevators to floors ranging from home furnishings to lingerie. But the busy square gets its name from a long-defunct newspaper, the *Herald*, and the small, leafy park here bustles during business hours thanks to a recent and much-needed

facelift. Don't bother with the two indoor malls south of Macy's on Sixth Ave, where you'll find a boring and suburban array of chain stores.

INTERNATIONAL CENTER OF PHOTOGRAPHY Map p226-7

☎ 212-857-0000; www.icp.org; 1133 Sixth Ave at 43rd St; adult/senior & student $10/7; ✆ 10am-5pm Tue-Thu, 10am-8pm Fri, 10am-6pm Sat & Sun; subway B, D, F, V to 42nd St–Bryant Park

Recently consolidated from two locations at its expanded Midtown space, this center remains the city's most important showcase for major photographers, especially photojournalists. Its past exhibitions have included work by Henri Cartier-Bresson, Man Ray, Matthew Brady, Weegee and Robert Capa, and have explored themes such as September 11 and the impact of AIDS. It's also a photography school, offering coursework for credit as well as a public-lecture series. And its gift shop is an excellent place to stock up on quality photo books or quirky, photo-themed gifts.

INTREPID SEA-AIR-SPACE MUSEUM

Map pp386-8

☎ 212-245-0072; www.intrepidmuseum.org; W 46th St; adult/senior & student/child $14.50/10.50/9.50; ✆ 10am-5pm Mon-Fri, 10am-6pm Sat & Sun Apr-Sep, 10am-5pm Tue-Sun Oct-Mar; subway A, C, E to 42nd St

At the western edge of Midtown, the Intrepid Sea-Air-Space Museum sits on an aircraft carrier at Pier 86. The flight deck of the USS *Intrepid*, which served in WWII and Vietnam, features several fighter planes, and the pier area contains the *Growler* guided-missile submarine, an *Apollo* space capsule, Vietnam-era tanks and the 900ft destroyer *Edson*. In 2003, an adjacent barge became home to a 204ft long, 88 ton Concorde jet. The *Intrepid* is the nexus for the **Fleet Week** (p10) celebrations each May, when thousands of the world's sailors descend on Manhattan. Free audio tours in French, German, Japanese, Russian and Spanish are available.

LITTLE KOREA Map pp386-8

Btwn 31st & 36th Sts & Broadway & Fifth Ave; subway B, D, F, N, Q, R, V, W to 34th St–Herald Sq

Herald Square's sorely lacking when it comes to good food; luckily, you can head for quality refueling at nearby Little Korea, a small enclave of Korean-owned restaurants, shops, salons and spas. Over the past few years, this neighborhood has seen an explosion of eateries serving Korean fare, with authentic Korean barbecues available around the clock at many of the all-night spots on 32nd St, some with the added treat of karaoke.

JACOB JAVITS CONVENTION CENTER
Map pp386-8

☎ 212-216-2000; www.javitscenter.com; Eleventh Ave btwn 34th & 38th Sts; subway A, C, E to 34 St–Penn Station then M11 crosstown bus

NYC's sole convention center is a four-block construction way on the outer reaches of Manhattan's west side. Designed by IM Pei, the behemoth of glass and steel – either totally loved or completely reviled by most New Yorkers – is host to hundreds of events each year, from auto shows and dentist conventions to travel expos and well-attended High Holiday services for the local gay and lesbian synagogue, Congregation Beth Simchat Torah.

TIME WARNER CENTER Map pp386-8
☎ 212-869-1890; www.wirednewyork.com/aol /default.htm; 1560 Broadway; ☺ 8am-8pm; subway N, Q, R, S, W, 1, 2, 3, 7 to Times Sq–42nd St

After three years of scaffolding, noisy construction and nightmare traffic, this much-discussed $1.8 billion project was completed in February 2004, revealing a pair of sleek towers hovering over the southwest corner of Central Park, replacing what had been the aging New York Coliseum. And so far, reviews have been mixed: while Columbus Circle neighborhood residents hate the increased foot and taxi traffic, mobs of locals and tourists alike love the

---

Jazz at Lincoln Center

As of October 2004, the jazz component of **Lincoln Center** (Map pp389-91; www.jazzatlincolncenter.com) left its old home for its grand new digs at the Frederick P. Rose Hall of Time Warner Center, a 100,000 sq ft, $128 million facility built specifically for jazz. The multi-room space, with a sleek and soaring glass design from Rafael Viñoly Architects, will also host opera, dance, theater and symphony shows, but its main theme is jazz, in the form of education, historical archiving and, of course, performance, with shows curated by its artistic director, none other than Wynton Marsalis. The place is perched high above Central Park – its ring of a glimmering skyline and the magnificent views will serve as a backdrop for jazz shows in glass-backed spaces such as the intimate **Allen Room** and **Dizzy's Club Coca-Cola** nightclub. 'The whole space is going to be dedicated to the feeling of swing,' Marsalis has said, 'which is a feeling of extreme coordination.'

---

seven-floor retail atrium (a glorified mall, really), with luxury shops including **Williams-Sonoma**, **Armani Exchange** and **Hugo Boss** (p274). There are no less than seven high-end eateries (see Towers of [Food] Power, p195) along with a 59000 sq ft wholefoods organic market. Burning off the eats isn't a problem here, either, as there's a sprawling new branch of the local Equinox gym chain, Olympic-size lap pool included.

MIDTOWN EAST
BRIDGEMARKET Map pp386-8
☎ 212-980-2455; 409 E 59th St at First Ave; subway E, F, 6 to 59 St–Lexington Ave

After decades in restoration, Bridgemarket – a vaulted, Guastavino-tiled space under the 59th St Bridge that served as a farmer's market in the early 20th century – was brought back to life in 1999 by design guru Sir Terence Conran. Now it's a thriving retail and dining complex, anchored by the Terence Conran Shop, alive with ingenious modern design accessories, and **Guastavino's** restaurant, a sweeping and dramatic space that serves killer brunches and cocktails, and turns into a dance club after the dinner crowd has cleared out for the night.

BRYANT PARK Map pp386-8
☎ 212-768-4242; www.bryantpark.org; W 42nd St btwn Fifth & Sixth Aves; subway B, D, F, V to 42 St–Bryant Park

Nestled behind the grand public library is this lovely square of green – yet another former patch of squalor, referred to as 'needle park' throughout the '80s – where local Midtown workers gather for lunchtime picnics on warm afternoons. Among its offerings are impressive skyscraper views, Europe-like coffee kiosks, a Brooklyn-constructed carousel offering rides for $1.50, and frequent special events: It's where the famed Fashion Week tent goes up every winter, and the site of a wonderful Monday-night summer outdoor film series, which packs the lawn with postwork crowds lugging cheese-and-wine picnics (for more information see Bryant Park Film Series, p230). **Bryant Park Grill**, a lovely restaurant and bar situated at the east end of the park, is the site of many a New York wedding come springtime.

CHRYSLER BUILDING Map pp386-8
Lexington Ave & 42nd St; subway S, 4, 5, 6, 7 to Grand Central–42nd St

The 1048ft Chrysler Building, just across from Grand Central Terminal, briefly reigned as the tallest structure in the world until it was superseded by the Empire State Building a few months later. An art deco masterpiece designed by William Van Alen in 1930, the building was constructed to be the headquarters for Walter P Chrysler and his automobile empire; fittingly, the facade's design celebrates car culture, with gargoyles that resemble hood ornaments, amorphous block cars and thatched steel designs, best viewed with binoculars. The 200ft steel spire (known as the 'vertex'), constructed in secret, was raised through the false roof as a surprise crowning touch – which shocked and dismayed a competing architect who was hoping that his new Wall St building would turn out to be New York's tallest skyscraper at the time (it wasn't). Lit up at night, there are few more poignant symbols than the Chrysler Building.

Nestled at the top was the famed Cloud Club, a former speakeasy. For a long time, developers have been planning to convert part of the building into a hotel, but so far that remains only a pipe dream.

Although the Chrysler Building has no restaurant or observation deck (and is filled with offices for unexciting companies including lawyers and accountants), it's worth wandering inside to admire the elaborately veneered elevators (made from slices of Japanese ash, Oriental walnut and Cuban plum-pudding wood) and the profusion of marble and the 1st floor ceiling mural (purportedly the world's largest at 97ft by 100ft) depicting the promise of industry.

GRAND CENTRAL TERMINAL
Map pp386-8
42nd St at Park Ave; www.grandcentralterminal.com; subway S, 4, 5, 6, 7 to Grand Central–42nd St
One of New York's most dramatic public spaces, Grand Central Terminal evokes the romance of train travel at the turn of the 20th century, while enduring the bustle of present-day New York. Thanks to a lovingly tendered 1998 renovation, its interior remains as impressive as ever.

Completed in 1913, Grand Central Terminal (also called Grand Central Station) is another of New York's stunning beaux arts buildings and boasts 75ft-high, glass-encased catwalks, with the constellations of the zodiac streaming across the vaulted ceiling – backwards (the designer made a boo-boo!). The balconies overlooking the main concourse afford an expansive view; perch yourself on one of these at around 6pm on a weekday to get a glimpse of the grace this terminal commands under pressure.

Timber house, City Island

Today, Grand Central's underground electric tracks only serve commuter trains en route to northern suburbs and Connecticut. But the old dame still merits a special trip for the fine dining, cool bars and occasional art exhibitions. The **Municipal Art Society** (☎ 212-935-3960; www .mas.org) leads weekly walks through Grand Central. During the hour-long tour, you'll learn all kinds of stuff about the terminal, but the best perk is that you get to cross the glass catwalk high above the concourse. Tours meet at the passenger information booth in the middle of the terminal. Also in Grand Central are a slew of shops, a tourist information booth, currency exchange and police post.

NEW YORK PUBLIC LIBRARY

Map pp386-8

☎ 212-930-0830; www.nypl.org; 42nd St at Fifth Ave; ⏰ 11am-7:30pm Tue & Wed, 10am-6pm Thu-Sat; subway S, 4, 5, 6 to Grand Central–42nd St, 7 to Fifth Ave
This main branch of the public library system is a monument to learning, housed in a grand beaux arts building and reflecting its big-money industrialist roots. When it was dedicated in 1911, New York's flagship library ranked as the largest marble structure ever built in the USA, with a vast 3rd-floor reading room designed to hold 500 patrons. This is not to mention the marble lions at the entrance, profligate use of gold leaf throughout, chandeliers, carved porticos and ceiling murals.

Today, this building, now called the Humanities and Social Sciences Library, is one of the best free attractions in the city. On a rainy day, hide away with a book in the airy reading room and admire the original Carre and Hastings lamps, or stroll through the Exhibition Hall, which contains precious manuscripts by just about every author of note in the English language, including a 'fair copy' of the Declaration of Independence and a Gutenberg Bible. Interesting exhibitions also rotate through here. The free building tour is a bonanza of interesting tidbits; it leaves from the information desk at 11am and 2pm Monday to Saturday.

PIERPONT MORGAN LIBRARY

Map pp386-8

☎ 212-685-0610; www.morganlibrary.org; 29 E 36th St at Madison Ave; closed for renovations until 2006; subway 6 to 33rd St
The Pierpont Morgan Library, closed to the public at the time of writing for extensive renovations, is part of the 45-room mansion owned by steel magnate JP Morgan. His collection features a phenomenal array of manuscripts, tapestries and books (with no fewer than three Gutenberg Bibles), a study filled with Italian Renaissance artwork, a marble rotunda and the three-tiered East Room main library. The rotating art exhibitions here are really top-notch – and, luckily, you can still catch traveling exhibitions, which are hosted by a whole range of host museums around the city. Check the website for the current schedule.

SUTTON PLACE Map pp386-8

Subway 4, 5, 6 to 59th St
This place encompasses several blocks of European-style luxury apartments that run parallel to First Ave from 54th to 59th Sts. The dead-end streets, which have pleasant benches looking out on the East River, served as the setting for Diane Keaton and Woody Allen's first date in the movie Manhattan. It's a lovely, quiet spot for gazing out at Queens and its 59th St Bridge.

UNITED NATIONS Map pp386-8

☎ 212-963-7539; btwn First Ave & 46th St; adult /senior & student/child $10.50/8/7; ⏰ 9:30am-4:45pm; subway S, 4, 5, 6, 7 to Grand Central–42nd St
The United Nations headquarters is technically located on a section of international territory overlooking the East River. Take a guided tour of the facility and you'll get to see the General Assembly, where the annual fall convocation of member nations takes place; the Security Council Chamber, where crisis management continues year-round; and also the Economic & Social Council Chamber. There is a park to the south of the complex which is home to Henry Moore's Reclining Figure as well as several other sculptures with a peace theme.

English-language tours of the UN complex depart every 30 minutes; limited tours in several other languages are also available. You may sometimes hear this area of Midtown East referred to as Turtle Bay, and even though the turtles are long gone, there are a number of interesting architectural examples around here, in particular among the permanent missions, such as those of **Egypt** (304 E 44th St, btwn First & Second Aves) and also **India** (245 E 43rd St, btwn Second & Third Aves).

FIFTH AVENUE

Immortalized in both film and song, Fifth Ave first developed its high-class reputation in the early 20th century, when a series of mansions on the avenue's uptown portion became known as Millionaire's Row. Today, the avenue's Midtown stretch still boasts upscale shops and hotels, including the garish but somehow endearing Plaza Hotel (N, R, W to Fifth Ave-59 St, F to 57 St) at Grand Army Plaza, overlooking Central Park and Fifth Ave. The historic institution doesn't have much of a grand lobby, but the stained-glass ceiling in the Palm Court is impressive. The fountain facing the hotel, with a statue of the Roman goddess Diana, is a good spot for a rest – provided you're not downwind from the horse-drawn carriages that line 59th St. Across the street, on the northwest corner of 59th St and Fifth Ave, don't miss the outpost of the venerable used-book purveyor, Strand (p268).

Most of the heirs to the millionaire mansions on Fifth Ave above 59th St sold them for demolition or converted them to the cultural institutions that now make up Museum Mile. The Villard Houses, on Madison Ave behind St Patrick's Cathedral, are a stunning exception. Financier Henry Villard built the six four-story townhouses in 1881, and they flaunt artistic details by the likes of Tiffany, John LaFarge and Auguste St-Gaudens; the mansion was later owned by the Catholic church and then sold to a series of hotel magnates.

While a number of the more exclusive boutiques have migrated to Madison Ave, several still line Fifth Ave above 50th St, including Cartier (p272), Henri Bendel (p273) and the movie-famous Tiffany & Co (p283).

AMERICAN FOLK ART MUSEUM

Map pp386-8

☎ 212-265-1040; www.folkartmuseum.org; 45 W 53rd St btwn Fifth & Sixth Aves; adult/senior & student $9/7; 10:30am-5:30pm Wed, Thu, Sat & Sun, 10:30am-7:30pm Fri; subway E, V to Fifth Ave–53rd St

With a focus on traditional arts tied to moments in history or personal milestones, the collection here features objects such as flags, liberty figures, textiles, weathervanes and decorative arts. Quilts, painted portraits and vases have been on display for recent exhibitions, which are ever-changing.

MUSEUM OF ARTS & DESIGN

Map pp386-8

☎ 212-956-3535; www.americancraftmuseum.org; 40 W 53rd St btwn Fifth & Sixth Aves; adult/senior/child under 13 yrs $9/6/free; 10am-6pm Tue, Wed & Fri-Sun, 10am-8pm Thu; subway E, V to Fifth Ave–53rd St

Directly across the street from Museum of Modern Art, the Museum of Arts & Design, which had its name switched from the American Craft Museum in order to boost its importance to art-world worthiness for those turned off by the term 'craft,' displays innovative and traditional, well, *crafts* in a spectacularly well-designed and airy space. The museum is currently hosting a 10-year series of exhibitions that examines American craft-making, and you can view works from the eight identified periods of artisanship.

MUSEUM OF TELEVISION & RADIO

Map pp386-8

☎ 212-621-6800; www.mtr.org; 25 W 52nd St btwn Fifth & Sixth Aves; adult/senior & student/child $10/8/5; noon-6pm Tue, Wed & Fri-Sun, noon-8pm Thu; subway E, V to Fifth Ave–53rd St

This couch potato's smorgasbord, between Fifth and Sixth Aves, contains a collection of more than 50,000 American TV and radio programs, all available from the museum's computer catalog with the click of a mouse. It's a great place to hang out when it's raining or when you're simply fed up with the real world. Nearly everybody checks out their favorite childhood TV programs and watches them on the museum's 90 consoles, but the radio-listening room is an unexpected pleasure. Your admission fee entitles you to two hours of uninterrupted audiovisual enjoyment. Special screenings are also held here on a regular basis.

NBC STUDIOS Map pp386-8

☎ 212-664-3700; www.shopnbc.com; subway B, D, F, V to 47th–50th Sts–Rockefeller Center

The NBC television network has its headquarters in the 70-story GE Building, which looms over the Rockefeller Center ice-skating rink (the rink doubles as a café in the summer months). The *Today* show broadcasts live 7am to 10am daily from a glass-enclosed street-level studio near the fountain.

Tours of the NBC studios leave from the lobby of the GE Building every 15 minutes; they're offered from 8:30am to 5:30pm Monday to Saturday, 9:30am to 4:30pm Sunday, with extended hours during the holiday season in November and December. Tours cost $17.75 for adults, $15 for seniors or children aged six to 16; children under six are not admitted. The walkabout lasts for about one hour and 10 minutes, but be advised that there is a strict policy of 'no bathrooms,' so be sure to empty your bladder beforehand!

Tickets to show tapings (eg *Saturday Night Live*, *Late Night with Conan O'Brien* etc) are no longer available by mail, but on a standby basis from 9am to 5pm Monday to Friday. Competition is stiff, so be sure to show up by 7am if you want even a remote chance of getting in. For other shows, visit www.tvticket.com for varying information.

RADIO CITY MUSIC HALL
Map pp386-8
☎ 212-247-4777; www.radiocity.com; 51st St at Sixth Ave; tours adult/senior/child $17/14/10; subway B, D, F, V to 47th–50th Sts–Rockefeller Center
This 6000-seat art deco movie palace had its interior declared a protected landmark and is looking fine, thanks to extensive renovation

work in 1999. In a triumphant restoration, the velvet seats and furnishings were returned to the exact state they were in when the building opened in 1932. (Even the toilets are elegant at the 'Showplace of the Nation.') Concerts here sell out quickly, and tickets to the annual Christmas spectacular featuring the hokey but enjoyable Rockette dancers now cost up to $70. (Samuel 'Roxy' Rothafel, the man responsible for the high-kicking chorus line, declared that 'a visit to Radio City is as good as a month in the country.')

You can see the interior by taking a tour, which leaves every half-hour between 11am and 3pm Monday to Sunday. Tickets are sold on a first-come, first-served basis.

ROCKEFELLER CENTER Map pp386-8
☎ 212-632-3975; www.rockefellercenter.com; btwn Fifth & Sixth Aves & 48th & 51st Sts; subway B, D, F, V to 47th–50th Sts–Rockefeller Center
Built during the height of the Great Depression in the 1930s, the 22-acre Rockefeller gave jobs to 70,000 workers over nine years and was the first project to combine retail, entertainment and office space in what is often referred to as a 'city within a city.'

Perhaps most impressively, Rockefeller Center features commissioned works around the theme 'Man at the Crossroads Looks Uncertainly But Hopefully at the Future' by 30 great artists of the day. One great artist, however, was looking skeptically at the future. Mexican muralist Diego Rivera, persuaded to paint the lobby of the 70-story RCA Building (now the GE Building), was outraged, along with the rest of the art world, when the Rockefeller family rejected his painting for containing 'Communist imagery' – namely, the face of Lenin. The fresco was destroyed and replaced with a Jose Maria Sert work depicting the more 'acceptable' faces of Abraham Lincoln and Ralph Waldo Emerson.

But even art neophytes will appreciate Prometheus overlooking the ice-skating rink, Atlas doing his thing in front of the **International Building** (630 Fifth Ave), which has a wacky sculpture inset into its lobby walls, and *News* by Isamu Noguchi above the entrance to the **Associated Press Building** (45 Rockefeller Plaza). Anyone interested in artworks within the complex should pick up the *Rockefeller Center Visitors Guide* in the GE lobby, which describes many of them in detail.

Architectural details around the complex are varied. Note the tile work above the Sixth Ave entrance to the GE Building, the three flood-lit cameos along the side of Radio City Music Hall and the back-lit gilt and stained-glass entrance

---

MoMA returns to Manhattan

After spending two years in exile at a temporary site in Long Island City Queens, the **Museum of Modern Art** (MoMA; Map pp386-8; ☎ 212-708-9400; www.moma.org; 11 W 53rd St btwn Fifth & Sixth Aves; adult/student $12/8.50, pay what you wish 4-7:45pm Fri; ☽ 10am-5pm Mon, Thu, Sat & Sun, 10am-7:45pm Fri; subway E, V to Fifth Ave–53rd St) reopened to the public in November of 2004 following the most extensive renovation project in its 75-year history. The project has doubled the museum's capacity to 630,000 sq ft on six floors, and added a sparkling new design by architect Yoshio Taniguchi. MoMA's permanent collection is back on view, which means you can be privy to its more than 100,000 paintings, sculptures, drawings, prints, photographs, architectural models, drawings and design objects. Highlights include works by masters including Cézanne, Van Gogh, Seurat, Gaugin, Rodin and Picasso. The museum's renovated sculpture garden is a joy to sit in, as is its cinema, where MoMA rotates screenings of its collection of more than 19,000 films. And the museum's top-notch temporary exhibitions are not to be missed; past shows have included *Roth Time: A Dieter Roth Retrospective*; *Kiki Smith: Prints, Books and Things*; *Ansel Adams at 100*; *Andy Warhol: Screen Tests*; and the much celebrated *Matisse/Picasso*.

Rock Center's Fir Ball

Perhaps the best-known feature of Rockefeller Center is its gigantic Christmas tree, which overlooks the skating rink during the holidays. (This tradition dates back to the 1930s when construction workers set up a small Christmas tree on the site.) The annual lighting of the Rockefeller Center Christmas tree during the week after Thanksgiving attracts thousands of visitors to the area, who cram around the felled spruce, selected each year with fanfare from an unlucky upstate forest. The scene is too crowded to be believed, but skating at the **Rink at Rockefeller Center** (Map pp386-8; ☎ 212-332-7654; Fifth Ave btwn 49th & 50th Sts; adult/child $8.50/7 Mon-Fri, $11/7.50 Sat & Sun, skate rental $6) under the gaze of Prometheus is unforgettable. Opening hours change weekly, so call for the schedule.

to the East River Savings Bank Building at 41 Rockefeller Plaza, immediately to the north of the skating rink.

The cluster of shops in Rockefeller Center is better than most, with outlets of the upscale cosmetic discounter **Sephora**, techie toy emporium **Sharper Image** and designer **Tommy Hilfiger**, among others.

ST PATRICK'S CATHEDRAL   Map pp386-8
☎ 212-753-2261; 50th St at Fifth Ave; ⏰ 6am-9pm; subway B, D, F, V to 47th–50th Sts–Rockefeller Center
It's worth checking out this cathedral just across from Rockefeller Center, as its elaborate interpretation of French Gothic styles is a feather in the cap of the Roman Catholic Church. The cathedral, built at a cost

of nearly $2 million during the Civil War, originally didn't include the two front spires, which were added in 1888. Although it seats a modest 2400 worshippers, most of New York's 2.2 million faithful will have been inside at one time or another. While it may seem like each and every one is there when you show up, muddle through to see some of the exquisite details inside.

After you enter, walk by the eight small shrines along the side of the cathedral, past the shrine to Nuestra Señora de Guadalupe and the main altar to the quiet Lady Chapel, dedicated to the Virgin Mary. From here, you can see the handsome stained-glass Rose Window above the 7000-pipe church organ. A basement crypt behind the altar contains the coffins of every New York cardinal and the remains of Pierre Touissant, a champion of the poor and the first black American up for sainthood (he emigrated from Haiti).

Unfortunately, St Patrick's is not a place for restful contemplation because of the constant buzz from baseball cap–wearing, videotaping, disrespectful visitors. It's also a regular protest site by gays who feel excluded by the church hierarchy. Since 1933, the exclusion of Irish gays from the St Patrick's Day Parade (an event not sponsored by the Catholic Church per se, but identified with Catholic traditionalists) has triggered protests near the cathedral every March; it also inspires participants in the spirited Gay Pride March to yell, 'Shame! Shame!' as they pass on by.

Frequent masses take place on the weekend, and New York's archbishop presides over the service at 10:15am Sunday. Casual visitors are only allowed in between services.

THEATER DISTRICT & TIMES SQUARE

Now enjoying a major renaissance – to the dismay of those who prefer to gripe about 'Disneyfication' and wax poetic about the prostitute-and-drug-drenched past – Times Square (subway N, Q, R, S, W, 1, 2, 3, 7 to Times Square–42nd St) can once again trumpet its reputation as the 'Crossroads of the World.' Smack in the middle of Midtown Manhattan, this area around the intersection of Broadway and Seventh Ave has long been synonymous with gaudy billboards and glittery marquees – before the advent of TV, advertisers went after the largest audience possible by

beaming their messages into the center of New York. With over 60 mega-billboards and 40 miles of neon, it's startling (and a bit alarming) how it always looks like daytime.

Times Square also continues to serve as New York's official theater district, with dozens of Broadway and off-Broadway theaters located in an area that stretches from 41st to 54th Sts, between Sixth and Ninth Aves (see p228). A few huge, multiplex movie theatres now line 42nd St, as well.

Up to a million people gather in Times Square every New Year's Eve to see an illuminated Waterford Crystal ball descend from the roof of One Times Square at midnight. While this event garners international coverage, it lasts just 90 seconds and, frankly, is something of a (very drunk) anticlimax.

Life & Times of Times Square

Once called Long Acre Square, Times Square took its present name from the famous newspaper, the *New York Times*, which is still located there. Though it's long been the site of bright lights and flashy behavior, Times Square dimmed quite a bit in the 1960s, as once-proud movie palaces that had previously shown first-run films turned into 'triple X' porn theaters. But in recent years, the city has reversed the area's fortunes by extending big tax breaks to businesses that relocated here (most notably Walt Disney) and legislating theaters to the hilt: under Mayor Giuliani an entertainment venue had to be at least 60% 'legitimate' theater to permit the other 40% to show or sell porn. Today, the square draws 27 million annual visitors, who spend something over $12 billion in Midtown.

The cacophony of color, zipping message boards (called 'zippers') that provide up-to-the-minute news updates and massive TV screens make Times Square seem like one big, blinding advertisement or video, and it was this blaring brightness that earned this portion of Broadway the nickname 'the Great White Way.' Television networks have opened studios in Times Square, and major companies, including Virgin Megastore and Reuters, have built headquarters in and around the square in recent years.

CONDE NAST Map p226-7
www.condenast.com; 4 Times Sq; subway N, Q, R, S, W, 1, 2, 3, 7 to Times Sq–42nd St

Though you won't be able to enter the high-security tower, it's kind of exhilarating to walk by this temple of publishing, which employs thousands of the puffed-up editor types you'll see networking and gossiping at the trendiest of downtown lounges. Magazine lovers should get a particular thrill, as this is home to the offices of no less than 17 titles, including the *New Yorker*, *Vogue*, *Gourmet*, *GQ*, *Conde Nast Traveler*, *Vanity Fair* and *Allure*.

MADAME TUSSAUD'S NEW YORK
Map pp226-7

☎ 800-246-8872; www.madame-tussauds.com; 234 W 42nd St btwn Seventh & Eighth Aves; adult/senior /child $25/22/19; 🕙 10am-8pm; subway N, Q, R, S, W, 1, 2, 3, 7 to Times Sq–42nd St

Cheesy and seriously touristy, but where else can you get so close to J.Lo, Robin Williams, the Rock, Susan Sarandon and other celebs? They're all faux, of course, as this is the NYC branch of the famous London wax museum. But still…

MTV STUDIOS Map pp226-7
www.mtv.com; 1515 Broadway at 45th St; subway N, Q, R, S, W, 1, 2, 3, 7 to Times Sq–42nd St

Among the television studios to have recently moved into the 'hood is this cross-generational favorite. While you can't enter the studios – unless you're between the ages of 18 and 24 and get tickets to be an audience member on

Total Request Live – you can shop till you drop from over-stimulation at the predictably bright and busy fan store. Or wave up to the TRL studios during a taping.

TIMES SQUARE VISITORS CENTER
Map pp226-7

☎ 212-869-5667; www.timessquarebid.org; 1560 Broadway btwn 46th & 47th Sts; 🕙 8am-8pm; subway N, Q, R, S, W, 1, 2, 3, 7 to Times Sq–42nd St

Sitting smack in the middle of this famous crossroads is the Times Square Visitors Center. More than one million visitors annually stop in to use the center's ATMs, video guides to the city and computer terminals with free Internet access. The center also offers free walking tours of the neighborhood at noon on Friday.

TKTS BOOTH Map pp226-7
☎ 212-768-1818; www.tdf.org; Broadway at 47th St; 🕙 3-8pm Mon-Sat, 11am-8pm Sun; subway N, Q, R, S, W, 1, 2, 3, 7 to Times Sq–42nd St

The Theater Development Fund is the largest nonprofit organization for theater in the country, and its most well-known project is making theater tickets available to audiences at half price. Its ticket-sales booths (another is located at the South Street Seaport on the corner of Front and John Sts), marked by huge, bright orange 'TKTS' signs, draw savvy crowds daily. Lining up at noon is the best way to get your pick of the offerings, posted each day at the ticket window like a *menu du jour*, based on what shows are still available as of that morning.

CENTRAL PARK

Walking Tour pp162–3

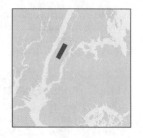

This 843-acre **park** (☎ 212-360-3444; www.centralparknyc .org), which celebrated its 150th anniversary in 2003 and sits smack-dab in the middle of Manhattan, is not to be missed. An oasis from the insanity, the downy lawns and meandering, wooded paths provide the bit of nature New Yorkers crave. There are acres of gardens, fathoms of freshwater ponds, miles of trails and innumerable secret pockets to explore here. While the park swarms with joggers, in-line skaters, musicians and tourists on warm weekends, there are quieter areas above 72nd St – recommended spots include the **Harlem Meer**, the **Lasker Rink & Pool** and the formal **Conservancy Gardens**. Meanwhile, winter exposes a different – though no less restorative – face of the park, as locals usually flock here during blizzards to cross-country ski, sled or simply stroll through the wonderland. Its sometimes-scary reputation as a dark and menacing place (especially for women runners and parade-goers) is generally not justified; today the park ranks as one of the safest parts of the city.

Like the subway, Central Park is the great leveler. Created in the 1860s and '70s by Frederick Law Olmstead and Calvert Vaux on the marshy northern fringe of the city, the immense park was designed as a leisure space for all New Yorkers, regardless of color, class or creed. Olmstead (who also created Prospect Park in Brooklyn) was determined to keep foot and road traffic separate and cleverly designed the crosstown traverses so the two would not meet, which makes the park an especially rewarding pedestrian destination. That such a large expanse of prime real estate has survived intact for so long again proves that in the end, nothing eclipses the heart, soul and pride that forms the foundation of New York's greatness. Today, this 'people's park' is still one of the city's most popular attractions, beckoning throngs of New Yorkers with free outdoor concerts, a zoo and the famous annual Shakespeare in the Park productions.

When Central Park was first created, wealthy New Yorkers had their wish granted for a quiet place for carriage rides. Some traditions never die – although today most New Yorkers wouldn't be caught dead in a horse-drawn carriage. But tourists love them, despite the expense and the stench in the summer. Carriages line up along 59th St (Central Park South; 1, 9, A, B, C, D to 59th St–Columbus Circle) and cost $35 for 20 minutes ($10 for every 15 minutes extra). Drivers expect tips.

Orientation

The expanse begins at 59th St at its south border and runs up to 110th St, while the east–west borders are Central Park West (the avenue just east of Columbus Ave) and Fifth Ave. For west-side access, take the B or C, which make stops at 72 St, 81 St, 86 St, 96 St, 103 St and 110 St. On the east side, the closest you'll get by subway is on the No 6 train, which makes stops along Lexington Ave (three avenues east of the park's border) at 68 St, 77 St, 86 St, 96 St, 103 St and 110 St. For park information, stop into the **Dairy**, which provides maps and tour guides, near the E 68th St entrance.

ARSENAL Map pp389–91

Built between 1847 and 1851 as a munitions supply depot for the New York State National Guard, the landmark brick building at E 64th St was designed to look like a medieval castle, and its construction predates the actual park. Today the building houses the City of New York Parks & Recreation and the Central Park Wildlife Conservation Center. The reason to visit here is not to see the building, though, but to view Olmstead's original blueprint for the park, treasured here under glass in a 3rd floor conference room.

Top Five Central Park

- **Bethesda Fountain** (p162) Sit and watch.
- **Delacorte Theatre** (p228) Catch some Shakespeare.
- **Great Lawn** (opposite) Lie down and stretch out.
- **Reservoir** (opposite) Take a brisk run all the way around.
- **Strawberry Fields** (opposite) Cast your mind back and remember John.

CENTRAL PARK ZOO & WILDLIFE CENTER Map pp389-91

☎ 212-861-6030; www.wcs.org; 64th St at Fifth Ave; ☺ 10am-5pm

The penguins are the main attraction at this modern zoo, though you'll find more than two dozen other species to visit, including polar bears and the endangered tamarin monkeys and red pandas. Feeding times are especially rowdy, fun times to stroll through: watch the sea lions chow down at 11:30am, 2pm and 4pm and see the penguins gobble fish at 10:30am and 2:30pm. The **Tisch Children's Zoo**, between 65th and 66th Sts, is perfect for smaller children.

GREAT LAWN Map pp389-91

Located between 72nd and 86th Sts, this massive emerald carpet was created in 1931 by filling in a former reservoir. It is the place for outdoor concerts (this is where Paul Simon played his famous comeback show, and also where you can watch the New York Philharmonic Orchestra each summer), and there are eight softball fields, basketball courts and a canopy of London plane trees. Not far from the actual lawn are several other big sites: the **Delacorte Theater**, which is home to the annual Shakespeare in the Park festival, and its lush Shakespeare Garden; the panoramic **Belvedere Castle**; the leafy **Ramble**, the epicenter of both birding and gay-male cruising; and the **Loeb Boathouse**, where you can rent rowboats for a romantic float in the middle of this urban paradise.

JACQUELINE KENNEDY ONASSIS RESERVOIR Map pp389-91

Don't miss your chance to run or walk around this 1.58 mile track, which draws a slew of joggers in the warmer months. The 106-acre body of water no longer distributes drinking water to residents, but serves as a gorgeous reflecting pool for the surrounding skyline and flowering trees, especially considering a new low, gleaming wrought-iron fence has replaced an ugly chain-link one around its circumference. The most beautiful time to be here is at sunset, when you can watch the sky turn from a brilliant shade of pink and orange to cobalt blue, just as the city's lights slowly flicker on.

STRAWBERRY FIELDS Map pp389-91

Standing just across from the famous Dakota building, where John Lennon was fatefully shot in 1980, is this poignant, tear-shaped garden, a memorial to the slain rock star. It's the most visited spot in Central Park, and maintained with some help from a $1 million grant from Lennon's widow Yoko Ono. The peaceful spot contains a grove of stately elms and a tiled mosaic that's often strewn with rose petals from visitors. It says, simply, 'Imagine.'

WOLLMAN RINK Map pp389-91

☎ 212-439-6900; btwn 62nd & 63rd Sts; ☺ Nov-Mar

Located on the park's east side, this is a romantic spot to strap on some rented ice skates and glide around, especially at night under the stars. Just try to tune out the blaring pop music, which tends to dampen the peaceful mood.

Neighborhoods – Central Park

Top Five Central Park Surprises

- **Fishing at Harlem Meer** (Map pp389-91) The Central Park Conservancy allows catch-and-release fishing here, even supplying you with rods and bait for luring in the bass and bluefish.
- **Horseback Riding** Enjoy the site of stately equines clomping along the park's ancient bridal path – or do it yourself with a private lesson from the **Claremont Riding Academy** (☎ 212-724-5100) for $55 per 30 minutes.
- **Shakespeare Garden** (Map pp389-91) Filled with blooming flowers and carved stone benches, this sanctuary sits high atop a hill, providing a meditative spot to enjoy tree-framed West Side views – and sunsets.
- **Time's Up! Moonlight Ride** On the first Friday of the month, this pro-bicycle environmental organization leads packs of riders through the beautiful night-time version of the park, with only the moon as your guide. Meet at Columbus Circle at 10pm (www.times-up.org).
- **Worthless Boulder** (Map pp389-91) Get a glimpse of the urban rock-climbing community, which flocks to this 10ft-tall rock at the Park's north end, near Harlem Meer.

UPPER WEST SIDE

Eating pp198-9, Drinking p220, Shopping pp284–5,
Sleeping pp303–6

This neighborhood is an architectural wonderland, with everything from opulent mansions-turned-apartment buildings, such as **Dorilton** (171 W 71st at Broadway) and **Ansonia** (2109 Broadway btwn 73rd and 74th Sts), to functional public buildings with succulent detail, such as the **McBurney School** (63rd St) off Central Park West and **Frederick Henry Cossitt Dormitory** (64th St) near Central Park West. Of course, almost every block up here sports gorgeous brownstones owned by the fiercely house-proud. On W 71st St, between Broadway and West End Ave, poets and dreamers will be inspired by **Septtuagesimo Uno park**; 'septtuagesimo' means 'seventy-one' in Latin. A spaghetti-strand oasis of just 0.4 acres, you can sense past and future impromptu marriage proposals here.

Orientation

The Upper West Side begins as Broadway emerges from Midtown at Columbus Circle and ends at the southern border of Harlem, around 125th St. Many hotels ring Central Park, and many celebrities live in the massive apartment buildings that line Central Park West up to 96th St.

AMERICAN MUSEUM OF NATURAL HISTORY Map pp389-91

☎ 212-769-5000; www.amnh.org; Central Park West at 79th St; suggested donation adult/senior & student/child $12/9/7, last hr free; ⊙ 10am-5:45pm; subway B, C to 81st St–Museum of Natural History, 1, 9 to 79th St

Founded in 1869, this museum started with a mastodon's tooth and a few thousand beetles; today, its collection includes more than 30 million artifacts, interactive exhibits and loads of taxidermy. It's most famous for its three large dinosaur halls, that underwent a complete overhaul several years ago and reflect current knowledge on how these behemoths behaved. Enthusiastic guides roam the dinosaur halls ready to answer questions, and the 'please touch' displays allow kids to handle many of the items, including the skullcap of a pachycephulasaurus, a plant-eating dinosaur that roamed the earth 65 million years ago.

Other treasures in the permanent collection include the enormous (but fake) blue whale that hangs from the ceiling above the Hall of Ocean Life and the Star of India sapphire in the Hall of Minerals & Gems. Newer exhibitions, such as the Hall of Biodiversity, feature a strong ecological slant, with a video display about the earth's habitats. The Butterfly Conservancy is a popular recurring exhibition, open from November to May and featuring 600 butterflies from all over the world (admission is extra). The building itself is amazing: turn the corner to admire the 77th St facade.

The museum let its imagination go wild dreaming up the new Rose Center for Earth & Space, featuring the state-of-the-art, 3D star show at the Hayden Planetarium. The big ball in the bigger glass box that contains the planetarium is a site to behold. It's called the Ecosphere and features hi-tech exhibitions tracing the development of the planet (rounding the ramps following the earth's creation and growth is a singular museum experience). Lasers and other special effects re-create the birth of the universe at the Big Bang Theater. (The star and laser shows cost extra, but admission to the Rose Center is included with the basic museum price.) The museum also has an IMAX theater.

The live jazz program called Starry Nights, which takes place in the Rose Center from 6pm to 8pm on Fridays, is highly recommended. Tapas, drinks and top jazz acts are all included with museum admission at these weekly gigs.

Transportation

Subway 1, 2, 3, 9, A, B, C, D.
Bus M10, M86, M96, M6, M7, M20.

CHILDREN'S MUSEUM OF MANHATTAN Map pp389-91

☎ 212-721-1234; www.cmom.org; 212 W 83rd St btwn Amsterdam Ave & Broadway; adult & child over 1 yr/senior $7/4; ⏱ 10am-5pm Wed-Sun; subway 1, 9 to 86th St, B, C to 81st St–Museum of Natural History

A favorite for area mommies, this museum features discovery centers for toddlers, a postmodern media center where technologically savvy kids can work in a TV studio, and the cutting-edge Inventor Center, where all the latest, cool tech stuff like digital imaging and scanners is made available. The museum also runs craft workshops on weekends and sponsors special exhibitions. Beware of the high-pitched cacophony. (**Brooklyn Children's Museum**, p138, has an affiliated children's museum.)

LINCOLN CENTER Map pp389-91

☎ 212-546-2656; www.lincolncenter.org; cnr Columbus Ave & Broadway; subway 1, 9 to 66th St–Lincoln Center

The 16-acre Lincoln Center complex includes seven large performance spaces built in the 1960s, which controversially replaced a group of tenements that inspired the musical *West Side Story*. During the day, Lincoln Center presents a demure face, but at night the interiors glow and sparkle with crystal chandeliers and the well-heeled. And it has just unveiled a $325 million transformation – a glass-walled restaurant with a grass roof, scrolling electronic billboards, spiffed-up buildings – with construction set to begin in 2006.

Upper West Side vs Upper East Side

These two uptown 'hoods may not seem so very different to the untrained eye. But to New Yorkers, they're as different as the USA and Paris. Upper West Siders would never consider moving to the other side of Central Park (like an ocean to locals on either side); and East Siders feel the same. So what's the big difference? None, really – though perceptions include the UWS having more children, liberals, Jews and artists and the UES having more conservatives, old folks and money. There is some truth to the images, though, truth be told: while the West Side's median income is $64,125, the cross-park average is $74,130; there are also more people of color living on the West Side, and slightly more registered Republicans in the East. Enter a which-is-better discussion with locals at your own risk.

Top Five Upper West Side

- **American Museum of Natural History** (opposite) Whale, dinosaur and space exhibits.
- **'Cesca** (p198) Eat, drink and be merry.
- **Fairway** (p171) Stroll the museum-like food aisles.
- **Lincoln Center** (left) Just about anything here is worth seeing.
- **Symphony Space** (p235 & p242) Catch a reading, dance piece or film.

If you have even a shred of culture vulture in you, Lincoln Center is a must-see, since it contains the Metropolitan Opera House, adorned by two colorful lobby tapestries by Marc Chagall, and the New York State Theater, home of both the New York City Ballet and the New York City Opera, the low-cost and more-daring alternative to the Met. The New York Philharmonic holds its season in Avery Fisher Hall.

The Lincoln Center Theater company performs at the 1000-seat Vivian Beaumont Theater, which also contains the smaller and more intimate Mitzi Newhouse Theater. To the right of the theaters stands the **New York Public Library for the Performing Arts** (☎ 212-870-1630), which houses the city's largest collection of recorded sound, video and books on film and theater.

The Juilliard School of Music, attached to the complex by a walkway over W 65th St, includes Alice Tully Hall, home to the Chamber Music Society of Lincoln Center, and the Walter Reade Theater, the city's most comfortable film-revival space and the major screening site of the New York Film Festival, held every September. On any given night, there are at least 10 performances happening throughout Lincoln Center – and even more on summer nights, when Lincoln Center Out of Doors (a series of dance and music concerts) and Midsummer Night Swing (ballroom dancing under the stars) lure those who love parks *and* culture.

Daily **tours** (☎ 212-875-5350; adult/senior & student/child $10/8.50/5) of the complex explore at least three of the theaters, which ones depend on production schedules. It's a good idea to call ahead for a space. They leave from the tour desk on the concourse level at 10:30am, 12:30pm, 2:30pm and 4:30pm. Another tour option ($16 for everyone; call ahead for times) visits the master piano-restorers of Klavierhaus.

NEW-YORK HISTORICAL SOCIETY

Map pp389-91

☎ 212-873-3400; www.nyhistory.org; 2 W 77th St at Central Park West; suggested donation adult/senior & student $8/5; ☺ 10am-6pm Tue-Sun; subway B, C to 81st St–Museum of Natural History, 1, 9 to 79th St

As the antiquated, hyphenated name implies, the New-York Historical Society is the city's oldest museum, founded in 1804 to preserve the city's historical and cultural artifacts. It was also New York's only public art museum until the Metropolitan Museum of Art was founded in the late 19th century.

The New-York Historical Society has suffered severe financial problems in recent years and, lamentably, most visitors don't even notice it on their way to its neighbor institution, the American Museum of Natural History. This is pure oversight, because the collection here is as quirky and unique as New York itself; only here can you see 17th-century cowbells and baby rattles and the mounted wooden leg of Gouverneur Morris. The special events and lecture series are also full of surprises and worth investigating.

RIVERSIDE PARK Map pp389-91

Btwn 72nd & 96th St along Hudson River (east of hwy); subway 1, 2, 3, 9 to 72 St

A great place to stroll, bike, run or simply gaze at the sun as it sets over the Hudson River, this skinny, lively greenspace is lined with cherry trees that blossom into puffs of pink in the spring. The park features an inspiring statue of Eleanor Roosevelt at its south entrance and a flower garden at about 94th St – a riot of color in balmy months. And, despite being along the highway, the 79th St **Boat Basin**, on the western edge of the park, is a fine spot from which to watch the sunset, especially while sipping a margarita from the adjoining bar/restaurant.

UPPER EAST SIDE

Walking Tour pp160–2, Eating pp199–200, Drinking pp220–1, Shopping pp285–8, Sleeping pp305–6

The Upper East Side (UES) is home to New York's greatest concentration of cultural centers, and many refer to Fifth Ave above 57th St as Museum Mile. The neighborhood, whose residents, by the way, are in a never-ending contest with those of the Upper West Side (UWS), just across the park (see Upper West Side vs Upper East Side, p121), also includes many of the city's most exclusive hotels and residences. The side streets

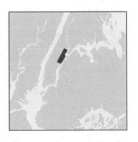

from Fifth Ave east to Third Ave between 57th and 86th Sts feature some stunning town houses and brownstones, and walking through this area at night offers opportunities to see how the other half lives – go ahead, peer inside those grand libraries and living rooms!

Orientation

You're on the UES when you are above 59th St and below 103rd St, between Fifth Ave and the East River. The sole subway line here is the 6, which explains why it's so damned crowded at rush hour, causing riders to often wait for two packed trains to pass them by until they can squeeze into one.

COOPER-HEWITT NATIONAL DESIGN MUSEUM Map pp389-91

☎ 212-849-8400; www.si.edu/ndm; 2 E 91st St at Fifth Ave; adult/senior & student/child $10/7/free; ☺ 10am-5pm Tue-Thu, 10am-9pm Fri, 10am-6pm Sat, noon-6pm Sun; subway 4, 5, 6 to 86th St

This museum is in the 64-room mansion built by billionaire Andrew Carnegie in 1901 in what was, in those days, way Uptown. Within 20 years, the bucolic surroundings that Carnegie craved disappeared as other wealthy men followed his lead and built palaces around him. Carnegie was an interesting character; an avid reader and generous philanthropist, he dedicated many libraries around the country and donated some $350 million in his lifetime. To learn more, hop on the 45-minute daily tour at noon or 2pm, included in the admission price.

Part of the Smithsonian Institution in Washington, this house of culture is a must for anyone interested in architecture, engineering, jewelry or textiles. Exhibitions have examined everything from advertising campaigns to Viennese blown glass. Even if none of this grabs you, the museum's garden and terrace are still worth a visit and the mansion is stunning.

Transportation

Subway 4, 5, 6.
Bus M1, M2, M3, M4, M101, M103.
Ferry New York Water Taxi (☎ 212-742-1969) zips to and from Brooklyn, Chelsea and the South St Seaport.

FRICK COLLECTION Map pp389-91

☎ 212-288-0700; www.frick.org; 1 E 70th St at Fifth Ave; adult/senior/student $12/8/5, child under 10 not admitted; 🕙 10am-6pm Tue-Thu & Sat, 10am-9pm Fri, 1-6pm Sun; subway 6 to 68th St–Hunter College

This stunning collection sits in a mansion built by businessman Henry Clay Frick in 1914, one of the many such residences that made up 'Millionaires' Row.' Most of these mansions proved too expensive for succeeding generations and were eventually destroyed, but the wily and very wealthy Frick, a Pittsburgh steel magnate, established a trust to open his private art collection as a museum.

It's a shame that the 2nd floor of the residence is not open for viewing, though the 12 rooms on the ground floor are grand enough and the garden beckons visitors – especially on Fridays after 6:30pm, when a cash bar opens for business. The Frick's Oval Room is graced by Jean-Antoine Houdon's stunning figure *Diana the Huntress*; the intimate museum also displays works by Titian and Vermeer, and portraits by Gilbert Stuart, El Greco, Goya, and John Constable. An audio tour is included in the price of admission and helps visitors to appreciate the art more fully; you can also dial up information on paintings and sculptures of your choosing on the ArtPhone. Perhaps the best asset here is that it's never crowded, providing a welcoming break from the swarms of gawkers at larger museums, especially on weekends.

GRACIE MANSION Map pp389-91

☎ 212-570-4751; East End Ave at 88th St; 🕙 Wed late Mar–mid-Nov; subway 4, 5, 6 to 86th St

Within the placid Carl Shurz Park, a favorite spot for a riverside stroll, is Gracie Mansion, the 1799 country residence where New York's mayors have always lived – except for Mr Bloomberg, who already had plush city digs when he landed the mayoral gig in 2002. To join one of the tours, which take place at 10am, 11am, 1pm and 2pm on Wednesday (adult/senior/student & child $3/2/free), you must call for a reservation.

JEWISH MUSEUM Map pp389-91

☎ 212-423-3200; www.jewishmuseum.org; 1109 Fifth Ave at 92nd St; adult/senior & student/child $10/7.50/free; 🕙 11am-5:45pm Sun-Wed, 11am-8pm Thu, 11am-3pm Fri; subway 6 to 96th St

Primarily featuring artwork examining 4000 years of Jewish ceremony and culture, this homage to Judaism also has a wide array of children's activities (storytelling hour, arts and crafts workshops etc). The building, a 1908 banker's mansion, houses more than 30,000 items of Judaica, as well as works of sculpture, paintings, numismatics, antiquities, prints, decorative arts and photography. The institution also offers frequent lectures and film screenings – especially in January, when it collaborates with Lincoln Center to present the annual **New York Jewish Film Festival**. On Thursdays between 5pm and 8pm the admission fee is on a pay-what-you-wish basis.

METROPOLITAN MUSEUM OF ART

Map pp389-91

☎ 212-535-7710; www.metmuseum.org; Fifth Ave at 82nd St; suggested donation adult/senior & student/child $12/7/free; 🕙 9:30am-5:30pm Tue-Thu & Sun, 9:30am-9pm Fri & Sat; subway 4, 5, 6 to 86th St

With more than five million visitors a year, the Met is New York's most popular single-site tourist attraction, with one of the richest coffers in the arts world. The Met is a self-contained cultural city-state, with two million individual objects in its collection and an annual budget of over $120 million. And, as the saying goes, the rich get richer – in 1999, the museum received a donated collection (worth $300 million) of modern masterpieces, including works by Picasso and Matisse. Additionally, the Met began a $155 million remodeling project in early 2004 that will put every inch of space to use; it will allow loads of works (including an Etruscan chariot) to come out from storage, renovate galleries of 19th-century and modern art, and add a new Roman Court (scheduled to open in 2007) that will increase the number of Hellenistic and Roman art works from 2500 to 7500.

Top Five Upper East Side

- **Beyoglu** (p199) Tuck into a postmuseum dinner.
- **Café Carlyle** (p233) Top-notch cabaret.
- **Frick Collection** (p123) Crowd-free galleries.
- **Metropolitan Museum of Art** (p123) Best collections in the world.
- **Neue Galerie** (p124) Admire the Gustav Klimt works.

Once inside the Great Hall, pick up a floor plan and head to the ticket booths, where you will find a list of exhibitions closed for the day, along with a lineup of special museum talks. The Met presents more than 30 special exhibitions and installations each year, and marked floor plans show you how to get to them. It's best to target exactly what you want to see and head there first, before museum fatigue sets in (usually after two hours). Then you can put the floor plan away and get lost trying to get back to the main hall. It's a virtual certainty that you'll stumble across something interesting along the way.

To the right of the Great Hall, an information desk offers guidance in several languages (these change depending on the volunteers) and audio tours of the special exhibitions ($6). The Met also offers free guided walking tours of museum highlights and specific galleries. Check the calendar, given away at the information desk, for the specific schedule. Families will want to see Inside the Museum: A Children's Guide to the Metropolitan Museum of Art and the kid-specific events calendar (both free at the information booth).

If you can't stand crowds, steer clear on a rainy Sunday afternoon in summer. But during horrible winter weather, you might find the 17-acre museum nearly deserted in the evening – a real New York experience. The roof garden is also a find, especially in the summer, when it adds a wine bar on weekend evenings.

MOUNT VERNON HOTEL MUSEUM & GARDEN Map pp389-91

☎ 212-838-6878; 421 E 61st St btwn First & York Aves; adult/senior & student/child $4/3/free; 🕙 11am-4pm Tue-Sun; subway 4, 5, 6 to 59th St

This 1799 carriage house, formerly known as the Abigail Adams Smith Museum, once belonged to a large riverside estate owned by the daughter of John Adams, the second US president. In the early part of the 19th century it became the Mount Vernon Hotel, and today it is a bizarrely old-fashioned sight, housing collections of American furniture, textiles, quilts, decorative arts, costumes and works on paper such as early NYC documents.

MUSEUM OF THE CITY OF NEW YORK Map pp389-91

☎ 212-534-1672; www.mcny.org; 1220 Fifth Ave btwn 103rd & 104th Sts; suggested donation family/adult/senior & student $12/7/4; 🕙 10am-5pm Wed-Sun; subway 6 to 103 St

Housed in a 1932 Georgian-Colonial mansion, the Museum of the City of New York offers

plenty of stimulation, both old-school and technology-based. You'll find Internet-based historical resources and a decent scale model of New Amsterdam shortly after the Dutch arrival, and the notable 2nd-floor gallery includes entire rooms from demolished homes of New York grandees, an exhibition dedicated to Broadway musicals and a collection of antique dollhouses, teddy bears and toys. Rotating exhibitions cast a clever eye on the city, with past subjects ranging from Harlem lost and found and the Roaring 20s to moving toward sustainable architecture in the 21st century and Magnum photos of New York.

NATIONAL ACADEMY OF DESIGN Map pp389-91

☎ 212-369-4880; www.nationalacademy.org; 1083 Fifth Ave at 89th St; adult/senior & student/child under 16 $8/4.50/free; 🕙 noon-5pm Wed & Thu, 11am-6pm Fri-Sun; subway 4, 5, 6 to 86th St

Cofounded by painter-inventor Samuel Morse, the National Academy of Design art-school complex includes a permanent collection of paintings and sculptures housed in yet another stunning beaux arts mansion, featuring a marble foyer and spiral staircase. The gem of a space was designed by Ogden Codman, who also designed the Breakers mansion in Newport, Rhode Island.

NEUE GALERIE Map pp389-91

☎ 212-628-6200; www.neuegalerie.org; 1048 Fifth Ave at 86th St; adult/senior $10/7, child under 12 not admitted; 🕙 11am-6pm Sat-Mon,11am-9pm Fri; subway 4, 5, 6 to 86 St

This showcase for German and Austrian art is a relative newcomer to the museum strip (it opened in 2000), but it stood out as a star right away. The intimate but well-hung museum, housed in a former Rockefeller mansion, features impressive works by Gustav Klimt, Paul Klee and Egon Schiele – not to mention a lovely street-level eatery, **Café Sabarsky**, serving Viennese meals, pastries and drinks. And, because of its no-children policy, you'll never encounter noisy stroller blockades, like in other area institutions.

NEW YORK ACADEMY OF MEDICINE Map pp389-91

☎ 212-822-7200; www.nyam.org; 1216 Fifth Ave at 103rd St; admission free; 🕙 9am-5pm Mon-Fri; subway 6 to 103rd St

With over 700,000 cataloged works, New York Academy of Medicine is the second-largest health library in the world (and in its holdings is the world's biggest cookbook collection). But skip all the books and head straight for the weirdly fascinating medical ephemera like the leper clapper (used by sufferers to warn a town of their arrival), a globule of the world's first penicillin culture, cupping glasses used in phlebotomy procedures, and George Washington's dentures.

ROOSEVELT ISLAND Map pp389-91

New York's anomalous, planned neighborhood sits on a tiny island no wider than a football field in the middle of the East River between Manhattan and Queens. Once known as Blackwell's Island after the farming family who lived here, the city bought the island in 1828 and constructed several public hospitals and a mental hospital. In the 1970s, New York State built housing for 10,000 people along Roosevelt Island's Main St, the island's only one. The planned area along the cobblestone roadway resembles an Olympic village or, as some observe more cynically, cookie-cutter college housing.

Museum Bargains

A terrific deal is the **CityPass** (www.citypass.com). Good for nine days, the pass covers admission to the **Empire State Building observatory** (p109), **American Museum of Natural History** (p120), **Intrepid Sea-Air-Space Museum** (p110), the **Circle Line** (p72), **Museum of Modern Art** (p115) and **Guggenheim Museum** (p125). The pass costs $45/39 per adult/child; without the pass, you would pay 30% to 50% more for admission to all these sites. As an added bonus, you can pick up the CityPass at the first attraction you visit.

Remember also, that many museums have 'pay-what-you-wish' days, usually on Thursday or Friday evenings.

Zipping across the river via the four-minute aerial tram is a trip in itself and worth the stunning view of the East Side of Manhattan framed by the 59th St Bridge. Instead of heading straight back like most, however, bring a picnic or a bike, as this quiet island is conducive to lounging and cycling.

Trams from the **Roosevelt Island tramway station** (☎ 212-832-4543; 60th St at Second Ave) leave every 15 minutes on the quarter-hour from 6am to 2am Sunday to Thursday, until 3:30am Friday and Saturday; the one-way fare is $1.50. Roosevelt Island has a subway station; from Manhattan, take the F train to Roosevelt Island.

SOLOMON R GUGGENHEIM MUSEUM Map pp389-91

☎ 212-423-3500; www.guggenheim.org; 1071 Fifth Ave at 89th St; adult/senior & student/child $15/10 /free; ☺ 10am-5:45pm Sat-Wed, 10am-8pm Fri; subway 4, 5, 6 to 86 St

A sculpture in its own right, Frank Lloyd Wright's sweeping spiral building almost overshadows the collection of 20th-century art housed in this museum. Because of its unusual design, the building sparked controversy during its construction in the 1950s, but today it's a distinctive landmark that architects fiddle with at their peril. An unpopular 1992 renovation added an adjoining 10-story tower that does indeed bear a striking resemblance to a toilet, just as the critics feared, despite being based on Wright's original drawings.

Inside, you can view some of the museum's 5000 permanent works (plus changing exhibitions) on a path that coincides with Wright's coiled design. Take the elevator to the top and wind your way down. The Guggenheim's collection includes works by Picasso, Chagall, Pollock and Kandinsky. In 1976, Justin Thannhauser's major donation of impressionist and modern works added paintings by Monet, Van Gogh and Degas. In 1992, the Robert Mapplethorpe Foundation gave 200 photographs to the museum, spurring curators to devote the 4th floor to photography exhibitions.

TEMPLE EMANU-EL Map pp389-91

☎ 212-744-1400; www.emanuelnyc.org; 1 E 65th St at Fifth Ave; ☺ 10am-5pm; subway N, R, W to Fifth Ave–59th St

Founded in 1845 as the first Reform synagogue in New York, this location was completed in 1929. It's now the largest Jewish house of worship in the world, and has a membership of some 3000 families. Stop by for a look at its notable Byzantine and Middle Eastern architecture. Its facade features an arch with symbols representing the 12 tribes of Israel, which are also depicted on the grand set of bronze doors. Inside the majestic, buttressed interior are Guastavino tiles, marble wainscoting and brilliant stained-glass windows.

WHITNEY MUSEUM OF AMERICAN ART Map pp389-91

☎ 212-570-3600, 800-944-8639; www.whitney.org; 945 Madison Ave at 75th St; adult/senior/child $12/9.50 /free; ☺ 11am-4:30pm Tue, 11am-6pm Wed, Sat & Sun, 11am-9pm Fri; subway 6 to 77th St

The Whitney makes no secret of its mission to provoke and it starts with the most brutal of structures housing the collection. Designed by Bauhaus architect Marcel Breur, the rock-like edifice is a fitting setting for the Whitney's style of cutting-edge American art. In recent years, high-profile exhibitions at **MoMA** (p115) and the **Brooklyn Museum** (p138) have overshadowed the Whitney's efforts to display innovative work, but it continues to stage its famous Biennial (next scheduled for 2006), an ambitious survey of contemporary art that rarely fails to generate controversy – though recent Biennials have been called shocking only for their mediocrity.

Established in the 1930s by Gertrude Vanderbilt Whitney, who began a Greenwich Village salon for prominent artists, the collection features works by Edward Hopper, Jasper Johns, Georgia O'Keeffe, Jackson Pollock and Mark Rothko.

YORKVILLE Map pp389-91
Subway 6 to 77 St
Known today as the one pocket of the Upper East Side with (relatively) affordable rental apartments, this area, east of Lexington Ave between 70th and 96th Sts, was once the settling point for new Hungarian and German immigrants. The only trace left of that heritage today are places like **Schaller & Weber**, an old-world German grocery, Heidelberg, a homey restaurant serving sauerbraten and other traditional goodies (both on Second Ave between 85th and 86th Sts) and the **Yorkville Meat Emporium** (Second Ave at 81st St), stocked with fresh meats and prepared Hungarian dishes.

Permanent Galleries of the Met

If you don't want to see anything in particular at the Metropolitan Museum of Art, then make a loop of the 1st floor – perhaps peeking at the Costume Institute, which shows a fascinating rotation of fashion-based exhibits – before heading to the 2nd-floor painting galleries. Entering the Egyptian art section in the north wing, you'll pass the tomb of Pernebi (c. 2415 BC), as well as several mummies and incredibly well-preserved wall paintings, before you come to the Temple of Dendur. The temple, threatened with submersion during the building of the Aswan Dam, found a home in New York under this glass enclosure – if you look closely at its walls, you can see the graffiti etched by European visitors to the site in the 1820s. There are pretty Central Park vistas from here.

If you can't make it to Cooperstown, home of America's Baseball Hall of Fame, then exit the gallery through the door behind the temple to behold the Met's collection of baseball cards, which includes the rarest and most expensive card in the world – a 1909 Honus Wagner worth some $200,000. Continue on to the left and you'll enter the American Wing of furniture and architecture, with a quiet, enclosed garden space that is a perennial favorite as a respite from the hordes. Several stained-glass works by Louis Comfort Tiffany frame the garden, as does an entire two-story facade of the Branch Bank of the US, preserved when the building was destroyed Downtown in the early 20th century.

After passing through the far door of the American Wing, you'll enter the gloomy galleries dedicated to medieval art. Turn right and walk across the European decorative arts section to the pyramid-like addition that houses the Robert Lehman Collection of impressionist and modern art, featuring several works by Renoir (including *Young Girl Bathing*), Georges Seurat and Pablo Picasso (including *Portrait of Gertrude Stein*). An unexpected bonus in this gallery is the rear terracotta facade of the original 1880 Met building, now completely encased by later additions and standing mutely on view as its own architectural artifact.

Continue on through the European decorative arts section and turn left into the Rockefeller Collection of arts of Africa, Oceania and the Americas, heading toward Fifth Ave. At the far end of the Rockefeller Collection, turn left and wander through the Greek and Roman art section. The museum has recently restored much of its Greek and Roman work, including the 2nd-floor Cypriot Gallery, which contains some of the finest pieces outside Cyprus.

Elsewhere on the 2nd floor, you'll see the Met's famous collection of European paintings, located in some of the museum's oldest galleries, beyond colonnaded entryways. The exhibition features works by every artist of note, including self-portraits by Rembrandt and Van Gogh and *Portrait of Juan de Pareja* by Velázquez. An entire suite of rooms focuses on impressionist and postimpressionist art. The new collection of modern masters is housed on this level, as well as the photographs recently purchased by the Met, and the museum's exquisite musical-instrument holdings. Also of interest up here are the treasures from Japan, China and Southeast Asia.

HARLEM & NORTHERN MANHATTAN

Walking Tour pp164–6, Eating pp201–2, Shopping pp288–9, Sleeping p306

From its origins as a 1920s black enclave until now, the heart of black culture has beat in Harlem. This neighborhood north of Central Park has been the setting for extraordinary accomplishments in art, music, dance, education and letters from the likes of Frederick Douglass, Paul Robeson, Thurgood Marshall, James Baldwin, Alvin Ailey, Billie Holiday, Jessie Jackson and many other African-American luminaries.

Harlem gets a bad, scary rap because, historically, some bad, scary things have gone down here. Nearly half the neighborhood was burned to the ground during riots in the 1960s. Two decades later, crack cocaine devastated families and empowered gangs, and a downward economic spiral just made matters worse. Fortunately, that's old news and Harlem is undergoing a renaissance that is bringing jobs, pride and tourism back Uptown.

First-time visitors will probably be surprised to discover that Harlem is just one subway stop away from the Columbus Circle–59th St station. The trip on the express A and D trains takes only five minutes, and both stop just one block from the Apollo Theater and two blocks from Malcolm X Blvd (Lenox Ave).

Transportation

Subway 1, 9, A, B, C, D, 2, 3, 4, 5, 6 to 125 St.
Bus M98, M100, M101, M103.

Despite its past reputation as a crime-ridden no-man's-land, today Harlem – with the exception of some still-abandoned, eerily empty side streets – shouldn't cause you to exercise any more caution than you would anywhere else in New York. For more details, see the Harlem Shuffle walking tour on p164.

Apartments, Harlem

Orientation

As you explore Harlem, you'll notice that the major avenues have been renamed in honor of prominent African Americans; however, many locals still call the streets by their original names, which makes finding your way around a little confusing. Eighth Ave (Central Park West) is Frederick Douglass Blvd. Seventh Ave is Adam Clayton Powell Jr Blvd, named for the controversial preacher who served in Congress during the 1960s. Lenox Ave has been renamed for the Nation of Islam leader Malcolm X. 125th St, the main avenue and site of many businesses, is also known as Martin Luther King Jr Blvd.

Walking in Harlem can be really tiring as the sites are pretty spread out and subway stations are few and far between; up here the crosstown buses can be handier than the train.

Harlem Renaissance Redux

There are two catalysts that have spurred Harlem's rebirth: the entire neighborhood was declared an Economic Redevelopment Zone in 1996, and tourists (mostly Japanese and European) have been flocking Uptown to check out the area's music and spiritual scene. While Harlem's development has attracted buckets of dollars, it has also brought Disney double-decker tour buses and disrespectful crowds clamoring for pews at Sunday services. Cheap rents for amazing spaces have also given rise to a burgeoning gay (white) ghetto, as always-first-to-arrive gay men have been snapping up brownstones quicker than you can say 'Malcolm X Blvd.' A balance has yet to be struck, and in the meantime everything is not coming up roses. Mom-and-pop stores are closing in the aftermath of the downturn in tourist revenue caused by September 11 and it's unclear how much longtime local residents are benefiting from Harlem's new boom.

City officials have aggressively promoted Harlem to developers, with the alarmingly huge **Harlem USA** (Map pp392-3; 300 West 125th St) entertainment and retail complex acting as the jewel in the crown. It features a dance club, 12-screen cinema, a rooftop skating rink and a HMV store. Oh, and even former president Bill Clinton staked a claim on 125th St, opening up his new offices here (to do exactly what, we're not sure, though there is a Krispy Kreme right close by to keep him occupied!). Don't expect to glimpse him in the 'hood, though; locals can never seem to.

Top Five Harlem

- **Apollo Theater** (below) Join the crowds for amateur night.
- **Copeland's** (p201) Enjoy a jazz brunch.
- **El Museo del Barrio** (p131) Latino masterpieces.
- **Shomberg Center for Research in Black Culture** (opposite) Discover African-American history.
- **Studio Museum in Harlem** (opposite) Catch fine black artwork.

HARLEM
APOLLO THEATER

Map pp392-3

☎ 212-531-5337; 5253 W 125th St at Frederick Douglass Blvd; subway A, B, C, D to 125th St

This has been Harlem's leading space for political rallies and concerts since 1914. Virtually every major black artist of note in the 1930s and '40s performed here, including Duke Ellington and Charlie Parker. After a desultory spell as a movie theater and several years of darkness, the Apollo was bought in 1983 and revived as a live venue. It was renovated in 2002, and the Apollo still holds its famous weekly Amateur Night, 'where stars are born and legends are made,' at 7:30pm on Wednesday. Watching the crowd call for the 'executioner' to yank hapless performers from the stage is often the best part. On other nights, the Apollo hosts performances by established artists like Whitney Houston and comedian Chris Rock. Tours cost $11/13 per weekday/weekend per person and leave at 11am, 1pm and 3pm Monday, Tuesday and Friday; 11am Wednesday; and 11am and 1pm Saturday and Sunday. Tour participants get to perform a number on the famed stage.

HARLEM MARKET

Map pp392-3

☎ 212-987-8131; 116th St; 🕙 10am-5pm; subway 2, 3 to 116th St

Vendors at the semi-enclosed Harlem Market, which is located between Malcolm X Blvd and Fifth Ave, do a brisk business selling tribal masks, oils, drums, traditional clothing and other assorted African bric-a-brac. You can also purchase cheap clothing, leather goods, music cassettes and bootleg videos of films that are still in first-run movie theaters. The market is operated by the Malcolm Shabazz Mosque, the former pulpit of Muslim orator Malcolm X.

SCHOMBURG CENTER FOR RESEARCH IN BLACK CULTURE

Map pp392-3

☎ 212-491-2200; www.nypl.org/research/sc/sc.html; 515 Malcolm X Blvd; admission free; ☺ noon-8pm Tue-Wed, noon-6pm Thu & Fri, 10am-6pm Sat; subway 2, 3 to 135th St

The nation's largest collection of documents, rare books, recordings and photographs relating to the African-American experience resides at this center near W 135th St. Arthur Schomburg, who was born in Puerto Rico, started gathering works on black history during the early 20th century while becoming active in the movements for civil rights and Puerto Rican independence. His impressive collection was purchased by the Carnegie Foundation and eventually expanded and stored in this branch of the New York Public Library. Lectures and concerts are regularly held in the theater here.

STUDIO MUSEUM IN HARLEM

Map pp392-3

☎ 212-864-4500; www.studiomuseum.org; 144 W 125th St at Adam Clayton Powell Jr Blvd; suggested donation adult/senior & student $7/3; ☺ noon-6pm Wed-Fri & Sun, 10am-6pm Sat; subway 2, 3 to 125th St

This showcase, a leading benefactor and promoter of African American artists for almost 30 years, provides working spaces for the up and coming. Its photography collection includes works by James VanDerZee, the photographer who chronicled the Harlem renaissance of the 1920s and '30s.

Going to the Gospel/Harlem Church Services

Harlem Sunday services, which are mostly Baptist, pack in the crowds with their deep spirituality and rocking gospel choirs. Unfortunately, the tour buses have been rolling in with their own crowds recently (some of the churches have side deals going with operators), which has resulted in a clash of cultures, with worshippers trying to get in touch with God and sightseers trying to snap the perfect photo. As the old saying goes, in Harlem 'there's a bar on every corner and a church on every block.' We've listed several churches here, but there are probably twice as many more in the immediate neighborhood, so instead of overwhelming the few we have space to mention, seek out your own – most church marquees proclaim 'all are welcome.' Services usually start at 11am.

Founded by an Ethiopian businessman, the **Abyssinian Baptist Church** (Map pp392-3; ☎ 212-862-7474; 132 W 138th St; services 9am & 11am Sun; subway 2, 3 to 135th St), near Adam Clayton Powell Jr Blvd called Odell Clark Pl, began as a Downtown institution but moved north to Harlem in 1923, mirroring the migration of the city's black population. Its charismatic pastor, Calvin O Butts III, is an important community activist whose support is sought by politicians of all parties. The church has a superb choir and the building is a beauty. Around the corner, **Mother African Methodist Episcopal Zion Church** (Map pp392-3; ☎ 212-234-1545; 146 W 137th St; subway 2, 3 to 135th St) usually takes the overflow from Abyssinian.

Canaan Baptist Church (Map pp392-3; ☎ 212-866-5711; 132 W 116th St; services 10:45am Sun Oct-Jun, 10am Jul-Sep; subway 2, 3 to 116th St), near St Nicholas Ave, is perhaps Harlem's friendliest church.

As the churches mentioned above see a lot of traffic, you might try one of the following instead:
- **Baptist Temple** (Map pp392-3; ☎ 212-996-0334; 20 W 116th St)
- **Metropolitan Baptist Church** (Map pp392-3; ☎ 212-663-8990; 151 W 128th St)
- **St Paul Baptist Church** (Map pp392-3; ☎ 212-283-8174; 249 W 132nd St)
- **Salem United Methodist Church** (Map pp392-3; ☎ 212-722-3969; 211 W 129th St)
- **Second Providence Baptist Church** (Map pp392-3; ☎ 212-831-6751; 11 W 116th St)

MORNINGSIDE HEIGHTS

This area between the Upper West Side and the way-north Washington Heights is generally the province of Columbia University, as is immediately evident from the scores of students and professors chilling in cafés, filling bookstores and darting to and from classes on the beautiful urban campus. But it's got other draws, too, namely affordable rents and a multi-ethnic population.

Orientation

Morningside Heights extends north from 110th to 125th St, between St Nicholas Ave and the Hudson River.

CATHEDRAL OF ST JOHN THE DIVINE

Map pp392-3

☎ 212-316-7540; Amsterdam Ave at 112th St; ⏰ 7:30am-6pm; subway B, C, 1 to Cathedral Pkwy

This is the largest place of worship in the USA – and it's not done yet. When it's finally completed, the 601ft-long Episcopal cathedral will rank as the third-largest church in the world (after St Peter's Basilica in Rome, Italy, and Our Lady at Yamoussoukro in Côte d'Ivoire). Sadly, a fire broke out here several years ago, irreparably damaging tapestries and other artifacts.

Though its cornerstone was laid in 1892, construction here is ongoing. Work has yet to begin on the stone tower on the left side of the west front and on the crossing tower above the pulpit. Other features shown on the church's cutaway floor plan near the front entrance, such as a Greek amphitheater, remain wistful visions.

Still, the cathedral is a flourishing place of worship and community activity, as well as the site of holiday concerts, lectures and memorial services for famous New Yorkers. Two quirky, popular services worth checking out are the annual **Blessing of the Animals**, a pilgrimage for pet owners that's held on the first Sunday of October, and the **Blessing of the Bikes**, on May 1, which draws helmeted folks with clunkers, sleek 10-speeds and mountain bikes. There's even a **Poet's Corner** just to the left of the front entrance – though, unlike at Westminster Abbey in London, no-one is actually buried here. Also check out the altar designed and built by the late Keith Haring, a popular artist in the 1980s pop-art world.

Other sights are the whimsical **Children's Sculpture Garden** on the south side, and the **Biblical Garden**, containing historically correct plants, out back. An intriguing **Ecology Trail** wends its way through the cathedral and the grounds, tracing the creation cycles (birth, life, death and rebirth) from a multicultural perspective.

Cathedral tours ($3 per person) are held at 11am Tuesday to Saturday and 1pm Sunday.

Top Five Northern Manhattan

- **Audubon Terrace** (p132) Wander around the myriad exhibit options.
- **Cathedral of St John the Divine** (above) Check out the vaulted ceilings.
- **Cloisters** (p132) Feel cultured and refreshed.
- **Columbia University** (above) Sit on the library steps.
- **El Museo Del Barrio** (opposite) Latin America awaits.

Transportation

Subway 1, 9, B, C to 110, 116 or 125 St.
Bus M104, M7, M10, M100.

COLUMBIA UNIVERSITY Map pp392-3

☎ 212-854-1754; Broadway; subway 1 to 116 St–Columbia University

When Columbia University, between 114th and 121st Sts, and the affiliated Barnard College moved to this site in 1897, their founders chose a spot far removed from the downtown bustle. Today, the city has enveloped and moved beyond Columbia's gated campus, but the school's main courtyard, with its statue **Alma Mater** perched on the steps of the Low Library, is still a quiet place to take some sun and read a book. Hamilton Hall, in the southeast corner of the main square, was the famous site of a student takeover in 1968, and has seen periodic protests and plenty of wild student parties since then.

RIVERSIDE CHURCH Map pp392-3

☎ 212-870-6700; www.theriversidechurchny.org; 490 Riverside Dr at W 120th St; ⏰ 7am-10pm; subway 1, 9 to 116th St–Columbia University

Built by the Rockefeller family in 1930, this Gothic beauty overlooks the Hudson River. In good weather, you can climb 355ft to the observation deck ($2) for expansive river views. The church rings its 74 carillon bells, the largest grouping in the world, with an extraordinary 20-ton bass bell (also the world's largest), at noon and 3pm on Sunday. Interdenominational services are held at 10:45am on Sunday.

GENERAL US GRANT NATIONAL MEMORIAL Map pp392-3

☎ 212-666-1640; www.nps.gov/gegr; Riverside Dr at W 122nd St; admission free; ⏰ 9am-5pm; subway 1, 9 to 125 St

Popularly known as Grant's Tomb, this landmark holds the remains of Civil War hero and president Ulysses S Grant and those of his wife, Julia. Completed in 1897 – 12 years after his death – the granite structure cost $600,000 and is the largest mausoleum in the country. Though it plagiarizes Mausoleus' tomb at Halicarnassus, this version doesn't qualify as one of the Seven Wonders of the World. The building languished as a graffiti-scarred mess for years until Grant's relatives shamed the National Park Service into cleaning it up by threatening to move his body elsewhere.

Neighborhoods – Harlem & Northern Manhattan

SPANISH HARLEM

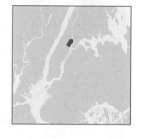

East of Harlem, Spanish Harlem (subway 6 to 103rd, 110th or 116th Sts) extends from Fifth Ave to the East River, above 96th St. This is one of the biggest Latino communities (Puerto Rican, Dominican and Cuban mostly) in the city and proud of it: Puerto Rican flags fly from vans blaring salsa, men play dominos in front of ramshackle *casitas* (houses) in the community gardens and people hang out on stoops, shouting to their neighbors in Spanglish.

Interesting stops include El Museo del Barrio, La Marqueta (both below), a colorful, ad hoc collection of produce and meat stalls on Park Ave above 110th St, and Duke Ellington Circle, with a statue of the man and his piano, where Fifth Ave and Central Park North (also known as Tito Puente Way) converge.

LA MARQUETA Map pp392-3

☎ 212-534-4900; E 115th St btwn Third & Park Aves; suggested donation adult/senior, student & child $6/free; ☾ 11am-5pm Wed-Sun; subway 6 to 103rd St
Managed by the NYC Economic Development Corporation, this market serves the local Latino community by hawking all manner of dairy, deli, produce, spices and meats from 30 stalls.

EL MUSEO DEL BARRIO Map pp389-91

☎ 212-831-7272; www.elmuseo.org; 1230 Fifth Ave btwn 104th & 105th Sts; suggested donation adult /senior & student/child $6/4/free; ☾ 11am-5pm Wed-Sun; subway 6 to 103rd St

The best starting point for exploring Spanish Harlem, this museum began in 1969 as a celebration of Puerto Rican art and culture. It has since expanded its holdings to include the folk art of Latin America and Spain. Its galleries now feature pre-Columbian artifacts and a collection of more than 300 *santos*, hand-carved wooden saints in the Caribbean Catholic tradition. Interesting temporary exhibitions feature the work of local artists and themes such as contemporary Brazilian art or the history of the Taínos. All signage and brochures are in both English and Spanish.

HAMILTON HEIGHTS & SUGAR HILL

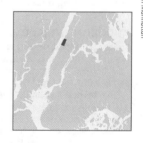

This area, which extends north of Harlem from about 138th to 155th Sts west of Edgecombe Ave, is loaded with off-the-beaten path delights. One of the greatest ways to get to a Yankees game is to head east on 155th St and walk across the Macombs Dam Bridge (which is also the best way to get to Yankee Stadium from Manhattan by car). In the summer, die-hard basketball fiends will want to check out the legendary competitions at Rucker Park (Map pp392-3; 155th St at Harlem River; subway B, D to 155 St). Unfortunately, this can't be recommended without a local escort, as the tight-knit community up here doesn't readily welcome outsiders.

JAMES BAILEY HOUSE Map pp392-3

10 St Nicholas Pl at W 150th St; subway C to 155 St
Architecture buffs will appreciate the former home of circus guru James A Bailey. Though it's now a funeral home, this 1880s, Gothic Revival mansion boasts granite facades and gabled roofs and is worth a look. The building next door at 14 Nicholas Pl is another stroke of structural whimsy with its cedar-shingled dome and wooden shutters with flower details.

HAMILTON GRANGE

Map pp392-3
☎ 212-283-5154; 141st St at Convent Ave; admission free; ☾ 9am-5pm Fri-Sun; subway A, B, C, D to 145th St
Once upon a time this was Alexander Hamilton's original country retreat. When the Federal-style home was moved to this too-small spot from its original location, it had to be turned sidewise and squeezed to fit, so now the facade actually faces inward! At the

time of writing, the ink had just dried on an agreement to relocate it once and for all to a permanent site somewhere in St Nicholas Park, where it will be restored and reoriented to exact historic specifications.

Nearby, the Hamilton Heights Historic District stretches along Convent Ave from the City College of New York campus (which has architectural marvels of its own) at 140th St to 145th St. This is one of the last remaining stretches of untouched limestone and brownstone townhouses in New York City, and it is simply gorgeous.

STRIVER'S ROW Map pp392-3
W 138th & 139th Sts btwn Frederick Douglass & Adam Clayton Powell Jr Blvds; subway B, C to 135th St
Also known as the St Nicholas Historic District, Striver's Row has prized row houses and apartments, many designed by Stanford White's firm in the 1890s. When whites moved out of the area, Harlem's black elite occupied the buildings. It's one of the most visited blocks in Harlem, so discretion is the better part of valor, as the locals are a bit sick of tourists. Plaques explain more of the area's history. Check out the alleyway signs advising visitors to 'walk their horses.'

WASHINGTON HEIGHTS
Near the northern tip of Manhattan (above 155th St), Washington Heights takes its name from the first US president, who set up a Continental Army fort here during the Revolutionary War.

An isolated rural spot until the end of the 19th century, Washington Heights is attracting new blood as New Yorkers discover its affordable rents. Still, this neighborhood manages to retain its Latino flavor, with a continual stream of Dominican immigrants settling here. Speaking Spanish comes in very handy in the Heights.

Most visitors to Washington Heights come to see the handful of museums, particularly the Cloisters in Fort Tryon Park, a beautiful spot in warm weather.

Free shuttle buses run among the area's museums between 11am and 5pm. (Call any one of the following museums to find out the schedule.)

AUDUBON TERRACE Map pp392-3
Broadway at 155th St; subway 1 to 157th St
Naturalist John James Audubon once lived in Audubon Tce, which now houses three fantastic and free museums set in a delightful plaza.

The **American Numismatic Society** (☎ 212-234-3130; admission free; ☺ 9am-4:30pm Tue-Fri) owns a large permanent collection of coins, medals and paper money.

A treasure of Spanish, Portuguese and Latin American art, the **Hispanic Society of America** (☎ 212-926-2234; www.hispanicsociety.org; admission free; ☺ 10am-4:30pm Tue-Sat, 1-4pm Sun) is housed in a two-level, ornately carved space hung with gold-and-silk tapestries.

The society has a substantial collection of works by El Greco, Goya, Diego Velázquez, and the formidable Joaquín Sorolla y Bastida, and a

library with over 25,000 volumes. Head upstairs for a bird's-eye view; all signage and brochures are bilingual in English and Spanish.

The **American Academy & Institute of Arts & Letters** (☎ 212-368-5900; admission free) opens its bronze doors to the public several times a year for temporary exhibitions; call ahead for the schedule.

CLOISTERS Map pp398-9
☎ 212-923-3700; 195th St; www.metmuseum.org; suggested donation adult/senior & student/child $12/7 /free; ☺ 9:30am-4:45pm Tue-Sun Nov-Feb, 9:30am-5:15pm Tue-Sun Mar-Oct; subway A to Dyckman St
The Met is a beautiful place to visit on any day, but if it's just too gorgeous to go inside, you might consider heading to its outside annex instead. Set in Fort Tryon Park overlooking the Hudson River, the Cloisters museum, built in the 1930s, incorporates fragments of old French and Spanish monasteries and houses the Metropolitan Museum of Art's collection of medieval frescos, tapestries and paintings. In summer, which is the best time to visit,

---

Transportation
Subway A, C, 1, 9 to 168 St–Washington Hts
Bus M98, M100, M4, M5

concerts take place in the grounds, and more than 250 varieties of medieval flowers and herbs are on view.

DYCKMAN FARMHOUSE MUSEUM
Map pp398-9
☎ 212-304-9422; 4881 Broadway at 204th St; admission $1; ☺ 10am-4pm Tue-Sun; subway A to 207th St
Built in 1784 on a 28-acre farm, the Dyckman House is Manhattan's lone surviving Dutch farmhouse. Excavations of the property have turned up valuable clues about colonial life, and the museum includes period rooms and furniture, decorative arts, a half-acre of gardens and an exhibition on the neighborhood's history. To get to the Dyckman House, take the subway to the 207th St station and walk one block south – many people mistakenly get off one stop too soon at Dyckman St.

MORRIS-JUMEL MANSION Map pp392-3
☎ 212-923-8008; www.morrisjumel.org; 65 Jumel Tce at 160th St; adult/senior, student & child $4/3; ☺ 10am-4pm Wed-Sun; subway C to 163rd St–Amsterdam Ave
Built in 1765, the columned Morris-Jumel Mansion is the oldest house in Manhattan. It served as George Washington's Continental Army headquarters. After the war, it returned to a country house for Stephen and Eliza Jumel, who had a sordid past, not limited to being the second wife of vice president Aaron Burr. Rumor has it that Eliza's ghost still flits about the place.

It's Free! Top Five
- **Bryant Park** (p230) Monday-night summer film series.
- **Chelsea gallery openings** (p158) Wine included.
- **Central Park SummerStage** (p239) A concert in the park.
- **Rudy's** (p219) Free happy-hour hot dogs.
- **Staten Island Ferry** (p149) Always free.

A designated landmark, the mansion's interior contains many of the original furnishings, including a 2nd-floor bed that reputedly belonged to Napoleon. The grounds are particularly attractive when the spring blossoms are out.

Leading east from St Nicholas Ave and 161st St to the mansion is lovely Sylvan Tce, a cobblestone lane lined with wooden-shuttered row houses. Perpendicular to this street is Jumel Tce, with some fine limestone houses; Paul Robeson once lived at No 16.

Down the block on the corner of 160th St is 555 Edgecombe Ave. In addition to being the address of Jackie Robinson, Thurgood Marshall and Paul Robeson at one time or another, current resident Marjorie Eliot hosts convivial, free-jazz jams in her home at **Apt 3F** (☎ 212-781-6595); held at 4pm on Saturday and Sunday, open to the public and warmly recommended.

Neighborhoods – Harlem & Northern Manhattan

Staten Island Ferry (p149)

Bald Eagles Have Landed – in Manhattan

Of all the ecological successes related to the recovery of the Hudson River Estuary, one soars above the flock: the reintroduction of bald eagles to Manhattan. Eagles once were common to the New York City area, but 20th-century development and toxic DDT combined to eradicate them from the area. After the September 11 attacks, the State of New York embarked on an ambitious five-year program to reintroduce the national symbol to New York City. Each June several young eaglets are brought from northern Wisconsin to their new treetop habitat, the thickly forested, 196-acre **Inwood Hill Park** (Map pp400-1) at the northern tip of Manhattan. Over the course of the summer, the eagles earn their wings, weaning themselves from the nest and taking flight over upstate New York, New Jersey and NYC itself. By September, the birds have matured enough to leave their habitat for faraway skies, but their nesting platform remains open for whatever other aviary visitors may drop by.

OUTER BOROUGHS

These four exciting neighborhoods – Brooklyn, Queens, the Bronx and Staten Island – may not be Manhattan, but don't tell them they're not New York. The Bronx has the attitude and the Yankees, Brooklyn the lore and the bridge, Queens the cutting-edge art and international eating, Staten Island the namesake ferry and – most exotic of all – Republicans. Actually, other than Brooklyn, not many Manhattanites venture out here; they're missing plenty. Lots of famous 'New Yorkers' grew up in 'the OB' too – Jennifer Lopez, Rudy Guiliani, Martin Scorsese, Woody Allen and Joey Ramone.

Previously cities and townships of various sorts, the four joined the New York City metropolis in 1898, something still lamented by at least a handful of the fiercely proud. At 280 sq miles total, the outer boroughs comprise over 92% of the New York City land area.

Top Five Outer Boroughs

- **Brooklyn Heights** (p136) New York City's oldest neighborhood, topped off with a walk across the city's best bridge.
- **Coney Island** (p141) The saucy prototype to Disney, with creaking boardwalk, big beaches and a rickety roller coaster.
- **International Express** (p144) Elevated No 7 subway line through ethnic pockets of New York.
- **Staten Island Ferry** (p149) New York Harbor rides, for free.
- **Yankee Stadium** (p148) The ultimate baseball sanctuary.

BROOKLYN

Walking Tour pp166–8, Eating pp202–4, Drinking pp221–2, Shopping pp289–90

Confident and cool, Brooklyn is the most popular and well-known outer borough, and attracts many a New Yorker across the East River. Park Slope is Central Park's less-known sister, Coney Island is the tacky-fun amusement park, Brooklyn Heights is the city's oldest neighborhood, Williamsburg is an edgy haven for scenesters looking for booze and grub. Even if you have just a few days in New York, at least walk across the borough's namesake bridge.

Much of the Brooklyn lore has been captured on film – Woody Allen's nostalgic nods to Jewish life, Italian 'goodfellas' looking for a score, Spike Lee doing the right thing. Plus there's the lingo. Seeping into all boroughs, the glamorized working-class 'New York accent' is sometimes just called 'Brooklynese' – the popular amalgam of Italian, Yiddish, Caribbean, Spanish and even Dutch influences on English: 'da' for the, 'hoid' for heard, 'dowahg' for dog, 'tree' for three, 'fugehdabboudit' for 'forget about it, kind sir.'

Orientation

Across the East River from Lower Manhattan, Brooklyn occupies the southeastern tip of Long Island and is connected to Manhattan by the Brooklyn, Manhattan and Williamsburg bridges (south to north, remember 'BMW'). The prestigious brownstone zone, Brooklyn Heights is nestled between the East River (and Brooklyn–Queens Expressway) to the west, Cadman Plaza West to the east, and Atlantic Ave to the south. Just east are the modern buildings of downtown, bordered by Flatbush Ave to the east.

Immediately south are a few quiet residential neighborhoods with excellent shopping and eating. Court and Smith Sts lead south from Atlantic Ave into Cobble Hill and the Italian neighborhood of Carroll Gardens. Boerum Hill, just east, is around Atlantic Ave, to the south of downtown.

To the north, along the river, Williamsburg is an up-and-coming 'downtown'-type neighborhood transformed from old warehouse spaces. Farther inland, huge Prospect Park's western neighbor is Park Slope (home to lots of families and shop-lined Fifth and Seventh Aves).

At the end of some subway lines are historic Coney Island and the predominantly Russian neighborhood of Brighton Beach.

Transportation

Sixteen subway lines crisscross between Manhattan and Brooklyn, and the G line goes to/from Queens. Here are a few useful stops, broken down by neighborhood:

Boerum Hill F, G to Bergen St, A, C, G to Hoyt Schermerhorn.

Brighton Beach B, Q to Brighton Beach.

Brooklyn Heights 2, 3 to Clark St.

Carroll Gardens F, G to Bergen St.

Cobble Hill F, G to Carroll St.

Coney Island D, F, Q to Coney Island–Stillwell Ave.

Downtown 2, 3, 4, 5 to Borough Hall, A, C, F to Jay St–Borough Hall, M, R to Court St.

Dumbo F to York St, A, C to High St.

Fort Greene B, M, Q, R to DeKalb Ave, C to Lafayette Ave.

Park Slope F to 7 Av, B, Q, 2, 3, 4, 5 to Atlantic Ave.

Prospect Heights B, Q to Prospect Park.

Prospect Park 2, 3 to Grand Army Plaza, B, Q to Prospect Park.

Williamsburg L to Bedford Ave.

BROOKLYN TOURISM & VISITORS CENTER Map p394
☎ 718-802-3846; www.brooklyn-usa.org; 209 Joralemon St, Borough Hall; ☺ 10am-6pm Mon-Fri; subway 2, 3, 4, 5 to Borough Hall

This new information center, on the ground floor of Borough Hall, is packed with brochures, walking-tour maps and shopping guides to all things Brooklyn. It also has a gift shop; a 'Fuhgeddaboudit' T-shirt is $12.

New Brooklyn?

Huge city-changing plans were hot topics around Brooklyn and New York as this book went to press. In January 2004, developer Bruce Ratner bought the New Jersey Nets NBA franchise, with the hope of moving it to Brooklyn by 2007. The move is contingent on the opening of the Atlantic Yards project – a sprawling 21-acre, $250 billion downtown overhaul (along Atlantic between Flatbush and Vanderbilt Aves) that got swollen thumbs-ups from much of city government (and even rapper Jay-Z, who was at the announcement). Part of the package would be a Frank Gehry–designed Brooklyn Arena for the Nets and luxe business and loft-living spaces.

Many locals feel less giddy about bringing back major-league sports to Brooklyn. The project would oust dozens, and worries of added traffic are other concerns.

Meanwhile, remote Red Hook is likely to see more action as Ikea plans to open a superstore in the waterfront hood.

Brooklyn Heights & Downtown

These side-by-side neighborhoods – the first you'll see in Brooklyn if crossing the Brooklyn or Manhattan bridges – could hardly be more different. Brooklyn Heights is New York's oldest neighborhood, its first designated historic district and (simply put) the boroughs at their most charming. Its 19th-century brownstones line (generally quiet) streets that were once home to literary figures like Thomas Wolfe, Henry Willer, Truman Capote and Thomas Paine. Don't miss its promenade view of Lower Manhattan.

Just east is modern, skyscraping downtown – with a few historical reminders (such as Borough Hall) and many office buildings.

See p166 for a walking tour that begins across the Brooklyn Bridge and takes in Brooklyn Heights, downtown and Cobble Hill and Carroll Gardens, to the south.

Farther east is the Fort Greene neighborhood, centered on restaurant-lined DeKalb Ave (which leads east past Fort Greene Park and Pratt Art School) and Lafayette Ave (near the Brooklyn Academy of Music, below).

BROOKLYN ACADEMY OF MUSIC

Map p394

☎ 718-636-4100; www.bam.org; 30 Lafayette Ave; subway 2,3,4,5, B, Q to Atlantic Ave

The oldest concert center in the USA, the Brooklyn Academy of Music has hosted such notable events as Enrico Caruso's final performance. Today, it continues to feature first-rate arts programs, including performances by visiting international opera companies and the resident Mark Morris dance troupe. The complex contains the **Majestic Theater**, the **Brooklyn Opera House** and the **Rose Cinema** (☎ 718-623-2770), the first outer-borough movie house dedicated to independent and foreign films. For more information see Culture Fixes in Brooklyn, p234.

BROOKLYN HISTORICAL SOCIETY

Map p394

☎ 718-222-4111; www.brooklynhistory.org; 128 Pierrepont St; adult/student/child $6/4/free; ☽ 10am-5pm Wed, Thu & Sat,10am-8pm Fri, noon-5pm Sun; subway M, R to Court St

Built in 1881, and renovated in 2002, this four-story Queen Anne–style landmark building houses a library, museum and auditorium. The museum has lots of old Dodger and Coney Island memorabilia. History nuts should schedule an appointment to peruse the 33,000 digitized photos from decades past. Call for info on the society-led walking tours.

NEW YORK TRANSIT MUSEUM

Map p394

☎ 718-694-1600; cnr Boerum Pl & Schermerhorn St; adult/child $5/3; ☽ 10am-4pm Tue-Fri, noon-5pm Sat & Sun; subway 2, 3, 4, 5 to Borough Hall, M, R to Court St

Down an old subway station's steps, the recently renovated museum is housed in an abandoned subway station built in 1936 and a fun place to explore 100-plus years of getting around the city. There are exhibits on subways and aboveground trolleys as well as how fare collection has evolved from token to subway card.

The museum's gift shop (and at its annex in **Grand Central Terminal**, p112) is good for gifts in subway-map prints.

Brooklyn Public Library (p139)

Boerum Hill, Cobble Hill & Carroll Gardens

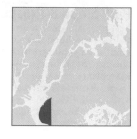

These three mostly residential neighborhoods, an easy walk south from Brooklyn Heights, are collectively known as (don't laugh) BoCoCa.

Boerum Hill, amidst office buildings and storefronts south of downtown, is on and south of Atlantic Ave between Smith and 3rd Sts; Cobble Hill (with shop-to-café-to-bar-lined Court St) is just west, south of Atlantic Ave from Brooklyn Heights. Once you get south of Union St, Cobble Hill turns into the old Italian neighborhood of Carroll Gardens. All cater to locals. Smith St's boutiques and bistros and Atlantic Ave's antique shops and Middle Eastern bakeries are worth poking around. Look for dining and shopping maps available at most.

Gowanus Canal

A couple blocks east of Smith St in Carroll Gardens, the quiet factory-lined **Gowanus Canal** (Map p395) won't win awards for beauty, but it carries a special victorious spirit for Brooklynites.

For much of the 20th century, the former creek (named for the Gouwane Native Americans who sold the area to the Dutch in 1636) roared with commercial life. Ships from New York Harbor came in to load/unload goods, and tens of millions of pounds of human waste were dumped in each year. The mess that ensured actually inspired poets and writers like Thomas Wolfe to make it a symbol of the city. Many say it was a favorite body dump for the Mafia too: nothing floats in black sludge.

In the past couple of decades, things have changed, largely due to the efforts of grassroots groups in the 'hood. The stench is gone, and – while not as quaint as the path-lined canals of London – it's worth a peek from one of the bridges (particularly the retractile bridge on Carroll St).

Dumbo

On the East River north of downtown, Down Under the Manhattan Bridge Overpass (Dumbo) – whatever happened to nonacronym neighborhoods? – is a small, arty loft-space district with incredible views of Manhattan from between the Brooklyn and Manhattan Bridges. Here, you'll find art galleries, cafés and a burgeoning music scene in a 10-block area that is easily seen visited after a Brooklyn Heights stroll.

DUMBO ARTS CENTER

☎ 718-694-0831; www.dumboartscenter.org; 30 Washington St; ⊗ noon-6pm Thu-Mon; subway A, C to High St, F to York St

Gallery space in the heart of artist-heavy Dumbo groups local artists with established curators for mixed-media exhibitions of fine arts. Each October, DAC organizes the **d.u.m.b.o. Art Under the Bridge Festival** (p12).

EMPIRE-FULTON FERRY STATE PARK

☎ 718-858-4708; www.nysparks.state.ny.us; 26 New Dock St; ⊗ 8am-7pm Thu-Mon, 7am-5pm Tue & Wed; subway A, C to High St, F to York St

Sweeping vistas of the Lower Manhattan skyline across the East River, snugly buttressed by the historic Brooklyn and Manhattan Bridges, make this small riverside spot a favorite of photographers and filmmakers, amateur and professional. Indeed, it's been featured in a good number of NYC films. Added sculptures during summer turn the park into an outdoor art gallery.

JACQUES TORRES CHOCOLATE

Map p394

☎ 718-875-9772; www.mrchocolate.com; 66 Water St; ⊗ 9am-7pm Mon-Sat; subway A, C to High St, F to York St

Chocolate factory-cum-café offering velvety, innovative artisan chocolates and open viewing of factory floor where all the candy goodness is getting made.

137

Park Slope & Prospect Park

East on Flatbush Ave from downtown, this leafy residential neighborhood has side-by-side brownstones, home to families and young professionals. Its two main arteries (5th and 7th Aves) run north–south, west of Prospect Park, and have plenty of laid-back shops and eating places. The area indeed slopes downward, but only a bit, on its way west towards the Gowanus Canal. Some dubbed it the 'Gold Coast ' in the early 1900s for the grand Victorians still facing Prospect Park

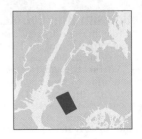

BROOKLYN BOTANIC GARDEN

Map p395

☎ 718-623-7200; www.bbg.org; 1000 Washington Ave; adult/senior & student/child $5/3/free ; ☯ 8am-6pm Tue-Fri, 10am-6pm Sat, Sun & holidays Apr-Sep, 8am-4:30pm Tue-Fri, 10am-4:30pm Sat, Sun & holidays Oct-Mar; subway 2, 3 to Eastern Pkwy–Brooklyn Museum, B, Q, S to Prospect Park

Behind the Brooklyn Museum (thus an easy combo visit), this garden features 12,000 plants in its 15 gardens. The Celebrity Path honors 150 Brooklyn-born (Spike Lee and Barbra Streisand among them). The Discovery Garden is a hands-on floral playground for kids. At the end of April, come for the **Sakuri Matsuri** (Cherry Blossom Festival; p10). The garden's also big on bonsai – the USA's oldest and biggest collection is here. Admission is free to all on Tuesday and 10am to noon Saturday.

BROOKLYN CHILDREN'S MUSEUM

Map p395

☎ 718-735-4400; www.brooklynkids.org; 145 Brooklyn Ave; admission $6; ☯ 1-6pm Tue-Fri, 11am-6pm Sat & Sun Jul & Aug, 1-6pm Wed-Fri, 11am-6pm Sat & Sun Sep-Jun; subway C to Kingston–Throop Ave, 3 to Kingston

The hands-on kids favorite was the world's first museum designed expressly for children, founded in 1899. Emphasizing art, music and ethnic cultures, the museum features a world playground that celebrates different cultures and a greenhouse designed to teach kids about environmental preservation. Each June the museum holds a balloon festival of custom-made balloons from around the world.

BROOKLYN MUSEUM

Map p395

☎ 718-638-5000; www.brooklynmuseum.org; 200 Eastern Pkwy; adult/senior & student/child $6/3/free; ☯ 10am-5pm Wed-Fri, 11am-6pm Sat & Sun, to 11pm 1st Sat of month; subway 2, 3 to Eastern Pkwy–Brooklyn Museum

The country's biggest art museum after the Met, with an incredible collection of 1.5 million pieces, sees far fewer visitors than its more-famous Manhattan friend. A 2004 renovation that yielded a lovely glass esplanade has made the museum all the more fetching. The five-floor building, open since 1897, is big, yet only a fifth of its originally planned size. It made news in 1999 when Rudy Giuliani attacked a work by Chris Ofili: a portrait of the Virgin Mary smeared in elephant dung.

The majority of the collection is less cutting-edge. Highlights are many, including the African Arts display on the 1st floor, featuring a Niger charm dance video. The Egyptian collection – the biggest in the Americas – occupies most of the 3rd floor; a dozen wall-tall Assyrian reliefs line one room, dating from 879 BC.

The 4th floor contains 28 period rooms, including the art deco Worgelt Study, a reconstruction of a 1930 Park Ave apartment. On the 5th floor, you'll find 58 sculptures by August Rodin, a collection of diverse American paintings, and a Thomas Edison film of a train ride over the Brooklyn Bridge in 1899.

GREEN-WOOD CEMETERY

Map p395

☎ 718-788-7850; www.green-wood.com; 500 25th St; admission free; ☯ 7am-7pm summer, 8am-5pm winter; subway M, R to 25 St

People in big cities die too, and New York is home to many sprawling cemeteries. Of the biggies, however, none beats the gorgeous and historic Green-Wood Cemetery, where 560,000 rest for the ages. (Head-to-toe, that's 520 miles of folks, minimum.)

Founded in 1838, Green-Wood was the plot where many big names wanted their bones to be. On this massive 478-acre plot (with ponds, lawns and trees), you can take nice strolls past the final resting places of folks like Leonard

Bernstein, Horace Greeley, FAO Schwarz, mobster Joey Gallo, Samuel FB Morse and many others. To get there, walk up the hill from the subway station to the 5th Ave entrance. Pick up a free map at the entrance.

Big Onion (☎ 212-439-1020; www.bigonion .com; adult/senior & student $12/10) runs terrific walking tours; see the Green-Wood website for others. Jeff Richmond's *Brooklyn's Green-Wood Cemetery: New York's Buried Treasure* is a comprehensive guide.

PROSPECT PARK Map p395

☎ 718-965-8951; www.prospectpark.org; subway B, Q, S to Prospect Park, 2, 3 to Grand Army Plaza, F to 15 St–Prospect Park

This 526-acre park was created in 1866 by Frederick Law Olmsted and Calvert Vaux (the masterminds behind Central Park). Prospect Park has many of the same activities in its broad meadows. Many come to lounge, run, boat, bike, skate or barbecue. For information on activities, stop by the **Audobon Center Boathouse** (☎ 718-965-8999; just west of B, Q subway station).

Just north of the boathouse is the **Children's Corner**. Here, you'll find a terrific 1912 **carousel** (admission $1; ☯ noon-5pm Thu-Sun Apr-Oct), which was a former Coney Island resident, and a small **zoo** (☎ 718-399-7339; adult/child $5/1; ☯ 10am-5pm Mon-Fri, to 5:30pm Sat & Sun Apr-Oct, to 4:30pm Nov-Mar), with sea lions

and 600 other animals. Kids also like the free **Lefferts Homestead Children's Historic House Museum** (☎ 718-789-2822; ☯ 1-4pm Fri-Sun Apr-Nov), an 18th-century Dutch farmhouse with toys and knick-knacks from the era to play with.

South of the boathouse, on the west edge of Propsect Lake, **Kate Wollman Rink** (☎ 718-287-6431; adult/senior & child $5/3, rental $5; ☯ Oct–mid-Mar, call for hrs) has enough ice to welcome hundreds of ice skaters. The nearby lake is open for **pedal boats** ($10; ☯ noon-6pm summer, noon-5pm Thu-Sun May–Memorial Day, noon-5pm Sat & Sun Labor Day–mid-Oct).

At the park's northwest entrance, **Grand Army Plaza** (cnr Eastern Pkwy & Flatbush Ave; near Grand Army Plaza station) is home to the 80ft arch, **Soldiers' & Sailors' Monument**, built in 1892 to commemorate the Union army's victory in the Civil War. At the base, where a farmer's market is held 8am to 4pm Saturdays year-round, note the bas-reliefs of war scenes. The fountain was restored in early 2004. The immense art deco **Brooklyn Public Library** faces the arch on its south side.

A free weekend **trolley** connects points of interest around the park (including the Brooklyn Museum) noon to 6pm in summer. You can rent **in-line skates** in Park Slope (p251).

Also see entries on the Brooklyn Museum and Brooklyn Botanic Garden, both at the park's northeastern edge.

Williamsburg

Edgy New York professionals in their 20s and 30s frequent Williamsburg to eat, shop, drink, and meet other edgy New York professionals. The 'new East Village' for about a decade, this neighborhood isn't gorgeous to look at (many new lofts and converted warehouses), but its main street, Bedford Ave, bustles with life. The Brooklyn Brewery, where those cute cursive 'B' beers you see in bars are born, offers Saturday tours.

Late-night taxis aren't always easy to find. You can also find late-night car services on Bedford Ave.

BROOKLYN BREWERY Map p395

☎ 718-486-7440; www.brooklynbrewery.com; 79 N 11th St; subway L to Bedford Ave

Since 1988, the Brooklyn Brewery has made its award-winning Brooklyn Lager under contract at breweries outside the borough. But the beer 'came home' to Brooklyn in 1996 with the opening of this microbrewery. Housed in a series of buildings that once made up the Hecla Ironworks factory (the firm that made

the structural supports for the Waldorf-Astoria Hotel), the brewery has become a Williamsburg institution. There is a nonsmoking tasting room with a display of historical beer bottles and monthly specials. Check for entertainment at night and a happy hour every Friday and Saturday between 6pm and 10pm. On Saturday,free tours take you backstage. Call for reservations and hours. For more details see the Beers in Brooklyn boxed text, p222.

Red Hook

Trivia question: what's the Statue of Liberty looking at? Well, here. South of Carroll Gardens, and far from the subway, burgeoning Red Hook is an old gritty waterfront working-class neighborhood (think *On the Waterfront* plus a few years) where Brooklyn's Gowanus Canal meets the harbor. At this point it's more urban adventure than straight-up attraction, but insiders are betting that Red Hook will become Brooklyn's next boom area, with locals actively debating neighborhood developmental, aka 'To Ikea or not to Ikea.'

For now, Red Hook is an untouristed, out-of-the-way spot with harbor sunset views, a water-taxi terminus, revolutionary history and an active local artist community. Now's the time to see it.

BROOKLYN WATERFRONT ARTISTS COALITION

☎ 718-596-2507; www.bwac.org; 499 Van Brunt St; ☽ noon-6pm Sat & Sun; water taxi to Beard St Pier

Gaze back at Liberty from the picturesque Van Brunt Pier, home to two warehouses of the pre–Civil War era and this artists collective, which hosts a rotating schedule of shows and exhibits, including a month-long show each May. Visit the website for upcoming events.

WATERFRONT MUSEUM & SHOWBOAT BARGE

☎ 718-624-4719; www.waterfrontmuseum.org; 701 Columbia St Marine Terminal; ☽ noon-6pm Sat & Sun; subway F, G to Smith & Ninth St, bus No 77 to Red Hook

Former juggler David Sharp dug up this sunken barge from under the George Washington Bridge, and now moors it near the Gowanus Canal, where he hosts appointment-only shows that are part circus act, part waterfront education. The barge, built in 1914, is listed on the National Register of Historic Places.

Coney Island & Brighton Beach

About 50 minutes by subway from Midtown, these two beachside neighborhoods sit on the calm Atlantic tides and are well connected by a beachside boardwalk. It's a fun day trip to visit both – Coney Island, the legendary amusement park with freak shows and hot dogs; Brighton Beach, for its Russian shops and bakeries.

July 4 sees a million visitors. The annual **Mermaid Parade**, held in late June, is a raucous affair where mermaid (and pirate) wannabes take to the streets. Contact **Sideshows by the Seashore** (☎ 718-372-5159; www.coneyisland.com) for more information.

ORIENTATON & HOURS

Many visitors start at Coney and return from Brighton Beach. Surf Ave runs parallel to the beach in Coney Island neighborhood, then turns inland as Ocean Pkwy. Brighton Beach's main thoroughfare is Brighton Beach Ave, which connects Ocean Pkwy with Coney Island Ave to the east.

Mermaids of Honor

The official start of the summer season in Coney Island is the wild, wet and wacky annual procession known as the Mermaid Parade, taking place during the last Saturday in June. The lineup of sequined and bejeweled revelers – mostly women (and some flamboyant men) who stuff themselves into teeny bikinis and colorfully freakish aquatic getups – moves chaotically along Surf Ave for an afternoon stroll every year, as wide-eyed observers of all stripes stand and cheer in the sun. Founded in 1983 by Coney Island USA (the arts organization that also produces the Coney Island Circus Sideshow), the Mermaid Parade honors Coney Island's forgotten Mardi Gras, which lasted from 1903 to 1954, and is hosted each year by a different celebrity King Neptune and Queen Mermaid; in 2004, music makers Moby and Theo (of the Lunachicks) presided over the madness. It's a truly unique, very New York spectacle-on-the-sea.

Coney Island's rides run daily between mid-June and Labor Day, usually from noon to 10pm, later on weekends. Most kick off the season in April on weekends only, and resume those hours after Labor Day for, as one park attendant says, 'as long as Mother Nature says it's OK.'

CONEY ISLAND Map p378
D, F to Coney Island-Stillwell Av

Across Surf Ave from the Coney Island/Stillwell Ave subway stop is **Nathan's** (p204), home to Coney's legendary hot dogs – and a belly-stuffing contest on July 4. Beyond (on Surf and Stillwell Aves) are many **games** (batting cages, mini golf, even 'shoot the freak'). Facing the water, to the right is **KeySpan Park**, where the Brooklyn Cyclones play minor-league baseball.

To the left, toward Brighton Beach, is the bulk of activity. Toward Surf Ave on 12th St (next to an army recruitment center) is the nonprofit **Sideshows by the Seashore** (☎ 718-372-5159; www .coneyisland.com; 1208 Surf Ave; adult/child

Transportation
Subway D, F, Q to Coney Island–Stillwell Av, or D, Q to Brighton Beach.

$5/3), which hosts a variety of 'nature's mistakes' (Insectavora, Sahar the Electric Lady etc). It also runs the **Coney Island Museum** (admission $1; ☺ 1pm-dusk Sat & Sun) upstairs.

Walking east, you'll find the **Deno's Wonder Wheel Amusement Park** (☎ 718-372-2592), with the long-standing pink-and-mint Ferris wheel (1920; $4) and a collection of kiddie rides (10 rides for $17). Beyond is its rival, the **Cyclone** (1927; under which Woody Allen grew up in *Annie Hall*), now part of the Astroland park. The coaster is $5 per ride (kiddie rides are $2 each, or 10 for $17). A clickety-clackety ride on the coaster winds around a wooden track, down nearly-vertical falls, and slamming around bends at nearly 60mph. Try for the front seat.

For good clean fun for the kids, visit the **Aquarium for Wildlife Conservation** (New York Aquarium; ☎ 718-265-3400; Surf Ave, btwn W 8th & 5th Sts; adult/child $11/7; ☺ 10am-4:30pm; subway F to W 8th St–NY Aquarium), which has a touch pool where kids can handle starfish, plus underwater views of baleen whales and popular feedings of sea lions and walruses. There are some 10,000 specimens.

All along the boardwalk, of course, is the **beach**. It's widely used, but still not too dirty. The water is off-limits when lifeguards are off duty during the low season. Plenty of shops sell water-related gear. The land you face? New Jersey.

BRIGHTON BEACH
Subway B, Q to Brighton Beach

Don't miss a stroll down the busy commercial strip of Brighton Beach Ave (lying under the shade of the subway line), about a 10-minute walk east of the aquarium. The area, also known as Little Odessa, is home to many emigrés who left the Soviet Union in the 1970s and 1980s. Most signs are in Russian and you'll see babushkas selling herbal teas, caviar and imported candies. Some delis sell meats and ready-to-go salads good for beach picnics. Plenty of Russian CD stores too; some offer Soviet-themed T-shirts and *matrushka* dolls from the motherland. Note: '*spasiba*' is 'thank you'.

How Coney Got Here

Coney Island brought the world fantasy fun long before Walt Disney was sketching mice. It's named for wild rabbits (*konijn* in Dutch), actually, which were pretty much all the first Europeans saw on the grassy shoreline in the 17th century. By the end of the 19th century, Coney Island had become a den for gamblers, hard drinkers, boxers, racers – some called it 'Sodom by the Sea.'

The 20th century brought a new era with late-night concerts (John Philip Sousa was a regular), settings of Buster Keaton films, and, best yet, amusement parks. The most famous, Luna Park, opened in 1903 and was a dream world of lagoons, live camels and elephants, rides to the moon and the Arctic – all lit by over a million bulbs (fire eventually took it down in 1946). Surviving gems of the time like the Wonder Wheel (1920) and Cyclone (1927) were mere players of a bigger game. On summer weekends, a million visited – and stuffed the beach full.

By the 1960s, Coney Island's pull had slipped (though long-time resident Woody Guthrie still considered it home) and the hood became a sad, crime-ridden reminder of past glories. During the 1980s, a slow, enduring comeback began, with new rides and 'freak shows' (sword swallowers, bearded women, folks with lizard skin etc) trickling in.

Rockaway Beach

For a quick urban getaway, head to the end of the line on the A train to Broad Channel and change to the Shuttle to 116th St and Rockaway Beach. This terrific beach is quieter and less crowded than Coney Island and though the train ride is about the same (under an hour from the Village or Chelsea), the scenery kicks ass. For most of the way the train is elevated, which is a delight in itself after so much belowground travel and once you hit the Gateway National Recreation Area and Jamaica Bay, your troubles will start melting away and you'll forget you're in New York. This neighborhood is a close-knit Italian and Irish enclave and the further you venture south on Beach Channel Dr and Rockaway Point Blvd, the more evident it will become that you're a day-tripper.

QUEENS

Eating pp204–5, Drinking p222

Queens is home to two major airports, the Mets, two World's Fairs, a budding modern art scene, dozens of jazz greats' former houses, the birthplace of the Ramones in Forest Hills, and an ethnic population so diverse that the chief subway line has become a 'historic trail' in itself. So why is it that New York's biggest borough is so often left out in the battle of the best? It is a bit drab, to be honest, and even many of its residents can't tell you what to do here. Yet there's heaps for urban adventurers to uncover.

Many popular Manhattan restaurants (Korean, Chinese, Vietnamese) test the ground here first, and the original locations still serve a loyal base of regulars.

Queens was named in the 17th century for the Queen Catherine of Braganza, married to Charles II of England. Braganzatown didn't have the same ring.

The **Queens Council on the Arts** (☎ 718-647-3377; www.queenscouncilarts.org) is a clearing-house for community events and publishes a few brochures. The website has a printable Art Loop map of Long Island City.

Orientation

Many of Manhattan's sunrise-watchers look over Queens. Between the Bronx and Brooklyn, Queens stretches eastward, roughly between Manhattan's 34th and 120th Sts. Queens is bounded by East River to the north and west (where the Astoria and Long Island City neighborhoods face Manhattan). Queens wraps around its southern neighbor, Brooklyn, to Jamaica Bay (home to JFK International Airport).

Northern Blvd leads east, passing through neighborhoods like Woodside, Jackson Heights, Corona and Flushing. Another main east–west artery is busy Roosevelt Ave, which runs under the No 7 subway line from Flushing and splits into Skillman and Greenpoint Aves just east of Long Island City.

Transportation

Subway Line No 7 stops at Long Island City, Jackson Heights, Corona and Flushing neighborhoods. Reach Astoria's 30 Av and Astoria–Ditmars Blvd stations by the N or W lines.

Long Island City

Queens' coolest pocket these days (though not its loveliest), Long Island City is just 10 minutes from Midtown by train and is home to some seriously good art amid the old warehouses and modern shimmer of the CitiCorp building. The elevated subway, graffiti and bustling diners imbue it with that old-school New York feel missing elsewhere.

Long Island City was indeed a city for a brief run, from 1874 to 1898, after which it joined the New York City metropolis.

Near **Court House Square** (Map p396; subway 7 to 45 Rd–Court House Sq, E, V to 23 St–Ely Ave, G to Long Island City–Court Sq), standing proud and kept-real, is one of the best collections of **graffiti** left anywhere in New York. Walk under the No 7 tracks on (unsigned) Davis St, just south of Jackson Blvd, to see the dazzling displays of wall-to-wall art on a cluster of industrial buildings. Tolerated space for this public art form has dwindled following the quality-of-life laws enacted by former mayor Giuliani – this is worth seeing.

ISAMU NOGUCHI GARDEN MUSEUM

Map p396

☎ 718-204-7088; www.noguchi.org; 32-37 Vernon Blvd; 🕙 10am-5pm Wed-Fri, 11am-6pm Sat & Sun; subway N, W to Broadway

Reopened in June 2004 (after three years of renovation), this museum is houses in a former factory near the river. The museum boasts the imaginative sculptures of the man who put curving steel pipes and red cubes in front of corporate buildings (such as at 140 Broadway in Manhattan).

MUSEUM FOR AFRICAN ART

Map p396

☎ 718-784-7700; www.africanart.org; 36-01 43rd Ave; adult/senior, student & child $6/3; 🕙 10am-5pm Mon, Thu & Fri, 11am-5pm Sat & Sun; subway 7 to 33 St

It's hard to see this amount (and quality) of African tribal crafts, masks, musical instruments and depictions of spirituality outside of that continent. (It's only one of two museums in the USA dedicated to African artists.) Previously in Soho, the museum is calling Queens home until 2006, when it's slated to move to Fifth Ave.

PS1 CONTEMPORARY ART CENTER

Map p396

☎ 718-784-2084; www.ps1.org; 22-25 Jackson Ave at 46th Ave; suggested donation adult/student $5/2; 🕙 noon-6pm Thu-Mon; subway E, V to 23 St–Ely Ave, 7 to 45 Rd–Court House Sq, G to Long Island City–Court House Sq

Many visitors to New York miss PS1, but its compelling alternative-space location (a closed 19th-century public school) and modern art (edgy and daring collections) with five sweeping galleries, makes good use of the dramatic, cement-wall garden out front.

The school had an interesting history. Built controversially after political scandal, it became a landmark for Long Island City, with its stone-tower clock and bell (both destroyed in 1964).

SOCRATES SCULPTURE PARK

Map p396

☎ 718-956-1819; cnr Broadway & Vernon Blvd; admission free; 🕙 10am-dusk; subway N, W to Broadway

Transformed from an illegal dumpsite in 1986, this open-air public space (near the Noguchi museum) displays sculptures and installations by local artists in a super location on the East River, with views of Roosevelt Island's tip and uptown. Past exhibits include an outdoor cubicle waiting room (with seats and a potted plant), green balls poking above the river surface, and the top few feet of a brownstone that seems buried in ground. From December to February, the park stages light-based installations, illuminating the Queens waterfront shortly after sunset.

Astoria

Named for millionaire fur merchant John Jacob Astor, this northwestern edge of Queens is home to the biggest Greek community in the country. Greek bakeries, diners and delis line many streets, particularly along Broadway (subway N, W to Broadway) and slightly more upscale on 31st St and Ditmars Blvd (subway N, W to Astoria–Ditmars Blvd). Before Greeks began moving here in the 1950s, it was primarily a neighborhood of factories (not to mention bridges – arched Hell Gate and towering Triboro still dominate the views west).

An easy walk northwest of the Astoria–Ditmars Blvd station, Astoria Park is home to the terrific art deco **Astoria Pool** (p252) and has nice paths along the river.

AMERICAN MUSEUM OF THE MOVING IMAGE Map p396

☎ 718-784-0077; www.ammi.org; 35th Ave & 36th St; adult/senior & student/child $10/7.50/5, free to all 4-8pm Fri; 🕙 noon-5pm Wed & Thu, noon-8pm Fri, 11am-6:30pm Sat & Sun; subway G, R, V to Steinway St

Set in the middle of Kaufman Astoria Studios (www.kaufmanastoria.com; one-time Paramount's east coast HQ, and the biggest and baddest film studio outside Hollywood), this fun museum features all sides of movie making and 90,000 recognizable items and props. You can see Yoda (the puppet from

Empire Strikes Back), *Seinfeld*'s 'puffy shirt,' and Charlton Heston's chariot from *Ben Hur*. The museum hosts interesting film retrospectives year-round in its Egyptian-themed theater. Check out the website for an up-to-date schedule.

The studios are closed to the public. The US army ran the site from 1945 to 1971, before becoming a film-production center once again. Many films and TV shows are shot here; this is where Big Bird, Grover and Elmo come to life for *Sesame Street*.

Ride on the International Express

The elevated, ultra-urban No 7 subway line cuts across the guts of Queens on an elevated track, connecting far-off Flushing with Midtown Manhattan. It not only offers views of the borough (and back) to Manhattan, but takes you on a 'national historic trail,' due to the longtime immigrant neighborhoods of Woodside (Irish), Jackson Heights (Indian, Filipino), Corona Heights (Italian, Peruvian, Colombian, Ecuadorian, Mexican) and Flushing (Chinese, Korean). A good day could be spent hopping on and off the burgundy-colored line, taking in some of New York's array of international flavor. Plan on two meals. Ride at the front or back car for clearest views.

One possible tour would be to take the No 7 from Times Square or Grand Central Terminal to the end of the line (Flushing–Main St), a 35-minute trip. Before you arrive, you'll pass the mammoth Flushing Meadows Corona Park to your right and Shea Stadium to your left.

In Flushing, get some Chinese, Taiwanese or Korean food, and ride back on the subway a stop to Willets Point–Shea Stadium for a walk through the park sights. Walk north to Roosevelt Ave, which runs under much of the 7 track. The **Louis Armstrong House** (p145) is a few blocks north.

Meander along Roosevelt Ave for 30 blocks west (venturing on side streets a bit) – past exciting shops and restaurants, all in Spanish – to 74th St, where things suddenly become quite Indian. Get a sari or eat. **Jackson Diner** (p205) is considered one of the best curry shops in the city.

Hop on the subway to Woodside–61 St to wander through an old Irish neighborhood, then get onto the subway's front car at the 52 St–Lincoln Ave or 46 St–Bliss St stations for a full views of Midtown as you inch closer. At Long Island City's 45 Rd–Court House Sq, get out for a look at the **PS1 Contemporary Art Center** (p143) and a serious show of **graffiti** (p142).

Flushing & Corona

The site of widely watched sports events at **Shea Stadium** (p244; the Mets) and the **USTA National Tennis Center** (p247; the US Open), the two otherwise little-known neighborhoods have active streets of locals-serving shops signed in Chinese, Korean, Spanish and Italian. In between the two areas is the bizarre but interesting Flushing Meadows Corona Park, dotted with buildings and monuments built to make statements for the 1939 and 1964 World's Fairs. They still do.

A lot has happened in this area. In the 17th century, Quakers met in Flushing to figure out how to avoid religious persecution from Dutch governor Peter Stuyvesant (which they did). Two hundred years later, many escaped slaves found freedom here (via the underground railroad).

By the 20th century, Flushing (in particular) had let itself go a bit. When F Scott Fitzgerald dissed the area as an ash heap in *The Great Gatsby* (1925), he was being kind. The World's Fairs helped turn things around, making the swampy area more attractive for the many jazz greats who lived here (as well as serving as the fictional home for the Bunkers of the '70s TV drama *All in the Family*).

Flushing – at the end of the No 7 line – is like Chinatown without the tourists. Clusters of shops and eateries center at Roosevelt Ave and Main St. Jazz buffs will want to visit **Flushing Cemetery** (46th Ave & 164th St, east of the Main St–Flushing station) to pay respects at the final resting places of Louis Armstrong (section 9, division A, plot 12B), Dizzy Gillespie (section 31, unmarked grave 1252) and others.

A couple subway stops west, Corona's southern reach is a quaint Italian neighborhood that looks like a town square from another era. At William F Moore Park (aka Spaghetti Park), the clink-clank of bocce balls sounds in summer, while passersby eat lemon ices (p205).

Just north, under the subway line on Roosevelt Ave, are rows of exciting restaurants and shops run by Latin American families.

It's possible to take in both neighborhoods and the park by foot in a few hours.

FLUSHING MEADOWS
CORONA PARK Map p397
Subway 7 to Willets Point–Shea Stadium

The area's biggest attraction, this 1225-acre park (built for the 1939 World's Fair) is dominated by monuments, such as Queens' most famous landmark, the stainless steel **Unisphere**, which at 120ft high and 380 tons is the world's biggest globe. Facing it is the former New York City Building, now home to the **Queens Museum of Art** (p146) and, on the southern side, the **World's Fair Ice Rink** (☎ 718-271-1996; ☽ Wed, Fri-Sun Oct-Mar, phone for hrs).

Just south are three weather-worn, Cold War–era **New York State Pavilion Towers**, which were part of the New York State Pavilion for the 1964 fair. More recently, these were used as spaceships in *Men in Black*. At its base is the **Queens Theater in the Park** (☎ 718-760-0064; www.queenstheatre.org), which hosts dance, drama and music shows.

Towards the No 7 line is the tall **Arthur Ashe Stadium**, and the rest of the **USTA National Tennis Center** (p247), and just beyond, **Shea Stadium** (p244); where the Mets play and the Beatles introduced the world to stadium rock).

West, over the Grand Central Parkway, are a few attractions, including the **New York Hall of Science** (right) and a small wildlife center.

The park actually has grounds too, on its eastern and southern edges. The top-quality astro-turf **soccer fields** are legendary for pick-up soccer. And Meadow Lake has boat and bike rentals at the **boathouse**.

The park is most easily reached from the walkway from the No 7 subway stop, Willets Point–Shea Stadium. Call ☎ 718-760-6565 for information.

Borough's Best Beaches

Many New Yorkers get out of the city for beach fun, but there are some good ones in the metropolis.

- **Brighton Beach, Brooklyn** (p141) Fewer bathers than at Coney Island just west.
- **Orchard Beach, the Bronx** (p148) Remote, hopping with locals.
- **Rockaway Beach, Queens** (Subway A to several 'Beach' stops at the end of line) The city's best; a 7-mile strip was where Joey wanted to hitch to in the Ramones song; Beach 90 St subway stop is a good starting place.
- **South Beach, Staten Island** (p149) Ferry-and-a-bus ride from Manhattan.

Queens Jazz Trail

They may have played over in Manhattan, but through the years Queens has been home to a hall of fame–caliber contingency of jazz greats. The lineup of locals includes such masters as Louis Armstrong, Dizzy Gillespie, Ella Fitzgerald, Lester Young, Count Basie, Billie Holiday, John Coltrane, Charles Mingus and Lena Horne. Forced by segregationist laws from buying or renting in other communities, they chose Queens for its sense of community and proximity to the clubs of Manhattan. Today, Flushing Town Hall helps spread the word by leading the **Queens Jazz Trail tour**, which travels the borough by foot and van pointing out relevant homes and clubs. Tickets cost $26, call ☎ 718-463-7700 for more information.

FLUSHING COUNCIL ON CULTURE & THE ARTS Map p397

☎ 718-463-7700; www.flushingtownhall.org; 137-135 Northern Blvd; admission free; ☽ 9am-5pm Mon-Fri, noon-5pm Sat & Sun; subway 7 to Flushing–Main St

Built in 1864, this Romanesque Revival building hosts year-round art shows and jazz and other music concerts. Ask about the $26 Queens Jazz Trail trolley tours by homes of greats who lived in the area: Louis Armstrong, Lena Horne, Ella Fitzgerald and many others. The council also has a jazz trail map plus other Queens-related brochures.

LOUIS ARMSTRONG HOUSE Map p397

☎ 718-478-8274; 34-56 107th St; tours $8; ☽ 10am-5pm Tue-Fri, noon-5pm Sat & Sun; subway 7 to 103 St–Corona Plaza

At the peak of his career, Louis chose this quiet Corona Heights home to live his last 28 years. Guides offer free 40-minute tours (leaving on the hour; the last goes at 4pm) through the home (past his gold records on the wall). He died in 1971. Call for information on the Louis Armstrong Archives.

NEW YORK HALL OF SCIENCE Map p397

☎ 718-699-0055; Flushing Meadows Corona Park, at 49th Ave; adult/student & child $9/6, free for all 2-5pm Fri Sep-Jun; ☽ 9:30am-2pm Tue-Thu, 9:30am-5pm Fri, noon-5pm Sat & Sun Sep-Jun, 9:30am-2pm Mon, 9:30am-5pm Tue-Fri, 10:30am-6pm Sat & Sun Jul & Aug; subway 7 to 111 St

Several buildings from different eras (including a wavy wall of concrete) join to make New York's only science-devoted museum. Best is the outdoor kids park, the **Science Playground** (☽ Apr-Dec).

QUEENS BOTANICAL GARDENS

Map p397

☎ 718-886-3800; www.queensbotanical.org; 43-50 Main St; admission free; ☼ 8am-6pm Tue-Fri, 8am-7pm Sat & Sun Apr-Oct, 8am-4:30pm Tue-Sun Nov-Mar; subway 7 to Flushing–Main St

This 39-acre garden – born for the 1939 World's Fair – includes a good variety of non-native flora. The expansive meadows are better picnic grounds than nearby Flushing Meadows Corona Park, and the pathways provide good cycling.

JAMAICA BAY NATIONAL WILDLIFE REFUGE Map p378

☎ 718-318-4340; www.nps.gov/gate; Cross Bay Blvd; admission free; ☼ 8:30am-5pm

Part of the Gateway National Recreation Area, Jamaica Bay is one of the northeast's largest bird sanctuaries, where hundreds of species fly through or lay over on the Atlantic Flyway.

Bird's-Eye NYC

Can't afford that helicopter tour? For a unique vantage of the city, check the super, detailed **Panorama of New York City**, a three tennis courts–sized room (9335 sq ft) of the New York metropolis in miniature. Housed at the **Queens Museum of Art** (Map p397; ☎ 718-592-9700; www.queensmuseum.org; Flushing Meadows Corona Park; adult/senior & student/child $5/2.50/free; ☼ 10am-5pm Wed-Fri, noon-5pm Sat & Sun; subway 7 to 111 St), a fine destination in itself, the Panorama features a descending walkway that encircles the 895,000 structures and details New York as it looks from an airplane. A lighted dawn-to-dusk simulation occurs every 15 minutes. This is New York circa 1992, when it was last updated (excepting alterations following the September 11 attacks). The rest of the museum, set in the former New York City Building built for the 1939 World's Fair, is now half devoted to that grand occasion and half to changing art exhibits.

THE BRONX

Eating pp205–6

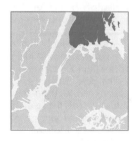

North of Manhattan, the Bronx is 'X-treme' New York. Here, the horn honking is a little louder, the graffiti a little more daring, the swagger a little sharper. All seemingly bent to justify that the dignifying article preceding its name – as with the Yucatán or the Hague – which helps make it more than just your ordinary living place. It is. Lots of famous folks have risen to fame from the Bronx (but from quite different blocks): J.Lo, C.Po and B.Jo are among them (Jennifer Lopez, Colin Powell and Billy Joel). Not to overlook those men in pinstripes, the Bronx Bombers themselves: the New York Yankees.

Like Queens, the Bronx is home to an ethnically diverse population. Nearly a quarter of the population is Puerto Rican, and there are growing numbers of Jamaicans, Indians, Vietnamese, Cambodians and Eastern Europeans.

A quarter of the Bronx is parkland, including Pelham Bay Park.

Bronx Tourism Council (☎ 718-590-3518; www.ilovethebronx.com) offers a visitors guide and regularly updates its website with area events. **Bronx County Historical Society** (☎ 718-881-8900; www.bronxhistoricalsociety.org) schedules many walking and bus tours in spring, summer and fall.

A good portion of a day could be spent seeing the zoo and botanical garden then walking to Belmont for an Italian dinner.

Orientation

The only borough on the mainland, the Bronx is just north of Manhattan and wedged between the Hudson, Harlem and East Rivers and Long Island Sound. The chief road of the 42-sq-mile Bronx is the north–south Grand Concourse, inspired by Paris' Champs Elysées, and still home to many fine art deco residences. Its meeting point with Fordham Rd, west of the Bronx Zoo and near the famous Italian neighborhood of Belmont, is the Bronx's main hub of commercial activity. It's flooded with pedestrians on weekends.

The Bronx is no pancake. Its hills come as a surprise to many visitors' legs.

ARTHUR AVE/BELMONT AVE

Map pp398-9

Subway B, D to Fordham Rd

Some argue that New York's 'real Little Italy' is here, on the blocks south of Fordham University between Bronx Park (to the east) and Third Ave (to the west) – clearly marked with 'Little Italy in the Bronx' banners. Here you'll find pizzerias, trattorias, bakeries (Arthur Ave Baking Co serves many of the city's restaurants), fishmongers selling clams on the half-shell, and butchers with bunnies in the window – all prepare their goods for locals and tend to sell them without breaking into English. It's good exploring. Do bring an appetite. Many New Yorkers claim that **Roberto's** (p205) is the finest Italian eating in the city.

The famous scene in the *Godfather* – where Al Pacino gets the gun from 'behind the toilet with the chain thing' and blasts his way into his new career – supposedly takes place at **Mario's** (2342 Arthur Ave).

From the Fordham Rd station, walk east 11 blocks downhill along Fordham (a busy commercial strip); turn right at Arthur Ave.

BRONX MUSEUM OF THE ARTS

Map pp398-9

☎ 718-681-6000; www.bxma.org; 1040 Grand Concourse at 165th St; suggested donation $5; ☀ noon-9pm Wed, noon-6pm Thu-Sun; subway B, D, 4 to 161 St–Yankee Stadium

Devoted to interesting, largely urban, contemporary art, the museum hosts a wide array of art (graffiti, video installations, paintings), usually by American artists with African, Latin American or Asian ancestry. From the subway station, walk east to the Grand Concourse, then north a few blocks.

BRONX ZOO Map pp398-9

☎ 718-367-1010; www.bronxzoo.com; adult/child $11/8 Apr-Oct, $8/6 Nov-Mar; ☀ 10am-5pm Mon-Fri, 10am-5:30pm Sat & Sun Apr-Oct, 10am-4:30pm daily Nov-Mar; subway 2, 5 to Pelham Pkwy

Also known as the Bronx Wildlife Conservation Society, this famous attraction is one of the country's best zoos and receives more than two million visitors a year. Opened in 1899, the 265-acre zoo has been a pioneer in creating naturalistic settings (re-creating African plains and forest, Himalayan mountains and Asian rainforests) for its nearly 5000 animals (gorillas, polar bears, penguins, zebras, giraffes – all sorts). The zoo's bison, acquired in the early 20th century, helped repopulate the animals in the Great Plains in recent years.

Big hits with kids include the hovering bats at the World of Darkness, and regularly scheduled penguin and sea-lion feedings. Look out for original structures that date from 1899, including the House of Reptiles. In winter, some animals live in sheltered areas and can't be viewed (but fewer visitors go).

A few attractions cost extra, including the Congo Gorilla Forest ($3), the 25-minute monorail journey *Bengali Express* ($3, May-Oct) and a Skyfari ride over some exhibits ($2). Combo tickets include everything.

Liberty Lines Express (☎ 718-652-8400) runs a Bx11 bus ($4) from Madison Ave (pick-ups include 26th, 39th, 47th, 54th and 63rd Sts) to the zoo. The trip runs every 10 or 20 minutes. Exact change or bills are required.

There are five entrances to the zoo. From the Pelham Parkway subway station, walk south on White Plains Rd, turn right on Lydig Ave. At Bronx Park East, turn right, then left to the Bronx River Parkway Gate (where the Bx11 bus drops off passengers).

Transportation

Subway The B, D, 2, 4, 5, 6 lines connect Manhattan with the Bronx with useful stops at Yankee Stadium (B, D, 4 to 161 St–Yankee Stadium), near the Bronx Zoo (2, 5 to Pelham Pkwy) and at the corner of Grand Concourse and Fordham Rd (B, D to Fordham Rd).

CITY ISLAND Map pp398-9

www.cityislandchamber.org; subway 6 to Pelham Bay Park, then bus No Bx29

About 15 miles from Midtown, and a world away, City Island is one of New York's most surprising neighborhoods. Founded by the English in 1685, the 1.5mile-long fishing community is filled with boat slips and six yacht clubs. If you're serious about diving, sailing or fishing, come here. On weekends (even in February), City Island Ave's two dozen seafood restaurants are mobbed by local families, including **Tony's Pier** (p206). On side streets, Victorian clapboard houses – definitely looking more New England than Bronx – overlook the water.

Several boats run excellent fishing trips into the calm Long Island Sound. The **Riptide III** (☎ 718-885-0236), at the island's north point, leaves daily from March to mid-December at 8am. If you're a first-timer, the mates help you out. Adult passage is $42, children $25.

Call about the summer party cruises around Manhattan.

Captain Mike's Dive Shop (☎ 718-885-1588; www.captainmikesdiving.com; 530 City Island Ave) has two-tank dive trips in the area for $55 to $88 on weekends. A popular one is to the wreckage of a WWI cruiser, the USS *San Diego*.

Just north of the island, in the surrounding Pelham Bay Park, is a pretty stretch of sand at **Orchard Beach**, once dubbed the 'Bronx Riviera.' The Bx12 bus goes here from the Pelham Bay Park subway stop (in summer only).

EDGAR ALLEN POE COTTAGE

Map pp398-9

☎ 718-881-8900; cnr Grand Concourse & E 193rd St; tours $3; ☺ 10am-4pm Sat, 1-5pm Sun; subway B, D to Kingsbridge Rd

Once an early-19th-century farm cottage, Poe's last home now sits in a small grassy plot in the heart of modern Bronx and towering apartment buildings and Grand Concourse traffic. Poe lived here from 1846 to 1849. There's a short guided tour and video.

NEW YORK BOTANICAL GARDEN

Map pp398-9

☎ 718-817-8700; www.nybg.org; adult/senior/student/child $6/3/2/1; ☺ 10am-6pm Tue-Sun Apr-Oct, 10am-5pm Tue-Sun Nov-Mar; subway B, D to Bedford Park Blvd

Spread across 50 acres of primary forest (just north of the Bronx Zoo), the New York Botanical Garden (opened in 1891) is home to several beautiful gardens and the restored Victorian Enid A Haupt Conservatory, a grand iron-and-glass edifice that is a New York landmark. You can also stroll through an outdoor rose garden, just next to the conservatory, and a rock garden with multi-tiered waterfall.

Metro-North (☎ 212-532-4900; www.mnr.org) trains leave hourly from Grand Central Terminal and stop right at the garden; the one-way fare is $4.50/6 at off-peak/peak hours. From the Bedford Park Blvd subway stop, walk east down the hill and seven blocks to the gate.

YANKEE STADIUM

Map pp398-9

☎ 718-293-6000; www.yankees.com; E 161st St & River Ave; tours $12-25; ☺ 10am-4pm Mon-Fri, 10am-noon Sat (when team is on road), 10am-noon Mon-Fri (when team is at home); subway B, D, 4 to 161 St–Yankee Stadium

The Yankees call their legendary ballpark (built in 1923) the 'most famous stadium since the Roman Coliseum,' and with 26 championships to their name, who's arguing? The Yankees play their home games here April to October (see p244 about tickets). Get to games early to take a stroll around **Monument Park**, behind left field, where plaques commemorate such baseball greats as Babe Ruth, Lou Gehrig, Mickey Mantle and Joe DiMaggio. The park closes 45 minutes before the game begins.

On hour-long guided tours, you can visit the dugout, press room, field and locker rooms. Individuals can show up at noon without reservations (adult/senior & child $12/$6), otherwise make a reservation in advance by calling ☎ 718-579-4531, or from the website. An expanded tour includes a 20-minute film ($17/12) or looks at the luxury suites and other areas ($25/15).

Also see The House that Ruth Built, left.

The House that Ruth Built

Pro baseball's biggest team plays in a stadium that brings chills of joy to fans and hatred to rival fans (supporters of the Boston Red Sox come to mind). It's possible, however, it may have had a different size, shape and location, if not for a fateful acquisition of a young pitcher named George Herman 'Babe' Ruth from the Red Sox in 1920.

In the days when pitchers could actually hit, Babe hit better than all of baseball. His home-run blasts brought in huge crowds, and the Yanks soon dwarfed the draws of the New York Giants (now in San Francisco), who served as landlord of the Yanks' field. So the Yanks got pushed out.

Opened in 1923, Yankee Stadium is said to facilitate Ruth's hitting style (not to mention the numbers of fans clamoring to get a glimpse of Babe in action). He led the Yanks in the stadium's debut season to win the Yanks' first World Series over the New York Giants (bah on those who say sports can't be poetic).

Renovations have changed the inside – the hard wood seats were replaced by soft plastic ones in the 1970s – but the outer facade is the same that Ruth fans rushed toward in the '20s.

In 1927, Ruth hit 60 homers, a single-season record until 1961, when North Dakota–born Yankee Roger Maris broke it with 61. Ruth's 714 career homers weren't surpassed until Hank Aaron beat it in 1974.

STATEN ISLAND

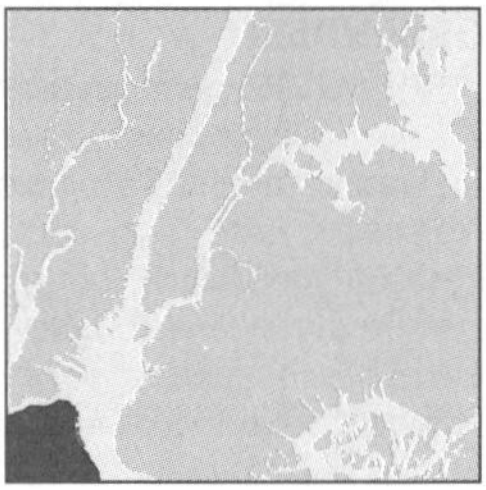

Though famed for the ferry, the starting point of the New York Marathon and a (now closed) dump taller than anything south on the East Coast, Staten Island is New York's 'forgotten borough.' Looking at a map, it's practically New Jersey (which is just a short jump across the Kill Van Kull, and in fact the island's first road connection with New York City and State only came in 1964, when the Verrazano Narrows Bridge opened.

Its population – wee, at under half a million – is largely middle-class Republicans, not always jiving with (predominately) Democratic politics in the city. Many residents entertain fantasies of secession from New York City, but have yet to go through with it.

Sandy Ground (in the island's south) is the country's oldest continuously inhabited African-American community. Ichabod Crane, the doomed rider in Washington Irving's *The Legend of Sleepy Hollow*, was real (actually Irving's schoolteacher); he's buried in the New Springfield Cemetery. Hip-hop's Wu-Tang Clan found their prose's inspiration from their beginnings in Clifton.

Many visitors don't leave the ferry, but if you're coming over, there are several surprisingly good attractions worth venturing to. With ferry time to/from Manhattan, and a couple hours at Snug Harbor Cultural Center by bus, plan on four hours.

If you're looking for a **beach**, bus S51 goes south to South Beach and Midland Beach, connected with a two-mile boardwalk.

The **Staten Island Chamber of Commerce** (☎ 718-727-1900; 130 Bay St; 🕘 9am-5pm Mon-Fri), three blocks east (left, if facing from the water) of the terminal, has a few brochures, but you're better off picking them up at the ferry terminal in Manhattan. The basic *St George Walking Tour* has a useful map of the ferry area. Pick up the free weekly, *Staten Island Source* (www.sisource.com).

Orientation

Staten Island is across the New York Harbor, south of Manhattan. The ferry unleashes passengers on downtown St George, just on the northern tip of a 58 sq mile island. Richmond Terrace runs along the water to the west.

Twenty-three bus routes converge on four ramps at St George Ferry Terminal (you can use your MTA Metrocard on any). Buses are timed to coincide with arrivals. Routes loosely cover the island, though some destinations require added walks to get there. Buses tend to run every 20 minutes during the day. Staten Island's train service, which departs from the ferry terminal, has less useful routes for attractions.

Staten Island Ferry

One of New York's greatest bargains, the free **Staten Island Ferry** (☎ 718-815-2628; www.siferry.com; 🕘 24hr) takes 70,000 passengers each day on the 25-minute five-mile journey from Lower Manhattan to Staten Island. Most of its passengers don't bat an eye at the knockout views of the harbor, Statue of Liberty or Ellis Island as they're commuting, and do so daily.

The island has long been concerned with getting its people to Manhattan efficiently (long before Melanie Griffith took the ferry to work in the film *Working Girl*). The Staten Island Ferry started its run in 1905, but many ferries worked the harbor before that. Some were adopted as Civil War boats, a few destroyed by Confederate capturees.

One of the eight-ferry fleet departs every 15 or 20 minutes Monday to Friday (every 30 minutes Saturday and Sunday) from 6am to 7pm, and about once an hour otherwise. It's a crapshoot, but the best ferries are the 'old' ones (dating from 1965), which have wooden benches and bigger outside decks. Try not to go during rush hour.

The ferries make 103 trips a day, and accidents are very rare. But there has been a handful in the past 25 years, capping on October 15, 2003, when, on a day of high winds, the ferry slammed into the St George pier, killing 10 and injuring dozens. The cause is still undetermined.

GREENBELT

☎ 718-667-2165; www.sigreenbelt.org; 200 Nevada Ave
In the heart of Staten Island, the 2800-acre Greenbelt – and its 32 miles of trails for hiking – crosses five ecosystems, including swamps and freshwater wetlands (bring bug spray). There are some easy and tougher hikes here (Staten Island has the highest elevation on the Atlantic seaboard south of Maine). Birders can track 60 species of birds here.

Check the website for many access points, reached (sometimes by transfer) on public bus. One good place is at High Rock Park, a hardwood forest spot-cut by six trails. Take Bus S62 from the ferry terminal to Victory Blvd and Manner Rd, and transfer to the S54.

HISTORIC RICHMOND TOWN

☎ 718-351-1611; www.historicrichmondtown.org; 441 Clarke Ave; adult/child $5/3.50; ☺ 1-5pm Wed-Sun Sep-May, 10am-5pm Wed-Sat, 1-5pm Sun Jun-Aug; bus No S74 to Richmond Rd & St Patrick's Pl
About 30 buildings (some dating back to a 1695 Dutch community) stand in this 100-acre preservation project maintained by the Staten Island Historical Society, including the former county seat of the island. The most famous building, the two-story 300-year-old redwood **Voorlezer's House**, is the country's oldest school-house, now fully restored and decorated with period pieces. Some of the buildings have been moved from around the island here, but 10 stand on the original site.

Every hour, a guide conducts tours and during July and August, folks in period garb roam the grounds and describe 17th-century colonial life in the sticks.

Hours are sometimes extended in summer; call before you go. A visit could easily be combined with a bus ride to the nearby **Jacques Marchais Center of Tibetan Art** below.

The bus ride takes 40 minutes from the ferry terminal.

JACQUES MARCHAIS CENTER OF TIBETAN ART

☎ 718-987-3500; www.tibetanmuseum.com; 338 Lighthouse Ave; adult/student/child $5/3/2; ☺ 1-5pm Wed-Sun; bus No S74 to Lighthouse Ave
Home to the largest collection of Tibetan art outside China, the Jacques Marchais Center was opened by art dealer Edna Koblentz year before her death in 1947. In it are many authentic objects and an amazing Tibetan temple center, the setting for many year-round events.

To get to the center, ask the S74 bus driver to let you off at Lighthouse Ave. The museum sits at the top of a hill and offers pretty views over the island.

While you're up here, you can see a **Frank Lloyd Wright home** – the only home he built in New York City. The cliffside Crimson Beech home (48 Manor Ct, across Lighthouse Ave), now a private residence, was built in 1959.

SNUG HARBOR CULTURAL CENTER

☎ 718-448-2500; www.snug-harbor.org; 1000 Richmond Tce; bus No S40 to Snug Harbor
Situated in a 19th-century sailors' retirement complex only a few short feet from the water, the Snug Harbor Cultural Center is more like an Ivy League school. In the 83-acre area, some 28 buildings house the Snug Harbor Cultural Center (which opened in 1976), several other cultural organizations, and a few gardens.

From the bus stop, you'll see five side-by-side buildings (built between 1833 and 1880) marking the front of the complex. The buildings are columned and seriously Greek Revival. The center one, the Main Hall, houses the terrific **Newhouse Center for Contemporary Art** (adult/student & child $2/1; ☺ 10am-5pm Tue-Sun), which hosts unique modern shows (and don't miss the old ceiling mural). Next door are sticking-with-the-sea exhibits at the **Noble Maritime Collection** (adult/child $3/free; ☺ 1-5pm Thu-Sun).

Behind the front five buildings, you'll find the glasshouse of the **Staten Island Botanical Garden** (☎ 718-273-8200; www.sibg.org; admission free) and a maze behind it. Just west, the soothing **New York Chinese Scholar's Garden** (adult/child $5/4, free 10am-1pm Tue; ☺ 10am-4pm Tue-Sun), built in 1999, offers a walk through ancient-styled pavilions and teahouses (with waterfalls running through), recapturing a place where long-ago scholars escaped from 'misguided rulers.' It gets busiest in April and May when much of the plants bloom.

To the east, past the botanical garden, is a small, chilling World Trade Center exhibit, which has some dug-up artifacts like a fire-fighter's helmet.

From the bus stop, go around the first five buildings to the right to get to the visitor center. There are a couple cafés serving food.

Get here from the ferry by bus S40. You can make the (rather grim) walk here along Richmond Tce in about 20 minutes.

Neighborhoods – Outer Boroughs

Walking Tours

Walking Tours

You can only know New York from its sidewalks. Make time to walk as much of the busy Midtown avenues, Downtown nooks and riverside trails as you can. You'll see what you can't see from the back of a blazing taxi (or subway car): 19th-century dates marking brownstone facades, storekeepers chatting over a smoke, historical plaques or secondary street names, sometimes even smiles. Manhattan is almost entirely flat, and the boroughs only swell up a little. So no excuses. These eight walks take in a lot – fashion, jazz, rock 'n' roll, architecture, skyscrapers, art, food, nature.

LOWER MANHATTAN

Jaws of bumpkins and city slickers alike drop daily amidst the financial district's canyons of historic art deco and modern skyscrapers, which tower over tight, crooked lanes that still follow the 300-year-old Dutch plan. For any walker, Lower Manhattan is a marvel.

Go on a weekday when business is afoot. Aim to walk before or after lunch hour (noon to 2pm), when it can be hectic on the

Walk Facts

Start Bowling Green station (subway 4 & 5)
End Chambers St/Brooklyn Bridge–City Hall station (subway J, M, Z, 4, 5 & 6)
Distance 3 miles
Time 2 to 3 hours
Fuel stop Sophie's Restaurant (p172)

narrow sidewalks, as can morning and evening rush hours. Dusk is an excellent time to be there, as skyscrapers start to light up. Note that most buildings are closed to the public.

From the Bowling Green subway station, go south to Battery Park, along Manhattan's

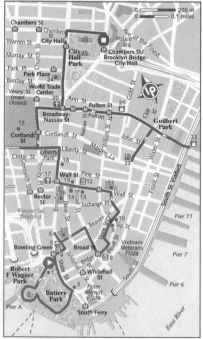

southern point. This is home to the **Sphere 1** (p80), a damaged sculpture that once stood in the World Trade Center plaza and now serves as a tribute to those lost in the attacks. Beyond stands **Castle Clinton 2** (p79), a fort built in 1811 to protect the city from the British. The only action it saw, however, came afterward as a domed concert hall and pre–Ellis Island immigration station. These days, it's home to the ticket office for the Statue of Liberty Ferry.

Walk east along the water (note fellow fort Castle Williams on Governor's Island to the southeast), then north to State St. The red-and-white **James Watson House 3** (1792) at 7–8 State St is the sole survivor of the Georgian mansions that once lined the street. This one is now the Shrine of the Blessed Elizabeth Seton, who once lived here.

Walk north on State St to the giant Custom House (1907) for a visit to the worthy **National Museum of the American Indian 4** (p77). Note the Works Progress Administration (WPA) murals from the 1930s inside. Out front is wee **Bowling Green 5** (p76), the city's oldest park (dating from 1733). The surrounding fence is original, though its original centerpiece (a bust of King George III) as well as many fence-post spires were melted down to make Revolutionary War bullets.

Charging Bull sculpture (p76)

At the park's north edge, the popular 1989 **Charging Bull sculpture 6** (p76) faces the country's longest avenue, Broadway. Across Broadway to the east stands the curving **Standard Oil Building 7** (26 Broadway), funded by John D Rockefeller's many dollars in 1922 and now home to the Museum of American Financial History (28 Broadway); you'll have to step back to see the setback top 27 stories with Greek temple–top.

Many Lower Manhattan street names link to history. Walk northeast on Beaver St (where pelts once were traded) to Broad St (unusually wide, as it was once a Dutch canal), then right to Pearl St (where Canarsie Indians once dug for clams and pearls). At Broad and Pearl Sts, visit the **Fraunces Tavern Museum 8** (p76; 54 Pearl St).

Go north on Pearl St, turn left on Coenties Alley to Stone St, the city's first cobbled lane, now home to several restaurants and pubs. At the block's north end, **India House 9** (1 Hanover Sq) is a pre–Civil War brownstone once home to the Cotton Exchange. Cross **Hanover Square 10** (former neighborhood of pirate Billy the Kid...arrrghhh!...), head left on winding Hanover Place, and follow Wall St (named for a long-gone wall that slaves of the Dutch made to protect New Amsterdam's northern border).

Turn left on Wall St. Across the street, note the green-topped **40 Wall St 11** (formerly the Bank of Manhattan, now owned by Donald Trump); in 1929 it battled the Chrysler Building for the honor of world's tallest building, but lost due to the Chrysler's surprise spire addition. A block further, a larger-than-life statue of George Washington stands atop the steps of the Doric **Federal Hall 12** (p76), the site where Washington took his presidential oath and the country's first Congress met. There's a free exhibit inside.

Across the street is the unassuming, unmarked, four-story **Morgan Guaranty Trust 13** (23 Wall St); its size made a serious anti-statement when it appeared in 1913 amidst the my-skyscraper-can-beat-up-your-skyscraper era. Only enter if you have millions to start an account. Just west is the **Stock Exchange 14** (p77), accessed from 20 Broad St. Back on Wall St, try to see the top of art deco **14 Wall St 15**, based on the Mausoleum of Halicarnassus (there are good views of this from the Staten Island Ferry). Continue west on Wall St to Broadway, noting the blazing red-and-gold mosaic entry of the **Bank of New York 16** (1 Wall St).

Impressively watching over Wall St is **Trinity Church 17** (p77), across Broadway, which dates from 1842. Of note in the church's cemetery is Alexander Hamilton, the face on the $10 bill, who lost his life in a duel to then vice president Aaron Burr in 1804. He's best known as former Secretary of Treasury.

North on Broadway, note the 41-story **Equitable Building 18** (120 Broadway). When it opened in 1915, its unapologetic hulking mass (1.2 million sq ft) prompted 1916 zoning laws, requiring building setbacks.

A block north, turn left at Liberty Plaza, where the sudden open space of the massive **World Trade Center site 19** (p81) can be seen. Posted signs along Liberty St straight ahead, and Church St to the right, tell the tale of its construction and other key buildings in the area. There's also an observation deck accessed from Liberty St, which leads to the modern World Financial Center across West St.

To the northeast of the site, at Church and Fulton Sts, the schist-and-brownstone **St Paul's Chapel 20** (p81), modeled after London's St-Martin-in-the-Fields, is the city's only pre–Revolutionary War building still standing. It houses an exhibit (☯ 10am-6pm Mon-Sat, 9am-4pm Sun) on the rescue efforts of September 11.

If food or shopping beckons, cross Broadway and continue east on Fulton St. Book-browse at the **Strand 21** (p257), at the corner of Gold St, or grab a Cuban sandwich at **Sophie's Restaurant 22** (p172). Continue on to the touristy but historic **South Street Seaport 23** (p81), with restaurants, shops and views of the Brooklyn Bridge.

Retrace your steps to Broadway and head north. At 792ft, the 60-story **Woolworth Building 24** (233 Broadway) was the world's tallest from 1913 to 1930, when the Chrysler nicked the title. Frank Woolworth, head of the nickel-and-dime chain, reputedly paid the $13.5 million construction costs in coins; note the gargoyle of Woolworth counting his change in the lobby.

Facing the building to the northeast is triangular City Hall Park, home to **City Hall 25** (p78) and, just behind, the recently restored **Tweed Courthouse 26** (52 Chambers St). The courthouse is a monument to late-19th-century corruption. An estimated $10 million of a $14 million budget ended up in the pockets of the scheming Mr Tweed. The final cost was twice what the US paid for Alaska Territory ($6.5 million) at around the same time. (It's not open to the public.)

From here, catch the subway to your next destination, walk a few blocks northeast to Chinatown for lunch or dinner, or walk across the **Brooklyn Bridge** (p166).

IMMIGRANTS' NEW YORK

This walk – through the Lower East Side (LES), Little Italy and Chinatown – covers some of the city's (and country's) most significant immigrant neighborhoods. In the past couple of centuries, millions of new arrivals (from places such as Ireland, Italy, Eastern Europe, China, Taiwan, Vietnam and the Dominican Republic) have called these blocks their first American home. And still do. These days, you're as likely to see a sign in Chinese, Vietnamese, Hebrew or Spanish as in English. Any day's fine for a walk here. Things are pretty busy on Chinatown sidewalks, particularly Canal St.

From the Delancey St–Essex St station (in the LES), walk west (away from the messy Williamsburg Bridge entry) a couple blocks, and turn left on Orchard St. This area, one of the world's most densely populated neighborhoods in the early 1900s, once was the center of Manhattan's Jewish garment industry (and home to composer Irving Berlin). Recent gentrification has inspired the makeover of many original tenements; take an hour-long tour of the real deal at **Lower East Side Tenement Museum 1** (p89).

A couple blocks south, turn left on Grand St (you'll see towering co-ops ahead). Go straight, past Essex St, and stop at **Kossar's 2** (p179) for the city's best 50¢ hot bialy (a bialy is the kid sister of the bagel, and one that never made much of a bang outside the LES).

Looking east along Essex St, you can see the redbrick **St Mary's Church 3** (Grand & Ridge Sts), on the left three blocks ahead; it's the city's oldest Catholic church, and in recent years added Spanish services for the local Dominican and Puerto Rican communities.

Return to Essex St and turn left. Along this strip, you'll see a number of rabbi-run Judaica shops selling new and antique items from Israel. A block south on the left is **WH Seward Park 4**, which was built in 1901 after the three blocks of the LES's most-crowded tenement houses were knocked down. In the years to come, unionized garment workers rallied here for better work conditions.

Along the park's southeastern edge is East Broadway, home to a few important sites for Jewish immigrants of the early 1900s. The **Forward Building 5** (175 E Broadway), towering over its neighbors, was home to a popular socialist-but-funny Yiddish daily. A block down, the orange-brick **Educational Alliance building 6** (197 E Broadway) once gave free English lessons to newly arrived Jews. Further down, the **Young Israel Synagogue 7** (225 E Broadway) began the modern 'Young Israel' movement in 1922, in which men shaved their beards and tried to Americanize.

Head back up East Broadway, noting the views of the Woolworth Building, behind the gold-topped Municipal Building (near where the tour ends).

Turn right on Essex St to Hester St and turn left. The next two blocks were the site of the (sarcastically named) '**Pig Market' 8** (btwn Essex & Orchard Sts), a Jewish-run market of street carts and shops that sold everything *but* pork.

Head straight on Hester St a few blocks to **Sarah D Roosevelt Parkway 9**, a seven-block park that was created in the 1930s by knocking down tenements. Walk north along the park to Grand St (where Chinatown begins its embrace), and bear left a few blocks to the Bowery.

Walk Facts

Start Delancey St–Essex St station (subway F, J, M & Z)
End Chambers St/Brooklyn Bridge–City Hall station (subway J, M, Z, 4, 5 & 6)
Distance 2.75 miles
Time 2 to 3 hours
Fuel Stops Sweet-n-Tart (p176), Mare Chiaro (p211)

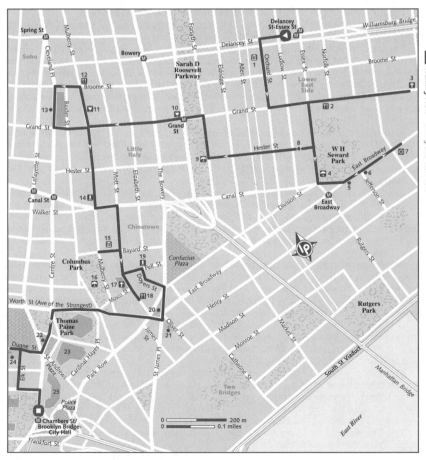

Walking Tours – Immigrants' New York

155

This long avenue was named by the Dutch for their word for 'farm' as it linked wee New Amsterdam to the farms in present-day East Village. In the early 1900s, the Bowery (then lined with rough bars and flophouses) was the de facto border between Jewish LES and Little Italy. Jewish gangster Meyer Lansky helped organize rival gangs on both sides.

Note the 1890 **Bowery Bank Building 10** (230 Grand St), just across the Bowery (now home to Capitale nightclub). Ahead on Grand St, turn right on Mulberry St, Little Italy's chief strip, all of one block long. Stop in for a gin and tonic at Frank Sinatra's old favorite drinking place **Mare Chiaro 11**(p211). In 1972, gangster Joey Gallo was gunned down at **Umberto's Clam House 12** (☎ 212-431-7545; 386 Broome St; previously at Mulberry & Hester Sts) when, as Bob Dylan sings in his 1975 song 'Joey,' he was 'picking up his fork.' A block west on Broome St, walk around the striking Renaissance-style 1909 **Police Headquarters Building 13** (240 Centre St), which became a luxurious apartment building in 1988.

Return on Grand St to Mulberry St and turn right, to trattorias, shops and red-white-and-green fire hydrants that mark Little Italy. A block or so down on the right, note the **Shrine of San Genarro 14** (109 Mulberry), which sponsors the famed namesake festival in September (p12).

On roaring Canal St, Chinatown returns with a boom. Cross Canal St, turn left a block to Mott St (the Chinatown version of Mulberry St), then right, where you'll see side-by-side gift shops and noodle houses.

Detour on Bayard St to visit the **Museum of Chinese in the Americas 15** (p86).

Facing the museum is one of New York's most intriguing public spaces, **Columbus Park 16** (p86). On nice days, you can see locals gently waking up with tai chi moves; wizened old geezers crouched over a game of mah-jongg (while onlookers place their bets); pet birds, brought to the park by their owners, whistling from their bamboo cages; and kids dribbling balls on the basketball courts. It was once a far different tale, when this was tough Irish turf in the early 1800s. At the time, this was a pond and reservoir for unwanted blood-and-guts from area butchers. When its stench became overpowering, its contents were removed by a canal, built for the purpose and now known as Canal St. (See also Five Points, later.)

Return to Mott St and turn right. Ahead, on the right, you'll see the **Church of the Transfiguration 17** (29 Mott St), a one-time Episcopal church (dating from 1801) that was transformed into a Catholic church in 1827 to attend to the needs of local Irish and Italian immigrants. These days services are also in Mandarin and Cantonese. If you're hungry, get a dumpling or two at **Sweet-n-Tart 18** (p176).

Head back up Mott St a few steps, and turn right on Pell St. Above the **Vegetarian Dim Sum House** (24 Pell St; p176) you'll see the red-and-green facade of Chinatown's last **wooden pagoda 19**.

Turn right on crooked Doyers St and proceed to **Chatham Square 20**, where 10 streets meet. From the square, bear right onto St James Pl, where on your left – edged behind a few buildings – is **First Shearith Israel Graveyard 21**, the USA's oldest Jewish cemetery (dating from the 1680s).

Retrace your steps to Chatham Square, and cross to Worth St and continue west till you reach the southern edge of Columbus Park. This point marks the (largely untraceable) center of the debauched Irish slum Five Points (as depicted in the Martin Scorsese film *Gangs of New York*, p87). Also in the area was Cow Bay, the largest neighborhood of freed African Americans in the early 19th century.

Go west on Worth St, past the New York County Courthouse, to Centre St and turn left to **Foley Square 22**, where a giant monument pays tribute to American slaves. Across Centre St from the square, note the **US Courthouse 23** (40 Centre St), where many high-profile trials are held (including Martha Stewart's in 2004).

Two blocks west of Centre St, along Duane St, the fenced-in plot of grass is the site of an **African Burial Ground 24** (p76), a cemetery for the city's early black residents (most of whom were slaves). Remains were found (over 400 bodies in all) in 1991 as construction crews began clearing the area for an impending project. Following much protest, construction ceased and the ground was declared a National Historic Site.

The Chambers St/Brooklyn Bridge–City Hall subway stations are two blocks south, just across from the **Municipal Building 25** (p78).

GREENWICH VILLAGE

Radicals, bohemians, poets, folk singers, rockers, freedom-seeking gays and lesbians – Greenwich Village has long been a hotbed for the alternative. A walk on these streets is not only gorgeous – it's Manhattan's most unruly street grid, with tight nooks winding and crisscrossing, very London-like – but historical. At weekends, sidewalks can feel like a bumper-car race with out-of-towners taking over (no offense, folks). If you want more elbow room, shoot for a weekday.

Walk Facts

Start Washington Sq Park (subway A, B, C, D, E, F, V to W 4 St)
End Washington Sq Park
Distance 2 miles
Time 1½ hours
Fuel Stops Chumley's (p215), John's Famous Pizzeria (p181)

The best place to start any tour of the village is the arch at **Washington Square Park 1** (p94), where, in the 1989 film *When Harry Met Sally*, the duo split after a road trip to New York and 'Mr Gigolo' David Lee Roth got busted for buying pot in 1993.

Head south across the park toward the tower of the ornate 1892 Greco-Romanesque **Judson Memorial Church 2** (p94), and continue south on Thompson St. Stop for a $1 game of chess – with some serious chess players – at **Village Chess Shop 3** (p269). Continue on to Bleecker St – a busy shop-filled street that cuts through most of the neighborhood – and go a block west to MacDougal St.

Across Minetta Lane is **Cafe Wha? 4** (☎ 212-254-3706; 115 MacDougal St), a past-its-prime music venue where Bob Dylan played early shows in 1961 (his song *Talkin' New York* re-tells the tale: 'you sound like a hillbilly, we want folk singers here') and Jimi Hendrix got 'discovered' in 1966.

Another block up, the three buildings at **127–131 MacDougal 5** became a HQ for the lesbian scene in the 1920s – probably not what original owner, dueling politician Aaron Burr, had in mind when he built it in 1829.

Retrace your steps to Minetta Lane and turn right and weave to the left along Minetta St. Quaint now, this was a big-time slum in the 18th century.

Cross Sixth Ave, toward the small, pigeon-filled square, perhaps stopping for a hot slice at **John's Famous Pizzeria 6** (p181), and walk up Bleecker St, past a three-block stretch of record stores and pastry shops. Cross Seventh Ave and make a quick right onto quiet Commerce St. In these alleys are some historic gems that conjure lottery-winning fantasies (and historic plaques are prolific – seemingly every four or five addresses). You may recognize some streets from various Woody Allen films.

Walking Tours – Greenwich Village

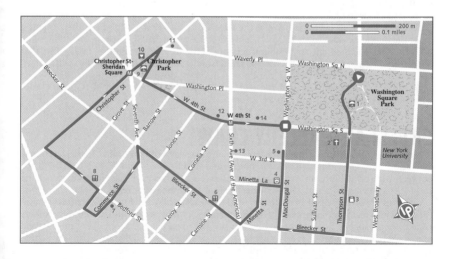

Ahead, at the corner of Commerce and Bedford Sts, you'll be standing a few yards from **75½ Bedford St 7**, a tighten-up-the-belt-to-enter 9.5ft-wide house where Cary Grant, John Barrymore and Pulitzer Prize–winning poet Edna St Vincent Millay lived over the years. Continue straight, winding (with Commerce St), then turn right on Barrow St, and left onto Bedford St.

Just on your right, the spare wooden door under an air-conditioning unit instead of a sign, is **Chumley's 8** (p215), the site of a prohibition-dodging socialist-run speakeasy. Its address (86 Bedford St) is said to have inspired the saying '86 it' – a shorthand imperative to get rid of something. When a police raid came, surely many a customer 86'ed their precious drink before rushing out the side exit (and onto Barrow St) to escape capture. Chumley's still serves meals and drinks.

Ramble on until Bedford St ends and turn right onto Christopher St, the lifeblood strip of the neighborhood's famed gay scene. Two blocks further, past more than a handful of sex shops, cross Seventh Ave to **Christopher Park 9**, where lifelike statues of two same-sex couples stand (*Gay Liberation*, 1992). Watching over the scene is a statue for Philip Sheridan, a 19th-century general who uttered the infamous phrase, 'the only good Indian is a dead Indian.' Facing it to the north, Christopher St is known as Stonewall Pl, and is the site of the 1969 gay rebellion (p67). **Stonewall Bar 10** (p216) is mid-block.

A block east – surrounded by the collision of Christopher and Grove Sts with (get this) Waverly Pl *and* Waverly Pl – stands the three-sided **Northern Dispensary 11** (165 Waverly Pl), built to fight cholera in 1831. It remained a health facility until 1989, when it closed.

Back toward the park, turn left onto W 4th St and gaze ahead. This is the stretch where Bob Dylan strolled with his gal for his album cover of *The Freewheelin' Bob Dylan*

Cafe Wha? (p157)

in 1963. His song 'Positively W 4th St' is a bitter recount of the times. He lived for four years at **161 W 4th St 12**.

Freewheel yourself over Sixth Ave. If the weather's nice, see if a dunking contest is going on at the public **basketball courts 13** (p94), a block south on W 3rd St. Back on W 4th St, radical John Reed churned out his firsthand account of the Russian Revolution in *The Day that Shook the World* in 1918 at **147 W 4th St 14**. This claim to fame, and his friendship with Lenin, helped him get entombed in the Kremlin wall upon his death from typhus in 1920.

Ahead is Washington Square Park, and another chance to reflect on Mr Gigolo's woes with weed. Sometimes all you can do is jump.

CHELSEA'S GALLERY CRAWL

It's said that works by tomorrow's masters are hung in today's galleries, and Chelsea has nearly 200 (and counting). Housed in old warehouses and storefronts – from W 20th to W 29th Sts, between Ninth and Eleventh Aves – most of Chelsea's galleries have been here only since the early 1990s when artists and gallery owners moved from the rising rents in Soho.

Galleries are usually open 10am to 6pm Tuesday to Saturday. All but a few are free to enter (don't go into residences marked 'this is not a gallery'). Many are on the ground floor; others tucked up on higher floors, accessed by elevator. Exhibits change about every month, and you're likely to find a bit of everything: daredevil cutting-edge installations, chin-scratching videos and sculpture, and more standard impressionistic paintings. For a complete list, grab a copy of *Chelsea Art* or the *New York Art World*, available for free at most galleries.

From W 23rd St, start at the infamous **Hotel Chelsea 1** (aka Chelsea Hotel; p296) for a look at the lobby. If it inspires the need for grilled meat, cross 23rd St for a hot dog at **F&B 2** (p185). Head west, turning left on Eighth Ave to 22nd St and the leafy, residential **Chelsea Historic District** (p97), from W 22nd to W 20th Sts, between Eighth and Tenth Aves. Turn right on W 22nd St, left at Ninth Ave and right onto W 21st St. Half a block south, go into the **General Theological Seminary 3** (p97), which has a garden popular for midday picnics.

Walk Facts

Start 23rd St station (subway C, E, 1 & 2)
End 23rd St station (subway C, E, 1 & 2)
Distance 2½ miles
Time 3 to 5 hours
Fuel Stops Empire Diner (p184), F&B (p185)

The art begins west on 21st St, past Tenth Ave. Peek into the well-established **Paula Cooper Gallery 4** (☎ 212-255-1105; 534 W 23 St; admission free; 🕑 10am-5pm Tue-Sat), which has another space across the street at 521 W 23 St. Just a few doors down, **Eyebeam 5** (☎ 212-252-5193; 540 W 21st St; www.eyebeam.org; admission free; 🕑 noon-6pm Wed-Sat) is a more experimental studio (gallery and school) often featuring videos of its students in a dark brick-wall space.

At the end of the block, across West End Ave (Eleventh Ave), you'll see the sprawling **Chelsea Piers 6** (p97), a sports complex along the Hudson River. North on West End Ave (Eleventh Ave), turn onto Chelsea's most popular gallery strip, W 22nd St (home to a dozen or so galleries). On the corner to your right is the **Chelsea Art Museum 7** (CAM; ☎ 212-255-0719; www.chelseaartmuseum.org; 556 W 22nd St; adult $5, student & senior $2; 🕑 noon-6pm Tue, Wed, Fri & Sat, noon-8pm Thu), which opened in 2002.

Head east on the block. On your right, see what's on at the long-time Soho staple, **Sonnabend 8** (☎ 212-627-1018; 536 W 22nd St; admission free; 🕑 10am-6pm Tue-Sat) and, just beyond, **Brent Sikkema 9** (☎ 212-929-2262; www.brentsikkima.com; 530 W 22nd St; admission free; 🕑 10am-6pm Tue-Sat) – both behind frosted glass and seemingly the ideal setting for a gallery spoof in a Woody Allen film.

Cross the street to browse art books at the nonprofit bookstore **Printed Matter Inc 10** (p271). Poke into a couple galleries just east, including **Max Protech 11** (☎ 212-633-6999; www.maxprotetch.com; 511 W 22nd St; admission free; 🕑 10am-6pm Tue-Sat). Even if you're not shopping, peek at **Comme des Garçons 12** (p270), a hip-luxe clothing shop with a jarring entrance. The bridge running over 22nd St (and many area streets) is a closed train line (note the weeds). Often art billboards, not ads, hang from it.

At the end of the block, turn left on Tenth Ave, perhaps stopping at **Empire Diner 13** (p184) for a snack. At the northeast corner of W 23rd St and Tenth Ave, note the mammoth **London Terrace Gardens 14** (1928), a ritzy art deco residence occupying an entire block.

Walking Tours – Chelsea's Gallery Crawl

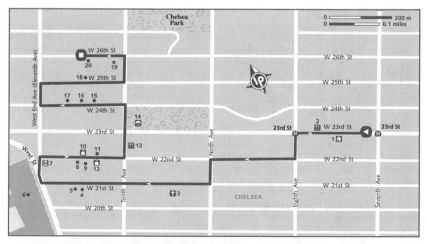

159

Head north and snake your way around the blocks to the north. Turn left on W 24th St. On the right-hand side of the street, see what's happening at a few risk-taking galleries, including **Metro Pictures 15** (☎ 212-206-7100; 519 W 24th St; admission free; ◷ 10am-6pm Tue-Sat). Further on, stop into **Luhring Augustine 16** (☎ 212-206-9100; www.luhringaugustine. com; 531 W 24th St; admission free; ◷ 10am-6pm Tue-Sat) – often showing large-format photography – and **Mary Boone Gallery 17** (☎ 212-752-2929; www.maryboonegallery.com; 541 W 24th St; admission free; ◷ 10am-6pm Tue-Sat).

A block north, on 25th St, stop by **Cheim & Read 18** (☎ 212-242-7727; www.cheimread.com; 547 W 25th St; admission free; ◷ 10am-6pm Tue-Sat). At W 26th St, you'll find a few smaller, edgier galleries, such as **Lucas Shoormans 19** (☎ 212-243-3159; 508 W 26th St; admission free; ◷ 10am-6pm Tue-Sat) on the 11th floor. A couple of posher ones (geared to sell) are down the block, including **Robert Miller 20** (☎ 212-366-4774; www.robertmillergallery.com; 524 W 26th St; admission free; ◷ 10am-6pm Tue-Sat), a former uptown institution that relocated here.

From here, retrace your steps to the 23rd St station, head south on Tenth Ave to the Chelsea Market (p96) in the Meatpacking District, and on to Greenwich Village for dinner.

SHOPPING ON FIFTH & MADISON AVES

Some of Manhattan's best, most famous (and most expensive) shopping can be found on Fifth Ave in Midtown and Madison Ave, extending far into the Upper East Side. Hundreds of shops, big and small, line these streets in sleek spaces intended to back up their clothing. This tour takes in some of the shopping highlights (and a few diversions to help re-energize the shopping maniac deep inside). Big windows invite peeps: see what grabs you.

Note that most stores here are open daily, and that most keep longer hours on Thursday nights.

From Rockefeller Center, exit to Sixth Ave (Avenue of the Americas) and walk east along W 47th St before turning left at Fifth Ave. This block is the **Diamond District 1** (p272), home to over 2000 diamond businesses and some 100 shops (traditionally run by Hassidic Jews). Packed amidst the jewelry is the historic **Gotham Book Mart 2** (p272).

At Fifth Ave, head north one block to **Rockefeller Center 3** (p115), with the towering GE Building (previously the RCA Building) standing behind the sunken Lower Garden, with the gold-leaf statue of Prometheus, and the famous ice rink open in winter. Before crossing Fifth Ave, go up a block, between W 50th and W 51st Sts, to admire the art deco **Atlas statue 4** in front of the International Building.

Across Fifth Ave, the flagship store for **Saks Fifth Avenue 5** (p274), on E 50th St, faces **St Patrick's Cathedral 6** (p116). Both are champs amidst many Midtown winners. After a look at both, walk east on E 50th St, past Madison Ave, to the **Villiard Houses 7** (451-455 Madison Ave, btwn 50th & 51st Sts), six Renaissance-style row houses, and home to Urban Center Books (p283), where you can thumb through architectural tomes.

On E 51st St, turn left (west) and cross Madison Ave, stopping off (as *Sex and the City*'s Carrie did) at **Jimmy Choo 8** (p273) for its top-shelf shoe selection. If you're ready to eat, the classic New York diner **Prime Burger** (☎ 212-759-4729; 5 E 51st St; burgers $3.50; ◷ 6am-7pm Mon-Fri, 7am-5pm Sat) is on this block.

Head back to Fifth Ave and turn right – Central Park's southeastern tip can be seen blocks ahead. A street north (on the corner of E 52nd St, known as 'Place de Cartier') is **Cartier 9** (p272), home to the French company's luxurious jewelry. Head up Fifth Ave to E 53rd St, and turn right. Mid-block, you'll find a five-piece fragment of the **Berlin Wall 10** (520 E 53rd St).

Return to Fifth Ave and turn right. Stay on the right-hand side of Fifth Ave past E 54th St, stop (at least for a green tea) at **Takashimaya 11** (p283), on the right-hand side past E 54th St.

Cross Fifth Ave, continue north and try on the glamorous offerings at the inviting store **Henri Bendel 12** (p273). A block north is where Audrey Hepburn ate her croissant, at **Tiffany & Co 13** (p283), E 57th St. Note the Atlas-supported clock above the door – a Tiffany trademark. One block up, on both sides of Fifth Ave, **Bergdorf Goodman 14** (p271) is a powerhouse store for Manhattan's formal wear. Men's stuff is on the right-hand side of Fifth, women's collections are on the left.

Across E 58th St, facing Central Park, is **FAO Schwartz 15** (p272), the king of toy stores that came upon tough financial times in early 2004 (at the time of writing it was closed for renovations).

Return to E 57th St, turn left – perhaps stopping to see what shoes **Prada 16** (p274) is displaying – and continue east to Park Ave. Several blocks to the right, you'll see the MetLife Building (near Grand Central Terminal). One block to the south, on the right, you can see a **Mercedes Benz dealership 17** (cnr Park Ave & E 56th St), designed by Frank Lloyd Wright. (Frank did car shops too.)

Turn back and proceed north on Park Ave to E58th St and turn left for a quick drink at **Tao 18** (p219), then turn north to E 59th St and turn right. Here, where the Upper East Side begins, peek at the high-end used bookstore **Argosy 19** (p271) to see what rare autographed books are available, then continue to Lexington Ave, where you'll find the famous **Bloomingdale's 20** (p286), where your purchases come in the trademark 'brown bag.'

Those seeking budget deals should go half a block north on Lexington Ave to **Tatiana's 21** (p287), across E 60th St.

Head west to Madison Ave, along E 60th St, to **Barneys 22** (p285), the most cutting-edge of Manhattan's luxe department stores. From here, looking up Madison Ave (New York's skinniest avenue), you'll see generally smaller boutiques than in Midtown. Every block to E 72nd St or so has at least a few shops that are worth checking out.

Across E 61st St (across Madison Ave), **Sherry-Lehman 23** (p287) is one of Manhattan's best places to pick up bottles of spirits. At the corner of E 64th St, stop in at **Givenchy 24** (p286) for formal French wear. At E 64th St, detour west towards Fifth Ave, which is residential here along the eastern edge of Central Park. The shopped-out can seep energy from the (real) critters at **Central Park Zoo & Wildlife Center 25** (p119) or from (bronze) critters atop the musical **Delacorte Clock 26** (p162) above the walkway.

Head back to Madison Ave and turn left. **Valentino 27** (p288) stocks his Oscar-worthy evening wear on the corner of E 65th St. One corner north (and across Madison Ave) is the four-floor store of **Giorgio Armani 28** (p286). Between E 68th and E 69th Sts are boutiques for **Versace 29** (☎ 212-744-6868; 815 Madison Ave; ⏰ 10am-6pm Mon-Sat), **Donna Karan 30** (☎ 212-861-1001; 819 Madison Ave; ⏰ 10am-6pm Mon-Wed, Fri & Sat, 10am-7pm Thu) and **Dolce & Gabbana 31** (p286), which are all on the east side of Madison Ave. One block north you'll arrive at **Gucci 32** (☎ 212-717-2619; 840 Madison Ave; ⏰ 10am-6pm Mon-Wed, Fri & Sat, 10am-7pm Thu, noon-5pm Sun) and **Prada 33** (p287).

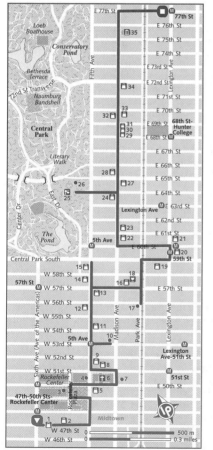

Walk Facts

Start 47th–50th Sts–Rockefeller Center station (subway B, D, F & V)
End 77th St station (subway 6)
Distance 3 miles
Time 2 hours (window shop) to 5 or 6 hours
Fuel Stop Tao (p219)

Shops start to tailor off around E 72nd St, at the corner of which **Ralph Lauren 34** (p287) occupies a 19th-century mansion, a rare remnant of when Madison Ave was home to homes not retailers.

Continue north on Madison Ave to see what art's on at the unmistakable **Whitney Museum of American Art 35** (p125) – cheapies can time their walk to arrive on pay-what-you-wish Friday evenings.

From here you can go up to E 77th St and right two blocks to the 77th St station at Lexington Ave. Alternatively, continue on to the **Metropolitan Museum of Art** (p123) or, after spending so much green, try soaking in some at **Central Park** (p118).

CENTRAL PARK

People come to this 843-acre park for sheer recreational pleasure; unlike other streets of Downtown Manhattan, Central Park Dr, a 6-mile loop road, has a lane for cyclists, skaters and runners. Central Park Dr is closed to traffic from 10am to 3pm and 7pm to 10pm Monday to Thursday, and from 7pm on Friday to 6am Monday, which offers your ears a break from Manhattan's ubiquitous noise pollution.

You can't really get lost in Central Park, except in the Ramble, but you should note that a wall encircles the entire park and you can only get in through designated 'gates' – breaks in the wall every five blocks or so.

A good walk in the park begins at the Columbus Circle entrance, at the park's southwest corner. If you're picnicking, fetch supplies at **Whole Foods** (p274) at Columbus Circle before going in. Pass through the Merchants' Gate and turn left on West Dr. On your left you'll see the **Umpire Rock 1**, which overlooks the Heckscher Ballfields to the north, the site of fun-to-watch softball league play in summer. Continue north on West Dr to **Sheep Meadow 2**, a wide green expanse that attracts sunbathers and Frisbee players (in good weather). This is a great place for a picnic amid stellar skyline views. A pathway leading to the right takes you along the south side of the meadow. Over the bridge to the right is an enclosed **carousel 3**, which boasts some of the largest hand-carved horses in the country ($1.25 a ride).

From the carousel walk east, through the tunnel, to the **Dairy 4**, which houses the park's visitor center (☎ 212-794-6564; www.centralparknyc.org; ☺ 10am-5pm Tue-Sun, 10am-4pm in winter), where you can pick up maps and information about park activities, and survey the gift shop.

From the Dairy, walk along East Dr south about 200m and then left to the **Central Park Zoo & Wildlife Center 5** (p119), a small zoo dating from the 1930s but still flaunting its 1980s makeover, which was designed to make the animals more comfortable. Zoo residents include a lazy polar bear and several sea lions, whose frequent feeding attracts squeals of delight from many a little one. Admission to the zoo includes entry to the **Tisch Children's Zoo 7**, a petting center for toddlers; you'll find it across 65th St from the main zoo. At the entrance, don't miss the **Delacorte Clock 6**, a timepiece festooned with dancing bears, monkeys and other similar furry friends, who spin and hammer out the time every 30 minutes on the half-hour.

After the children's zoo, walk north on the path that parallels East Dr, to a group of statues (including Christopher Columbus and William Shakespeare) that marks the beginning of **the Mall 8**, an elegant promenade lined with benches and a collection of 150 American elms, believed to be the largest surviving stand in the country.

At the north end of the Mall, you'll come to the **Naumburg Bandshell 9**. After years of disuse, the bandshell and the area immediately facing it are alive again with occasional performances and a DIY roller-disco. (Just behind is the Pergola wisteria-festooned walkway and the Rumsey Playfield, site of the wildly popular Central Park SummerStage series, p238.)

Continuing north of the bandshell and across the 72nd St Transverse brings you to **Bethesda Fountain 10**, a hippie hangout in the 1960s (nattily depicted in the film *Hair*, which has many scenes set in the park). The fountain, with its *Angel of the Waters* sculpture at the center, has been restored and ranks as one of Central Park's most uplifting sights.

Continue on the path west of the fountain until you reach **Bow Bridge** 11. Cross the bridge and enter **the Ramble** 12, a lush wooden expanse that serves as a decent bird-watching pocket. If you manage to emerge from the Ramble without being hopelessly turned around, continue north to the 79th St Transverse. Directly across the transverse, you'll come to the 19th-century **Belvedere Castle** 13, and you will enjoy excellent views of the **Delacorte Theater** 14 (p119; the site of Joseph Papp Public Theater's free Shakespeare productions, which are held in summer).

Walk Facts

Start 59th St–Columbus Circle station (subway A, B, C, D, 1 & 2)
End 72nd St station (subway B & C)
Distance 3.75 miles
Time 2 to 4 hours
Fuel Stops Whole Foods for picnic supplies (p274), Josie's (p198)

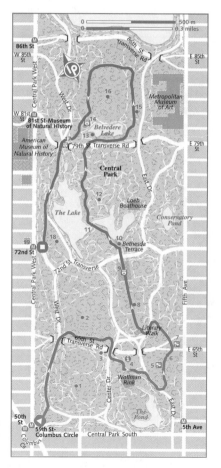

Walk east along the Turtle Pond and north to **Cleopatra's Needle** 15, an Egyptian obelisk dating from 1600 BC; facing it to the east is the massive Metropolitan Museum of Art. Just west is the grand (and appropriately named) **Great Lawn** 16 (p119), where some free concerts take place (including open-air shows by the New York Philharmonic and Metropolitan Opera in June and July). Rock concerts used to be staged here, but the lawn couldn't handle the audiences of 75,000, so these events have been banished to the North Meadow above 97th St.

Cut west across the lawn (or around it when it's closed during winter) and go south. Past the lawn, nearly to the 79th St Transverse, is the 19th-century **Swedish Cottage** 17, a sweet little chalet that is home to the **Marionette Theater** (☎ 212-988-9093; adult/child $6/5; ☺ performances 10:30am & noon Mon-Fri Jul & Aug, 10:30am & noon Tue-Fri & 1pm Sat Sep-Jun). Reservations are required for these well-attended shows.

Continuing to the W 72nd St park entrance brings you to legendary **Strawberry Fields** 18 (p119), the three-acre landscape dedicated to the memory of John Lennon; it contains plants from more than 100 nations and motley offerings from fans. This spot was frequently visited by the former Beatle, who resided in the **Dakota** 19 across the street, where he was fatally shot in 1980. The famished can top it all off a block west at **Josie's** (p198).

The 72nd St subway station is just across Central Park West.

Walking Tours – Central Park

HARLEM SHUFFLE

Harlem, the USA's most famous African-American neighborhood, has changed more in the past decade than any other part of New York City. This walking tour leads past once boarded-up buildings, many of which have been restored in recent years by an expansive 'Spruce-Up Project,' and new construction sights along 125th St,

Walk Facts

Start 135th St station (subway B & C)
End 125th St station (subway A, B, C & D)
Distance 2 miles
Time 2 to 3 hours
Fuel Stops Sylvia's (p201), Strictly Roots (p202)

where new retail complexes are rapidly overseeing the latest 'renaissance' of the neighborhood. It's not the first renaissance, as this tour goes past historic civil rights and jazz-era sites of decades past.

Any daytime hours are good to take the walk, though Harlem buzzes with more life at weekends, particularly Sunday, when you can take advantage of Sylvia's 'gospel brunch' (see p201).

From the 135th St station, make your way north on Edgecombe Ave to 138th St, and then turn right for a block to reach **Striver's Row** 1 (p132), on W 138th St and W 139th St,

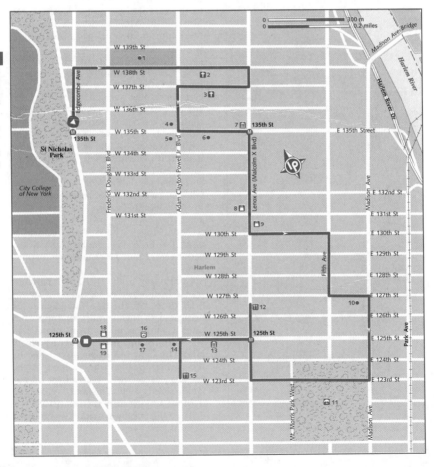

between Frederick Douglas Blvd and Adam Clayton Powell Jr Blvd. These two blocks of 1890s townhouses got their nickname in the 1920s, when aspiring African Americans first moved in here. Note the alley between the blocks is where trash was (and still is) collected.

A couple of nearby churches have been (and remain) big community players. West of Adam Clayton Powell Jr Blvd on 138th St, the **Abyssinian Baptist Church 2** (136–142 W 138th St) has its origins from 1808, when a Lower Manhattan church was formed by African Americans in response to segregated services. It moved here in 1920. Previous pastor (and namesake of the nearby boulevard) Adam Clayton Powell Jr became the first African-American congressman (1944 to 1970).

On the other side of the block, you'll see the city's oldest African-American church (originally in Lower Manhattan), the **Mother African Methodist Episcopal Zion Church 3** (140–146 W 137 St), which played an important role establishing the underground railroad in the mid-1800s.

Walk south on Adam Clayton Powell Jr Blvd to W 135th St, which was a very hopping corner from the 1920s to the 1940s. The northwest corner (now Teiz Supermarket) was the site of the **Big Apple Jazz Club 4**, sometimes credited for how New York got its nickname. The southwest corner was the site of **Ed Small's Paradise 5**, the 'hottest spot in Harlem' – management once fired a young waiter here named Malcolm Little (later known as Malcolm X). It's now an office building.

In those days (between the 1920s and 1940s), 125th St was the commercial heart of Harlem, but its shops were white-run. Not so here on 135th St, the first home for many just-arrived African Americans. The **Harlem YMCA 6** (☎ 212-630-9600; ymcanyc.org/harlem; 181 W 135th St), here since 1919, provided rooms for those denied a room in segregated hotels. Notable guests include James Baldwin, Jackie Robinson, Jesse Owens and (in the branch across the street) Malcolm Little. Go in to see the mural and find out what's happening in the independently run theater downstairs.

Head a block east and see the archives and photos at the **Schomburg Center for Research in Black Culture 7** (p129) to learn more about Harlem's past.

South on Lenox Ave (Malcolm X Blvd), browse at **Liberation Bookstore 8** (p289) or the **Scarf Lady 9** (p289), then pick your own route east – perhaps on 130th St, a row of 1880s brick homes built by William Astor – to Fifth Ave. Here quickly look north to see Yankee Stadium in the Bronx, where one-time Harlem resident Jackie Robinson and the Brooklyn Dodgers beat the Yanks in the 1955 World Series.

Go south on Fifth Ave and turn east on E 127th St, stopping to see the last **home of poet Langston Hughes 10** (20 E 127th St), who died in 1967. Walk east to Madison Ave and south to E 124th St to **Marcus Garvey Park 11**, named for the unique Jamaica-born founder of the 'Back to Africa' movement who lived in Harlem from 1916 to 1927. His speeches and newspaper *Negro World* sought to promote racial pride. Climb the park's central hill – where the city's last fire watchtower stands.

Leave the park, heading west to Lenox Ave (Malcolm X Blvd) and head back north to W 125th St, the main hub of Harlem activity (and site of Bill Clinton's offices; top floor of 55 W 125th St). If you're hungry, Harlem's most famous soul food is at **Sylvia's 12** (p201).

Walking west on 125th St, you'll come across a number of sites, as well as signs of Harlem's 'new renaissance' (department stores and chains); the famed street peddlers are a thing of the past. Stop at the **Studio Museum in Harlem 13** (p129), just across from the towering, rather out-of-place State Office Building (1973). The giant white building at the southwest corner of 125th St and Adam Clayton Powell Jr Blvd was once **Hotel Theresa 14**, sometimes known as the 'black Waldorf-Astoria.' Entertainers playing the nearby Apollo (such as Count Basie and Duke Ellington) stayed here. Fidel Castro insisted on staying here in 1960 and met with Malcolm X and Soviet Premier Nikita Khrushchev here. Get vegetarian meals at **Strictly Roots 15** (p202), situated a couple blocks south, before heading west on 125th St to the historic and famous **Apollo Theater 16** (p128), which hosts many performances, including the Wednesday Amateur's Night. Opposite the theater, you will notice the sign for **Blumstein's 17**, a (now closed) store that finally began hiring African-Americans following an eight-week boycott in 1934. Later on, the first black Santa appeared here.

Around the corner on Frederick Douglas Blvd, you gotta stop at 125th St's first African-American–run shop **Bobby's Happy House 18** (p288) to pick up a gospel or blues CD. While back on 125th St, **Harlem USA! 19** (p128) – a (controversial) complex of chain department stores and a theater owned by NBA great Magic Johnson – opened in 2000.

From here, take the 125th St subway, or walk further east to explore **Columbia University** (p130) or **Riverside Park** (p122).

(Note: *Harlem Shuffle* is a 1963 song by Los Angeles duo Bob & Earl.)

BROOKLYN: BRIDGE & BROWNSTONES

Many visitors skip Brooklyn, which is a shame, considering neighborhoods like Brooklyn Heights and Cobble Hill are considered by many to be 'what New York used to look like.' The area, just across the Brooklyn Bridge, is flat-out gorgeous, lined with pre–Civil War brownstones on shady (almost quiet) streets with views of the Manhattan skyline. Brooklyn Heights, actually, is New York's oldest neighborhood and was once home to literary figures who were escaping higher rents across the East River. These days it's a very fashionable address for those who can afford it.

It's best to venture to Brooklyn (particularly for your first time) on the Brooklyn Bridge, though some may wish to walk *back* to Manhattan for the better views. If so, pick up the tour from Brooklyn's Clark St station (1 & 2), then walk back.

From City Hall Park in Manhattan, walk across the East River on the **Brooklyn Bridge 1** (p79) pedestrian walkway (elevated over the traffic), looking back for views of Woolworth and Municipal Buildings.

After 25 minutes the walkway forks: bear right (going left heads to Dumbo; p137) and continue till the walkway's end (at the corner of Adams and Tillary Sts) and turn right on Tillary St. To your left, notice **Columbus Park 2** and (in the distance) the Brooklyn Borough Hall (see below). Head south (into Brooklyn Heights) on Clinton St to Pierrepont St, and go towards Manhattan a couple blocks and to the **Brooklyn Historical Society 3** (p136) to see photos of Brooklyn's past.

Head north and west a few blocks to Willow St and **Truman Capote's home 4** (70 Willow St, btwn Pineapple & Orange Sts), where he wrote books like *Breakfast at Tiffany's*.

A block west is the **Brooklyn Heights Promenade 5**, which overhangs the (out of sight) Brooklyn Queens Expressway (BQE) but has full-frontal views of Manhattan and the Hudson Bay.

Stroll south along the promenade to Montague St and turn left. One block east, turn left on Montague Terrace to see **Thomas Wolfe's home 6** (5 Montague Terrace), where he wrote *Of Time and the River*. Return to Montague St and bear left. This street (once Brooklyn's 'Bank Row') had trolleys roaring down it until the 1930s; pedestrians dodging the wrath of the trolley wheels prompted the name of the famed baseball team, Brooklyn Dodgers. These days Montague St is Brooklyn Heights' main strip of shops and cafes and a good place to grab a coffee, or browse in **Heights Books 7** (p290).

From Montague St, wind your way right on Henry St and left on Joralemon St to **133 Clinton St 8**, the former HQ for the Brooklyn Excelsiors, a champion baseball team credited for nationalizing the sport during the Civil War.

A block south, turn left on Schermerhorn St. Two blocks further (and into downtown Brooklyn) pop down into the **New York Transit Museum 9** (p136), housed in an old subway station. Afterwards, you can take a peek two blocks north at the **Brooklyn Borough Hall 10** (☎ 718-875-4047; 209 Joralemon St); there are free tours at 1pm Tuesday. (Or if your sweet-tooth is aching for, many say, the world's best cheesecake, detour eight blocks east to Junior's (p204).

Retrace your steps to Clinton St and go south to Atlantic Ave, the border between Brooklyn Heights and Cobble Hill. Between Court and Henry Sts on Atlantic are several Arabic restaurants and delis. Stop at **Damascus Bread & Pastry Shop 11** (☎ 718-625-7070; 195 Atlantic Ave; ☺ 7am-7pm) for a pastry or **Sahadi's 12** (☎ 718-624-4550; 187 Atlantic Ave; ☺ 9am-7pm Mon-Fri, 8:30am-7pm Sat) for various gourmet foods, including over 20 fresh choices at the olive bar.

Walk back to Court St, and south into Cobble Hill, an Italian neighborhood. Court St features a good mix of shops, pizza joints, bars and cafés, with brownstone residences on surrounding streets.

Turn right on Congress St (three blocks south) to see quiet **Cobble Hill Park** 13. Walk south along Clinton St eight blocks, into the Carroll Gardens neighborhood, stopping at the **Rankin Residence** 14 (cnr Clinton & Union Sts), an 1840 redbrick Greek Revival building, once the lone house in a farm (it's now a funeral home, alas).

Walk east on Carroll St two blocks to Smith St. Look right on Smith St a couple blocks (past the schoolyard, atop a small hill), where **Ft Box** 15 once stood. Nothing remains (there's a parking lot actually), but this is where General George Washington watched the disastrous

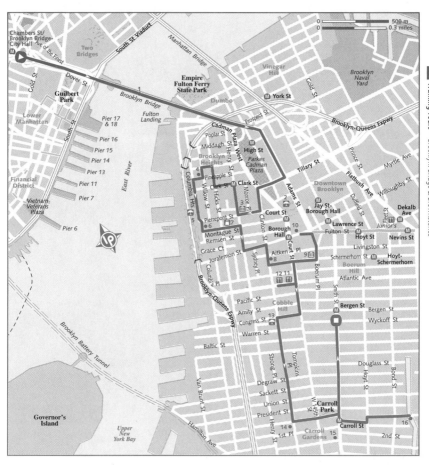

start of the Revolutionary War during the Battle of Long Island. If the gumption arises, detour over a couple more downtrodden blocks to the infamous **Gowanus Canal 16** (p137) via Carroll St. Back on Smith St, an up-and-coming strip of smart boutiques and French bistros (mostly between Sackett and Baltic Sts), head north before catching a subway back to Manhattan from Bergen St.

Alternatively, meander northward to Adams St, and return to Manhattan on foot.

Eating

Eating

Where do you start in a city that's home to nearly 13,000 restaurants, with new ones opening every single day of the year? We suggest you begin with whatever you're craving, because you'll find it – probably right down the street – and it's bound to be some of the best you've ever had. Whether it's a hot dog, tempeh reuben, plate of moules frites, heap of green-tea risotto or slab of foie gras you're hankering for, it's waiting for you, and then some. And don't settle for taste alone. Because the city's ambient eateries have enough rose-petal–strewn stairways, pressed-tin ceilings, top-notch jazz bands, mermaid-moored fish tanks, belly dancers, waterfalls, live DJs and passed hookah pipes to keep you entertained before, during and after your meal.

You'll find plenty to suit your fancy in this chapter – as well as from local sources including the listings of *New York Magazine*, Wednesday's Dining & Wine section of the *New York Times* and the fun-to-read but not wholly trustworthy *Zagat Survey*, a popular compendium of average-Joe opinions. Just listen to your stomach, pick a neighborhood and do your research. Then prepare for a true foodie's adventure.

Pastries, Greenwich Village

Takeout & To Go

For all the ambient locations, sometimes you just want to stuff your face with lo mein in the privacy of your room, with nothing but the TV to distract you. Other times you want to create your own stylized atmosphere, be it a picnic in Central Park or a packed lunch on the train to Long Island. That's nothing new in a city where folks can't stay still for long, and it's why virtually every place – from cheap Chinese storefronts to the most high-class dining rooms – offers not only takeout, but door-to-door delivery.

Opening Hours

Most places are open daily; those that do have days off usually close on Monday. Mealtimes for the varied schedules of New Yorkers are quite fluid, with restaurants complying: many diner-type spots serve breakfast all day or at least start as early as 3am, to accommodate club-goers who rely on stacks of pancakes to sober up. Loosely speaking, though, you can usually find breakfasts served till noon. Lunchtime overlaps a bit, often starting at 11:30am and ending at 4pm, and dinnertime is anywhere from 5pm or 6pm until 10pm during the week and about 11pm on weekends. That said, there are scores of eateries that serve until midnight, 1am or even 2am or 3am; many stay open round-the-clock. Prime time for dinner is between 8pm and 9pm. Brunch, usually limited to Sundays, is generally served from 11am until 3pm or 4pm.

How Much?

If you're on a super-strict budget – or if you have money burning a hole in your pocket – you've come to the right place. You can grab a falafel sandwich, hot dog, fresh fruit, curry, crepe or soup from street vendors (skip those tasty-smelling roasted nuts; they're never as good as they smell) for between $2 and $4, a slice of pizza for $1.50, or ethnic meals (Chinese, Middle Eastern, Indian, Turkish, Japanese, Korean, Vietnamese) for as cheap as $4 a plate. Mid-range restaurants charge about $17 on average per entree, while the most upscale spots in town have entrees for upwards of $35, or tasting menus for about $75 per person. A treat for foodies who lack expendable incomes is NYC and Company Restaurant Week, a 10-day stretch in winter and again in summer in which top-notch restaurants offer three-course lunch menus for $20 and dinner menus for $30.

Booking Tables

Most restaurants take reservations for lunch and/or dinner, although some do not accept them unless you have four or more in your party. For those places that refuse reservations altogether (eg **Blue Ribbon Brooklyn**, p203), expect rowdy waits that could last a half-hour or more. But hey, it's all part of the experience.

Tipping

Just as in the rest of the USA, you are expected to tip your server an average of 15% of your bill before tax. You can leave slightly less for poor service and slightly more (20% is the standard reward) if it's excellent. Some coffee bars have tip jars next to the register; these are optional, and best fed with a quarter or two.

LOWER MANHATTAN

While food is not so easy to find here after the workers have gone home, it's much improved in the past couple of years, with more upscale bistro-type spots taking root to serve the buttoned-up brokers, attorneys and politicians who gather in these parts. The lunch offerings are varied and usually on the cheap-and-quick side.

BRIDGE CAFÉ

Map pp380-1   *American Creative*
☎ 212-227-3344; 279 Water St at Dover St; entrees $15-18; ☽ lunch Mon-Fri, dinner Mon-Sat; subway 4, 5, 6 to Brooklyn Bridge–City Hall

Certified as the oldest pub in the city (the building dates from 1794). The restaurant, located underneath the Brooklyn Bridge, offers an extensive wine list and dressed-up standard American fare including pastas, seafood, roasted meats and a killer key lime pie. In spite of its old-world flavor – or because of it, perhaps – the historic dining room retains a romantic-hideaway vibe.

CABANA

Map pp380-1   *Nuevo Latino*
☎ 212-406-1155; 89 South St Seaport; entrees $13-20; ☽ lunch & dinner; subway 1, 2, 4, 5, J, M, Z to Fulton St–Broadway Nassau

This branch of the mini-chain (you'll find others on the Upper East Side and in Queens) is a fabulously flavorful addition to the mall-like Seaport staples. The fresh grub includes Cuban *ropa vieja* (dish of shredded beef and tomatoes), Jamaican jerk chicken, grilled seafood salad marinated in tangy citrus mojo, and thick slabs of *arepa con queso* (thick corn cakes topped with white cheese). The sweeping view of New York Harbor makes it worth the wait at this bustling haven.

LES HALLES

Map pp380-1   *French*
☎ 212-285-8585; 15 John St btwn Broadway & Nassau St; entrees $18-22; ☽ lunch & dinner; subway A, C to Broadway–Nassau St or J, M, Z, 2, 3, 4, 5 to Fulton St

Celebrity chef Anthony Bourdain reigns at this packed and serious bistro where vegetarians need not apply. You'll find the expected onion soup, escargot and moules frites on the menu, but raves point to the top-shelf meats: NY strip steak, *cote de boeuf, choucroute garnis* and *steak au poivre*.

SALAAM BOMBAY

Map pp380-1   *Indian*
☎ 212-226-9400; 317 Greenwich St btwn Duane & Reade Sts; entrees $17-23; ☽ lunch & dinner; subway 1, 2, 3, 9 to Chambers St

Squeeze into the long communal banquette and rub elbows with financial types at this low-lit, maroon-and-gold dining room to sample upscale Indian cuisine from all over the subcontinent. Usual *saag panir* (spinach dish) and chicken *tikka* (tomato based curry) dishes are replaced by northern-style tandoori lobster, Goan chicken with coconut, and Kashmiri lamb slow-cooked in a tender, tangy yogurt marinade. And the daily lunch buffet, a mere $12.95, is a delicious afternoon bargain.

Top Five Street Eats

- **Donuts & coffee** Every neighborhood has several come morning, stocked with sticky donuts, fresh coffee and even some pre-buttered bagels, with nothing costing more than $1.
- **Gyros & falafel** They're ubiquitous – especially around business Midtown and shoppers' Soho (try Broadway between Houston and Lafayette Sts) – but they are delicious.
- **Roasted chestnuts** It's a seasonal treat, proffered all over town right around Christmas time, and the scent is heavenly.
- **Soup** Thick homemade corn chowder, lobster bisque and cream of potato soup can be found at carts all over the city, but especially in Soho (Prince and Mercer Sts) and Midtown (34th St at Ninth Ave).
- **Tacos** Some of the city's best Mexican tacos, *tortas* (Mexican sandwiches) and *horchatas* (cold rice-water drinks) are doled out of trucks parked on Upper West Side corners – 98th St and Broadway and 104th St and Broadway.

Cheap Eats
SOPHIE'S RESTAURANT

Map pp380-1   *Cuban*
☎ 212-269-0909; 205 Pearl St btwn Maiden Ln & Platt St; entrees $6-8; ☽ lunch Mon-Fri; subway 2, 3 to Wall St

Downtown nine-to-fivers cram into this bare-bones storefront, and it's no wonder: the steaming plates of rice and beans topped with onion and cilantro have a perfectly zesty garlic-to-hot-pepper ratio, *tostones* (flattened, fried slices of plantains) are crisp and not too greasy, and the thick, strong *café con leche* (coffee with milk) makes everything right and bright again before venturing back to that dreary office. Imagine what it'll do for someone on vacation.

TRIBECA

While Tribeca's businesses were in a financial jam in the months, and even years, following September 11, the ones that survived seem to be doing so with gusto. And they are a top-of-the-line bunch indeed, serving everything from basic comfort food to glitzy French grub.

BOULEY Map pp380-1 *French*
☎ 212-694-2525; 120 West Broadway at Duane St; entrees $30-36 or dinner tasting menu $75; ☽ lunch & dinner; subway A, C, 1, 2, 3, 9 to Chambers St

The home base of celebrity chef David Bouley is the stuff of legend: tender roasted monkfish with a fragrant stew of razor clams and asparagus; lobster with broad beans and haricot verts in a succulent port-wine and blood-orange sauce; Mediterranean rouget with rose olives and saffron; even a rare kobe beef option, a serious splurge at $110 for a decadent 10oz slab. It's all served in one of two elegant rooms – the red room or the white room – to some of the most discriminating eaters in New York. And that's saying something. So book early, or be prepared to accept a 10:30pm or later dinner seating.

BUBBY'S Map pp380-1 *Comfort Food*
☎ 212-219-0666; 120 Hudson St at N Moore St; entrees $10-16; ☽ breakfast, lunch & dinner daily, brunch Sun; subway 1, 9 to Franklin St

This old Tribeca standby is known as something to every New Yorker: to tabloid readers as a lunch favorite of J.Lo and the late JFK Jr, to locals as a great place to bring the kids for brunch on Sunday, and to foodies as home of some of the best mac 'n' cheese in the city. To you it should be known as *the* place for simple, big, delicious food: slow-cooked barbecue, grits, matzo-ball soup, buttermilk potato salad and fried okra – all melt-in-your-mouth good.

DUANE PARK CAFE
Map pp380-1 *Elegant American*
☎ 212-732-5555; 157 Duane St btwn Hudson St & West Broadway; entrees $18-22; ☽ lunch Mon-Fri, dinner daily; subway 1, 9 to Franklin St

Can't snag a prime-time table at Bouley? This unassuming neighbor and beloved local secret plates fresh and fancy feasts at a fraction of the price. The small and romantic dining room is filled not with trendoids but folks who love good eatin'. Sample luscious beef fillet topped with eye-watering horseradish, homemade rabbit sausage and bass seeped in cumin broth.

NAM Map pp380-1 *Vietnamese*
☎ 212-267-1777; 110 Reade St btwn Church St & West Broadway; entrees $13-18; ☽ lunch Mon-Fri, dinner daily; subway 1, 9 to Franklin St

The sleek, bamboo-lined dining room here was a popular newbie when it opened in this ethnic-starved 'hood back in 2001, and it's still going strong. House specialties cooked by a trio of female chefs, such as the soft rice-paper rolls stuffed with jicama and sweet sausage and shrimp-and-chicken coconut crepes, are delectable, and steps above the cheapie Chinatown alternatives.

Top Five Eats in Tribeca & Soho

- **Bubby's** (left) Hip comfort food and a kid-friendly vibe.
- **Duane Park Café** (left) A locals' secret gem.
- **Hoomoos Asli** (p175) Fresh Israeli salads with bite.
- **Public** (p174) An eclectic, space-age dining experience.
- **Souen** (p174) Macrobiotic deliciousness.

NOBU Map pp380-1 *Japanese*
☎ 212-219-0500; 105 Hudson St at Franklin St; entrees $15-20; ☽ lunch Mon-Fri, dinner daily; subway 1, 9 to Franklin St

At 10 years old, this place is still over-the-top trendy, luring in an ever-present rotation of top celebrities and spawning a culinary empire, with outposts in Miami, LA, Las Vegas and London. Some customers do come for the unbelievably toothsome, creative fare, though, such as the signature black cod in miso, quirky sushis prepared with everything from chilies to aioli and Matsuhisha shrimp and caviar. At times Nobu gets almost nauseatingly trendy. Nobu's tasting menu *(omakase)* is a multicourse chef's choice starting at $80; for a more affordable and less rowdy taste, go next door to **Next Door Nobu** (☎ 212-219-0500), which doesn't take reservations but does offer many of the same menu options.

Cheap Eats
PAKISTAN TEA HOUSE
Map pp380-1 *Pakistani*
☎ 212-240-9800; 176 Church St btwn Duane & Reade Sts; meals $6-8; ☽ lunch & dinner; subway A, C, 1, 2, 3, 9 to Chambers St

Follow the South Asian cabbies here for authentic curries and rotis, heated in microwaves but offering a delicious bang for your buck. Plus, the place serves until 4am, providing a unique post-clubbing option of savory *palak panir* (a dish of spinach with a specific type of Indian cheese) or chicken *tikka* to help you sober up.

SOHO

Formerly known for being long on pretension and short on quality cuisine, Soho is now something of a food destination in its own right. Sure enough, stuck between cosmetics chains, shoe boutiques and low-rise office buildings are some creative and delicious bistros, cafés and ethnic kitchens.

BALTHAZAR

Map pp382-5 *French Bistro*
☎ 212-965-1414; 80 Spring St btwn Broadway & Crosby St; entrees $18-28; ☽ breakfast, lunch & dinner; subway 6 to Spring St

You'd think folks would be over this bustling (OK, *loud*) bistro, but it retains its superstar status, attracting A-listers mixed in with the locals and tourists. Perhaps it's the location, which makes it a convenient shopping-spree rest area. Or it could be the uplifting ambience, with big, mounted mirrors, cozy high-backed booths or the airy high ceilings and wide windows. But it's most likely the something-for-everyone menu, which features a stellar raw bar, steak frites, salad nicoise, roasted beet salad and prawn risotto with sage and butternut squash. The kitchen stays open till 2am Thursday to Saturday.

DOS CAMINOS SOHO

Map pp382-5 *Nouveau Mexican*
☎ 212-277-4300; 475 West Broadway at Houston St; entrees $15-23; ☽ lunch & dinner; subway F, V, Grand St S to Broadway–Lafayette St or 1, 9 to Houston St

The din is deafening at this always-mobbed fiesta, and waits for tables can be lengthy. But chill out at the bar with one of the fruity, *fuerte* margaritas and hang tough, because the food is worth it. Steve Hanson's take on Mexican food is creative and palate-pleasing, and includes roasted tomato chipotle meatballs, pan-roasted sea bass flavored with jalapeños and fresh oregano, and a grilled chicken torta topped with zippy manchego cheese and smoky, roasted poblano peppers. The made-fresh-to-order guacamole is an addictive swirl of garlicky green goodness. You'll never be able to decide on dessert, as every single one from the warm chocolate empanada to the pineapple upside-down *tres leche* cake – are swoon-inducing.

FANELLI'S CAFÉ

Map pp382-5 *American*
☎ 212-226-9412; 94 Prince St at Mercer St; entrees $9-13; ☽ lunch & dinner; subway N, R to Prince St

This is the grizzled old-timer of the neighborhood, predating all the chain stores, swarms of weekend shoppers and hints of gentrification. Once a speakeasy, Fanelli's Café is New York's second-oldest restaurant, established way back in 1872. The dark, century-old dining room is topped with a pressed-tin ceiling and full of tables covered in red checkered cloths. The burgers are particularly scrumptious, although you can always count on quality specials such as ravioli and grilled fish. Late-night hours – the kitchen serves till 2:30am Monday to Thursday and till 3am Friday and Saturday – make it a great post–Downtown-theater option.

PUBLIC Map pp382-5 *Eclectic*
☎ 212-343-7011; 343-7011; 210 Elizabeth btwn Rivington & Stanton Sts; entrees $18-25; ☽ lunch & dinner daily, brunch Sat & Sun; subway N, R, W to Prince St or 6 to Spring St

This new kid on the block is open to all – all those who like high-concept gourmet grub with a healthy dose of strange wild game thrown in, that is. The place, designed to honor the concept of public spaces, features a mix of futuristic and old-fashioned details. The clientele is decidedly modern, though, and the menu covers the entire gamut of *whatever:* chestnut risotto cake with pickled squash and pine nuts; striped bass with parsnips and edamame; grilled venison with fennel; and a strikingly odd appetizer of grilled kangaroo. But Public is a delicious, if newfangled, experience, to be sure.

SOUEN

Map pp382-5 *Vegetarian/Macrobiotic*
☎ 212-807-7421; 219 Sixth Ave at Prince St; entrees $8-16; ☽ lunch & dinner; subway C, E to Spring St

The city's longtime purveyor of healthful, substantial meals serves extensive vegetarian and fish options that hark back to the old-school 1970s time of what it meant to eat well. But the sleek, understated style of the place and the emphasis on basic, but stunning, flavors will make you grateful that someone is still doing food this way, and doing it very well. Salmon and vegetables steamed in ginger-tamari broth; a soba-noodle, bean and tahini platter; and fat, fresh futomaki rolls are all simple joys.

Cheap Eats

HAMPTON CHUTNEY CO

Map pp382-5   *Indian Fusion*

☎ 212-226-9996; 68 Prince St btwn Crosby & Lafayette Sts; meals $7-9; ☽ lunch & dinner; subway 6 to Spring St

What started as a small hut serving South Indian *dosas* out in the Hamptons town of Amagansett has wound up a similarly-sized storefront in the center of Soho. Popular with trendy publishing types who work in the neighborhood, the deliciously Westernized versions of the thin rice crepes come stuffed not only with traditional masala mixtures, but with options from grilled asparagus and goat cheese to chicken and Monterey Jack. It's a bit like fancy fast food – even the counter servers wear plucky, matching uniforms.

HOOMOOS ASLI

Map pp382-5   *Kosher Israeli*

☎ 212-966-0022; 100 Kenmare St at Cleveland Pl; entrees $4-8; ☽ lunch & dinner; subway 6 to Spring St

Not all Middle Eastern fare is alike. The folks here will remind you of that with the way they chat in Hebrew with loyal regulars, wait tables with an unmistakably sabra sass and firmly correct you if you order 'hummus' rather than 'hoomoos,' which is, folks here claim, the correct pronunciation. Anyhoo…along with the endearing quirkiness is an across-the-board delicious menu of casual salads, sandwiches and phyllo-wrapped entrees. Try a bit of everything with the $8.50 salad combo, which could include minty carrots, lemony tabouleh, garlicky baba ghanoush and creamy, caper-studded potato salad. Everything comes with some of the softest pita around.

Ñ Map pp382-5   *Spanish Tapas*

☎ 212-219-8856; 33 Crosby St btwn Broome & Grand Sts; tapas $3-6; ☽ dinner till very late; subway 6 to Spring St

This tiny, crowded hideaway is the perfect place to relax after a day of exploring. Get some spicy Spanish olives, cod empanadas and a goblet of bold rioja and you'll be good to go. Live flamenco bands on Wednesday nights lure in quite a crowd, and could transport you to Barcelona, if that sounds tempting.

SNACK Map pp382-5   *Greek*

☎ 212-925-1040; 105 Thompson St btwn Prince & Spring Sts; entrees $6-12; ☽ lunch & dinner; subway C, E to Spring St

Everything's just so good! This teensy little five-table storefront is more popular with to-go

customers, who like to munch on the gratis Jordan almonds that sit in a tiny bowl near the counter. But whether you squeeze into a seat along the wall or take it to one of the nearby postage-stamp–sized parks, you'll find yourself grinning widely as you stuff your face with plates of veal meatballs riddled with pine nuts and swimming in stewed prunes or sandwiches such as vegetarian souvlaki, fat butter beans in a garlicky creamy yogurt sauce that get stuffed into a fresh pita.

CHINATOWN & LITTLE ITALY

CHINATOWN

This is the place for bargains – and for mobs of diners, many of them tourists. While the stroll through streets and alleys crammed with fish vendors and herbal-medicine shops is a fascinating sensory overload, you'll find a scene that's both more mellow and more authentic than in the Chinatowns of Brooklyn or Queens (see Keepin' It Real, p177). In recent years, it's actually the Vietnamese offerings that make Manhattan's Chinatown most worth the trip. Take note that almost every place is a Cheap Eat – whether you need it to be or not. To reach any of the following spots, take the subway to the Canal St stations at Broadway, Lafayette or Center Sts (J, M, N, Q, R, W, Z, 6 to Canal St).

DOYERS VIETNAMESE RESTAURANT

Map pp380-1   *Vietnamese*

☎ 212-513-1521; 11 Doyers St btwn Bowery & Pell St; entrees $6-9; ☽ lunch & dinner

Everything about this place is an adventure: its location, on the curvy little barber-shop-lined street of Doyers; its ambience, in a cave-like, below-street-level hideaway with old-school charm; and the lengthy menu, with curiously yummy dishes including crispy fried tilapia, shrimp-papaya salad, curried eel and a slew of vegetarian offerings, from fried rice stick with vegetables to curried watercress.

FUNKY BROOME Map p378-9   *Cantonese*

☎ 212-941-8628; 176 Mott at Broome St; entrees $10-18; ☽ lunch & dinner; subway J, M, Z to Bowery, 6 to Spring St

Young Asian trendies congregate here for the tacky-cool zebra-print decor and some seriously authentic delicacies, happily paying the slightly higher prices for the hipper than old-school Chinatown ambience. Flavorful soups, such as the sliced pork, mustard green and salted egg concoction, are excellent, as are the mini-woks – satay meatballs and vermicelli, stuffed fried tofu – kept warm at your table over blue Sterno flames.

MEI LAI WAH COFFEE HOUSE

Map pp380-1   *Chinese Bakery*
☎ 212-925-5438; 64 Bayard St at Elizabeth St; buns 60¢; ☺ breakfast, lunch & dinner

You must get here in the morning to witness the true splendor of this teeny, battered old storefront bakery. The city's best steamed pork and sesame buns are doled out warm and fresh to the throngs of Filipinos and Chinese who work in the neighborhood, shoving and yelling to get their morning fix of these heavenly puffs of dough. The coffee is excellent, too – a Chinatown rarity.

NHA TRANG Map pp380-1   *Vietnamese*
☎ 212-233-5948; 87 Baxter St at Bayard St; entrees $5-8; ☺ lunch & dinner

This popular, basic Chinatown joint attracts a lunchtime crowd of cops, jurors and lawyers from the nearby courthouses. Classics such as rice noodles with fish balls, chicken with chilies and lemongrass or spicy veggies with bean curd. For a legal speedball, chase your meal with the super-rich and delicious Vietnamese-style coffee, made thick and sweet with condensed milk.

SHANGHAI CAFÉ

Map pp380-1   *Chinese*
☎ 212-732-5533; 100 Mott St btwn Bayard & Canal Sts; entrees $6-9; ☺ lunch & dinner

If the family-style, weary dining rooms with red threadbare carpeting and black cushioned chairs of this neighborhood are getting you down, the sleek and modern dance-club–like atmosphere of Shanghai Café will lift you right back up. Enjoy steamed soup dumplings and other authentic standards with young locals and feel as though you're in hipster Hong Kong.

SWEET-N-TART

Map pp380-1   *Chinese/Dim Sum*
☎ 212-964-0380; 20 Mott St btwn Park Row & Pell St; entrees $4-8; ☺ lunch & dinner

Chinese locals flock to the mesmerizingly cheesy purple downstairs dining room or the bright-red banquet hall upstairs, and walking in feels a bit like crashing a private, very fun party. You'll be given a warm welcome, though, as patient waiters guide you through the massive menu of authentic tasty treats. Stick to one of the consistently delicious main dishes such as broiled fish-ball soup or minced beef and pre-served vegetable congee; or order a variety of little dim-sum specialties, so you can get nut-filled glutinous dumplings, butterfly shrimp with sliced almonds, stir-fried turnip cake and boiled edamame all on one table.

VEGETARIAN DIM SUM HOUSE

Map pp380-1   *Dim Sum*
☎ 212-577-7176; 24 Pell St; meals $8-12; ☺ breakfast, lunch & dinner

Similar to its two pure-veg competitors in the 'hood (Vegetarian Paradise 1 and 2), this tiny crowd-pleaser offers long lists of mock-meat specialties, with not a drop of the real stuff in da house. But this one's got the freshest, most consistent offerings, such as sweet yam soup, and faux 'spareribs' and 'chicken,' made of various forms of bean curd and often tasting alarmingly real.

Top Five Eats in Chinatown & Little Italy

- **Da Genarro** (opposite) Worth wading through the tourists.
- **Ferrara's Pasticceria** (opposite) Orgasmic can-nolis and tiramisu.
- **Mei Lai Wah Coffee House** (left) The pork buns send locals into a frenzy!
- **Nha Trang** (left) Unbelievably cheap and tasty Vietnamese.
- **Sweet-n-Tart** (left) Tasty, traditional Chinese treats.

LITTLE ITALY

It's pretty much one big tourist trap here, where gussied-up waiters stand on side-walks hawking eateries to tourists who didn't take time to do their research. Still, there's a certain charm to the slowly fad-ing 'hood, quickly being taken over by the ever-expanding Chinatown and Soho. And some of the food – the desserts, es-pecially – are surprisingly delicious. Take the Grand St S to Grand St to reach all of the following outposts.

DA GENNARO

Map pp382-5   *Italian*

☎ 212-431-3934; 129 Mulberry St btwn Grand & Hester Sts; entrees $20; ⏱ lunch & dinner

The most consistently excellent red-sauce joint on the strip, this slightly upscale option attracts a more discerning breed of tourists who appreciate its casual atmosphere and classic pasta, seafood, steak and meatball-laden offerings.

Keepin' It Real: NYC's Most Authentic Ethnic 'Hoods

Sure, Manhattan's Little Italy and Chinatown are fine – if you like mobs of tourists desperately seeking authenticity. But you can truly find it in the outer boroughs, where the latest waves of immigrants have settled and continue to arrive. Below, a guide going 'round the world in neighborhoods:

- **China:** Sunset Park, Brooklyn (Map p395), instead of Chinatown. Instead of mobs of New Jersey tourists buying Hello Kitty wallets you get Asian crowds, top-notch eateries (including 24-hour dim sum spots) and a feeling that you're far, far away. Take the N train to Eighth Ave.
- **India:** Jackson Heights, Queens (Map p396), instead of E 6th Street. The dirt-cheap chicken *tikka* can't beat sari shops, *thali* plates and Bollywood theater. Take subway 7, E, F, G, R to Roosevelt Ave.
- **Ireland:** Woodlawn in the Bronx (Map pp398-9) over Manhattan's Third Ave Irish bars. Say goodbye to drunken frat boys and hello to correctly-poured pints of Guinness, authentic bangers 'n' mash, just-arrived youngsters and, of course, about a dozen great pubs. Take the 4 subway to Woodlawn.
- **Italy:** Belmont in the Bronx (Map pp398-9), instead of Little Italy. Trade in mediocre restaurants for excellent eateries, samples of fresh mozzarella in the Arthur Avenue Retail Market, to-die-for-cannoli and serious Soprano-character dead ringers. Take the B, D, 4 subway to Fordham Rd, then the Bx 12 bus to Hoffman St.
- **Korea:** Flushing, Queens (Map p397), instead of Koreatown. Goodbye Macy's shoppers, hello kimchi buyers. Take the 7 train to Flushing–Main St.
- **Russia:** Brighton Beach, Brooklyn, instead of Midtown restaurants. No more vodka-tinis, please – just the rudely staffed food markets, bustling nightclubs and boardwalk that feels like Odessa on the sea. Take subway D to Ocean Pkwy.

FERRARA'S PASTICCERIA

Map pp382-5   *Italian Bakery*

☎ 212-226-6150; 195 Grand St btwn Mott & Mulberry Sts; desserts $3-6; ⏱ afternoon & evening dessert

This old-school institution, open since 1892, creates an eye-popping array of cannoli, napoleons, *sfogliatelle* (cheese-filled pastry) and myriad cookies in its ovens. The creamy gelati, in chocolate, hazelnut and vanilla, are luscious, as are the espressos and cappuccinos that folks have been pouring in for since way before Starbucks was a twinkle in its CEO's eye.

PELLEGRINO'S

Map pp382-5   *Italian*

☎ 212-226-3177; 138 Mulberry St btwn Grand & Hester Sts; entrees $20; ⏱ lunch & dinner

Consistent Northern Italian fare such as linguini with lobster, lasagna and rich tiramisu for dessert keep folks piling into this Mulberry Street staple. The house special is a classic take on the Italian-American scene around here: 'linguini Sinatra,' with lobster, shrimp, clams and pignoli.

LOWER EAST SIDE

It's impossible to keep up with the offerings in these parts, where slinky lounges with elaborate nouveau-fusion menus and instant A-list crowds seem to pop up daily – in spots that used to be dilapidated tenements, no less! It's an irony not lost on the businesses, as attested to by spots such as Tenement (serving so-so 'old-world' cuisine) and Lansky Lounge (a homage to local 1930s gangster Meyer Lansky).

CUBE 63

Map pp382-5   *Sushi*

☎ 212-228-6751; 63 Clinton St btwn Rivington & Stanton Sts; entrees $18-30, rolls $4-11; ⏱ lunch & dinner; subway F to Delancey St, J, M Z to Delancey–Essex Sts

The fare at this space-age, glowing refuge among the low-lit cubicle dining rooms on this culinary row is outrageously good. You will find standard sushi rolls and sashimi, all fresh and wonderful, plus signature fusions, such as the Mexican roll (jalapeño, spicy sauce and whitefish), volcano (crab meat, toasted shrimp and eel sauce) or the decadent 63 roll (spicy tuna, avocado and lobster salad). The clientele here is as decidedly hip and sassy as the menu.

'INOTECA

Map pp382-5   *Italian Snacks*
☎ 212-614-0473; 98 Rivington at Ludlow St; entrees $9-13; ⓨ lunch & dinner daily, brunch Sat & Sun; subway F, V to Lower East Side–Second Ave

Tuck yourself in at one of the chunky square tables of this airy, dark-wood–paneled corner haven and choose from *tramezzini* (small sandwiches on white or whole wheat bread), *panini* (pressed sandwiches) and bruschetta options – or get one of each. The nibbly bits and pressed sandwiches are all delicious and affordable. The truffled egg toast, a square of bread hollowed out in its center and filled with egg, truffles and fontina cheese, is a signature favorite. But you can't go wrong, whether you choose the beet-orange-mint salad, vegetable lasagna built with layers of eggplant rather than pasta, or a plate of garlicky mussels. Best of all is the list of 200 wines, 25 of them available by the glass.

Top Five Eats in the Lower East Side & East Village

- **Bereket** (right) For that 2am stuffed-grape-leaf hankering.
- **'Inoteca** (above) Perfect wine, panini and ambience.
- **Patio Dining** (p180) Organic feasts and open-air cocktails.
- **Prune** (p180) Bloody Mary brunches to make your head spin.
- **WD 50** (right) Star chef thinks way outside the box.

PALADAR

Map pp382-5   *Nuevo Latino*
☎ 212-473-3535; 161 Ludlow St at Stanton St; entrees $12-18; ⓨ dinner daily, brunch Sat & Sun; subway F, V to Lower East Side–Second Ave

Chef Aaron Sanchez combines tropical flavors in revolutionary ways for the diners squeezed in under the dark pressed-tin ceiling and sconce lighting. That results in casual treats such as the fat chicken empanadas, and halibut bathed in an orange vinaigrette, sparkling ceviche, lentil salad with plantains and hanger steak rubbed with adobo spices. What's more, the kitchen stays open until 2am from Thursday to Saturday.

SUBA

Map pp382-5   *Nuevo Latino*
☎ 212-982-5714; 109 Ludlow St btwn Delancey & Rivington Sts; entrees $18-23; ⓨ dinner; subway F to Delancey St, J, M Z to Essex–Delancey Sts

Capitalizing on the popularity of its Paladar neighbor but taking the cuisine to a more

sophisticated level is Suba, where a boisterous tapas bar reigns upstairs and a soothing little dining room, surrounded by an actual moat, lies in wait. The kicky dishes are impressive, especially the sumptuous saffron-laced duck breast and chipotle-marinated slab of tuna. Desserts are outstanding, as are the convoluted mixologies (such as the lime pie cocktail) that many of the gorgeous diners are sipping.

WD 50

Map pp382-5   *American Creative*
☎ 212-477-2900; 50 Clinton St at Stanton St; entrees $20-25; ⓨ dinner Mon-Sat; subway F to Delancey St, J, M Z to Delancey–Essex Sts

Wylie Dufresne, the genius behind 71 Clinton Fresh Foods (just a few doors down) and one of the leaders in the full-throttle gentrification of this part of the 'hood, added this crowd-pleaser to his growing empire in 2003. It drew in VIPs and wannabes alike in a stream that hasn't slowed. Bamboo floors, a fireplace and exposed beams all highlight the provocative fare in this casual fine-dining hot spot: oysters with apples, olives and pistachios; skate served with preserved-lemon gnocchi and smoked scallions. Get ready to discover all the foods you never knew you loved.

Cheap Eats

BEREKET

Map pp382-5   *Turkish*
☎ 212-475-7700; 187 E Houston St at Orchard St; entrees $4-7; ⓨ 24hr; subway F, V to Second Ave

You'll feel like you've stepped into Istanbul here, where club kids, local workers and folks working the graveyard shift gather for excellent stuffed grape leaves, kebabs, bean and leek stews and fresh salads.

KATZ'S DELI

Map pp382-5   *Jewish Deli*
☎ 212-254-2246; 205 E Houston St at Ludlow St; entrees $8; ⓨ breakfast, lunch & dinner; subway F, V to Lower East Side–Second Ave

This was where Meg Ryan faked her famous orgasm in *When Harry Met Sally*, and, while the classic deli grub may not have the same effect on you, it'll probably come pretty close. The vast, worn-out room is infused with old-world nostalgia – especially the WWII 'Send a salami to your boy in the army' – as are the crusty guys behind the counter who dole out crisp kosher dills, frothy chocolate egg creams and pastrami and corned beef piled high on fresh rye. It's a true New York experience – especially at 2am, when trendy clubbers pile in for sobering sandwiches.

KOSSAR'S BIALYSTOKER KUCHEN BAKERY Map pp382-5 *Bakery*

☎ 212-260-2252; 367 Grand St; 2-dozen $22; ☺ breakfast, lunch & dinner Sun-Thu; subway B, D to Grand St

This small, 75-year-old bakery is the best bialy maker in the city. It's got old-world charm, a heavenly scent and knows just how to churn out the bialy, a cousin of the bagel, that's made of dough smeared with onion-garlic paste and then baked for exactly seven minutes. Pop in for a couple – or a couple of dozen.

TEANY Map pp382-5 *Vegan Teahouse*

☎ 212-475-9190; 90 Rivington St btwn Ludlow & Orchard Sts; entrees $6-12; ☺ breakfast, lunch & dinner till late; subway F to Delancey St, J, M Z to Delancey–Essex Sts

This teeny-tiny café, tucked below street level on a quietly hip block, is co-owned by famously vegan pop star Moby – which accounts for the animal-friendly fare served in the mellow, candlelit spot. The book-like menu boasts close to 100 teas, all served in individual teapots and ranging from the typical (spearmint, Irish breakfast) to the sublimely exotic (green sea anemone, white peony). You can also choose from frothy soy-infused coffees, beer and wine, and delicious little foods including muffins, tea sandwiches (the cheddar-pickle and peanut butter–chocolate ones rock), excellent salads and scrumptious desserts.

YONAH SHIMMEL BAKERY

Map pp382-5 *Knishes*

☎ 212-477-2858; 137 E Houston St btwn Eldridge & Forsyth Sts; knishes $2; ☺ 9:30am-7pm; subway F, V to Lower East Side–Second Ave

Shimmel has been selling baked, fist-sized knishes for 92 years and knows how it's done. Choose from varieties including potato, sweet potato, red cabbage, cheese and kasha, all stellar. You'll also find bagels, blintzes and cookies inside the diminutive old storefront, just a couple doors away from the wonderful **Landmark Sunshine Cinemas** (p231) and the perfect pre- or post-movie nosh.

EAST VILLAGE

This is the epitome of what's beautiful about the New York dining scene – cheap-ass, high-class, meat-heavy, vegan and ethnic restaurants on every block, elbow-to-elbow, offering abundant, exciting options no matter what your scene, taste or budget.

ANGELICA KITCHEN

Map pp382-5 *Vegan*

☎ 212-228-2909; 300 E 12th St btwn First & Second Aves; entrees $8-13; ☺ lunch & dinner; subway L to First Ave

This way-popular, light-filled eatery has come a long way since its humble hippie roots. Started as an herb shop by a few free spirits in 1978, it evolved into a homey café that served just a few basic items to no more than 20 customers at a time. But now Angelica, named after the flowering herb said to cure digestive ailments, is loved by hippies, scenesters and omnivores alike, serving creative, organic, animal-free fare to each and every one of them behind a floor-to-ceiling glass storefront. The dragon bowls, an original-menu holdover, are budget-priced macrobiotic piles of fresh veggies, grains, protein and sea vegetables. An ever-changing roster of specials has chefs turning these same ingredients into stews, soups, casseroles and elegant salads. Dining alone? Make a friend over dinner at the big community table in the middle of the room.

COUNTER

Map pp382-5 *Vegetarian Comfort Food*

☎ 212-982-5870; 105 First Ave btwn 6th & 7th Sts; entrees $9-14; ☺ lunch & dinner Tue-Sat; subway F, V to Lower East Side–Second Ave

Get po'boys, burgers and jambalaya sans the meat at this lovely wine-and-snack bar in the heart of the East Village. Sit at the airy counter in the center of the space and order one of several organic wines with an elegant plate of cashew-kalamata pâté, or settle in at one of the tables, where you'll have more room to dig into a lentil loaf with mashed potatoes or grilled organic peanut butter and banana sandwich. Either way, the sleek ambience, friendly servers and bird's-eye view of the First Ave parade of hipsters will have you loving this place right away.

GAIA

Map pp382-5 *Turkish*

☎ 212-358-1166; 98 Ave B btwn 6th & 7th Sts; entrees $12-17; ☺ dinner; subway F, V to Lower East Side–Second Ave

This new sultry spot is loungey, with billows of fabric and complimentary mezes. But it's just enough to whet your appetite for all the rest that's offered here, including luscious vegetable dishes swimming in fruity olive oil, stuffed chickpea balls, swanky cocktails and occasional belly dancers.

PATIO DINING

Map pp382-5   *Creative American*

☎ 212-460-9171; 31 Second Ave btwn 1st & 2nd Sts; entrees $14-19; ◷ dinner Mon-Sun, brunch Sun; subway F, V to Lower East Side–Second Ave

Chef-owner Eric Korsh has been turning out stunners from his tiny kitchen ever since he opened the place in the early '90s. The restaurant has since doubled in size, and you no longer have to squeeze past the sweating stove to get to the toilet, but the intimate atmosphere has remained. Seasonal, organic ingredients get transformed into flavorful stews, juicy braised chops and rich pasta dishes. The northern half of the eatery is a patio-like (get it?) cocktail lounge, attracting flocks of beautiful locals who swill martinis in what used to be a parking lot.

PRUNE

Map pp382-5   *Creative American*

☎ 212-677-6221; 54 E 1st St btwn First & Second Aves; entrees $18-23; ◷ lunch & dinner daily, brunch Sat & Sun; subway F, V to Lower East Side–Second Ave

Rich meals are the order of the day here, as you'll find hearty offerings including roast suckling pig, rich sweetbreads and sausage-studded concoctions. The cramped dining room is well-lit and wide open, bistro-style, on warm evenings, providing a lovely vantage point onto the quaint stretch of 1st St. It's always crowded – especially for Sunday brunch, when late sleepers rouse themselves for top-notch Bloody Marys (in nine varieties), lox and oysters.

SANCTUARY

Map pp382-5   *Vegetarian & Indian*

☎ 212-780-9786; 25 First Ave btwn 1st & 2nd Sts; entrees $8-13; ◷ dinner Tue-Sun, lunch Sat & Sun; subway F, V to Lower East Side–Second Ave

Don't be confused – you are still in New York, even though the slatted-wood booths, live New Age music and mini-market of crystals and dream catchers will make you think you've wound up in Haight Ashbury. The meditative vibe, along with the prominent Indian flavor on the menu, comes from the fact that the place is run by the swami-headed Interfaith League, which meets upstairs. Food is fresh and clean but extremely tasty, with a wide variety of options ranging from tofu, cauliflower and zucchini in creamy spinach-yogurt sauce to faux-meat treats such as fabulous Chick-None drumsticks.

TSAMPA

Map pp382-5   *Tibetan*

☎ 212-614-3226; 212 E 9th St btwn Second & Third Aves; entrees $9-14; ◷ dinner; subway 6 to Astor Pl

The dark and sultry space lulls you into a Zen-like state before wowing you with tastes: soft dumplings are sublime, while grilled trout sings with ginger sauce and the stir-fry of a dozen vegetables is a goldmine for herbivore types.

Cheap Eats

B&H DAIRY

Map pp382-5   *Kosher Dairy*

☎ 212-505-8065; 127 Second Ave btwn St Marks Pl & 7th St; emtrees $5; ◷ breakfast, lunch & dinner; subway 6 to Astor Pl

This is a classic lunch counter with some of the most authentic New York food and crusty old 'tude around. Everything is homemade, fresh and vegetarian, including the six types of soups on offer daily, which, along with a pillowy slice of fresh-baked challah, will fill you up for about five bucks.

DAWGS ON PARK

Map pp382-5   *Hot Dogs*

☎ 212-598-0667; 178 E 7th St btwn Aves A & B; hot dogs $4; ◷ lunch & dinner; subway F, V to Lower East Side–Second Ave

Hot dogs sold in cafés, a step up from the dirty-water dogs you'll find at street carts, were all the rage a few years ago, when places such as Dawgs sprang up in various Downtown locales. This is one of the best, with its counter that looks out onto Tompkins Square Park, photos of local canines (who can often be found lounging on the floor of the place), and scrumptious dogs topped with corn salsa, vegan bean chili or traditional mustard and kraut. Toppings are available on beef, turkey or tofu weiners, and salty snacks, from onion rings to sweet potato fries, are just a couple of bucks extra.

SEA

Map pp382-5   *Thai*

☎ 212-228-5505; 75 Second Ave btwn 4th & 5th Sts; entrees $6-11; ◷ lunch & dinner; subway F, V to Lower East Side–Second Ave

SEA, an acronym for South East Asian, is a cheap, mobbed maker of outstanding Thai grub. Best of all (or worst of all, depending on your preference), the glowing red space is so hipped out you'll think you're in a nightclub. It's loud and there's always a wait, but you'll be glad you stuck it out when one of your slim hottie waiters loads you up with yummy plates of pad Thai, green curry and sweet Thai iced teas, and your bill for four is less than it would be for two – or even three – at some comparable spots around town.

SECOND AVE DELI

Map pp382-5 *Jewish Deli*
☎ 212-677-0606; 156 Second Ave btwn 9th & 10th Sts; entrees $7-10; ⊙ lunch & dinner daily, till 3am Fri & Sat; subway 6 to Astor Pl

This is one of the last great Jewish delis in this part of New York (along with **Katz's**, p178). Head here for matzo-ball soup, garlicky dills, tangy slaw and hot pastrami and turkey sandwiches built so high you won't be able to fit your mouth around them.

In Search of the Perfect Slice

It's pretty hard to find a *bad* slice of pizza in NYC, where everything from greasy, floppy triangles to thick, whole-wheat squares topped with goat cheese and fennel are fresh, hot and delicious anytime of day or night. But sometimes you're just not satisfied until you can find the best. And so, armed with an empty belly and a fistful of dollars, that's just what we set out to do. First stop was John's Famous Pizzeria (Map pp382-5; ☎ 212-243-1680; 278 Bleecker St), the much-ballyhooed West Village outpost, where pies were thin but chewy, saucy but sweet. Next came two neighbors, **Arturo's Pizzeria** (Map pp382-5; ☎ 212-677-3820; 106 W Houston St), with a bustling dining room featuring live piano music, and **Stromboli Pizzeria** (Map pp382-5; ☎ 212-255-0812; 112 University Pl), for takeout only. Arutro's had matzo-thin, crispy crusts and fresh toppings, while Stromboli makes an impression with spicy, plentiful sauce. **Lombardi's** (Map pp382-5; ☎ 212-941-7994; 32 Spring St), a Soho fave, had tangy sauce, fresh mozzarella, sky-high toppings and a thick crust embedded with sesame seeds, while the 72-year-old **Patsy's Pizzeria** (Map pp382-5; ☎ 212-534-9783; 2287 First Ave), the original of five locations, offered extra-large, coal-fired triangles. To shake things up a bit, we hit one of several **Two Boots Pizzerias** (Map pp382-5; ☎ 212-254-1919; 42 Ave A) for slices topped with stuff from marinated chicken and plum tomatoes to barbecued shrimp, crawfish andouille and jalapeños, all with cornmeal-dusted crusts. So who's the winner? Crispy, thin and delicate enough to make you feel OK about downing an entire pie, we pick Arturo's. And the party-down atmosphere there didn't hurt, either.

WEST (GREENWICH) VILLAGE

BAR PITTI Map pp382-5 *Italian*
☎ 212-982-3300; 268 Sixth Ave btwn Bleecker & Houston Sts; entrees $15-22; ⊙ lunch & dinner; subway 1, 9 to Houston St

Stylish *Sex and the City* types cram into tiny blond-wood tables set against warm ochre walls – and belly up to a slew of sidewalk seats when the warm-weather café takes over the wide swath of sidewalk out front – for classy pasta concoctions such as the house rigatoni Pitti, with a creamy sausage-and-pea-studded sauce. Sea bass, veal and other hearty offerings keep the sleek set coming back over and over again.

DELICIA Map pp382-5 *Brazilian*
☎ 212-242-2002; 322 W 11th St btwn Greenwich & Washington Sts; entrees $12-15; ⊙ dinner Tue-Sat; subway 1, 9 to Christopher St–Sheridan Sq

Duck your head and step below street level into this cozy, homey room that'll make you feel as if you're being welcomed into someone's private home. Service is slow enough to let you savor minty *caipirinhas* (traditional rum concoctions) and appetizers including melt-in-your-mouth fried yucca and tender codfish croquettes. Just when you think you've been forgotten, a friendly server – often one of the down-to-earth owners – is there to make gentle suggestions, and serve up whatever treat you settle on: butternut squash baked with shrimp and cilantro in coconut milk, chicken roasted in passion-fruit juice, or the vegetarian *feijoada*, a classic black-bean stew with fresh veggies and yucca and topped with fresh oranges (the classic pork-studded option is there, too) are all excellent choices. For groups of three or more, go for the three-course fixed-price sampler and get a taste of it all.

DO HWA Map pp382-5 *Korean Barbecue*
☎ 212-414-2815; 55 Carmine St; entrees $12-20; ⊙ dinner; subway A, C, E, F, V, Grand St S to W 4th St

Quentin Tarantino's investment in Do Hwa has no doubt helped to boost the popularity of this Korean barbecue spot in the heart of the Village. Harvey Keitel, Wesley Snipes and Uma Thurman have stopped by for a taste of the flavorful beef ribs and kimchi in the spare Asian dining room, where DJs spin nightly. It also explains why pan-Asian fusion foods, such as pan-grilled chicken breast with sesame marinade and grilled snapper, are mixed in among the traditional offerings.

Top Five Eats in the West Village

- **Bar Pitti** (p181) See-and-be-seen Italian goodness.
- **Delicia** (p181) Brazilian flavor hits the Village.
- **Manna Bento** (opposite) Big Korean flavor, diminutive prices.
- **Paradou** (right) A French-bistro hideaway.
- **Pearl Oyster Bar** (opposite) The lobster rolls and oysters pack 'em in.

FLORENT Map pp382-5 *French Diner*
☎ 212-989-5779; 69 Gansevoort St btwn Greenwich & Washington Sts; meals $9-13; ☺ breakfast & lunch Mon-Wed, 24hr Fri-Sun; subway A, C, E to 14th St, L to Eighth Ave

This all-night cool-person's hang colonized the Meatpacking District in the far West Village many moons ago. It's a bustling spot that draws clubbers at all hours with its hangar steak, burgers and breakfast selections, as well as its praiseworthy blood sausage or pork chops. On the weekend closest to July 14, Florent takes over Gansevoort St for an open-air Bastille Day celebration.

FRENCH ROAST Map pp382-5 *French Bistro*
☎ 212-533-2233; 458 Sixth Ave at W 11th St; entrees $10-18; ☺ 24hr; subway L to Sixth Ave, F, V to 14th St

The airy dining room, manned by doting, fey waiters and filled with all manner of hipsters who are out so late they've run out of options, serves up quite tasty renditions of croque madame, salad nicoise, duck confit, steak frites – even a tofu stir-fry and grilled vegetable plate. There's another branch on **Broadway** (☎ 212-799-1533; 2340 Broadway at 86th St; ☺ 24hr; subway 1, 9 to 86th St).

JAPONICA Map pp382-5 *Japanese*
☎ 212-243-7752; 100 University Pl at 12th St; sushi meal $20; ☺ lunch Mon-Sat, dinner daily; subway L, N, Q, R, W, 4, 5, 6 to 14th St–Union Sq

This sushi institution, located in the heart of NYU-land, doles out huge fresh portions to locals and tourists alike who seem willing to suffer through long waits for a taste of the fat cubes of *nigiri* (oval-shaped sushi), fluke and yellowtail sushi, plus a range of veggie hand rolls stuffed with fresh spinach, asparagus and pickled squash. Steaming bowls of traditional soba stews are rich and satisfying. Plenty of newer, sleeker, more fashionable sushi spots have sprouted up since Japonica opened more than 20 years ago, but this bedrock still holds its own.

LE PETIT AUBEILLE
Map pp382-5 *Belgian*
☎ 212-727-1505; 400 W 14th St at Ninth Ave; entrees $12-16; ☺ breakfast, lunch & dinner; subway A, C, E to 14th St, L to Eighth Ave

It was one of the Meatpacking District pioneers way before the models and high-fashion boutiques pushed out the sex clubs and hookers. And it remains one of the few places left with character. The small storefront, serving Belgian bistro standards such as moules frites, chicken stew and sweet waffles, is the perfect antidote to the mall-like, tourist-packed Markt (serving similar fare) across the street. Colorful children's Tintin books line the walls and blue-checked tablecloths lend the space a whimsical air, as do jovial waiters and more than 30 varieties of Belgian bottled beer.

LITTLE HAVANA Map pp382-5 *Cuban*
☎ 212-255-2212; 30 Cornelia St btwn Bleecker & W 4th Sts; entrees $13-16; ☺ lunch & dinner Tue-Sun; subway A, C, E, F, V, Grand St S to W 4th St

A tiny Village gem on this short but sweet restaurant row, where owner Lydia Sharpe turns out earthy and filling dishes in a cozy setting. Try the first-rate black beans, spicy roast pork with tomatillo sauce, and roasted salmon.

PARADOU
Map pp382-5 *French Bistro*
☎ 212-463-8345; 8 Little West 12th St btwn Ninth Ave & Washington St; entrees $12-18; ☺ dinner; subway A, C, E to 14th St, L to Eighth Ave

Skip the trendy mob scene of Pastis across the street and settle into this minuscule haven instead. The hydrangea-heavy garden out the back is a mini-miracle in springtime, while the romantic little dining room is lovely all year-round. Service is well-paced and supportive, not to mention performed by a handsome crew which doles out tasty buckwheat crepes, panini and grilled fish dishes with a flourish. The wine list is stellar, with plenty of affordable options and by-the-glass pours served in individual mini-carafes.

PEARL OYSTER BAR

Map pp382-5 *Seafood*

☎ 212-691-8211; 18 Cornelia St btwn Bleecker & W 4th Sts; entrees $17-23; ⏱ lunch Mon-Fri, dinner Mon-Sat; subway A, C, E, F, V, Grand St S to W 4th St

This recently expanded (thank heaven!) destination is an upscale version of a seafood shack – think Maine coast meets Manhattan. Owner Rebecca Charles turns out top-notch stews, grilled seasonal fish, pan-roasted oysters, steamers, chowders and the all-around star: a succulent lobster roll, the northeast's name for creamy lobster salad stuffed into a fresh hot-dog roll and served with homemade fries. Go super-early or super-late for dinner, or prepare for a mega-wait.

TERRA 47 Map pp382-5 *Seasonal Organic*

☎ 212-358-0103; 47 E 12th St btwn Broadway & University Pl; entrees $13-18; ⏱ lunch & dinner; subway L, N, Q, R, W, 4, 5, 6 to 14th St–Union Sq

One of the latest spots to attempt ambience, gourmet cooking and quality vegetarian and carnivorous selections on the same menu, Terra 47 is off to a good start. The stylish space, decorated with tile and stained-glass touches, is intimate but not too diminutive. And both free-range venison *and* baked tempeh are getting rave reviews. Some folks don't appreciate the fact that every dessert is vegan, but the cakes are still surprisingly moist and tasty.

Cheap Eats

MANNA BENTO Map pp382-5 *Korean*

☎ 212-473-6162; 289 Mercer St btwn Waverly Pl & Eighth St; entrees $5-8; ⏱ lunch & dinner Mon-Sat; subway N, R to 8th St–NYU

Blink and you might miss this obscure gem, known almost exclusively by NYU students who sit solo hunched over steaming plates and thick textbooks as a sweet lady in a little white bonnet doles out homemade meals. It's the best place around for delicious, bargain, home-style eats such as vegetables, spicy tofu, glass noodles and kimchi served over fluffy white rice for $5 every afternoon.

PEANUT BUTTER & CO

Map pp382-5 *Peanut Butter Sandwiches*

☎ 212-677-3995; 240 Sullivan St btwn Bleecker & W 3rd Sts; sandwiches $4-6; ⏱ lunch & dinner; subway A, C, E, F, V, Grand St S to W 4th St

Just like chocolate, french fries and bagels, peanut butter is a foodstuff that ignites both desperate cravings and passionate opinions.

Fans of the creamy beige ambrosia will be in heaven here, where several varieties – crunchy, smooth, spicy, cinnamon-raisin – get slapped on white or wheat, paired with jelly, bananas and honey or green-apple slices, and served with potato chips and celery sticks, inspiring landslides of lunchroom nostalgia for Americans, and unmitigated joy for just about anyone else.

CHELSEA, UNION SQUARE, FLATIRON DISTRICT & GRAMERCY PARK

These comprise one of New York's newest gourmet ghettos, offering a stunning variety of dining options for all budgets. But lovers of exotic flavors, beware: it's mostly takes on American cuisine that you'll find in these parts. Chelsea is starting to offer some health-minded, high-protein-options to suit the tastes of the pumped-up 'Chelsea boys' who want to work out, cruise and eat, all in the same 'hood.

AMUSE

Map pp382-5 *Creative American*

☎ 212-929-9755; 108 W 18th St btwn Sixth & Seventh Aves; entrees $13-18; ⏱ lunch & dinner Mon-Sat; subway 1, 9 to 18th St

The sleek outpost of creative comfort food, from owners of older favorites Aureole and Tribeca Grill, organizes its offerings into $5, $10, $15 and $20 categories, letting you stay within your budget with ease and discretion. But it's all good here, where the cheap stuff always has a little something extra to make it fancy (such as the bearnaise sauce on the $5 fries), and the pricier options, such as succulent duck and fresh-fish creations, make you glad you shelled out.

CITY BAKERY

Map pp382-5 *Bakery & International Salad Bar*

☎ 212-366-1414; 3 W 18th St btwn Fifth & Sixth Aves; salad bar $12 per lb; ⏱ breakfast & lunch; subway L, N, Q, R, W, 4, 5, 6 to 14th St–Union Sq

The perfect place to take a load off after trolling the **Greenmarket Farmers' Market** (p107), the pricey salad-bar offerings here are actually priceless: tofu-skin salad, roasted beets, fresh grilled chicken with sugar-snap peas, soy beans with cabbage. Though hard to snag at lunchtime, there are plenty of tables lining the perimeter of the place. After enjoying the health-bent offerings at the bar, you won't likely be able to escape without sampling some of the rich bakery fare, from top-notch chocolate-chip cookies to thick, molten hot chocolate, served with or without a serving of chubby homemade marshmallow squares.

Top Five Eats in Chelsea-Flatiron

- **Amuse** (p183) Comfort food in sleek surroundings.
- **Bonobos** (opposite) It's raw, it's vegan, it's delicious!
- **City Bakery** (p183) Fresh food by the pound, plus the best hot chocolate around.
- **Madras Mahal** (right) South Indian fare at its best.
- **Tabla** (opposite) Indian-fusion with a view.

EMPIRE DINER Map pp382-5 — *Diner*
☎ 212-243-2736; 210 Tenth Ave at 22nd St; entrees $12-16; ☺ 24hr; subway C, E to 23rd St

Housed in a deco Pullman car, the menu here verges on the eclectic by throwing lentil burgers and mesclun and fine beers in with its burger-and-omelette standards. It offers opportunities for some fabulous people-watching (though why anyone would want to choke on exhaust fumes while dining *en plein air* at this corner is a puzzle – yet the sidewalk tables are always taken).

FOOD BAR Map pp382-5 — *American*
☎ 212-243-2020; 149 Eighth Ave btwn 17th & 18th Sts; entrees $13-18; ☺ breakfast, lunch & dinner; subway A, C, E to 14th St, L to Eighth Ave

The epicenter of said Chelsea-boy refueling, this dark and sexy sceney hub will lull you with ambient techno, coy and comely waiters and a hunky clientele – especially during weekend brunch hours, when sweaty, sleepy men arrive by the truckload to sober up from all-night clubbing by slurping up egg-white omelettes and strong coffee. The takes on simple favorites – Caesar salad with grilled chicken, vegetable lasagna, grilled salmon and big burgers – are consistently delicious, as are the chilly fresh-watermelon margaritas, served in jelly glasses that are fun to wrap your hands around.

GRAMERCY TAVERN
Map pp382-5 — *Creative American*
☎ 212-477-0777; 42 E 20th St btwn Broadway & Park Ave S; entrees $20-26, 3-course prix fixe $68; ☺ lunch Mon-Fri, dinner daily; subway N, R, W, 6 to 23rd St

This is a superstar on the restaurant scene. Though it can be tough to get a table here (reserve early), you'll be forever grateful that you planned ahead, as some of the best servers in the city spoil you with rotating treats from the kitchen to whet your appetite to start, and anything from braised rabbit over shallots to a portobello mushroom tart to linger over, all from celebrity chef Tom Colicchio. Sinful pastries are baked by an in-house pastry chef, and creative cocktails get stirred and shaken by a well-educated crew of mixologists.

MADRAS MAHAL
Map pp386-8 — *South Indian*
☎ 212-684-4010; 104 Lexington Ave btwn 27th & 28th Sts; entrees $11-14; ☺ lunch & dinner; subway 6 to 28th St

A favorite among the dozen or so Indian eateries in this Little-India stretch of Lexington Ave. It was one of the first places in Manhattan to offer the now-trendy South Indian *dosas* – huge, paper-thin rice crepes folded around flavorful mixtures of masala potatoes, peas, cilantro and other earthy treats. You'll also find reasonably priced North Indian dishes, such as the requisite *saag panir* or fried samosas, but the Southern eats are what shine here. The place is not only vegetarian but kosher, which explains the preponderance of devoted Orthodox customers who wash their hands at a small communal sink at the edge of the dining room.

SUEÑOS Map pp382-5 — *Mexican*
☎ 212-243-1333; 311 W 17th St; entrees $16-20; ☺ dinner Tue-Sun; subway A, C, E to Eighth Ave, L to 14th St

Chef-owner Sue Torres, who also runs nearby favorite Rocking Horse Café, touts her bright fuchsia-and-orange space as a proud purveyor of authentic Mexican food. While that claim may be questionable (empanadas stuffed with goat cheese? A 'tortilla lady' who cranks out fresh rounds of cornmeal upon a raised corner stage fit for a DJ?), the upper-crust fusion offerings *are* delicious. Quesadillas topped with *huitlacoche*, a fascinating corn fungus that's a popular north-Mexico delicacy, as well as pan-seared snapper with mango salsa, will thrill your taste buds. Reserve early.

TABLA Map pp386-8   *Indian-American Fusion*
☎ 212-889-0667; 11 Madison Ave at 25th St; prix fixe
$57-88; ☟ lunch Mon-Fri, dinner daily; subway N, R,
W 6 to 23rd St

Ascend the sweeping stairway to this 2nd-floor
expanse of light and divine aromas, where some
of the best tables in the house overlook placid
Madison Square Park. Everything created by the
Goa-raised and France-trained chef Floyd Car-
doz sparkles with intelligence and love, from
lobster and haricot verts in coconut curry to
a wild mushroom kebab with braised fennel,
all served with fruity, flowery flourishes. Desserts, such as Tahitian vanilla-bean kulfi and soft
cheese with roasted figs and poached quinces,
are unsurpassed. For a breezier, hipper experience, head to the more casual **Bread Bar** on the
ground floor, where food is straight-up Indian
(tandoori meats, curries, buttery naan) and just
as exquisite.

UNION SQUARE CAFE
Map pp382-5   *American*
☎ 212-243-4020; 21 E 16th St btwn Fifth Ave & Union
Sq W; entrees $23-28; ☟ lunch & dinner; subway L, N,
Q, R, W, 4, 5, 6 to 14th St–Union Sq

This 20-year-old neighborhood hottie is considered one of New York's best, and with good
reason. Formally-clad waiters dote on you, the
wine list is dizzying, and the cuisine, a solid,
elegant cornucopia of falling-off-the-bone
tender lamb, rich risotto and plump gnocchi,
just never gets old – even if the most dedicated, sophisticated regulars must.

Cheap Eats
BETTER BURGER
Map pp382-5   *Organic Burgers*
☎ 212-989-6688; 178 Eighth Ave at 19th St; burgers
$5-10; ☟ lunch & dinner; subway A, C, E to 14th St, L
to Eighth Ave

Catering to all the muscled, protein-loving
boys in the 'hood is this brilliant new take on
the tired old burger, brought to you by the
same folks who own **Josie's** (p198). This sleek,
bright, fast-food joint offers organic, hormone-
free burgers made from your choice of beef,
ostrich, turkey, chicken, tuna, soy or mashed
veggies. All come on homemade whole
wheat buns and are topped with homemade
'tomato zest,' a more sophisticated version of
ketchup. To really treat yourself, add an order
of the air-baked 'fries,' which are so delicious
you'll swear they were dunked in grease.

BONOBOS
Map pp382-5   *Raw Vegan*
☎ 212-505-1200; 18 E 23rd St at Madison Ave; entrees
$5-8; ☟ lunch; subway N, R, 6 to 23rd St

Bringing life in the form of 'live food' to this
uninspired block along the south side of
Madison Square Park is this new veggie café,
which does a swift takeout business. You can
create your own salad with elements from
sun-dried tomatoes and beets to ground
flaxseed crackers to pumpkin seeds, or discover one of the wholesome entrees: the
veggie nut patty platter with homemade
ketchup and the spiral-cut squash topped
with pesto sauce are particularly satisfying.
Live honey dates or almond banana pudding
provide the sweetness.

F&B Map pp386-8   *European Street Food*
☎ 646-486-4441; 269 W 23rd St btwn Seventh &
Eighth Aves; entrees $3-6; ☟ lunch & dinner; subway
C, E, 1, 9 to 23rd St

Yet another result of the recent hot-dog craze
(see **Dawgs on Park**, p180), this bright blue and
white little cubicle, with stool seating around
its perimeter, offers 10 types of toppings
(hummus and grated carrots, feta cheese
and roasted peppers, the ol' kraut 'n' mustard
combo) on beef or smoked-tofu dogs. More
outrageous options include a salmon sausage covered in fresh tomato and lemon or
a smoked-chicken hot dog with corn relish.
Non-dog offerings include haricot-verts frites,
Swedish meatballs, salads, apple beignets and
a range of bottled beers.

POP BURGER
Map pp382-5   *Burgers*
☎ 212-414-8686; 58-60 Ninth Ave; burgers $5-10;
☟ lunch & dinner; subway A, C, E to Eighth Ave,
L to 14th St

It seems the good folks of Chelsea have gone
a little crazy for the humble hamburger. And
if Better Burger, earlier in this section, is a
bit too wholesome for you, then this is the
place to pop into. The gimmick here is that
you get two teensy little burgers instead of
just one – delicious, thick beef burgers
served on fresh challah-like rolls with fresh
lettuce and tomato. And vegetarians have a
magnificent option in the portobello burger,
a big fried meaty-thick mushroom served
on a big version of the tiny buns. The scene
is strictly nightclub; it's open late, for post-
clubbing sustenance, and the back room is
a dark cocktail lounge.

REPUBLIC Map pp382-5 *Pan-Asian*
☎ 212-627-7168; 37 Union Sq West btwn 16th &17th Sts; entrees $4-9; ✆ lunch & dinner; subway L, N, Q, R, W, 4, 5, 6 to Union Sq
It's a delicious bargain. So who cares if it's deafening? Start with a salmon sashimi salad or coconut-crusted shrimp for a few bucks and move on to a tofu udon soup or spinach noodles with soy lime sauce. The restaurant's big, airy space gives diners slurping room.

Top Five 24-Hour Eateries
- **Bereket** (p178) Some of the best Turkish food in the city, available 24/7 and wedged between the East Village and the Lower East Side.
- **Empire Diner** (p184) Dine alfresco, in the fumes, with Chelsea boys and other beauts.
- **Florent** (p182) Join clubbers, locals and plain ol' hungry folk for some steak frites at 4am.
- **French Roast** (p182) Strong coffee, sure. But complete bistro offerings, to boot.
- **Kang Suh** (p195) We're supposed to grill our own meats at 5am? Yep. And sing karaoke, too.

MIDTOWN
AQUAVIT

Map pp386-8 *Scandinavian*
☎ 212-307-7311; 13 W 54th St btwn Fifth & Sixth Aves; 3-course prix fixe $69, tasting menu $90; ✆ lunch & dinner; subway E, V to Fifth Ave–53rd St
Scandinavian cuisine is hard to come by in this city – as is presentation and quality of such high standard as you'll thrill over here. The nearly 25-year-old landmark of streamlined Swedish succulence is still a destination, and even more so in recent years, as proprietor Marcus Samuelsson just won the coveted James Beard award. Enjoy elaborate creations, including veal stew with roasted sunchokes and foie gras ganache with duck sour cherry sausage and apple gelée in the expansive dining room, soothed by a two-story waterfall.

CHO DANG GOI Map pp386-8 *Korean*
☎ 212-695-8222; 55 W 35th St btwn Fifth & Sixth Aves; entrees $10-15; ✆ lunch & dinner; subway B, D, F, V, N, Q, R, W to 34th St–Herald Sq
Groups of Korean youngsters flock to this authentic eatery, located in the area of Midtown known as Koreatown, for meals studded with bits of the signature, homemade tofu.

Traditional *bibimbops* (dish of rice, veggies and/or meat served with a fried egg on top), sticky-rice dishes and pork stews are all among the best in the 'hood, as are the tiny plates of kimchi surprises (including a pile of teensy dried fish, eyes intact) you'll get showered with before your meal begins.

DAWAT Map pp386-8 *Indian*
☎ 212-355-7555; 210 E 58th St btwn Second & Third Aves; entrees $17-23; ✆ lunch Mon-Sat, dinner daily; subway N, R, W to Lexington Ave–59th St
Famed chef, cookbook author and actress Madhur Jaffrey runs this Nirvana outpost, which transforms Indian favorites, including spinach *bhajia* (type of fritter) and fish curries, into exotic masterpieces. Sea bass and lamb chops each get royal treatments with marinades made of various blends of yogurt, mustard seeds, saffron and ginger, and charming, cardamom-flecked desserts cool your palate.

FRANCHIA
Map pp386-8 *Vegan Teahouse*
☎ 212-213-1001; 12 Park Ave btwn 34th & 35th Sts; entrees $11-17; ✆ lunch & dinner; subway 6 to 33rd St
The stunningly stark, black and white, three-level space is evocative of a traditional Korean teahouse, with takeout on the ground floor, a casual café scene on the 2nd floor and an all-out low-tabled lounge on top. Shiny floors, intricately carved wooden sliding doors, grass-green accents and tableware inscribed with tea poems will immediately relax you, as will the 30 types of teas, from black to fruit, available on the substantial menu. Fill yourself up on the Mongolian hot pot, green-tea pancakes, tofu steak or the amazing vegetarian fondue for two with seaweed balls, tofu squares and veggie cakes for double-dipping.

Top Five Eats in Midtown
- **Aquavit** (left) High-class Scandinavian palace of eatin'.
- **Cho Dang Goi** (left) Authentic Korean goodness.
- **Dawat** (above) A star of India mans (womans?) this kitchen.
- **Per Se** (p195) A Time Warner Center creative-American highlight.
- **Russian Samovar** (p197) Blini, caviar and flavored vodkas, oh my!

(Continued on page 195)

Eating – Midtown

1 Roast ducks, Chinatown (p175) **2** Bagels (p54) **3** Hot-dog pushcart (p53)

1 *Prometheus statue (p115), Rockefeller Center* **2** *Pasta, Little Italy (p175)* **3** *Pizza star (p181), East Village*

1 *B Bar & Grill (p213)*
2 *Galapagos (p221)*
3 *BB King's Joint (p240)*

New Amsterdam Theater
225) **2** Ed Sullivan Theater
09) **3** Bowlmor Lanes (p250)

1 *Smalls (p241)* **2** *Times Square (p116)* **3** *Vazac's (p21.*

1 Roller blading, Chelsea Piers (p248) **2** Kayaking (p247), Hudson River **3** Baseball (p44), Yankee Stadium

1 *Prospect Park (p139)* **2** *Che Bryant Park (p111)* **3** *Boating (p247), Central Park*

Sociable Games
Arranged
Please See Director

(Continued from page 186)

GRAND CENTRAL OYSTER BAR
& RESTAURANT Map pp386-8 *Seafood*

☎ 212-490-6650; Grand Central Terminal, Lower Concourse, 42nd St at Park Ave; entrees $17-24; ☽ lunch & dinner Mon-Sat; subway S, 4, 5, 6, 7 to 42nd St–Grand Central

This 90-year-old landmark, sprawled in the basement of Grand Central, is the jewel in the crown of the recently refurbished train station's eateries (Mexican, Italian and Middle Eastern are among the other offerings). Two huge, high-ceilinged dining rooms get filled regularly with lovers of bivalves, served in many varieties with a dollop of mignonette sauce. Cooked fish and bowls of chowder are fine but not stellar, but if you're an oyster fan, you'll be completely satiated.

Towers of (Food) Power

The glitzy new **Time Warner Center** (p111) shopping towers that loom over Central Park at Columbus Circle are home not to one, but to seven impressive high-end restaurants. Among the offerings: **Rare** (☎ 212-823-9500; entrees $25-28), the sprawling steakhouse filled with gilded trees and chandeliers, from Jean-Georges Vongerichten, who made his mark at favorites including Mercer Kitchen and Vong; American creative at the homey **Per Se** (☎ 212-823-9335; entrees $11-28); French-Asian fusion at **Café Gray** (☎ 212-823-6338; entrees $50-75), where Gray Kunz, of the defunct Lespinasse, will reign over an open kitchen; and **Masa** (☎ 212-823-9800; tasting menu $300), a Japanese rich-person's lair complete with a celebrity following that easily rivals Nobu.

KANG SUH

Map pp386-8 *Korean*

☎ 212-564-6845; 1250 Broadway at 32nd St; entrees $10-15; ☽ 24hr; subway B, D, F, V, N, Q, R, W to 34th St–Herald Sq

This Koreatown barbecue joint has a few things that set it apart from the rest: for one, you do your own cooking over piles of hot coals that your server brings to you by the bucket. Plus, it's got karaoke to make it a rowdy draw for party-lovin' young folk. Couple that with the fact that the place stays open all night, and you'll have more excitement to go along with your grilled prime steak and chicken than you'd ever bargain for.

HELL'S KITCHEN (CLINTON)

Not exactly known as a culinary destination, Hell's Kitchen has lately begun developing a true kitchen culture of its own. You'll find old, cheap standards on these gritty stretches, plus a burgeoning crop of nouveau-American hot spots, thanks to the northern creep of Chelsea and the growing development west of Ninth Ave.

44 & X HELL'S KITCHEN

Map pp386-8 *American*

☎ 212-977-1170; 622 Tenth Ave at 44th St; entrees $19-24; ☽ dinner daily, brunch Sat & Sun; subway A, C, E to 42nd St–Port Authority

The South Beach vibe here – thanks to its hunky, well-groomed, cell-phone–lovin' clientele – provides a warm welcome on an otherwise bleak stretch of Tenth. Tables are packed tightly, but the simply white and beige decor and wide front windows make it airy and light; the menu, with a mix of updated comfort foods (mushroom-and-herb-crusted halibut, creamy mac 'n' cheese, chili-rubbed pork loin), are even better.

LANDMARK TAVERN

Map pp386-8 *American*

☎ 212-757-8595; 626 Eleventh Ave at 46th St; ☽ lunch & dinner; subway A, C, E to 42nd St–Port Authority

This 1868 structure once housed the tavern owner's family (see the 2nd-floor living room); this means that you can enjoy your steak, Irish soda bread and grilled fish in a historic setting, complete with fireplace and period furniture. But don't expect a cramped, dull replica of bygone days. This spacious eatery buzzes with the energy of modern-day Manhattan.

MARKET CAFÉ Map pp226-7 *American*

☎ 212-564-7350; 496 Ninth Ave btwn 37th & 38th Sts; entrees $10-14; ☽ lunch & dinner Mon-Sat; subway A, C, E to 34th St–Penn Station

The Formica tables, white tile walls and bright teal booths will make you think 'old-school diner.' But the charming service, cool steel chandeliers and chic lounge music – not to mention the fresh menu – will show you that this is a special, Downtown-hip kinda place. A serving of steak frites is succulent, cod roasted in veal broth is divine and salads are verdant and refreshing. Expect to wait on weekends.

Eating – Midtown

SOUL FIXINS

Map pp386-8   *Southern American*

☎ 212-736-1345; 371 W 34th St at Ninth Ave; entrees $8-14; ☺ breakfast, lunch & dinner; subway A, C, E to 34th St–Penn Station

It's a tiny storefront that's hot and humid inside no matter what the weather, due to the simmering pots of collards, mac 'n' cheese, candied yams and other down-South specialties that cook all day long. Treat yourself to a $5 breakfast of fish or eggs with grits, and sample all the veggie sides with a lunch combo plate. At dinner, prices and offerings rise with barbecued chicken or ribs, meatloaf and heaped servings of chicken and dumplings. Customers are harried in-and-outers who work in nearby office buildings; you can lounge for as long as you want in the close, steamy quarters.

Pizza restaurant

SPLASHLIGHT STUDIOS

Map pp386-8   *Creative American*

☎ 212-268-7247; 529-535 W 35th St btwn Tenth & Eleventh Aves; entrees $16-20; ☺ lunch Mon-Fri; subway A, C, E to 34th St–Penn Station

So you're in town for a weekend-long convention at the Siberia-based Jacob Javits Center and it's lunchtime. Do you: a) settle for stale, plastic-wrapped hoagies from the pitiful Javits Center vendors; b) hike three avenues east to scare up some decent grub; or c) lounge over a decadent meal in a sexy, sunny, secret

space just across the street? Pick c, and you'll be rewarded with artistic nouveau creations, including miso-glazed salmon with *yuzu* (type of citrus), sesame crawfish and a luscious glass of one of the excellent wines. Housed in a stylishly modern photography studio, you'll most likely get a glimpse of a 10ft-tall exquisite model on your way to the loo.

Cheap Eats
MANGANARO'S

Map pp386-8   *Italian Deli*

☎ 212-947-7325; 492 Ninth Ave at 37th St; meals $6-9; ☺ lunch Mon-Sat; subway A, C, E to 34th St–Penn Station

Fresh mozzarella and prosciutto sandwiches, penne with vodka sauce and meatball parm heroes are among the best in the city at this family-owned gourmet food shop.

TIMES SQUARE & THEATER DISTRICT

Pizza joints, Irish pubs and mid-range ethnic restaurants fill up the side streets off Times Square. But in recent years, thankfully, some restaurateurs have figured out that theatergoers would like to get some quality grub before or after a show, and now you'll find a rich offering of top-notch eateries, as well.

✱ BARBETTA Map pp226-7   *Italian*

☎ 212-246-9171; 321 W 46th St; entrees $25-30; ☺ lunch & dinner

Barbetta is steeped in history, from its townhouse digs once belonging to the Astors, to the fact that it has been family owned and operated since 1906. The baroque dining room, serene garden and impeccable service (not to mention their Piemonte specialties such as crespelle alla Savoiarda, a vegetable- and cheese-filled crepe with veal essence, and liberal use of fancy flavorings such as white truffles) will no doubt keep it around for another century.

✱ JOE ALLEN Map pp226-7   *American*

☎ 212-581-6464; 326 W 46th St; entrees $15-20; ☺ lunch & dinner

Joe does simple food with flair, such as a gigantic chicken salad or pan-roasted sole. The brick walls of the dining room reverberate loudly when it's crowded, which is almost every night. It's impossible to get a table for dinner without a reservation unless you wait until the theater starts at 8pm.

LAKRUWANA Map p226-7 *Sri Lankan*

☎ 212-957-4480; 358 W 44th St at Ninth Ave; entrees $13-17; dinner daily, brunch Sun; subway A, C, E to 42nd St–Port Authority

Step out of the bustling theater-district fray and into the slightly cheesy glitz of this authentic Sri Lankan dining room. It's a welcome relief from the steaks and salads that are more easily found in these parts, as your taste buds will be wowed by sweet-sour-spicy delicacies such as rice and coconut crepes filled with egg, and a steamed banana leaf filled with rice, plantain, eggplant, caramelized onions, and curry. The tastes prove that Bernadette Peters isn't the only one on Broadway who can sing.

MESKEREM Map p226-7 *Ethiopian*

☎ 212-664-0520; 468 W 47th St btwn Ninth & Tenth Aves; entrees $10-15; ☺ lunch & dinner; subway C, E to 50th St

Sop up huge and fiery, berbere-sauce-flecked dishes with the spongy, expands-in-your-stomach flatbread called *injera* at this small, dimly-lit dining room located on a placid side street. Meat eaters will love the garlicky chunks of beef and chicken-meets-egg concoction, while vegetarians will love the spicy lentil or chickpea stews.

RUSSIAN SAMOVAR Map pp226-7 *Russian*

☎ 212-757-0168; 256 W 52nd St btwn Broadway & Eighth Ave; entrees $19-25; ☺ lunch Tue-Sat, dinner daily; subway C, E, 1, 9 to 50th St

Co-owner Mikhail Baryshnikov isn't the only lure at this chicken Kiev palace. Russians come in droves for the upscale, authentic dining room, accented by hanging fringed lamps and live music on some nights. And it's easy to gorge yourself with dignity here: caviar and blini or smoked salmon appetizers melt on the tongue, rack of lamb or grilled steak is succulent, and chicken Kiev, seasoned with dill and mustard seeds, is best as it comes. Top off your tank with a cup of traditional cherry tea.

UNCLE NICK'S Map pp226-7 *Greek*

☎ 212-245-7992; 747 Ninth Ave btwn 50th & 51st Sts; entrees $10-16; ☺ lunch Sun-Thu, dinner daily; subway C, E to 50th St

Tourists jam in here on weekends, but for good reason: the brick-walled space is home to some excellent standards. Try the *tsatsiki* (zingy yogurt and cuke) or *skordalia* (garlicky potato) dips, pork kebabs or grilled sardines swimming in lemon and oil. Next door is the calmer and hipper **Ouzaria**, where flavored ouzo cocktails are the focus. It's a great place for a small party of pals.

ZEN PALATE Map pp226-7 *Asian Vegan*

☎ 212-582-1669; 663 Ninth Ave at 46th St; entrees $11-16; ☺ lunch & dinner; subway A, C, E to 42 St–Port Authority

Long before many of the current veggie, faux-meat purveyors hit the restaurant scene, this Midtown joint was doling out fanciful feasts – shredded heaven, basil vegetarian ham, rose petals, moo shu Mexican style – that make creative use of smoked tofu cubes and fresh veggies. And tiny, tapas-like treats make perfectly healthy, post-theater snacks. There's another branch on **Union Square** (☎ 212-614-9291; 34 Union Sq E at 16th St; ☺ lunch & dinner).

Restaurant Row

Officially the block of W 46th St between Eighth and Ninth Aves, Restaurant Row generally refers to almost all the restaurants west of Times Square. To reach any of the following places, take the subway (N, Q, R, S, W, 1, 2, 3, 7, 9) to Times Square–42nd St. Most restaurants in this area keep 'theater hours,' opening for pre-matinee meals at around 11:45am Wednesday, Saturday and Sunday and closing until around 5pm, when they reopen for dinner. Barbetta and Joe Allen are absolute classics.

Cheap Eats

AFGHAN KEBAB HOUSE

Map pp226-7 *Afghan*

☎ 212-768-3875; 155 W 46th St btwn Sixth & Seventh Aves; entrees $10-14; ☎ lunch & dinner; subway F, V to 47th-50th Sts–Rockefeller Ctr

Flavor in da house! Part of a delicious mini-chain, the unique flavors here – a seamless marriage of Indian and Middle Eastern tastes and textures – come in the form of beef kofta, tender stewed pumpkin and rice dishes, or *palau* (a rice dish) topped with goodies from seasoned lamb to orange rind and pistachios.

ISLAND BURGERS & SHAKES

Map pp226-7 *Diner*

☎ 212-307-7934; 766 Ninth Ave btwn 51st & 52nd Sts; burgers $6-8; ☺ breakfast, lunch & dinner; subway C, E to 50th St

Recently closed down for a couple of months due to a fire, the surf-themed Island is quickly swimming back. You'll find such eclectic options here as Thai chicken salad, fajitas and classic BLTs, but the reason to come is for, duh, the burgers and shakes. Fat, expertly grilled beef patties (as well as *churascos*, or grilled chicken breasts) come in a whopping 50 disguises – Bourbon Street (blackened, served on sourdough and topped with bacon, jack and Bajou mayo) and Pop and Top's (with Thai sauce, jalapeño and roasted peppers) among them. And the shakes, in vanilla, chocolate, strawberry or black & white, are thick and rich.

KEMIA Map pp226-7 *Moroccan Tapas*
☎ 212-582-3200; 630 Ninth Ave at 44th St; small plates $5-8; ☷ dinner Mon-Sat; subway A, C, E to 42nd St–Port Authority
A rose-petal–strewn floor, cushy ottomans, tapestries billowing from the ceilings, excellent DJs, a multi-culti crowd and killer cocktails would be enough of a draw. But excellent and affordable tapas, too? Try the Lebanese cheese trio, zingy hummus plate, crispy polenta with goat cheese or merguez sausage with tahini. They're all excellent.

UPPER WEST SIDE
This huge swath of neighborhood – from the classic-arts Lincoln Center 60s to the well-heeled, residential 70s and 80s blocks to the more eclectic 90s – has plenty of good grub to mine. But it wasn't particularly destination-worthy until the last few years, when Tom Valenti made a splash with his creative-American stunner **Ouest** (p199) and other greats followed. Now it's got everything.

A Map pp389-91 *Caribbean Fusion*
☎ 212-531-1643; 947 Columbus Ave btwn 106th & 107th Sts; entrees $8-13; ☷ dinner Tue-Sat; subway B, C to 103rd St
This closet-sized find is a tiny miracle: delicious food served at unbelievably low prices, made even better by its BYO policy. The crowd is cool, the space is adorable (especially the subway maps that adorn the walls) and the staff as friendly as folks in little towns.

AIX Map pp389-91 *French*
☎ 212-874-7400; 2293 Broadway at 88th St; entrees $26-35; ☷ dinner daily, brunch Sat & Sun; subway 1, 9 to 86th St
Part of the stellar-cuisine new wave, chef Didier Virot is wowing New Yorkers with his upscale versions of updated Gallic classics. Roasted halibut gets dressed up in a sweet garlic cream and paired with an oatmeal porcini cake while boneless pork short ribs get braised with fennel seed and lemon and

nestled with smashed sweet potatoes. Even a bar experience in this warm, two-storey palace – try the swoon-inducing cosmo – is a special treat indeed.

Top Five Eats on the Upper West Side
- **Aix** (left) French destination for uptown foodies.
- **'Cesca** (below) Upscale Italian, luscious wines.
- **Josie's** (below) Dairy-free, organic dining with style.
- **Mana** (opposite) Clean food, precious flavor.
- **Ouest** (opposite) Valenti's original UWS magnet.

'CESCA Map pp389-91 *Italian*
☎ 212-787-6300; 164 W 75th St btwn Columbus & Amsterdam Aves; entrees $17-26; ☷ dinner; subway 1, 9, 2, 3 to 72nd St
It wasn't enough for Tom Valenti to reign in the 80s, so he opened a place in the 70s, too – to the joy of foodies there and everywhere, who were jonesing for some classy Italian food. The handsome, comforting place (stained wood, candelabra, sumptuous leather banquettes) is the setting for mackerel, chicken ragout, wild game and ravioli classics, as well as clever antipasti options such as marinated baby artichokes with fresh ricotta and tiny veal meatballs with pastina. The impressive wine list offers mainly Italian bottles and plenty of by-the-glass choices, which you could opt to sip at the classy up-front bar, while nibbling serious bar snacks such as spicy parmigiana fritters.

JOSIE'S Map pp389-91 *Organic*
☎ 212-769-1212; 300 Amsterdam Ave at 74th St; entrees $10-16; ☷ lunch & dinner; subway 1, 9, 2, 3 to 72nd St
The shtick here – not that it needs one – is dairy-free. There are plenty of treats for meat-eaters (roasted chicken breast, burgers) and veggies alike (roasted yams, beets, greens and tempeh; vegetarian meatloaf), and all ingredients are farm-fresh and organic. The only thing absent is cheese and milk (soy and rice milk stand in for coffee), and with all the clever salads, stews and toothsome desserts – not to mention the excellent organic-wine list – you'll never miss 'em. There's another branch at **Third Ave** (Map pp389-91; ☎ 212-490-1558; 565 Third Ave at 37th St; ☷ lunch & dinner; subway 6 to 33rd St). For healthful but slightly more traditional and upscale food after a show at Lincoln Center, try **Josephina**, at 1900 Broadway between 63rd and 64th Sts, from the same owners.

MANA Map pp389-91 *Vegetarian/Macrobiotic*
☎ 212-787-1110; 646 Amsterdam Ave btwn 91st & 92nd Sts; entrees $9-15; ◷ lunch & dinner, brunch Sat & Sun; subway 1, 9, 2, 3 to 96th St

The clean and simple atmosphere is like a second home to many healthful locals, who come for the welcoming service and pure, delicious meals. Greens, grains and beans change daily, as do entree specials, which include Asian-influenced stews and noodle dishes and organic-fish options for those needing a big dose of protein. Vegan chocolate cake, paired with a luscious cup of grain 'coffee' with maple syrup and soy milk, is a perfect way to end.

OUEST Map pp389-91 *Modern American*
☎ 212-580-8700; 2315 Broadway btwn 83rd & 84th Sts; entrees $19-33; ◷ dinner daily, brunch Sun; subway 1, 9 to 86th St

Chef-owner Tom Valenti is widely credited as the man who brought a foodie revolution to the Upper West Side, which was known as a gourmet's wasteland for years. But his lively, upscale ambience and eclectic menu – with stunners such as braised lamb shank and pan-roasted sturgeon with risotto – changed all that for good. Ouest is the pioneer food-destination that still reigns, along with its delicious followers.

TAVERN ON THE GREEN
Map pp389-91 *Modern American*
☎ 212-873-3200; Central Park West at 67th St; entrees $10-20; ◷ brunch & dinner; subway B, C to 72 St

This world-famous restaurant, nestled into the western edge of the park, is basically a glitzy, overpriced tourist destination. Still, with a half-million patrons annually, it must be doing something right. Judge for yourself with a sunset cocktail at the bar after a (well-dressed) day in the park. If you like the vibe, go for the gusto. Pricey menu offerings range from penne with eggplant and tomatoes ($20) to filet mignon ($37).

TURKUAZ Map pp389-91 *Turkish*
☎ 212-665-9541; 2637 Broadway at 100th St; entrees $10-16; ◷ lunch & dinner; subway 1, 9 to 103rd St

A transporting atmosphere highlighted by tapestry-draped ceilings and weekend belly dancers comes at exceptionally reasonable prices here – as do authentic, Istanbul-style mezes and big dishes, including pine-nut studded stuffed grape leaves, marinated lamb kebabs, skewered swordfish and a fragrant vegetable casserole. The candlelit front lounge is a great setting for shots of raki, plates of mezes and romance.

Cheap Eats

CAFÉ VIVA Map pp389-91 *Vegetarian Pizza*
☎ 212-663-8482; 2578 Broadway at 97th St; entrees $3-8; ◷ lunch & dinner; subway 1, 2, 3, 9 to 96th St

It looks like a regular pizzeria, but look closely at the offerings and you'll see it's anything but. Thick pizza slices come in such healthful options as spelt crust with roasted peppers, shiitake mushrooms and soy cheese; cornmeal crust with sweet peppers, corn and mozzarella; and whole wheat crust with miso-marinated tofu, eggplant, tomatoes and spinach. They've got traditional pies, too, as well as calzones, salads, sandwiches and pasta dishes.

SAIGON GRILL Map pp389-91 *Vietnamese*
☎ 212-875-9072; 620 Amsterdam Ave at 90th St; entrees $6-12, lunch special $5-6; ◷ lunch & dinner; subway 1, 2, 3 to 96th St

Locals pack the place – or call for incessant takeout orders, which arrive so fast you'll swear they were cooked on the back of the delivery guy's bicycle – for traditional noodle, curry and rice dishes. For dessert, don't miss Grandma's sweet rice dumplings, glutinous little balls stuffed with sugary peanut butter.

UPPER EAST SIDE

Although this neighborhood tends to be tony and relatively conservative, you'll find dozens of casual and ethnic little eateries in the mix.

✈BEYOGLU Map pp389-91 *Turkish*
☎ 212-650-0850; 1431 Lexington Ave at 81st St; entrees $11-15; ◷ lunch & dinner; subway 6 to 77th St

This is one of restaurateur Orhan Yegen's spots – a charismatic, loungey space where yogurt soup, doner kebabs and feta-flecked salads are elegant and excellent. Get in early for your pick of a good table; it's within strolling distance of the Met, making for a tasteful way to end an artistic afternoon.

⚜ CAFÉ SABARSKY Map pp389-91 *Austrian*
☎ 212-288-0665; Neue Galerie, 1048 Fifth Ave at 86th St; entrees $12-17; breakfast, lunch & dinner; subway 4, 5, 6 to 86th St

Located on the ground floor of the gorgeous, Klimt-filled Neue Galerie museum and across the street from leafy Central Park, this airy café couldn't be in a better spot. Luckily, the meals and pastries are just as good. Try warming beef goulash, cod strudel or a tangy herring sandwich, or rich little cakes served with strong coffee or hot chocolate. Sometimes, quality acts take over the room, turning it into a high-end cabaret supper club.

Top Five Brunch Places

- **Balthazar** (p174) Sour cream hazelnut waffles, smoked salmon with crème fraîche and brioche, and hangover drinks such as the potent Ramos Fizz… What's not to love?
- **Copeland's** (p201) Chicken 'n' waffles mixed with live gospel music make a Harlem magnet.
- **Lakruwana** (p197) Jumpstart a Sunday matinee with some jackfruit curry, rice crepes and other Sri Lankan goodies.
- **Mana** (p199) Vegans tired of shunning omelettes for dry toast will rejoice in multigrain waffles, excellent tofu scrambles and creamy rice porridge.
- **Prune** (p180) It's all about the nine types of over-garnished Bloody Marys – but the oysters, lox, fresh pastries and handsome hipsters don't hurt, either.

CANDLE CAFE Map pp389-91 *Vegetarian*
☎ 212-472-0970; 1307 Third Ave btwn 74th & 75th Sts; entrees $12-15; ⏱ lunch & dinner; subway 6 to 77th St
In a 'hood where quality veggie selections are hard to come by, Candle is a light at the end of a carnivorous cave – it's sandwiched, in fact, by a popular steakhouse and a burger joint. Wealthy New Age types are the norm in this simple storefront, permeated by the constant, clean scent of wheatgrass due to the juice bar stationed up front. Offerings range from the most simplistic – Good Food plates, a custom-made spread of greens, roots, grains and soy-based protein – to the more complex concoctions, such as the beloved Paradise Casserole, a feast of layered sweet potatoes, black beans and millet topped with mushroom gravy. Vegan cakes are surprisingly moist.

DANIEL Map pp389-91 *French*
☎ 212-288-0033; 60 E 65th St btwn Madison & Park Aves; prix fixe $88; ⏱ dinner; subway F to Lexington Ave–63 St, 6 to 68th St–Hunter College
The biggest draw here is celebrity chef Daniel Boulud and his cult of personality. His ornate and mind-boggling cuisine takes a close second, though. Amid elaborate floral arrangements and wide-eyed foodies are plates of peeky toe crab and celery-root salad, foie gras terrine with gala apples and black-truffle crusted lobster – and that's just for first course. Stunning entrees range from cod confit with fennel, grapefruit, chickpeas and cardamom to a duo of beef, which gets you short ribs braised in red wine paired with roasted tenderloin dressed up with creamy celery mousseline.

ETHIOPIAN RESTAURANT

Map pp389-91 *Ethiopian*
☎ 212-717-7311; 1582 York St btwn 83rd & 84th Sts; entrees $10-14; ⏱ lunch & dinner; subway 4, 5, 6 to 86th St
It's got a simple name and atmosphere, but it's a gem – especially if you happen to be this far east anyway. Use your endless servings of springy *injera* bread to mop up every last bite here, as all things – spicy lentils, peppery beef cubes, stew-like collard greens – leave you wanting more. Traditional honey wine complements it all with a sweet, refreshing bite.

Cheap Eats
LEXINGTON CANDY SHOP

Map pp389-91 *Diner*
☎ 212-288-0057; 1226 Lexington Ave at E 83rd St; entrees $5-10; ⏱ breakfast, lunch & dinner; subway 4, 5, 6 to 86th St
This picture-perfect lunch spot is complete with an old-fashioned soda fountain. Here, schoolkids suck up primo egg creams and malteds while neighborhood folks nurse a

Balthazar (p174)

coffee or a famed lime rickey. Best of all, this place sells burgers and other classic diner fare at reasonable prices in one of the city's most expensive neighborhoods.

HARLEM & NORTHERN MANHATTAN

Justifiably famous for its traditional soul food, the latest wave of gentrification has brought the f-word – fusion – to these parts in recent years. Get ready for more atmospheric options than ever before.

HARLEM

AMY RUTH'S RESTAURANT

Map pp392-3   *Soul Food*

☎ 212-280-8779; 114 W 116th St btwn Malcolm X Blvd (Lenox Ave) & Adam Clayton Powell Jr Blvd (Seventh Ave); entrees $11-16; ☽ breakfast, lunch & dinner, 24hr Fri & Sat; subway B, C, 2, 3 to 116th St

Locals know to choose this place over the tour-bus frequented soul-food spot with that other woman's name. While Sylvia's is delicious, not to mention legendary, this less frenzied gem has all the standards – candied yams, smoked ham, corn pudding, fried okra, you name it – but has a particular specialization in waffles. Choose from chocolate, strawberry, blueberry, smothered in sautéed apples, or paired with fried chicken. You'll be glad you strayed.

COPELAND'S

Map pp392-3   *Soul Food*

☎ 212-234-2357; 547 W 145th St btwn Amsterdam Ave & Broadway; entrees $15-20; ☽ dinner daily, brunch Sun; subway A, B, C, D, 1, 9 to 145th St

The pastel-colored dining room, hung with oil portraits of famous African Americans, has all the classics: fried chicken, catfish and barbecued chicken and ribs. Sunday's gospel brunch gets packed, so reserve early.

NATIVE Map pp392-3   *Caribbean*

☎ 212-665-2525; 101 W 118th St at Malcolm X Blvd (Lenox Ave); entrees $10-14; ☽ lunch & dinner; subway 2, 3 to 116th St

The scenesters lounging on the animal-print banquettes here are just as hip as the grub, including cumin-flecked fried chicken, plantain fritters, red curry coconut shrimp and pan-seared catfish. It's one of the newer offerings on the young-Harlem scene.

ORBIT Map pp392-3   *Eclectic*

☎ 212-348-7818; 2257 First Ave at 116th St; entrees $10-15; ☽ lunch & dinner; subway 6 to 116th St

This bohemian eatery from Minnie Rivera, Sofina Terzo and Angelique Irrizary – the latter two promoters for two of the biggest lesbian parties in town (Lovergirl and Shescape, respectively) – boasts exposed-brick walls, a classy oak bar, hand-painted tables and a massive mural of Marilyn Monroe. And its party roots show: you can enjoy live jazz, blues or Brazilian vocalists nightly along with a mixed bag of festive meal options, including everything from roasted duck rolls and edamame to chicken pot pie and steak au poivre.

Top Five Eats in Harlem-Morningside Heights

- **Amy Ruth's** (left) Southern standards – minus the tour-bus masses.
- **Charles' Southern Style Kitchen** (p202) Cheap and crispy fried chicken and fixins.
- **Copeland's** (left) *The* place for a soulful jazz brunch.
- **Native** (left) A hip fusion outpost.
- **Strictly Roots** (p202) Soul food for vegans.

SUGAR HILL BISTRO

Map pp392-3   *Southern American*

☎ 212-491-5505; 458 145th St btwn Amsterdam & Convent Aves; entrees $19-26; ☽ dinner daily, brunch Sat & Sun; subway A, C, B, D, 1, 9 to 145th St

Welcome to the Harlem Renaissance. Within the walls of this landmark, two-story Victorian brownstone, you'll find artworks by notable African-American artists (for sale), live jazz on weekend nights, R&B brunch on Saturday and a popular gospel brunch on Sunday. And then there's the food, served in the elegant upstairs dining room: chicken and dumplings, Louisiana-style jambalaya, herb-crusted lamb chops and spaghetti with black-angus meatballs.

SYLVIA'S Map pp392-3   *Southern American*

☎ 212-996-0660; 328 Malcolm X Blvd; entrees $10-15; ☽ lunch & dinner; subway 2, 3 to 125th St

Open since 1962, this famous Harlem eatery is overrun with tour buses these days. But original owner Sylvia Woods still sweats in the kitchen herself some days, one of a slew who help to churn out massive portions of buttery collards, fried catfish and excellent banana pudding.

Cheap Eats
CHARLES' SOUTHERN
STYLE KITCHEN Map pp392-3   *Soul Food*
☎ 212-926-4313; 2839 Frederick Douglass Blvd
(Eighth Ave) btwn 151st & 152nd Sts; entrees $5-7;
☯ lunch & dinner; subway B, D to 155th St

Along with some of the best fried chicken
in Harlem, you'll find salmon cakes and tasty
macaroni and cheese, all part of the rotating
daily special lineup at this tiny takeout joint. The
all-you-can-eat buffet in the dining room ($10
lunch, $12 dinner) is an astounding bargain.

STRICTLY ROOTS

Map pp392-3   *Jamaican Vegan*
☎ 212-864-8699; 2058 Adam Clayton Powell Jr Blvd
(Seventh Ave) btwn 122nd & 123rd Sts; entrees $6-9;
☯ lunch & dinner; subway A, B, C, D, 2, 3 to 125th St
This Rastafarian-loved haven promises to serve
'nothing that crawls, walks, swims or flies.' And
the cafeteria-style spot does quite well with
the ingredients that remain, offering a rotating
menu of fried plantains, faux-beef curry, stews
and stir-fried veggies, along with fresh juices
and thick smoothies.

MORNINGSIDE HEIGHTS
Columbia and its charges have colonized
much of this part of Manhattan and you'll
stumble across plenty of cheap and late-night
diners and bars geared to students. There are
a few pearls in the detritus, though.

TERRACE IN THE SKY

Map pp392-3   *French*
☎ 212-666-9490; 400 W 119th btwn Morningside
Dr & Amsterdam Ave; entrees $29-36 & prix fixe $45
Tue-Thu; ☯ lunch Sun-Fri, dinner daily; subway 1, 9 to
116th St–Columbia University
This penthouse suite of Columbia's Butler Hall
is where smarty-pants students get mom and
dad to take them on parents' weekend. What
the vast dining room lacks in stuffy, overly-
simple decor (white tablecloths, red velvet
chairs, pockmarked drop ceiling), it makes up
for in view: a 16th-floor stunner of the precious
city and its endless sky. The dishes, courtesy
of Jason Potanovich, don't disappoint, either.
Salmon is encrusted in mustard seeds and
nestled against smoky lentil jus and finger-
ling potatoes, while partridge is served with
quinoa, chanterelles, caramelized turnips and
foie gras sauce.

TOMO
Map pp392-3   *Japanese*
☎ 212-665-2916; 2850 Broadway at 111th St; meals
$13-17; ☯ lunch & dinner; subway 1, 9 to 110th
St–Cathedral Pkwy
Fresh, reasonably priced sushi is a big draw
for students and scores of locals. But equally
appealing are the warming options of chicken
katsu (dish of sliced boneless chicken), noodle
bowls, tempura, bento boxes and salmon teri-
yaki. Vegetarians love the *futomaki* (mixed-
veggie sushi roll) and shiitake-cucumber
hand rolls.

Cheap Eats
OLLIE'S NOODLE SHOP
& GRILLE Map pp392-3   *Chinese*
☎ 212-932-3300; 2957 Broadway; entrees $6-10;
☯ lunch & dinner; subway 1, 9 to 116th St
This bright, bustling, late-night favorite is an
all-glass peephole onto frenetic Broadway.
Similar to other branches of this city chain,
with a massive menu offering all manner of
noodle soups, stir-fries, dumplings, salads –
even pastas and burgers, oddly enough.

TOM'S RESTAURANT
Map pp392-3   *Diner*
☎ 212-864-6137; 2880 Broadway at W 112th St;
entrees $5-8; ☯ breakfast, lunch & dinner; subway 1,
9 to 116th St
Once an ordinary Greek diner, this hangout
shot to pseudo-stardom twice: first, when
Suzanne Vega's 'Tom's Diner' was released
(although many believe the Tom's in Brooklyn was the true inspiration for that song)
and second, when the exterior started appearing regularly as the hangout for TV's
Seinfeld crew. Menu options – omelettes,
burgers, Greek salads and the like – are still
ordinary, but at least as good as any other
beloved greasy spoon in town.

OUTER BOROUGHS
BROOKLYN
In Brooklyn's eateries, there's less rush to
finish your meal than at some Manhattan
restaurants. Smith St in Cobble Hill and
Carroll Gardens has undergone a renaissance in the past decade, with many French

bistros. Williamsburg's younger scene welcomes a new restaurant or two seemingly every month. Mingle with the locals on Fort Greene's DeKalb Ave, a few blocks east of Flatbush Ave.

ALMA

Map p394 _Mexican_
☎ 718-643-5400; 187 Columbia St at DeGraw St; entrees $12-18; ☯ dinner; subway F, G to Bergen St

Hugging the edge of the former no-man's-land area – the part of Carroll Gardens that's cut off from the quaint area by the Brooklyn-Queens Expressway – Alma is party central in this hoppin' new scene. The three-level energy nexus is home to a mellow bar on its ground floor, a dramatic dining space in the middle and a marvelous roof garden on top, where you can gaze at sweeping views of the Manhattan skyline while you dive into your specialty margarita and delicious Mexi-fusion meal. Choose from spice-rubbed tuna, grilled-veggie fajitas, succulent ceviche, grilled duck with a luscious tomato-peanut sauce and the richest cube of flan this side of the border.

BANANIA CAFE

Map p394 _French & International_
☎ 718-237-9100; 241 Smith St; entrees $13-20; ☯ dinner daily, brunch Sat & Sun; subway F, G to Bergen St

At this cozy bistro, one of many on the street, waitstaff with accents serve well-prepared fish dishes (try the potato-crusted skate) and a _very_ tender braised lamb shank. There's always at least one vegetarian option, such as the

cheese-covered pumpkin ravioli. It positively buzzes at brunch on weekends – a basket of pastries and breads is plopped on your table before you even get a chance to cast your eyes at a menu.

BLUE RIBBON BROOKLYN

Map p394 _American_
☎ 718-840-0404; 280 Fifth Ave; entrees $13.50-28.50; ☯ dinner till late; subway M, R to Union St

A spin-off of the Manhattan location, this buzzing Park Slope restaurant has a wild array of meats (rack of lamb, pigeon, New York strip) plus lobster, fish and a super vegetarian k-bob. Those waiting for a seat slurp up oysters at the bar (half a dozen for $12). Things keep going late. Next door is Blue Ribbon's **sushi restaurant** (☎ 718-840-0408) with sleek wooden benches and an impressive show of raw fish.

DINER

Map p394 _American_
☎ 718-486-3077; 85 Broadway; entrees $10-20; ☯ lunch & dinner; subway J, M, Z to Marcy Ave

The stylin' low-lit dining car from 1927, nearly under the Williamsburg Bridge, is one of Williamsburg's most-loved and best eating places. The small menu has standard fare; better to go with one of the daily specials. Always several fish dishes and a veggie option along with steaks and super grilled pork loin – all artfully prepared. Often a DJ sits at the fully stocked bar. Brunch is big with late-morning stumblers-in.

GRIMALDI'S

Map p394 _Pizzeria_
☎ 718-858-4300; 19 Old Fulton St; pizzas $12-14; ☯ lunch & dinner; subway A, C to High St, 2, 3 to Clark St

Known as Patsy's in another life – and still widely recognized as the makers of one of New York's best pies – Grimaldi's beats most of them with its brick-oven, tomato-slice-thin pizzas served in its 'under the Brooklyn bridge' family-style location. This place is perfect for pizza: red-and-white checkered tabletops, star-studded photo collection on the walls, and half a dozen greatest hits collections by Frank Sinatra (plus a Slade album) on the jukebox.

Top Five Eats in the Outer Boroughs

- **Grimaldi's** (right) Perfect pies under the bridge.
- **Jackson Diner** (p205) All-you-can-eat Indian meals every day.
- **Junior's** (p204) Heavenly cheesecake.
- **River Cafe** (p204) Luxe meals overlooking Midtown lights.
- **Roberto's** (p205) The best of the real Little Italy.

JUNIOR'S

Map p394   *Cheesecakes & American*

☎ 718-852-5257; 386 Flatbush Ave; cheesecake $4.50, breakfast $5-8.50, sandwiches $4-12; ⏰ breakfast, lunch & dinner till late; subway B, M, Q, R to DeKalb Ave

Maybe cheesecakes begin as ancient hovering spirits, perhaps of the slain from Celtic battlefields, spending centuries roaming the earth, searching for *the* ideal baker and their re-entry into the physical. This is it. Junior's is cheesecake's Xanadu. If this sounds overly dreamy, you haven't tried it. Open since 1950, Junior's also serves breakfasts and sandwiches.

Nathan's Famous Hot Dogs

If you eat 'em, this is *the* place to try an all-beef dog with sauerkraut and mustard. It's a bite of history: Nathan's (☎ 718-946-2202; 1310 Surf Ave; hot dogs $2.25; ⏰ breakfast, lunch & dinner till late; subway D, F to Coney Island/Stillwell Ave) has been serving the Coney Island invention here since 1916. Every July 4, Nathan's holds a dog-eating contest – the record (held by a *small* Japanese man) is 50½. Also on the menu are fried fish, fried chicken, burgers and clams. No veggie alternatives.

LIQUORS

Map p394   *Cajun/American*

☎ 718-488-7700; 219 DeKalb Ave; entrees $10-16; ⏰ breakfast, lunch & dinner Sat & Sun, dinner till late Mon-Fri; subway B, M, Q, R to DeKalb Ave

One-time liquor store now dressed up like weather-worn bayou bistro, Liquors serves Cajun-inspired meals (jambalaya with sausage and rum chicken, cornmeal-crusted catfish) and a mean prix-fixe brunch on weekends ($12.50). In good weather, the back courtyard is open. It's a highlight along DeKalb's busy-with-locals dining scene.

NATIONAL

Russian

☎ 718-646-1225; 273 Brighton Beach Ave; prix-fixe dinner $60; ⏰ dinner till late; subway B, Q to Brighton Beach

Raucous and thoroughly Russian, the National nightclub storms to life on weekend nights, when the vodka flows and dancing begins. Pick Russian or French dishes from the prix-fixe menu. It's hearty stuff: spinach blintzes, roasted duck, eel with rice, cornish game hen, but not much for vegetarians. All tables in the

two-leveled floor, of course, face the on-stage, over-the-top live shows.

PETER LUGER STEAKHOUSE

Map p394   *Steak*

☎ 718-387-7400; 178 Broadway; steaks $28-37; ⏰ lunch & dinner; subway J, M, Z to Marcy Ave

A Williamsburg meat-eating haven since 1887, Peter Luger serves up some of the city's juiciest sirloin cuts (as well as lamb chops, grilled salmon and – for beginners – burgers). It's timeless dining, from its Bavarian design and rather brusque waitstaff in aprons. No major credit cards accepted.

RIVER CAFE

Map p394   *International*

☎ 718-522-5200; 1 Water St; prix-fixe brunch $35 & dinner $70; ⏰ lunch & dinner; subway A, C to High St, 2, 3 to Clark St

This famous question-popping high-class restaurant gazes over Brooklyn Bridge and Lower Manhattan and has food to match the view: duck breast smothered in foie gras, caviar services, fresh seafood and at least one vegetarian option. Dinners and Sunday are prix fixe. Gentlemen must wear jackets in the main dining room after 5pm.

TOM'S RESTAURANT

Map p395   *Diner*

☎ 718-636-9738; 782 Washington Ave; entrees $2.75-$8; ⏰ breakfast & lunch Mon-Sat; subway 2, 3 to Eastern Pkwy–Brooklyn Museum

Three blocks from the Brooklyn Museum of Art, this happy greasy spoon woos locals with its all-day breakfasts and egg creams. Open since 1936, much of the decor (floral in all possible forms) has been picked up along the way. It's good and it's cheap: two eggs, toast, coffee, home fries or grits costs $2.75. Friendly staff bring by 'cold orange slices' and cookies during your meal or while you wait.

QUEENS

Queens' ethnically diverse neighborhoods (see p142) are packed with shameful-to-omit restaurants serving an array of cheap, international meals. Some of Manhattan's biggest restaurants are offshoots of the originals out here.

Astoria's 31st St at Ditmars Blvd (subway N, W to Astoria–Ditmars Blvd) is a hubbub of Greek restaurants. Flushing (subway 7 to Flushing–Main St) has scores of Chinese, Taiwanese, Japanese and Korean eateries. Jackson Heights (subway 7 to 74th St–Broadway) has many Indian and Filipino restaurants. In Corona, walk along Roosevelt Ave between 74th St and 103rd St (under the No 7 line) to find fantastic Mexican, Peruvian, Colombian and Ecuadorian *restaurantes*.

For hearty European fare (and Czech beer), visit **Bohemian Hall & Beer Garden** (p222).

JACKSON DINER   *Indian*
☎ 718-672-1232; 3747 74th St, Jackson Heights; entrees $9-22; ☽ lunch & dinner; subway 7 to 74th St–Broadway

Widely touted as the city's best Indian food, this diner-convert curry house delivers the goods with south Indian specialties (such as the veggie-filled *masala dosas* or *uthapam* lentil pancakes) and big selection of lamb and chicken curries (no beef, things are kept real here). A lunch buffet runs 11:30am to 4pm daily ($6.95 Monday to Friday, $8.95 Saturday and Sunday). Walk north a block, past the sari shops, from the subway station (and Roosevelt Ave).

KUM GANG SAN
Map p397   *Korean & Japanese*
☎ 718-461-0909; 138-28 Northern Blvd, Flushing; entrees $8-50; ☽ 24hr; subway 7 to Flushing–Main St

Dressed up like an old Korean teahouse, Kum Gang San is one of Flushing's nicest (and busiest) eateries, packing in a full house for the DIY table barbecue (sirloin steak, ribs, shrimp), sushi, maki rolls and Korean stews and soups. Weekday lunch specials, such as a bowl of bibimbops with beef and vegetables, run $7 to $13.

LEMON ICE KING OF CORONA
Map p397   *Italian Ice*
☎ 718-699-5133; 52-02 108th St, Corona; cups $1-2; ☽ lunch & dinner Sep-Jun, lunch & dinner till late Jul–Aug; subway 7 to 103rd St–Corona Plaza

Across from Spaghetti Park's bocce court, the old-time King gives the area its timeless aura. The tasty ices come in 25 flavors; the best are ones with real chunks of lemon, watermelon, cherry and other fruits. The King is about half a mile south from the subway, also reached via Flushing Meadows Corona Park.

UNCLE GEORGE
Map p396   *Greek*
☎ 718-626-0593; 33-19 Broadway; entrees $7-16.50; ☽ 24hr; subway N, W to Broadway, G, R, V to Steinway St

This simple, corner bistro-style diner, overlooks Astoria's Greek bakeries and shops. Uncle George serves up lots of meat (eg plump beef-filled grape leaves with egg-lemon sauce) and fish dishes (not much for the vegetarian). There are plenty of daily specials, such as rabbit stew.

WATER'S EDGE
Map p396   *American*
☎ 718-482-0033; 44th Dr & East River, Long Island City; entrees $24-36; ☽ lunch & dinner Mon-Sat; subway 7 to 45 Rd–Court House Sq, E, V to 23rd St–Ely Ave

Floating impressively on an East River barge, Water's Edge is high-class and romantic dining with views of the beaming Manhattan skyline – the dining's alfresco in good weather. The food's impressive too. Seasonal menus are balanced between fish dishes (eg fresh Atlantic halibut with artichokes and fennel) and standard fare such as grilled filet mignon. Best of all is arriving by boat; the restaurant offers free boat service from its E 34th St pier on the East River (boats leave from 6pm to 10:45pm).

THE BRONX

Belmont, or 'Little Italy in the Bronx,' is the borough's most famous culinary enclave with tempting trattorias and pizzerias spilling onto side streets. It's centered on Arthur Ave, just south of Fordham University (subway B, D to Fordham Rd). Walk east on Fordham Rd from the subway station, then right on Arthur Ave. City Island (p147) has scores of fresh seafood choices.

ROBERTO'S
Map pp398-9   *Italian*
☎ 718-733-2868; 632 E 186th St at Belmont Ave; entrees $8-26; ☽ lunch & dinner Tue-Fri, dinner Sat; subway B, D to Fordham Rd

Often sworn by its fans, with frightening passion, as New York's (not just Belmont's) best Italian restaurant, friendly Roberto's fills its small, inviting space early, and stays that way. Do as many regulars do and forgo the wine-splattered menus, and ask *'per cortesia, vorrei provare la scelta del cuoco'* ('I'd like to try the chef's choice please'). Daily specials are many: swordfish steaks, veal cutlets, with pasta sides. In nice weather, sidewalk seating is the way to go. Afterward linger unhurried over wine, espresso and dessert.

TONY'S PIER

Map pp398-9   *Seafood*

☎ 718-885-1424; 1 City Island Ave; entrees $9-22; ☾ dinner till late; subway 6 to Pelham Bay Park then bus No Bx29

On City Island's southern tip, Tony's Pier is pure mayhem. Enough so that signs are posted, in English and *Español*, to help get you to the right queue (one says, 'read the signs to find out where to order your food'). One line leads to a fried world: calamari, lobster tails, scallops, porgy (all come with fries); in another is raw stuff (clams, oysters). Dining's simple – plastic cups and plates, Formica tabletops – and the bar bustles till late.

Drinking

Drinking

Like everything else in this fair city – eateries, shops, cultural institutions, personality types – watering holes come in endless incarnations. You can pick your poison and let that be your guide, leading you to swank martini lounges, sweaty beer halls, drunk-ass shots-of-whiskey dives or sophisticated wine bars. Or you can choose by scene, sipping elixirs with model-gorgeous gay men, a buttoned-up after-work crowd, hooting sports fans, greasy-haired hipsters or knowledgeable wine tasters.

Whatever your taste, keep a couple of points in mind: first, thanks to the city's smoking ban, there's absolutely no lighting up in bars anymore. Unless you're in a specified cigar bar (which, curiously enough, are still allowed, even though the smoke stinks even more…) or at one of the places lucky enough to have outdoor patios or roof decks, you'll be banished to the sidewalk for your tobacco breaks, rain or no rain. Second, be aware that bars must legally close at 4am, and some close at 2am. So plan ahead for last call. Finally, know that many of the bars listed here are actually called *lounges* – living-room-cum-bars with DJs, plush couches and super-low lighting, which popped up everywhere when former mayor Rudy Giuliani started enforcing NYC's arcane cabaret laws. They're the moody places of choice for folks who don't care for blaring jukes and seedy pool-table areas. But don't worry – there are still *plenty* of those at hand, too.

Top Five Drinking Spots

- **Bar Veloce** (p213) A skinny wine bar with panache.
- **Chibi's Bar** (p211) Sake's the thing at this Soho gem.
- **Louis** (p213) Impromptu jazz and tasty cocktails in the East Village.
- **Pravda** (p210) A cave of infused-vodka goodness.
- **xl** (p217) For gay men and their friends, a space that's befittingly dramatic.

Dublin House (p220)

LOWER MANHATTAN

Like its minimal restaurant scene, you won't find a slew of bars to belly up to down here. What you will find are financial types unwinding at much-anticipated happy hours and a couple of slick lounges.

JEREMY'S ALE HOUSE Map pp380-1
☎ 212-964-3537; 254 Front St at Dover St; ☾ 8am-11pm Mon-Fri, 10am-midnight Sat, noon-7pm Sun; subway J, M, Z to Chambers St, 2, 3 to Fulton St, 4, 5, 6 to Brooklyn Bridge–City Hall

An odd mix of frat house and quirky dive bar. You'll find bras hung over the bar, cheap pints served in Styrofoam cups and a lovely view of the Brooklyn Bridge – not to mention frighteningly early opening hours.

PUSSYCAT LOUNGE Map pp380-1
☎ 212-349-4800; 96 Greenwich St at Rector St; ☾ noon-3am Mon-Wed, noon-4am Thu-Sat; subway N, R, W, 1, 9 to Rector St

For some unknown reason, this battered go-go bar has become a hip place for slumming. Most nights bring young financial types, but a fabulous gay crowd turns the place queer on Monday.

REMY LOUNGE Map pp380-1
☎ 212-267-4646; 104 Greenwich St btwn Carlisle & Rector Sts; ☾ 5pm-4am Wed-Sat; subway N, R to Rector St

This down-to-earth two-level lounge is loco with salsa and other tropical rhythms heating up the dance floor nightly, as well as '80s disco on Friday. It's refreshingly free of hipsters at all times.

RISE Map pp380-1
☎ 212-344-0800; Ritz-Carlton New York, 14th fl, 2 West St at Battery Pl; ☾ 4pm-midnight Mon-Thu, 4pm-1am Fri & Sat, 5:30-11pm Sun; subway N, R, W to Rector St

Even $13 martinis won't make you think twice about hanging at this Ritz-Carlton view bar, where the sleek, high-up lounge affords spectacular vistas of sunsets over the Hudson, tasty martinis and amusing people-watching opportunities.

TRIBECA & SOHO

Though the super-trendies have moved on to the Lower East Side, you'll still find several see-and-be-seen bars in these parts.

Lounges abound, but seek and ye shall find basic, real-people pubs aplenty, too.

TRIBECA

BUBBLE LOUNGE Map pp380-1
☎ 212-431-3433; 228 West Broadway btwn Franklin & White Sts; ☾ 5pm-2am Mon-Thu, 6pm-4am Fri & Sat; subway 1, 2 to Franklin St

Patronized by well-heeled Wall St types getting giddy on 280 varieties of champagne and sparkling wine, this is the place to drop $2000 on a bottle of champagne. Luckily, you can also order bubbly by the glass for around $12.

CHURCH LOUNGE Map pp380-1
☎ 212-519-6600; 2 Sixth Ave btwn Walker & White Sts; ☾ 8-4am; subway A, C, E to Canal St, 1, 9 to Franklin St

Located in the swanky lobby of the Tribeca Grand Hotel, it's the epitome of lounge: low lighting, cozy nooks, beautiful patrons and sweet elixirs.

LIQUOR STORE BAR Map pp380-1
☎ 212-226-7121; 235 West Broadway at White St; ☾ noon-4am; subway A, C, E to Canal St

In a Federal-style building that its owners proudly claim has been in commercial use since 1804, and with big windows and outdoor tables offering plenty of people-watching. The bar takes its name from a previous business at the same site, and offers a down-to-earth respite from Tribeca trendies.

LUSH Map pp380-1
☎ 212-766-1275; 110 Duane St btwn Broadway & Church St; ☾ 5pm-4am Tue-Fri, 9pm-4am Sat; subway A, C, 1, 2, 3, 9 to Chambers St

Top-shelf liquors, Belgian brews and weekend DJs lure refined patrons to its red couches and elevated banquettes.

PUFFY'S TAVERN Map pp380-1
☎ 212-766-9159; 81 Hudson St btwn Harrison & Jay Sts; ☾ noon-4am; subway 1, 9 to Franklin St

This oft-empty, old-school tavern is worn and lovely, with jazz on its juke and locals on its stools.

RACCOON LODGE Map pp380-1
☎ 212-776-9656; 59 Warren St btwn Church St & West Broadway; ☾ 10-4am Mon-Fri, 3pm-4am Sat & Sun; subway A, C, 1, 2, 3, 9 to Chambers St

The Downtown branch of this watering hole (there's also a branch on the **Upper West Side**, p220) has excellent atmosphere – the hooch is strong, the popcorn free and the fireplace, pool table and pinball machine are unbeatable on any given winter night. After work it's a little stiff with suits, but as the evening progresses the neighborhood and biker regulars come out.

WALKER'S Map pp380-1
☎ 212-941-0142; 16 North Moore St at Varick St; ☾ noon-4am; subway 1, 9 to Franklin St
Sunday night jazz is the only scene going on here – unless you count the no-frills pints at the bar, beef-heavy menu and down-to-earth folks hanging in this unpretentious tavern. A TV in the front room pulls in big crowds for the World Series and other major sporting events.

SOHO

BAR 89 Map pp382-5
☎ 212-274-0989; 89 Mercer St btwn Broome & Spring Sts; ☾ noon-2am Mon-Thu, noon-3am Fri-Sun; subway N, R, W to Prince St
Models and model wannabes flock here for scotches and other fine liquors, but the biggest attraction is the bathrooms – unisex stalls with see-through doors that fog into an opaque shield when you lock yourself in.

BRITTI CAFFÉ BAR Map pp382-5
☎ 212-334-6604; 110 Thompson St btwn Prince & Spring Sts; ☾ noon-2am; subway N, R, W to Prince St
Cocktails at this airy, big-windowed Italian café have names inspired by Italian cars, and the hot-pressed panini and sexy crowd here are just as racy.

CAFE NOIR Map pp382-5
☎ 212-431-7910; 32 Grand St at Thompson St; ☾ noon-4am; subway A, C, E to Canal St
Probably best known for its hot bathroom sex scene in the 2002 film *Unfaithful*, this sultry, sophisticated spot has less-carnal treats, such as its North African and Mediterranean inspired appetizers. Munch away while watching the passing Soho parade from the open-air bar railing.

CIRCA TABAC Map pp382-5
☎ 212-941-1781; 32 Watts St btwn Sixth Ave & Thompson St; ☾ 6pm-2am Mon-Wed, 6pm-4am Thu-Sat; subway A, C, E, 1, 9 to Canal St
One of the few places left where you not only can smoke, but are encouraged to do so, Tabac

offers more than 150 types of smokes, mainly global cigars. The lounge is sumptuous, just like much of its fine-cut tobacco.

EAR INN Map pp382-5
☎ 212-226-9060; 326 Spring St btwn Greenwich & Washington Sts; ☾ noon-4am; subway C, E to Spring St
A block from the Hudson River, this great old dive sits in the old James Brown House (the James Brown who was an aide to George Washington, not Soul Brother No 1), which dates back to 1817. Patrons range from sanitation workers and office dweebs to bikers and poets – and all of them love it, as well as the bar's famous shepherd's pie.

PRAVDA Map pp382-5
☎ 212-226-4944; 281 Lafayette St btwn Prince & Houston Sts; ☾ 5pm-1am Mon-Wed, 5pm-2:30am Thu, 5pm-3:30am Fri & Sat, 6pm-1am Sun; subway B, D, F, V to Broadway–Lafayette St
Pravda tried to remain on the down low, but lines out the door leaked the secret to the entire city. If you dress hip enough and look sufficiently intense, you'll make it past the gatekeepers and enter clouds of cigar smoke in this mock East European speakeasy. The martinis make all the hassle worth it, though; the two-page vodka list includes Canada's Inferno Pepper, a home-grown Rain Organic and a slew of specialty martinis.

PUCK FAIR Map pp382-5
☎ 212-431-1200; 298 Lafayette St btwn E Houston & Prince Sts; ☾ 11-4am Mon-Fri, noon-4am Sat & Sun; subway B, D, F, V to Broadway–Lafayette St
Pints of Guinness and plates of bangers and mash reign at this two-level Irish pub, which has a slick and modern air about it. Round corner tables are perfect for big groups, and the downstairs room, complete with DJs and little snugs, is good for canoodlers.

SAVOY Map pp382-5
☎ 212-219-8570; 70 Prince St at Crosby St; ☾ noon-11:30pm Mon-Thu, noon-midnight Fri & Sat, 5-11pm Sun; subway N, R, W to Prince St
The horseshoe-shaped bar, just inside a vast window, is the perfect place to perch yourself for a glass of wine and a small plate of olives after a hard day of doing whatever. The warm, inviting atmosphere and excellent people-watching opportunities complete the lovely picture.

CHINATOWN & LITTLE ITALY

Drinking in these nabes is a mixed bag – offering a strange mix of old-man dives and hyper-trendy hideaways.

CHIBI'S BAR Map pp382-5
☎ 212-274-0025; 238 Mott St btwn Prince & Spring Sts; ☾ 6pm-midnight Tue-Thu, 5pm-2am Fri, 2pm-2am Sat, 2pm-midnight Sun; subway 6 to Spring St
This tiny, romantic sake bar works its magic through smooth jazz sounds and the dangerously delicious flavors of specialty sakes and saketinis. The best part is the host, Chibi, a sweet little bulldog.

DOUBLE HAPPINESS Map pp382-5
☎ 212-941-1282; 173 Mott St btwn Broome & Grand Sts; ☾ 6pm-2am Sun-Wed, 6pm-3am Thu, 6pm-4am Fri & Sat; subway J, M, Z to Bowery, 6 to Spring St
This tiled, basement-level bar tunnels through an old apartment with a narrow skylight room and tables tucked into candlelit corners. Pretty girls scan the crowd for a well-dressed Romeo among the wrinkled bards. It's too cool to be signed, but look for the steep stone steps.

GOOD WORLD BAR & GRILL Map pp382-5
☎ 212-925-9975; 3 Orchard St btwn Canal & Division Sts; ☾ 11-4am; subway F to East Broadway, B, D to Grand St
Here, in the thick of Chinatown, is this sleek, wooden Swedish bar, of all things. It's got nice high barstools and a sweet back patio and is the perfect example of how worlds collide in this unpredictable city.

MARE CHIARO Map pp382-5
☎ 212-226-9345; 176½ Mulberry St btwn Broome & Grand St; ☾ 10-1am Mon-Thu, 10-2am Fri & Sat, noon-1am Sun; subway B, D to Grand St
Frank Sinatra liked this 100-year-old Little Italy hang, which was also used as a backdrop for scenes in *The Godfather*.

SWEET & VICIOUS Map pp382-5
☎ 212-334-7915; 5 Spring St btwn Bowery & Elizabeth St; ☾ 4pm-4am; subway J, M to Bowery, 6 to Spring St
This wide-open bar with hardwood floors and hard-ass benches will leave your butt sore if you don't get up and shake your thang to the good music – or at least down plenty of the reasonably priced cocktails.

WINNIE'S Map pp382-5
☎ 212-732-2384; 104 Bayard St btwn Baxter & Mulberry Sts; ☾ noon-4am; subway J, M, Z, N, Q, R, W, 6 to Canal St
Performing drunken, embarrassing karaoke at this Chinatown dive is a rite of passage for New Yorkers. The place is tiny and always packed, the disgusting cocktails (such as the Abortion, a mixture of Sambuca and Baileys) are potent, and the weird karaoke videos, flashed behind you on a movie screen, are hopelessly stuck in the '80s.

LOWER EAST SIDE

Ludlow St and environs used to be a dingy, fringe neighborhood populated by old-timers and newcomers until the early '90s, when the entire area exploded with bars, unmarked lounges, restaurants and live-music clubs. Now it's a convenient and overpopulated spot for a pub crawl, with endless variety of scenes in a very condensed area.

ADULTWORLD Map pp382-5
☎ 212-253-0035; 116 Suffolk St btwn Delancey & Rivington St; ☾ 9pm-4am Tue-Sun; subway J, M, Z to Delancey–Essex Sts
No, it's not a porn palace, but more like a funhouse for grown-ups, with strangely convoluted stairways (one that goes to nowhere), blaring music and booths good for making big groups feel cozy. The entrance, as you may have guessed, is yet another too hip to have a sign.

ANGEL Map pp382-5
☎ 212-780-0313; 174 Orchard St btwn Houston & Stanton Sts; ☾ 7pm-3am Sun-Thu, 6pm-4am Fri, 7pm-4am Sat; subway F, V to Lower East Side–2nd Ave
DJs turn the beat around night after night at this tiny lounge, soothing chic fans of high-quality cocktails with anything from R&B to electronica.

BARRAMUNDI Map pp382-5
☎ 212-529-6900; 147 Ludlow St btwn Stanton & Rivington Sts; ☾ 5pm-4am Mon-Fri, 6pm-4am Sat, 7pm-4am Sun; subway F, J, M, Z to Delancey St
This is an Australian-owned arty place featuring convivial booths, reasonably priced drinks and a lovely, shady garden.

HAPPY ENDING Map pp382-5

☎ 212-334-9676; 302 Broome St btwn Eldridge & Forsyth Sts; ☯ 6pm-2am Tue-Wed, 6pm-3am Thu, 6pm-4am Fri & Sat, 9pm-4am Sun; subway F to Delancey St, J, M, Z to Delancey–Essex Sts

Formerly an Asian massage parlor and bathhouse, this underground den of former iniquity still has showerheads in its walls and a feeling of immersion. Guys cruise the perimeter for dolled-up gals and precious elixirs.

MAGICIAN Map pp382-5

☎ 212-673-7851; 118 Rivington St btwn Essex & Norfolk Sts; ☯ 5pm-4am; subway F to Delancey St, J, M, Z to Delancey–Essex Sts

An unassuming storefront with the requisite low lighting and well-mixed drinks. You'll find an unpretentious crowd, wonderfully eclectic jukebox and plenty of space to put your elbows on the bar.

ORCHARD BAR Map pp382-5

☎ 212-673-5350; 200 Orchard St btwn Stanton & E Houston Sts; ☯ 8:30pm-4am Tue-Sat; subway F, V to 2nd Ave

This unmarked place is populated by mostly drunk, mostly beautiful urbanites kicking back on the banquettes and grooving to DJs spinning deep house and techno-type beats.

PARKSIDE LOUNGE Map pp382-5

☎ 212-673-6270; 317 E Houston St at Attorney St; ☯ 1pm-4am; subway F, V to Lower East Side–2nd Ave

It's the dive bar of choice for many hipsters, who like to slum it every once in a while when they OD on sleek lounges. You'll find no such nonsense here – just cheap drinks, pool and a weekly comedy show on Tuesday.

SCHILLER'S LIQUOR BAR Map pp382-5

☎ 212-260-4555; 131 Rivington St at Norfolk St; ☯ 4pm-2am; subway F to Delancey St, J, M, Z to Delancey–Essex Sts

This oasis on an otherwise gritty corner is part bistro (witness the extensive menu, with steak frites and welsh rarebit) and part liquor lounge (hence the name). Its upbeat, bohemian, upscale feel is lovely, as are its cocktails.

SUBA Map pp382-5

☎ 212-982-5714; 109 Ludlow St btwn Delancey & Rivington Sts; ☯ 6pm-1am Sun-Wed, 6pm-2am Thu, 6pm-4am Fri & Sat; subway F to Delancey St, J, M, Z to Delancey–Essex Sts

Determined to top other trendy hotspots in the neighborhood, Suba's got an actual water-filled moat around its downstairs dining room, where you can get top-notch Spanish food along with your cocktails. Head to the noisy and crowded upstairs lounge for blood-orange margaritas, and you can choose a free tapas with every drink during happy hour.

WELCOME TO THE JOHNSONS
Map pp382-5

☎ 212-420-9911; 123 Rivington St btwn Essex & Norfolk Sts; ☯ 3:30pm-4am Mon-Fri, noon-4am Sat & Sun; subway F to Delancey St, J, M, Z to Delancey–Essex Sts

When this Brady Bunch–like theme bar opened several years ago, former suburbanites couldn't get enough of its tacky '70s living-room vibe. It's still a bit of a novelty, but less so, making it a great place to expect a seat along with your Pabst Blue Ribbon beer, especially on weeknights.

WHISKEY WARD Map pp382-5

☎ 212-477-2998; 121 Essex St btwn Delancey & Rivington Sts; ☯ 5pm-4am Mon-Sat, 5pm-2am Sun; subway F to Delancey St, J, M, Z to Delancey–Essex Sts

This boozers' boîte, a dark and simple watering hole, is for folks who can hold their liquor and like to, as shots and beers are the standard order.

EAST VILLAGE

Just like eating options, drinking choices run the complete gamut here, from skankiest dive to loveliest lounge. You can't walk a block without tripping over a bar – or one of its stumbling patrons, especially on weekends – so it's definitely *the* 'hood for imbibing.

2A Map pp382-5

☎ 212-505-2466; 25 Ave A at 2nd St; ☯ 4pm-4am; subway F, V to Lower East Side–2nd Ave

It's a two-level place with a split personality: bare-bones pub downstairs and homey lounge up. The best part is its name, as you can always remember where to find it.

ANGEL'S SHARE Map pp382-5

☎ 212-777-5415; 2nd fl, 8 Stuyvesant St btwn Third Ave & 9th St; ☯ 6pm-3am; subway 6 to Astor Pl

Sneak through the Japanese restaurant on the same floor to discover this tiny gem of a hideaway, with creative cocktails, well-suited waiters and a civilized policy that states you cannot stay and drink if there's not room enough for you to sit.

B BAR & GRILL Map pp382-5
☎ 212-475-2220; 40 E 4th St at Bowery;
🕑 11:30-3am Mon-Fri, 10:30-3am Sat & Sun; subway 6 to Bleecker St

This place packs in a mixed, moneyed crowd, especially on hot summer nights when the outdoor patio, featuring trees festooned with hot-pink strings of lights, provides sweet relief. Tuesday at B Bar means the notorious Beige party, for which the fabulously queer only need apply.

BAR VELOCE Map pp382-5
☎ 212-260-3200; 175 Second Ave btwn 11th & 12th Sts; 🕑 5pm-3am; subway L to 3rd Ave

A narrow, candlelit wine bar, this refreshingly sophisticated spot serves a mix of uptown and Downtown patrons, all thirsting for the same quality vino, Italian tapas and polite bartenders. Just look for the white Vespa parked permanently outside its entrance.

CHEZ ES SAADA Map pp382-5
☎ 212-777-5617; 42 E 1st St btwn First & Second Aves; 🕑 6pm-midnight Mon-Thu, 6pm-2:30am Fri & Sat; subway F, V to Lower East Side–2nd Ave

This two-level lounge has a Moroccan theme, strewn rose petals and some of the mintiest *mojitos* around.

D.B.A. Map pp382-5
☎ 212-475-5097; 41 First Ave btwn 2nd & 3rd Sts; 🕑 1pm-4am; subway F, V to Lower East Side–2nd Ave

A dark and bare-bones pub, the draw here is the massive menu, hand-scrawled on a big chalkboard, announcing about 125 beers, 130 single-malt scotches and 50 tequilas.

ESPERANTO Map pp382-5
☎ 212-505-6559; 145 Ave C at 9th St; 🕑 6pm-midnight Sun-Thu, 6pm-1am Fri & Sat; subway L to 1st Ave, 6 to Astor Pl

This open-air, pan-Latin bar and café, serving a mouthwatering mix of margaritas and Cuban rice and beans, is best visited in summer. Sidewalk seating is perfectly situated across the street under the massive weeping willow tree of a neighborhood garden, and the frequent live music from inside wafts softly out to you.

FEZ Map pp382-5
☎ 212-533-2680; 380 Lafayette Ave btwn Great Jones & W 4th Sts; 🕑 4pm-3am; subway 6 to Bleecker St

Lush darkness, potted plants and couches are the draws at this, yet another Moroccan-tinged lounge. This one sits off the bright and airy dining room; one flight down is the intimate performance space, home to acts from jazz bands to Joan Rivers.

HOLIDAY COCKTAIL LOUNGE Map pp382-5
☎ 212-777-9637; 75 St Marks Pl btwn First & Second Aves; 🕑 5pm-4am; subway 6 to Astor Pl

You want dive bar? You've got it, right here. The old-school, battered, charming place feels as if it's from another era – and with $3 drinks, it might as well be.

IL POSTO ACCANTO Map pp382-5
☎ 212-228-3562; 190 E 2nd St btwn Aves A & B;
🕑 6pm-2am Tue-Sun; subway F, V to Lower East Side–2nd Ave

Opened as a waiting lounge by the owners of the always mobbed Il Bagatto restaurant next door, this lovely little open-air Italian wine bar has 120 different pours, plus excellent snacks to tide you over.

KGB Map pp382-5
☎ 212-505-3360; 85 E 4th St btwn Second & Third Aves; 🕑 7pm-4am; subway F, V to Lower East Side–2nd Ave

Dipped in a Commie-red mood, KGB is one of the few bars in which you can actually have a conversation; literary meetings and other artistic endeavors are sponsored here as well, and it's a favorite hang for staffers at the *Village Voice*, housed just around the corner.

LOUIS Map pp382-5
☎ 212-673-1190; 649 E 9th St btwn Aves B & C;
🕑 6pm-3am; subway F, V to Lower East Side–2nd Ave

Named for Louis Armstrong, this tiny lounge serves up excellent wines, cocktails and panini, not to mention free, quality, live jazz music most nights.

MARION'S CONTINENTAL RESTAURANT & LOUNGE Map pp382-5
☎ 212-475-7621; 354 Bowery btwn Great Jones & E 4th Sts; 🕑 5:30pm-2am; subway 6 to Bleecker St

Thought most come to eat at the kitschy 1950s supper club – or drink and dance at the wildly popular gay bar Slide, just next door – the romantic front bar here should not be overlooked. It's the perfect spot for a relaxing martini.

MARS BAR Map pp382-5
☎ 212-473-9842; 25 E 1st St at Second Ave; ⏲ 5pm-4am; subway F, V to Lower East Side–2nd Ave
A scruffy relic from the heyday of East Village punk, Mars Bar is a graffiti-covered hollow where tattooed kids caress bottles of beer and headbang to their favorite speed-metal riffs.

MEOW MIX Map pp382-5
☎ 212-254-0688; 269 E Houston St; ⏲ 7pm-4am; subway F, V to Lower East Side–2nd Ave
Legendary lesbo bar filled with baby dykes and rocker chicks, staying strong long after the *Chasing Amy* scene made it better known. Sexy femmes pour in on Thursday for Gloss, a huge and messy weekly go-go affair for the young and sassy. Some will tell you that life begins after your first Xena Night, held in early June and December. Happy hour is 5pm to 8pm nightly.

ODESSA CAFÉ Map pp382-5
☎ 212-253-1470; 110 Ave A btwn St Marks Pl & E 7th St; ⏲ 24hr; subway 6 to Astor Pl
You may not have to be buzzed into the bathrooms for security reasons anymore, but this Polish-diner-turned-bar, right on Tompkins Square Park, is classic East Village scruff. The decor has never been updated (witness the gaggy red, bumpy ceiling), even though liquor was just added into the mix a few years ago, and the clientele is pure tattooed, grungy fun. You definitely enjoy your $4 cocktail and plate of rib-sticking pierogi.

PATIO DINING Map pp382-5
☎ 212-460-0992; 31 Second Ave btwn 1st & 2nd Sts; ⏲ 5pm-2am Sun-Thu, 5pm-3am Fri & Sat; subway F, V to Lower East Side–2nd Ave
This former parking lot is now like a lovely outdoor patio at your pal's – even though it's technically inside. It's got floor-to-ceiling windows, slick couches, excellent mixologists, and top-notch grub in the adjoining restaurant.

PRESSURE (AT BOWLMOR LANES) Map pp382-5
☎ 212-255-8188; 110 University Pl btwn E 12th & E 13th Sts; ⏲ 11-4am Mon, Fri, Sat, 11-1am Tue, Wed, Sun, 10-2am Thu; subway L, N, Q, R, W, 4, 5, 6 to 14th St–Union Sq
The dome-covered lounge, featuring a Twister game and other playthings, is an annex to the

hip alleys, boasting a disco soundtrack and glow-in-the-dark bowling, with a retro atmosphere that's popular for large groups. (For Bowlmor Lanes information see p250).

SCRATCHER Map pp382-5
☎ 212-477-0030; 209 E 5th St at Third Ave; ⏲ 11:30-4am; subway 6 to Astor Pl
This watering hole attracts a large Irish clientele because it looks like a true Dublin pub. It's a quiet place to sip coffee and read the newspaper during the day but a crowded and raucous spot at night.

SLIDE Map pp382-5
☎ 212-420-8885; 356 Bowery; ⏲ 5pm-4am; subway F, V to Lower East Side–2nd Ave, 6 to Astor Pl
It's shenanigans galore (eg naked go-go boys) at this newcomer East Village bar, run by new hot promoter Daniel Nardicio. Attitude-free vibe: skinny boys with beards, tattoos, some dykes in the mix – you name it. Drag queens get chatty with mics on Friday, and the all-out queen show is after midnight on Saturday. And there's $2 beers during happy hour (5pm to 9pm daily) and an open bar from 5pm to 6pm. Whoa now, Dan!

STARLIGHT BAR & LOUNGE Map pp382-5
☎ 212-475-2172; 167 Ave A; ⏲ 7pm-3am Tue-Thu, 7pm-4am Fri & Sat; subway L to 1st Ave
This is a sultry, loud, straight-friendly lounge with a devoted following of Downtown cuties – boys and girls. But Sunday means Starlette, a long-running lesbians-flirting cosmo-sipping party.

SWIFT HIBERNIAN LOUNGE Map pp382-5
☎ 212-242-9502; 34 E 4th St btwn Bowery & Lafayette St; ⏲ noon-4am; subway 6 to Bleecker St
You could stage a cattle raid from the wooden tables of this medieval hall-like pub; instead you should just have another pint of Guinness and enjoy the live bands. Church pews and candles complete the Irish atmosphere.

UNCLE MING'S Map pp382-5
☎ 212-979-8506; 225 Ave B btwn 13th & 14th Sts; ⏲ 6pm-4am Mon-Fri, 8pm-4am Sat; subway L to 1st Ave
This sexy bar on the 2nd floor over a liquor store has upholstered couches for languidly sipping designer cocktails. The bar is unsigned, adding to its mystery.

VAZAC'S Map pp382-5

☎ 212-473-8840; 108 Ave B at E 7th St; 🕑 5pm-4am; subway L to 1st Ave, 6 to Astor Pl

A local favorite at the southeast end of Tompkins Square Park, it's got sticky floors, a horseshoe-shaped bar and plenty of pinball. Also called 7B's, it's been featured in films, including *The Verdict* and *Crocodile Dundee*.

WAIKIKI WALLY'S Map pp382-5

☎ 212-673-8908; 101 E 2nd St at First Ave; 🕑 6pm-3am Sun-Thu, 6pm-4am Fri & Sat; subway 6 to Bleecker St

A kitschy tiki bar, this theme-crazy funhouse gives you leis, bamboo thatching, Hawaiian-shirted bartenders and fruity drinks.

WEST (GREENWICH) VILLAGE

This area's bohemian coffeehouse legend still prevails – hence the preponderance of earthy, homey bar-cafés – but the clientele has devolved to one that's often a mix of frat boys and bridge-and-tunnel visitors. Still, old-school charm, gay or straight, can be found if you get off the beaten paths.

APT Map pp382-5

☎ 212-414-4245; 419 W 13th St btwn Ninth Ave & Washington St; 🕑 10pm-4am; subway A, C, E to 14th St, L to Eighth Ave

This way-chic, bi-level lounge features sleek design, glowing light in fiery red and yellow tones, and pretty patrons. The upstairs reservations-only level feels like a private, wealthy living room.

BAR D'O Map pp382-5

☎ 212-627-1580; 29 Bedford St at Downing St; 🕑 6pm-3am Mon-Fri, 7pm-4am Sat & Sun; subway 1, 9 to Houston St

This plush lounge features drag acts several nights a week and attracts a chic mixed crowd of gays and straights (except on Monday, which is the long-running lesbian party Pleasure).

BLIND TIGER ALEHOUSE Map pp382-5

☎ 212-675-3848; 518 Hudson St at W 10th St; 🕑 1pm-4am; subway 1, 9 to Christopher St–Sheridan Sq

Gregarious and without pretension, this old-timers' joint keeps the good feelings flowing with daily specials on Brooklyn microbrews, plus plenty of free bar grub.

CHUMLEY'S Map pp382-5

☎ 212-675-4449; 86 Bedford St btwn Grove & Barrow Sts; 🕑 4pm-midnight Sun-Thu, 4pm-2am Fri & Sat; subway 1, 9 to Christopher St–Sheridan Sq

This is a hard-to-find, storied speakeasy that serves decent pub grub along with 11 beers on tap. Look for the unmarked brown door in a white wall.

CORNER BISTRO Map pp382-5

☎ 212-242-9502; 331 W 4th St btwn Jane & W 12th Sts; 🕑 11:30-4am Mon-Sat, noon-4am Sun; subway 1, 9 to Christopher St–Sheridan Sq

It's a famous bar from the bygone beat era where you can eat charred hamburgers until 2am at carved wooden tables. Many consider the enormous, half-pound bistro burger with bacon and onions the best in the city.

COWGIRL/BAR K Map pp382-5

☎ 212-633-1133; 519 Hudson St at 10th St; 🕑 11-2am; subway 1, 9 to Christopher St–Sheridan Sq

It's a strange confluence of culture here: urbanites mingling among cowgirl paraphernalia, eating Fritos smothered in melted cheese and sipping okra martinis. Choose from the TV-outfitted front bar and restaurant, the back loungey area or the back-back sprawling bar.

HELL Map pp382-5

☎ 212-727-1666; 59 Gansevoort St btwn Greenwich & Washington St; 🕑 7pm-4am Sat-Thu, 5pm-4am Fri; subway A, C, E to 14th St, L to Eighth Ave

One of the original lounges in the area, this dark, high-ceilinged spot gets a mixed queer-straight crowd that's never hellish.

HENRIETTA HUDSON Map pp382-5

☎ 212-924-3347; 438 Hudson St; 🕑 4pm-3am Mon & Tue, 4pm-4am Wed-Fri, 1pm-4am Sat & Sun; subway 1, 9 to Houston St

Bridge-and-tunnel lesbians with big hair and lipstick and gym-teacher wannabes put on their hard-drinking hats and dance to Melissa Etheridge on the juke or line up to play some pool.

HUDSON BAR & BOOKS Map pp382-5

☎ 212-229-2642; 636 Hudson St btwn Horatio & Jane Sts; 🕑 5pm-2am Mon-Thu, 5pm-4am Fri & Sat; subway A, C, E to 14th St, L to Eighth Ave

A re-creation of a men's club, this is where you'll find a country-library feel, a James Bond drink theme, and plenty of chess games to choose from.

MARIE'S CRISIS Map pp382-5
☎ 212-243-9323; 59 Grove St btwn Seventh Ave S & Bleecker St; ☽ 4pm-4am; subway 1, 9 to Christopher St–Sheridan Sq
Aging Broadway queens and other fans of musicals assemble around the piano and take turns belting out campy numbers, often joined by the entire crowd.

OTHER ROOM Map pp382-5
☎ 212-645-9758; 143 Perry St btwn Greenwich & Washington Sts; ☽ 5pm-2am Sun & Mon, 5pm-3am Tue-Thu, 5pm-4am Fri & Sat; subway 1, 9 to Christopher St–Sheridan Sq
This beer-and-wine-only hideaway, on the very western edge of the Village, is a small, civilized sanctuary.

RHÔNE Map pp382-5
☎ 212-367-8440; 63 Gansevoort St btwn Greenwich & Washington Sts; ☽ 6pm-4am Mon-Sat; subway A, C, E to 14th St, L to Eighth Ave
This massive, concrete, industrial space (warmed up with creative lighting, of course) is one of the sleekest spots for wine imbibing, as you'll find 300 bottles and almost 40 choices by the glass.

Henrietta Hudson (p199)

STONEWALL BAR Map pp382-5
☎ 212-463-0950; 53 Christopher St; ☽ 3pm-5am; subway 1, 9 to Christopher St–Sheridan Sq
The site of the Stonewall riots in 1969, when drag queens fought back during a police raid, the Stonewall Bar is a drinking place (with some feisty events) for leathermen, drag queens and lesbians – you know, everyone.

WHITE HORSE TAVERN Map pp382-5
☎ 212-989-3956; 567 Hudson St;
☽ 11-2am Sun-Thu, 11-4am Fri & Sat; subway 1, 9 to Christopher St–Sheridan Sq
This handsome bar was Dylan Thomas' last drinking hole and has seen almost every New York–based writer while away an evening. If your plan is for quiet journal writing and scotch sipping, though, get here nice and early; late-nights belong to the noisy frat-boy crowd nowadays.

CHELSEA
Thought mostly the domain of sleek cruising lounges (and massive nightclubs) for gorgeous gay men, there's still some variety to be found here, whether it's for old-school jazz or a plain ol' pint.

BONGO Map pp386-8
☎ 212-947-3654; 299 Tenth Ave btwn 27th & 28th Sts; ☽ 5pm-2am Mon-Wed, 5pm-3am Thu-Sat; subway C, E to 23rd St
This pint-sized lounge has an upscale design that's punctuated by Eames chairs, and is a perfect location for a post–gallery-opening cocktail.

CAJUN Map pp382-5
☎ 212-691-6174; 129 Eighth Ave btwn 16th & 17th Sts; ☽ noon-2am; subway A, C, E to 14th St, L to Eighth Ave
Hear Dixieland jazz, free of cover, nightly at this New Orleans–style bar-restaurant, where folk sip on-tap beers and chow down on shrimp gumbo or catfish as modern boys swish by the open-air facade on their way to clubs.

CHELSEA BREWING COMPANY
Map pp386-8
☎ 212-336-6440; Chelsea Piers, Pier 59, West Side Highway at 23rd St; ☽ noon-2am; subway C, E to 23rd St
Enjoy one of the quality microbrews, waterside, in the expansive outdoor area of this way-west beer haven – a perfect place to re-enter the world after a day of swimming, golfing or rock climbing at the sports center here.

EAGLE NYC Map pp386-8

☎ 646-473-1866; www.eaglenyc.com; 554 W 28th St;
🕒 10pm-4am Mon-Sat, 5pm-4am Sun; subway 1, 9 to
28th St, C, E to 23rd St

Leather-clad men descend on the Eagle (a reopened version of the historic original) for leather/fetish fun and thematic nights that include live S&M action. **Leatherman** (p267) runs a second shop from inside here.

GLASS Map pp386-8

☎ 212-904-1580; 287 Tenth Ave btwn 26th & 27th
Sts; 🕒 6pm-4am Tue-Fri, 8pm-4am Sat; subway 1, 9
to 28th St

Brought to you by the owners of Bottino, a small wine bar in the 'hood, this lounge is a work of art, filled with white benches, egg-shaped seats and a romantic red glow.

GREEN TABLE Map pp382-5

☎ 212-741-9174; Chelsea Market, 75 Ninth Ave btwn
15th & 16th Sts; 🕒 noon-9pm Tue-Sat, 11am-5pm
Sun; subway A, C, E to 14th St, L to Eighth Ave

Sip on an early-evening biodynamic or organic wine or beer at this little natural café and wine bar, featuring guilt-free snacks like ancho-chili popcorn.

HALF KING Map pp386-8

☎ 212-462-4300; 505 W 23rd St at Tenth Ave;
🕒 9-3:30am; subway C, E to 23rd St

A unique marriage of bare-bones tavern and sophisticated writers' lair; you'll often catch literary readings in this wood-accented, candlelit watering hole.

SBNY Map pp382-5

☎ 212-691-0073; 50 W 17th St; 🕒 4pm-4am Sun-Thu,
4pm-6am Fri & Sat; subway L to 6th Ave, F, V to 14th St

Still called by its old name Splash, SBNY dance club still has the hot shirtless bartenders and top-circuit DJs. Theme nights change constantly and go-go guys with fig leaf–sized towels hop about. SB? South Beach of course. Happy hour runs from 4pm to 8pm Monday to Saturday.

SERENA Map pp382-5

☎ 212-255-4646; Chelsea Hotel, 222 W 23rd St btwn
Seventh & Eighth Aves; 🕒 6pm-4am Mon-Fri, 7pm-
4am Sat; subway C, E, 1, 9 to 23rd St

The lush, underground lounge of the Chelsea Hotel, this is dark and sultry with an array of couches, make-out corners and chill-out DJs; weekdays are better than weekends, when beefy doormen will make you sweat at the velvet ropes for a while before letting you in.

TRAILER PARK LOUNGE & GRILL
Map pp386-8

☎ 212-463-8000; 271 W 23rd St btwn Seventh &
Eighth Aves; 🕒 noon-2am Sun-Wed, noon-4am
Thu-Sat; subway C, E, 1, 9 to 23rd St

White trash is elevated to the level of hipster-worthy theme at this bar, a mint-green–fronted dark cave filled with kitschy *tchochkes* (knick-knacks), a mix of gay and straight hipsters and cheesy drinks topped with those little paper umbrellas.

VICEROY Map pp382-5

☎ 212-633-8484; 160 Eighth Ave at 18th St;
🕒 11-1am Mon-Fri, 9-1am Sat & Sun; subway A, C, E
to 14th St, L to Eighth Ave

The grand dark-wood bar here is a lovely spot to start off an evening with a top-shelf pour, steamed artichoke appetizer and a friendly chat with one of the adorable bartenders.

XL Map pp382-5

☎ 646-336-5574; 357 W 16th St; 🕒 4pm-4am;
subway A, C, E to 14th St, L to Eighth Ave

After-work beautiful boys loom over froofy cocktails at this expansive (you know, XL) high-ceilinged lounge. Wall TVs blare music videos, except for Monday drag queen and cabaret shows, and a massive fish-tank provides a wall in the WC (if those fish could speak...). Martinis are $3 from 4pm to 7pm.

UNION SQUARE, FLATIRON DISTRICT & GRAMERCY PARK

You'll find flavors of the East Village and more staid upper reaches of the east in this confluence of nabes, known mostly for taverns and stylish hotel bars.

BREAD BAR Map pp386-8

☎ 212-889-0667; 11 Madison Ave at 25th St;
🕒 noon-11pm Mon-Thu, noon-11:30pm Fri, 5:30-
11:30pm Sat, 5:30-11pm Sun; subway N, R, W, 6 to
23rd St

The park-side, hip bar downstairs from the top-notch Tabla eatery. The drinks here have a delicious South Asian flavor, as twists on martinis get flavored with pineapple juice and lemongrass and the Bloody Marys get a dose of masala.

DOS CAMINOS Map pp386-8

☎ 212-294-1000; 373 Park Ave S btwn 26th & 27th St; ⏰ 11:30am-11:30pm Sun & Mon, 11:30am-midnight Tue-Thu, 11:30-12:30am Fri & Sat; subway 6 to 28th St

The stylish crowd of professionals at the bar of this massive Mexican joint go loco for prickly-pear margaritas and more than 100 types of fine tequila.

FLUTE Map pp382-5

☎ 212-529-7870; 40 E 20th St btwn Broadway & Park Ave S; ⏰ 5pm-4am Mon-Fri, 6pm-4am Sat, 5pm-2am Sun; subway N, R, W to 23rd St

A dark and lush underground lounge, the specialty of the house here is the bubbly – four pages worth, actually, with options ranging from $8 flutes of sweet stuff to $300 bottles of DP. Cheers!

LIVE BAIT Map pp382-5

☎ 212-353-2400; 14 E 23rd St btwn Broadway & Madison Ave; ⏰ 11:30-1am Mon-Wed, 11:30-2am Thu-Sat, noon-midnight Sun; subway N, R, W to 23rd St

A slice of New Orleans on this otherwise un-kitschy stretch of 23rd St, this fisherman-themed beer bar offers up Tabasco-spiked oyster shooters and other spicy, lethal mixes.

OLD TOWN BAR & GRILL Map pp382-5

☎ 212-529-6732; 45 E 18th St btwn Broadway & Park Ave S; ⏰ 11:30-12:30am Mon-Wed, 11:30-1am Thu & Fri, 12:30pm-1:30am Sat, noon-midnight Sun; subway L, N, Q, R, W, 4, 5, 6 to 14th St–Union Sq

A legendary tavern that bears some similarity to Pete's (below) for its hard drinking and local tenor. Old Town's been on the block since 1892.

PETE'S TAVERN Map pp382-5

☎ 212-473-7676; 129 E 18th St at Irving Pl; ⏰ 11-2:30am; subway L, N, Q, R, W, 4, 5, 6 to 14th St–Union Sq

This dark and atmospheric watering hole is a New York classic – all pressed tin and carved wood and an air of literary history. You can get a respectable burger here, plus choose from more than 15 draft beers.

MIDTOWN

Something for everyone – cheesy tourist, barely-legal suburbanite, high-class hipster, buttoned-up businessman – is what defines this wide swath of city when it comes to imbibing. Following is, just a tiny taste to whet your thirst.

BRITISH OPEN Map pp386-8

☎ 212-355-8467; 320 E 59th St btwn First & Second Aves; ⏰ noon-3am Mon-Sat, noon-1am Sun; subway 4, 5, 6 to 59th St

In a city packed with Irish pubs, the British Open, in the shadow of the Queensboro Bridge, fills the sports bar niche; come here for football, cricket and golf on the TV.

BRYANT PARK CAFÉ & GRILL Map pp226-7

☎ 212-840-6500; 25 W 40th St btwn Fifth & Sixth Aves; ⏰ 11:30am-11pm; subway B, D, F, V to 42nd St–Bryant Park

Sure, you can sneak a bottle of wine into the Monday-night open-air film screenings come summer. Or you can enjoy a legit cocktail in this swanky, park-side setting – barstool included.

CAMPBELL APARTMENT Map pp386-8

☎ 212-953-0409; 15 Vanderbilt Ave at 43rd St; ⏰ 3pm-1am Mon-Sat, 3-11pm Sun; subway S, 4, 5, 6, 7 to Grand Central

Take the lift beside the Oyster Bar or the stairs to the West Balcony and head out the doors to the left to reach this sublime spot for a cocktail. This used to be the apartment of a landed railroad magnate and has the velvet, mahogany and murals to prove it. Cigars are welcome, but sneakers and jeans are not.

CHERRY Map pp386-8

☎ 212-519-8505; W New York–The Tuscany, 120 E 39th St btwn Park & Lexington Aves; ⏰ 5pm-3am; subway 4, 5, 6, 7, S to 42nd St–Grand Central

The all-red Randy Gerber playpen even has a ruby-hued pool table and crimson velvet ropes at its swanky entrance.

COSMO Map pp226-7

☎ 212-582-2200; 359 W 54th St btwn Eighth & Ninth Aves; ⏰ 6pm-2am; subway C, E to 50th St, B, D to 7th Ave

A teeny-tiny two-level lounge, this former gay bar is now a mixed local favorite, with romantic lighting, a high ceiling and specialty martinis galore.

FILM CENTER CAFE Map pp226-7

☎ 212-262-2525; 635 Ninth Ave btwn 44th & 45th Sts; ⏰ noon-4am; subway A, C, E to 42nd St

A lively local place decorated with film posters, this basic place with a vintage feel sees its fair share of Broadway stars, plus offers a raw bar, stiff drinks and an American-cuisine kitchen that stays open till last call.

GUASTAVINO'S Map pp386-8

☎ 212-980-2455; 409 E 59th St btwn First & York Aves; ⏰ 5:30-10pm Sun-Thu, 5:30-9pm Fri, 5-11:30pm Sat (club 11pm-4am Thu-Sun); subway N, R, W to Lexington Ave–59th St, 4, 5, 6 to 59th St

Set into the soaring granite columns of the Queensboro Bridge, this Terence Conran special is all sky-high ceilings and awe-inspiring design. The tiny bar serves tasty, fancy cocktails, and the upstairs dining room turns into a trendy nightclub once the kitchen closes.

HEARTLAND BREWERY Map pp226-7

☎ 646-366-0235; 127 W 43rd St btwn Sixth Ave & Broadway; ⏰ 11:30am-midnight Mon-Sat, noon-8pm Sun; subway N, Q, R, W, S, 1, 2, 3, 9, 7 to 42nd St–Times Sq

Smack in the heart of crazy Times Square, this massive outpost of a small local chain makes its brews onsite, churning out tasty pints from oatmeal stout to lager.

HUDSON BARS Map pp226-7

☎ 212-554-6343; 356 W 58 St btwn Eighth & Ninth Aves; ⏰ 4pm-2am Mon-Sat, 4pm-1am Sun; subway A, B, C, D, 1, 9 to 59th St–Columbus Circle

No less than three bars, one hipper than the next, grace the 2nd-floor lobby of Ian Schrager's Hudson hotel. The sleek Hudson Bar is difficult to get into, but you can peer past the velvet rope to see who's mingling on the glass floor. Try the Library bar's pool table and leather sofas, or the lovely outdoor garden bar, where you can smoke in peace.

KEMIA Map pp226-7

☎ 212-333-3410; 630 Ninth Ave at 44th St; ⏰ 5:30pm-2am Tue-Sat; subway A, C, E to 42nd St–Port Authority

The perfect pre- or post-theater cocktail spot, Kemia displays plenty of drama of its own: a rose-petal–strewn staircase whisks you down to the underground hideaway, where you'll find low ottomans, billowing tapestries, more roses, excellent DJs, delicious cocktails and Moroccan tapas.

LOVERGIRL NYC Map pp386-8

☎ 212-252-3397; www.lovergirlnyc.com; 20 W 39th St, Club Shelter; admission $10 before midnight, $12 after; ⏰ 10pm-5am Sat; subway B, D, F, V to 42nd St–Bryant Park

This Saturday dance party gets hoppin' at 1am, packed to the rafters with women of color: rap star–lookin' butches and their fly, tight-jeaned femmes. No sneakers, no work clothes – you're expected to dress to impress. Hot go-go goddesses dance to great R&B and hip-hop from long-time scene favorite DJ Mary Mac. Get a sample from the website.

RAINBOW GRILL Map pp386-8

☎ 212-632-5000; 30 Rockefeller Plaza; ⏰ 5pm-midnight Sun-Thu, 5pm-1am Fri-Sun; subway B, D, F, V to 47th-50th Sts–Rockefeller Center

This 65th-floor bar and eatery ranks as one of the most romantic spots in New York as the views (including a bird's-eye of the Empire State Building) are dreamy. The connected Rainbow Room is open Friday nights and some Saturdays for dinner and dancing; jackets and reservations are required.

RUDY'S BAR & GRILL Map pp226-7

☎ 212-974-9169; 627 Ninth Ave btwn 44th & 45th Sts; ⏰ 8-4am; subway A, C, E to 42nd St

This dive practically glories in its reputation as a spot for sots. Wash down that $2 pint o' piss with free hot dogs and you'll no doubt be hooked like the rest of us.

STONE ROSE Map pp386-8

☎ 212-823-9796; Time Warner Center, Columbus Circle at 59th St; ⏰ 6pm-2am; subway A, B, C, D, 1, 9 to 59th St–Columbus Circle

The newest high-rise cocktail lounge, this one owned by the famous Rande Gerber and sitting in the chi-chi Time Warner Center, overlooks Central Park and has already started attracting the nearby publishing crowd for post-work poison.

TAO Map pp386-8

☎ 212-888-2288; 42 E 58th St btwn Madison & Park Aves; ⏰ 11:30am-midnight Mon & Tue, 11:30-1am Wed-Fri, 5pm-1am Sat, 5pm-midnight Sun; subway N, R, W to 5th Ave–59th St, 4, 5, 6 to 59th St

A design thriller in every sense, this Eastern-themed lounge gives you paper lanterns, bamboo, theme drinks and a massive, 16ft Buddha statue, just in case all the excitement zaps your zen.

XTH AVE LOUNGE Map pp386-8

☎ 212-245-9088; 642 Tenth Ave btwn 45th & 46th Sts; ⏰ 6pm-4am; subway A, C, E to 23rd St–Port Authority

A dark and spiffy little storefront, this chic and tiny lounge is proof that Hell's Kitchen's scary days are over.

UPPER WEST SIDE

A neighborhood for grown-ups, many with children (witness the new trend of happy hours for mommies and their babies), is not exactly the No 1 destination for hardcore drinkers. Or, on second thought, perhaps it is… Judge for yourself at one of the many basic bars.

BROADWAY DIVE Map pp389-91

☎ 212-865-2662; 2662 Broadway btwn 101st & 102nd Sts; ☾ noon-4am; subway 1, 9 to 103rd St

It's just what it says it is, with sticky floors and a dartboard. Or you might try the affiliated **Dive Bar** (☎ 212-749-4358; 732 Amsterdam Ave; subway 1, 2, 3 to 96th St), between 95th and 96th Sts, which is a little more upscale, but not much.

CAFÉ DEL BAR Map pp389-91

☎ 917-863-5200; 945 Columbus btwn 106th & 107th Sts; ☾ 6pm-2am; subway B, C to Cathedral Pkwy (110 St)

This tiny, red-lit Jamaican spot is the perfect place to wait for your table at the tiny **A** (p198) restaurant next door (from the same owners). Enjoy Red Stripe beers, rum concoctions and reggae beats.

DUBLIN HOUSE Map pp389-91

☎ 212-874-9528; 225 W 79th St btwn Amsterdam Ave & Broadway; ☾ noon-4am; subway 1, 9 to 79th St

An old-school Irish bar; it shouldn't be remarkable but is, thanks to the odd combination of old men and undergrads who patronize the place.

EVELYN LOUNGE Map pp389-91

☎ 212-724-5145; 380 Columbus Ave at 78th St; ☾ 6pm-4am; subway 1, 9 to 79th St

A roomy, cellar-level space with plenty of couches, Evelyn includes a classy cigar lounge and a martini list with more options than the dinner menu. A laid-back crowd frequents this spot during the week but is shoved aside by hobnobbing students on the weekend.

POTION LOUNGE Map pp389-91

☎ 212-721-4386; 370 Columbus Ave btwn 77th & 78th Sts; ☾ 6:30pm-4am; subway B, C to 81st St–Museum of Natural History

The specially illuminated bar-top lights up the layers of the specialty cocktails here, making your lava-lamp–like concoction seem all the more exotic. It's a good ending to a daylong visit to the Museum of Natural History.

RACCOON LODGE Map pp389-91

☎ 212-874-9984; 480 Amsterdam Ave at 83rd St; ☾ 4pm-4am; subway 1, 9 to 86th St

It's as cool as its Downtown counterpart (see p209). There's a mixed crowd, rocking jukebox, pool table and groovy bartenders to boot.

SHALEL Map pp389-91

☎ 212-799-9030; 65 W 70th St btwn Central Park West & Columbus Ave; ☾ 5:30pm-2am Sun-Thu, 5:30pm-4am Fri & Sat; subway B, C, 1, 2, 3, 9 to 72nd St

Craving some Downtown style? Then visit this underground Moroccan joint, with low couches, flickering votives and even an in-house waterfall.

UPPER EAST SIDE

Not exactly the most hoppin' area to party in; elegant hotel lounges with a sprinkling of dives is the order of the evening over here.

BEMELMAN'S BAR Map pp389-91

☎ 212-570-7109; The Carlyle, 35 E 76th St at Madison Ave; ☾ noon-2am; subway 6 to 77th St

Waiters wear white jackets, a baby grand piano is always being played and Ludwig Bemelman's Madeleine murals surround you. It's a classic spot for a serious cocktail.

KINSALE TAVERN Map pp389-91

☎ 212-348-4370; 1672 Third Ave btwn 93rd & 94th Sts; ☾ noon-4am; subway 6 to 96th St

This classic pub/sports bar attracts rugby and soccer fanatics with its live-satellite broadcasts of European matches and more than 20 on-tap beers.

MARK'S LOUNGE Map pp389-91

☎ 212-744-4300; Mark Hotel, 25 E 77th St btwn Madison & Fifth Aves; ☾ 4pm-1am; subway 6 to 77th St

The quiet lounge at this hotel epitomizes Upper East Side elegance.

METROPOLITAN MUSEUM OF ART BALCONY BAR Map pp389-91

☎ 212-535-7710; 1000 Fifth Ave at 82nd St; ☾ 4-8pm Fri & Sat; subway 4, 5, 6 to 86th St

Just past the Chinese ceramics on the 2nd-floor balcony, this is the most culturally elegant spot to sip in the city, made even more so by a live string quartet. A garden bar on the museum's rooftop, open from May to October, is just as exquisite.

PARK VIEW AT THE BOATHOUSE
Map pp389-91

☎ 212-517-2233; Park Drive North at E 72nd St, Central Park; ⏰ noon-9:30pm; subway 6 to 68th St

For unobstructed lakeside views sashay on over to the boathouse with the crowd of yuppies, tourists and after-work suits to enjoy a pricey waterside cocktail, with a dose of fresh air on the side.

SUBWAY INN Map pp389-91

☎ 212-223-8929; 143 E 60th St btwn Lexington & Third Aves; ⏰ 8-4am; subway 4, 5, 6 to 59th St

This is a classic old-geezer watering hole with cheap drinks and loads of authenticity, right down to the barmen's white shirts and thin black ties. It's an amusing place to recover from a shopping spree at posh Bloomingdale's, just around the corner.

OUTER BOROUGHS
BROOKLYN

Williamsburg is Brooklyn's biggest party zone, with new hipster bars in and off Bedford Ave – on a weekend just follow the groups of 20- and 30-somethings trolling for booze. (The days of coke bars here are long gone.)

Many bars in residential pockets like Park Slope (start with Fifth Ave) and Smith St in Cobble Hill and Carroll Gardens are more laid-back than the bustling check-out scene of many of Manhattan's slurping holes.

EXCELSIOR Map p395

☎ 718-832-1599; 390 Fifth Ave; ⏰ 6pm-4am; subway F, M, R to 4th Ave–9th St

One-room gay bar with candlelit, street-facing tables, dim lights, an everything's-game and a make-out porch and garden in the back. Open to straights. Things stay pretty mellow.

FREDDY'S Map p395

☎ 718-622-7035; 485 Dean St; ⏰ 11-4am Mon-Sat, noon-4am Sun; subway 2, 3 to Bergen St

Potentially on the chopping block of the proposed Atlantic Yards stadium, this pub classic – $4 drafts, booze, a grill and free live music nightly – has become a de facto HQ for neighborhood dissent of the plan. Express your support by seeing its various shows (open mic, Lou Reed tributes), or downing hard liquor in an inviting two-room place lined with bric-a-brac, art and wood-paneled walls. Go while you can.

GALAPAGOS Map p394

☎ 718-384-4586; www.galapagosartspace.com; 70 N 6th St, btwn Kent & Wythe Aves; admission free-$10; ⏰ 6pm-2am Sun-Thu, 6pm-4am Fri & Sat; subway L to Bedford Ave

In a former mayonnaise factory in Williamsburg, this jazzed-up modern art space/bar indeed warrants its Darwinian name for its mix and match of ever-changing, ever-surprising performances. Vaudeville on Friday includes burlesque numbers and tango dancers on a trapeze wire, perhaps followed by up-and-coming alt rockers staging a CD-release party. Or a small theater troupe testing out a new play. There's drinking too, of course. It's located three blocks west (toward the river) from the subway stop.

GINGER'S Map p395

☎ 718-778-0924; 363 Fifth Ave; ⏰ 5pm-4am Mon-Fri, 2pm-4am Sat & Sun; subway F, M, R to 4th Ave–9th St

Let-love-rule lesbian bar with ruby-red walls that sees a lot of gays and straights at its long bar up front and big garden in the back. More laid-back than Manhattan's lesbian bars? Sure, this is Brookburg, baby.

IONA Map p394

☎ 718-384-5008; 180 Grand St, btwn Bedford & Driggs Ave; ⏰ 2pm-4am; subway L to Bedford Ave

Super Irish-style beer garden in Williamsburg with wooden tables used by chatty hipster locals, lingering for hours over a beer or three. Plus there's ping pong (!) and outdoor grills in good weather. Walk south on Bedford to Grand St and turn left.

LUNATARIUM Map p394

☎ 718-813-8404; www.lunatarium.com; 10 Jay St; admission free-$25; subway F to York St, A, C to High St

This Dumbo warehouse space, with river views and exposed rafters inside, can pack in 1500 moving bodies for its DJ who's who shows (DJ Spooky among the list) and blasting drum 'n' bass, techno and house music. Check the website for special events and hours.

SUNNY'S

☎ 718-625-8211; 253 Conover St btwn Beard & Reed Sts; ⏰ 8pm-4am Wed, Fri & Sat; subway F, G to Smith St–9th St, then bus B77 to Conover St

This old, out-of-the-way longshoreman bar in Red Hook, gazed at directly by the Statue of Liberty offshore, comes right out of On the Waterfront. Except it's not Marlon Brando here, but writers, debaters, musicians – generally bohos of various ages – who bring in instruments to play bluegrass, Celtic or jazz tunes. Sunny, the owner, stresses its communal environment, and much cross-table banter gets going over a couple of beers. As soon as you walk in, you're a part.

Beers in Brooklyn

With its heightened profile among 20- and 30-somethings, Brooklyn has become a drinking and entertainment destination in its own right. Lovers of hops, barley and malt will be happy up at these spaces:

BROOKLYN ALE HOUSE Map p394

☎ 718-302-9811; 103 Berry St at N 8th St; ☽ 3pm-4am; subway L to Bedford Ave

Bustling with what feels like a pre-boom Williamsburg crowd, the Ale House serves several ales and beers on tap, including Boddington's, and some hefty portions of liquor in mixed drinks. Space fills up on weekends with singles and couples' minglers, mostly professionals in their 30s. (The TV is only there so the bartender can watch Oklahoma football games on mute.) It's a block west of Bedford Ave.

BROOKLYN BREWERY Map p394

☎ 718-486-7422; www.brooklynbrewery.com; 79 N 11th St; free tours; ☽ noon-5pm Sat; subway L to Bedford Ave

In an 1860s ironworks factory, Brooklyn Brewery is the sole beer-maker in a neighborhood that was home to a dozen brewers in the pre-Prohibition days. (The street is now known as 'Brewers Row.') Tours (with tastings) run all year, but fill up in summer; call ahead. Happy hours are held here from 6pm to 10pm Friday. Check the website for events. From the subway, walk north to N 11th St, turn left and walk a couple of blocks.

QUEENS

Queens' diverse population (more than 100 ethnicities are represented in this borough) ensures a wide range of internationally-themed bars and nightspots where you can explore a new side of New York City. Following are two watering holes that are particularly noteworthy.

BOHEMIAN HALL & BEER GARDEN
Map p396

☎ 718-274-0043; 29-19 24th Ave; ☽ 5pm-2am Mon-Thu, 5pm-3am Fri, noon-3am Sat & Sun; subway N, W to Astoria Blvd

Miss the beer in Prague? Never been? Bohemian Hall – run by staff with clipped Czech accents – is the real deal. Dating from 1919, when New York was home to some 800 beer gardens, this happy drinking place has hearty East European food, barbecue and – of course – mouthwatering beers on tap. Kids can stay till 9pm.

NIXTERIDES
Map p396

☎ 718-267-8700; 37-22 Ditmars Blvd; ☽ 8-4am; subway N, W to Astoria–Ditmars Blvd

Mix up a dive bar, a cup of espresso and a 1970s movie set in Athens and you get something like Nixterides (meaning 'bat'). This gathering place, in Queens' Greek-American burg of Astoria, is not your usual place to unwind. There are framed paintings of flowers facing hanging plastic plants, and a loud crew of regulars chatting in Greek across tables. Many tables face out the full front windows. Everything comes with a bottle of water, no questions asked.

Entertainment

Entertainment

As hard as New Yorkers work, they tend to play even harder. Some mixture of theater, concerts, dance performances, movies and clubbing usually has a place in residents' lives – and even if it doesn't, just the *potential* for so much fun is a reason why many reside here.

So how to get a handle on it all? No single source could possibly list everything going down in the city, but the weekly *Time Out* does its damnedest. For high-culture events, check out the Friday and Sunday editions of the *New York Times*, as well as *New York* magazine and the *New Yorker*. Dance clubs and smaller music venues take out numerous ads in free weeklies like the *Village Voice* and *New York Press*. The **Department of Cultural Affairs** (☎ 212-643-7770) has a hotline that lists events and concerts at major museums and other cultural institutions, while **NYC/On Stage** (☎ 212-768-1818), a 24-hour information line, publicizes music and dance events.

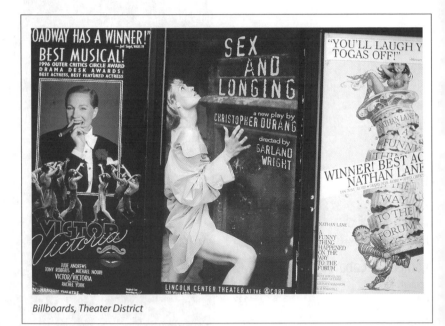

Billboards, Theater District

Tickets & Reservations

To purchase tickets for shows, you can either head to the box office, or use one of several ticket-service agencies to order by phone or Internet.

Broadway Line (☎ 212-302-4111; www.broadway.org) provides descriptions of plays and musicals both on and off the Great White Way, and lets you charge tickets. **Telecharge** (☎ 212-239-6200; www.telecharge.com) sells tickets for most Broadway and off-Broadway shows (though there's a per-ticket surcharge); for strictly off Broadway, try **SmartTix.com**, **Theatermania.com**, **Ticketcentral.com** or **Ticketmaster.com**.

THEATER

Everything about New York City is theatrical, but you'll find real performances at hundreds of showcases citywide, from big Broadway hit factories to tiny little Downtown theaters that make you feel like you've invaded someone's living room.

The most celebrated scene is Broadway, of course, the heart of which runs right through Times Square. Though this area used to proffer plenty of lascivious performances – peep shows, porn-film palaces etc – that all came to an end during the Giuliani administration in the 1990s. Hizzoner got rid of the sleazy scene, replacing it with theaters hawking Disney musicals, from *The Lion King* to *Beauty and the Beast*. Frankly, some theater fans have a lot more respect for the former.

Cheesy, bright-lights musicals aside, Broadway offerings have become more diverse than ever lately. The newest wave of innovative, musical works include *Avenue Q* (about cheap rents and the meaning of life), *The Boy From Oz* (the Peter Allen story) and *Wicked* (a *Wizard of Oz* prequel starring the witches). Repackaged movie hits like *The Producers* and *Hairspray* have taken the town by storm, redeeming and legitimizing the theater scene. A few classic revivals – including *King Lear* and *Twentieth Century* – starring big-name film actors have attracted burgeoning, enthusiastic crowds to Broadway, and revived musicals such as *Chicago* and *Little Shop of Horrors* have also garnered acclaim.

More adventurous stage buffs should definitely investigate what is happening off-Broadway, Downtown and even in the outer boroughs, as some of the freshest, most accomplished stage work is happening far from the renowned Theater District.

BROADWAY

In general, 'Broadway' productions are staged in the lavish, early-20th-century theaters surrounding Times Square. Major venues follow, although most times you'll be making your choice based on the production, not the theater. Evening performances begin at 8pm. You can reach all of these theaters on the subway by taking N, Q, R, S, W, 1, 2, 3, 7 to Times Sq–42nd St.

MAJESTIC THEATER Map pp226-7
247 W 44th St at Eighth Ave
Arguably Broadway's best theater, the Majestic has staged blockbuster musicals including *Carousel*, *South Pacific* and *Camelot* with Julie Andrews. Its legendary current production, *Phantom of the Opera*, opened in January 1988 and may play until the sky falls down. Most of the 1600 seats here offer good views.

NEIL SIMON THEATER Map pp226-7
250 W 52nd St btwn Broadway & Eighth Ave
Currently blessed with the hit *Hairspray*, based on the film by John Waters, this large venue is named after America's most successful playwright – although its original name, which it held until 1983, was the Alvin.

NEW AMSTERDAM THEATER Map pp226-7
214 W 42nd St btwn Seventh & Eighth Ave
This 1771-seat jewel was rescued from decrepitude by the Disney corporation, which stages upbeat, kid-friendly productions such as *The Lion King* here. The lobby, restrooms and auditorium are lavish, but the seating is a bit cramped.

NEW VICTORY THEATER Map pp226-7
209 W 42nd St btwn Seventh & Eighth Ave
Another former triple-X palace that was rescued from the wrecking ball and refurbished. It now produces theater exclusively for children.

What's On Where

For the latest dish (from trash talking to recommendations) on Broadway performances, check out All That Chat (talkinbroadway.com/forum), which has audience members' reviews of new shows, and Broadway World (BroadwayWorld.com).

- **Broadway Line** (☎ 212-302-4111; www .livebroadway.com) Plays and musicals both on and off the Great White Way.
- **Clubfone** (☎ 212-777-2582; www.clubfone .com) Cabaret events, live music and dance.
- **NYC/On Stage** (☎ 212-768-1818; www.tdf.org) A 24-hour information line for music and dance events.
- **NYC Theatre** (www.nyc.com/theatre) Reviews of on- and off-Broadway plays.
- **Sheckys** (www.sheckys.com) Reviews of bars and clubs.

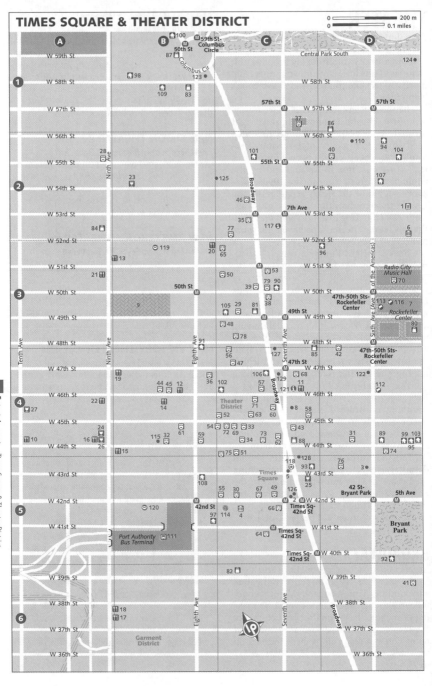

TIMES SQUARE & THEATER DISTRICT

Entertainment – Times Square & Theater District

ST JAMES THEATER Map pp226-7
246 W 44th St btwn Broadway & Eighth Ave
Now showing *The Producers*, a wildly popular remake of Mel Brooks' classic 1968 film, the landmark building has shown past hits such as *The King and I* and *My One and Only*.

VIRGINIA THEATER Map pp226-7
245 W 52nd St btwn Broadway & Eighth Ave
Little Shop of Horrors is reigning at this lavishly designed space, seating 1275 and inaugurated by President Coolidge.

WINTER GARDEN THEATER Map pp226-7
1634 Broadway at 50th St
The Winter Garden dropped the curtain on *Cats* in September 2000 after an 18-year run. The theater recently emerged with *Mamma Mia!*, an over-the-top musical extravaganza celebrating the music of Swedish super-group ABBA.

Half-price Broadway TKTS

An essential NYC experience – a night at the theater – needn't break the bank. Tailormade for the traveler's timetable, and easy to find in Times Square (look for the queues by the bright red 'TKTS' sign), the **TKTS booth** (☎ 212-768-1818; Broadway & W 47th St) sells cut-rate, same-day tickets to Broadway and off-Broadway shows. Tickets sell at 25% or 50% off box-office rates, plus a $3 fee. Check the electric marquee for what's available. There's often plenty of choices, but be flexible. The booth is courtesy of the Theatre Development Fund, an arts advocacy group that sells 2.5 million theater seats annually. If you can't find TKTS, ask the singing naked cowboy, a man whose presence as, well, a singing naked cowboy (he actually wears boots, underwear, a cowboy hat and a sign with his nickname), has stopped many tourists – and locals – in their tracks

OFF-BROADWAY

Off-Broadway simply refers to shows performed in smaller spaces (200 seats or fewer), and you'll find many theaters just around the corner from Broadway venues, as well as elsewhere in town. Off-Broadway events include readings, experimental and cutting-edge performances and improvisations held in spaces with fewer than 100 seats. Some of the world's best theater happens in these more intimate venues: recent notable productions have included Eve Ensler's *The Vagina Monologues*, the Pulitzer Prize-winning *Wit* and the airborne, trippy *De La Guarda*.

ASTOR PLACE THEATER Map pp382-5
☎ 212-254-4370; 434 Lafayette St btwn W 4th St & Astor Pl; subway R to 8th St–NYU, 6 to Astor Pl
This spot is on the map because of the phenomenal **Blue Man Group** (www.blueman.com), a trio of bald, blue guys who get wild with all manner of props and paint while poking fun at the art mob mentality. Audience participation is required (whether you like it or not!).

CHASHAMA Map pp386-8
☎ 212-391-8151; www.chashama.org; 217 E 42nd St at Third Ave; subway 4, 5, 6, 7 to Grand Central–42nd St
This avant-garde space, which has just moved east to this new location, churns out fascinating dramas and cabaret productions.

CIRCLE IN THE SQUARE THEATER
Map pp226-7
☎ 212-307-2705; 1633 Broadway at 50th St; subway 1, 9 to 50th St
Circle staged groundbreaking productions like Eugene O'Neill's *The Iceman Cometh* at its original 159 Bleecker St premises. The company takes an active role in New York's thespian scene and trains new actors at its theater school.

CULTURE PROJECT Map pp382-5
☎ 212-253-7017; 45 Bleecker St at Lafayette St; subway 6 to Bleecker St, B, D, F to Broadway–Lafayette St
This intimate theater had a long and successful run with the brilliant *Exonerated*, and is now hosting Sarah Jones's *Bridge and Tunnel*. The Women Center Stage Festival, a spotlight of female playwrights, takes over for two weeks each summer.

DARYL ROTH THEATRE
Map pp382-5
☎ 212-239-6200; 20 Union Sq East at 15th St; subway L, N, Q, R, W, 4, 5, 6 to 14th St–Union Sq
This is another theater hosting sold-out shows thanks to the innovative work of its presenting company, **De La Guarda** (www.delaguarda.com). De La Guarda is a high-flying team of Argentineans exploring the energy and ecstasy of dancing and prancing while soaring above the crowds standing below. They like to get the audience involved.

EAGLE THEATER
☎ 718-205-2800; 73-07 37th Rd, Jackson Heights, Queens; tickets $5; subway 7 to 74th St–Broadway
King of Bollywood cinema in New York (with hot samosas for sale), the Eagle plays Indian films – with all the bells and whistles – nightly; most action, with locals dressed to impress, is on Friday. English subtitles run on many films, but it's not that important.

JOSEPH PAPP PUBLIC THEATER
Map pp382-5
☎ 212-260-2400; www.publictheater.org; 425 Lafayette St btwn E 4th St & Astor Pl; subway N, R to 8th St–NYU, 6 to Astor Pl
One of the city's most important cultural centers, the Papp presents its famous and fabulous Shakespeare in the Park productions at Central Park's Delacorte Theater every summer. Meryl Streep, Robert DeNiro and Kevin Kline are among the many stars to perform here.

MITZI E NEWHOUSE THEATER AT
LINCOLN CENTER Map pp389-91
☎ 212-239-6200; 150 W 65th St at Broadway; subway 1, 9 to 66th St–Lincoln Center
This intimate, 299-seat space is part of the Lincoln Center Theater organization, and produces high-quality dramas.

NEW YORK THEATER WORKSHOP
Map pp382-5
☎ 212-460-5475; 79 E 4th St btwn Second & Third Aves; subway F, V to Lower East Side–Second Ave
This innovative production house originated two big Broadway hits – *Rent* and *Urinetown* – and offers a constant supply of high-quality drama, including recent works by Paul Rudnick and Michael Cunningham.

ORPHEUM THEATER Map pp382-5
☎ 212-477-2477; 126 Second Ave at Eighth St; subway 6 to Astory Pl

Located in the East Village, this 349-seat house was a premier Yiddish theater at the beginning of the 20th century. It gained offbeat fame in the '80s with its highly popular musical *Little Shop of Horrors* (now on Broadway), and is the current home of the long-running beat-fest *Stomp*.

PS 122 Map pp382-5
☎ 212-477-5288; www.ps122.org; 150 First Ave at E 9th St; subway R to 8th St–NYU, 6 to Astor Pl

This former schoolhouse has been committed to fostering new artists and their far-out ideas since its inception in 1979. Its two stages have hosted such performers as Meredith Monk, Eric Bogosian, Blue Man Group and the late Spalding Gray.

DANCE

New York City is home to more than half a dozen world-famous dance companies, plus plenty of avant-garde, lesser-known experimentalists.

ALVIN AILEY AMERICAN DANCE THEATER Map pp226-7
☎ 212-767-0590; www.alvinailey.org; W 55th St at Ninth Ave; subway C, E to 50th St

After years of fractured existence and performing at various host theaters, the Ailey company has just recently moved into its new 77,000-sq-ft home – the largest facility devoted exclusively to dance in the USA. The glass-cube structure, purchased in 2001 and designed by architects Natan Bibliowicz and Carolyn Lu, contains 12 dance studios, a black box theater, costume shop, concession area, physical therapy center, administrative offices and the Ailey School.

BROOKLYN ACADEMY OF MUSIC (BAM) Map p394
☎ 718-636-4139; 30 Lafayette Ave at Ashland Pl, Ft Greene, Brooklyn; subway D, M, N, R to Pacific St (M Sat & Sun only), B, Q, 2, 3, 4, 5 to Atlantic Ave

Bill T Jones, Pina Bausch and the Nederlands Dans Theater are among those who have graced the stage here. To catch the most experimental performers, check out the annual Next Wave Festival, held in spring.

CITY CENTER Map pp226-7
☎ 212-581-1212; www.citycenter.org; 131 W 55th St btwn Sixth & Seventh Aves; subway N, R, Q, W to 57th St

This Midtown venue hosts the energized and original Alvin Ailey American Dance Theatre every December, as well as a steady stream of engagements by renowned companies like the premier classical company **Dance Theatre of Harlem** (below), and **American Ballet Theatre** (p230).

DANCE THEATRE OF HARLEM
Map pp392-3
☎ 212-690-2800; www.dancetheatreofharlem.org; Everett Center for the Performing Arts, 456 W 152nd St btwn St Nicholas & Amsterdam Aves; subway A, B, C, D to 145th St

The Harlem company's home theater stages frequent open houses, as well as performances by students of the Harlem school and visiting dancers from around the world.

DANCE THEATER WORKSHOP
Map pp382-5
☎ 212-924-0077; 219 W 19th St btwn Seventh & Eighth Aves; subway 1, 9 to 18th St

You'll find experimental, modern works here, usually by local Downtown up-and-comers.

DANSPACE PROJECT AT ST MARK'S CHURCH Map pp382-5
☎ 212-674-8194; Second Ave at 10th St; subway F, V to Lower East Side–Second Ave

An intimate space with high ceilings, this church-cum-performance-venue presents frequent, edgy showcases of young breakout locals.

JOYCE THEATER Map pp382-5
☎ 212-242-0800; www.joyce.org; 175 Eighth Ave at W 19th St; subway A, C, E to 14th St, L to Eighth Ave

An offbeat, intimate venue located in Chelsea, the Joyce offers noncommercial companies the chance to shine. The Merce Cunningham and Pilobolus dance companies make annual appearances at this renovated cinema, which seats 470.

KITCHEN Map pp382-5
☎ 212-255-5793; 512 W 19th St btwn Tenth & Eleventh Aves; subway A, C, E to 14th St, L to Eighth Ave

A tiny experimental space in west Chelsea where you'll find new, progressive pieces and works-in-progress on most nights.

METROPOLITAN OPERA HOUSE
Map pp386-8

☎ 212-477-3030; Lincoln Center, Amsterdam Ave at 64th St; subway 1, 9 to 66th St–Lincoln Center

American Ballet Theatre (www.abt.org) presents its largely classical season during the late spring and summer at this grand theater.

NEW YORK STATE THEATER Map pp386-8

☎ 212-870-5570; Lincoln Center, Broadway at 63rd St; subway 1, 9 to 66th St–Lincoln Center

New York City Ballet (www.nycballet.com), established by Lincoln Kirstein and George Balanchine in 1948, features a varied season of premieres and revivals, always including a production of *The Nutcracker* during the Christmas holidays. The company performs at this 2755-seat theater of Lincoln Center. Student-rush tickets ($10) are made available online and at the box office on the day of the performance; you must be under 29 and a full-time high school or university student. For more information call the **student-rush hotline** (☎ 212-870-7766).

CINEMAS

Cinephiles can sate any film cravings in New York, from the latest Japanese animation import to versions of saucy European films banned elsewhere in the US. While it might seem strange to come to New York City and go to the movies, a lot of New Yorkers consider film to be just as evolved an art form as opera or Broadway drama. Besides, nothing beats an air-conditioned movie theater in the thick of the summer's dog days. Frequent film festivals – the New York, Jewish, Lesbian & Gay and Asian-American among them – are special events that give added weight to your movie-watching.

Even though movie tickets cost at least $10, long lines on evenings and weekends are not uncommon, testifying to New Yorkers' devotion to film. Unfortunately, the 'bargain matinee' known throughout the rest of the country is virtually unheard of in New York, though some arthouses still show double features. You're likely to have to stand in one line to buy a ticket and another to get into the theater, and most first-run films sell out 30 minutes early on date nights (Friday and Saturday). Avoid long lines (and sold out showings) by calling ☎ 212-777-3456 and by visiting the websites www.moviefone.com and www.fandango.com, and prepaying for the movie of your choice for an extra charge of $1.50 per ticket.

Film Festivals

With so many film festivals in New York – 30 at last count – chances are you'll be able to hit one no matter when you visit. Many credit the highly publicized and quickly growing Tribeca Film Festival (p10) for upping the ante on quality of films and screening locations. The topics of New York's film festivals are as varied as the city itself. There's Dance on Camera (January), a celebration of movies about dance, and the Jewish Film Festival (January), which explores Jewish culture and religion onscreen. The old fave New York Film Festival (January) highlights up-and-coming directors every year, and the African-American Women in Film Festival (March) is about, well, you guessed it! The Williamsburg Film Festival (March) has brought the fun to that artsy-trendy Brooklyn neighborhood, and screens local filmmakers, while the Lesbian & Gay Film Festival (June), a highlight of Gay Pride month, has added filmmaker panels in striving to make the queer showcase better than ever. Meanwhile, the Human Rights Watch Film Festival (June) enlightens locals to the evils of global societies, while the New York Hawaiian Film Festival (May), the Asian-American International Film Festival (June) and the Israeli Film Festival (June) focus on those varied cultures.

Free Fun, Part I: Bryant Park Film Series

Summers in **Bryant Park** (www.bryantpark.org) take a celluloid focus, with the return of the outdoor, Monday-night Film Series. Films, both modern and classic, are projected onto a massive screen that goes up every June on the west side of the tree-lined, European-style patch of green. Folks show up as early as 3:30pm to get a good spot for their blanket, picnics and bottles of wine in tow, with an anxious after-work crowd zipping in by 6pm to enjoy the remaining late-afternoon rays. The movies start at about 9pm, and each summer's series has a different theme, though most are classics or New York–based. Recent screenings have included *Splendor in the Grass*, *Whatever Happened to Baby Jane*, *Sleepless In Seattle*, *42nd Street*, *An Affair to Remember* and *Breakfast at Tiffany's*.

REVIVAL THEATERS

ANTHOLOGY FILM ARCHIVES
Map pp382-5

☎ 212-505-5181; 32 Second Ave at 2nd St; subway F, V to Lower East Side–Second Ave

This East Village theater screens low-budget European and fringe works, plus revives classics such as *From Here to Eternity* and puts on festivals like the 'World of Werner.' It also hosts the Underground Film Festival each winter.

CINEMA CLASSICS Map pp382-5
☎ 212-677-5368; 332 E 11th St btwn First Ave & Ave A; subway L to First Ave

A tiny, cramped venue that's also a bar-café. Cinema Classics is where you can catch flicks such as *Modern Times, Annie Hall* or the *Manchurian Candidate* for a mere $8.

CLEARVIEW'S CHELSEA Map pp382-5
☎ 212-777-3456; 260 W 23rd St btwn Seventh & Eighth Aves; subway C, E to 23rd St

In addition to showing first-run films, this multi-screen complex hosts midnight showings of the *Rocky Horror Picture Show*, as well as a great Thursday-night series, *Chelsea Classics*, which has local drag star Hedda Lettuce hosting old-school camp from Joan Crawford, Bette Davis, Barbra Streisand etc.

FILM FORUM Map pp382-5
☎ 212-727-8110; 209 W Houston St btwn Varick St & Sixth Ave; subway 1, 9 to Houston St

This is a three-screen cinema in Soho featuring independent films, revivals and career retrospectives. Theaters are small, as are the screens, so get there early for a good viewing spot. There's a great little café in the lobby.

LEONARD NIMOY THALIA Map pp389-91
☎ 212-864-1414; Symphony Space, 2537 Broadway at 95th St; subway 1, 2, 3, 9 to 96th St

This small, just-renovated theater screens quality double features of a variety of time periods and genres.

MAKOR Map pp389-91
☎ 212-601-1000; 35 W 67th St btwn Central Park West & Columbus Ave; subway 1, 9 to 66th St –Lincoln Center

An outpost of the 92nd St Y, this Jewish cultural center geared toward the 30-something set has frequent film screenings, based around Israeli and Jewish themes.

MUSEUM OF MODERN ART
GRAMERCY THEATRE Map pp382-5
☎ 212-777-4900; 127 E 23rd St btwn Park Ave South & Lexington Ave; subway R, W, 6 to 23rd St (W Mon-Fri only)

This wonderful theater is the site of constant, high-quality retrospectives and some foreign festivals.

WALTER READE THEATER Map pp389-91
☎ 212-875-5600; Lincoln Center, 165 W 65th St; subway 1, 9 to 66th St–Lincoln Center

The Walter Reade can boast some good wide, screening-room-style seats. The New York Film Festival takes place here every September, and at other times of the year you can catch independent films, career retrospectives and themed series.

NEW-RELEASE THEATERS

ANGELIKA FILM CENTER Map pp382-5
☎ 212-995-2000; 18 W Houston St at Mercer St; subway B, D, F, V to Broadway–Lafayette St

An old favorite, the Angelika specializes in foreign and independent films and is often over-crowded despite the fact that screens can be annoyingly small and you can hear the rumble of the subway during screenings. The roomy café here serves gourmet grub. If you've time to kill before the screening, check out the Stanford White–designed beaux arts building that houses Angelika. Called the Cable Building (the miles of cable here moved the country's first and last cable cars ever installed), it features an oval window and caryatids on its Broadway facade.

BAM ROSE CINEMA Map p394
☎ 718-623-2770; 30 Lafayette Ave at Flatbush Ave; subway M, N, R, W to Pacific St, Q, 1, 2, 4, 5 to Atlantic Ave

The gorgeous Fort Greene theater at the Brooklyn Academy of Music shows independent and foreign films in spaces that are blessed with excellent seating, huge screens and a lovely, landmark design. Also catch mini-festivals and revivals here.

LANDMARK SUNSHINE CINEMAS
Map pp382-5

☎ 212-358-7709; 143 East Houston St; subway F, V to Lower East Side–Second Ave

A renovated Yiddish theater, the wonderful Landmark shows foreign and mainstream art films on massive screens and is a welcome addition to the neighborhood.

LINCOLN PLAZA CINEMAS Map pp389-91

☎ 212-757-2280; 1886 Broadway at 62nd St; subway A, B, C, D, 1, 2 to 59th St–Columbus Circle

This underground, six-screen venue is the place to go for artsy independent films on the Upper West Side.

LOEWS 42ND ST E-WALK THEATER

Map pp226-7

☎ 212-505-6397; 42nd St btwn Seventh & Eighth Aves; subway N, Q, R, S, W, 1, 2, 3, 7 to Times Sq

A massive, 13-screen theater in Times Square, the E-Walk dishes out all the latest Hollywood pabulum in state-of-the-art facilities.

TV Tapings

You can become part of a studio audience for one of the many TV shows taped in town and, though most are booked long in advance, you can always stand on line the day of the taping and keep your fingers crossed for standbys or cancellations.

Saturday Night Live (p42), one of the most popular NYC-based shows, is known for being difficult to get into. That said, you can try your luck by getting your name into the mix in the fall, when seats are assigned by lottery. Simply send an email to snltickets@nbc.com in August, or line up by 8:15am the day of the show at 50th St between Fifth and Sixth Aves (at NBC studios) for standby lottery tickets (16 years and older only). Another late-night show that draws crowds is the *Late Show with David Letterman*. You can try to request tickets for a specific date at www.cbs.com/lateshow, or else secure a standby ticket by calling ☎ 212-247-6497 at 11am on the day of the taping, which begins at 5:30pm Monday to Thursday. Get on the *Daily Show with John Stewart* on Comedy Central by reserving tickets at least three months ahead of time by calling ☎ 212-586-2477, or call at 11:30am the Friday before you'd like to attend for a chance at last-minute seats.

Audience members at *Total Request Live* must be at least 16 years old; line up at **MTV studios** (Map pp226-7; 1515 Broadway btwn 43rd & 44th Sts) by noon for weekday tapings, which begin at 3:30pm, or call the **MTV hotline** (☎ 212-398-8549) to try and snag a specific reservation. For *Last Call with Carson Daly*, visit www.1iota.com for reservations, or call ☎ 800-452-8499; you can try your hand at standbys by lining up at the 49th St entrance of 30 Rockefeller Plaza (NBC studios) by 11am. Daytime fans, join the scandal-loving viewers of the *Ricki Lake Show* by filling out a request for tickets at www.sonypictures.com /tv/shows/ricki/index.htm.

For more show ticket details, visit the websites of individual TV stations, or try www.tvtickets.com.

LOEWS LINCOLN SQUARE

Map pp389-91

☎ 212-336-5000; 1992 Broadway at 68th St; subway 1, 2, 3, 9 to 72nd St

This Upper West Side behemoth includes a 3D IMAX theater and 12 large screens that play first-run features.

COMEDY & CABARET

Laughter can be a good therapy in a city of eight million people. Luckily, there's no shortage of funny folks or fun venues to help you do so.

COMEDY CLUBS

BOSTON COMEDY CLUB

Map pp382-5

☎ 212-477-1000; 82 W 3rd St btwn Sullivan & Thompson St; subway A, C, E, B, D, F, V to W 4th St

A standard, well-known club on the comedy circuit. The folks at this Village spot have been cracked up by the likes of Janeane Garofalo and Dave Chapelle; you may also discover someone new at the New Talent Showcase.

CAROLINES ON BROADWAY Map pp226-7

☎ 212-757-4100; 1626 Broadway at 50th St; subway N, R, W to 49th St, 1, 9 to 50th St

This is a big and bright venue in Times Square. Comedy specials are frequently filmed here, reflected by the caliber of the talent.

COMEDY CELLAR Map pp382-5

☎ 212-254-3480; www.comedycellar.com; 117 MacDougal St btwn 3rd & Bleecker Sts; subway A, C, E, F, V, S to W 4th St

This long-established basement club in Greenwich Village features mainstream material and showcases high-profile comics (eg Jon Lovitz and Jon Stewart), a number of whom like to make surprise visits. Drop-ins are of the star-studded variety, including Robin Williams, Jerry Seinfeld and Chris Rock.

GOTHAM COMEDY CLUB

Map pp382-5

☎ 212-367-9000; 34 W 22nd St btwn Fifth & Broadway; subway F, V, R, W to 23rd St (W Mon-Fri only)

A lovely, intimate venue in the Flatiron District, and the breakout up-and-comers here are a scream. The last Thursday of the month is Homocomicus, a comedy series dedicated to queer comics.

PARKSIDE LOUNGE Map pp382-5

☎ 212-673-6270; 317 E Houston St at Attorney St; subway F, V to Lower East Side–Second Ave

Providing a much-loved alternative to the big mainstream venues, this dive bar hosts a weekly comedy show, the *Tuesday Night Train Wreck*, which is just as wild as it sounds.

STAND-UP NY Map pp389-91

☎ 212-595-0850; 236 W 78th St at Broadway; subway 1, 9 to 79 St

A small, mainstream club on the Upper West Side, the shows here range from *Raw Thursdays* (crude comics) to newcomer nights for gay, Latino and other types of specialized humor. Some big guns (Robin Williams, *Comedy Central* stars etc) have been known to come by.

STARLIGHT BAR & LOUNGE
Map pp382-5

☎ 212-475-2172; 167 Ave A btwn 10th & 11th Sts; subway L to First Ave

Funnyman Keith Price hosts queer comics every Wednesday night at this lovely gay bar's sofa-strewn rear lounge.

UPRIGHT CITIZENS BRIGADE
THEATRE Map pp386-8

☎ 212-366-9176; 307 W 26th St btwn Eighth & Ninth Aves; subway C, E to 23rd St

Pros of comedy sketches and outrageous improvisations reign at this small venue, which offers its weekly Wednesday show *Hump Night* to help get you through the week.

CABARET

Take a city with loads of Broadway stars and gay men and what do you get? Plenty of top-notch cabaret venues. Following is just a sample.

CAFÉ CARLYLE Map pp389-91

☎ 212-744-1600; 35 E 76th St at Madison Ave; subway 6 to 77th St

The legendary Bobby Short reigns at this swanky spot at the Carlyle hotel, drawing audiences that often feature stars of their own (Tony Bennett likes the shows here). Woody Allen has been known to play his clarinet here on Mondays.

DANNY'S SKYLIGHT ROOM Map pp226-7

☎ 212-265-8133; 346 W 46th St btwn Eighth & Ninth Aves; subway A, C, E to 42nd St–Port Authority

This piano lounge for sophisticates, part of Danny's Grand Sea Palace restaurant, features all manner of cabaret pros, from all-original quirky folks to no-frills masters of standards.

DON'T TELL MAMA Map pp226-7

☎ 212-757-0788; 343 W 46th St btwn Eighth & Ninth Aves; subway A, C, E to 42nd St–Port Authority

This art deco room, named for a song in *Cabaret*, features some high-quality camp – Tommy Femia doing a jaw-dropping rendition of Judy Garland, for example – as well as the serious stuff, such as green (but talented) performers from nearby music schools.

DUPLEX CABARET Map pp382-5

☎ 212-255-5438; 61 Christopher St at Seventh Ave South; subway 1, 9 to Christopher St–Sheridan Sq

It's way gay at this tiny spot, where you'll find drag queens weekly, plus piano-bar shows from some of the brightest up-and-comers on the circuit.

FEINSTEIN'S AT THE REGENCY
Map pp389-91

☎ 212-339-4095; 540 Park Ave at 61st St; subway F to Lexington Ave–63rd St, N, R, W to Lexington Ave–59th St (W Sat & Sun only)

You'll be puttin' on the ritz at this high-class joint, which features uniformed waiters, a reservations-only policy and performers ranging from Anne Hampton Callaway to Linda Eder.

OAK ROOM Map pp226-7

☎ 212-840-6800; 59 W 44th St btwn Fifth & Sixth Aves; subway B, D, F, V to 42nd St–Bryant Park

Order a martini, settle in and get the Dorothy Parker vibe at this **Algonquin** (p299) piano lounge, which is known for launching the careers of Harry Connick Jr, Diana Krall and others.

OPERA

Just like the other classics, you won't be hard-pressed to find good opera here. Although the prestigious Metropolitan Opera is what most people want, you can see equally top-shelf, although less-luxurious, productions at New York State Theater by New York City Opera. The budget options are Downtown.

AMATO OPERA THEATER Map pp382-5

☎ 212-228-8200; 319 Bowery at 4th St; subway 6 to Astor Pl

To see classics without all the glitz, head to this small, alternative opera house, which regularly puts on favorites including *Die Fledermaus*, *The Marriage of Figaro* and *La Bohéme*.

METROPOLITAN OPERA HOUSE

Map pp386-8

☎ 212-362-6000; www.metopera.org; Lincoln Center, W 64th St at Amsterdam Ave; subway 1, 9 to 66th St–Lincoln Center

New York's premier opera company, the Metropolitan Opera offers a spectacular mixture of classics and premieres. It's nearly impossible to get into the first few performances of operas that feature such big stars as Jessye Norman and Plácido Domingo, but once the B-team moves in, tickets become available. The season runs from September to April. Though ticket prices start at $55 and can get close to $200, the $12 standing-room tickets are one of NY's greatest bargains. They go on sale at 10am Saturday for the following week's performances. For a season schedule, visit the website.

NEW YORK STATE THEATER

Map pp386-8

☎ 212-870-5630; www.nycopera.com; Lincoln Center, Broadway at 65th St; subway 1, 9 to 66th St–Lincoln Center

This is the home of the New York City Opera, a more daring and lower-cost company than the Metropolitan Opera. It performs new works, neglected operas and revitalized old standards in the Philip Johnson–designed space. The split season runs for a few weeks in early fall and once again during early to late spring.

Culture Fixes in Brooklyn

Highbrow entertainment doesn't stop at Manhattan's shoreline. Brooklyn's offerings are top-rate and often more cutting edge. See what's happening at **Galapagos** (p221) in Williamsburg. If you find yourself in Queens, check out **Queens Theater in the Park** (p145).

Barge Music

Only in Brooklyn can you find an old barge transformed into a chamber-music setting on a pier facing the tip of Manhattan. **BargeMusic** (Map p394; ☎ 718-624-4061; wwwbargemusic.org; Fulton Ferry Landing, Brooklyn; adult/student $35/20; ☺ 7:30pm Thu-Sat, 4pm Sun; subway A, C to High St, 2, 3 to Clark St) was Olga Bloom's brilliant plan, which started in 1977 atop an old flat-bottomed barge. BargeMusic still rotates classical musicians for quality shows in an unbeatable location. Reserve ahead.

Brooklyn Academy of Music

Brooklyn Academy of Music (Map p394; ☎ 718-636-4100; www.bam.org; 30 Lafayette Ave, Brooklyn; subway B, Q, 2, 3, 4, 5 to Atlantic Ave) is a powerhouse in cutting-edge theater, dance and film in downtown Brooklyn, BAM – as it's always called – helped put Brooklyn on the arts map, when it dared to break free in the 1970s from more conventional performances held at Manhattan institutions. Founded in 1861, and struggling for much of the 20th century, the BAM complex features the Majestic Theater, the Brooklyn Opera House and the four-screen **Rose Cinema** (☎ 718-623-2770), the first outer boroughs movie house dedicated to indie and foreign films. Try to catch its Next Wave Festival, a major series of opera, dance, theater and orchestral music held in fall. In June 2004, BAM unveiled its new makeover – a multimillion dollar restoration to bring back the multipastel facade from its original incarnation. The subway here's simple, but you can also reserve a spot on the **BAMbus**, which leaves from 120 Park Ave, at E 42nd St, in Manhattan, an hour before most performances. One-way fare is $5.

Brooklyn Center for the Performing Arts

On the Brooklyn College campus, at the end of the subway line, **Brooklyn Center for the Performing Arts** (☎ 718-951-4500; www.brooklyncenter.com; 290 Campus Rd; subway 2, 5 to Brooklyn College–Flatbush Ave) hosts headliners like Santana and Pavarotti as well as top-level dance performances.

St Ann's Warehouse

St Ann's Warehouse (Map p394; ☎ 718-858-2424; www.artsatstanns.org; 38 Water St, Brooklyn; subway A, C to High St, F to York St) is a cool concert and theater venue. It's been in Dumbo since 2001 (but active in Brooklyn for a couple of decades) and hosts innovative, interesting shows. Lou Reed and John Cale staged their tribute to Andy Warhol at St Ann's. Other performances include a puppet version of *The Barber of Seville* and tribute concerts featuring David Byrne and others.

READINGS/SPOKEN WORD

For all the highly stimulating theatrics in town, New Yorkers still can't help but be drawn to hear a good old-fashioned literary reading. Though the multitudinous Barnes & Nobles around town offer a constant calendar of big-name writers, there are plenty more intimate and unique venues, from indie bookstores to pubs.

92ND ST Y Map pp389-91
☎ 212-415-5500; 1395 Lexington Ave at 92nd St; subway 6 to 96th St
The Y is a bastion of literary greatness, hosting frequent readings, plus a Biographers and Brunch lecture series on Sundays, from top-shelf authors. Recent appearances have included Doris Lessing, Martin Amis and Jane Smiley.

BLUESTOCKINGS Map pp382-5
☎ 212-777-6028; 172 Allen St btwn Stanton & Rivington Sts; subway F, V to Lower East Side–Second Ave
A small, independent feminist bookstore and café, Bluestockings hosts frequent readings and spoken-word performances, usually with a feminist, political bent.

BOWERY POETRY CLUB
Map pp382-5
☎ 212-614-0505; 308 Bowery btwn Bleecker & Houston St; subway 6 to Bleecker St
Just across from CBGB in the East Village, this large café and performance space has eccentric readings of all genres, from plays to fiction, and frequent themed poetry slams.

CORNELIA ST CAFÉ Map pp382-5
☎ 212-989-9319; 29 Cornelia St btwn Bleecker and W 4th Sts; subway A, C, E, B, D, F, V to W 4th St
This intimate café is known for its various reading series, including Poetry and Prose on Sundays and a jazz-poetry combo on Thursdays.

HALF KING Map pp386-8
☎ 212-462-4300; 505 W 23rd St btwn Tenth & Eleventh Aves; subway C, E to 23rd St
It looks like a standard-issue Irish pub on the outside, but inside you'll find flickering votives, high-quality fiction and poetry readings, and a literary crowd along with the pints of Guinness.

KGB Map pp382-5
☎ 212-505-3360; 84 E 4th St btwn Second & Third Aves; subway F, V to Lower East Side–Second Ave
This Commie-themed bar, one flight above street level, hosts readings most nights, with frequent appearances from lit stars such as Rick Moody and Luc Sante, plus its popular Drunken! Careening! Writers! Series on Thursdays.

SMALL PRESS CENTER Map pp226-7
☎ 212-764-7021; 20 W 44th St btwn Fifth & Sixth Aves; subway B, D, F, V to 42nd St–Bryant Park
A nonprofit group that promotes independent book publishing, the Center, housed in a small, landmark library, hosts lectures on literary subjects from Dorothy Parker and her Algonquin cronies to the legacy of James Thurber. An annual book fair happens every March.

SYMPHONY SPACE Map pp389-91
☎ 212-864-1414; 2537 Broadway at 95th St; subway 1, 2, 3, 9 to 96th St
In addition to hosting innovative films, music concerts and dance performances, Symphony Space is home to the beloved Selected Shorts series, hosted by Isaiah Sheffer and broadcast on National Public Radio stations across the country, on frequent Wednesdays in spring. The evening entails high-quality short stories read by celebrities that have included Alec Baldwin, David Sedaris, James Naughton, Susan Orlean and Walter Mosley.

CLUBBING

New York's club scene is constantly changing. That's partly because New York partiers get bored easily. It's also because club promoters have found themselves in an unending battle with the city over drug activity, noise and myriad other violations; for that reason, some of the biggest spots – Sound Factory, Avalon (née Limelight) – are often closing down and reopening.

Not to be confused with bars and lounges, clubs are generally larger spaces that feature dance floors and DJs. The definition is more crucial these days, as Mayor Bloomberg tries to decide exactly how to do away with (or at least update) the city's archaic Cabaret Law, which stipulates where dancing is and is not legal based on neighborhood zoning restrictions. The law has raised the ire of many club owners, who have even formed an alliance, **Legalize Dancing NYC** (www.legalizedancingnyc.com), to make sure it goes away.

For up-to-the-minute news, check out the 'clubs' section of the weekly *Time Out New York* magazine, the always updated website of the monthly magazine *Paper* (www.papermag.com), and, for gay soirees, either *HX* or *Next* magazine, two monthly bar rags found at most queer clubs. You should also keep an eye out for club and band flyers on walls and billboards while strolling the East Village – sometimes that's the best way to find out about clubs that don't have phones and don't advertise. Oh, and don't even think about going to any of these places before 11pm, even on a weeknight; things don't truly pick up until 1am or later.

AVALON Map pp382-5
☎ 212-807-7780; 660 Sixth Ave at 20th St; subway F, V, R, W to 23rd St (W Sat & Sun only); admission $25

The latest incarnation of Limelight, troubled club-kid lair of deported scene king Peter Gatien. The parties housed at this labyrinthine church space are attracting attention for the prog-house, techno and trance DJs who spin here, mainly on Saturday. Sunday nights are big gay affairs.

CIELO Map pp382-5
☎ 212-645-5700; 18 Little West 12th St btwn Ninth Ave & Washington St; subway A, C, E to Eighth Ave, L to 14th St; admission $10

Known for its intimate space and free or low-cost parties, this Meatpacking District newcomer packs in a fashionable, multi-culti crowd for its blend of tribal, Latin-spiced house and soulful grooves, especially on Monday with DJ Francois K's 'outerplanetary' sounds at Deep Space.

CLUB SHELTER Map pp386-8
☎ 212-719-4479; 20 W 39th St btwn Fifth & Sixth Aves; subway B, D, F, V to 42nd St–Bryant Park; admission $10-20

The night to check out this multilevel behemoth is Saturday, for the beloved, long-running deep-house party Shelter with DJ legend Timmy Regisford. Meanwhile, Lovergirl packs in lesbian homegirls on a couple of its other floors – on the same night – for a party known more for its cruising than its sounds.

CROBAR Map pp386-8
☎ 212-629-9000; 530 W 28th St btwn Tenth & Eleventh Aves; subway C, E to 23rd St; admission $25

A brand-new megaclub, this massive venue, a local sibling of Crobars in Miami and Chicago,

caters to a largely suburban crowd on weekends, but holds plenty of queer-tinged bashes with super-DJs including Victor Calderone.

DEEP Map pp382-5
☎ 212-229-2000; 16 W 22nd St btwn Fifth & Sixth Aves; subway F, V, R, W to 23rd St (W Sat & Sun only); admission $12-25

This new house and hip-hop venue isn't the trendiest spot, but it does house the monthly 718 Sessions, a riot of old-school dancing to deep, soulful house from DJ Danny Krivit. House parties rage on Friday with DJ Marc Anthony.

Top Five Clubs

- **Cielo** (left) It's intimate, with cutting-edge DJs.
- **Club Shelter** (left) House music lives on here.
- **Opaline** (below) For East Village freaks, there's no place like this home.
- **Roxy** (opposite) The epitome of Chelsea-boy dance-floor humping.
- **Volume** (opposite) It's new, it's massive, it's so Williamsburg.

EXIT2 Map pp386-8
☎ 212-582-8282; 610 W 56th St btwn Eleventh & Twelfth Aves; subway A, B, C, D, 1, 9 to Columbus Circle; admission $25

This four-floor multiplex king of all clubs is where the world's most famous DJ, Junior Vasquez, spins at his Saturday-night soiree Earth – from a private, $8-million booth, no less. You'll get lost in the maze of theme rooms on every floor, each equipped with leopard-patterned sofas and its own DJ playing specialty music. Whatever music you're craving, it's in there somewhere. Also check out the roof garden.

LOTUS Map pp382-5
☎ 212-243-4420; 409 W 14th St btwn Ninth & Tenth Aves; subway A, C, E to 14th St, L to Eighth Ave; admission $10-20

The big night at this slick, VIP-crowd club is Friday, when GBH (not to be confused with GHB) rocks the house. Resident DJ Angola spins a fresh mix of house, disco and garage.

OPALINE Map pp382-5
☎ 212-995-8684; 85 Ave A btwn 5th & 6th Sts; subway F, V to Lower East Side–Second Ave; admission $10

This lush lounge, below street level in the heart of the East Village, becomes Area 10009 on Fridays. Hosts Amanda Lepore,

Sophia Lamar and Dee Finley suck in a queer and queer-friendly crowd for a decadent evening, set to various beats from DJs Nita and Formika.

PYRAMID Map pp382-5
☎ 212-228-4888; 101 Ave A btwn 6th & 7th Sts; subway F, V to Lower East Side–Second Ave
You'll find a happening soiree on just about any night of the week at this mainly gay party cave. Fridays, offering the long-running '80s party, 1984, draw the biggest mobs.

ROXY Map pp382-5
☎ 212-627-0404; 515 W 18th St btwn Tenth & Eleventh Aves; subway A, C, E to 14th St, L to Eighth Ave; admission $15-25
This legendary megaclub keeps the good times rolling with the freewheeling Tuesday roller disco. John Blair promotes the big Saturday-night bash, a Circuit Party–like massive gathering of shirtless gay men, humping to the sounds of big names from Manny Lehman to Susan Morabito.

SAPPHIRE Map pp382-5
☎ 212-777-5153; 249 Eldridge St at E Houston St; subway F, V to Lower East Side–Second Ave, admission $5
This tiny, hoppin' venue has survived the crowds of the mid-'90s Ludlow St boom with its hip factor intact. Come here for some steamy dancing on a tightly packed dance floor.

VOLUME Map p394
☎ 718-388-3588; 99 North 13th St at Wythe Ave, Williamsburg, Brooklyn; subway L to Bedford Ave, admission $5-20
This 12,500ft former paint factory is a brand-new Billyburg superclub, hosting massive parties that fuse art installations, visual effects and a range of electronic-beat DJs for an eclectic, extraordinary experience.

MUSIC
Though it's no Austin or Seattle, NYC does have an impressive indie music scene, and has given rise to favorites including The Strokes, Yeah Yeah Yeahs, Rufus Wainwright and Babe the Blue Ox in recent years. Dedicated fans make it their business to chart the latest sounds, following their favorites to intimate venues around the city, many of which mix up their genres and billings. More traditional sounds are also constants,

as a slew of jazz clubs, cabaret houses and classical venues book gigs steadily, and whether you enjoy piano soloists or full symphonies, New York offers the full range of high culture, performed by renowned house companies and highly regarded touring artists. Megastars rarely tour without hitting the New York area – they'll pack Madison Square Garden, the city's main arena, and, in summer, Jones Beach (p315), a fantastic outdoor amphitheater on the Long Island seashore.

ROCK, HIP-HOP & INDIE
ARLENE GROCERY Map pp382-5
☎ 212-358-1633; www.arlene-grocery.com; 95 Stanton St at Orchard St; subway F, V to Lower East Side–Second Ave
This convenience-store-turned-club was just pre-curve enough of the LES's '90s explosion to entitle it to a snooty vibe. The one-room hothouse incubates local talent, with great live shows for free every night – plus cheap beer, happily.

BEACON THEATER Map pp389-91
☎ 212-496-7070; 2124 Broadway btwn 74th & 75th Sts; subway 1, 2, 3, 9 to 72nd St
This Upper West Side venue has a pretty cool atmosphere for such a large, mainstream space. It hosts big acts for folks who want to see shows in a more intimate environment than that of a big concert arena. Moby, Aimee Mann and the Allman Brothers have all played this stage, though the theater seating here usually inhibits dancing.

BOWERY BALLROOM Map pp382-5
☎ 212-533-2111; www.boweryballroom.com; 6 Delancey St at Bowery; subway J, M to Bowery
This terrific, medium-sized venue has the perfect sound and feel for seeing acts like Jonathan Richman, American Music Club, the Delgados and other bands demanding audience attention.

CBGB Map pp382-5
☎ 212-982-4052; www.cbgb.com; 315 Bowery btwn E 1st & 2nd Sts; subway 6 to Bleecker St
This dark little den is still going strong after nearly three decades. The name stands for 'Country, Bluegrass and Blues,' but since the mid-'70s the place has heard more rock than anything else. Some of the luminaries who've sweated through legendary sets here include

Blondie, Talking Heads and the B52s. Today, the bands experiment with rock, Motown, thrash and everything in between. The recent addition of the Downstairs Lounge doles out quality jazz, readings and other such diversions.

CONTINENTAL Map pp382-5

☎ 212-529-6924; www.continentalnyc.com; 25 Third Ave at St Marks Pl; subway N, R to 8th St–NYU, 6 to Astor Pl

This beer-sticky rocker space is famous for cheap drink specials and unannounced gigs by the likes of Iggy Pop and Jakob Dylan. It built its following by not charging a cover for quality rock and roll and is often still the case.

FEZ Map pp382-5

☎ 212-533-2680; www.feznyc.com; 380 Lafayette St at Great Jones St; subway B, D, F, V to Broadway–Lafayette St, 6 to Bleecker St

Underground, below the airy Time Café and the couch-strewn cocktail lounge, is this dark supper club surrounding a small stage. Some views are blocked by basement pillars, but the diverse range of acts – everything from the jazzy Howard Fishman Quartet to the pop-folk of Mila Drumke – makes it worth settling in.

IRVING PLAZA Map pp382-5

☎ 212-777-1224; www.irvingplaza.com; 17 Irving Pl at 15th St; subway L, N, Q, R, W, 4, 5, 6 to Union Sq

In the Union Square area, Irving Plaza is probably the best club of its size hosting mainstream indie acts like Stereolab, Jane's Addiction and the Flaming Lips. Just be prepared to stand – either on the cramped floor in front of the stage or on the balcony up above the entire scene.

JOE'S PUB Map pp382-5

☎ 212-539-8770; www.joespub.com; Public Theater, 425 Lafayette St btwn Astor Pl and E 4th St; subway R, W to 8th St–NYU (W Mon-Fri only), 6 to Astor Pl

Part cabaret theater, part rock and new-indie venue, this supper club has hosted Toshi Reagon, Jonatha Brooke and Diamanda Galas.

LUNA LOUNGE Map pp382-5

☎ 212-260-2323; 171 Ludlow St at Stanton St; subway F, V to Lower East Side–Second Ave

With a mellow bar and pool table up front and a small back room especially for live shows, Luna hosts garage bands, local musicians and up-and-coming indie darlings every single night of the week. The Strokes, Kid Rock and Madder Rose have all graced the teeny stage here with their presence.

Free Fun, Part II: Central Park SummerStage

Among New Yorkers, one of summer's most highly anticipated musical pleasures is the return of the **Central Park SummerStage** (Map pp389-91; ☎ 212-360-2756; www.summerstage.org), an annual series of mostly free concerts that take place at Rumsey Playfield in the center of the park. A program of the City Park Foundation, SummerStage presents eclectically billed music concerts (eg Sonic Youth and Wilco, Devo and Yeah Yeah Yeahs), dance performances and readings from a wide variety of artists, free of charge except for the annual blockbuster benefit concerts (which featured the Strokes in its sold-out May 2004 event). Admission to shows, via the park's Fifth Ave and 69th St entrance, is on a first-come, first-served basis, and though most shows get seriously crowded (especially on weekends), you should always be able to squeeze your way into the back of the throngs. When the summer schedule is released at the end of every May, New Yorkers clamor to see which of their faves will be onstage, as there's always something for everyone. Past performers, for example, have included Ani DiFranco, De La Soul, Elvis Costello, Indigo Girls, Jack Johnson and Lucinda Williams.

MADISON SQUARE GARDEN
Map pp386-8

☎ 212-465-6741; www.thegarden.com; Seventh Ave at W 33rd St; subway A, C, E, 1, 2, 3, 9 to 34th St–Penn Station

Perched above Penn Station in Midtown, this 19,000-seat venue is known as 'the world's most famous arena,' and seeing blue-chip rock, pop and rap here, in a sea of energized fans, is an unforgettable experience.

MEOW MIX Map pp382-5

☎ 212-254-0688; www.meowmixchix.com; 269 E Houston St at Suffolk St; subway F, V to Lower East Side–Second Ave

Though its biggest claim to fame is being a popular lesbian bar, the Mix also hosts frequent indie bands, all-woman rockers and otherwise.

MERCURY LOUNGE Map pp382-5

☎ 212-260-4700; www.mercuryloungenyc.com; 217 E Houston St btwn Essex & Ludlow Sts; subway F, V to Lower East Side–Second Ave

Big names will turn up (Lou Reed or John Popper, for example), but this beloved club on the Lower East Side almost always has something worth hearing. Intimate and comfy, with tables and ample dance space facing the riser stage, the Mercury can also boast of a quality sound system – a great combination for local and touring groups, and their audiences.

NORTH SIX Map p394
☎ 718-599-5103; www.northsix.com; 66 North 6th St, Brooklyn; subway L to Bedford Ave
Catch local up-and-comers and occasional name bands at this room just across the river in Brooklyn.

PETE'S CANDY STORE Map p394
☎ 718-302-3770; www.petescandystore.com; 709 Lorimer St, Williamsburg, Brooklyn; subway L to Lorimer St, G to Metropolitan Ave
A slick performance lounge in the middle of hyper-trendy Williamsburg, Pete's hosts local indie rock and rockabilly bands, burlesque shows and group Scrabble nights. It also has a new reading series: Pete's Big Salmon, presenting local poets and fiction writers every other Monday at 7:30pm.

PIANOS
☎ 212-505-3733; www.pianosnyc.com; 106 Norfolk St; subway F, V to Lower East Side–Second Ave
An old piano shop turned hipster's musical haven serving mixed-genre bills (hip-hop, cowpunk, electronica, Asian rock) and pouring plenty of Rheingold for an appreciative Lower East Side crowd.

RADIO CITY MUSIC HALL Map pp226-7
☎ 212-247-4777; www.radiocity.com; Sixth Ave at W 51st St; subway B, D, F, V to 47-50 Sts–Rockefeller Center
An iconic strip of neon in the middle of Midtown, this grand art deco concert hall, built in 1932, hosts performances such as kd lang, Neil Young, Mary J Blige, Prince and the Gipsy Kings. Just touring the gorgeous facility is a thrill in itself.

SOUTHPAW Map p395
☎ 718-230-0236; www.spsounds.com; 125 Fifth Ave btwn Sterling & St John's Pls, Park Slope, Brooklyn; subway D, M, N, R to Pacific St (M Mon-Fri only), subway B, Q, 2, 3, 4, 5 to Atlantic Ave
This popular rock venue moved right in to the list of favorite spots not long after it opened its doors in 2002. The innovative design gives you a clear view of the stage from wherever you're sitting, whether at the long bar or in one of the comfy banquettes around the perimeter. The top-notch sound system is perfect for piping the tunes of local rock, funk and world musicians.

CLASSICAL

BARGEMUSIC Map p394
☎ 718-624-2083; Fulton Ferry Landing, Brooklyn Heights, Brooklyn; subway A, C to High St, 2, 3 to Clark St
Chamber-music concerts on this 125-seat docked ferryboat are an intimate affair. For almost 30 years it's been a beloved venue, with beautiful waterfront views and performances throughout the year, from Thursday to Sunday.

CARNEGIE HALL Map pp226-7
☎ 212-247-7800; www.carnegiehall.org; 154 W 57th St at Seventh Ave; subway N, R, Q, W to 57th St
Since 1891, this historic performance hall has hosted Tchaikovsky, Mahler and Prokofiev, among others. Today it hosts visiting philharmonics, the New York Pops orchestra and various world-music performers, including Cesaria Evora and Sweet Honey in the Rock.

GRACE CHURCH Map pp382-5
☎ 212-254-2000; 802 Broadway at 10th St; subway R to 8th St
Programs such as Bach at noon (Tuesday to Friday, except in summer), frequent concerts by the Choir of Men and Boys as well as organ and orchestra recitals are an excellent reason to visit this magical, beautiful Episcopal church in the heart of the Village.

LINCOLN CENTER Map pp386-8
☎ 212-875-5000; Lincoln Center Plaza, Broadway at W 64th St; subway 1, 9 to 66th St–Lincoln Center
At Avery Fisher Hall, the showplace of the **New York Philharmonic** (www.newyorkphilharmonic .org), expect the highest standards of the classic repertoire that continues to define it. Tickets can be purchased through **Center Charge** (☎ 212-721-6500). **Alice Tully Hall** (☎ 212-721-6500) is home to the American Symphony Orchestra and the Little Orchestra Society.

MERKIN CONCERT HALL Map pp389-91
☎ 212-501-3330; 129 W 67th St btwn Amsterdam Ave & Broadway; subway 1, 9 to 66th St–Lincoln Center
This 457-seat hall, part of the Kaufman Cultural Center, is one of the city's more intimate venues for classical music.

TOWN HALL Map pp226-7

☎ 212-840-2824; www.the-townhall-nyc.org; 123 W 43rd btwn Sixth & Seventh Aves; subway B, D, F, V to 42nd St–Bryant Park

Classical ensembles regularly play at this landmark venue, as do folk, jazz and blues artists – and even Garrison Keilor, when he brings his radio show to town.

TRINITY CHURCH Map pp380-1

☎ 212-602-0800; www.trinitywallstreet.org; Broadway & Wall St; subway 2, 3 4, 5 to Wall St, N, R to Rector St

This former Anglican parish church offers an excellent Concerts at One music series (also held at St Paul's Chapel, Broadway at Fulton St) for just a $2 suggested donation. Call the concert hotline (☎ 212-602-0747) for a schedule.

JAZZ & BLUES

The West Village is a veritable jazz ghetto, with many clubs offering long jams, cheap cover charges and a hot buffet of all flavors of jazz. Midtown has plenty of excellent venues, too. But Uptown is still the granddaddy of jazz joints, so old-school enthusiasts might want to hop up to Harlem. The only thing missing nowadays at all these places is that classic cloud of smoke.

55 BAR Map pp382-5

☎ 212-929-9883; www.55bar.com; 55 Christopher St at Seventh Ave; subway 1, 9 to Christopher St–Sheridan Sq

This West Village joint hosts jazz, blues and fusion nightly, with regular performances by quality artists-in-residence and stars passing through. Cover ranges from next-to-nothing to about $15 (but that includes two drinks).

BAM CAFÉ Map p394

☎ 718-636-4139; www.bam.org; 30 Lafayette Ave at Ashland Pl, Ft Greene, Brooklyn; subway D, M, N, R to Pacific St (M Sat & Sun only), B, Q, 2, 3, 4, 5 to Atlantic Ave

A high-ceilinged restaurant and lounge in the Brooklyn Academy of Music complex, this venue gives you a healthy helping of live jazz – and sometimes R&B, cabaret or spoken word – along with your supper.

BB KING'S JOINT Map pp226-7

☎ 212-997-4144; www.bbkingblues.com; 237 W 42nd St; subway N, R, 1, 2, 3, 7, 9 to Times Sq–42nd St

Catch old-school rock, blues and reggae acts like Etta James and Merle Haggard at this two-tiered, horseshoe-shaped room in the heart of the new Times Square, with cool secondary bills at the adjacent Lucille's Grill.

BIRDLAND Map pp226-7

☎ 212-581-3080; www.birdlandjazz.com; 315 W 44th St btwn Eighth & Ninth Aves; subway A, C, E to 42nd St–Port Authority

This landmark club was named for Charlie Parker, or 'Bird,' and has been turning out big-name acts since 1949, when Parker often headlined (at the original location, on 52nd St), as did Thelonious Monk, Miles Davis, Stan Getz and everyone else. Today you're likely to catch the Duke Ellington Orchestra (directed by Paul Mercer Ellington), the James Moody Quartet and Stanley Jordan.

BLUE NOTE Map pp382-5

☎ 212-475-8592; www.bluenote.net; 131 W 3rd St btwn Sixth Ave & MacDougal St; subway A, C, E, F, V, S to W 4th St

This is by far the most famous (and expensive) of the city's jazz clubs. Covers as high as $75 get you in to hear big stars play short sets to a serious jazz audience (which means no talking – ever!).

CHICAGO BLUES Map pp382-5

☎ 212-924-9755; 73 Eighth Ave at W 14th St; subway A, C, E to 14th St, L to Eighth Ave

This West Village venue hosts visiting blues masters nightly. The up-and-coming also perform at this none-too-flashy club, and if you've got a harmonica in your pocket, you can jump in for Monday night's blues jam.

CLEOPATRA'S NEEDLE Map pp389-91

☎ 212-769-6969; www.cleopatrasneedleny.com; 2485 Broadway btwn W 92nd & 93rd Sts; subway 1, 9, 2, 3 to 96th St

Late-night and open-mic jams are a hallmark at Cleopatra's Needle and the music goes until 4am. Some of the best band views are from the bar, where you can take a pint on tap and nosh on Mediterranean-influenced fare; there's never a cover, but mind the $10 drink and/or food minimum.

C-NOTE Map pp382-5

☎ 212-677-8142; www.thecnote.com; 157 Ave C at 10th St; subway F, V to Lower East Side–Second Ave

This bare-bones, obscure East Village space feeds thrifty music-lovers with an endless stream of free jazz and blues. Trios frequent the early end of the night (usually before 7pm), while open jams take over on Saturdays.

IRIDIUM Map pp226-7
☎ 212-582-2121; www.iridiumjazzclub.com; 1650 Broadway at 51st St; subway 1, 9 to 50th St

The tables are really tight here, but the sound is good and the sight lines fairly clear. High-quality, big-ticket traditional jazz acts play two sets a night from Sunday to Thursday, and three sets on weekends. Monday night is reserved for the talented and hilarious Les Paul trio, as it has been for the past several decades. There's also a Sunday jazz brunch here.

KNITTING FACTORY Map pp380-1
☎ 212-219-3055; www.knittingfactory.com; 74 Leonard St btwn Church St & Broadway; subway 1, 9 to Franklin St

This Tribeca favorite has a long and influential history in the realm of NYC jazz, folk and experimental music, spoken word and performance. Its four performance spaces host all manner of music, from cosmic space jazz to Tokyo shock rock and the occasional traditional gig, plus rock and hip-hop. Listen to bands on the main floor, balcony, lounge or in the bar downstairs.

LENOX LOUNGE Map pp392-3
☎ 212-427-0253; www.lenoxlounge.com; 288 Malcolm X Blvd btwn 124th & 125th Sts; subway 2, 3 to 125th St

The Lounge is an old favorite of local jazz cats and has recently blipped onto the radar of further-flung enthusiasts (especially Japanese expats and visitors). Don't miss the lux Zebra Room in the back. Sunday nights the place turns itself over to a soulful gay soiree.

ST NICK'S PUB Map pp392-3
☎ 212-283-9728; 773 St Nicholas Ave at 149th St; subway A, B, C, D to 145th St

This is an amazing place to hear raw jazz created by musicians for musicians. Monday nights feature an open jam starting at 9:30pm, when axe- and horn-toting tourists take up the creative gauntlet. Later in the evening, big-name jazz cats come from their bigger gigs around town, keeping it real and live here at the Pub.

SMALLS Map pp382-5
☎ 212-929-7565; 183 W 10th St at Seventh Ave; subway 1, 9 to Christopher St–Sheridan Sq

It has only a sliver of a lit doorway that's easy to miss, but don't. This place hosts smoking 10½-hour jazz marathons every night from 10pm to 8:30am. Descend the stairs and grab a couch, pop whatever beverage of choice you've

brought along (Small's has no liquor license, meaning it's all ages, adding to the nice mix on stage and in the audience) and sit back for quality jazz, from straight ahead to far out.

SMOKE Map pp389-91
☎ 212-864-6662; www.smokejazz.com; 2751 Broadway btwn 105th & 106th Sts; subway 1, 9 to 103rd St

Unobstructed sight lines and plush sofas have hardcore fans of top-notch talent lining up around the block to get in on weekends. During the week it's not such a mob scene and there's no cover charge.

SWEET RHYTHM Map pp382-5
☎ 212-255-3626; www.sweetrhythmny.com; 88 Seventh Ave South btwn Bleecker & Grove Sts; subway 1, 9 to Christopher St–Sheridan Sq

This supper club, formerly Sweet Basil's, has lost some of its cachet. But it still features top-notch musicians, many toting instruments (and talents) all the way from Brazil, Cuba and Africa.

TONIC Map pp382-5
☎ 212-358-7501; www.tonicnyc.com; 107 Norfolk St btwn Delancey & Rivington; subway F to Delancey St

Expect avant-garde, creative and experimental music at this Lower East Side room, known for inspired improvisational jams from performers such as John Zorn, Kim Gordon, John Medeski and Marc Ribot.

UP OVER JAZZ CAFÉ Map p395
☎ 718-3998-5413; www.upoverjazz.com; 351 Flatbush Ave at Seventh Ave, Park Slope, Brooklyn; subway B, Q to Seventh Ave, 2, 3 to Grand Army Plaza

Straight-up piano jazz, quintets and Latin jazz are the orders of the night at this Park Slope hot spot, one flight above busy Flatbush Avenue. Nightly open jams during the week start at 9:30pm.

Entertainment – Music

VILLAGE VANGUARD Map pp382-5

☎ 212-255-4037; www.villagevanguard.net; 178 Seventh Ave at W 11th St; subway 1, 9 to Christopher St–Sheridan Sq

This basement-level venue in the West Village could possibly be the world's most prestigious jazz club, as it has hosted literally every major star of the past 50 years. There's a two-drink minimum.

FOLK & WORLD

It's not such a folkie scene here these days, but the multi-culti population ensures that you can always get a good dose of world sounds.

BACK FENCE Map pp382-5

☎ 212-475-9221; 155 Bleecker St btwn MacDougal & Sullivan Sts; subway A, C, E, F, V, S to W 4th St

This surprisingly laid-back venue is stuck on a depressingly rowdy, college-student-mobbed strip of the Village. It offers fine folk and blues during the week, classic rock on weekends.

LQ Map pp386-8

☎ 212-593-7575; 511 Lexington Ave btwn 47th & 48th Sts; subway 4, 5, 6, 7, S to 42nd St–Grand Central

This brand-new Latin club is bringing much-needed flavor to this staid part of town, with nationally renowned salsa bands playing live music to the throngs of dancers every Wednesday night.

PADDY REILLY'S MUSIC BAR Map pp386-8

☎ 212-686-1210; 510 Second Ave at 29th St; subway 6 to 28th St

It's the place to be for serious pints and even more serious Irish folk bands throughout the week.

PEOPLE'S VOICE CAFÉ Map pp386-8

☎ 212-787-3903; 45 E 33rd St btwn Madison & Park Aves; subway 6 to 33rd St

Members of the group Songs of Freedom and Struggle founded this good old-fashioned peacenik coffeehouse in 1979. Today it's a nonprofit collective of musicians and activists who host shows from political folkies, storytellers and dancers.

SOB'S Map pp382-5

☎ 212-243-4940; 204 Varick St btwn King and Houston Sts; subway 1, 9 to Houston St

SOB's stands for Sounds of Brazil, but it isn't limited to samba: you can shake it to Afro-Cuban music, salsa and reggae, both live and on the turntable. SOB's hosts dinner shows nightly but it doesn't start jumping until 2am.

SYMPHONY SPACE Map pp389-91

☎ 212-864-1414; 2537 Broadway at 95th St; subway 1, 2, 3, 9 to 96th St

The refurbished theater here, the gem of the upper–Upper West Side, hosts world-music concerts. Recent groups have performed gypsy, Scottish, Indian and Greek music.

Sports, Health & Fitness

Sports, Health & Fitness

Hailing a cab may feel like a game, and subway stations in August can resemble saunas, but New York City is filled with more-traditional ways to get your kicks on fields, courts, stadiums and in gyms, pools and spas. Rather watch than play? With more professional sports teams than any other American metropolis, NYC can punch your ticket in a number of ways.

WATCHING SPORTS

With so many teams and overlapping seasons, a game is rarely a day away. Other than football, tickets are generally available. **Ticketmaster** (☎ 800-462-2849, 212-307-7171; www.ticketmaster.com) sells individual tickets and the teams handle package deals. Another consideration is **StubHub** (☎ 866-788-2482; www.stubhub.com), a service for ticket-holders to sell tickets.

Look out for the funny, irreverent *New York Sports Express* (www.nysportsexpress .com), a free weekly.

BASEBALL

In the years after WWII, New York had three teams, all powerhouses: the New York Yankees, Giants and the Brooklyn Dodgers. Thirteen times, two of them met in the finals for the heralded Subway Series. The unthinkable came in 1957 when both the Dodgers and Giants bolted for California (did it *have* to be California?). The arrival of the Mets in Queens a few years later was welcomed, but didn't quite dull the sense of betrayal felt by many fans (including ones not yet born in 1957). In 2000, the Yanks beat the Mets in a reprise of the Subway Series, adding more lore for the ages.

Teams play 162 games during the regular season from April to October, when the real action starts – the playoffs.

NEW YORK YANKEES Map pp392-3
☎ 718-293-6000; www.yankees.com; Yankee Stadium, cnr 161st St & River Ave; tickets $8-70; subway B, D, 4 to 161st St–Yankee Stadium
It would be an Empire State–sized understatement to call the Yanks a baseball dynasty. Playing in the American League, the Bronx Bombers have won 26 World Series championships since 1900 – four times in the past decade. Watch Alex Rodriguez and the boys at **Yankee Stadium** (p148), 15 minutes from Midtown by subway. Bleacher seats are almost always available. It's not a good idea to wear your Red Sox hat.

NEW YORK METS Map p397
☎ 718-507-8499; www.mets.com; Shea Stadium, 123-01 Roosevelt Ave, Flushing, Queens; tickets $5-48; subway 7 to Willlets Point–Shea Stadium
New York's 'new' baseball team has represented the National League since 1962. Fans still hold onto the magic of '86, when the Mets last won the World Series in a miraculous comeback. Their blue-and-orange logo shows select buildings from different boroughs. The trip to Shea is 35 minutes by subway.

Central Park (p118)

BROOKLYN CYCLONES

☎ 718-449-8497; www.brooklyncyclones.com; Key-Span Park, cnr Surf Ave & W 17th St, Coney I; tickets $6-10; ☯ ticket office 10am-4pm Mon-Fri, 10am-3pm Sat; subway F, D to Coney I–Stillwell Ave

The Mets' new farm team plays minor-league ball for the Brooklyn faithful at their shiny stadium, just a few steps from the Coney Island boardwalk.

STATEN ISLAND YANKEES

☎ 718-720-9265; www.siyanks.com; Richmond County Bank Ballpark, 75 Richmond Tce, Staten I; tickets $10; ☯ ticket office 9am-5pm Mon-Fri, 10am-3pm Sat; Staten I Ferry

Catch the Bombers of tomorrow, or at least some fabulous Manhattan skyline views at this stylish waterfront stadium across New York Harbor.

BASKETBALL

Two NBA teams, the Knicks and the Nets, call the New York metropolitan area home. The season lasts from October to May or June. Individual game tickets are available through **Ticketmaster** (opposite) and **StubHub** (opposite) or by visiting the ticket office.

Book way ahead if you're hoping to see either squad play the star-laden Los Angeles Lakers.

NEW YORK KNICKS Map pp386-8

☎ 212-465-5867; www.nyknicks.com; Madison Square Garden, btwn Seventh Ave & 33rd St; tickets $52-1605; subway A, C, E, 1, 2, 3, 9 to 34th St–Penn Station

The beloved Knickerbockers play hoops in front of Spike Lee and 18,999 others at the Garden. In recent years, hard times have come to Knicks basketball: a championship has eluded the team since 1973 (when Willis Reed and politician Bill Bradley played); even Patrick Ewing, star center of the '80s and '90s, never claimed the ring (damn you, Michael Jordan!). Some (maniacal) fans believe that, with the recent addition of Brooklyn native Stephen Marbury, the ever-elusive victory may be within reach.

NEW JERSEY NETS

☎ 800-765-6387; www.njnets.com; Continental Airlines Arena, Meadowlands Sports Complex, NJ; tickets $40-480

Overshadowed, stuck in the Jersey Meadowlands but – in recent years – plainly better than the Knicks, the Nets play exciting ball, though their closest championship call was being runners-up in the 2001–02 and 2002–03 championship finals. Perhaps what the Nets have needed – other than a new name (Nets? c'mon) – is a total relocation. In January 2004, Bruce Ratner bought the team and announced plans to move it to Brooklyn by 2007. Meanwhile, with players like slick point guard Jason Kidd, the Nets seem poised to contend for Eastern Conference champion each year. (See Is Your Game in Jersey?, below, for directions.)

NEW YORK LIBERTY Map pp386-8

☎ 212-465-6293; www.nyliberty.com; Madison Square Garden; tickets $10-65; subway A, C, E, 1, 2, 3 to 34th St–Penn Station

Women's basketball has become another hot ticket since the WNBA league's outset in 1997. The Liberty plays from May to September or October.

Is Your Game in Jersey?

Home games for the Giants, Jets, Nets, Devils and MetroStars are held at the Meadowlands Sports Complex in East Rutherford, New Jersey. The easiest way to reach the complex is by public bus service from the Port Authority Bus Terminal in Midtown. The 20-minute trip is $3.25 each way. Buses run continuously from two hours before a game or event until one hour afterward.

By car from Manhattan, take the Lincoln Tunnel from Midtown to Route 3 West and follow signs to Exit 4, Route 120.

FOOTBALL

Both of New York's NFL teams play in New Jersey at Giants Stadium from August to December; they play on alternate weekends (16 games per season), but tickets are expensive ($200 and up) and scarce. Try **StubHub** (p244) and www.craigslist.com for available tickets. In addition, the Giants have a free ticket-exchange program; see their website or call for details. (See Is Your Game in Jersey? on p245 for details on getting to the games.)

NEW YORK GIANTS
☎ 201-935-811, 201-935-8222; www.giants.com; Giants Stadium, East Rutherford, NJ

One of the NFL's oldest teams, the Giants (part of the NFC conference) have stumbled in recent years, last playing at the Super Bowl in 2000. Once again, they are rebuilding, this time banking on young quarterback Eli Manning. Seeing ex-coach Bill Parcells in division-rival Dallas Cowboys' gear is hard for many Giants fans to take.

NEW YORK JETS
☎ 516-560-8200 ext 1; www.newyorkjets.com; Giants Stadium, East Rutherford, NJ

The Jets, generally less popular than the Giants (hell, they play in Giants Stadium), have yet to return to the big time since the fabled 1969 Super Bowl when flashy quarterback Joe Namath 'guaranteed' a victory. He was right, and it started an era when AFC teams dominated the once too-tough-to-beat NFC teams. That said, the Jets have been playing badly in recent years.

NEW YORK DRAGONS
☎ 516-794-9303; www.newyorkdragons.com; Nassau Veterans Memorial Coliseum, Uniondale, Long I; tickets $15-110; Long I Railroad Hempstead station, then bus No N70, N71 or N72 to the coliseum

If you're looking to get silly, see New York's arena football team play the miniversion of gridiron in Long Island. The season runs from February to June.

HOCKEY

Of all things, there are more major-league hockey teams in the metropolis than any other sport. The season lasts from September to April; each team plays three or four games a week.

NEW JERSEY DEVILS
☎ 201-935-6050; www.newjerseydevils.com; Continental Airlines Arena, East Rutherford, NJ; tickets $20-90

The Devils may not be New Yorkers, but they play some premier hockey, and have won the Stanley Cup three times in the past decade (1995, 2000 and 2003).

NEW YORK RANGERS Map pp386-8
☎ 212-465-6741; www.nyrangers.com; Madison Square Garden; tickets $30-155; subway A, C, E, 1, 2, 3, 9 to 34th St–Penn Station

Manhattan's favorite hockey squad ended a 54-year dry spell by hoisting the Stanley Cup in 1994. Though 'iffy' play has plagued recent seasons, the Rangers' fans still raise the MSG roof, especially when the Blueshirts play arch rivals, the New York Islanders.

NEW YORK ISLANDERS
☎ 631-888-9000; www.newyorkislanders.com; Nassau Veterans Memorial Coliseum, Uniondale, Long I; tickets $31-160

New York's other NHL hockey team plays in Long Island.

HORSE RACING

Horse fans can find a few tracks in the area. Thoroughbreds race Wednesday to Sunday at **Aqueduct Race Track** (Howard Beach, Queens; subway A to Aqueduct Racetrack) from October to early May, and at **Belmont Race Track** (Belmont, Long Island; Long Island Railroad to the Belmont Race Track stop) from May to mid-July, and September and October. Belmont hosts the famous Belmont Stakes in June. For information on either, contact the **New York Racing Association** (☎ 718-641-4700; www.nyra.com).

The track at **Meadowlands** (☎ 201-935-8500; www.thebigm.com; Meadowlands Sports Complex, East Rutherford, NJ) has harness racing December to August and thoroughbreds September to November. Wednesday to Saturday races begin at 7:30pm, Sunday at 1:10pm. See Is Your Game in Jersey? on p245 for directions.

SOCCER

Yes, the US *does* play soccer; unfortunately the women's professional soccer league, which included the New York Power, folded in 2003.

NEW YORK/NEW JERSEY METROSTARS

☎ 201-583-7000; www.metrostars.com; Giants Stadium, East Rutherford, NJ; tickets $18-38

The MetroStars' 30-game soccer season runs from April to October. A diverse crowd of soccer loyalists make the games fun. (See Is Your Game in Jersey? on p245 for directions.)

TENNIS

The pro tennis circuit's final Grand Slam event each year, the US Open (www.usopen .org), takes place over two weeks at the end of August at USTA National Tennis Center (Map p397; ☎ 718-760-6200; www.usta.com; Flushing Meadows Corona Park, Queens; subway 7 to Willets Point–Shea Stadium). Tickets go on sale at Ticketmaster in April or May, but marquee games (held at Arthur Ashe Stadium) are hard to get. Most who see the games know someone or resort to scalpers.

OUTDOOR ACTIVITIES

New York's activities vary with the season. In summer, parks fill with soccer and basketball players; the river with kayaks and sailboats. In winter, many lace up their ice skates or (after about six inches of snow) cross-country ski the Sheep Meadow in Central Park.

BIRD-WATCHING

One of the country's most important birding areas (no, seriously) is Central Park. Its diverse habitat helps draw some 15% of all migrating birds (some 200 species) to the Big Apple in spring and fall. At those times, the New York City Audubon Society (Map pp386-8; ☎ 212-691-7483; www.nycas.org; 71 W 23rd St; subway F, V to 23rd St) holds four-session Beginner's Birding courses (adult $75), which include two field trips. Also, Starr Saphir leads three-hour walking tours (Audubon members/nonmembers $3/6) of Central Park. On Monday and Wednesday, she leaves from W 81st St and Central Park West at 7:30am, Tuesday from W 103rd St and Central Park West at 9am.

Kids enjoy the free Discovery Kit birding backpacks (binoculars, sketchbook etc) available for use at Central Park's Belvedere Castle (Map pp389-91; ☎ 212-772-0210; ☯ 10am-5pm Tue-Sun).

BOATING & KAYAKING

With only one landlocked borough (can you guess? It's the Bronx), New York City offers plenty of chances to liaise with water. The free Staten Island Ferry (p149) is New York's ultimate recreational boating trip. Central Park and Brooklyn's Prospect Park have rowboats to rent, and City Island, a fully fledged fishing community in the Bronx, has charter opportunities. Manhattan's Circle Line (p72) offers classic round-the-island boat cruises, while the new-fangled yellow-and-black New York Water Taxis (p338) provide hop-on, hop off Manhattan and Brooklyn access. For a true adventure, try Manhattan Kayak Company (p247), and paddle over to Jersey for a sushi lunch.

DOWNTOWN BOATHOUSE Map pp389-91

☎ 646-613-0740; www.downtownboathouse.org; Pier 26, btwn Chambers & Canal Sts; admission free; ☯ 9am-6pm Sat & Sun May 15–October 15, also open some weekday evenings; subway 1, 9 to Franklin St

This terrific public boathouse offers 20-minute kayaking (including equipment) in the protected embayment in the Hudson River. You don't need to book tours, just walk up. Tips are given to first-timers and, after a few times, you can go on the five-mile harbor kayak trip (show up before 8am on weekends and holidays). The boathouse has two other locations: in Chelsea (Map pp386-8; Pier 66A, west of W 22nd St); and at Riverside Park (Map pp389-91; W 72nd St).

LOEB BOATHOUSE Map pp389-91

☎ 212-557-2233; Central Park, btwn 74th & 75th Sts; $10 per hr; ☯ 10am-5:30pm; subway B, C to 72nd St, 6 to 77th St

Central Park's boathouse rents row boats from April to October (weather permitting). (The water is really not as dirty as Woody Allen suggests in the boat scene in *Manhattan*.)

MANHATTAN KAYAK COMPANY
Map pp386-8

☎ 212-924-1788; www.manhattankayak.com; Pier 63, btwn W 23rd St & West Side Hwy; rates $25-250; phone for tour times; subway C, E to 23rd St

With over 30 tours spanning more than 150 nautical miles of New York Harbor, Manhattan Kayak Company (see also p71) offers a huge swathe of waterborne options, including brunch, sunset and full-moon tours, Statue of Liberty loops, and rigorous journeys around Manhattan and out to Coney Island. All levels of paddlers are accommodated.

Chelsea Piers

New York's biggest sporting center is at the historic **Chelsea Piers** (Map pp382-5; ☎ 212-336-6666; www.chelseapiers .com; West Side Hwy, btwn W 16th & 22nd Sts; subway C, E to 23rd St), a 30-acre sporting village where you can golf, work out, play soccer and basketball, get a massage, swim, box and bowl – and more.

Chelsea Piers served as New York's chief port during the heyday of transatlantic ocean voyages. Constructed in 1910 by the makers of Grand Central Terminal, Chelsea Piers was where the *Titanic* was hoping to land in 1912 and the de-embarkation point for many Europe-bound WWII soldiers. Its pier days ended in 1967. Opened in 1995, the project transformed the last four piers of the original nine piers.

Today it's easy to overlook the 100-year-old lore, with the red, white and blue makeover, not to mention all the sporting options that leave first-timers' jaws dropping. Hundreds of bodies get fully exercised here each day. Following is a selection of activities that you can do.

Batting Cages (☎ 212-336-6500; Field House, Pier 59; 10 pitches $2; ☺ 11am-10pm Mon-Fri, 9am-9pm Sat & Sun) Four modern cages offer fast, medium and slow-pitch baseball and softball. Call for hourly rentals.

Golf (☎ 212-336-6400; Golf Club, Pier 59; ball cards from $20, golf simulator games per hr $35; ☺ 6:30am-11pm) Manhattan's only driving range has four levels of weather-protected tees in nets –you can aim for New Jersey! Golf clubs are available.

Ice Skating & Hockey (☎ 212-336-6100; Sky Rink, Pier 61; adult/child general skating $13/9.50, skate rental $6, helmets $3) There are two year-round rinks. Schedules vary, usually beginning at 11:30am or noon. Open hockey hours are limited, usually weekday lunches and Saturday nights ($25, goaltenders are free). Phone ahead for opening hours.

In-line Skating (☎ 212-336-6200; the Roller Rinks, Pier 62; adult/child skating $7/6, rental $18/13, pad rental $7; ☺ outdoor rinks May-Aug) For more excitement (ramps, obstacles), 'extreme' skating is $20 for three- or four-hour sessions. Phone for opening hours.

Soccer (☎ 212-336-6500; Field House, Pier 62) Mostly for indoor soccer and basketball leagues and gym classes. You can play pick-up indoor soccer from noon to 1:30pm Monday to Thursday ($8).

Spa (☎ 212-336-6780; Pier 60; massage $45-130, facials $80-95, body scrubs $65; ☺ 10am-9pm Mon-Fri, 10am-7pm Sat & Sun) Massage comes in plenty of forms and there's also other treatments available. Package deals include full-day treatment for $288. Any purchase over $75 gives you free Sports Center access.

Sports Center (☎ 212-336-6000; Pier 60; per day $50; ☺ 6am-11pm Mon-Fri, 8am-9pm Sat & Sun) Indoor running track, swimming pool, work out equipment, basketball, boxing, kick boxing, volleyball, yoga classes, rock climbing, great views from inside and sundecks.

SCHOONER ADIRONDACK Map pp382-5
☎ 646-336-5270; Chelsea Piers, Pier 62, btwn W 23rd St & West Side Hwy; daytime/sunset & night tours $35/45; ☺ daytime 1pm, sunset 5:30pm, night 7:30pm; subway C, E to 23rd St

The two-masted 'Dack hits the Hudson and New York Harbor with four two-hour sails daily from May to October – be sure to book. Exciting stuff.

CYCLING

Unless you're an experienced city cyclist, you may prefer limiting your New York rides to designated bike areas. The few bike lanes on city streets (Lafayette St, Broadway, Second Ave) are frequently blocked by double-parked cars or cars weaving around slower ones to make a turn.

On streets, wear a helmet and signal your turns. Don't ride on sidewalks. It's possible to take a bike on the last door of subways, but avoid rush hours and stand with your bike. Most city bridges have bike lanes (Brooklyn Bridge is the most fun). See **Bike Network Development** (http://www.ci.nyc.ny.us /html/dcp/html/bike/home.html) for more information on New York biking.

Where to Ride

Central Park is a natural choice for New York biking. Wide, well-paved roads run north-south and in between, making excellent 1.7-, 5.2- and 6.1-mile loops (see Map p163). Roads have a bike lane and are always open to cyclists; roads are closed to traffic between 10am to 3pm and 7pm to 10pm Monday to Friday, and all day Saturday and Sunday.

Rides along the rivers are possible (and popular) along much of Manhattan's 32-mile perimeter. The best stretches are along

Hudson River from Battery Park in Lower Manhattan up the west side to Riverside Park in the Upper West Side. Alternatively, take the bumpier east side route, south from E 37th St towards Battery Park.

Brooklyn's gorgeous **Prospect Park** (p138) has a 3.35-mile Park Dr to ride anytime. Note the road is open to traffic 7am to 9am and 5pm to 7pm Monday to Friday.

The more ambitious can ride the 15-mile Shore Parkway Bike Path from Coney Island to Queens. The best bit faces Manhattan. Ask at a bike shop for details.

Staten Island's **Greenbelt** (☎ 718-667-2165; www.sigreenbelt.org) has miles of developed bike paths (and some hills), and you can take a bike over on the ferry.

Some clubs sponsor various rides. The **Five Borough Bicycle Club** (☎ 212-932-2300 ext 115; www.5bbc.org; 891 Amsterdam Ave; subway 1, 2, 3 to 96th St) leads free trips for its members ($20 annual fee). Another good club is the **New York Cycle Club** (☎ 212-828-5711; www .nycc.org).

Several hundred cyclists (and in-line skaters) promote safer streets and bike lanes in Critical Mass, a traffic-halting ride leaving from Union Square at 7pm the last Friday of the month. See **Time's Up** (www.times-up.com) for more information.

Bike Rental

BICYCLE HABITAT Map pp382-5
☎ 212-431-3315; www.bicyclehabitat.com; 244 Lafayette St; bike hire 1st/2nd day $30/25; ⏰ 10am-7pm Mon-Thu, 10am-6:30pm Fri, 10am-6pm Sat & Sun; subway 6 to Spring St

Knowledgeable staff can help plan bike routes and rent bikes (you'll need a $300 deposit); see website for city biking tips.

CENTRAL PARK BICYCLE TOURS & RENTALS Map pp386-8
☎ 212-541-8759; www.centralparkbiketour.com; 2 Columbus Circle; bike hire per day $35, tours $35; subway A, B, C, D, 1, 9 to 59 St–Columbus Circle

This place rents mountain bikes and leads various tours of the park – one tour takes in movie sights. Call ahead during winter, when the stand's closed. Tour prices include bike rental.

LOEB BOATHOUSE Map pp389-91
☎ 212-557-2233; Central Park, btwn 74th & 75th Sts; bike hire per hr $9-15; subway B, C to 72nd St, 6 to 77th St

Bikes are available from April to October.

GOLF

Golfing New York City? But of course. New York's only golf courses are outside Manhattan. They all have slightly higher fees at weekends and you'll need to reserve a tee-off time. If you feel like belting a few balls without the walking, head to the driving range at **Chelsea Piers** (opposite).

BETHPAGE ST PARK
☎ 516-249-0707; Farmingdale, Long I; green fees $24-39, club rental $30

Four public courses, including the Black Course, which was the first public course to host the US Open (2002).

DYKER BEACH GOLF COURSE
☎ 718-836-9722; cnr 86th St & 7th Ave, Dyker Beach, Brooklyn; green fees $28-34; subway R to 86th St

This is a scenic public course and is the easiest to reach by subway. No rental clubs are available.

FLUSHING MEADOWS PITCH & PUTT
Map p397
☎ 718-271-8182; Flushing Meadows Corona Park, Queens; green fees $11.50; subway 7 to Willets Point–Shea Stadium

Eighty yards is the longest of the 18-hole minicourse. Rental clubs are available.

LA TOURETTE
☎ 718-351-1889; 1001 Richmond Hill Rd, Staten I; green fees $29-34, club rental $15

This public course is on Staten Island. Take a taxi from the ferry.

VAN CORTLANDT PARK GOLF COURSE Map p398-9
☎ 718-543-4595; Bailey Ave, The Bronx; green fees $33-43; subway 1, 9 to Van Cortlandt Park

This is the USA's oldest 18-hole public golf course.

ICE SKATING

Outdoor rinks are open during the winter months, though the rink at **Chelsea Piers** (opposite) is open all year. See also p138 for skating at Brooklyn's Prospect Park, and p145 for Queens' Flushing Meadows Corona Park.

Ten-Pin Mania

Among retro-crazed New Yorkers (and Americans in general, for that matter), a night of bowling qualifies as quite a hoot. Maybe it's the shoes, or all the pitchers of beer. Go with a group to get goofy (and drunk).

Amf Chelsea Pier Lanes (Map pp382-5; ☎ 212-835-2695; AMF Chelsea Pier Lanes, btwn Piers 59 & 60; 🕙 9am-midnight Sun-Thu, 9-2am Fri & Sat) Forty lanes for $5.50 per game ($3 shoe rental) before 5pm weekdays. The price jumps to $7.50 per game ($4.50 shoe rental) at other times.

Bowlmor Lanes (Map pp382-5; ☎ 212-255-8188; 110 University Pl; 🕙 11-4am Mon & Fri, 11-1am Tue & Wed, noon-2am Thu, noon-4am Sat, noon-1am Sun; subway L, N, Q, R, W, 4, 5, 6 to 14th St-Union Sq) Open since 1938, Bowlmor is New York bowling. Games cost $6.45 before 5pm weekdays, $7.95 after 5pm weekdays, $8.45 on weekends. Shoe rental is $5. After 10pm Sunday, it's all glow-in-the-dark bowling, with live DJs.

Leisure Time Bowling Center (Map pp386-8; ☎ 212-268-6909; 625 8th Ave, 2nd floor, Port Authority Bus Terminal; 🕙 10am-11pm Sun-Thu, 10-1am Fri & Sat; subway A, C, E to 42nd St) Thirty lanes; $6 per game before 5pm weekdays, $7 at other times; shoes are $4 to rent. The last Saturday of the month is disco night.

ROCKEFELLER CENTER ICE RINK

Map pp386-8

☎ 212-332-7654; Rockefeller Center, cnr 49th St & Fifth Ave; adult/child Mon-Thu $8.50/7, Fri-Sun $11/7.50, skate rental $6; 🕙 9am-10:30pm Mon-Thu, 8:30am-midnight Fri & Sat, 8:30am-10pm Sun; subway B, D, F, V to 47th–50th Sts–Rockefeller Center

The famous rink, under the gaze of the gold statue of Prometheus in the art deco plaza, is an incomparable location for a twirl on ice, but it gets sardine-busy at evenings and weekends. Call for skating schedules.

WOLLMAN SKATING RINK

Map pp389-91

☎ 212-439-6900; Central Park, near 59th St & 6th Ave entrance; adult weekday/weekend $8.50/11, child $4.25/4.50, skate rental $4.75; 🕙 10am-2:30pm Mon & Tue, 10am-10pm Wed & Thu, 10am-11pm Fri & Sat, 10am-9pm Sun; subway F to 57 St, N, R, W to 5th Ave–59th St

Larger than Rockefeller's, this rink is at the southern edge of Central Park. Your slides, stops and slips will be in full view of the buildings peeking over Central Park; skating here is best at night.

JOGGING

You'll find several goods spots for a run in Manhattan. Central Park's loop roads are best during traffic-free hours (see p248), though you'll be in the company of many cyclists and in-line skaters. The 1.6-mile path surrounding the Jacqueline Kennedy Onassis Reservoir (where Jackie O used to run) is for runners and walkers only; access it between 86th and 96th Sts. Running along the Hudson River is a popular path, best from W 23rd St to Battery Park in Lower Manhattan. The Upper East Side has a path that runs along FDR Drive and the East River (from E 63rd St to E 115th St). Brooklyn's Prospect Park has plenty of paths.

The **New York Road Runners Club** (Map pp389-91; ☎ 212-860-4455; www.nyrrc.org; 9 E 89th St; 🕙 10am-8pm Mon-Fri, 10am-5pm Sat, 10am-3pm Sun; subway 6 to 96th St) organizes weekend runs citywide, including the **New York Marathon** (opposite).

ROCK CLIMBING

Central Park contains a couple of rocks that attract boulderers' attention, including Chess Rock, just north of Wollman Rink, and the more challenging Rat Rock, north of Heckscher Playground (around 61st St) – however, the best is City Boy, a 20-footer around 107th St, west of the Harlem Meer.

CITY CLIMBERS CLUB Map pp389-91

☎ 212-974-2250; Parks & Recreation Center, 533 W 59th St; 🕙 5-10pm Mon-Fri, noon-5pm Sat; subway A, B, C, D, 1, 9 to 59th St–Columbus Circle

New York's first climbing wall still serves as a key HQ for climbers, with 11 belay stations and 30 routes, plus a climbing cave. The first Tuesday and last Thursday of the month are for members only.

New York City Street Sports

Who needs lawns? With all that concrete around, New York has embraced a number of sports and events played on it.

Handball

Irish immigrant Phil Casey built New York's first four-wall handball court in 1882, and following his rise in the sport (he challenged, and whipped, the Irish world champ in 1887), it quickly became big in New York. In the early 20th century, South Brooklyn started putting up one-wall handball courts around Coney Island, reviving an Irish tradition that had died out long before. It led to one-wall paddleball, still widely played around town. These days, you'll find one-wall courts in outdoor parks all over the city (there are 260 courts in Manhattan alone). See www.nycgovparks.org for a list of handball courts.

In-line Skating

Freestyle skaters have flaunted their footwork in a disco skate circle near the Naumberg Bandshell in Central Park for decades. Of course in-line skating is a popular mode of recreation (and transport) around the city: notably, the counter-clockwise loop at Central Park, Brooklyn's Prospect Park, and along Hudson River Park from Battery Park to Chelsea Piers (or further north). **Blade Night Manhattan** (8pm Wed May–Oct) is a free group skate (up to 200 go) that leaves Chelsea Piers at 23rd St.

Rent skates at **Blades West** (Map pp389-91; ☎ 212-787-3911; 120 W 72 St; per day incl pads $22; subway 1, 2, 3 to 72nd St); **Blades Chelsea Piers** (Map pp382-5; ☎ 212-336-6199; Pier 62, cnr W 22nd St & West Side Hwy; per day $22; subway C, E to 23 St) and near Brooklyn's Prospect Park at **3rd Street Skate Co** (Map p395; ☎ 718-768-9500; 207 Seventh Ave; per 2 hrs/day $10/20 Mar–Oct; subway F to 7th Ave).

New York Marathon

Equally as awe-inspiring as the runners chugging through New York's streets is how the world's most famous marathon grew from a $1000 budget race with 55 finishers in 1970, to a premier running event that spans New York's five boroughs. However, you need a little luck, not just conditioning and strength, to run the race. The final list of 30,000 runners is completed by lottery; applications are accepted until April or May of each year (see www.nycmarathon.org for more information). Held on the first Sunday of November, it's easy to watch the spectacle of over a million people lining the streets, but the best vantage may be its end point – **Tavern on the Green** (p199) in Central Park.

Pick-up Basketball

People with hoop dreams, small and large, hit the city's courts throughout the year. The most famous are the courts at W 3rd St and Sixth Ave (Map pp382-5), which draw summer audiences on the weekends, and games sometimes fade into elongated dunk-a-thons. You can also find games at **Tompkins Square Park** (p91) in the East Village and at **Riverside Park** (p122) in the Upper West Side. You probably should know how to dribble, pass and shoot (well) before telling someone to 'throw you the rock.'

Stickball

Nothing is more street than stickball, New York's decades-old offshoot of English games like 'old cat' and 'town ball.' It's essentially a crude form of baseball – but the pitcher usually throws off the bounce, batters hit with a broom handle, the bases are manhole covers, and parked cars and fire escapes serve as obstacles. Back in the day, a pink Spalding ball (a 'spaldeen'), which was used for the game, was a coveted possession.

Stickball has stormed its way back in the past 20 years and is popular with various New York leagues. Of the most successful is the Bronx-based **Emperors Stickball League** (☎ 212-591-0165; www.nyesl.org), which plays 10am to 2pm or 3pm Sunday at Stickball Blvd, between Seward and Randall Aves; call for directions. Compared with baseball, one player said, 'It's louder, more in your face; we taunt...but with respect.' The best time to watch the sport is at the international Memorial Day tournament, when teams from San Diego, Florida and Puerto Rico are on scene.

One-time league leader and firefighter Steve Mercado, who died at the World Trade Center in 2001, is still known around New York City as 'Mr Stickball' for his sporting play and efforts to revive the game. Read his poem *Our Game* on the Emperors' website.

SOCCER

Soccer leagues generally don't allow drop-in, single-game players. You can find pick-up soccer games in Central Park's East Meadow around E 97th St and the North Meadow at weekends during the season (April to October). Games at **Flushing Meadows Corona Park** (Map p397) are legendary and are in action whenever the weather allows (even February); **Chelsea Piers** (p248) has games of the indoor variety.

TENNIS

Playing on New York's nearly 100 public tennis courts requires a permit ($50 annual fee) from April to November; it's free at other times. Call ☎ 212-360-8133 or visit the Central Park permit center at **Arsenal** (Map pp389-91; E 65th St & Fifth Ave). **Paragon Athletic Goods** (p270) also sells permits. **Riverbank State Park** (Map pp392-3) also has courts.

CENTRAL PARK TENNIS CENTER

Map pp389-91

☎ 212-316-0800; west of W 96 St & Central Park West; ✆ 6:30am-dusk Apr-Oct; subway B, C to 96th St

The daylight-hours-only facility has 30 good courts (the most of any of Manhattan's parks), open to those with permits or single-play tickets ($7), which are available at the snack bar. Least-busy times are early afternoon weekdays.

USTA NATIONAL TENNIS CENTER

Map p397

☎ 718-760-6200; www.usta.com; Flushing Meadows Corona Park, Queens; per hr outdoor court $16-24, indoor court $32-48; ✆ 6am-midnight Mon-Fri, 8am-midnight Sat, 8am-11pm Sun Oct-Jul; subway 7 to Willets Point–Shea Stadium

Be like Serena, Venus or Andre on the courts where the US Open is staged every year – no one minds if you wear a headband. USTA takes reservations up to two days in advance for the 22 outside courts and nine indoor ones. Walk-ins can play indoors for $16 per hour from 6am to 8am weekdays (when available). After-dark lights for outside courts are $8 extra.

HEALTH & FITNESS
GYMS & SWIMMING POOLS

Manhattan alone has 17 recreation centers. Most of these centers have gym facilities and an indoor or outdoor swimming pool. See www.nycgovparks.org for more information, or try calling ☎ 212-408-0204. Check out the *Village Voice* for other gym listings. **Chelsea Piers** (p97) sports center is a beauty.

ASPHALT GREEN

Map pp389-91

☎ 212-369-8890; 555 E 90 St; gym or pool $20, both $25; ✆ gym 5:30am-10:30pm Mon-Fri, 8am-8pm Sat & Sun, pool 5:30am-4pm & 8-10pm Mon-Fri, 11am-8pm Sat, 8am-8pm Sun; subway 4, 5, 6 to 86th St

This super nonprofit fitness center in the Upper East Side is known for its excellent 50m Olympic-sized pool (and its underwater observation window). Many programs cater to kids.

ASTORIA POOL

Map p396

☎ 718-626-8620; cnr Astoria Park, 19th St & 23rd Dr, Queens; ✆ 11am-7pm summer; subway N, W to Astoria Blvd

This Works Progress Administration Olympic-size outdoor pool, built in 1936, is an art deco wonder, with views of Manhattan and the Triborough Bridge, not to mention about 1000 visitors a day. If New York gets the 2012 Olympic Games, swimmers will take the plunge here.

CARMINE RECREATION CENTER

Map pp382-5

☎ 212-242-5228; 1 Clarkson St; ✆ 7am-10pm Mon-Fri, 9am-5pm Sat & Sun; subway 1, 9 to Houston St

This Greenwich Village center has one of the city's best public pools. There's an indoor and outdoor swimming pool (the latter was used for the pool scene in *Raging Bull*) and a gym that's open to the public.

CRUNCH Map pp386-8

☎ 212-594-8050; www.crunch.com; 555 W 42nd St; day pass $24; ✆ 6am-10pm Mon-Fri, 9am-7pm Sat

& Sun; subway A, C, E to 42nd St–Port Authority Bus Terminal

This popular fitness center has several locations throughout town, and is equipped with a full fitness center, sauna and spa. This is New York City's only Crunch location with a pool.

RIVERBANK STATE PARK

Map pp392-3

☎ 212-694-3600; 679 Riverside Dr, at W 145th St; adult/child pool $2/1; ⏰ park 6am-11pm (call for activity hrs); subway 1 to 145th St

This modern five-building facility, perched atop a waste refinery (not as crazy as it sounds), has an indoor Olympic-size pool, an outdoor lap pool, a fitness room, basketball and handball courts, a running track around a soccer/football field and a softball field. It's a good spot for pick-up games.

MASSAGE & DAY SPAS

Make an appointment at the following places in advance.

BODY CENTRAL

Map pp382-5

☎ 212-677-5633; www.bodycentralnyc.com; 99 University Pl; ⏰ 12:30-9pm Mon & Wed, 8:30am-9pm Tue & Thu, 8:30am-5pm Fri, 10am-4pm Sat; subway L, N, Q, R, W, 4, 5, 6 to 14th St–Union Sq

Relieve pavement-pounded feet with the relaxing 30-minute 'Standing Ovation' foot massage ($50) or treat the rest of the body with a choice of nine other clarity-inducing massages. Body Central also offers chiropractic and nutritional services.

GRACEFUL SERVICES

Map pp386-8

☎ 212-593-9904; 1097 Second Ave; ⏰ 10am-10pm; subway 4, 5, 6 to 59 St, N, R, W to Lexington Ave–59 St

Heaps of New Yorkers looking for relief, not frills, go to barebones Grace for a Qi Gong massage. The cost is $50/60 per 45/60 minutes for the full body, or $35/60 per 30/60 minutes for the feet.

PAUL LABRECQUE EAST

Map pp389-91

☎ 212-988-7816; www.paullabrecque.com; 171 E 65th St, the Chatham; ⏰ 8am-9pm Mon-Fri,

9am-8pm Sat, 10am-8pm Sun; subway 6 to 68th St–Hunter College

Sit back with the stars at this swank Uptown spa (with a salon just for the guys), which has enticed Reese Witherspoon to add a translucent sheen to her locks with a color varnish ($50) and 'I don't take coffee, I take tea' Sting for an indulgent shave ($65). Paul also offers 10 types of facials ($95 to $160) and 14 different massages.

YOGA

BIKRAM YOGA NYC

Map pp382-5

☎ 212-206-9400; 182 Fifth Ave, 3rd fl; per class $20; ⏰ 7am-8:15pm, call for schedule; subway N, R, W to 23rd St

So very Hollywood (but taking off in Manhattan), Bikram is hot stuff: striking the 26-pose asana in a heated room (in the Flatiron Building, no less) means you're going to sweat into shape. There are showers. Bikram has three other locations.

JIVAMUKTI Map pp382-5

☎ 212-353-0214; www.jivamuktiyoga.com; 404 Lafayette St, Suite 3; per class $19; ⏰ 8am-8:30pm Mon-Thu, 8am-6:45pm Fri, 9am-5:30pm Sat & Sun; subway 6 to Bleecker St

Quite posh, hip and large for a yoga house – there's a wall waterfall – Jivamukti sees many hipster locals and celebs striking halasana poses in the vinyasa and hatha classes. Not all classes are open to drop-ins. There are showers and a shop.

LAUGHING LOTUS

Map pp382-5

☎ 212-414-2903; 59 W 19th St; per class $15; ⏰ 7:30am-8:15pm Mon-Thu, 7:30am-10pm Fri, 8:30am-5pm Sat, 9am-7pm Sun; subway F, V to 23rd St

Happy, popular and pink, the Laughing Lotus has drop-in 1½-hour classes, ranging from devotional sun celebrations, basic stretching/breathing classes, more advanced vinyasa and family hour.

OM YOGA CENTER

Map pp382-5

☎ 212-254-9642; 826 Broadway; per class $15; ⏰ 7:30am-8pm Mon, Wed & Fri, 7am-8pm Tue & Thu, 9am-8pm Sat & Sun; subway L, N, Q, R, W, 4, 5, 6 to 14th St–Union Sq

This inviting space – with redwood floors, high ceilings and showers – has popular vinyasa classes run by former dancer (and choreographer of videos like *Girls Just Want to Have Fun*!) Celia Lee. The MTV days are behind her.

Shopping

Shopping

What do you want to buy? New York has it. The city's thousands of shops satisfy all desires, quirks and interests: mammoth megastores at Times Square (and increasingly around town) shine their 21st-century sheen as decades-old mom-and-pop shops hold their ground. You can buy a durian ('stinky fruit') from a Chinatown sidewalk vendor who speaks Cantonese, get a camera or diamond necklace at a shop run by Orthodox Jews, browse through old photos from a streetside stall, thumb through a book or two at shops devoted to old travel guides or mysteries or architecture, and lower those turned-up noses at uptown boutiques by buying that Oscar-worthy gown. Then break for lunch. This is just the beginning, and there really is no end.

Shopping Areas

Midtown's Fifth Ave and the Upper East Side's Madison Ave have the famous high-end fashion and clothing by international designers, while Downtown's coolest offerings are in Soho's loft stores. Times Square has a few super-size stores to match the giant flashing screens and light-up-the-night ads, while grand dame department store Macy's has long made Midtown's Herald Square one of the city's busiest shopping zones. Downtown, the East Village and the Lower East Side have funky shops selling music, gifts and clothing for a younger crowd, while Greenwich Village has an eclectic mix of antiques, high-end fashion and shops catering to gays and lesbians. Chelsea's flea markets are a popular weekend draw for locals. Brooklyn's Smith St and Atlantic and Fifth Aves can make an East River shop-hop worthwhile.

Most museums – the Met, MoMa etc – have super shops if you're looking for NYC gifts. For junky souvenirs (T-shirts, cheap Yankees hats), Chinatown and Times Square are the best bets.

Opening Hours

With the exception of Lower Manhattan and shops run by Orthodox Jews (which are closed Saturdays), nearly all stores, boutiques and megastores are open daily. Few stores open before 10am, though many stay open to 7pm or 8pm. Things open a little later (at 11am or noon) in more residential pockets (such as the East Village, Lower East Side and Brooklyn). Many stores, particularly on Madison Ave, open longer hours on Thursday.

Sales

Sample sales run year-round – though the popularity of them has made 'sale' an overused buzzword – but some sales still offer canyon-deep drops in price. Check **NY Sale** (www.nysale.com) and **Lazar Shopping** (www.lazarshopping.com) for weekly updates about what's selling for what and where. Always wear knickers that you don't mind people seeing as dressing rooms are a no-go – people drop their trousers right in the action.

Many stores (department stores, shoe stores, boutiques) have end-of-the-season sales starting in January and July. Designer clothes and shoes sell for discounts of around 50% (or higher); Barneys' warehouse sale is legendary (though women's clothes still sell at higher until the very end).

Top Five Shopping Streets

- **Fifth Ave** (Map pp386-8) Midtown, 42nd St to Central Park South. A little money lasts no time at these ultra-classy department stores.
- **Madison Ave** (Map pp389-91) Upper East Side, 50th St to 75th St. Ritzy boutiques and designers' classiest shops cater to the catwalks.
- **Bleecker St** (Map pp382-5) Greenwich Village. The big three: rock 'n' roll records, thematic condoms, Marc Jacobs bags.
- **West Broadway & Prince St** (Map pp382-5) Soho. Big names represent sportier versions of high-style lines on Soho's brick streets.
- **Mott St** (Map pp386-8) Nolita. Second-hand boutiques, teensy shoe shops – follow it south to where Chinatown puts its spin on Mott.

LOWER MANHATTAN

Not many people venture to Manhattan's financial zone for the shopping, but there are a few worthy places to check out.

HAGSTROM MAP & TRAVEL CENTER

Map pp380-1   *Travel*

☎ 212-785-5343; 125 Maiden Lane; ☿ 8:30am-6pm Mon-Fri; subway 2, 3 to Wall St

Busy travel store packing a wide assortment of travel guides, maps and accessories.

J&R MUSIC & COMPUTER WORLD

Map pp380-1   *Music & Electronics*

☎ 212-238-9000; 15-23 Park Row; ☿ 9am-7:30pm Mon-Sat, 10:30am-6:30pm Sun; subway A, C, J, M, Z, 2, 3, 4, 5 to Fulton St–Broadway Nassau

Nearly a block full of J&R shops devoted to cameras, computers, CDs, DVDs, stereos and electronics lines Park Row, each with big selections and sometimes very good deals.

SHAKESPEARE & CO

Map pp380-1   *Bookstore*

☎ 212-742-7025; 1 Whitehall St; ☿ 8am-7pm Mon-Fri; subway R, W to Whitehall St, 4, 5 to Bowling Green

The lower Manhattan branch of this popular New York bookstore chain. Other stores can be found in **Greenwich Village** (p268), **Midtown** (p274) and the **Upper East Side** (p287).

SOUTH STREET SEAPORT

Map pp380-1   *Mall*

☎ 212-732-7678; 12 Fulton St; ☿ 10am-9pm Mon-Sat, 11am-8pm Sun; subway A, C, J, M, Z, 2, 3, 4, 5 to Fulton St–Broadway Nassau

Unless you don't have a mall back home, you'll probably only want to visit this 100-shop mall for its location: an East River pier, overlooking the Brooklyn Bridge and Manhattan's lower end. Do go for that (and the public restrooms) and a wander around the stores set up in the historic buildings just west on Fulton St.

STRAND BOOK STORE

Map pp380-1   *Used Bookstore*

☎ 212-732-6070; 95 Fulton St; ☿ 9:30am-9pm Mon-Fri, 11am-8pm Sat & Sun; subway A, C, J, M, Z, 2, 3, 4, 5 to Fulton St–Broadway Nassau

Inducing used-book mania, this offspring of the famous **Downtown** (p268) flagship has more elbow room between its aisles. Many cheap deals await, but – as far as book-browsing adventures go – nothing beats the original.

Viva Century 21

It's not often that a store – four walls, a ceiling, a door and a few things to buy tucked in – becomes a symbol of survival and strength in the wake of unspeakable tragedy. But, standing stoic next to the split-open guts of the World Trade Center site, **Century 21** (Map pp380-1; ☎ 212-227-9092; 22 Cortland St at Church St; ☿ 7:45am-8pm Mon-Wed & Fri, to 8:30pm Thu, 10am-8pm Sat, 11am-7pm Sun; subway A, C, 4, 5 to Fulton St–Broadway Nassau) isn't your normal store. Many saw its reopening five months after the September 11 attacks (and its renewed commitment to the location, not a lucrative Midtown move) as New York started to get back on its feet. Good on ya, 21.

The four-level, marble-floor department store continues to win over its fans by offering deep discounts on men's and women's designer clothes, accessories, shoes, perfumes (sometimes at less than half the original price). Big design names – Donna Karen, Marc Jacobs, Armani, you name it – can be found here.

There's a catch: *everyone* in the city knows about it. On weekends, the place gets jam-packed with all sorts of bargain hunters elbowing for room. The casual shopper (ie 'it's something to do') will either convert to fanaticism or run for cover. It's hard to leave without finding something.

TENT & TRAILS

Map pp380-1   *Sporting Goods*

☎ 212-227-1760; 21 Park Pl, west of Broadway; ☿ 9:30am-6pm Mon-Wed & Sat, 9:30am-7pm Thu & Fri, noon-6pm Sun; subway 2, 3 to Park Pl

Fantastic outdoor outfitter with top-of-the-line gear and knowledgeable staff.

SOHO

Once New York's gallery capital, Soho's loft spaces have undergone a retailers' boom in recent years. It's a virtual shopping party along Soho's some 25 sq blocks of brick lanes, with all the big-name designers and retailers pouring the champagne. Most of these stores have main locations in Midtown or the Upper East Side too, with the more casual (and affordable) selections in branches clustered here.

The following entries are only a taste of what's on offer. Along Broadway, you'll find small shops and chains like Armani Exchange and Banana Republic, Sephora for beauty products, and Puma for shoes.

A few blocks west (via shop-lined streets such as Prince St), West Broadway has shops including (north to south) fcuk, DKNY, Diesel Style Lab, Eileen Fisher, Miss Sixty, Anthropologie and Tommy Hilfiger.

In-between streets include Greene St, where you can find Louis Vuitton, Agnes B, Vivienne Tam, Agnes B Homme, Lucky Brand's jeans store and some larger furnishings stores. On Mercer St, look for APC and several children-related shops.

East of Broadway, Lafayette St has several shops catering to the DJ and skate crowd. A couple more blocks east, the up-and-coming shopping district of Nolita (North of Little Italy) centers around Mott, Mulberry and Elizabeth Sts (between Houston and Kenmare St) – it's good for shoes. Listed here are a few of our favorites.

ALICE UNDERGROUND

Map pp382-5 *Vintage Clothing*
☎ 212-431-9067; 481 Broadway; ☼ 11am-7pm; subway J, M, N, Q, R, W, Z, 6 to Canal St
Well-organized vintage store that's light on the labels, but offers plenty of shirts, slacks, dresses, suits and hats in good condition.

ANNA SUI Map pp382-5 *Clothing*
☎ 212-941-8406; 113 Greene St; ☼ 11:30am-7pm Mon-Sat, noon-6pm Sun; subway N, R, W to Prince St
Anna's long-live-rock designer clothing fill this fun space, south of Prince St. Come to dress yourself as the child that Stevie Nicks and Jim Morrison never had. (Or did they?)

APPLE STORE SOHO

Map pp382-5 *Computers & Electronics*
☎ 212-226-3126; 103 Prince St; ☼ 10am-8pm Mon-Sat, 11am-7pm Sun; subway N, R, W to Prince St
Apple's uplifting, airy flagship location – with translucent stairway and upstairs walkway – bustles with Soho shoppers picking up an iPod and other Mac gear, or checking email for free. Very helpful staff, plus free computer-tips discussions upstairs.

BARNEYS CO-OP

Map pp382-5 *Clothing*
☎ 212-965-9964; 116 Wooster St; ☼ 11am-7pm Mon-Sat, noon-6pm Sun; subway N, R, W to Prince St
The youngest in the litter of Barneys' classic digs. Also visit Co-Op in **Chelsea** (p270) and, for the full collection, the main store in the **Upper East Side** (p285).

BLOOMINGDALE SOHO

Map pp382-5 *Clothing*
☎ 212-729-5900; 504 Broadway; ☼ 10am-9pm Mon-Fri, 10am-8pm Sat, 11am-7pm Sun; subway N, R, W to Prince St
Brand-new Bloomies for the Downtown set, delivering the latest goods from Zak Posen, Diane Von Furstenberg, Marc Jacobs and other drop-worthy names.

BROADWAY PANHANDLER

Map pp382-5 *Kitchenware*
☎ 212-966-3434; 477 Broome St; ☼ 10:30am-7pm Mon-Fri, 10:30am-7pm Sat, 11am-6pm Sun; subway A, C, E to Canal St
Chefs-at-home love this packed-to-the-brim shop of stylish and sturdy kitchen gear to drool over, including those cute Le Creuset pans from France..

CALYPSO

Map pp382-5 *Women's Clothing*
☎ 212-965-0990; 280 Mott St; ☼ 11:30am-7:30pm Mon-Sat, noon-6:30pm Sun; subway B, D, F, V to Broadway–Lafayette St
It's summer forever at this St Bart's–born shop, which stocks tropical clothing – light dresses, Dr Boudoir swimwear, flip-flops and slinky blouses – year-round. Calypso has several boutiques (the jewelry shop is a few doors down on Mott St), including another boutique at 74th St and Madison Ave in the Upper East Side. Call for details.

Top Five Local Designers

- **Hotel Venus** (opposite) Patricia Fields' spandex and neon fun.
- **Triple 5 Soul** (p261) Indulge your inner DJ.
- **Vlada** (p263) Dress up like the first MTV video stars.
- **A Cheng** (p264) Funked-up but still smart ladies' wear for work.
- **Eidolon** (p289) Trendy women's clothing made by trendy Brooklyn women.

CAMPER Map pp382-5 *Shoes*
☎ 212-358-1841; 125 Prince St; ☼ 11am-8pm Mon-Sat, noon-6pm Sun; subway N, R, W to Prince St
Spare collection of Camper's cool, distinctive casual shoes (lots of rubber soles and corduroy patterns) in a pleasingly jarring space.

CATHERINE Map pp382-5   *Women's Clothing*
☎ 212-925-6765; 468 Broome St; ⊙ 11am-7pm
Mon-Sat, noon-7pm; subway C, E to Spring St
French designer Catherine Malandrino's lux-but-hip party dresses, frocks, slacks and blouses at this boutique have gotten nods from the likes of *Sex and the City* and Mary J Blige. Catherine recently opened a new Meatpacking District location at Hudson and 13th Sts; call for details.

D&G Map pp382-5   *Clothing*
☎ 212-965-8000; 434 W Broadway; ⊙ 11am-8pm
Mon-Sat, noon-6pm Sun; subway N, R, W to Prince St
For Dolce & Gabbana's funkier D&G line, this shop packs in teeny bikinis, distressed jeans, leather pants and logo T-shirts. For formal stuff, visit the branch on the **Upper East Side** (p286).

EMPORIO ARMANI Map pp382-5   *Clothing*
☎ 646-613-8099; www.emporioarmani.com; 410 W Broadway; ⊙ 11am-7pm Mon-Wed, Fri & Sat, 11am-8pm Thu, noon-6pm Sun; subway N, R, W to Prince St
Armani's good taste comes at affordable prices too. This shop is middle of the line, between the Giorgio Armani posh pickings in the **Upper East Side** (p286) and a bit swankier than Armani Exchange. See website for other locations.

ENCHANTED FOREST Map pp382-5   *Toys*
☎ 212-925-6677; 85 Mercer St; ⊙ 11am-7pm
Mon-Sat, noon-6pm Sun; subway N, R, W to Prince St, 6 to Spring St
For toys that ignite the imagination (rather than plug movies or other commercial tie-ins), this small, devoted store is one of a few Mercer St shops geared to little ones. Lots of hand puppets and teddy bears here.

FIRESTORE Map pp382-5   *Clothing & Gifts*
☎ 212-698-4520; 263 Lafayette St; ⊙ 10am-6pm
Mon-Sat, noon-5pm Sun; subway 6 to Spring St, N, R, W to Prince St
Get New York Fire Department gifts – caps, T-shirts, hooded 'Keep Back 200Ft' sweat-shirts – at this small shop. Next door is NY911, a shop with September 11–related items and many New York Police Department wares.

HELMUT LANG Map pp382-5   *Clothing*
☎ 212-925-7214; 80 Greene St; ⊙ 11am-7pm
Mon-Sat, noon-6pm Sun; subway N, R, W to Prince St, 6 to Spring St
Slide through the stark reception area up front and enter the hidden world of Mr Lang's

edgy-yet-luxurious, ready-to-wear collection. You'll certainly get sidewalk points by carrying a Lang bag around.

HOTEL VENUS
Map pp382-5   *Clothing*
☎ 212-966-4066; 382 W Broadway; ⊙ 11am-8pm; subway C, E to Spring St
Previously a longtime W 8th St staple and now still as wild as ever in Soho, Patricia Field's bright, bizarre fashion collection now puts a wham-bam in Soho. Implausibly colored frizzy wigs, all sorts of spandex and lingerie, sequins, Hello Kitty comforters, key chains and to-be-noticed dresses. There's a hair salon at the back.

INA Map pp382-5   *Consignment Clothing*
☎ 212-334-9048; 21 Prince St; ⊙ noon-7pm Sun-Thu, noon-8pm Fri & Sat; subway N, R, W to Prince St, B, D, F, V to Broadway–Lafayette St
Locals love this super consignment shop that stocks choice designer clothes for women (the men's shop is around the corner at 262 Mott St). Usually you can find a big-name suit or dress for under $100, or a marked-down pair of Prada shoes.

Kate Spade (p242)

JACK SPADE Map pp382-5 *Handbags*

☎ 212-625-1820; 56 Greene St; ⊙ 11am-7pm
Mon-Sat, noon-7pm Sun; subway N, R, W to Prince St

Kate Spade and hubby Andy sell a popular collection of snappy bags, briefcase and laptop cases for men. The women's collection is at Kate Spade (see below).

JOHN FLEUVOG

Map pp382-5 *Shoes*

☎ 212-431-4484; 250 Mulberry St; ⊙ noon-8pm
Mon-Sat, noon-6pm Sun; subway N, R, W to Prince St

John's ever-funky, ever-urban soles have long put the heel-click in Downtown swagger. Many designs: thick-soled, pointed tips, two-tone arrow stitch etc. Usually the sales rack has a dozen or so pairs that dip under the $100 mark.

JONATHAN ADLER

Map pp382-5 *Home*

☎ 877-287-1910; 47 Greene St; ⊙ 11am-7pm
Mon-Sat, noon-6pm Sun; subway J, M, N, Q, R, W, Z, 6 to Canal St

Pick up Jonathan's curvy, geometric pottery (vases and lamps) and accessories for the home (furnishings and throws).

KATE SPADE Map pp382-5 *Handbags*

☎ 212-274-1991; 454 Broome St; ⊙ 11am-7pm
Mon-Sat, noon-6pm Sun; subway N, R, W to Prince St, 6 to Spring St

See the latest collection from Kate of her famed, '50s-inspired nylon and leather bags and accessories, plus shoes and sunnies. Men's bags are at Jack Spade on Greene St (see above).

KATE'S PAPERIE Map pp382-5 *Stationery*

☎ 212-941-9816; 561 Broadway; ⊙ 10am-8pm
Mon-Sat, 11am-7pm Sun; subway N, R, W to Prince St

A New York classic with its inspired selection of handmade stationery and journals. See also the **Midtown** (p273) location.

MOSS Map pp382-5 *Home Furnishings*

☎ 212-204-7100; 146 Greene St; ⊙ 11am-7pm
Mon-Sat, noon-6pm Sun; subway N, R, W to Prince St

Converted from a gallery space, Moss' two showrooms prop industrial designs – slick, modern and fun – behind glass, exhibit-like, but they're definitely for sale. It's easy to find something, for an empty corner or spot on your desk that you won't find elsewhere.

OTTO TOOTSI PLOHOUND

Map pp382-5 *Shoes*

☎ 212-925-8931; 413 W Broadway;
⊙ 11:30am-7:30pm Mon-Fri, 11am-8pm Sat, noon-7pm Sun; subway N, R, W to Prince St

New York hipsters looking for designer-label deals frequent one of Tootsi's four shops (see also p270). It usually has sales on some selections, including Miu Miu, Helmut Lang, Paul Smith and Prada Sport. Tootsi gets jammed full during its famous $99 sales.

PAUL FRANK STORE

Map pp382-5 *Clothing & Gifts*

☎ 212-965-5079; 195 Mulberry St; ⊙ 11am-7pm;
subway 6 to Spring St

The monkey guy's corner shop is stuffed full with the grinning monkey logo on T-shirts, satchels, wallets and even ladies' undies. The selection of new '70s-style T-shirts may be a bit obvious, but are fetching nevertheless.

PEARL RIVER MART

Map pp382-5 *Chinese Dept Store*

☎ 212-431-4770; 477 Broadway; ⊙ 10am-7pm;
subway J, M, N, Q, R, W, Z, 6 to Canal St

This one-stop Canal St classic, now in its fancier Broadway location, is still Chinatown's best shop. Find everything Asian here – cheap Chinese and Japanese teapots, dragon-print dresses, paper lanterns, pecking chicken wind-up clocks that look like something from the Mao era, and various (loud) Asian instruments. Eastward ho!

POP SHOP Map pp382-5 *Clothing & Gifts*

☎ 212-219-2784; 292 Lafayette St; ⊙ noon-7pm
Mon-Sat, noon-6pm Sun; subway N, R to Prince St, B, D F, V to Broadway–Lafayette St

Find the appealing pop art of Keith Haring on T-shirts, cards and other gift items. A popular shop for browsing out-of-towners looking for something for cousin Edward.

PRADA Map pp382-5 *Clothing*

☎ 212-334-8888; 575 Broadway; ⊙ 11am-7pm
Mon-Sat, noon-6pm Sun; subway N, R, W to Prince St

The Italian designers' ever-chic outfits and shoes are one thing, but the space! Transformed from the old Guggenheim Soho location by Dutch architect Rem Koolhaas, this shop, with sweeping wooden floors and tucked-away downstairs rooms, is a marvel to see. For a thrill, try something on – the clear glass walls of the fitting rooms fog when the door closes.

Shopping – Soho

RALPH LAUREN Map pp382-5 *Clothing*
☎ 212-625-1660; 381 W Broadway; ☽ noon-8pm
Mon-Sat, noon-6pm Sun; subway C, E to Spring St
Ralph's Soho branch stocks more casual, sporty wear than at the bigger store in the **Upper East Side** (p287).

RESURRECTION
Map pp382-5 *Vintage Clothing*
☎ 212-625-1374; 217 Mott St; ☽ 11am-7pm
Mon-Sat, noon-7pm Sun; subway 6 to Spring St
Fine vintage collection of designer labels for men and women (eg Pucci, Halston) and a bit posher than what you'll find at East Village vintage shops on the other side of Houston St.

SCOOP Map pp382-5 *Clothing*
☎ 212-925-2886; 532 Broadway; ☽ 11am-8pm
Mon-Sat, 11am-7pm Sun; subway N, R, W to Prince St
Scoop carries Marc by Marc Jacobs and Theory dresses, plus a good collection of designer cords and other casual wear. There's a men's store in the **Upper East Side** (p287).

SWISS ARMY
Map pp382-5 *Luggage & Accessories*
☎ 212-965-5714; 136 Prince St; ☽ 11am-7pm
Mon-Sat, noon-6pm Sun; subway N, R, W to Spring St
Love the knives and watches? This shop stocks those, plus great red or black luggage and handbags by Victorinox at this Prince St location. If you're prone to getting lost, get a compass here (they point north).

TRAVELER'S CHOICE
Map pp382-5 *Travel Bookstore*
☎ 212-941-1535; 2 Wooster St; ☽ 9am-5pm
Mon-Fri, noon-5pm Sat; subway A, C, E to Canal St
A good place to get equipped for the next trip, or start dreaming about it. Plenty of guides, phrasebooks, dictionaries, maps and travel accessories.

TRIPLE 5 SOUL
Map pp382-5 *Urban Clothing*
☎ 212-431-2404; 290 Lafayette St; ☽ 11am-7:30pm; subway N, R, W to Prince St, B, D, F, V to Broadway–Lafayette St
For hooded sweatshirts with block lettering of 'Triple 5 Soul' (looks good on the subway) and other '70s-style wear for the sidewalk pounder of the new era, check the Soul. Also you'll find T-shirts stickered with 'I [heart] soul' – but ain't that a given?

USED BOOK CAFÉ
Map pp382-5 *Used Bookstore*
☎ 212-334-3324; 126 Crosby St; ☽ 10am-9pm
Mon-Fri, noon-9pm Sat, noon-7pm Sun; subway B, D, F, V to Broadway–Lafayette St
With the look of a real library, with mezzanine, this café positively crawls with locals – even Bulgarian-language tutors – at weekends. Browse through over 45,000 used books and CDs. Prices are good, and all proceeds benefit Housing Works, a charity serving New York City's HIV-positive and AIDS homeless communities.

VICE Map pp382-5 *Urban Clothing*
☎ 212-219-7788; 252 Lafayette St; ☽ 11:30am-8pm
Mon-Sat, noon-6pm Sun; subway 6 to Spring St
Street urban meets Thanksgiving, or an uptown dinner with Uncle Louis. Vice carries what DJs and skateboarders can put on to look good without compromising those inner core beliefs (Fred Perry, Stüssy, Zoo York etc). Great shoe selection too.

Top Five Shoes

- **Camper** (p258) Casual shoes made of Spanish corduroy.
- **Jeffrey New York** (p267) Select top-shelf mix.
- **Jimmy Choo** (p273) Sells high-class women's pumps.
- **Nolita shoe stores** (p258) Several shoes stores are clustered at Mott & Prince Sts, a discount zone for stylish shoes.
- **Otto Tootsi Plohound** Classy, but funkier than Fifth Ave at **Chelsea** (p270) & **Soho** (opposite).

CHINATOWN

Chinatown sprawls for many blocks, but you'll find most of everything along Canal and Mott Sts. Sidewalk-spilling stores line busy Canal St between the Bowery and 7th Ave, offering T-shirts, jewelry (not all pieces are tacky – poke around) and light electronics (it's best for extension cords and plugs).

The (slightly) more relaxed Mott St has more tourist-oriented shops, where you can find fun imports (lacquerware, Chinese-style ornaments, silk dresses, teas, toys etc). Chinatown's shops open daily, generally from 9am till sometime after dusk.

On Canal St, avoid buying anything that requires a warranty (such as stereo equipment or cameras). Keep your purse in front of you, and your wallet in your front pocket – snatchings on Canal St do occur.

Note that Chinatown's best shop, **Pearl River Mart** (p260) is no longer in the 'hood, but is now a few blocks north on Broadway.

BEAUTY Map pp382-5 *Clothing*
☎ 212-385-9966; 81 Mott St; ☽ noon-9:30pm; subway J, M, N, Q, R, W, Z, 6 to Canal St

Up a few stairs from busy Mott, this small boutique stocks small-size women's wear and shoes, imported from Hong Kong, Japan and Korea. Some knockoffs, some originals – all at lesser prices than Midtown.

CHINATOWN ICE CREAM FACTORY
Map pp382-5 *T-Shirts & Ice Cream*
☎ 212-608-4170; 65 Bayard St; ☽ 11am-10pm; subway J, M, N, Q, R, W, Z, 6 to Canal St

A busy ice-cream shop in its own right, the Factory sells ridiculously cute trademark yellow T-shirts ($10) with an ice cream–slurping happy dragon on it. The scoops are pretty good, too.

KAM MAN Map pp382-5 *Kitchenware*
☎ 212-571-0330; 200 Canal St; ☽ 9am-9pm; subway J, M, N, Q, R, W, Z, 6 to Canal St

Head past hanging ducks to the basement of the classic Canal St food store for cheap Chinese and Japanese tea sets, plus other kitchen products.

PEARL PAINT COMPANY
Map pp382-5 *Art Supplies*
☎ 212-431-7932; 308 Canal St; ☽ 10am-7pm Mon-Fri, 10am-6:30pm Sat, 10am-6pm Sun; subway J, M, N, Q, R, W, Z, 6 to Canal St

Artists looking for supplies come to this sprawling, multilevel, red-and-white warehouse.

LOWER EAST SIDE

Before the neighborhood's recent hipster makeover, shopping in the Lower East Side (LES) was generally limited to Orchard St's (largely cheesy) $99 leather-jacket shops or the Judaica shops on Essex St, between Grand and Canal Sts. They're still there today (and can be fun to browse in). Joining these are new boutiques, vintage shops and antique stores, catering to a largely younger crowd.

The densest concentration of new shops is on Orchard and Ludlow Sts, between Houston and Delancey Sts.

Stop by the **LES visitor center** (Map pp382-5; ☎ 866-224-0206; 261 Broome St at Orchard St; ☽ 10am-5pm) to pick up a Go East card, which offers discounts of 5% to 50% on some 100 stores around the neighborhood.

TOYS IN BABELAND
Map pp382-5 *Sex Toys*
☎ 212-375-1701; www.babeland.com; 94 Rivington St; ☽ noon-10pm Mon-Sat, noon-7pm Sun; subway F, J, M, Z to Lower East Side–Essex St

Sex toys and staff who know how to use them – advice is cheerfully given. Lots of colors, lots of shapes, lots of belts. There's also a new Soho location on Mercer St intended to shake up the tourist circuit a bit; see website for details.

BLUESTOCKINGS
Map pp382-5 *Lesbian Bookstore & Café*
☎ 212-777-6028; 172 Allen St; www.bluestockings.com; ☽ 1-10pm; subway F, V to Lower East Side–Second Ave

This independent bookstore is owned by women and strong on dyke lit-and-crit, and assorted radical readings. The gathering spot also has a fair-trade café and puts on regular special events, such as poetry jams and teach-ins on various political subjects.

BREAKBEAT SCIENCE
Map pp382-5 *DJ Music*
☎ 212-995-2592; 181 Orchard St; ☽ 1-8pm Sun-Wed,1-9pm Thu-Sat; subway F, V to Lower East Side–Second Ave

The namesake music label's shop stocks drums-and-bass and jungle vinyl, with turntable stations to preview, as well as proper T-shirt attire for the DJ crowd.

DOYLE & DOYLE
Map pp382-5 *Antique Jewelry*
☎ 212-677-9991; 189 Orchard St; ☽ 1-7pm Tue & Wed, Fri-Sun, 1-8pm Thu; subway F, V to Lower East Side–Second Ave

For select pickings of antique jewelry (swinging '60s necklaces, Cartier earrings), this shop puts a little more sparkle into the Lower East Side than the vintage shops. Prices rise (quickly) from $100 into the thousands.

KLEIN'S OF MONTICELLO

Map pp382-5   *Women's Clothing*

☎ 212- 966-1453; 105 Orchard St; 🕐 10am-5pm Sun-Thu, 10am-4pm Fri; subway F, J, M, Z to Delancey St–Essex St

A bit more swank – more uptown – than most LES boutiques, Klein's stocks high-end clothing at discount prices. There's a good collection of light cashmere sweaters by Malo, as well as Jil Sanders' leather coats.

LAS VENUS

Map pp382-5   *Vintage Furniture*

☎ 212-982-0608; 163 Ludlow St; 🕐 noon-9pm Mon-Thu, noon-midnight Sat & Sun, noon-8pm Sun; subway F, J, M, Z to Delancey St–Essex St

Down a couple steps from the street, for furnishings back a few decades, this colorful shop packs in cool Danish modern furniture (from the 1950s, '60s and '70s) and other vintage furnishings. Much of it edges towards the pricey line, but some deals await the prodder (as well as old *Playboys*, if that's your thing). Las Venus stocks its chrome furnishings at the 2nd floor of **ABC Carpet & Home** (p269).

LUDLOW GUITARS

Map pp382-5   *Music Store*

☎ 212-353-1775; 164 Ludlow St; 🕐 11am-7pm Mon-Fri, 11am-6pm Sat & Sun; subway F, J, M, Z to Delancey St–Essex St

Amid women's clothing boutiques, this fun-filled shop is all about rock. New and used guitars, basses, amps and pedals.

MARY ADAMS

Map pp382-5   *Women's Clothing*

☎ 212-473-0237; 138 Ludlow St; 🕐 1-6pm Wed-Sat, 1-5pm Sun or by appointment; subway F, J, M, Z to Delancey St–Essex St

Drop by to see what lacy, romantic, boldly colored dresses and gowns Mary has done lately, or you can collaborate with the designer to get one made from scratch.

PICKLE GUYS   Map pp382-5   *Pickles*

☎ 212-656-9739; 49 Essex St; 🕐 9am-6pm Sun-Thu, 9am-4pm Fri; subway F, J, M, Z to Delancey St–Essex St

Yes, pickles! Pickles have been a part of Essex St and LES for decades. The guys run this shop smiling, and sell all sorts of pickles, tomatoes, olives and relishes – all made with an 'old Eastern European recipe.' One pickle is 50¢, but – go wild – opt for a quart.

VLADA   Map pp382-5   *Women's Clothing*

☎ 212-387-7767; 101 Stanton St; 🕐 1-8pm Sun-Fri, noon-8pm Sat; subway F, J, M, Z to Delancey St–Essex St

Taking its cue from early MTV looks – back when MTV ruled! – this small corner shop sells Vlada's vintage-inspired women's clothing – sweaters, dresses, jackets etc.

YU   Map pp382-5   *Clothing Boutique*

☎ 212-979-9370; 151 Ludlow St; 🕐 noon-7pm Wed-Sat, noon-6pm Sun; subway F, V to Lower East Side–Second Ave

Small consignment boutique carries funky Japanese designs and Amy Downs' locally loved hatwear.

Travelers Gear Galore

Left something at home? Rest assured. NYC's got plenty of places where travelers can replenish supplies.

- **Apple Store Soho** (p258) Check your email while changing laptop batteries.
- **Complete Traveller** (p272) Stacks and stacks of used travel books.
- **Flight 001** (p267) Stylish travel gear for the retro-class jetsetter.
- **Hagstrom Map & Travel Center** (p257) Packed with maps, guidebooks and accessories.
- **Swiss Army** (p261) In case your pocketknife was confiscated at JFK.
- **Tent & Trails** (p257) Get outfitted for the great outdoors beyond NYC.
- **Traveler's Choice** (p261) Stock up for your next destination.

EAST VILLAGE

A couple blocks east of Broadway, the East Village's main strip (and entry point) is St Marks Pl (between E 7th and 9th Sts) – a street so punk rock that it breaks the city's numbered-street grid (it oughta be 8th St). It's lined with all the budding or bonafide rocker will want or need: profane T-shirts, rare vinyl and CDs, piercing shops, egg creams and guitars.

But the East Village's offerings do venture beyond this crusted rock-core mold. E 7th and (particularly) E 9th St are lined with new and vintage boutiques selling designer clothing, lingerie, high-end dresses made by local designers as well as, well, T-shirts with bad words on them.

A CHENG

Map pp382–5   *Women's Clothing*
☎ 212-979-7324; 443 E 9th St; ☽ noon-8pm
**Mon-Fri, noon-7pm Sat & Sun; subway L to 1st Av,
6 to Astor Pl**
A hit with East Village girls in recent years, local designer A Cheng stocks her latest collection of fun work-type wear for women. You can also find Jack Spade bags and other accessories.

AMARCORD

Map pp382–5   *Women's Clothing*
☎ 212-614-7133; 84 E 7th St; ☽ noon-7:30pm
Tue-Sun; subway N, R, W to 8 St–NYU, 6 to Astor Pl
High-quality (and highly seasonal) vintage clothing for women that looks new. Its **Brooklyn** (p289) shop has a bigger collection, including things for men too.

ATOMIC PASSION

Map pp382–5   *Vintage Clothing*
☎ 212-553-0718; 430 E 9th St; ☽ 1:30-8pm; subway
L to 1 Ave, 6 to Astor Pl
A longtime E 9th St resident, Atomic Passion's front shrine (of plastic wise men and flowers) shouts, 'Vintage is fun!' and its floor-to-ceiling stock of (mostly women's) wear from the '50s, '60s and '70s backs it up. There are always plenty of pumps to try on.

COBBLESTONES

Map pp382–5   *Vintage Clothing & Accessories*
☎ 212-673-5372; 314 E 9th St; ☽ 1-7pm Tue-Sun;
subway 6 to Astor Pl
Built from love, this vintage collection dips further back than many East Village vintage shops (that is, into the '40s and '50s). It's up-to-the-neck full, with an even split between clothing and knick-knacks. Don't be alarmed when the shopkeeper sings along with her retro soundtrack. It's OK; she does that.

DINOSAUR HILL

Map pp382–5   *Toys*
☎ 212-473-5850; 306 E 9th St; ☽ 11am-7pm;
subway 6 to Astor Pl
A wonderful toy store with an amazing puppet selection including Czech marionettes, Three Little Pigs finger-puppet sets, unique jack-in-the-boxes and clothes for infants.

FABULOUS FANNY'S

Map pp382–5   *Vintage Eyewear*
☎ 212-533-0637; 335 E 9th St; ☽ noon-8pm; subway
6 to Astor Pl
A good variety of vintage wire and plastic frames.

FOOTLIGHT RECORDS

Map pp382–5   *Music*
☎ 212-533-1572; 113 E 12th St; ☽ 11am-7pm
**Mon-Fri, 10am-6pm Sat, noon-5pm Sun; subway N, R,
W to 8 St–NYU, 6 to Astor Pl**
A well-chosen collection of out-of-print Broadway and foreign-movie soundtracks. Footlight is also big on jazz, vocalists and (brace yourself) documentaries, all on the good ol' LP format. Vinyl hounds must visit.

GOOD, THE BAD & THE UGLY

Map pp382–5   *Women's Clothing*
☎ 212-473-3769; 437 E 9th St; ☽ 1-9pm Mon-Sat,
1-8pm Sun; subway L to 1 Av, 6 to Astor Pl
Visit for the always intriguing made-in-the-back retro-inspired women's clothing and accessories, such as lingerie made from cotton banjo-playing clown fabric. Let's call that The Good.

KIEHL'S Map pp382–5   *Beauty Products*
☎ 212-677-3171, 800-543-4571; 109 Third Ave;
☽ 10am-7pm Mon-Sat, noon-6pm Sun; subway N, Q,
R, W, 4, 5, 6, to 14th St–Union Sq, L to Third Ave
Making and selling skincare products since 1851, Kiehl's (under L'Oréal ownership since 2000) has doubled its shop size, but its personal touch remains (as well as the generous sample sizes). Pick up some of Kiehl's Musk Oil, a popular product now past its 100th birthday, and moisturizers, masks and emollients. Or just peek in to admire the late owner's eccentric collection of antique Harley-Davidson motorcycles.

KIM'S VIDEO & MUSIC

Map pp382–5   *CDs & Videos*
☎ 212-598-9985; 6 St Marks Pl; ☽ 9am-midnight;
subway 6 to Astor Pl
Forever the St Marks Pl's staple, left-of-the-dial Kim's has a fringe collection of videos & DVDs (indie directors, foreign films), CDs (rock and alt-rock, sure, but also avant-jazz, electronica, dub etc) and literature (anarchist journals, zines). There are plenty of used CD bins too. If you're just looking for a new copy of **The Ramones**, you're likely to get it cheaper at Sounds (see opposite).

LOVE SAVES THE DAY

Map pp382–5   *Kitsch*
☎ 212-228-3802; 119 2nd Ave; ☽ noon-8pm Mon-
Fri, noon-9pm Sat & Sun; subway 6 to Astor Pl
As the waves of change engulf the East Village, Loves Saves the Day stays true to its original

form. Its campy collection of old polyester clothes, GI Joes, *Star Wars* '77 figurines and other dolls is not much changed since the days when Rosanna Arquette bought Madonna's pyramid jacket here in the viva-los-'80s film *Desperately Seeking Susan.*

MANHATTAN PORTAGE

Map pp382-5 *Handbags*
☎ 212-995-5490; 333 E 9th St; ☉ noon-7pm Sun-Tue, noon-8pm Wed-Sat; subway 6 to Astor Pl
If not content with Army-Navy satchels, check out longtime off-the-edge-cool Manhattan Portage's collection of cell-phone cases, laptop bags and DJ bags with reflective stripes. These guys just make you want to carry stuff wherever you go.

OTHER MUSIC Map pp382-5 *Indie Music*
☎ 212-477-8150; 15 E 4th St; ☉ noon-9pm Mon-Fri, noon-8pm Sat, noon-7pm Sun; subway 6 to Bleecker St
Facing Tower Records (tsk, that mecca for mainstream conformistas!), this indie-run CD store has won over a loyal fan base with its informed selection of, well, other types of music: offbeat lounge, psychedelic, electronica, indie-rock etc. It stocks new and used CDs. Friendly staff mean what they do, and may be able to help translate your inner musical whims and dreams to actual CD reality.

PHYSICAL GRAFFITI

Map pp382-5 *Vintage Clothing*
☎ 212-477-7334; 96 St Marks Pl; ☉ 1-9pm; subway 6 to Astor Pl
Yesteryear's best polyester and other casual greats always have a home at this small, hip used-clothing shop. If it feels a little gritty, well, what do you expect for a shop housed in the building Led Zeppelin used for the album of the same name?

ST MARKS BOOKSHOP

Map pp382-5 *Bookstore*
☎ 212-260-7853; 31 Third Ave; ☉ 10am-midnight Mon-Sat, 11am-midnight Sun; subway 6 to Astor Pl
Around the corner from St Marks, this bookshop specializes in political literature, poetry and academic journals.

SCREAMING MIMI'S

Map pp382-5 *Vintage Clothing*
☎ 212-677-6464; 382 Lafayette St; ☉ noon-8pm Mon-Sat, 1-7pm Sun; subway 6 to Bleecker St
A big selection of '60s and '70s wear. Up the front are shoes in good shape and a collection of big earrings and watches. Out the back are clothes – no labels (though you can find Edith Collins purses), but it's all in great condition.

SELIA YANG

Map pp382-5 *Women's Clothing*
☎ 212-254-9073; 328 E 9th St; ☉ noon-7pm Tue-Fri, noon-6pm Sat & Sun; subway 6 to Astor Pl
Here's a switch for the East Village: high-end, luxe formal evening wear. Selia also has custom bridal wear available.

SOUNDS

Map pp382-5 *New & Used CDs*
☎ 212-677-3444; 20 St Marks Pl; ☉ noon-8pm Wed-Sun; subway 6 to Astor Pl
Sounds doesn't have St Marks' biggest CD selection, but usually has the best deals; new CDs (rock, alt-rock and a decent backlog of jazz and blues) start at $9.99. Sounds runs a smaller store at **St Marks Place** (☎ 212-677-2727; 16 St Marks Pl), where some cash attendants have been known to burst into impromptu lectures of the merits of Chuck Berry the man, the guitar hero, the god.

TOKIO 7

Map pp382-5 *Consignment Store*
☎ 212-353-8443; 64 E 7th St; ☉ noon-8:30pm Mon-Sat, noon-8pm Sun; subway 6 to Astor Pl
This high-holy hip-consignment shop, down a few steps on a shady stretch of E 7th St, has good-condition designer labels for men and women at some 'come again?' prices. Best is the selection of men's suits – nearly always something tip-top worth trying on in the $100 to $150 range.

TOKYO JOE

Map pp382-5 *Consignment Store*
☎ 212-473-0724; 334 E 11th St; ☉ noon-9pm; subway 6 to Astor Pl
This Japanese-run consignment shop – a hole in the wall, really – is crammed full with women's and men's designer clothing and shoes (not to mention browsing 20-something shoppers aiming to honor our new century in style). Not for the claustrophobic.

VILLAGE X Map pp382-5 *T-Shirts*
☎ 212-777-9550; 36 St Marks Pl; ☉ 11am-11pm Sun-Thu, 11-1am Fri & Sat; subway 6 to Astor Pl
If St Marks Pl is the capital of rock 'n' roll T-shirts, then Village X is its commissar. Come for anything you've seen a rock legend wear (eg John Lennon's famed NYC shirt) or the classic 'New York: it ain't Kansas' (with gun) variety.

WEST (GREENWICH) VILLAGE

The crookedest neighborhood in Manhattan makes for fun, rather offbeat, shopping strolls. A good entry point (from Broadway) is via Bleecker St, which passes between three chief phases: rock 'n' roll (CD and guitar shops, between Broadway to Seventh Ave), gay New York (around Christopher St), then swankier clothing and antiques (from Charles St to Eighth Ave).

So-called 'Doc Martin's alley' is along W 8th St, between Fifth and Sixth Aves, where you can find a (slightly diminishing) number of knockoff and discount shoe stores. Diagonal Greenwich Ave is lined with shops. The Meatpacking District, a renovated area of warehouses just north and south of W 14th St between Ninth and Tenth Aves, is home to more high-end designer clothing shops and furnishings.

AEDES DE VENUSTAS

Map pp382–5 *Bath & Beauty*
☎ 212-206-8674; www.aedes.com; 9 Christopher St; ☷ noon-8pm Mon-Sat, 1-7pm Sun; subway A, B, C, D, E, F, V to W 4 St, 1, 9 to Christopher St–Sheridan Sq

Plush and inviting, Aedes de Venustas ('Temple of Beauty' in Latin, if you want to impress the staff) offers 35 brands of luxury European perfumes, as well as other bath and beauty products. Stars come here (the Liv Tylers and Madonnas) to shop.

AUTO Map pp382–5 *Furnishings*
☎ 212-229-2292; 805 Washington St; ☷ noon-7pm Tue-Sat, noon-6pm Sun; subway A, C, E to 14th St, L to Eighth Ave

For the houseproud swank set, Auto, in the Meatpacking District, stocks modern furnishings (bedding, pillows, throws etc) and jewelry items.

BLEECKER BOB'S

Map pp382–5 *Used Music*
☎ 212-475-9677; 118 W 3rd St; ☷ noon-midnight; subway A, B, C, D, E, F, V to 4 St

On creaky wooden floors, Bob stacks a glorious selection of old vinyl ('60s garage, vintage house, NYC sections, plus standard genres), CDs, Led Zeppelin posters, stickers and a few bongs.

CHEAP JACK'S VINTAGE CLOTHING

Map pp382–5 *Vintage Clothing*
☎ 212-777-9564; 841 Broadway; ☷ 11am-8pm Mon-Sat, noon-7pm Sun; subway L, N, Q, R, W, 4, 5, 6 to 14th St–Union Sq

Though 'Moderately Priced Jack's' might be a more accurate name, the shop packs its three sprawling floors (are we still in Manhattan, dear?) with orderly displays (dear?) of used jeans, shirts, blouses, hats, suits and dresses. Watch for occasional 'buy one, get one free' sales.

CONDOMANIA Map pp382–5 *Sex Shop*
☎ 212-691-9942; 351 Bleecker St; ☷ 11am-11pm Sun-Thu, 11am-midnight Sat & Sun; subway 1, 9 to Christopher St–Sheridan Sq

Step right up, we've got every type of colored condom, glow-in-the-dark condoms, sized-to-fit condoms, flavored condoms, twisted-form condoms…oh, and regular ones too. Plus other sex-related gear.

CREATIVE VISIONS/GAY PLEASURES

Map pp382–5 *Gay & Lesbian Bookstore*
☎ 212-255-5756; 548 Hudson St; ☷ noon-9pm Sun-Thu, noon-10pm Sat & Sun; subway 1, 9 to Christopher St–Sheridan Sq

Pick up gay, lesbian and transgender books and videos, and various Pride wear, at this shop. The shop hosts various events and readings too; call or drop by to check the schedule.

EAST-WEST BOOKS

Map pp382–5 *Spiritual Bookstore*
☎ 212-243-5994; 78 Fifth Ave; ☷ 10am-7:30pm Mon-Sat, 11am-6:30pm Sun; subway L, N, Q, R, W, 4, 5, 6 to 14th St–Union Sq

This bookstore stocks a wide array of books on Buddhism and Asian philosophies, plus to-gel-by music, yoga props and jewelry.

FLIGHT 001 Map pp382-5 *Travel Gear*
☎ 212-691-1001; 96 Greenwich Ave; ☻ 11am-8:30pm Mon-Fri, 11am-8pm Sat, noon-6pm Sun; subway A, C, E to 14th St, L to Eigth St

Travel's fun, sure, but it's really only about getting fun travel gear. Flight 001 has ice-cold cool travel accessories in Pan Am sky-blue, M&M green and other colors: bags, passport holders, jetlag pills, miniclocks, tiny flashlights and Lonely Planet guides.

Flight 001

FORBIDDEN PLANET
Map pp382-5 *Books & Games*
☎ 212-473-1576; 840 Broadway; ☻ 10am-10pm Mon-Sat, 11am-8pm; subway L, N, Q, R, W, 4, 5, 6 to 14th St–Union Sq

Indulge your inner sci-fi nerd. Find heaps of comics, books, video games and figurines (ranging from Star Trek to Shaq). Fellow Magic and Yu-Gi-Oh! card-game lovers play upstairs in the public sitting area.

FUNHOUSE Map pp382-5 *Goth Clothing*
☎ 212-674-0983; 61 W 8th St; ☻ 11:30am-9pm Mon-Thu, 11am-9pm Fri & Sat, noon-8pm Sun; subway A, B, C, D, E, F, V to W 4 St

For everything goth but the hearse, visit the Funhouse for velvet black-and-red dresses (from $70), ruffled tie-up blouses (à la Mr Mojo

Risin), swords, fake blood, giant ceiling webs and usually some clearance items.

GENERATION RECORDS
Map pp382-5 *New & Used Music*
☎ 212-254-1100; 210 Thompson St; ☻ 11am-Mon-Thu, 11-1am Fri-Sat, noon-10pm Sun; subway A, B, C, D, E, F, V to W 4th St, 6 to Bleecker St

Excellent collection of punk, heavy metal, indie rock, regular ol' rock CDs and vinyl, including many hard-to-finds and bootlegs. Great value on the used CDs downstairs (eg Stones from $4).

JEFFREY NEW YORK
Map pp382-5 *Designer Clothing*
☎ 212-206-1272; 449 W 14th St; ☻ 10am-8pm Mon-Wed & Fri, 10am-9pm Thu, 10am-7pm Sat, 12:30-6pm Sun; subway A, C, E to 14th St, L to Eigth Ave

One of the pioneers in the recent Meatpacking District makeover, Jeffrey sells several high-end designer clothing and accessories in a roomy modern space. It's known, also, for its edgy, but pricey, shoe selection (Prada, Versace, Gucci etc).

LEATHERMAN Map pp382-5 *Sex Shop*
☎ 212-243-5339; 111 Christopher St; ☻ noon-10pm, noon-8pm; subway 1, 9 to Christopher St–Sheridan Sq

Famous for window displays, this longtime sex shop stocks a lot of leather, clothes, toys, jockstraps and videos in its little frame. Mostly for LeatherMen, but friendly staff help anyone. Make sure you see the rowdier stuff downstairs.

L'IMPASSE Map pp382-5 *Clothing*
☎ 212-533-3255; 29 W 8th St; ☻ 11am-9pm Mon-Fri, 11am-10pm Sat, 11:30am-8:30pm Sun; subway A, B, C, D, E, F, V to W 4 St

Party dresses and spandex outfits g-a-l-o-r-e for disco girls and drag queens. Sing it loud, sing it strong: bring back Studio 54!

MARC JACOBS
Map pp382-5 *Designer Clothing*
☎ 212-924-0026; 405 Bleecker St, 403 Bleecker St & 385 Bleecker St; ☻ noon-8pm Mon-Sat, noon-7pm Sun; subway 1, 9 to Christopher St–Sheridan Sq, A, C, E to 14th St, L to Eigth Ave

With three small shops on just over a block, each with ginormous windows for easy peeking, Marc has made a Bleecker St hopscotch of himself: his famous leather bags and other accessories are at No 385, men's clothing is at No 403, and his newish Marc by Marc Jacobs women's line at No 405.

MATT UMANOV GUITARS

Map pp382-5   *Musical Instruments*
☎ 212-675-2157; 273 Bleecker St; ☷ 11am-7pm Mon-Sat, noon-6pm Sun; subway A, B, C, D, E, F, V to W 4 St, 1, 9 to Christopher St–Sheridan Sq

Friendly g uitar house that goes easy on the blaring distortion (though they do sell the pedals). The shop stocks and services an excellent collection of our fretted friends (including some mouth-watering Gibson, Fender and Gretsch guitars, plus steel guitars and banjos).

MCNULTY'S TEA & COFFEE CO, INC

Map pp382-5   *Coffee & Tea*
☎ 212-242-5351; 109 Christopher St; ☷ 10am-9pm Mon-Sat, 1-7pm Sun; subway 1, 9 to Christopher St–Sheridan Sq

Next to the LeatherMan's sex toys, sweet McNulty's flaunts a different era of Greenwich Village. It's been selling gourmet teas and coffees here since 1895.

OSCAR WILDE MEMORIAL BOOKSHOP

Map pp382-5   *Gay & Lesbian Bookstore*
☎ 212-255-8097; 15 Christopher St; ☷ 11am-7pm; subway A, B, C, D, E, F, V to W 4 St, or 1, 9 to Christopher St–Sheridan Sq

The world's oldest bookshop geared to gay and lesbian literature (open since 1967) stocks books, rainbow flags and other gifts. It nearly closed in 2003, but has been rescued from the brink of collapse by a longtime fan who is now its new manager. Go buy something.

PARTNERS & CRIME

Map pp382-5   *Specialty Books*
☎ 212-243-0440; 44 Greenwich Ave; ☷ noon-9pm Mon-Thu, noon-10pm Fri & Sat, noon-7pm Sun; subway 1, 2 to Christopher St–Sheridan Sq, F, V, 1, 2, 3, 9 to 14th St

Cozy bookshop offering new and out-of-print whodunits, plus talks with mystery authors and live performances of old radio broadcasts (with live organists and taped sound effects) on the first Saturday of most months (call for reservations ☎ 212-462-3027; admission $5).

RALPH LAUREN

Map pp382-5   *Women's Clothing*
☎ 212-645-5513; 380 Bleecker St; ☷ noon-8pm Mon-Fri, 11am-7pm Sat & Sun; subway 1, 2 to Christopher St–Sheridan Sq, A, C, E to 14th St, L to Eigth Ave

Ralph's new Greenwich Village post sports a more casual edge than the **Upper East Side** (p287) shop. Here you can also find Ralph's cheapest line, Blue Label, plus plenty of polos.

REBEL REBEL Map pp382-5   *Music*

☎ 212-989-0770; 319 Bleecker St; ☷ noon-8pm Sun-Wed, noon-9pm Thu-Sat; subway 1, 9 to Christopher St–Sheridan Sq

Tight-fit, tiny music store with CDs and rare vinyl defying limits of space. Ask for what you don't see – there's loads more in the back.

SHAKESPEARE & CO

Map pp382-5   *Bookstore*
☎ 212-529-1330; 716 Broadway; ☷ 10am-11pm Sun-Thu, 10am-11:30pm Fri-Sat; subway N, R, W to 8 St, 6 to Astor Pl

The Greenwich branch of the citywide independent bookshop chain. With NYU's Tisch film school across the street, this one stocks many theater and film books and scripts. Other shops are in **Lower Manhattan** (p257), **Midtown** (p274) and the **Upper East Side** (p287).

STRAND BOOK STORE

Map pp382-5   *Used Books*
☎ 212-473-1452; 828 Broadway; ☷ 9:30am-10:30pm Mon-Sat, 11am-10:30pm Sun; subway L, N, Q, R, W, 4, 5, 6 to 14th St–Union Sq

Book fiends – or even those who have casually skimmed one or two – shouldn't miss New York's most-loved used bookstore. Operating since 1927, the Strand's towering aisles display (a bit confusingly) 'eight miles' of books (that's well over two million, if you're counting). Check out the changing sales racks – of recent hardbacks, travel books and reference items – or the staggering number of reviewers' copies in the basement. This is *the* place to lose yourself in the cleansing powers of book browsing.

The Strand buys or trades books from 9:30am to 6pm Monday to Saturday. The Strand has a store in **Lower Manhattan** (p257) and an open-air outlet at the **Grand Army Plaza** entrance to Central Park, at the corner of Fifth Ave and 59th St.

SUSAN PARRISH ANTIQUES

Map pp382-5   *Antiques*

☎ 212-645-5020; 390 Bleecker St; ☟ noon-7pm Mon-Sat (or by appointment); subway 1, 9 to Christopher St–Sheridan Sq

On a block of antiques dealers, Susan Parrish's impressive selection of Americana (a rarity in New York City) includes quilts and various one-of-a-kind peeling-paint furnishings.

THREE LIVES & COMPANY

Map pp382-5   *Bookstore*

☎ 212-741-2069; 154 W 10th St; ☟ noon-8pm Mon-Tue, 11am-8:30pm Wed-Sat, noon-7pm Sun; subway 1, 9 to Christopher St–Sheridan Sq

Relaxed independent bookstore tucked away on a quiet corner with carefully selected new books.

TOWER RECORDS Map pp382-5   *Music*

☎ 212-505-1500; 692 Broadway; ☟ 9am-midnight; subway 6 to Bleecker St

Three floors of CDs with collections of most music types, notably rock on the ground floor, and jazz and blues on the 2nd; singles are in the basement. Keith Richards used to live above it. As they say, coolness seeps downward.

VILLAGE CHESS SHOP LTD

Map pp382-5   *Games*

☎ 212-475-9580; 230 Thompson St; ☟ 11am-midnight; subway A, B, C, D, E, F, V to W 4 St

A crusty crew of chess-perts frequent this hole-in-the-wall chess shop for $1 games in a no-frills sitting area. Come to play, buy a book to study up, or buy one of the chess sets (the best ones are thematic: Aztec, Crusades, Vegas etc). There's coffee on, too.

VILLAGE COMICS

Map pp382-5   *Comics & Sci-Fi*

☎ 212-777-2770; 215 Sullivan St; ☟ 10:30am-7:30pm Mon & Tue, 10:30am-8pm Wed-Sat, 10:30am-7pm Sun; subway A, B, C, D, E, F, V to W 4 St

Near New York University, this shop does a brisk business with its taken-seriously sci-fi gear, comics and trading cards. There's also a good collection of mounted death masks. Wicked.

VIRGIN MEGASTORE

Map pp382-5   *Music & Videos*

☎ 212-598-4666; 52 E 14th St; ☟ 9-1am Mon-Sat, 10am-midnight Sun; subway L, N, Q, R, W, 4, 5, 6 to 14th St–Union Sq

This Union Sq branch has big collections of CDs and DVDs. There's another Virgin at **Times Square** (p284).

CHELSEA & UNION SQUARE

Other than a handful of gems scattered about, Chelsea's shopping scene can be a bit ho-hum compared to other parts of Manhattan – during the week, that is. On weekends Chelsea really lights up, when flea marketeers hit the area around the **Annex Antique Fair & Flea Market** (p270) to comb bins and tables packed with furnishings, accessories, CDs, clothing and plain weird stuff from past eras.

Elsewhere, you'll find a few chains on Fifth Ave (Daffy's, Victoria Secret, Armani Exchange) and Seventh Ave (Bed, Bath & Beyond, Barnes & Noble). The Flower District runs along Sixth Ave between 26th and 30th Sts.

ABC CARPET & HOME

Map pp382-5   *Home Furnishings*

☎ 212-473-3000; 888 Broadway; ☟ 10am-8pm Mon-Thu, 10am-6:30pm Fri & Sat, noon-6pm Sun; subway L, N, Q, R, W, 4, 5, 6 to 14th St–Union Sq

Home designers and decorators stroll here to brainstorm ideas. Set up like a museum on six floors, ABC is filled with all sorts of furnishings, small and large, including easy-to-pack knick-knacks and more bulky antique furnishings and carpet.

ACADEMY RECORDS & CDS

Map pp382-5   *Used & New Music*

☎ 212-242-3000; 12 W 18th St; ☟ 11:30am-8pm Mon-Sat, 11am-7pm Sun; subway N, R, W, 6 to 23 St

'Frank' or Haydn blares in this *great* music shop as a wall-to-wall crew of serious shoppers (the beret ratio is seriously 4:1) rifle through stacks of classical vinyl, all sorts of new and used CDs, and – especially – the $1.99 bargain CD bins (most types). Academy sells its rock and jazz vinyl at its E 19th St shop; call for details.

BARNES & NOBLE

Map pp382-5   *Books*

☎ 212-253-0810; www.barnesandnoble.com; 33 E 17th St; ☟ 10am-10pm; subway L, N, Q, R, W, 4, 5, 6 to 14th St–Union Sq

One of several Manhattan Barnes & Noble locations, this has the largest collection. You can find books to get some background on New York City as well as Lonely Planet titles in the travel sections. Plus there's music and a café where you can read magazines. Check the website for other locations.

BARNEYS CO-OP

Map pp382-5 — *Designer Clothing*

☎ 212-593-7800; 236 W 18th St; ☀ 11am-8pm Mon-Fri, 11am-7pm Sat, noon-6pm Sun; subway 1, 9 to 18th St

This Barneys outlet has cheap deals, plus its famous warehouse sale in February and August. There's also a branch in **Soho** (p258) but Barneys' mother superior is in the **Upper East Side** (p285).

BOOKS OF WONDER

Map pp382-5 — *Children's Bookstore*

☎ 212-989-3270; 16 W 18th St; ☀ 11am-7pm Mon-Sat, 11:45am-6pm Sun; subway L to 6 Av, F, V to 14th St

Chelsea-ites love this small, indie, funloving bookstore devoted to children's and young-adult titles.

CHELSEA MARKET

Map pp382-5 — *Food & Wine*

www.chelseamarket.com; 75 Ninth Ave btwn 15th & 16th St; ☀ 8am-8pm Mon-Fri, 10am-8pm Sat & Sun; subway A, C, E to 14th St, L to Eighth Ave

This 800ft-long shopping concourse, a former cookie factory, is filled with 25 minimarkets,

---

Antiquing Chelsea

A nation of collectors converges on Chelsea on weekends, making up one of the favorite browsing spots for New Yorkers. The open-air emporium of **Annex Antiques Fair & Flea Market** (Map pp386-8; ☎ 212-243-5343; 107-111 W 25th St; admission $1; ☀ dawn-dusk Sat & Sun; subway F, V, 1, 9 to 23rd St), past the turnstile, has dozens of dealers hawking all sorts of goods to loyal a New York crowd. Come here for hit-or-miss knick-knacks, furnishings, watches, cameras and whatnot. Spillover flea markets are in surrounding parking lots on weekends – notably the excellent free-access stands a block south at Sixth Ave and 24th St (furniture, jean jackets, CDs, bikes etc).

Garage Antique Fair (Map pp386-8; 112 W 25th St; ☀ dawn-dusk Sat & Sun; subway F, V, 1, 9 to 23rd St) is the place to go if you're antiquing in Chelsea on a weekend. Save some time and energy from the Annex market half a block east to browse these 150 vendors' offerings, set up on two levels of this covered parking lot. Plenty of old photos, posters, eyewear and assorted furnishings.

---

offering goods such as fresh flowers, luscious baked goods, organic snacks and top-shelf wines sold by knowledgeable staff. It's like a European covered market, but a bit snazzy and NYC-paced.

COMME DES GARÇONS

Map pp382-5 — *Designer Clothing*

☎ 212-604-9200; 520 W 22nd St; ☀ 11am-7pm Tue-Sat, noon-6pm Sun; subway C, E to 23 St

Amid Chelsea's galleries, this store is kinda art in itself. A twisting, aluminum tunnel leads to a pear-shaped glass door that's disorienting to walk through. Inside, you'll find white Plexiglas walls, à la *2001*, and slick high-end Italian clothing and shoes.

HOUSING WORKS THRIFT SHOP

Map pp382-5 — *Thrift Store*

☎ 212-366-0820; 143 W 17th St; ☀ 10am-6pm Mon-Sat, noon-5pm Sun; subway 1, 9 to 18th St

This thrift shop – with its swank window displays – looks more boutique than thrift, and its selections of clothes, accessories, furniture and books are great value. All proceeds benefit the charity serving the city's HIV-positive and AIDS homeless communities.

LOEHMANN'S Map pp382-5 — *Dept Store*

☎ 212-352-0856; www.loehmanns.com; 101 7th Ave at 16th St; ☀ 9am-9pm Mon-Sat, 11am-7pm Sun; subway 1, 9 to 18th St

A starting point for local hipsters looking for designer labels on the cheap (though some may not admit it), Loehmann's is a five-story department store that, it is said, inspired a wee-young Calvin Klein to make clothes good. The original store of the successful chain is in the Bronx; see the website for other locations.

OTTO TOOTSI PLOHOUND

Map pp382-5 — *Shoes*

☎ 212-460-8650; 137 Fifth Ave; ☀ 11:30am-7:30am Mon-Fri, 11am-8pm Sat, noon-7pm Sun; subway N, R, W to 23rd St

Great New York minichain for designer shoes (Prada, Miu Miu, Costume National etc) – this branch is Tootsi's standout location (see also the **Soho** branch, p260). Tootsi gets backed at its bi-annual sales (starting in January and July).

PARAGON ATHLETIC GOODS

Map pp382-5 — *Sporting Goods*

☎ 212-255-8036; 867 Broadway; ☀ 10am-8pm Mon-Sat, 11:30am-7pm Sun; subway L, N, Q, R, W, 4, 5, 6 to 14th St–Union Sq

Paragon offers a comprehensive collection of sports merchandise, with better prices than the chains and an excellent selection of in-line skates. Watch for end-of-season sales.

PRINTED MATTER INC

Map pp382-5   *Art Books*
☎ 212-925-0325; 535 W 22nd St; ⊙ 10am-6pm Tue-Fri, 11am-7pm Sat; subway C, E to 23 St
A popular stop on Chelsea's busiest art gallery strip, this nonprofit bookstore stocks many art books and products published by artists themselves.

REVOLUTION BOOKS

Map pp382-5   *Radical Bookstore*
☎ 212-691-3345; 9 W 19th St; ⊙ 10am-7pm Mon-Sat, noon-5pm Sun; subway 1, 9 to 18th St
The Rev has New York's biggest and best radical collection of books, leaflets and journals. You'll find bookshelves devoted to Lenin, Mao and Marx; many books in *Español*; as well as cute red-star earrings ($7). The shop also hosts talks.

MIDTOWN

Midtown sprawls, and shopping options along with it. Fifth Ave, from 42nd St to Central Park South, is a famed strip, with flagship stores of international designers, followed by high-style department stores like Bergdorf Goodman and Henri Bendel, and jewelers like Tiffany & Co and Cartier. Herald Square – where Broadway, Sixth Ave and 34th St meet – is home to Macy's and one of the city's busiest shopping zones.

See p160 for a guided walk from Midtown to the Upper East side. For shopping in the Times Square and Theater District, see p283.

ARGOSY Map pp386-8   *Used Bookstore*
☎ 212-753-4455; www.argosybooks.com; 116 E 59th St; ⊙ 10am-6pm Mon-Fri, 10am-5pm Sat; subway 4, 5, 6 to 59th St, N, R, W to Lexington Ave–59th St
Since 1925, this landmark used bookstore has stocked fine antiquarian items such as leather-bound books, old maps, art monographs and other classics picked up from high-class estate sales and closed antique shops. Books range from a Matisse-illustrated 1935 copy of James Joyce's *Ulysses*, signed by the artist, for $4000, to less expensive clearance items.

Top Five Department Stores

- **Barneys** (p285) Best cutting-edge, high-end designs.
- **Saks Fifth Avenue** (p274) Classy collection and friendly staff.
- **Bergdorf Goodman** (below) Highest-end formal wear.
- **Henri Bendel** (p273) Inviting Fifth Ave shop.
- **Century 21** (p257) High-end designs at discount prices.

Check the website for other featured items stored away.

B&H PHOTO-VIDEO

Map pp386-8   *Cameras & Electronics*
☎ 212-502-6200 photo, 212-502-6300 video; www .bhphotovideo.com; 420 Ninth Ave; ⊙ 9am-7pm Mon-Thu, 9am-1pm Fri, 10am-5pm Sun; subway A, C, E to 34th St–Penn Station
Visiting B&H, the city's most popular camera shop can be an experience in itself. Its shop is bigger than its previous location, but still suffers from zoo-like crowding and a pay-first, pick-up-second bureaucracy. Come for film, cameras and other electronics, including some used items. Linguistically adept staff (mostly Orthodox Jews), helpful for international clients, can offer some assistance, but it's good to have an idea of what you want before showing up.

BANANA REPUBLIC

Map pp386-8   *Clothing*
☎ 212-974-2350; www.bananarepublic.com; 626 Fifth Ave; ⊙ 10am-8pm Mon-Sat, 11am-7pm Sun; subway B, D, F, V to 47th–50th Sts–Rockefeller Center
Good ol' Banana Republic sells its slick stylish wear in (are you sitting?) 12 Manhattan stores; check the website for locations. This branch, at Rockefeller Center, has one of the bigger selections.

BERGDORF GOODMAN

Map pp386-8   *Dept Store*
☎ 212-753-7300; 754 Fifth Ave; ⊙ 10am-7pm Mon-Wed & Fri, 10am-8pm Thu, noon-8pm Sun; subway N, R, W to Fifth Ave, F to 57th St
If you wake up in one of those 'must spend millions to inherit millions' type movies, come here first to re-outfit yourself in elegant clothing, shoes and jewelry. The men's collection is at 745 Fifth Ave. It's 100% class.

BORDERS Map pp386-8 *Books*

☎ 212-980-6785; www.bordersstores.com;
461 Park Ave; 9am-10pm Mon-Fri, 10am-8pm Sat,
11am-8pm Sun; subway 4, 5, 6 to 59th St, N, R, W to
Fifth Ave–59th St

This bookstore chain has three other Manhattan stores and offers a wide assortment of books, including Lonely Planet titles. Check the website for other locations.

BROOKS BROTHERS

Map pp386-8 *Clothing*
☎ 212-682-8800; 346 Madison Ave; 9am-7pm
Mon-Wed, Fri & Sat, 9am-8pm Thu, noon-6pm Sun;
subway S, 4, 5, 6, 7 to Grand Central–42nd St

Brooks still sell the blue blazers that delighted prep school kids (and grads) for so many years, but also more recent splashier clothing too. Collections for men, women and children.

CARTIER Map pp386-8 *Jewelry*

☎ 212-753-0111; www.cartier.com; 653 Fifth Ave;
10am-5:30pm Mon-Sat, noon-5pm Sun; subway E,
V to Fifth Ave–53rd St

For sheer class, Cartier's first-rate jewelry and accessories is as good as it gets. Here, or in the **Upper East Side** (p286) boutique you'll find the French company's rings, watches, glasses and bags; check its website for other locations.

CHRISTIE'S Map pp386-8 *Auction House*

☎ 212-636-2000; www.christies.com; 20 Rockefeller
Center; subway B, D, F, V to 47th–50th Sts–Rockefeller
Center

This top-level auction house has sold former belongings of John F Kennedy, Marilyn Monroe and Frank Sinatra. Auctions are held here frequently; check the website for the calendar.

COMPLETE TRAVELLER

Map pp386-8 *Used Travel Bookstore*
☎ 212-685-9007; 199 Madison Ave at E 35th St;
10am-6:30pm Mon-Fri, 10am-6pm Sat, noon-5pm
Sun; subway 6 to 33 St

Stocking two rooms full with travel guides and maps from the travelways of days past, the Complete Traveller arranges its stock by destination. Perfect browsing ground for travel bugs: old Baedeker guides, the complete WPA series of US state guides (three Oklahomas on shelf!), maps and some newer titles.

COMPUSA Map pp386-8 *Computers*

☎ 212-764-6224; 420 Fifth Ave; 8:30am-8pm
Mon-Fri, 10am-7pm Sat, 11am-6pm Sun; subway B, D,
F to 34th St--Herald Sq

A huge store with computer software, printers and accessories. There's also another branch in **Midtown** (☎ 212-262-9711; 57th & Broadway; 8:30am-8pm Mon-Fri, 10am-7pm Sat, 11am-6pm Sun).

DISNEY STORE Map pp386-8 *Toys*

☎ 212-702-0702; 711 Fifth Ave; 10am-8pm
Mon-Sat, 11am-7pm Sun; subway E, V to Fifth Ave–53rd St,
N, R, W to Fifth Ave–59th St

Three floors just bursting with Disney-related merchandise. Sorry kids, no life-size Mickeys, Goofys or Tiggers to shake paws with.

FAO SCHWARTZ Map pp386-8 *Toys*

☎ 212-644-9400; www.fao.com; 767 Fifth Ave;
noon-7pm Mon-Wed, noon-8pm Thu-Sat, 11am-6pm Sun; subway 4, 5, 6 to 59th St, N, R, W to Fifth
Ave–59th St

The toy-store giant – where Tom Hanks played footsy piano in the movie *Big* – had closed its doors for renovation during research of this book, but was scheduled to re-open before this book hits the shelves. Call ahead.

GOTHAM BOOK MART

Map pp386-8 *Bookstore*
☎ 212-719-4448; 41 W 47th St; 9:30am-6:30pm
Mon-Fri, 9:30am-6pm Sun; subway B, D, F, V to
47th–50th Sts–Rockefeller Center

Overflowing with choice lit since 1920, the Gotham Book Mart is what bookstores are meant to be. It's historic too. Frances Stelof (who died in 1989) founded the James Joyce Society here in 1947, and snuck some of his books and other naughty ones like Henry Miller's *Tropic of Cancer* past US obscenity laws. Located in the middle of the Diamond District, the mart may be moving in the future. Call ahead.

Diamonds Are Forever

In need of some bling-bling? On 47th St, between Fifth & Sixth Aves, is the Diamond District, home to some 100 cooperative stalls selling discount diamonds, pearls and other jewelry. Haggling's in effect, but you can get far better prices here than at a regular shop. As Orthodox Jews run many of the stores, the street shuts down early Friday and is closed weekends.

GUCCI Map pp386-8 *Designer Clothing*
☎ 212-826-2600; www.gucci.com; 685 Fifth Ave; ☾ 10am-6:30pm Mon-Fri, 10am-7pm Sat, noon-6pm Sun; subway E, V to Fifth Ave–53rd St

The super swank, thoroughly modern five-floor Gucci store reflects the style of chic men's and women's ready-to-wear clothing that's on offer. You can also pick up Gucci's famed handbags and shoes here. Gucci has an Upper East Side boutique; see the website for details.

H&M Map pp386-8 *Dept Store*
☎ 646-473-1164; www.hm.com; 1328 Broadway at 34th St; ☾ 10am-10pm Mon-Sat, 11am-8pm Sun; subway B, D, F, N, Q, R, V, W to 34th St–Herald Sq

The flagship H&M, at Herald Sq, is one of five of the Swedish knockoff discount clothing in Manhattan. Check the website for locations (note the number of directors whose names end in 'sen' or 'son'). This store and the branch at 51st St and Fifth Ave have large selections.

HENRI BENDEL Map pp386-8 *Dept Store*
☎ 212-247-1100; 712 Fifth Ave; ☾ 10am-7pm Fri-Wed, 10am-8pm Thu; subway E, V to Fifth Ave–53rd St, or N, R, W to Fifth Ave–59th St

As boutique-cozy as a big-name, high-class department store can be, Bendel's makes for an easy pop-in-and-out. Its European collections include curious, stylish clothing of established and up-and-coming designers, as well as cosmetics and accessories. Look out for the original Lalique windows.

JIMMY CHOO Map pp386-8 *Shoes*
☎ 212-593-0800; 645 51st St; ☾ 10am-6pm Mon-Sat, noon-5pm Sun; subway E, V to Fifth Ave–53rd St, 6 to 51 St

Elegant shoes for the stars. Madonna picked her bridal digs here and *Sex and the City* gals loved the nonmatrimonial luxurious high heels – some heels don't stop. Prices start around $400. A second (bigger) shop is in the **Upper East Side** (p286).

J LEVINE JEWISH BOOKS & JUDAICA
Map pp386-8 *Jewish Bookstore*
☎ 212-695-6888; 5 W 30th St; ☾ 9am-6pm Mon-Wed, 9am-7pm Thu, 10am-5pm Sun; subway B, D, F, N, Q, R, V, W to 34th St–Herald Sq

The Levine family has been churning out the Talmud, menorahs and a wide range of Jewish-related books since 1890.

KATE'S PAPERIE Map pp386-8 *Stationery*
☎ 212-459-0700; 140 W 57th St; ☾ 10am-8pm Mon-Fri, 10am-7pm Sat, 11am-6pm Sun; subway F, N, Q, R, W to 57 St

New York's terrific stationery chain is popular for wedding announcements and the handmade journals. There are a few locations, including one in **Soho** (p260).

LEDERER DE PARIS
Map pp386-8 *Handbags*
☎ 212-355-5515; 654 Madison Ave; ☾ 9:30am-6pm Mon-Wed, Fri & Sat, 9:30am-6:30pm Thu; subway 6 to 51 St

This place has top-quality handwoven handbags and accessories.

LORD & TAYLOR
Map pp386-8 *Dept Store*
☎ 212-391-3344; 424 Fifth Ave; ☾ 10am-8:30pm Mon-Fri, 10am-7pm Sat, 11am-7pm Sun; subway 6 to 33 St, 7 to Fifth Ave, S, 4, 5, 6, 7 to Grand Central–42nd St

Staying true to its traditional roots (Ralph Lauren, Donna Karen, Calvin Klein etc), this 10-floor store tends to let shoppers browse pressure-free (even in cosmetics), and has a great selection of swimwear.

MACY'S Map pp386-8 *Dept Store*
☎ 212-695-4400; 151 W 34th St at Broadway; ☾ 10am-8:30pm Mon-Sat, 11am-7pm Sun; subway B, D, F, N, Q, R, V, W to 34th St–Herald Sq

The world's largest department store has a bit of everything – clothing, furnishings, food, hair salons. It's less high-end than many Midtown department stores but it's useful if you're looking for simpler things, like a good pair of jeans or work shirt, and not necessarily an only-from-Manhattan 21st-century outfit.

NBA STORE
Map pp386-8 *Sporting Goods*
☎ 212-644-9400; 767 Fifth Ave; ☾ 10am-7pm Mon-Sat, 11am-6pm Sun; subway E, V to Fifth Ave–53rd St

Amid posh department stores and designer outlets, why not hoops? Pick up team jerseys, b'balls and other (rather marked-up) memorabilia, or shoot some free baskets inside before slam-dunking your way to Takashimaya or Saks Fifth. Wheee-haaa!

NEW YORK TRANSIT MUSEUM SHOP

Map pp386–8   *Gifts*

☎ 212-878-0106; Shuttle Passage at Grand Central Station; ☾ 8am-8pm Mon-Fri, 10am-6pm Sat & Sun; subway S, 4, 5, 6, 7 to Grand Central–42nd St

This annex of the **Brooklyn Museum** (p138) sells gifts with subway map prints – T-shirts, umbrellas, table cloths, purses and more.

PRADA

Map pp386–8   *Designer Clothing*

☎ 212-664-0010; 724 Fifth Ave; ☾ 10am-6pm Mon-Wed, Fri & Sat, noon-6pm Sun; subway N, R, W to Fifth Ave–59th St

Midtown has two Prada shops not far from each other. The Fifth Ave store carries the Italian designer's men's and women's clothing, while its shoe store is at 45 E 57th St. Prada also has stores in the **Upper East Side** (p287) and in **Soho** (p260).

RIZZOLI

Map pp386–8   *Bookstore*

☎ 212-759-2424; 31 W 57th St; ☾ 10am-7:30pm Mon-Fri, 10:30am-7pm Sat, 11am-7pm Sun; subway F to 57th St

This handsome store of the Italian bookstore/publisher sells great art, architecture and design books (as well as general-interest books). There's also a good collection of foreign newspapers and magazines.

SAKS FIFTH AVE

Map pp386–8   *Dept Store*

☎ 212-753-4000; 611 Fifth Ave at 50th St; ☾ 10am-7pm Mon-Wed, Fri & Sat, 10am-8pm Thu, noon-6pm Sun; subway B, D, F, V to 47th–50th Sts–Rockefeller Center

Anyone heard of Saks? Here's where it started. This lovely flagship offers its updated collection of high-end women's and men's clothing. Famous for its January sale. (Note the good view of Rockefeller Center from its upper floors.)

SALVATORE FERRAGAMO

Map pp386–8   *Clothing*

☎ 212-759-3822; 655 Fifth Ave at 52nd St; ☾ 10am-7pm Mon-Sat, noon-6pm Sun; subway E, V to Fifth Ave–53rd St

Opened in 2003, Salvatore's flagship store fills its two floors with the Italian designer's glamorous men's and women's collections.

SEPHORA

Map pp386–8   *Bath & Beauty*

☎ 212-823-9383; www.sephora.com; 10 Columbus Circle at 59th St; ☾ 10am-9pm; subway A, B, C, D, 1, 9 to 59th St–Columbus Circle

Amid the chic hubbub at the Time Warner Center (see Shops at Columbus Circle below), visit this branch of Sephora for high-quality cosmetics (Clinique, Lancôme etc) at discount prices. There are several branches around town, including Times Square and on Broadway in Soho; see website for information.

SHAKESPEARE & CO

Map pp386–8   *Books*

☎ 212-505-2021; 137 E 23rd St; ☾ 9am-9pm Mon-Thu, 9am-8pm Fri, 11am-7pm Sat, noon-6pm Sun; subway 6 to 23rd St

The Midtown branch of this popular New York bookstore chain. It's indie and the selection's good. Other shops are in **Lower Manhattan** (p257), **Greenwich Village** (p268) and the **Upper East Side** (p287).

SHOPS AT COLUMBUS CIRCLE

Map pp386–8   *Mall*

☎ 212-823-6300; 10 Columbus Circle; subway A, B, C, D, 1, 9 to 59th St–Columbus Circle

Still shining from its February 2004 opening, this remarkable four-floor 'retail center' (at the base of the two-towered Time Warner Center) is home to 50 largely upscale shops and several restaurants. Shops include Coach, Williams-Sonoma, Hugo Boss, Thomas Pink, Sephora, J Crew, Borders Books & Music, Armani Exchange and Inside CNN. If you're bent on a Central Park picnic, visit **Whole Foods** (☾ 8am-10pm) in the basement for ready-to-go salads and sandwiches.

Top Five Cheap NYC Souvenirs

- **Subway-print umbrella** From the New York Transit Museum in Brooklyn (p136) and at Grand Central Terminal (left).
- **Chinatown Ice Cream Factory T-shirt** (p262) Dragons *do* smile when eating dessert.
- **Mug from Zabar's** (p285) Very insider, plus that wacky font.
- **Knick-knacks from China** Pearl River Mart (p260) is a catch-all shop, but smaller stands are a bit cheaper.
- **I love NY T-shirts** Widely available for $3 at Times Square.

(Continued on page 283)

Shopping – Midtown

1 *Souvenir stall (p274)* 2 *Taxis (p341), Third Ave* 3 *Stilt walkers, West Indian American Day Carnival Parade (p12)*

1 *Strand Book Store (p268)*
2 *Mannequin, Henri Bendel (p273)* **3** *Antique furniture sale, Greenwich Village (p92)*

1 Greenmarket Farmers' Market (p107) 2 Barneys (p28
3 Mural, East Village (p90)

NO. 2

1 *Gramercy Park Hotel (p298)*
2 *Peninsula hotel window (p3*
3 *Waldorf-Astoria hotel (p30*

THE WALDORF-ASTORIA

e Cyclone (p141), Coney
nd **2** TKTS booth (p117)
aiting tables, Greenwich
age (p92)

1 *Trump Taj Mahal (p323), Atlantic City* 2 *Elfreth's Alley (p332), Philadelphia* 3 *Vanderbilt Mansion (p320) Hyde Park*

(Continued from page 274)

TAKASHIMAYA Map pp386-8 *Dept Store*
☎ 212-350-0100; 693 Fifth Ave; ⏱ 10am-7pm Mon-Sat, noon-5pm Sun; subway E, V to Fifth Ave–53rd St

The Japanese owners upped the ante on Fifth Ave's elegant, minimalist style with this stunning store, which sells high-end furniture, clothing and (less costly) homewares from all over the world. Purchases come gorgeously packaged. Even if you're *not* shopping today, don't miss the ground-floor floral arrangements and have a green tea at the relaxing **Tea Box café** in the basement.

TIFFANY & CO Map pp386-8 *Jewelry*
☎ 212-755-8000; 727 Fifth Ave; ⏱ 10am-7pm Mon-Fri, 10am-6pm Sat, noon-5pm Sun; subway F to 57th St

This famous jeweler, with the trademark clock-hoisting Atlas over the door, has won countless hearts with its fine diamond rings, watches, necklaces and more – not to mention its football (Tiffany's did the Vince Lombardi Super Bowl trophy in 1970). The thrifty-but-curious can window-browse and consider a key chain (very touristy), cuff link or money clip. But don't bring in a croissant in a bag for a joke 'breakfast at Tiffany's' photo; staff don't have a sense of humor on this.

Actually you're probably carrying a Tiffany design with you at the moment; the Great Seal of the USA (found on all $1 bills) is a Tiffany product.

URBAN CENTER BOOKS
Map pp386-8 *Architecture Bookstore*
☎ 212-935-3592; 457 Madison Ave; ⏱ 10am-7pm Mon-Thu, 10am-6pm Fri, 10am-5:30pm Sat; subway 6 to 51 St

This impressive shop, in the courtyard of the historic Villlard Houses at 51st St, carries 7000 new (and some out-of-print) architecture books.

TIMES SQUARE & THEATER DISTRICT

Like it or not, Times Square is no longer the 'porn, pimp and drug zone' it was in the not-too-distant past. These days, MTV, ABC Television, Reuters and Nasdaq call it home, and some giant – really giant – shops have opened their doors, including Toys 'R' Us, which will make your kids slobber.

On W 48th St, you'll find several musical-instrument shops (such as Manny's and Sam Ash), where rock stars come to pick up a pedal or a new beast-slaying axe.

COLONY Map pp226-7 *Music*
☎ 212-265-2050; 1619 Broadway; ⏱ 9:30am-midnight Mon-Sat, 10am-midnight Sun; subway N, R, W to 49 St

Located in the Brill Building (the onetime home of Tin Pan Alley song-crafters), the historic Colony once sold sheet music to the likes of Charlie Parker and Miles Davis. Its collection remains the city's largest. Plus there's a giant collection of karaoke CDs (show tunes, mariachi, AC/DC etc) and cases of memorabilia (Beatles gear, original Broadway posters, unused Frank and Sammy tickets etc) – all for sale.

DRAMA BOOKSHOP
Map pp226-7 *Bookstore*
☎ 212-944-0595; www.dramabookshop.com; 250 W 40th St; ⏱ 10am-8pm Mon-Sat, noon-6pm; subway A, C, E to 42nd St–Port Authority Bus Terminal

Treasures in print for Broadway fans are shelved at this expansive bookstore, which has taken its theater (plays and musicals) seriously since 1917. Staff are good at recommending worthy selections. Check out the website for regular events, such as talks with playwrights.

MANNY'S MUSIC
Map pp226-7 *Musical Instruments*
☎ 212-819-0576; 156 W 48th St; ⏱ 10am-7pm Mon-Sat, noon-6pm Sun; subway N, R, W to 49 St

Guitar junkies and gear-heads should pay tribute to W 48th St's most famous music shop, Manny's. Here's where Jimi Hendrix regularly stopped to get a few new guitars, the Stones bought the distortion pedal they used on 'Satisfaction,' the Ramones rhythm section first equipped themselves, and (before all that) jazz greats like Benny Goodman picked up a reed or two. Wall photos tell the tale, and Manny's still stocks all the goods (guitars, basses, drums, keyboards) for you to make your band. Hey ho!

Sam Ash (☎ 212-719-2299; 160 W 48 St; ⏱ 10am-8pm Mon-Fri, to 7pm Sat, noon-6pm Sun) is another top notch music outfitter on the block.

MYSTERIOUS BOOKSHOP
Map pp226-7 *Mystery Bookstore*
☎ 212-765-0900; www.mysteriousbookshop.com; 129 W 56th St; ⏱ 11am-7pm Mon-Sat; subway F, N, R, Q, W to 57th St

If murder, suspense or good ol' fashioned crime-ridden thrillers gets your goat, stop to browse this shop's huge collection of signed copies and first editions. Read the comprehensive monthly newsletter online.

TOYS 'R' US

Map pp226-7 *Toys*
☎ 800-869-7787; 1514 Broadway; ☻ 10am-10pm Mon-Sat, 11am-8pm Sun; subway N, Q, R, S, W, 1, 2, 3, 7, 9 to Times Sq–42nd St

Sure you have one of these at home, but this super-size Toys 'R' Us is its greatest bastion, with three thematic floors including a huge video-game area downstairs, an alley of stuffed animals and an indoor Ferris wheel (per ride $2.50).

VIRGIN MEGASTORE

Map pp226-7 *Music & Video*
☎ 212-921-1020; 1540 Broadway; ☻ 9-1am Sun-Thu, 9-2am Fri & Sat; subway N, Q, R, S, W, 1, 2, 3, 7, 9 to Times Sq–42nd St

Virgin's huge Times Square branch is hard to miss – it claims to be the world's largest music store – and, in addition to selling CDs and merchandise, it hosts many big-name signings (yes, ladies, even Josh Groban!). Note that lines can take hours. You can usually find cheaper CDs on Bleecker St in Greenwich Village or St Marks Pl in the East Village. Virgin also has a store at **Union Square** (p269).

UPPER WEST SIDE

Not a record-breaking shopping area, the residential Upper West Side has, nevertheless, stacks of shops catering to its well-to-do, sporty (OK, yuppie) residents along its three main avenues (Broadway, Amsterdam and Columbus). Best for the shop-and-walk is by far Columbus Ave, particularly between W 66th St and W 82nd St (or so), where you can find high-end boutiques and shops. Also, staff here tend to be a bit less pushy than on the other side of Central Park.

APPLAUSE BOOKS

Map pp389-91 *Theatrical/Film Bookstore*
☎ 212-496-7511; 211 W 71st St; ☻ 10am-9pm Mon-Sat, noon-6pm Sun; subway 1, 2, 3, 9 to 72nd St

Tennessee Williams? He goes by 'T-dub' here. Celebrating all things theater, film, directing

and design, Applause is the first stop before your own fame and fortune rushes in. There's a full wall paperback plays and screenplays.

GRYPHON RECORDS

Map pp389-91 *Used Music*
☎ 212-874-1588; 233 W 72nd St; ☻ 9:30am-7pm Mon-Fri, 11am-8pm Sat & Sun; subway 1, 2, 3, 9 to 72 St

Messy and wonderful, Gryphon is filled with a veritable firetrap of vinyl treasure (some 50,000 found in hidden nooks) and some intense clients silently browsing through the largely classical and old-time vocalists' collections. There's also some used books up the front – ask about the ultra-rare Lonely Planet title that eludes you.

KANGOL

Map pp389-91 *Hats*
☎ 212-724-1172; 196 Columbus Ave; ☻ 10:30am-9pm; subway A, B, C, D, 1, 9 to 59th St–Columbus Circle

Back in the 1980s, rappers like LL Cool J made this British company's little kangaroo label cool, but it took till 2003 for the US to get its first Kangol shop. Stop by for the latest tweed and pastel knit caps and berets. Note the sign, 'No, we're English.'

MAXILA

Map pp389-91 *Fossils, Bones & Dung*
☎ 212-724-6173; 451 Columbus Ave; ☻ 11am-7pm Mon-Sat & 1-5pm Sun Oct-Dec, 11am-7pm Tue-Sat Jan-Mar, 11am-7pm Mon & Wed-Sat & 1-5pm Sun Apr-Jun; subway B, C to 81st St–Museum of Natural History

Lovers of fossils must visit the world's only osteological shop, which stocks and sells many similar specimens you'll see at the nearby **American Museum of Natural History** (p120). It's all real. The wonderful collection includes prehistoric fish, coyote skulls, anatomy posters and (hey, kids) 10 million-year-old fossilized dung ($18).

MURDER INK/IVY'S BOOKS

Map pp389-91 *Mystery Bookstore*
☎ 212-362-8905; 2486 Broadway; ☻ 10am-7:30pm Mon-Sat, 11am-6pm Sun; subway 1, 2, 3, 9 to 96th St

The city's first shop devoted to crime and mystery fiction has been stocking everything of the genre – plus stacks of out-of-print titles – since 1972. Its space-partner, Ivy's Books, carries a broad selection of new and used books. Gus the dog works here.

NEW YORK LOOK

Map pp389-91   *Women's Clothing*

☎ 212-245-6511; 30 Lincoln Plaza, on Broadway btwn W 62nd & 63rd Sts; ⌚ 10am-9pm Mon-Thu, 10am-8pm Fri, 11am-9pm Sat, noon-7pm Sun; subway A, B, C, D, 1, 9 to 59th St–Columbus Circle

This minichain has stylish contemporary work outfits, evening wear and swimsuits of various designer labels (Theory, Tahari, Whistles etc). Next door is Look's small shoe shop, with good pickings of Italian pumps. Call for locations.

REALLY GREAT THINGS

Map pp389-91   *Clothing*

☎ 212-787-5354; 284 Columbus Ave; ⌚ 11am-7pm Mon-Sat, 1-6pm Sun; subway B, C, 1, 2, 3, 9 to 72 St

The name's a little trite at this friendly, ultra-classy shop but the changing collection of (mostly women's) clothing by hot European designers and top-rate knockoffs (not to mention their own shoe line for women) is – um, err, crikey – really great.

THEORY Map pp389-91   *Women's Clothing*

☎ 212-362-3676; 230 Columbus Ave; ⌚ 11am-7pm Mon-Sat, noon-5pm Sun; subway 1, 2, 3, 9 to 72 St

Fans of Theory – the clothing – should visit their new shop, where you can find the popular hip work outfits and plush blazers, as well as some items not available elsewhere, including Theory's leather boots.

ZABAR'S Map pp389-91   *Kitchenware*

☎ 212-787-2000; 2245 Broadway; ⌚ 8:30am-7:30pm Mon-Fri, 8am-8pm Sat, 9am-6pm Sun; subway 1, 9 to 79th St

A New York classic gourmet emporium, Zabar's is famous not only for its food, but also its large 2nd-floor kitchenware department. A $2.49

Top Five Bookstores

- **Argosy** (p271) Rare books, photographs and autographs.
- **Gotham Book Mart** (p272) Bypassed profane laws in name of literature.
- **Mysterious Bookshop** (p283) Who, what, when, where, why and how?
- **Oscar Wilde Memorial Bookshop** (p268) The world's oldest gay & lesbian bookshop.
- **Strand Book Store** (p268) Eight miles of used books.

Zabar's mug – with its distinctive orange lettering, kind of an uptown Dodge City font – is a cheap insiders-type gift from New York.

UPPER EAST SIDE

The glamour of Midtown's designer shops and department stores slides its way along Madison Ave into the Upper East Side, a posh neighborhood filled with residents who can actually afford shopping at places like – oh – Gucci, Prada, Barneys, J Paul Gaultier, Cartier, Versace, and maybe Valentino. The main shopping is on, and just off, Madison Ave from Midtown to about E 75th St.

Of course, these folks are more likely to cast away their finds from last season ('that old thing?') in nearby consignment shops than one Downtown, so budgeteers should venture the Upper East Side too.

See p160 for a walk that takes in the Upper East Side and Midtown's shopping highlights.

A SECOND CHANCE

Map pp389-91   *Consignment Clothing*

☎ 212-744-6041; 1109 Lexington Ave; ⌚ 11am-7pm Mon-Fri, 11am-6pm Sat; subway 6 to 77 St

A small shop with excellent pickings for recent women's designer-label clothing, handbags and accessories.

BANG & OLUFSEN

Map pp389-91   *Electronics*

☎ 212-879-6161; 952 Madison Ave; ⌚ 10am-6:30pm Mon-Wed & Fri & Sat, 10am-7pm Thu, noon-5pm Sun; subway 6 to 77th St

Come here for Bang & Olufsen's tip-top, Danish-designed audio and video equipment. It performs as well as it looks.

BARNEYS Map pp389-91   *Dept Store*

☎ 212-826-8900; 660 Madison Ave; ⌚ 10am-8pm Mon-Fri, 10am-7pm Sat, 11am-6pm Sun; subway N, R, W to Fifth Ave–59th St

Maybe Manhattan's best designer clothing selection, Barneys justifies its occasionally nose-raised staff (as if nostrils could say: 'too fat!' 'too poor!' 'too straight!') with its spot-on choice collections of the '00s' best designer duds (Marc Jacobs, Prada, Helmut Lang, Paul Smith and Miu Miu shoes). For less expensive deals (geared to a younger market), check out Co-Op Barneys on the 7th and 8th floors, or

Soho (p258), or at **Chelsea** (p270) with frantic 'I-got-it-first!' warehouse sales held in February and August.

BIG CITY KITE CO

Map pp389-91 *Kites*
☎ 212-472-2623; 1210 Lexington Ave; ⊙ 11am-6:30pm Mon-Wed & Fri, 11am-7:30pm Thu, 10am-6pm Sat; subway 4, 5, 6 to 86th St

Even the harshest kite skeptics – you know who you are – swoon over this small shop, a few blocks east of Central Park. The shop loves kiting, and will help you find one for same-day flight: lots of trick and sport kites, and more traditional ones. Favorites include the Wind Clipper Pirate Ship ($26) and the Martin Lester Legs Kite ($88) – a soccer bloke from the waist down.

BLOOMINGDALE'S

Map pp389-91 *Dept Store*
☎ 212-705-2000; 1000 3rd Ave at 59th St; ⊙ 10am-8:30pm Mon-Thu, 9am-10pm Fri & Sat, 11am-7pm Sun; subway 4, 5, 6 to 59th St, N, R, W to Lexington Ave–59th St

Massive 'Bloomies' is something like the Metropolitan Museum of Art to the shopping world: historic, sprawling, overwhelming and packed with bodies, but you'd be sorry to miss it. Navigate the mass (and dodge the dozens of automaton types trying to spray you with the latest scent) to browse and buy clothing and shoes from a who's-who of designers, including an increasing number of 'new-blood' collections. Note: please resist the temptation to make 'bloomer' jokes about the store's name with occasionally impatient staff.

CALVIN KLEIN

Map pp389-91 *Designer Clothing*
☎ 212-292-9000; 654 Madison Ave; ⊙ 10am-6pm Mon-Wed & Fri & Sat, 10am-7pm Sat, noon-6pm Sun; subway 4, 5, 6 to 59th St

Here's the two-floor showcase store for CK: the casual king, in all its faded-denim yet refined royal glory. You'll find more high-end wear here than at department stores elsewhere.

CARTIER Map pp389-91 *Jewelry*
☎ 212-472-6400; 828 Madison Ave; ⊙ 10am-6pm Mon-Wed & Fri, 10am-7pm Thu, 10am-5:30pm Sat; subway 6 to 68th St–Hunter College

A boutique selling Cartier's ultra-classy jewelry and accessories. Cartier has another location in **Midtown** (p271).

CHRISTIAN LOUBOUTIN

Map pp389-91 *Shoes*
☎ 212-396-1884; 941 Madison Ave; ⊙ 10am-6pm Mon-Sat; subway 6 to 77 St

Try on the trademark red-soled high-heeled shoes from this French (very French) designer who's not afraid of purple or emulating Louis XV styles. What else would you expect from a man who says black and beige soles are 'dull'?

CHUCKIES Map pp389-91 *Women's Shoes*
☎ 212-593-9898; 1073 Third Ave; ⊙ 10:45am-7:45pm Mon-Fri, 10:45am-7pm Sat, 12:30-7pm Sun; subway F to Lexington Av–63rd St

This is no pizza place. Chuckies features some top-tier, cutting-edge shoes from designers like Jimmy Choo, Miu Miu, Dolce & Gabbana, Stella McCartney and from its private label.

DOLCE & GABBANA

Map pp389-91 *Clothing*
☎ 212-249-4100; 825 Madison Ave btwn 68th and 69th Sts; ⊙ 10am-6pm Mon-Wed & Sat, 10am-7pm Thu, noon-5pm Sun; subway 6 to 68th St–Hunter College

Try on Dolce & Gabbana's formal wear here. The **Soho** (p259) branch carries the more casual D&G line.

GIORGIO ARMANI

Map pp389-91 *Designer Clothing*
☎ 212-988-9191; 760 Madison Ave; ⊙ 10am-6pm Mon-Wed & Fri & Sat, 10am-7pm Thu; subway F to Lexington Av–63rd St

Four slick, airy floors – looking more Midtown than most boutiques around here – where you can see the world-famous designer's most formal and classy offerings.

GIVENCHY

Map pp389-91 *Designer Clothing*
☎ 212-772-1040; 710 Madison Ave; ⊙ 10am-6pm Mon-Wed, Fri & Sat, 10am-7pm Thu, noon-6pm Sun; subway N, R, W to Fifth Ave–59th St, 4, 5, 6 to 59th St

Givenchy sells its traditional suits – with clean lines and quite French – and accessories for women, men and kids. Pick up one of their trademark bags.

JIMMY CHOO Map pp389-91 *Shoes*
☎ 212-759-7078; 716 Madison Ave; ⊙ 10am-6pm Mon-Wed & Fri & Sat, 10am-7pm Thu, noon-5pm Sun; subway F to Lexington Av–59th St

Head to Manhattan's second location for Jimmy Choo's highly elegant, high-heeled and high-priced shoes (and handbags). The original shop you've seen on *Sex and the City* is in **Midtown** (p273).

MISSONI Map pp389-91   *Designer Clothing*
☎ 212-517-9339; www.missoni.it; 1009 Madison Ave; ☽ 10am-6pm; subway 6 to 77th St
A boutique displaying the latest collection by the Italian family of designers famed for geometric striped knitwear and off-the-shoulder fringed sweaters. Preview the look on their fun website (or you can dance to its electronica soundtrack).

MORGENTHAL FREDERICS
Map pp389-91   *Spectacles*
☎ 212-838-3090; 699 Madison Ave; ☽ 9am-7pm Mon-Fri, 10am-6pm Sat, noon-6pm Sun; subway N, R, W to Fifth Ave—59th St, 4, 5, 6 to 59th St
Come for inventive, modern frames – some are bigger than life (like the celebs who wear them); the best are the two-tone plastic frames. There are other locations in town, including Soho at **Bergdorf Goodman** (p271) and **Shops at Colombus Circle** (p274). Call for details.

NELLIE M BOUTIQUE
Map pp389-91   *Women's Clothing*
☎ 212-996-4410; 1309 Lexington Ave; ☽ 10am-8pm Mon-Fri, 11am-8pm Sat, 11am-7pm Sun; subway 4, 5, 6 to 86th St
Off Madison, this inviting boutique carries upscale-but-hip clothing from smaller designer labels (such as Rebecca Taylor) than are found at most Upper East Side giants. Plenty of evening wear and accessories, as well as more sporty finds.

PRADA Map pp389-91   *Designer Clothing*
☎ 212-327-4200; 841 Madison Ave; ☽ 10am-6pm Mon-Wed, Fri & Sat; subway 6 to 68th St—Hunter College
Showcases the Milan company's expensive and ever-trendy offerings. There's another shop in **Soho** (p260) and two in **Midtown** (p274), one devoted to Prada's shoe line.

RALPH LAUREN
Map pp389-91   *Designer Clothing*
☎ 212-606-2100; 867 Madison Ave; ☽ 10am-6pm Mon-Wed & Fri, 10am-7pm Thu, noon-5pm Sun; subway 6 to 68th St—Hunter College
Housed in a beautiful 1890s mansion (one of Manhattan's few remaining residences of that era), Ralph's flagship store rewards the long stroll up Madison Ave, even if you've already stocked up on Polo gear elsewhere or at the smaller branch in **Greenwich Village** (p268). There's a big selection here, with an emphasis on more formal wear (particularly for men).

SCOOP MEN
Map pp389-91   *Men's Clothing*
☎ 212-535-5577; 1275 Third Ave; ☽ 11am-8pm Mon-Fri, 11am-7pm Sat, noon-6pm Sun; subway 6 to 77 St
This outpost of the **Soho** (p261) shop carries just the men's offerings. A bit more downtown/casual – designer jeans, shirts and sweaters – than most of the Upper East Side shops.

SHAKESPEARE & CO
Map pp389-91   *Bookstore*
☎ 212-570-0201; 939 Lexington Ave; ☽ 9am-8:30pm Mon-Fri, 10am-7pm Sat, 10am-5pm Sun; subway 6 to 68th St—Hunter College
Near Hunter College, this branch of this popular New York bookstore chain has a good academic selection. You'll also find branches in **Lower Manhattan** (p257), **Greenwich Village** (p268) and **Midtown** (p274).

SHERRY-LEHMAN
Map pp389-91   *Wine*
☎ 212-838-7500; 679 Madison Ave; ☽ 9am-7pm Mon-Sat; subway 4, 5, 6 to 59th St
This atmospheric store sells world-class wines and spirits.

SOTHEBY'S
Map pp389-91   *Auction House*
☎ 212-606-7000; www.sothebys.com; 1334 York Ave; subway 6 to 68th St—Hunter College
This famous auction house holds sales at least every week (the schedule is on the website). Thematic sales vary, including fine books, clocks, rugs, Russian art and period furniture.

TATIANA'S
Map pp389-91   *Consignment Clothing*
☎ 212-755-7744; 767 Lexington Ave; ☽ 11am-7pm Mon-Fri, 11am-6pm Sat; subway N, R, W to Lexington Ave—59th St, 4, 5, 6 to 59th St
One of the Upper East's best consignment shops, Tatiana's (just a couple of steps from Bloomingdale's) is stocked with women's designer-label evening wear, suits, skirts, tops and shoes. Often you can find last year's luxury pieces, practically new, at much lower prices.

VALENTINO

Map pp389-91   *Designer Clothing*

☎ 212-772-6969; 747 Madison Ave; ⏰ 10am-6pm Mon-Wed & Fri & Sat, 10am-7pm Thu; subway F to Lexington Ave–63rd St

Going to the Oscars? And you have several thousand dollars? This Italian designer's boutique, with sky-high prices, sells creations for the runway. Lots of red (dresses, ruffled blouses, cardigans etc) and genius-smart suits for men. If you're taking the train to the world of glamour, this is the end of the line.

Silk chemises, Pearl River Mart (p260)

VERA WANG

Map pp389-91   *Bridal Wear*

☎ 212-628-3400; 991 Madison Ave; ⏰ 9:30am-6pm Mon, Tue & Fri, 11am-7pm Wed & Thu, 9am-6pm Sat by appointment only; subway 6 to 77 St

For the best in bridal, many consider Vera to be the queen of the wedding-dress designers. Call ahead to arrange an hour-long session of trying on wedding dresses, evening wear and high-society couture. Bridesmaids should proceed directly to **Vera Wang** (☎ 212-628-9898; 980 Madison Ave; ⏰ by appointment only), the shop that's devoted entirely to them.

HARLEM

Harlem's main shopping strip has always been 125th St; it's just the shopkeepers that have changed. The recent and ongoing 'Harlem renaissance' is evident in new malls and big-time chains popping up (HMV, Old Navy, Nine West and H&M). NBA great Magic Johnson has opened an eponymous cinema and a Starbucks. Small businesses are still there, but are increasingly finding themselves 'priced out' of Harlem. The (unsigned) Harlem USA! mall (where you'll find HMV, Magic Theatres and Old Navy) is at 125th St and Frederick Douglass Blvd. More memorable finds can be found at smaller shops run by locals, including the following entries.

BOBBY'S HAPPY HOUSE

Map pp392-3   *Gospel & Blues Music*

☎ 212-663-5240; 2335 Frederick Douglass Blvd; ⏰ 11am-8pm; subway A, B, C, D to 125th St

This fantastic shop has a small but cherished collection of gospel ('ooolllddd-time gospel'), R&B and blues videos, CDs and cassettes. When it opened (on 125th St) in 1946 it was the first African American business on the street – original owner Bobby Robinson, who has produced blues artists like Elmore James, still runs the place (he's usually there Sunday afternoons, and is happy to have a chat). These days, you're likely to hear the shop before you see it, as the Happy House sets up blaring gospel videos in its can't-miss window showcase to attract passersby. If you stop to sway or sing along, you may not be the only one.

HARLEM MARKET

Map pp392-3   *Arts & Crafts*

☎ 212-987-8131; 116th St; ⏰ 10am-5pm; subway 2, 3 to 116th St

Enjoy some alfresco shopping at this popular marketplace, where you'll find items including African crafts, essential oils, incense, traditional clothing, CDs and bootleg videos.

HARLEM UNDERGROUND

Map pp392-3   *T-Shirts*

☎ 212-987-9385; 2027 Fifth Ave; ⏰ 10am-7pm Mon-Thu, 10am-8pm Fri & Sat; subway 2, 3 to 125th St

For 'Harlem' embroidered T-shirts and sweatshirts, stop in at this small shop, a couple of doors north of 125th St. Everything is made on location.

LIBERATION BOOKSTORE

Map pp392-3   *Bookstore*

☎ 212-281-4615; 421 Lenox Ave at 131st St;
⏰ 3-7pm Tue-Fri, noon-4pm Sat; subway 2, 3 to
125th St

This small bookstore has the city's best selection of African and African American history,
literature and art, though its opening hours
are a little loose.

SCARF LADY Map pp392-3   *Scarves & Hats*

☎ 212-862-7369; 408 Lenox Ave; ⏰ 11:30am-7pm
Tue-Sat; subway 2, 3 to 125th St

Mystery revealed: Paulette Gay *is* the Scarf
Lady. Her small boutique is crammed with
hundreds of her handmade, colorful scarves,
hats and other accessories.

Woodbury Common

Sounds like sacrilege to suggest leaving New York to
shop, but many locals (and tourists) do. **Woodbury
Common Premium Outlets** (☎ 845-928-4000;
www.premiumoutlets.com; 498 Red Apple Court,
Central Valley, NY), 90 minutes north of the city,
is home to over 200 top-tier stores selling (often)
marked-down clothing. All the designers have
shops (Gucci, Christian Dior, Versace, Prada, Marc
Jacobs etc), and you can find over 30 shoe outlets,
and plenty of sports gear and luggage. The colonial-
style 'village' is connected by pedestrian lanes and
surrounded by parking lots.

You can drive there (see website for directions) or
go by bus or train. The easiest way is to take a **Gray
Line New York** (☎ 212-445-0848, 800-669-0051
ext 3; adult/child $35/17.50; ⏰ departs 8:30am-
2:45pm, returns 3:30pm-9:25pm) bus, which has
daily trips for shoppers.

BROOKLYN

Across the East River, Brooklyn has a well-
established shopping scene, notably in three
neighborhoods. Williamsburg's youthful
hipster district centers along Bedford Ave,
with side-by-side shops and cafes. Several
vintage shops are here, including a thrift
store, as well as more upscale boutiques.

Atlantic Ave, running east–west near
Brooklyn Heights, has long been heralded as
a mecca for antique and furnishings shops,
and heading south from Atlantic, Smith St
is lined with local designers' boutiques. Pick

up shopping guides to Atlantic and Bococa
for neighborhood shops. Residential Park
Slope, just west of Prospect Park, has a good
selection of laid-back clothing shops and
bookstores along Fifth Ave (slightly more
hip than Lower East Side) and Seventh Ave
(slightly more Upper West Side).

AMARCORD Map p394   *Vintage Clothing*

☎ 718-963-4001; 223 Bedford Ave, Williamsburg;
⏰ 1-8pm; subway L to Bedford Ave

On Williamsburg's chief artery (between S 4th
and S 5th Sts, a couple blocks from the Bedford
Ave subway station), this Amarcord (unlike its
East Village, p264) cousin, stocks men's classic
vintage clothing in addition to women's.

BEACON'S CLOSET

Map p394   *Vintage Clothing*

☎ 718-486-0816; 88 N 11th St, Williamsburg;
⏰ noon-9pm Mon-Fri, 11am-8pm Sat & Sun; subway
L to Bedford Ave

Twenty-something hipsters find this giant
Williamsburg warehouse of vintage clothing
part goldmine, part grit. Lots of coats, polyester tops and '70s-era T-shirts are handily
displayed by color, but the sheer mass can
take time to conquer. From the L Station, walk
along Bedford Ave from 7th St to 11th St, turn
left (toward Manhattan), and go two blocks;
it's between Berry and White Sts.

The smaller, more manageable branch on
Fifth Ave (Map p395; ☎ 718-230-1630; 220 Fifth
Ave) stocks the cream of the crop only.

BREUKELEN/BARK

Map p394   *Gifts & Accessories*

☎ 718-246-0024, 718-625-8997; 369 Atlantic Ave;
⏰ noon-7pm Tue-Sat, noon-6pm Sun; subway A, C, G
to Hoyt Schermerhorn

These two modern accessories shops – selling
swank products for the home and body, many
not found elsewhere in town – share a space
on Atlantic Ave. Check out Bark's cameras that
(willfully) distort images with color lenses and
softened corners.

EIDOLON Map p395   *Women's Clothing*

☎ 718-638-8194; 233 Fifth Ave; ⏰ noon-8pm
Tue-Sat, noon-7pm Sun; subway M, R to Union St

This popular boutique is a Fifth Ave highlight
for its selection of women's clothing (work
suits, dresses, tops, hats, shoes etc) made by
local designers. The stylish Gentle Souls pumps
and boots are tip-top.

Shopping – Brooklyn

HEIGHTS BOOKS Map p394 *Used Books*

☎ 718-624-4876; 109 Montague St; ◷ 10am-11pm Sun-Thu, 10am-midnight Fri & Sat; subway M, R to Court St, 2, 3 to Clark St

It's tight book-browsing at Heights as floor space is given over to fully-stocked shelves rather than aisles, but it's well organized, and there are tons of books.

Clothing Sizes
Measurements approximate only, try before you buy

Women's Clothing
Aus/UK	8	10	12	14	16	18
Europe	36	38	40	42	44	46
Japan	5	7	9	11	13	15
USA	6	8	10	12	14	16

Women's Shoes
Aus/USA	5	6	7	8	9	10
Europe	35	36	37	38	39	40
France only	35	36	38	39	40	42
Japan	22	23	24	25	26	27
UK	3½	4½	5½	6½	7½	8½

Men's Clothing
Aus	92	96	100	104	108	112
Europe	46	48	50	52	54	56
Japan	S		M	M		L
UK/USA	35	36	37	38	39	40

Men's Shirts (Collar Sizes)
Aus/Japan	38	39	40	41	42	43
Europe	38	39	40	41	42	43
UK/USA	15	15½	16	16½	17	17½

Men's Shoes
Aus/UK	7	8	9	10	11	12
Europe	41	42	43	44½	46	47
Japan	26	27	27½	28	29	30
USA	7½	8½	9½	10½	11½	12½

JACQUES TORRES CHOCOLATE

Map p394 *Chocolate*

☎ 718-875-9772; www.mrchocolate.com; 66 Water St; ◷ 9am-7pm Mon-Sat; subway A, C to High St, F to York St

Serious chocolatier JT runs this small European-style store in Dumbo, with three-table café, filled with the most velvety and innovative chocolates ever crafted. Take a few to the nearby Empire Fulton Ferry State Park for a snack and a view between the Brooklyn and Manhattan bridges. The shop also does a brisk Internet business.

OLIVE'S VERY VINTAGE

Map p394 *Vintage Clothing*

☎ 718-243-9094; 434 Court St; ◷ noon-8pm Mon-Fri, 11am-8pm Sat, 11am-7pm Sun; subway F, G to Carroll St

Past most of the Court St shops, this excellent Carroll Gardens boutique is well worth the walk if you're after women's vintage clothing (such as shoes, tops, dresses, coats, gloves and other accessories) dating as far back as the 1940s.

SPACIAL ETC

Map p394 *Clothing & Accessories*

☎ 718-599-7962; 199 Bedford Ave, Williamsburg; ◷ 11am-9pm; subway L to Bedford Ave

This eye-catching Williamsburg corner shop, at N 6th St, has select pickings of various clothing and gear for the young professional's home. There's always a few tempting pairs of shoes, or some knitwear made by a local designer. It's one block south from the L station.

Sleeping

Sleeping

Hotels in NYC have become so swanky and cool that even New Yorkers themselves clamor to stay in them – for bar scenes, high-end eateries and the general see-and-be-seen world of their lobbies and lounges. Stylish 'boutique' inns are the result of a still-exploding trend that was ushered in by celeb hotelier Ian Schrager, who opened Morgans in 1985, followed by the Paramount, Royalton and Hudson. Today, New York has a larger percentage of independent hotels than any big city in the country, making it an excellent place to put some thought into your choice and find a spot that really suits your personality and needs.

While boutique hotels may get the most play, there is definitely something for everyone, in nearly every neighborhood: the business-class luxury of the **Ritz-Carlton** (p293), the country-B&B charm of **Inn on 23rd Street** (p297), the trendsetting style of the slick **W** (p298) chain, and the budget comfort and character of the **Gershwin Hotel** (p298). There are even companies that will get you into someone's apartment, part of a system of house shares and short-term sublets (p299), which has blossomed in recent years. Still, even though the city offers more than 75,000 hotel rooms, reservations are highly recommended.

The accommodations industry suffered an economic blow after September 11 but has since rebounded, with prices back up to their average of $275 a night and visitors quick to fill the spaces. That said, it's not too hard to find a budget room – that's less than $150 by New York's definition – or even a space for $50 or less in a youth hostel, if that's your scene. If $275 sounds cheap to you, not to worry: the sky's the limit, with some tricked-out, best-view-in-town suites going for an audacious $15,000 nightly! (Be aware that prices quoted in this book do not include city hotel taxes, which are a steep 13.25%. Prices also fluctuate depending on the season.)

LOWER MANHATTAN

Most hotels around the Financial District and Battery Park City cater to the business set, so it's not necessarily the place to book if you're looking for boutique style or hoppin' scenes at weekends, when businesses close and the streets get quiet. Some folks will love the weekend deals, though, as well as the proximity to some big tourist attractions, such as the Statue of Liberty, Battery Park waterfront area and the South Street Seaport. Beware of the preponderance of big-name chains in these parts; unfortunately, the place with the most flair, Regents Wall Street, closed up shop in early 2004.

Brave New Rooms

Finding bargains is really not such a skill anymore – as long as you know how to use the Internet and decide on a price that's right for you, you're in. It's thanks to the slew of websites that help you find discounted quarters and even name your own prices, just like the mega-popular sites that do the same for discounted airline tickets.

Priceline.com is a straightforward site that lets you choose the area of Manhattan you'd like to stay in, the level of hotel room (one to five stars) and bid on the price you'd like to pay. A different version of this is **Hotwire.com**, which allows you to pick a neighborhood and tells you a price, but not the hotel. (Some hotels offer helpful feedback reviews from prior users.) The catch, on all such sites, is that you must enter your credit card information before you know where you'll be staying; if the type of hotel you requested agrees to match your price, you'll automatically be charged for the room and notified that you indeed have a reservation. So if you're not so picky, and price is your biggest concern, this is the way to go.

Travelers who want to know where they'll be up front are better off browsing the offerings at one of the following discount sites: **Orbitz.com**, which lets you choose your hotel's star rating and amenities and then gives you several options, as do **Hotels.com**, **Hoteldiscounts.com** and **Travelzoo.com**, all claiming prices that are up to 70% less than the rack rates. **Justnewyorkhotels.com**, **Newyork.dealsonhotels.com**, **Newyorkcityhotelstoday.com** and **NYC-hotels.net** work the same way, but are focused strictly on NYC. Checking individual hotel websites is also worth a shot, especially during slow seasons like midwinter, as discounts that are on par with Internet prices are sometimes offered directly from the inn.

BATTERY PARK CITY RITZ-CARLTON

Map pp380-1   *Deluxe International*

☎ 212-344-0800; www.ritz-carlton.com; 2 West St at Battery Pl; s/d/ste from $240/400/800; subway 4, 5 to Bowling Green

It's hard to pick the best amenity of this luxurious, 38-story glass and brick tower, but if pressed perhaps the sweeping harbor and city views would reign; they're best seen through the telescopes that sit in all waterside rooms and suites. Then again, maybe the big marble baths (and 'bath butler' service, of all things), goose-down pillows, on-site spa and gym, two top-notch restaurants (with stunning tableside views at Rise), 'technology butler,' or a complimentary Downtown car service would be most exciting. Regardless, this is the life.

BEST WESTERN SEAPORT INN

Map pp380-1   *Chain Hotel*

☎ 212-766-6600, 800-468-3569; www.seaportinn.com; 33 Peck Slip btwn Front & Water Sts; s/d $160/180; subway A, C to Broadway–Nassau St, J, M, Z, 2, 3, 4, 5 to Fulton St

Despite its blah chain style, the Seaport Inn offers some striking water views from its terrace rooms, and it sits in the shadow of the grand Brooklyn Bridge. It's got a small on-site gym, high-speed Internet and services for assisting deaf patrons. Plus, the rate can't be beat, and neither can its waterfront feel.

HOLIDAY INN WALL STREET

Map pp380-1   *Business Hotel*

☎ 212-232-7700; www.holidayinnwsd.com; 15 Gold St at Platt St; s/d/ste from $175/300/500; subway A, C to Broadway–Nassau St, J, M, Z, 2, 3, 4, 5 to Fulton St

Office-equipped rooms featuring wired desktop computers and complimentary cell phones make it clear this recent addition is courting a serious business crowd – but special weekend rates starting at $99 are pretty welcoming to anyone looking for that combo of budget and class. The decor is minimal – boring brick building, staid lobby and standard-order hotel-chain room – but beds are comfy and the high-tech aspect makes contacting home damn easy.

MILLENIUM HILTON

Map pp380-1   *Business Hotel*

☎ 212-693-2001; www.hilton.com; 55 Church St; r from $350; subway N, R to Cortland St

Reopened after its post-September 11 renovation (the hotel is set directly across from the World Trade Center site), the Millenium is better than ever, thanks to a $32 million infusion. Rooms have dramatic views (including some eerie ones overlooking the World Trade Center site), plasma TVs and all the high-tech amenities you'll ever need. Plus there's a gorgeous workout facility, a glass-enclosed heated swimming pool, and fine dining in the Church & Day restaurant.

WALL STREET INN

Map pp380-1   *Business Boutique*

☎ 212-747-1500, 800-695-8284; www.thewallstreetinn.com; 9 South William St at Broad St; s/d $250/450, from $159 Fri-Sun; subway 2, 3 to Wall St, 4, 5 to Bowling Green

It's nice to have a smaller, more personal option in Lower Manhattan, especially when it's housed in an intimate, renovated landmark building in the historic Stone Street district. The primary target here is, once again, the businessperson. Weekend rates lure in families and traveling couples who like the on-site fitness center, included breakfast and lovely marble bathtubs.

Top Five Boutique Hotels

- **Chambers** (p300) A marvel of modern design.
- **Hotel Gansevoort** (p295) The sexiest Meatpacking District arrival yet.
- **Hudson** (p301) Ian Schrager's latest is the epitome of inn style.
- **Mercer** (p293) It's so, Soho cool.
- **On the Ave** (p304) Uptown style at way-Downtown prices.

TRIBECA & SOHO

You'll find plenty of flash and style in these parts, which serve as home to some of the coolest little inns in town. Plus the location cannot be beat, as you're in walking distance to not only most harbor highlights, but serious dining, drinking and dancing options as well. Most of the hotel lobbies down here will get you as excited as your very own room.

MERCER Map pp382-5   *Boutique Hotel*

☎ 212-966-6060; 147 Mercer St at Prince St; s/d/ste from $400/575/1100; subway N, R, W to Prince St

It's sleek and grand and so cool that it (annoyingly) doesn't even have a sign. But you'll spot the Mercer right away as it's the place where thin and stylish hipsters are entering, their Tumi bags rolling quietly at their heels. The hushed lobby features a library, the excellent restaurant is an eatery for discerning locals, and the rooms – wooden-floored lofts with flooding sunlight and exposed brick – evoke the once-upon-a-time artist's way the 'hood was known for.

60 THOMPSON

Map pp382-5   *Boutique Hotel*

☎ 212-431-0400, 877-431-0400; www.60thompson .com; 60 Thompson St btwn Broome & Spring Sts; s/d/ste $370/450/550; subway C, E to Spring St
Another snazzy boutique hotel, this 100-room gem is distinguished by its gorgeous rooftop terrace (with views of the Empire State Building), an intimate courtyard, and rooms featuring wrought-iron balconies, down duvets, leather-paneled walls and the high-backed custom-designed Thompson Chair. The intimate Thom restaurant – with circular booths, steak frites and homemade ice cream – is also a winner.

SOHO GRAND HOTEL

Map pp382-5   *Deluxe International*

☎ 212-965-3000, 800-965-3000; www.sohogrand.com; 310 West Broadway; s/d/ste $260/400/1600; subway A, C, E to Canal St
The nondescript outside belies the Soho Grand's striking interior, where a glass and cast-iron stairway carries you to the sleek and airy lobby. Since the hotel first opened in 1996, it has maintained its high status and models and publishing types can always be found in the slick Grand Bar and Lounge. Its 367 rooms feature cool, clean lines, plus Frette linens and Kiehl's grooming products. Its newer sister location is the **Tribeca Grand** (Map pp380-1; ☎ 212-519-6600; www.tribecagrand.com; 2 Sixth Ave at Church, Walker & White Sts; subway 1, 9 to Franklin St) with 203 gorgeous rooms and similar amenities.

Cheap Sleeps
COSMOPOLITAN HOTEL

Map pp382-5   *Budget Hotel*

☎ 212-566-1900, 888-895-9400; www.cosmohotel .com; 95 West Broadway; s/d $109/149; subway 1, 2, 3, 9 to Chambers St
The 105 pastel-hued rooms of this inn are lacking in decor, but the hotel is affordable and spotless, and sitting in a prime Tribeca location.

LOWER EAST SIDE

Having a friend with a cool extra bed used to be the closest you'd get to trendy digs in this part of town. But the hotel craze has finally hit here, thanks to a new option from the folks at design magazine *Surface*. Two other options, both with low rates, let you stay right in the midst of all the clubs, lounges and eateries that make the Lower East Side so impossibly hip – just don't expect their linens to be as stylish as your meal.

HOWARD JOHNSON EXPRESS INN

Map pp382-5   *Chain Hotel*

☎ 212-358-8844; www.hojo.com; 135 E Houston St at Forsyth St; s/d $129/$169; subway F, V to Lower East Side–Second Ave
Sure, it's bland and not so hip but it's only a few years old, and the newness makes it clean and fresh, and the location is prime. Beds are comfy, water pressure is excellent, photos from local artists adorn the walls of the teeny lobby and you get free bagels and pastries in the morning. If that doesn't suit you, hit the classic **Yonah Shimmel Bakery** (p179) next door for a knish.

SURFACE HOTEL

Map pp382-5   *Boutique Hotel*

☎ 212-475-2600; www.surfacehotel.com; 107 Rivington St btwn Essex & Ludlow Sts; r from $250; subway F to Delancey St, J, M, Z to Delancey–Essex Sts
This sleek, $30 million high-rise was plagued by construction setbacks, which kept delaying its anticipated grand opening. But it finally opened its doors in 2004, making this 20-story luxury inn the place for Downtowners. Its steel-and-glass tower, designed by Paul Stallings, and owned by the California-based *Surface* mag, affords excellent views, and an on-site restaurant and nightclub give you all the excitement you need right at one address.

Cheap Sleeps
OFF SOHO SUITES

Map pp382-5   *Budget Hotel*

☎ 212-979-9815, 800-633-7646; www.offsoho.com; 11 Rivington St btwn Chrystie St & Bowery; r/ste $79/150; subway B, D to Grand St, J, M, Z to Bowery
If you can endure the cheap and nausea-inducing interior decoration and focus on the money you're saving, you'll be just fine. Suites have kitchenettes, there's a 10% discount for

stays of a week or more, and the excellent location straddles Chinatown and the Lower East Side.

EAST VILLAGE

Not much going on, bed-wise, in this part of town. The two options below are both Cheap Sleeps – that's all you'll find here – but both have their share of perks, the primary one being the completely cool location.

EAST VILLAGE B&B

Map pp382-5   B&B
☎ 212-260-1865; 244 E 7th St btwn Aves C & D, apt 5-6; r $100; subway F, V to Second Ave–Lower East Side
This lesbian-owned find is a popular oasis for Sapphic couples who want peace and quiet in the midst of the noisy East Village scene (**Meow Mix**, p238, is right nearby). Housed in a residential apartment building on a lovely block, the three rooms (one single and two double) are way stylish – bold linens, modern art, gorgeous wooden floors – and the huge (by NYC standards) shared living room space is filled with light, beautiful paintings from around the globe, exposed brickwork and a big-screen TV. Breakfast is included – as is use of the washing machine!

ST MARKS HOTEL

Map pp382-5   Budget Hotel
☎ 212-674-2192; 2 St Marks Pl at Third Ave; s/d $90/100; subway 6 to Astor Pl
It's still a bit rough around the edges (though it's had a recent facelift) and is perched on a noisy block, but snag a room in the back, enjoy the front-desk clerk's charms and settle in: all the Downtown culture you desire is right outside the door.

WEST (GREENWICH) VILLAGE

Old-school charm, intimate quarters, reasonable prices and lots of gay-friendliness are what you'll find here – not to mention a couple of slick, impressive newcomers. It's a perfect Downtown lodging location for those who want the comforts of Midtown and coolness of below 14th Street, without the edginess of the East Side.

ABINGDON GUEST HOUSE

Map pp382-5   B&B
☎ 212-243-5384; www.abingdonguesthouse.com; 13 Eighth Ave at Jane St; s/d $160/190; subway A, C, E to 14th St, L to Eighth Ave
Without looking out the window, you'll swear you've landed in a New England country inn. Elegant, comfortable rooms feature four-poster beds, fireplaces, scads of exposed brick and billowing curtains. Each room has a slightly different style – one is clean whites and lavenders while another is deep earth tones with handsome furniture – but each one is a score. Do peer outside though, and the lovely bustle of this stretch of Eighth Ave will assure you you're in New York City.

HOTEL GANSEVOORT

Map pp382-5   Boutique Hotel
☎ 212-206-6700; www.hotelgansevoort.com; 18 Ninth Ave at 13th St; s/d/ste $395/500/625; subway A, C, E to 14th St, L to Eighth Ave
This 187-room luxury hotel in the trendy Meatpacking District opened its doors in January 2004, and was an instant hit. Could it be the 400-thread-count linens? Hypoallergenic down duvets? Plasma TVs? Steam showers? Yes, yes and more yesses. But we'd also credit the jaw-dropping views (especially from the rooms with balconies), luscious spas, pet-friendly floors and a fitness center. Not to mention the simple fact that it's in the fastest gentrifying 'hood in Manhattan, now saturated with trendy bistros and shops rather than yesterday's trannie hookers and slippery suet from sides of beef.

INCENTRA VILLAGE HOUSE

Map pp382-5   B&B
☎ 212-206-0007; 32 Eighth Ave at 12th St; r $120-199; subway A, C, E to 14th St, L to Eighth Ave
These two redbrick, landmark townhouses were built in 1841 and later became the city's first gay inn. Today, its 12 rooms get booked way in advance by queer travelers; call early to get in on its gorgeous Victorian parlor (featuring a baby grand piano that's often the site of a show-tune sing-along) and antique-filled rooms, some with fireplaces and four-poster beds.

SOHO HOUSE Map pp382-5 Boutique Hotel
☎ 212-627-9800; www.sohohouseny.com; 29-35 Ninth Ave at 13th St; r $250-795; subway A, C, E to 14th St, L to Eighth Ave
A new sibling of London's Soho House, this private social club for the high-fashion VIP

crowd has 24 guest rooms for nonmembers – but don't expect to snag one easily in this serious hot spot. If you do get beyond the proverbial velvet ropes, you'll find stylin' cribs with a mix of antique and modern furniture, steam showers, Grey Goose minibars, plasma TVs and complimentary condoms. Guests also gain entry to the private screening room and luxurious Cowshed Spa.

WASHINGTON SQUARE HOTEL

Map pp382-5   *Budget Hotel*
☎ 212-777-9515, 800-222-0418; www.washington squarehotel.com; 103 Waverly Pl btwn MacDougal St & Sixth Ave; s/d $130/165; subway A, C, E, B, D, F, V to W 4 St
This intimate lodge sits right off the corner of Washington Square Park and practically on the campus of NYU. The lobby is unexpectedly elegant, rooms off the skinny hallways are cramped and basic but recently renovated, and the vibe is a lovely sort of grown-up bohemian. An attached restaurant and lounge offers a jazz brunch on Sundays.

Cheap Sleeps
LARCHMONT HOTEL

Map pp382-5   *Indie Inn*
☎ 212-989-9333; www.larchmonthotel.com; 27 W 11th St btwn Fifth & Sixth Aves; s/d $80/109; subway F, V to 14th St
This European-like inn is cozy and affordable, with shared bathrooms and communal kitchens. The hotel's 52 rooms include sinks and perks such as robes and slippers, plus a plum spot on a beautiful, leafy Fifth Ave block. Reserve early, as it fills up fast.

CHELSEA

Plenty of options here, most with indie charm, local lore and gay-friendliness. You're bound to find something, especially if you're sick of massive lobbies, high-rises or cutting-edge technology. It's a great location for circuit boys who don't want to be too far from all the entertainment.

CHELSEA HOTEL Map pp382-5   *Indie Inn*
☎ 212-243-3700; 222 W 23rd St; s & d from $135, ste from $325; subway C, E, 1, 9 to 23rd St
This infamous inn is a literary and cultural landmark brimming with New York nostalgia and art by past and present residents. The list

of noteworthy guests and residents is long, from Dylan Thomas and Bob Dylan to Arthur Miller and Arthur C Clarke. This is also where Sid Vicious killed Nancy Spungen (that should help you sleep easy) and where *The Professional* was filmed. The cheapest rooms have a shared bathroom and the most expensive suites have a separate living room, dining area and kitchen; every room has high ceilings, air-con and its own unique style.

CHELSEA LODGE Map pp382-5   *B&B*
☎ 212-243-4499; www.chelsealodge.com; 318 W 20th St btwn Eighth & Ninth Aves; s & d from $105-195, ste $225; subway C, E to 23rd St
A European-style inn housed in a landmark brownstone of Chelsea's historic district. The small, Americana-appointed rooms have hardwood floors, comfy beds and plenty of light. You'll get lots of charm and attention for a reasonable price, not to mention a room in the loveliest part of the neighborhood.

CHELSEA PINES INN Map pp382-5   *B&B*
☎ 212-929-1023; www.chelseapinesinn.com; 317 W 14th St btwn Eighth & Ninth Aves; r $99-139, winter special $79; subway A, C, E to 14th St, L to Eighth Ave
It's gay-man central at this sweet, unique little inn, where vintage movie posters plaster the walls, a greenhouse and small back patio provide peaceful nooks and the cute and friendly desk guys dole out advice on where to eat, party and cruise. Rooms are small but homey.

COLONIAL HOUSE INN

Map pp382-5   B&B

☎ 212-243-9669; www.colonialhouseinn.com; 318 W 22nd St btwn Eighth & Ninth Aves; r $80-125, with bathroom $125-160; subway C, E to 23rd St

This friendly gay inn is serene and graceful, but with all the upbeat charm you'd expect from proprietor Mel Cheren, who ran the legendary hip-hop club Paradise Garage. The airy lobby doubles as a modern-art gallery, and rooms range from economy (bed, dresser) to deluxe (fireplace, fridge). A rooftop deck has great views and nude sunbathers.

INN ON 23RD ST

Map pp386-8   B&B

☎ 212-463-0330; www.innon23rd.com; 131 W 23rd St btwn Sixth & Seventh Aves; s & d $179-259, ste from $329; subway C, E, 1, 9 to 23rd St

This B&B is a true find: the hushed lobby exudes Victorian charm but is not without quirks, such as the slumped-over 'dead' mannequin that scares you when you first walk in. Rooms are luxurious and swathed in fanciful fabrics, and breakfast is served in an elegant parlor.

MARITIME HOTEL

Map pp382-5   Boutique Hotel

☎ 212-242-4300; www.themaritimehotel.com; 363 W 16th St btwn Eighth & Ninth Aves; s & d $195-260, ste $395-1100; subway A, C, E to 14th St, L to Eighth Ave

Originally the site of the National Maritime Union headquarters (and more recently a shelter for homeless teens), this white tower dotted with portholes has been transformed into a marine-themed luxury inn by a hip team of architects. It feels like a luxury ocean-liner, as its 120 rooms, each with their own round window, are compact and teak-paneled; the most expensive quarters feature outdoor showers, a private garden and sweeping Hudson views. An eatery and outdoor cocktail lounge are precious perks.

Cheap Sleeps

CHELSEA CENTER HOSTEL

Map pp382-5   Hostel

☎ 212-643-0214; www.chelseacenterhostel.com; 313 W 29th St btwn Eighth & Ninth Aves; dm $25; subway A, C, E to 34th St–Penn Station

This 18-bed hostel is a quiet, affordable favorite for backpackers and European budget travelers.

CHELSEA INN

Map pp382-5   B&B

☎ 212-645-8989, 800-640-6469; www.chelseainn.com; 46 W 17th St btwn Fifth & Sixth Aves; s/d/ste $89/140/190; subway L, N, R, 4, 5, 6 to 14th St–Union Sq

Made up of two adjoining townhouses, this funky-charming hideaway has small but comfortable rooms that look like they were furnished entirely from flea markets or grandma's attic. It's character on a budget, just a bit east of the most desirable part of this happening 'hood. Special winter rates go as low as $79.

CHELSEA INTERNATIONAL HOSTEL

Map pp382-5   Hostel

☎ 212-647-0010; www.chelseahostel.com; 251 W 20th St btwn Seventh & Eighth Aves; dm/r $25/60; subway C, E, 1, 9 to 23rd St

A festive, international scene defines this hostel, where the back patio serves as party central. Bunk rooms sleep four to six and amenities include communal kitchens and laundry facilities. You must show your passport when you check in, but you don't need to be from abroad, and there's a two-week maximum stay.

CHELSEA STAR HOTEL

Map pp386-8   Hostel

☎ 212-244-7827; www.starhotelny.com; 300 W 30th St at Eighth Ave; dm/r $30/70; subway A, C, E to 34th St–Penn Station

A European-style hostel with a twist in the form of private rooms done up in various themes, from *Star Trek* to *Absolutely Fabulous*. You'll also find a patio, bike and skate rentals and a lovely mixed crowd at this popular spot.

UNION SQUARE, FLATIRON DISTRICT & GRAMERCY PARK

Though often overlooked, this area is prime lodging ground for two main reasons: it's quiet, and because of the location. You'll find inns that feel like you have discovered them, leafy, residential streets, and close proximity (in walking distance) to both Midtown and East Village attractions. It's long on character and short on space, so book early.

GRAMERCY PARK HOTEL

Map pp382-5 *Indie Inn*

☎ 212-475-4320, 800-221-4083;
www.gramercyparkhotel.com; 2 Lexington Ave at 21st
St; s/d/ste from $150/160/200; subway 6 to 23rd St

This New York institution is where JFK Jr lived as a boy, Humphrey Bogart married Helen Mencken (on the roof garden) and Babe Ruth drank to excess (and then some) in the bar. If you stay here, you'll overlook Gramercy Park and even receive a key to that private garden haven. Rooms were recently renovated, and the lively piano bar off the lobby is a must-see.

Peninsula (p302)

INN AT IRVING PLACE

Map pp382-5 *B&B*

☎ 212-533-4600; www.innatirving.com; 56 Irving Pl
at E 17th St; r from $325; subway L, N, R, 4, 5, 6 to 14th
St–Union Sq

A charming 11-room landmark townhouse just a few blocks south of Gramercy Park, it's got an excellent location, smooth ambience and a reputation for romance (all the rooms have fireplaces and beds craving more action than sleep). Think an Edith Wharton novel.

MARCEL Map pp386-8 *Boutique Hotel*

☎ 212-696-3800; www.nychotels.com; 201 E 24th St
at Third Ave; s/d $100/200; subway 6 to 23rd St

Minimalist and chic, with earth-tone touches, this inn is popular with the fashion-industry

crowd. Rooms on the avenue have great views, and the sleek lounge, Spread, is a great place to unwind from a day of touring. Other classy inns run by Amsterdam Hospitality group are **Bentley** (p305), **Moderne** (Map pp226-7; ☎ 212-397-6767; 243 W 55th St) and **Amsterdam Court House** (Map pp226-7; ☎ 212-459-1000; 226 W 50th St).

PARK SOUTH HOTEL

Map pp386-8 *Boutique Hotel*

☎ 212-448-0888; www.parksouthhotel.com; 122 E
28th St; r $179-395; subway 6 to 28th St

Housed in a historic 1906 building, the classic-meets-contemporary style features a high-ceilinged lobby, sweet views of the Chrysler Building, and richly hued, handsome quarters. The on-site restaurant, the Black Duck, serves classy bistro fare.

W NEW YORK – UNION SQUARE

Map pp382-5 *Classy Chain Hotel*

☎ 212-253-9119, 877-946-8357; www.whotels.com;
201 Park Ave South at 17th St; r from $319; subway L,
N, Q, R, 4, 5, 6 to 14th St–Union Sq

This hipster pad demands a black wardrobe and a platinum credit card. Like all the W hotels, everything is top of the line, comfortable and classy here, and its location right on bucolic Madison Square Park is a big perk. But reserve early if you want to stay at this ultra-popular place. The W has several Manhattan outposts, including the **W New York – Tuscany** (Map pp386-8; ☎ 877-946-8357; 120 E 39th St at Lexington Ave) and **W New York – Times Square** (Map pp226-7; ☎ 877-946-8357; 1567 Broadway at 47th St); visit their website for more details.

Cheap Sleeps
CARLTON ARMS HOTEL

Map pp386-8 *Budget Hotel*

☎ 212-679-0680; www.carltonarms.com; 160 E 25th
St at Third Ave; s/d/tr $70/85/100; subway 6 to 23rd St

Europeans flock to this quirky, affordable spot that features artist-designed rooms with various themes, from rhinos to English cottage. Weekly stays bring further discounts.

GERSHWIN HOTEL

Map pp386-8 *Indie Inn*

☎ 212-545-8000; www.gershwinhotel.com; 7 E 27th
St at Fifth Ave; dm/r $35/99; subway 6 to 28th St

Just four blocks north of the Flatiron Building, this popular and funky spot (half youth hostel, half hotel) is full of original artwork (starting with its pod-like structures adorning the entrance), touring bands and other fabulousness. It has a cool new lobby bar, and sits right next door to the **Museum of Sex** (p108). In some ways, it feels more bohemian than the more historic, classic and pricey Chelsea Hotel, and because young travelers dig it so much beds can be hard to come by. Reservations and reconfirmations are a must.

HOTEL 17 Map pp382-5 *Budget Hotel*
☎ 212-475-2845; www.hotel17ny.com; 225 E 17th St btwn Second & Third Aves; s/d/tr $70/87/110; subway N, Q, R, 4, 5, 6 to 14th St–Union Sq, L to Third Ave
This popular spot has serious character – and that's not even counting its past as a location for Woody Allen's *Manhattan Murder Mystery* and a Madonna photo shoot. There's an old-fashioned lift, a cool chandelier in the lobby, vintage wallpaper and a worn but chic charm to the small, quiet rooms.

MIDTOWN

Options are endless in Midtown, the accommodations capital of New York City. Prices can go as high as several thousand dollars and as low as $75. You'll find massive high-rise chains, fabulous boutiques, charming inns and closet-like cheapos. Best of all, you're perfectly situated to get to any attraction in the city in about 20 minutes or less.

ALEX Map pp386-8 *Boutique Hotel*
☎ 212-867-5100; 205 E 45th St btwn Second & Third Aves; r $375-1500; subway 4, 5, 6, 7, S to Grand Central–42nd St
The brand-new 33-story luxury inn from celeb architect David Rockwell features bamboo furnishings, terrazzo floors, original photographs, huge suites, flat-screen TVs and a way-hyped restaurant, Riingo, from the same stars that brought New Yorkers **Aquavit** (p186).

ALGONQUIN Map pp226-7 *Luxury Hotel*
☎ 212-840-6800, 800-555-8000; www.algonquin hotel.com; 59 W 44th St btwn Fifth & Sixth Aves; r $189-699; subway B, D, F, V to 42nd St, 4, 5, 6, 7 to Grand Central
This is the storied classic of Dorothy Parker's Algonquin Round Table fame. It still attracts visitors with its upscale wood and chintz decor, and classic 1902 lobby with handsome sconces and carpets. It's got a 24-hour fitness center, and well-lit and comfortable (though cramped) quarters.

Private Apartments

The tight hotel market – not to mention the massive expense of renting an apartment here – has given birth to a cottage industry of sorts, with enterprising New Yorkers turning into part-time innkeepers. After getting approved by one of several rental agencies, a residence – usually that of a part-time New Yorker or someone who travels frequently – becomes available for long or short stays. It's often excellent value, plus a way to fly below the radar as a tourist, coming and going as you please without being forced to make any strained conversation around a B&B's breakfast table. It'll make you feel like you actually live here. The following companies offer a range of apartments in neighborhoods all over the five boroughs:

CitySonnet (☎ 212-614-3034; www.westvillagebb .com; hosted rooms from $80, studios from $135) Rents private apartments or (hosted) guest rooms in an occupied apartment, many in the hippest Downtown locations.

Gamut Realty Group (☎ 212-879-4229, 800-437-8353; www.gamutnyc.com; studios from $125, 1-bedroom apt from $150, apt per week $800-1450) Handles a number of short- and long-term apartment rentals, in spaces such as high-rises with doorman, and townhouses. From Herald Square north.

A Hospitality Company (☎ 212-965-1102, 800-987-1235; www.hospitalityco.com; apt per night from $165, per week from $995) Rents fully furnished apartments with features such as data ports, cable TV and fully equipped kitchens in whatever neighborhood might float your boat. Its website is available in six languages.

Manhattan Lodgings (☎ 212-677-7616; www .manhattanlodgings.com; apt per night from $125, per month from $1550, hosted stays $105-140) A selection of studio, one-bedroom and two-bedroom apartments, plus hosted B&B facilities.

Servas (☎ 212-267-0252; www.usservas.org; annual membership $65) An innovative worldwide program where members stay in approved host homes (there are around 140 in the tristate area) for two-night stays, free of charge. Call or visit the website for an application form and program details.

BRYANT PARK
Map pp226-7 *Boutique Hotel*
☎ 212-642-2200; www.bryantparkhotel.com; 40 W 40th St btwn Fifth & Sixth Aves; s & d from $295-395; subway B, D, F, V to 42nd St, 7 to Fifth Ave
You'll be the happiest visitor in town if you snag one of the 11 rooms with terraces overlooking

stately Bryant Park. But you'll be rewarded here nonetheless, in stylish rooms designed with clean lines and modern furnishings, featuring Tibetan rugs, hardwood floors, deep soaking tubs and luxurious goose-down comforters.

CASABLANCA HOTEL

Map pp226-7   *Boutique Hotel*
☎ 212-869-1212, 888-922-7225; www.casablancahotel .com; 147 W 43rd St; standard/deluxe r $275/295, ste $375; subway N, Q, R, S, W, 1, 2, 3, 7 to Times Sq
Casablanca is a low-key, high-class 48-room place done out in North African motifs – tiled hallway floors, bold statues and vases and carved wooden headboards. Nice touches include a complimentary breakfast, all-day snacks and espresso, free wine and appetizers (weekdays only), fresh flowers and plush robes.

CHAMBERS Map pp226-7   *Boutique Hotel*
☎ 212-974-5656; www.chambershotel.com; 15 W 56th St btwn Fifth & Sixth Aves; s $275-350, d $350-400, ste $650-1600; subway F to 57th St, N, R, W to Fifth Ave–59th St
This high-style inn has rooms with track lighting, stainless-steel fixtures, all-glass showers, cushy club chairs, wooden floors and clean jute rugs. Shared space is just as attractive, with high ceilings, buckets of light, tucked-away reading nooks and a permanent exhibition of more than 500 pieces of original modern artwork.

CITY CLUB HOTEL

Map pp226-7   *Boutique Hotel*
☎ 212-921-5500; www.cityclubhotel.com; 55 W 44th St btwn Fifth & Sixth Aves; r $225-495, ste $975; subway B, D, F, V to 42nd St–Bryant Park
This small treasure sits in the shadows of both the Algonquin and Royalton hotels, but it's certainly not overshadowed. An intimate, noscene lobby with slick furniture leads you to expansive rooms with Frette bed linens, TVs hidden behind wall mirrors, original artwork, marble bathrooms with bidets and, attached to some, high-ceilinged terraces with excellent views. Daniel Boulud's DB Bistro Moderne serves three exquisite meals per day.

DYLAN Map pp386-8   *Boutique Hotel*
☎ 212-338-0500; www.dylanhotel.com; 52 E 41st St btwn Madison & Park Aves; s/d $295/395, ste $650-1200; subway S, 4, 5, 6 to 42nd St–Grand Central
The 1903 beaux arts building, featuring a restored, grand marble staircase that swirls up from the lobby, once housed the Chemists

Club. After extensive renovations, it's now a house of style, with simple yet luxurious rooms awash in white walls, steel-blue carpets and soft lighting that seeps out of boxy fixtures.

FLATOTEL Map pp226-7   *Boutique Hotel*
☎ 212-887-9400; www.flatotel.com; 135 W 52nd St btwn Sixth & Seventh Aves; r $199-495; subway B, D, F, V to 47-50th Sts–Rockefeller Center
Transformed from a condominium complex in the early '90s, Flatotel offers 288 rooms and suites with an interesting blend of bland and luxurious – lots of taupe, glossy wood, amazing views, flat-screen TVs, super-comfy beds and modern furniture. Full apartments are also available.

FOUR SEASONS

Map pp386-8   *International Chain Hotel*
☎ 212-758-5700, 800-487-3769; www.fourseasons .com/newyorkfs/index.html; 57 E 57th St btwn Madison & Park Aves; r from $495, ste $1300-9500; subway N, R, W to Fifth Ave–59th St
This stellar branch of the worldwide chain was designed by renowned architect IM Pei. This limestone monolith has 52 floors, all full of spacious rooms with a handsome earth-tone design that's simple yet deluxe. The blond-wood lobby lounge serves tiered trays of crustless sandwiches for tea, and the bar at the restaurant Fifty Seven Fifty Seven gets mobbed with upscale after-work scenesters.

HOTEL 41 Map pp226-7   *Boutique Hotel*
☎ 877-847-4444; www.hotel41.com; 206 W 41st St btwn Seventh & Eighth Aves; r $149-249, penthouse ste $389; subway N, Q, R, W, 1, 2, 3, 7, 9 to Times Sq–42nd St
Everything about this big Times Square bargain is stylish and unique – from its winding steel terrace/staircase on the facade to its crisp, white, attractive quarters and its sexy, lowlit lounge bar. And oh, those excellent rates!

HOTEL ELYSÉE Map pp386-8   *Indie Inn*
☎ 212-753-1066; www.elyseehotel.com; 60 E 54th St btwn Madison & Park Aves; s & d from $295-345, ste $500; subway E, V to Lexington Ave–53rd St, 6 to 51st St
It often gets votes from travel magazines for being the most romantic little inn in NYC, and it's no wonder. The old-fashioned, French-style charm comes through in its heavily curtained, dated rooms and suites, but fans of newer boutique hotels may find it stuffy.

HOTEL METRO

Map pp386-8   *Bargain Hotel*

☎ 212-947-2500, 800-356-3870; fax 279-1310; 45 W
35th St btwn Fifth & Sixth Aves; r $150-350; subway B,
D, F, N, Q, R, V, W to 34th St–Herald Sq

This stylish bargain combines 1930s art deco
(its lobby features movie posters from Hollywood's golden era) with the comfort of a
gentlemen's club in its attractive lounge and
library area. Upstairs you'll find rather plain
rooms, but the price, location (near the Morgan Library, Madison Square Garden and Penn
Station) and friendly staff make this 160-room
hotel a worthy choice.

HUDSON

Map pp226-7   *Boutique Hotel*

☎ 212-554-6000; www.ianschragerhotels.com;
356 W 58th St btwn Eighth & Ninth Aves; s & d $175-275,
ste $300-3500; subway A, C, B, D, 1, 9
to 59th St–Columbus Circle

More like a nightclub than a place you'd think
of for sleeping, this most recent property from
boutique-hotel king Ian Schrager is the jewel
in his crown. The lobby bars are always jam-
min' with a too-cool VIP crowd (and plenty of
wannabes), the rooftop terrace has Hudson
views, and the rooms are just as highly stylized
and cushy as you'd expect. Schrager's other
local lodges are the **Royalton** (Map pp226-7;
☎ 212-869-4400; 44 W 44th St), the place that
put him on the map, and **Morgans** (Map pp386-
8; ☎ 212-686-0300; 237 Madison Ave), where
Morgans Bar and the restaurant sensation, Asia
de Cuba, are all the rage.

IROQUOIS

Map pp226-7   *Indie Inn*

☎ 212-840-3080, 800-332-7220; www.iroquoisny
.com; 49 W 44th St btwn Fifth & Sixth Aves; r $345-445,
ste $570-1090; subway B, D, F, V to 42nd St, 4, 5, 6, 7
to Grand Central

This 1920s-era hotel has undergone a complete renovation that's spared no detail. All-
marble bathrooms, fat and cushy beds, Frette
bathrobes and soothing color schemes are all
here, as well as the James Dean Suite, with
sporting memorabilia of the actor who lived
here from 1951 to 1953. Its sister property, **Le
Marquis** (Map pp386-8; ☎ 212-889-6363; www
.lemarquis.com; 12 E 31st St btwn Fifth & Madison Aves), is a lovely, refurbished 1906 space,
with endearingly mismatched rooms featuring
black-and-white checked floors, pure white
comforters and froofy curtains.

IVY TERRACE   Map pp386-8   *B&B*

☎ 516-662-6862; www.ivyterrace.com; E 58th
St btwn Lexington & Third Aves; s & d $175-200;
subway 4, 5, 6 to 59th St, N, R, W to Lexington
Ave–59th St

This lesbian-owned urban B&B is popular with
couples who don't want to stay in the fray
of the Downtown scene. But with gay bars –
Townhouse and OW Bar – right on the block,
there's still plenty of nearby entertainment, not
to mention Bloomingdale's and the rest of the
shopping district for all guests, straight or gay.
The three rooms have Victorian charm – lace
curtains, sleigh beds and hardwood floors – and
fill up fast, so call ahead.

KITANO   Map pp386-8   *Deluxe Indie Inn*

☎ 212-885-7000; www.kitano.com; 66 Park Ave at
38th St; s/d $480/600, ste $750-2100; subway S, 4, 5, 6,
7 to 42nd St–Grand Central

This one-time Rockefeller property was formerly known as the Murray Hill Hotel. The
Japanese Kitano firm took it over in the 1970s,
and today its sleek and hushed Eastern vibe
still feels fresh. Museum-quality artwork sits
throughout the space and rooms are simple
and large – especially the high-end Tatami
Suite, featuring futons, wooden floors, shoji
paper screens and tatami mats.

LIBRARY HOTEL

Map pp386-8   *Boutique Hotel*

☎ 212-983-4500; www.libraryhotel.com;
299 Madison Ave at 41st St; r $229-300, ste $350;
subway S, 4, 5, 6 to 42nd St–Grand Central

Each of the 10 floors in this cleverly themed
space is dedicated to one of the 10 major
categories of the Dewey Decimal System:
Social Sciences, Literature, Philosophy, and
so on, with a total of 6000 volumes split up
between quarters. The handsome style here
is bookish, too: mahogany paneling, hushed
reading rooms and a gentlemen's-club
atmosphere, thanks largely to its stately 1912
brick mansion home.

MANDARIN ORIENTAL NEW YORK

Map pp386-8   *International Chain Hotel*

☎ 212-885-8800; www.mandarinoriental.com; 80
Columbus Circle at 60th St; r $595-895, ste $1600-
12, 595; subway A, B, C, D, 1, 9 to 59th St–Columbus Circle

Yep, that's twelve *thousand*. But it's for the
Presidential Suite, reserved for A-list celebs, so
don't worry about bucking up. New York's most
opulent option yet is in the newly unveiled **Time**

Warner Center (p111), towering over the southern end of Central Park. Amenities range from soaking tubs overlooking the park or the Hudson, flat-screen TVs and an unrivalled, sophisticated style. Curiously, though, the linen thread-count is a low 280, while most upscale inns use 400. The nerve!

MANSFIELD Map pp386-8 *Boutique Hotel*
☎ 212-944-6050, 877-847-4444; www.mansfieldhotel .com; 12 W 44th St btwn Fifth & Sixth Aves; s & d $230-265; subway B, D, F, V to 42nd St, 7 to Fifth Ave

A 1904 building renovated according to historic specifications, the Mansfield provides a great deal in an excellent location. Everything is top of the line, from the EO bath products to the Belgian linens. The M Bar here has a fabulous domed glass-and-lead ceiling. The Mansfield is run by the Boutique Hotel Group, and sister locations include the **Franklin** (p305), **Hotel Wales** (Map pp389-91; ☎ 212-876-6000; 1295 Madison Ave btwn 92nd & 93rd Sts), **Shoreham** (Map pp386-8; ☎ 212-247-6700; 33 W 55th St btwn Fifth & Sixth Aves) and the **Roger Williams** (Map pp386-8; ☎ 888-448-7788; 131 Madison Ave at 31st St), popular with fashion types.

PENINSULA
Map pp386-8 *International Chain*
☎ 212-956-2888, 800-262-9467;
www.newyorkpeninsula.com; 700 Fifth Ave at 55th St; s/d $395/500; subway E, F to Fifth Ave

This grand dame dates back to 1904, making it one of the oldest surviving major hotels in Midtown. The totally renovated space includes an elegant stairway sweeping up from the lobby, and a sprawling spa and athletic club, with a pool almost big enough for laps. For rates and information, skip the mess of a website and just phone.

PLAZA HOTEL Map pp386-8 *Boutique Hotel*
☎ 212-759-3000, 800-527-4727; www.fairmont .com/theplaza/; 768 Fifth Ave btwn 58th & 59th Sts; r $289-1000; subway N, R, W to Fifth Ave–59th St

The fabled 100-year-old Plaza has attracted some high-profile customers, including the Beatles, Cary Grant and Grace Kelly, and Tony Soprano (after Carmela kicked him out). It's been featured in films from *The Way We Were* to *Lost in New York*, and is home to Kay Thompson's Eloise character in her popular children's book series. Try to snag a promotional special to get your foot in the door, as the sprawling rooms, choice restaurant, new spa and famous Oak Bar are absolutely divine, in an old-school

glamour sort of way. Suites are decadent affairs costing up to $15,000.

TIME Map pp226-7 *Boutique Hotel*
☎ 212-320-2900; www.thetimeny.com; 224 W 49th St btwn Broadway & Eighth Ave; s & d $179-500; subway C, E, 1, 9 to 50th St

This palace of modern design was inspired by Alexander Theroux's book, *The Primary Colors*, which explains the obsessive red, blue and yellow schemes that vary from room to room. The red room, in addition to being crimson, features red candy and a bottled 'red scent' to really beat you over the head. The design is really sumptuous, though, and if the hues start getting to you, you can head downstairs to the lovely lounge for some tapas and a specialty martini.

WALDORF-ASTORIA
Map pp386-8 *Legendary Chain*
☎ 212-355-3000, 800-925-3673;
www.waldorfastoria.com; 301 Park Ave btwn 49th & 50th Sts; s & d $200-500; subway 6 to 51st St, E, F to Lexington Ave

The legendary hotel – now part of the Hilton chain – needs no introduction. Housed in a landmark art deco building, it has an elegant lobby and plenty of large rooms, though their outdated style is a bit dowdy. Middle-aged executives frequent the smoky Bull & Bear restaurant, and the Cocktail Terrace above the lobby is a fine place to sip a Manhattan to the strains of piano sonatas.

WARWICK
Map pp226-7 *International Chain Hotel*
☎ 212-247-2700, 800-223-4099; www.warwickhotels .com; 65 W 54th St at Sixth Ave; r $200-500; subway B, D, F, V to 47th-50th Sts–Rockefeller Center

The slightly stuffy classic, built by William Randolph Hearst for his celebrity pals, had a great facelift recently, and its elegant rooms feature mahogany armoires, marble bathrooms and plenty of space.

WESTIN AT TIMES SQUARE
Map pp226-7 *International Chain Hotel*
☎ 888-627-7149; www.westinny.com; 270 W 43rd St at Eighth Aves; s & d $290-450, ste $500-1600; subway A, C, E to 42nd St–Port Authority

Since its opening in 2002, the gleaming, 45-story Westin has added a unique form to the Midtown skyline. Its Gothamesque tower's facade is a mosaic of purple and rose-colored

Sleeping – Midtown

mirrors featuring a strip of white that alights continuously from top to bottom once the sun goes down. It's just as flashy inside the hotel, where you'll find a jazzy lobby, rooms with amazing views (above the 15th floor) and a clean, modern aesthetic, bathed in tones of slate and steel-blue.

WESTPARK HOTEL

Map pp226-7   *Boutique Hotel*
☎ 212-445-0200, 866-937-8727;
www.westparkhotel.com; 308 W 58th St btwn Eighth & Ninth Aves; r from $150; subway A, B, C, D, 1, 2 to 59th St–Columbus Circle

Near Central Park, this understated charmer is popular for its individually decorated rooms, complimentary breakfast, cocktail hour, DVD library and international feel.

Cheap Sleeps

HOTEL 31 Map pp386-8   *Budget Hotel*
☎ 212-685-3060; 120 E 31st St btwn Park Ave South & Lexington Ave; s/d/tr $60/75/100; subway B, D, F, N, Q, R, V, W to 34th St–Herald Sq

Brought to you by the same folks responsible for Hotel 17, this Midtown version isn't quite as hip, but it has small, comfortable rooms and is just a short stroll from the Empire State Building.

MANHATTAN INN

Map pp386-8   *Budget Hotel*
☎ 212-629-9612; fax 629-9613; 303 W 30th St btwn Eighth & Ninth Aves; r $90; subway A, C, E to 34th St–Penn Station

This is a genuine New York bargain. The rooms are tidy, with private bathrooms, satellite TV, air-conditioning and continental breakfast.

MURRAY HILL INN

Map pp386-8   *Budget Hotel*
☎ 212-683-6900, 888-996-6376;
www.murrayhillinn.com; 143 E 30th St btwn Lexington & Third Aves; d without/with bathroom $75/100; subway 6 to 33rd St

On a peaceful side block, this inn is a safe, good-value place with clean, small rooms.

THIRTYTHIRTY

Map pp386-8   *Boutique Hotel*
☎ 212-689-1900; www.stayinny.com; 30 E 30th St btwn Park & Madison Aves; r $125-150; subway 6 to 33rd St

Part of the Citylife hotel group, this unbelievably sleek bargain is the best way to get in

on the boutique-hotel scene without going broke. Its two other area properties, just as stylish and affordable, are the **Habitat Hotel** (Map pp386-8; ☎ 212-753-8841; 130 E 57th St at Lexington Ave) and **On the Ave** (p304).

WOLCOTT HOTEL

Map pp386-8   *Budget Hotel*
☎ 212-268-2900; www.wolcott.com; 4 W 31st St btwn Fifth Ave & Broadway; s/d $100/120; subway B, D, F, N, Q, R, V, W to 34th St–Herald Sq

John Duncan, the architect of Grant's Tomb, designed this 280-room beaux-arts hotel. Rooms are small but a great deal, and the gilded lobby is stunning.

UPPER WEST SIDE

You'll find a good selection of mid-range and budget hotels in this part of town, but none of the fanfare you'd find in the hipster inns to the south. It's strictly old-school New York – character, bargain and no-nonsense grandeur.

COUNTRY INN THE CITY

Map pp389-91   *B&B*
☎ 212-580-4183; www.countryinnthecity.com; 270 W 77th St btwn Amsterdam & Columbus Aves; apt $150-210; subway 1, 9 to 79th St

Just like staying with your big-city friend: the 1801 limestone townhouse sits on a stellar, tree-lined street, and the four self-contained apartments are cool and sophisticated, with

Top Five Suites

- **Carlyle** (p305) Carlyle Suite. In addition to 1000 square feet and antique furniture, this pad comes with its very own grand piano.
- **Dylan** (p300) Alchemy Suite. This magnificent 1932 Gothic chamber boasts vaulted ceilings, slender columns and a stunning stained-glass window depicting a chemistry theme.
- **Iroquois** (p301) James Dean Suite (suite 803). Sports photos and memorabilia of the Rebel heartthrob, who lived here from 1951 to 1953.
- **Kitano** (p301) Tatami Suite. Tricked out with Japanese paper lanterns, screens, futons and tatami mats, the hotel can even turn this suite into the site of your very own traditional tea ceremony.
- **Lowell** (p306) Gym Suite. The in-room gym, plus two private bathrooms, was enough to lure even Arnold Schwarzenegger here once upon a time.

four-poster beds, glossed wooden floors, warm color schemes and lots of light. Plus, there's a minimum stay of three nights – just like your best pal would probably have it. No credit cards.

EMPIRE HOTEL

Map pp389-91 *Budget Hotel*
☎ 212-265-7400; 44 W 63rd St btwn Broadway & Columbus Ave; s/d/ste $130/240/450; subway 1, 9 to 66th St–Lincoln Center

Its standard, no-frills rooms are small, clean and chintz-filled. Culture-vultures will love having Lincoln Center on one side of the building and an excellent indie film house on the other.

EXCELSIOR HOTEL

Map pp389-91 *Budget Hotel*
☎ 212-362-9200; www.excelsiorhotelny.com; 45 W 81st St at Columbus Ave; r $129-229, ste $239-539; subway B, C to 81st St–Museum of Natural History

This is an old, 169-room place that overlooks the beautiful American Museum of Natural History. It's old-school, with flowered bedspreads, carpeting and striped wallpaper, but it's got a small fitness center and is near the park and biggie museums.

HOTEL BELLECLAIRE

Map pp389-91 *Budget Hotel*
☎ 212-362-7700; www.hotelbelleclaire.com; 250 W 77th St at Broadway; economy r/s/d/ste $109/169/179/249; subway 1, 9 to 79th St

Another neighborhood bargain, the difference here is in the design: frilly bed ruffles have been replaced by smooth white comforters, cheesy framed prints and old wallpaper by bolts of slate-gray fabric and wood-framed mirrors. There's still carpeting, but hey, at least no flowered curtains.

INN NEW YORK CITY

Map pp389-91 *B&B*
☎ 212-580-1900; www.innnewyorkcity.com; 266 W 71st St at West End Ave; ste $300-600; subway 1, 2, 3, 9 to 72nd St

Four massive, quirky suites in this 1900 townhouse let you live in a mansion. It's far west, and close to both Riverside Park and Central Park, and its rooms feature antique chestnut furnishings, Jacuzzis and stained-glass panels, if just a bit too much flowered carpeting. It's stately, massive and heavy with history.

LUCERNE

Map pp389-91 *Budget Hotel*
☎ 212-875-1000; www.newyorkhotel.com; 201 W 79th St at Amsterdam Ave; s & d $180-290; subway 1, 9 to 79th St

Part of the Empire Hotel Group, known for affordability and good locations. The Lucerne's decor is frilly and old-fashioned, but it's clean, and its rooftop patio has beautiful views of Central Park and the Hudson River. Sibling hotels include the **Belvedere** (Map pp226-7; ☎ 212-245-7000; 319 W 48th St) and the **Newton** (opposite).

ON THE AVE

Map pp389-91 *Boutique Hotel*
☎ 212-362-1100, 800-509-7598; www.stayinny.com; 2178 Broadway at 77th St; r $159-309, ste from $475; subway 1, 2, 3, 9 to 79th St

Another excellent City Life property, this one boasts a sleek design composed of warm earth tones, stainless steel and marble baths, and sunny rooms hung with original artwork. And don't miss the 16th-floor all-guest balcony, with stunning views. Highly recommended.

PHILLIPS CLUB

Map pp389-91 *Business Hotel*
☎ 212-835-8800; www.phillipsclub.com; 155 W 66th St btwn Broadway & Amsterdam Ave; ste $420-1000, per month $6600-15,000; subway 1, 9 to 66th St–Lincoln Center

Most often used for long stays – one month or more – but the suites are also available nightly. They're classy and spacious, with high-end linens and original framed photographs, and they offer business amenities including data ports, multiphone lines with voicemail and conference spaces. All guests get access to the exclusive Reebok Sports Club gym.

Cheap Sleeps

HOSTELLING INTERNATIONAL – NEW YORK Map pp389-91 *Hostel*
☎ 212-932-2300; www.hinewyork.org; 891 Amsterdam Ave at 103rd St; dm $29-32, nonmembers extra $3, d without/with bathroom $120/135; subway 1, 9 to 103rd St

With clean, safe and air-conditioned rooms, the dorm beds at HI–New York go fast in the summer (book ahead!). That may also be because of its popular, sprawling and shady patio and way-friendly vibe.

Sleeping – Upper West Side

Top Five Luxury Stays

- **Battery Park City Ritz-Carlton** (p293) 'Bath butler, bring me some lavender bubbles. Oh, and technology butler…why won't this jpg open?' Talk about service.
- **Four Seasons** (p300) IM Pei designed the Louvre Pyramid in Paris, Bank of China in Hong Kong, East Wing of DC's National Gallery – and this lux lodge.
- **Mandarin Oriental New York** (p301) Where else can you gaze down at Central Park from an in-house soaking tub?
- **Soho House** (p295) Celebs of all stripes clamor to get into one of the two dozen rooms here, with VIP perks from a sprawling spa to a private film screening room.
- **Westin at Times Square** (p302) Killer views from a skyline-altering palace.

JAZZ ON THE PARK HOSTEL

Map pp389-91 *Hostel*
☎ 212-932-1600; www.jazzhostel.com; 36 W 106th St btwn Central Park West & Manhattan Ave; dm $27-37, d $80-130; subway B, C to 103rd St
This recently refurbished flop is way cool for a hostel. Rooms are small, with standard wood-frame bunks, but there's a beautiful roof deck and exposed-brick lounge that hosts local jazz acts. Double rooms are done up with bold paint jobs and firm beds. Its newest property, **Jazz on the Town** (Map pp386-8; ☎ 212-351-3260; 130 E 57th St btwn Lexington & Park Aves), also has a fun atmosphere and great roof deck.

NEWTON Map pp389-91 *Budget Hotel*
☎ 212-678-6500; www.newyorkhotel.com/newton; 2528 Broadway btwn 94th & 95th Sts; s & d $85-160; subway 1, 2, 3, 9 to 96th St
There's nothing exciting about the property itself – rooms with drab chain-like decor and wall-to-wall carpeting, plus that ubiquitous disinfectant smell in the bare-bones lobby. But it's cheap and clean and in a primo location, with **Symphony Space** (p235) theater just across the street, Central Park a couple of blocks east and the 2, 3 express trains a block away.

UPPER EAST SIDE

Some of New York's poshest, most elegant hotels are up here, allowing you to stay near some of the city's wealthiest residents and greatest cultural institutions, such as the Met and Central Park. Rooms run upwards of $300 on average, and nightlife is pretty much a non-happening event, so be prepared to crawl Downtown (or cross-town) for any action.

BENTLEY Map pp389-91 *Boutique Hotel*
☎ 212-644-6000, 888-664-6835; www.nychotels.com; 500 E 62nd St at York Ave; r/ste $135/235; subway F to Lexington Ave–63rd St
You can't stay any further east than in this chic boutique hotel, boasting a swanky lobby, down comforters and some of New York's most spectacular views. If you don't stay here, though, at least grab a cocktail at the rooftop restaurant.

CARLYLE Map pp389-91 *Deluxe Indie Inn*
☎ 212-744-1600; www.thecarlyle.com; 35 E 76th St btwn Madison & Park Aves; s & d $495-795, ste from $850; subway 6 to 77th St
This New York classic epitomises old-fashioned luxury: a hushed lobby, antique boudoir chairs and framed English country scenes or Audubon prints in the rooms, some of which have terraces and baby grand pianos. If you don't have a pad with a piano, though, you can get your fix downstairs at the classy Bemelman's Bar, decorated with murals from Ludwig Bemelman's *Madeline* book series, or Café Carlyle, home to cabaret legend Bobby Short.

FRANKLIN

Map pp389-91 *Boutique Hotel*
☎ 212-369-1000, 877-847-4444; www.franklinhotel .com; 164 E 87th St btwn Lexington & Third Aves; standard/superior r $275/295; subway 4, 5, 6 to 86th St
This is a friendly hotel with 48 rooms featuring fresh flowers and Belgian white bed linens with swatches of creamy fabric billowing overhead. Its sibling in the nabe is **Hotel Wales** (p302), a century-old place that was returned to its former glory a few years ago. Don't miss the provocative Puss in Boots canvasses in the Franklin's lobby.

HOTEL PLAZA ATHÉNÉE

Map pp389-91 *Luxury Indie Inn*
☎ 212-734-9100; www.plaza-athenee.com; 37 E 64th St btwn Madison & Park Aves; s & d $515-675, ste $1200-3600; subway F to Lexington Ave–63rd St
Tucked away on a residential street, the stately lobby (marble floors, luscious tapestries etc)

and elegant rooms (beige tones, balconies, marble bathrooms etc) ensure an understated yet royal getaway.

LOWELL HOTEL

Map pp389-91   *Boutique Hotel*

☎ 212-838-1400; 28 E 63rd St btwn Madison & Park Aves; s & d $445-600; subway F to Lexington Ave–63rd St

It's intimate and quiet and one of New York's hot-spot hotels, favored by super celebrities including Brad Pitt, Madonna and Arnold Schwarzenegger, who chose the gym suite (with a personal gym) to stay buff while traveling. Most rooms in this stunning art deco building have kitchenettes, fireplaces and terraces.

MARK NEW YORK

Map pp389-91   *Luxury Indie Inn*

☎ 212-744-4300; www.mandarinoriental.com; Madison Ave at E 77th St; s & d $570-730, ste $760-2500; subway 6 to 77th St

Run by the super-glitzy Mandarin Oriental, the regal, neoclassical Italian-style rooms with tree-like potted plants, deeply hued carpets and black wooden furniture will thrill those who like to be spoiled.

MELROSE HOTEL

Map pp389-91   *Luxury Indie Inn*

☎ 212-838-5700; www.melrosehotelnewyork.com; 140 E 63rd St btwn Lexington & Third Aves; r $199-340, ste from $500; subway N, R, W to Lexington Ave–59th St, 4, 5, 6 to 59th St

The gilded lobby and high-gloss marble floor will seduce you right away, as will the entire refurbished legend, reopened in 2002 after service as an A-list women-only hotel until 1981 (putting up stars from Joan Crawford to Candace Bergen), when its life as the Barbizon Hotel came to an end. Today its splendor remains, especially in its light-filled, modernized suites with original artwork and spectacular views.

PIERRE HOTEL

Map pp389-91   *International Chain*

☎ 212-838-8000; www.fourseasons.com/pierre; 2 E 61st St at Fifth Ave; r $385-700; subway N, R, W to Fifth Ave–59th St

The sumptuous boudoirs feel like secret oases, all space and dim lighting, massive beds

and towering potted ferns. It's run by Four Seasons, and is like the dark and sexy cousin of the IM Pei property a few blocks downtown.

HARLEM

With gentrification comes waves of visitors, and the smartest entrepreneurs have capitalized on that fact – but in a classy, quirky way. You won't find a ton of options up here, but what you will find are intimate inns with character, which is quite a relief. All are Cheap Sleeps. Just be aware that some side streets may feel slightly menacing after dark.

Cheap Sleeps
HARLEM FLOPHOUSE

Map pp392-3   *B&B*

☎ 212-662-0678; www.harlemflophouse.com; 242 W 123rd St btwn Adam Clayton Powell & Frederick Douglass Blvds; s/d $65/90; subway A, B, C, D to 125th St

There's nothing cluttering the four gorgeous bedrooms at this place – large spaces with antique light fixtures, glossed-wood floors and massive beds – and that's a very good thing. The tin ceilings, wooden shutters and decorative moldings inside this restored brownstone building are good enough on their own.

SUGAR HILL INTERNATIONAL HOUSE

Map pp392-3   *Hostel*

☎ 212-926-7030; www.sugarhillhostel.com; 722 St Nicholas Ave; dm/d $25/$60; subway B, C to 145th St

Bare-bones but clean and cheap, Sugar Hill offers standard bunk beds in a renovated limestone home that dates back to the 19th century.

URBAN JEM GUEST HOUSE

Map pp392-3   *B&B*

☎ 212-831-6029; 2005 Fifth Ave btwn 124th & 125th Sts; r $115-185; subway 2, 3 to 125th St

This restored 19th-century brownstone features 14ft-high ceilings, marble fireplace mantels, detailed woodwork and African-themed art.

Excursions

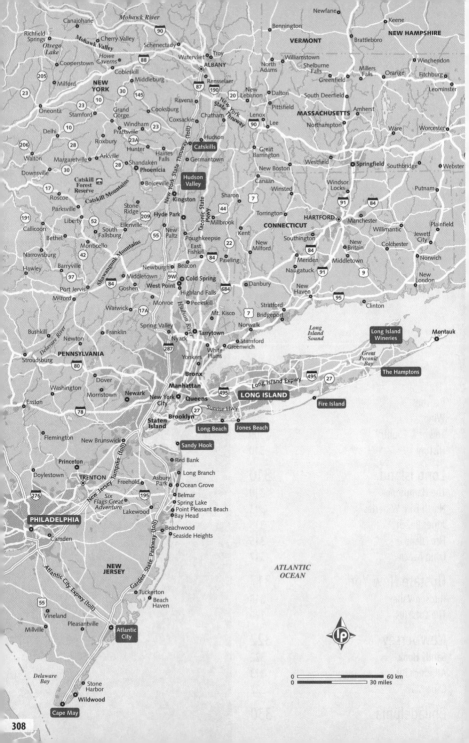

Excursions

Some New Yorkers tend to get stuck in ruts, often not leaving the city for months at a time. 'There's nowhere tranquil nearby,' they moan. 'There's too much traffic – and it's too inconvenient without a car.' Don't believe it for a minute! The surrounding environs – New York's Hudson Valley and the mountainous Catskills, New Jersey's refreshing beaches and glitzy casinos, Long Island's ritzy Hamptons and plentiful wineries, and Philadelphia's rich history – offer a slew of wonderful options, from beaches and country towns to wine trails and nature preserves. You can get to just about any excursion in this chapter via public transportation (which, if combined with cycling, gives you even more options), but if you want or need a car, simply plan your escape during a weekday, when most of the city is stuck at work. Beating traffic is one of the advantages of being on vacation, after all!

Coney Island (p140)

BEACHES

It may seem surprising, but New York City is surrounded by beaches – sandy stretches of parkland that abut the frothy Atlantic Ocean. While the closest lie within the city limits (Coney Island, the Rockaways, City Island), urban beaches can be crowded, noisy and dirty, and heading out of town will definitely be a more tranquil experience. Long Island has several options: **Jones Beach**, the sprawling city of sand; **Fire Island**, a peaceful, car-free gem; hip **Long Beach**, a quick train ride from Manhattan; and the **Hamptons**, with miles of white beaches edging the area's tony towns. In New Jersey you'll find the entire Jersey Shore, with highlights including **Sandy Hook** and **Cape May**.

WINE

While New York's Finger Lakes region, way upstate, is the state's most renowned wine producer, Long Island is quickly catching up. You'll find more than 30 vineyards on Long Island's eastern end, with most on the **North Fork** and more and more uncorking on the **South Fork** (the Hamptons) as well.

TOWNS & COUNTRY

Leisurely paced villages surrounded by nature are closer than you may think. New York State's **Hudson Valley** has endless little hubs great for exploring, and the area is laced with historic mansions and small museums. Further north are the mountainous **Catskills**, dotted with artsy hamlets, scenic hiking and camping spots and antique shops galore. On Long Island, the **Hamptons** truly offer a bit of everything, in a series of quaint towns known for picture-perfect Main Streets, high-end boutiques and a five-star restaurant scene (with plenty of celeb sightings). Connected to the Hamptons by a ferry is the **North Fork** of Long Island, which is a more low-key version of its Hamptons' counterpart known more for its mellow B&Bs and myriad wineries.

HISTORY

A quick bus ride takes you to the historic heart of the nation. **Philadelphia** – a smaller, mellower city than NYC – has plenty of its own offerings, such as the Liberty Bell, Independence Hall, the US Mint and tasty cheese steaks, to name but a few.

LONG ISLAND

The largest island in the US (120 miles long), Long Island begins with Brooklyn (Kings County), and Queens (Queens County) on its western shore. New York City then gives way to the suburban housing, strip malls and working-class heroes in neighboring Nassau County. You might hear reference to the north and south shores here; the north is the ritzy part. The terrain becomes flatter, less crowded and more exclusive in rural Suffolk County, which comprises the eastern end of the island. Suffolk County itself contains two peninsulas – commonly called the North and South Forks – divided by Peconic Bay. It's the South Fork that lures the most visitors, as it's what's also known as the East End – or, commonly, the Hamptons.

THE HAMPTONS

What began as a tranquil hideaway for city artists, musicians and writers has developed into a frenetic summer getaway mobbed with jet-setters, celebrities and throngs of curious wannabes. That said, there is still plenty of the original peace and beauty to discover. The beaches and farmlands (what's left of them) are indeed stunning and there's plenty of opportunity for outdoor activity, from kayaking to mountain biking. You can easily combine your peace-seeking with some boutique shopping and serious dining, as both the shops and restaurants are top notch. You're also quite likely to spot celebs if you're here in the summer. But bargain

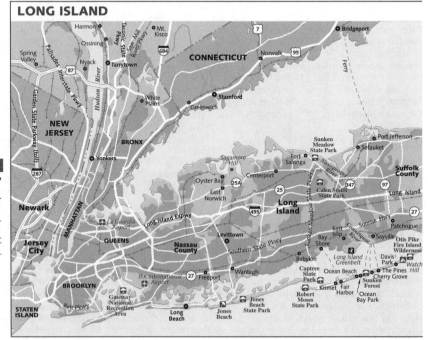

LONG ISLAND

travelers be warned: absolutely everything costs a pretty penny out here, with most inns charging well over $200 a night. Summer is high season; prices do drop a wee bit and traffic jams disappear about a month after Labor Day. This lessening of crowds, combined with the balmy weather of the fall harvest season make autumn the most beautiful time for a visit.

The Hamptons is actually a series of villages, most with 'Hampton' in the name. Those at the western end – or 'west of the canal,' as locals call the places that are on the other side of the Shinnecock Canal – include Hampton Bays, Quogue and Westhampton, and are less frenzied than those to the east, which start with the village of **Southampton**. This is an old-moneyed and rather conservative spot compared to some of its neighbors, home to sprawling old mansions, a Main Street with a slew of 'decency' rules (such as no 'beach wear' allowed to be worn in town) and some lovely beaches. Pick up maps and brochures about the town at the **Southampton Chamber of Commerce office**, squeezed among a group of high-priced artsy-crafty shops and decent restaurants. Within the town is a small Native American reservation, home to the Shinnecocks, who run a tiny **Shinnecock Museum** with unpredictable hours. The **Parrish Art Museum** has quality exhibitions (and be sure to pick up a copy of *The East Hampton Star* or *The Southampton Press* for local arts listings). For an excellent meal that won't empty your wallet, join the locals at **La Parmigiana** for huge plates of pasta and meatballs.

To the east, **Bridgehampton** has the shortest of all the main drags, but it's packed with trendy boutiques and restaurants. You'll also find the **Enclave Inn**, a relative bargain that's stylish and comfortable, and just a short walk from the beach.

Seven miles north of Bridgehampton on Peconic Bay is the old whaling town of **Sag Harbor**. There are bunches of historic homes and points of interests here and you can pick up a historic walking tour map at the **Windmill Information Center** on Long Wharf at the end of Main Street. **Sag Harbor Whaling Museum** is fascinating, its tiny Cape Cod–style streets are a joy to stroll along and there are several excellent restaurants worth checking out. The **Bike Hampton** shop rents bicycles and sells excellent maps of area cycling trails. **Espresso** is a small Italian deli tucked into a quiet

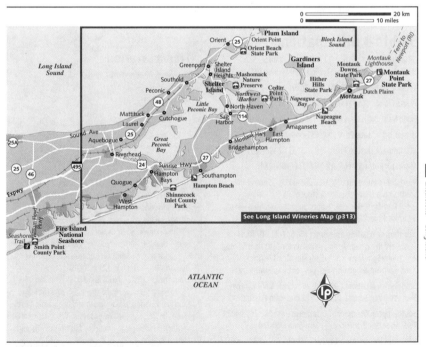

residential street; pick up outrageously good sandwiches and desserts for a beach picnic; **Sen** is a popular sushi den. **American Hotel**, right on Main Street, has eight luxurious rooms and a highly regarded restaurant catering to scotch-and-cigar types from the city.

A quick ferry ride from the edge of North Haven, which borders Sag Harbor, will take you to sleepy Shelter Island, nearly a third of which is dedicated to the **Mashomack Nature Preserve**, dotted with biking and hiking trails.

Long Island's trendiest town is **East Hampton**, where you can catch readings and art exhibitions at **Guild Hall**. **Babette's** is an outstanding organic and mostly vegetarian eatery where former President Clinton stopped in to visit the active Democratic owner when he was in town. The eateries where you'll most likely spot celebrities are **Della Femina** and **Nick & Toni's**, where the Italian-influenced meals are, in fact, flawless. **Mill House Inn**, a renovated property in East Hampton run by Dan and Katherine Hartnett, offers eight lovely rooms (the prices are the same regardless of the season).

More honky-tonk than the rest of the Hamptons, **Montauk** has relatively reasonable restaurants and a louder bar scene, largely because all the service personnel – mainly students – live here in communal housing. For a kitschy 'bargain,' try staying at the **Memory Motel**, a scruffy but comfortable spot where Mick Jagger often stayed in the 1970s and was inspired to write the Rolling Stones song of the same name. To get pampered, book a room at the beachfront and spa-equipped **Gurney's Inn Resort**. For some real beachy eatin', head to the **Lobster Roll ('Lunch')** for what else but a lobster roll – rich lobster-meat salad stuffed into a fresh hot-dog roll.

Covering the eastern tip of the South Fork is **Montauk Point State Park**, with its impressive Montauk Lighthouse. You can camp in the sand nearby at windswept **Hither Hills State Park** or hike the nearby mountainous **Walking Dunes** of sand, with 80ft peaks that overlook the bay. Or try pitching a tent at **Cedar Point Park** in the Springs section of East Hampton on the calm Northwest Harbor. Just be sure to call ahead, as sites tend to fill up fast. Montauk retains a strong **fishing** tradition and there are many opportunities to cast a line here. You can contract charter boats at the dock for a day of fishing or jump on one of the party cruises (about $30 per person for a half-day). Captain Fred E Bird's **Flying Cloud** comes highly recommended for fluke fishing May to September and sea bass, porgies and striper fishing September to November.

Sights & Information

Bike Hampton (☎ 631-725-7329; 36 Main St, Sag Harbor; rental per day depending on bike $25-40)

Cedar Point Park (☎ 631-852-7620)

Flying Cloud (☎ 631-668-2026; 67 Mulford Ave, Montauk)

Guild Hall (☎ 631-324-0806; 158 Main St, East Hampton)

Hither Hills State Park (☎ 631-668-2554)

Mashomack Nature Preserve (☎ 631-749-1001)

Montauk Point State Park (☎ 631-668-3781)

Parrish Art Museum (☎ 631-283-2111; 25 Jobs Lane, Southampton; adult/senior & student $5/3; ☯ 11am-5pm Mon-Sat, 1-5pm Sun Memorial Day–Sept 14, closed Tue-Wed rest of year)

Sag Harbor Whaling Museum (☎ 631-725-0770; Main St at Garden St, Sag Harbor; adult/senior & student $5/3; ☯ 10am-5pm Mon-Sat, 1-5pm Sun May 17–Oct 1, noon-4pm Sat & Sun only Oct-Dec, or by appointment)

Shinnecock Museum (☎ 631-287-4923; Montauk Hwy, Southampton; admission $5; ☯ 11am-4pm Fri-Sun)

Southampton Chamber of Commerce (☎ 631-283-0402; 76 Main St, Southampton; ☯ 9am-5pm Mon-Fri)

Windmill Information Center (☎ 631-692-4664; Long Wharf at Main St, Sag Harbor; ☯ 9am-4pm Sat & Sun)

Transportation

Distance from New York City 100 miles (East Hampton)
Direction East
Travel time 2¼ hours
Car Take the Midtown Tunnel out of Manhattan, which will take you onto Interstate 495/Long Island Expwy. Follow this for about 1½ hours to exit TK, which will take you onto TK East. Take it for about 5 miles and then merge onto the Montauk Highway/Rte 27, which will take you directly into Southampton. Follow Rte 27 to get to all towns east.
Bus The Hampton Jitney (☎ 800-936-0440; www .hamptonjitney.com; one-way $27, roundtrip $47) is a luxury express bus. It departs from Manhattan's East Side – 86th St; 40th St between Lexington and Third Aves; 69th St; and 59th St at Lexington Ave – and makes stops at villages along Rte 27 in the Hamptons.
Train The Long Island Rail Road (LIRR; ☎ 718-217-5477; www.mta.nyc.ny.us/lirr; one-way $16) leaves from Penn Station in Manhattan and the Flatbush Ave station in Brooklyn, making stops in West Hampton, Southampton, Bridgehampton, East Hampton and Montauk.

Eating

Babette's (☎ 631-537-5377; 66 Newtown Lane, East Hampton; entrees $12-18)

Della Femina (☎ 631-329-6666; N Main St, East Hampton; entrees $18-30)

Espresso (☎ 631-725-4433; 184 Division St, Sag Harbor; entrees $7-11)

La Parmigiana (☎ 631-283-8030; 48 Hampton Rd, Southampton; entrees $11-18)

Lobster Roll ('Lunch') (☎ 631-267-3740; 1980 Montauk Hwy, Montauk; entrees $12-20)

Nick & Toni's (☎ 631-324-3550; 136 N Main St, East Hampton; entrees $18-30)

Sen (☎ 631-725-1774; 23 Main St, Sag Harbor; entrees $15-25)

Sleeping

American Hotel (☎ 631-725-3535; Main St, Sag Harbor; r $195-325)

Enclave Inn (☎ 631-537-0197; Montauk Hwy, Bridgehampton; r $99-349)

Gurney's Inn Resort (☎ 631-668-2345; 290 Old Montauk Hwy, Montauk; s & d 190-380, ste $200-425)

Memory Motel (☎ 631-668-2702; 692 Montauk Hwy, Montauk; r $95-120)

Mill House Inn (☎ 631-324-9766; 31 N Main St, East Hampton; r from $200)

NORTH FORK WINERIES

In just over 25 years, Long Island's wine scene has grown from one small winery to a thriving industry that takes up more than 3000 acres of land. A vast majority of the 50-plus vineyards are at the East End's North Fork, where distinctive green 'wine trail' road signs mark the way along Rte 25 once you pass the town of Riverhead, where the two forks split. If you want to include the few South Fork stops in your travels (**Duck Walk Vineyards** and **Wölffer Estate**), you can explore the Hamptons and then continue on to the North Fork via the Shelter Island Ferry (see earlier). But staying out of the paparazzi-filled fray and just settling into the easy pace of the North Fork is a worthy trip in itself. Harvest time is in fall,

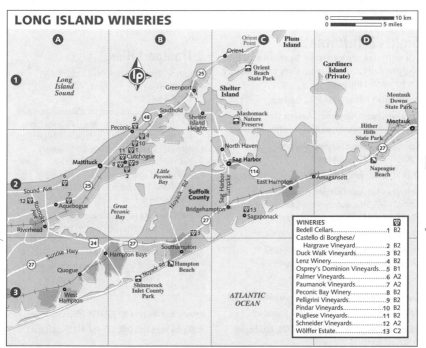

LONG ISLAND WINERIES

WINERIES	🍷
Bedell Cellars	1 B2
Castello di Borghese/ Hargrave Vineyard	2 B2
Duck Walk Vineyards	3 B2
Lenz Winery	4 B2
Osprey's Dominion Vineyards	5 B1
Palmer Vineyards	6 A2
Paumanok Vineyards	7 A2
Peconic Bay Winery	8 B2
Pellegrini Vineyards	9 B2
Pindar Vineyards	10 B2
Pugliese Vineyards	11 B2
Schneider Vineyards	12 A2
Wölffer Estate	13 C2

which, coupled with foliage and pumpkin-picking opportunities, makes it an ideal time to visit, however most places remain open year-round. Several wineries offer full-scale tours of their facilities. The following (all on Map p313) are just some of the wineries that offer tastings: **Bedell Cellars**, **Castello di Borghese/Hargrave Vineyard**, **Lenz Winery**, **Osprey's Dominion Vineyards**, **Palmer Vineyards**, **Paumanok Vineyards**, **Peconic Bay Winery**, **Pelligrini Vineyards**, **Pindar Vineyards**, **Pugliese Vineyards**, **Schneider Vineyards** and **Wölffer Estate**. For individual winery information, as well as maps for touring the wine trail, contact the **Long Island Wine Council**.

However, there's plenty to do beyond sipping and spitting. **Greenport** is friendly and more affordable than South Fork villages, and you'll find plenty of open-air restaurants clustered around the marina. **Claudio's** is a landmark that gets noisy at the long wooden bar as tourists clamor for lobster dinners. **Aldo's** is a more refined option. It serves sublime food and is known for its home-baked biscotti. Reservations are essential. Stop at **Greenport-Southold Chamber of Commerce** for maps and other information, and take a spin on the restored waterfront **carousel**.

Also worth a visit is the tiny hamlet of **Orient**, about 3 miles from the Orient Point ferry terminal. There's not much of a business district in this 17th-century hamlet, just an old wooden post office and a general store, but Orient features a well-preserved collection of white clapboard houses and former inns. Further out of town, you can bike past the Oyster Ponds just east of Main Street and see the beach at **Orient Beach State Park**.

A drive along the back roads of the North Fork affords some beautiful, unspoiled vistas of farms and rural residential areas. But if you're too bushed to make the trip out and back in one day (a doable, but tiring, prospect), you'll find plenty of classic inns to rest your head for the night. Two good options are the **Always In Bed & Breakfast**, an elegant, cozy B&B in the woods of **Southold**, and the **Quintessentials B&B Spa**, an 1840s Victorian place outfitted with a full-service spa, plush quarters and peaceful, flowering grounds. If you do wind up driving out, a stop in **Riverhead** is worthwhile – both for the **Tanger Outlet Center**, a massive tangle of factory outlet stores such as Banana Republic and Nautica, and for its **Polish Town**, a tiny, insular community of Polish immigrants with various ethnic bakeries and restaurants such as **Polonez Polish Russian Restaurant**.

Sights & Information

All wineries are generally open from 11am to 5pm daily, with closing time extended by an hour in summer.

Bedell Cellars (☎ 631-734-7537; Cutchogue)

Carousel (Front St, Greenport; admission $1; ☸ 10am-10pm summer, weather permitting rest of year)

Castello di Borghese/Hargrave Vineyard (☎ 631-734-5158; Cutchogue)

Duck Walk Vineyards (☎ 631-726-7555; Southampton)

Greenport-Southold Chamber of Commerce (☎ 631-765-3161; www.greenportsouthchamber.org; Rte 25, Southold; ☸ 9am-4pm Mon-Fri)

Lenz Winery (☎ 631-734-6010; Peconic)

Long Island Wine Council (☎ 631-369-5887; www.liwines.com; 104 Edwards Ave, Calverton)

Orient Beach State Park (☎ 631-323-3400)

Osprey's Dominion Vineyards (☎ 631-765-6188; Peconic)

Palmer Vineyards (☎ 631-722-9463; Riverhead)

Paumanok Vineyards (☎ 631-722-8800; Aquebogue)

Peconic Bay Winery (☎ 631-734-7361; Cutchogue)

Pelligrini Vineyards (☎ 631-734-4111; Cutchogue)

Transportation

Distance from New York City 100 miles
Direction East
Travel Time 2¼ hours
Car Take the Midtown Tunnel out of Manhattan, which will take you onto Interstate 495/Long Island Expwy. Take this until it ends, at Riverhead, and follow signs onto Rte 25. Stay on Rte 25 for all points east.
Bus Sunrise Coach Lines (☎ 800-527-7709; www.sunrisecoach.com; one-way $16) picks up passengers at 44th St at Third Ave in Manhattan and makes stops along the North Fork.

Train The Long Island Rail Road (LIRR; ☎ 718-217-5477; www.mta.nyc.ny.us/lirr) has a North Fork Line, with trips leaving from Penn Station and Brooklyn. Tickets, which can be bought at the station from agents or automatic machines, range from $13 to $19 roundtrip.

Pindar Vineyards (☎ 631-734-6200; Peconic)

Pugliese Vineyards (☎ 631-734-4057; Cutchogue)

Schneider Vineyards (☎ 631-727-3334; Riverhead)

Tanger Outlet Center (☎ 631-369-2732; 1770 W Main St, Riverhead)

Wölffer Estate (☎ 631-537-5106; Sagaponack)

Eating

Aldo's (☎ 631-477-1699; 103-105 Front St, Greenport; entrees $15-25)

Claudio's (☎ 631-477-0715; 111 Main St, Greenport; entrees $18-30; ✔ mid-Apr–Jan 1)

Polonez Polish Russian Restaurant (☎ 631-369-8878; 123 W Main St, Riverhead; entrees $12-20)

Sleeping

Always In Bed & Breakfast (☎ 631-765-5344; 14580 Soundview Ave; r $135-150)

Quintessentials B&B Spa (☎ 631-477-9400; 8585 Main Rd, East Marion; r $175-275)

JONES BEACH

Jones Beach State Parks offerings are simple: 6½ miles of clean sand covered with bodies. The type of character differs depending on which 'field' you choose – for example, 2 is for the surfers and 6 is for families, and there is a gay beach followed by a nude beach – but it's a definite scene no matter where you choose to spread your blanket. The ocean gets quite warm by mid-summer, up to about 70°F, and there are plenty of lifeguards. In between sunning and riding waves, though, you might also hop into one of the two massive on-site pools for a swim, play shuffleboard or basketball on beachside courts, stroll the 2-mile boardwalk, visit the still waters of the bay beach or, at the Castles in the Sand museum, learn how master builder Robert Moses transformed Long Island with the creation of Jones Beach in the 1940s. Burgers, nachos, ice cream and other beach foods are available at snack bars, located at each beach field, and there's a sit-down eatery, the Boardwalk Restaurant, with ocean views and serious fare, from seared tuna to buckets of steamers. When the sun goes down, you can grill at one of the many barbecues in the sand, or head to the Tommy Hilfiger Jones Beach Theater (recently bought and renamed to serve as a constant advertisement, unfortunately), where alfresco concerts under the stars feature headliners along the lines of David Bowie, Kid Rock and Britney Spears.

Sights & Information

Castles in the Sand (☎ 516-785-1600; admission $1; ✔ 10am-4pm Sat & Sun Memorial Day–Labor Day)

Jones Beach State Park (☎ 516-785-1600)

Tommy Hilfiger Jones Beach Theater (☎ 516-221-1000) Phone for opening hours and admission.

Eating

Boardwalk Restaurant (☎ 516-785-2420; entrees $10-15)

Transportation

Distance from New York City 33 miles
Direction East
Travel Time 45 minutes
Car Take the Midtown Tunnel from Manhattan onto I-495/Long Island Expwy. Take this to exit TK and get on the Northern State Pkwy or Southern State Pkwy until the Wantagh Pkwy, which will take you directly to Jones Beach State Park.
Train The Long Island Rail Road (LIRR; ☎ 718-217-5477; www.mta.nyc.ny.us/lirr; roundtrip $14) offers roundtrips from Penn Station and Brooklyn's Flatbush Avenue station to the Freeport station on Long Island; the trip takes less than 40 minutes and, between Memorial Day and Labor Day, includes a shuttle bus to Jones Beach.

FIRE ISLAND

This skinny barrier island of sand runs parallel to Long Island, and contains much wonder, beauty and flaming adventure along its scant 32 miles. Federally protected as the Fire Island National Seashore, the land offers sand dunes, forests, white beaches, camping, hiking trails, inns, restaurants, 15 hamlets and two villages. Its scenes range from car-free residential villages of summer mansions and packed pubs to stretches of sand where you'll find nothing but pitched tents, deer (overpopulation is a big problem here) and some mosquitoes. Robert Moses State Park, the only part of the island that's accessible by car, lies at the westernmost end, and features wide, soft-sand beaches with mellower crowds than those at Jones Beach. It's also home to the **Fire Island Lighthouse**, which houses a history museum. Walk way east along the shore here and you'll stumble upon a lively nude beach.

The gemlike parts of Fire Island, though, are found further east, in the tranquil, car-free villages. Davis Park, Fair Harbor, Kismet, Ocean Bay Park and Ocean Beach combine small summer homes with tiny towns that have groceries, bars, nightclubs and restaurants – just keep in mind that almost everything in every town shuts down a couple of weeks after Labor Day. A good place to stay is **Ocean Beach Hotel**; you can rely on the **South Bay Water Taxi** service to shuttle you between villages. Each village has slightly different crowds – some more geared toward singles, others family-friendly; to find out more, check out the town guide at www.fireisland.com. Perhaps the most infamous villages, though, are those that have evolved into gay resorts: **Cherry Grove** and **the Pines**. These, too, attract different crowds – Cherry Grove a more down-to-earth, rainbow-flag–touting person who likes burgers, beers and nude sunbathing. Cherry Grove attracts lesbians, too, while the Pines is exclusively men – affluent men, with sculpted bodies, Manhattan apartments and a taste for drug-fueled soirees, either at each others' large houses or at **Pines Pavilion** nightclub. The boys from either side often meet in the middle, of course, namely for an anonymous encounter at the tangle of forest that separates the two villages (nicknamed 'the meat rack'). While day trips are easy to Fire Island, staying on this oasis, where boardwalks serve as pathways between the dunes and homes, is wonderful. If you can't stay in someone's summer share-house, there are few options: **Belvedere**, for men only, **Holly House**, and **Grove Hotel**, all in the Grove; Grove Hotel offers the main source of entertainment with its nightclub.

None of the eateries are worth writing home about, but **Rachel's/Jack's Place** has great ocean views, while **Cherry's Pit** sits on the bay. Both are popular Grove gathering places.

If you want to skip the scene altogether and just get back to nature, you can enjoy a hike through the **Sunken Forest**, a 300-year-old forest, with its own ferry stop (called Sailor's Haven). At the eastern end of the island, the 1300-acre preserve of **Otis Pike Fire Island Wilderness** includes a beach campground at **Watch Hill** (reservations are a must, as sites fill up a year in advance).

Sights & Information

Cherry Grove (☎ 914-844-7490; www.cherrygrove.com)

Fire Island Information (www.fireisland.com)

Fire Island Lighthouse (☎ 631-681-4876)

Fire Island National Seashore (☎ 631-289-4810; www.nps.gov/fiis)

Otis Pike Fire Island Wilderness/Watch Hill (☎ 631-289-9336; camp sites $20)

Pines (www.fipines.com)

Pines Pavilion (☎ 631-597-6677; admission $5-20)

Robert Moses State Park (☎ 631-669-0449; www.nysparks.state.ny.us)

South Bay Water Taxi (☎ 631-665-8885; www.southbaywatertaxi.com; fares $10-20)

Sunken Forest (☎ 631-289-4810)

Eating

Cherry's Pit (☎ 631-597-9736; entrees $10-15)

Rachel's/Jack's Place (☎ 631-597-4174; entrees $8-12)

Sleeping

Belvedere (☎ 631-597-6448; r from $200)

Grove Hotel (☎ 631-597-6600; r $40-$500, ste $80-500)

Holly House (☎ 631-597-6991; r from $200)

Ocean Beach Hotel (☎ 631-583-9600; r $225)

Transportation

Distance from New York City 60 miles

Direction East

Travel Time 2 hours (including ferry ride)

Car Take the Midtown Tunnel out of Manhattan onto I-495/Long Island Expwy. For Sayville ferries (to Pines, Cherry Grove and Sunken Forest), get off at exit 57 onto the Vets Memorial Highway. Make a right on Lakeland Ave and take it to the end, following signs for the ferry. For Davis Park Ferry from Patchogue (to Watch Hill) take the Long Island Expwy to exit TK. For Bay Shore ferries (all other Fire Island destinations), take the Long Island Expwy to exit 30E, then get onto the Sagtikos Pkwy to exit 42 south, to Fifth Ave terminal in Bay Shore. You can also take **Tommy's Taxi Service** (☎ 631-665-4800), with pick-up points in Manhattan and takes you directly to the Bay Shore ferry for $16. To get to Robert Moses State Park by car, take exit 53 off the Long Island Expwy and travel south across the Moses Causeway. **Train** The **Long Island Rail Road** (LIRR; ☎ 718-217-5477; www.mta.nyc.ny.us/lirr) makes stops in both Sayville and Bay Shore, and has a connecting summer-only shuttle service to the **Fire Island Ferry Service** (☎ 631-665-3600; Bay Shore), **Sayville Ferry Service** (☎ 631-589-0810; Sayville) and **Davis Park Ferry** (☎ 631-475-1665, Davis Park). One-way tickets from Manhattan and Brooklyn are about $12; roundtrip ferry tickets average $15.

LONG BEACH

Beautiful Long Beach, closer to the city than either Jones Beach or Fire Island, is one of the best stretches of sand within an hour of the city. It's easily accessible by train, has clean beaches, a hoppin' main town strip with shops and eateries within walking distance of the ocean, a thriving surfers' scene and many city hipsters; even rock-n-roll bad girl Joan Jett calls the town home (as does renowned Long Island tabloid queen, Amy Fisher). Pick up information at the **Long Beach Chamber of Commerce** and the official **City of Long Beach** office to help navigate around the area.

You'll probably do just fine on your own, though, as Long Beach is compact and easily negotiated. **Lincoln Beach**, at the end of Lincoln Blvd, is the main spot for surfing; you can rent boards or even sign up for a surfing lesson at **Unsound Surf**. The skinny sand strip sits in front of this wave-churned spot in the Atlantic, with plenty of other sunning and swimming areas along

> ## Transportation
>
> **Distance from New York City** 30 miles
> **Direction** East
> **Travel Time** 45 minutes
> **Car** Follow the Grand Central Pkwy east to the Van Wyck Expwy, toward JFK Airport. Take exit 1E to the Nassau Expwy, which heads right into Long Beach.
> **Train** The **Long Island Rail Road** (LIRR; ☎ 718-217-5477; www.mta.nyc.ny.us/lirr; roundtrip $12) goes directly to Long Beach from both Penn Station and Flatbush Ave in Brooklyn.

either side. Behind the beach scene is a sweet residential 'hood, made up of cute beach houses and larger year-round homes, seemingly all equipped with porches and wind chimes. Strolling or biking through is a nice break from the surf and sun; you can also bike along the boardwalk that fronts the beach, which has lanes reserved for cyclists. You can rent bikes at **Buddy's**.

There's plenty of good eats in the town around the beach. Stroll around and find whatever suits your fancy, or make a beeline for one of the following: **Baja California Grille**, serving up tasty Mexican fare; **San Remo Pizzeria** or **Kitchen Off Pine Street**, a great place for an eclectic dinner before heading back to the city – just be sure to dust all the sand out of your hair and put your shoes back on first. Long Beach doesn't have much in the way of hotels – just the scrappy **Long Beach Motor Inn** in nearby Island Park – but getting back to NYC is so easy, it doesn't really matter anyway.

Sights & Information

Buddy's (☎ 516-431-0804; 907 W Beech St; 3-hr bike hire $15)

City of Long Beach (☎ 516-431-1000; www.long beachny.org; 1 West Chester St; ☺ 9am-4pm Mon-Fri)

Lincoln Beach (☎ 516-431-1810)

Long Beach Chamber of Commerce (☎ 516-432-6000; 350 National Blvd; ☺ 9am-4pm Mon-Fri)

Unsound Surf (☎ 516-889-1112; surf-report line ☎ 516-892-7972; 359 East Park Ave; lessons per hr $50)

Eating

Baja California Grille (☎ 516-889-5992; 1032 W Beech St; entrees $6-10)

Kitchen Off Pine Street (☎ 516-431-0033; 670 Long Beach Blvd; entrees $13-22)

San Remo Pizzeria (☎ 516-432-4038; 1085 W Beech St; entrees $2-6)

Sleeping

Long Beach Motor Inn (☎ 431-5900; 3915 Austin Blvd, Island Park; r $79)

UPSTATE NEW YORK

Heading north from New York City the landscape quickly mellows into a long lush stretch of historic riverfront towns and thickly treed hills, the dynamic colors of which set New York City folks scrambling each fall to locate their driver's licenses so they can rent a car and peep at the leaves.

HUDSON VALLEY

Winding roads along the Hudson River take you by picturesque farms, Victorian cottages, apple orchards and old-money mansions built by New York's elite. **Hudson Valley Tourism** has regional information about sites and events. Painters of the Hudson River school romanticized these landscapes – you can see their work at art museums as well as those in the city. Autumn is a particularly beautiful time for a trip up this way, either by car or train (though having a car makes site-hopping much easier); cyclists also love the beauty and challenge of riding through the area (for further information, read *Ride Guide: Mountain Biking in the NY Metro Area* by Joel Sendek, Anacus Press, or *25 Mountain Bike Tours in the Hudson Valley* by Peter Kick, Backcountry Books). The season's changing foliage and opportunities for pumpkin- and apple-picking make this excursion a classic Americana experience. **Trapani's Blackberry Rose Farm** in Milton is a family-run stand selling fresh produce, jams, baked goods and cider.

On the west side of the river, 40 miles north of NYC, **Harriman State Park** covers 72 sq miles and offers swimming, hiking, camping and a visitor center. Adjacent **Bear Mountain State Park** offers great views from its 1305ft peak. The Manhattan skyline looms beyond the river and surrounding greenery. You can enjoy hiking in summer, wildflowers in spring, gold foliage in fall and cross-country skiing in winter. The **Storm King Art Center**, in Mountainville, is well worth a visit. It showcases stunning avant-garde sculpture by Calder, Moore and Noguchi, among others. Tucked among rolling hills, this outdoor park occupies 400 acres, successfully combining art and nature. The nearby **B&B at Storm King Lodge** is a stately 1800s home with tasteful rooms featuring private bathrooms and fireplaces.

The largest town on the Hudson's east bank, **Poughkeepsie** (puh-*kip*-see) is famous for **Vassar**, a private liberal-arts college that admitted only women until 1969. Its modern **Francis Lehman Loeb Art Center** features Hudson River–school paintings and contemporary work. **Dutchess County Tourism Office** has regional information. Cheap motel chains in Poughkeepsie are clustered along Rte 9, south of the Mid-Hudson Bridge. But for a stay with some character, try the **Copper Penny Inn**, a well-run B&B in a converted 1860s farmhouse.

Hyde Park has long been associated with the Roosevelts, a prominent family since the 19th century. The **Franklin D Roosevelt Library & Museum** features exhibits on the man who created the New Deal and led the USA into WWII. Eleanor Roosevelt's cottage, **Val-Kill**, was her retreat from Hyde Park, her mother-in-law and FDR himself. The **Vanderbilt Mansion** is a national historic site 2 miles north on Rte 9, is a spectacle of lavish beaux arts and eclectic architecture. A **combination ticket** (☎ 800-967-2283; adult $18) is available for the three sites; reservations are recommended. There are plenty of other grand mansions to explore – **Kykuit**, a Rockefeller home with antique carriages and gardens sits in Tarrytown along with the Gothic Revival mansion Lyndhurst Castle; **Olana**, built with Moorish touches by Hudson

Transportation

Distance from New York City 95 miles (to Hyde Park)

Direction North

Travel Time 1¾ hours

Car To leave Manhattan, take the Henry Hudson Pkwy to I-95 to the Palisades Pkwy. Follow this to the New York State Thruway to Rte 9W or Rte 9, the principal scenic river routes. Most towns can also be reached by taking the faster Taconic State Pkwy, which runs north from Ossining and is considered one of the state's prettiest roads when the leaves turn in the autumn.

Bus Short Line Buses (☎ 212-736-4700; www .shortlinebus.com; roundtrip $28) runs regular trips to Hyde Park and Rhinebeck.

Train While Amtrak (☎ 212-582-6875, 800-872-7245; www.amtrak.com) trains run the length of the river and connect with several communities on the eastern shore, your best and cheapest bet from New York City is the **Metro-North commuter train** (☎ 212-532-4900, 800-638-7646; www.mnr.org; one-way off-peak $5.50-9.50), which departs from Grand Central Terminal (take the 'Hudson Line'). On weekends, Metro-North runs special summer and autumn tourist packages that include train fare and transportation to and from specific sites such as Hyde Park and the Vanderbilt Mansion.

Boat One of the most relaxing and pleasant ways to take in several sites strung along here is by the **NY Waterway** (☎ 800-533-3779; www.nywaterway .com; tours from $40), which offers ferry trips up the Hudson River. Full-day tours on offer include many of the area's mansions and historic sites.

Excursions – Upstate New York

River–school artist Frederic Church is in Hudson; and **Springwood**, in Hyde Park, was FDR's boyhood country home.

If military history is your thing, know that generations of American soldiers have been groomed at the United States Military Academy since its establishment in 1802, including US Grant, Douglas MacArthur and Dwight Eisenhower. Today, the cadet corps are made up of men and women who live on a campus comprised of redbrick and gray-stone buildings, churches and temples. For maps and tour information, go to **West Point Visitors Center**, which is actually in Highland Falls, about 100 yards south of the military academy's Thayer Gate.

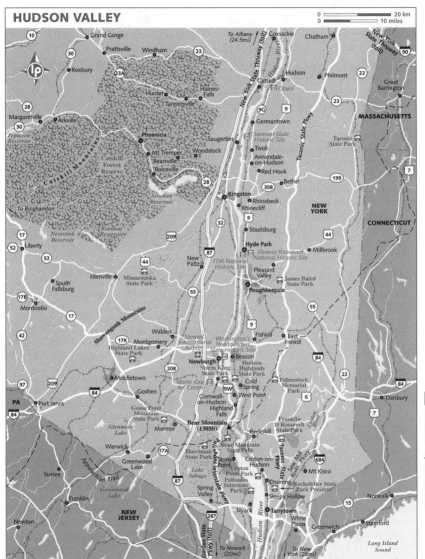

HUDSON VALLEY

319

Sights & Information

Bear Mountain State Park (☎ 845-786-2701)

Dutchess County Tourism (☎ 800-445-3131; www
.dutchesscountytourism.com; 3 Neptune Rd, Poughkeepsie)

Franklin D Roosevelt Library & Museum (☎ 845-229-
8114; www.fdrlibrary.marist.edu; 511 Albany Post Rd/Rte
9, Hyde Park; admission $10; ⊗ 9am-5pm;)

Harriman State Park (☎ 845-786-5003)

Trapani's Blackberry Rose Farm (☎ 845-795-5830; 1636
Rte 9W, Milton; ⊗ 9am-5pm)

Hudson Valley Network (www.hvnet.com)

Hudson Valley Tourism (☎ 800-232-4782;
www.hudsonvalley.org)

Kykuit (☎ 914-631-9491; Pocantico Hills, Tarrytown;
adult/senior/child $22/20/18; ⊗ tours 9:45am,
1:45pm, 3pm)

Olana (☎ 518-828-0135; Rte 9G, Hudson)

Springwood (☎ 800-967-2283; Albany Post Rd, Hyde
Park; admission $14; ⊗ 9am-5pm)

Storm King Art Center (☎ 845-534-3115;
www.stormkingartcenter.org; Old Pleasant Hill Rd,
Mountainville; admission $9; ⊗ Apr-Nov)

Vassar/Francis Lehman Loeb Center (☎ 845-437-5632;
Poughkeepsie; admission free; ⊗ 10am-5pm Tue-Sat,
1-5pm Sun)

Val-Kill (☎ 845-229-9115; www.nps.gov/elro; Albany
Post Rd, Hyde Park; admission $8; ⊗ 9am-5pm daily
May-Oct, Thu-Mon Nov-Apr)

Vanderbilt Mansion (☎ 800-967-2283; www.nps
.gov/vama; Rte 9, Hyde Park; admission $8; ⊗ 9am-5pm)

West Point Visitors Center (☎ 914-938-2638, Rte 9W,
Highland Falls; ⊗ 9am-4:45pm)

Sleeping

B&B at Storm King Lodge (☎ 845-534-9421;
Mountainville; r $150-175)

Copper Penny Inn (☎ 845-452-3045; Poughkeepsie;
r $90-150)

The Other CIA

Also in Hyde Park, the renowned **Culinary Institute of America** (☎ 800-285-4627; www.ciachef.edu) trains future chefs and can satisfy anyone's gastronomic cravings. Its four student-staffed restaurants are formal, but **St Andrew's Cafe** (☎ 845-471-6608; dinner around $30) is more casual and the least expensive – reservations are required. A nearby inn, the **Village Square** (☎ 845-229-7141; 4159 Albany Post Rd; r $40-100) has exceptional country-style rooms.

THE CATSKILLS

This scenic region of small towns, farms, resorts and forests has become the latest playground for NYC publishing types and various celebs who have tired of the Hamptons glitz. They've been snapping up historic houses here to serve as second-home getaways, but so far, the rural feel of the area has not been compromised. You'll still find quaint towns and antiquing opportunities galore, plus gorgeous countryside: Catskill Forest Park, established in 1904, comprises 700,000 acres of forest preserve, private land and artsy villages.

In the southern Catskills, the town of **Woodstock** symbolizes the tumultuous 1960s, when US youth questioned authority, experimented with freedom and redefined popular culture. Today it's a combination of quaint and hip. The town has been an artists' colony since 1900, and you'll see an eclectic mix of young Phish fans sporting dreadlocks, and old-time, graying hippie throwbacks. The **Woodstock Guild** is a good source for finding out the latest goings-on in the arts and culture scene – such as the annual Woodstock Film Festival, in October, which attracts film fans from all over. The famous 1969 Woodstock music festival actually occurred in **Bethel**, a town over 40 miles southwest, where a simple plaque marks the famous spot. Two not-so-peaceful spin-offs, also named 'Woodstock,' took place in nearby Saugerties (1994) and Rome (1999). **Saugerties**, just a few miles from the town of Woodstock, offers a similar downtown area, with a smaller offering of galleries, cafés and eateries. Area dining is plentiful, and includes the **Blue Mountain Bistro**, which serves four-star French–Mediterranean cuisine and Spanish tapas to a sophisticated crowd; and **New World Home Cooking Co**, focusing on fresh and tasty organic food in a quirky setting. **Heaven** is a hip coffee hang, offering organic blends, affordable soups and sandwiches and scrumptious baked goods.

You'll find plenty of fine inns in the area, but only a couple stand out from the frilly Victorian masses. The **Villa at Saugerties**, run by a young ex-city couple who escaped the rat race, is the sleekest place around. The four amazing rooms are more urban boutique hotel than country B&B. In Woodstock, **Twin Gables Guesthouse** is central, with nicely furnished rooms with shared bathroom. Backpackers should head to the nearby **Rip Van Winkle Campground** for cheap, well-maintained sites. But for a true adventure, stay at the remote **Saugerties Lighthouse**, an 1869 lighthouse that sits on a small island in the Esopus Creek. The Saugerties Lighthouse Conservancy operates it as a year-round B&B, boating guests out to one of the three spare and tidy rooms, all with sweeping water views.

South of Saugerties, Rte 28 crosses the Catskills west of Woodstock, then winds past the Ashokan Reservoir and through the 'French Catskills.' Along this way are excellent restaurants, camping, inexpensive lodging, antique shops and character galore. In Mt Tremper is the **Kaatskill Kaleidoscope**, the world's largest. The 60ft tube, an old farm silo, is touristy, but the 10-minute presentation is worthwhile, featuring US history, psychedelic colors and, of course, images of marijuana leaves. In Arkville, take a scenic ride on the historic **Delaware and Ulster Rail Line**. Nearby Fleischmanns hosts a good, old-fashioned **auction** every Saturday night, where locals pack the rafters to snap up bargains from cheap old records to furniture. Take a load off at the **River Run Bed & Breakfast**, which has beautiful oak floors, stained-glass windows, a big porch and comfortable rooms.

Go even further north if it's good winter skiing you're looking for. Rtes 23 and 23A lead to **Hunter Mountain Ski Bowl**, a year-round resort with challenging runs and a 1600ft vertical drop, and **Windham Mountain**, with more intermediate runs.

Sights & Information

Delaware and Ulster Rail Line (☎ 845-652-2821; www.durr.org; Hwy 28, Arkville; adult/senior/child $10/8/6; ☺ May-Aug)

Hunter Mountain Ski Bowl (☎ 518-263-4223; www.huntermtn.com; Hunter)

Kaatskill Kaleidoscope (☎ 888-303-3936; Mt Tremper; adult/child under 12 $7/free; ☺ 10am-5pm Sun-Thu, 10am-7pm Fri-Mon)

Windham Mountain (☎ 518-734-4300; www.skiwindham.com; Windham)

Woodstock Guild (☎ 845-679-2079; www.woodstock guild.org; Woodstock; ☺ 9am-5pm Mon-Fri)

Eating

Blue Mountain Bistro (☎ 845-679-8519; Glasco Tpke, Saugerties; entrees $15-25)

Heaven (☎ 914-679-0111; 17 Tinker St, Woodstock; entrees $2-5)

New World Home Cooking Co (☎ 845-246-0900; Rte 212, Woodstock; entrees $10-20)

Sleeping

Rip Van Winkle Campground (☎ 845-246-8334; Woodstock; tent sites $24-28)

River Run Bed & Breakfast (☎ 845-254-4884; www.catskill.net/riverrun; 882 Main St, Fleischmanns; r $75-165)

Saugerties Lighthouse (☎ 847-247-0656; www .saugertieslighthouse.com; Saugerties; r $135-160)

Twin Gables Guesthouse (☎ 845-679-9479; 73 Tinker St, Woodstock; s/d $59/69)

Villa at Saugerties (☎ 845-246-0682; www.thevillaatsaugerties.com; 159 Fawn Rd, Saugerties; r $95-160)

Transportation

Distance from New York City 110 miles (Saugerties)

Direction North

Travel Time 2 hours

Car Take the New York State Thruway (via the Henry Hudson Highway north from Manhattan), or I-87, to Rte 375 for Woodstock, Rte 32 for Saugerties or Rte 28 for other points north.

Bus Adirondack Trailways (☎ 800-858-8555; average roundtrip $45) operates daily buses to Kingston, the Catskills' gateway town, as well as to Saugerties, Catskill, Hunter and Woodstock.

NEW JERSEY

New Jersey is often the butt of jokes – for its preponderance of suburbanite-filled malls, its nasal dialect and, most of all, for its polluted (and very smelly) manufacturing district off the Jersey Turnpike. But when you take the time to exit the highways and flee the malls, you are privy to a beautiful side of NJ: a surprising 40% of the state is forest, and a quarter is farmland. It has extensive parkland, beautiful Victorian buildings and a full 127 miles of beaches.

SANDY HOOK

Sandy Hook's 1665-acre natural wonderland comprise 7 miles of beach. Like Jones Beach on Long Island, the area blends massive ocean beaches with bay beaches and history. But here, in **Sandy Hook Gateway National Recreation Area**, you'll also find the nation's oldest lighthouse, the Maritime Holly Forest with plentiful opportunities for observing birds (such as the endangered plover), outstanding views of Manhattan's skyline on clear days, a nude beach alongside a gay beach (area G), and a complex system of paved bike paths, which wend their way through the abandoned forts of historic Ft Hancock and white sand-dune peaks. Best of all, you can get here via the **SeaStreak Ferry**, which leaves from Lower Manhattan and gets you here in a cool and salty 45 minutes. Bring your bike along for the ride, and you can pedal to various Jersey Shore areas, including the nearby towns of **Atlantic Highlands** and **Highlands**. The **Atlantic Highlands Chamber of Commerce** can provide you with several eating and sleeping options in the area.

If you get hungry on the beach, you'll find plenty of standard concession stands serving snacks such as hot dogs and nachos. For better grub, hit **Seagull's Nest**, a restaurant in the stand that serves fresh salads, seafood and ice-cold beers. You could try the **Harborside Grill** for seafood or **Indigo Moon** for French cuisine, both in Atlantic Highlands. The closest place to stay is the gay-owned **Sandy Hook Cottage**, done up with tasteful, beach-house decor. Also nearby is the **Grand Lady By the Sea Bed and Breakfast**, a historic, romantic inn that overlooks the beach.

Transportation

Distance from New York City 45 miles
Direction West
Travel Time 1 hour
Car Take the Garden State Pkwy to exit 117 and follow Rte 36 east to the beach.
Bus You can take a **New Jersey Transit** (☎ 973-762-5100; www.njtransit.com) bus from Port Authority to Red Bank, NJ, and then switch to the local M24, which stops at Sandy Hook.
Ferry The **SeaStreak Ferry** (☎ 732-872-2628; www.seastreak.com; 2 First Ave, Atlantic Highlands; one-way $19, roundtrip $34, one-way bike extra $3) leaves from Pier 11 near Wall St and also from a pier at E 34th St. It's the best option.

Sights & Information

Atlantic Highlands Chamber of Commerce
(☎ 732-872-8711; www.atlantichighlands.org; 🕓 9am-4pm Mon-Fri)

Sandy Hook Gateway National Recreation Area
(☎ 732-872-5970)

Eating

Harborside Grill (☎ 732-291-0066; 40 First Ave, Atlantic Highlands; entrees $8-14)

Indigo Moon (☎ 732-291-2433; 171 First Ave, Atlantic Highlands; entrees $12-25)

Seagull's Nest (☎ 732-872-0025; Sandy Hook Area D; entrees $5-10)

Sleeping

Grand Lady By the Sea Bed and Breakfast
(☎ 732-708-1900; www.grandladybythesea.com; 254 Rte 36, Highlands; r $100-150)

Sandy Hook Cottage (☎ 732-708-1923; www.sandyhookcottage.com; 36 Navesink Ave, Highlands; r $100-200)

ATLANTIC CITY

When the railway arrived on Absecon Island in the 1850s, city dwellers came here for the wide white beach and seaside atmosphere. By 1900 the resort was a hot spot that catered to the affluent; in the 1920s it was a hotbed of vice, with smuggled liquor, speakeasies and illegal gambling. After WWII, faster transportation made other destinations more accessible, and Atlantic City went into steep decline. In 1977 the state approved casinos to revitalize the place, and since then, Atlantic City (or 'AC' as it's known locally), has become one of the country's most popular tourist destinations, with 33 million annual visitors spending some $4 billion at its 12 casinos and numerous restaurants. The part of town that sits in the shadows of the oceanfront casinos has been largely left behind – it's rife with empty lots, rough-looking bars and abandoned warehouses. However, AC is still an interesting stopover on your way to Cape May and you may find the anthropology of the surreal scene intriguing. If you're a gambler, you can't beat the selection of nearly 1000 blackjack tables and more than 30,000 slot machines in town.

Caesar's Atlantic City

As in Las Vegas, the hotel–casinos have themes, from the Far East to Ancient Rome, but they're very superficially done here. Inside they're still all basically the same, with clanging slot machines, flashing lights and gluttonous all-you-can-eat food buffets. This is changing, however, as big developers like Donald Trump and Steve Wynn vie for supremacy. The latest addition – the **Borgata Hotel Casino & Spa** – from Boyd Gaming and MGM Mirage, has really upped the ante, offering plush rooms, a full-service spa and five-star restaurants galore. Staying in any of the towering hotels can be cheap or extravagant, depending on the season, with rooms ranging from $50 in winter to $400 in summer. (For bargain sleeps that don't have casinos, try **Comfort Inn** or the **Holiday Inn Boardwalk**.)

There are plenty of hotel–casinos. The southernmost casino, **Atlantic City Hilton**, has over 500 hotel rooms. **Bally's Park Place & Wild West Casino** occupies the site of the 1860 Dennis Hotel, which is incorporated into the newer, 1200-room facility. **Caesar's Atlantic City** contains 1000 rooms and Atlantic City's Planet Hollywood theme restaurant, which is just off the gaming area.

Popular with low-rolling senior citizens, the **Claridge Casino Hotel**, between Pacific Ave and the Boardwalk, is accessible by a moving walkway that operates in one direction only – into the casino. **Harrah's Marina Hotel Casino** is considered the friendliest casino in town. Newbie gamblers might try its floor, which has gracious and instructive dealers. **Resorts Casino Hotel** is a 670-room Victorian hotel that served as a hospital during WWII. Near the Boardwalk, **Sands Hotel, Casino & Country Club** looks like a big, black, glass box. This is Atlantic City's oldest casino.

One of the more affordable casinos in which to bunk down is **Showboat Casino**, which has a riverboat-theme interior going on in its 700 rooms. **Tropicana Casino & Entertainment Resort** is one of the biggest places in town, with its own indoor theme park (Tivoli Pier), a 90,000-sq-ft casino and 1020 rooms. Trump's properties include **Trump's Marina Resort**, with an art deco theme; **Trump Plaza Casino Hotel**; and the **Trump Taj Mahal**, where nine two-ton limestone elephants welcome visitors, and 70 bright minarets crown the rooftops. The buffet here is one of the best in town.

Each of the casinos offers a full schedule of entertainment, ranging from ragtime and jazz bands in hotel lobbies to top-name entertainers in the casino auditoriums. Some of

ATLATIC CITY

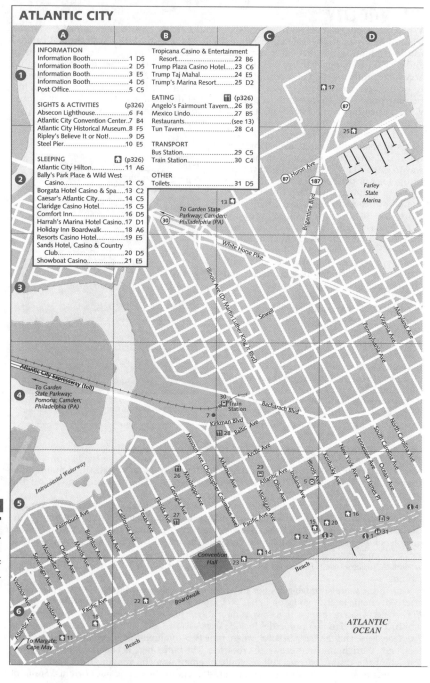

To Garden State
Parkway; Camden;
Philadelphia (PA)

White Horse Pike

Illinois Ave (Dr Martin Luther King Jr Blvd)

Sewell

Brigantine Blvd

Huron Ave

Farley
State
Marina

Atlantic City Expressway (toll)

To Garden
State Parkway;
Pomona; Camden;
Philadelphia (PA)

Intracoastal Waterway

Bacharach Blvd

Train
Station

Kirkman Blvd

Baltic Ave

Arctic Ave

Atlantic Ave

Pacific Ave

Missouri Ave (Christopher Columbus Ave)

Arkansas Ave

Florida Ave

Georgia Ave

Texas Ave

California Ave

Iowa Ave

Brighton Ave

Morris Ave

Chelsea Ave

Montpelier Ave

Sovereign Ave

Boston Ave

Ventnor Ave

Fairmount Ave

Pacific Ave

Ohio Ave

Michigan Ave

Indiana Ave

Illinois Ave

Kentucky Ave

New York Ave

Tennessee Ave

St James Pl

Ocean Ave

South Carolina Ave

North Carolina Ave

Pennsylvania Ave

Virginia Ave

Maryland Ave

Convention
Hall

Boardwalk

Beach

Beach

*ATLANTIC
OCEAN*

To Margate;
Cape May

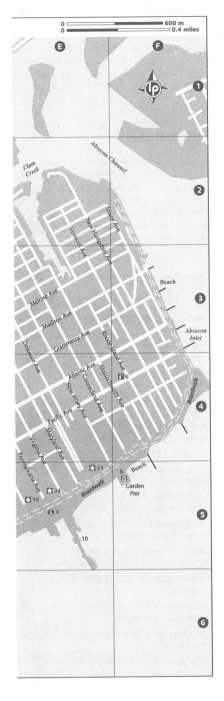

this stuff is way over the top, but worth it for the cheese factor alone; think sequins and feathers.

However, there is some life outside of the casinos. Built in 1870, the **Boardwalk** was the first in the world. Enjoy a walk or a hand-pushed **rolling chair ride** (adult $20) and drop in on the informative **Atlantic City Historical Museum**, run by a quirky old-timer. The Miss America Pageant, held every September in the city's Convention Hall – which is worth a visit if only for its claim of 'world's largest' pipe organ (with 33,000 pipes, it weighs 150 tons) – remains a very popular draw. The **Steel Pier** amusement pier, directly in front of the Trump Taj Mahal, belongs to Donald Trump's empire. It used to be the place where the

Transportation

Distance from New York City 130 miles
Direction South
Travel Time 2¼ hours
Car Leave Manhattan via one of the Hudson River crossings (Holland Tunnel, Lincoln Tunnel, George Washington Bridge). Take the NJ Turnpike to the Garden State Pkwy; Atlantic City is exit 38 off the Parkway. The Atlantic City Expwy runs directly to Atlantic City from Philadelphia. Casino parking garages cost about $2 per day, but they waive the fee if you have a receipt showing you spent money inside.
Bus Greyhound (☎ 800-231-2222), **Academy** (☎ 800-442-7272) and **New Jersey Transit** (☎ 973-762-5100; www.njtransit.com) buses run from Port Authority; a roundtrip costs around $25. **Gray Line** (☎ 212-397-2620) operates from 900 Eighth Ave between W 53rd and 54th Sts in Midtown. A casino will often refund the fare (in chips, coins or coupons) if you get a bus directly to its door. Fares are cheaper Monday to Thursday.
Train New Jersey Transit (☎ 973-762-5100; www.njtransit.com) doesn't go direct to AC, so a train trip requires two connections and about twice the money as a bus trip. From Penn Station, switch in Trenton to Philadelphia; from Philly, switch to the Atlantic City Line.
Air The **Atlantic City International Airport** (☎ 609-645-7895), off Tilton Rd in Pomona, is used by airlines servicing the city's casino industry. **Spirit Airlines** (☎ 800-772-7117) and **US Airways Express** (☎ 800-428-4322) connect the town with Boston, Cleveland, Detroit, Newark, Philadelphia and several Florida cities.

famous diving horse plunged into the Atlantic before crowds of spectators, but today it's a collection of small amusement rides, games of chance, candy stands and 'the biggest Go-Kart track in South Jersey!' The Ripley's Believe It or Not museum offers odd and grotesque displays in a theme park–style setting. It's basically a touristy rip-off, but may be a useful diversion for tiny tots. The Visitor Information Center, under the giant tepee in the middle of the Atlantic City Expwy, can provide you with maps and accommodation deals, as can the various other information booths on or near the Boardwalk.

The Absecon Lighthouse dates from 1857 and, at 171ft high, ranks as the tallest in New Jersey and the third-tallest in the country. It's been restored to its original specifications (including the Frensel lens) and you can climb the 228 steps to the top for phenomenal views.

Aside from the Borgata, good food can be found away from the casinos. A few blocks inland from the Boardwalk, Mexico Lindo is a favorite among Mexican locals, while Angelo's Fairmount Tavern is a beloved family-owned Italian restaurant. Tun Tavern, attached to the Sheraton, is AC's only microbrewery. The outdoor patio makes a nice spot to take in the sunset and have a pint and a burger. If you've got a car, try Hannah G's, an excellent breakfast and lunch spot in nearby Ventnor; or Maloney's, a popular seafood-and-steak place. Ventura's Greenhouse Restaurant, in next-door Margate City, is an Italian restaurant loved by locals.

Sights & Information

Atlantic City Historical Museum (☎ 609-347-5839; www.acmuseum.org; Garden Pier; admission free; ☺ 10am-4pm)

Ripley's Believe It or Not (☎ 609-347-2001; New York Ave at Boardwalk; adult/senior/child $11/9/7; ☺ 10am-10pm daily May-Aug, 11am-5pm Mon-Fri, 10am-8pm Sat & Sun Sep-Apr)

Visitor Information Center (☎ 609-449-7130; www.atlanticcitynj.com; Garden State Pkwy; ☺ 9am-4pm)

Absecon Lighthouse (☎ 609-449-1360; cnr Rhode Island & Pacific Aves)

Eating

Angelo's Fairmount Tavern (☎ 609-344-2439; Mississippi Ave at Fairmount Ave; entrees $12-20)

Hannah G's (☎ 609-823-1466; 7310 Ventnor Ave; entrees $4-12)

Maloney's (☎ 609-823-7858; 23 S Washington Ave; entrees $14-25)

Mexico Lindo (☎ 609-345-1880; 2435 Atlantic Ave; entrees $5-11)

Tun Tavern (☎ 609-347-7800; 2 Ocean Way; entrees $10-25)

Ventura's Greenhouse Restaurant (☎ 609-822-0140; 106 Benson Ave, Margate City; entrees $12-22)

Sleeping

Rates at all of the following places fluctuate hugely, from around $65 to $400 a night, depending on weekend events, time of year, vacancy etc.

Atlantic City Hilton (☎ 609-340-7111; Boston Ave at the Boardwalk)

Bally's Park Place & Wild West Casino (☎ 609-340-2000; Park Place at the Boardwalk)

Borgata Hotel Casino & Spa (☎ 866-692-6742; One Borgata Way)

Caesar's Atlantic City (☎ 609-348-4411; Arkansas Ave at Boardwalk)

Claridge Casino Hotel (☎ 609-340-3400; Indiana Ave)

Comfort Inn (☎ 609-348-4000; 154 Kentucky Ave)

Harrah's Marina Hotel Casino (☎ 609-441-5000; Brigantine Blvd)

Holiday Inn Boardwalk (☎ 609-348-2200; the Boardwalk at Chelsea Ave)

Resorts Casino Hotel (☎ 609-344-6000; North Carolina Ave at the Boardwalk)

Sands Hotel, Casino & Country Club (☎ 609-441-4000, 800-227-2637; Indiana Ave)

Showboat Casino (☎ 609-343-4000; Delaware Ave & Boardwalk)

Tropicana Casino & Entertainment Resort (☎ 609-340-4000; Iowa Ave at Boardwalk)

Trump Plaza Casino Hotel (☎ 609-441-6000; Mississippi Ave at Boardwalk)

Trump Taj Mahal (☎ 609-449-1000; 1000 Boardwalk)

Trump's Marina Resort (☎ 609-441-2000; Huron Ave)

CAPE MAY

Founded in 1620, Cape May is on the state's southern tip and is the country's oldest seashore resort. Its sweeping beaches get crowded in summer, but the stunning Victorian architecture is attractive year-round. The entire town was designated a National Historic Landmark in 1976. In addition to its attractive architecture, accommodations (many of them B&Bs in historic homes) and restaurants, Cape May boasts a lovely beach, famous lighthouse, antique shops, and opportunities for whale-watching, fishing and superlative bird-watching. It's the only place in New Jersey where you can watch the sun both rise and set over the water. The quaint area attracts everyone from suburban families to a substantial gay crowd, who are drawn to the many gay-friendly inns.

Transportation

Distance from New York City 150 miles
Direction South
Travel Time 2¾ hours
Car Same as directions to Atlantic City, but continue on to the end of the Garden State Pkwy.
Bus Vehicles to and from New York City are run by New Jersey Transit (☎ 973-762-5100; www.njtransit.com).

While summer is high season, when places are hoppin' and beaches can be enjoyed at their full potential, the rest of the year is also great for settling into one of the romantic lodgings, strolling on the deserted beach and enjoying some fine-dining. The **Cape May Jazz Festival** is a biannual affair, and the **Cape May Music Festival** is highlighted by outdoor jazz, classical and chamber music concerts. For comprehensive information on Cape May county attractions, stop at the **Welcome Center**.

The white, sandy beaches are the main attractions in summer months. The narrow **Cape May Beach** requires passes sold at the lifeguard station on the boardwalk at the end of Grant St. The **Cape May Point Beach** (admission free) is accessible from the parking lot at Cape May Point State Park near the lighthouse. **Sunset Beach** (admission free) is at the end of Sunset Blvd and is the spot to watch the sunset with a 100% uninterrupted horizon line. This is also the place to begin your hunt for the famed Cape May Diamonds – pure quartz crystals that are tumbled smooth by the rolling surf. If you're here between May and September, don't miss the pomp and ceremony of the flag-lowering ceremony at Sunset Beach. Offshore, **Cape May Whale Watcher** 'guarantees' sighting a marine mammal on one of its ocean tours.

The 190-acre **Cape May Point State Park**, just off Lighthouse Ave, has 2 miles of trails, plus the famous **Cape May Lighthouse**. Built in 1859, the 157ft lighthouse recently underwent a $2 million restoration, and its completely reconstructed light is visible as far as 25 miles out to sea. You can climb the 199 stairs to the top in the summer months.

The Cape May peninsula is a resting place for millions of migratory birds each year, and the **Cape May Bird Observatory** (☎ 609-898-2473) maintains a hotline offering information on the latest sightings and is considered one of the country's 10 birding hot spots. Fall is the best time to glimpse some of the 400 species that frequent the area, including hawks, but from March through May you can see songbirds, raptors and other species. The bird observatory also offers tours of **Reed's Beach**, 12 miles north of Cape May on Delaware Bay, where migrating shorebirds swoop down to feed on the eggs laid by thousands of horseshoe crabs each May. Also visit the 18-acre **Nature Center of Cape May**, which features a ` site with open-air observation platforms over the marshes and beaches.

In town, the **Emlen Physick Estate**, an 18-room mansion built in 1879, now houses the **Mid-Atlantic Center for the Arts**, which books tours for Cape May historic homes, the lighthouse or nearby historic Cold Spring Village. The . dates from WWI, when 12 experimental concrete ships were built to compensate for a shortage of steel. *Atlantis*, with a 5-inch concrete aggregate hull, began its seagoing life in 1918, but eight years later it broke free in a storm and ran aground on the western side of the Cape May Point coast. A small chunk of the hull still sits a few feet from shore on Sunset Beach at the end of Sunset Blvd.

CAPE MAY

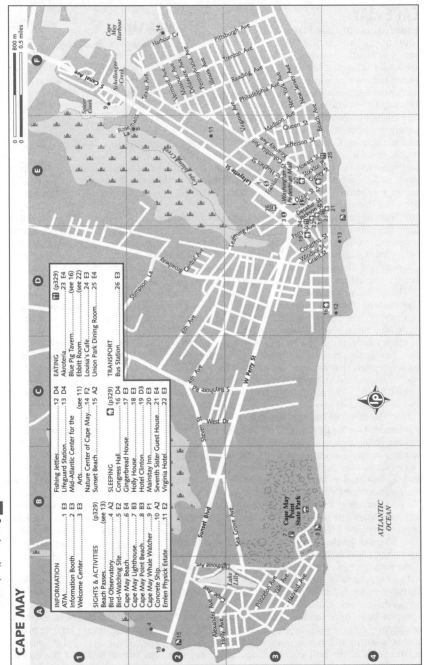

INFORMATION		**EATING**	(p329)
ATM...................................1 E3	Fishing Jetties.....................12 D4	Akroteria...........................23 E4
Information Booth................2 E3	Lifeguard Station................13 D4	Blue Pig Tavern.................(see 16)
Welcome Center..................3 E3	Mid-Atlantic Center for the	Ebbitt Room.....................(see 22)
	Arts...............................(see 11)	Louisa's Cafe......................24 E3
SIGHTS & ACTIVITIES (p329)	Nature Center of Cape May...14 F2	Union Park Dining Room.......25 E4
Beach Passes.....................(see 13)	Sunset Beach.....................15 A2	
Bird Observatory..................4 A2		**TRANSPORT**
Bird-Watching Site................5 E2	**SLEEPING** (p329)	Bus Station........................26 E3
Cape May Beach...................6 E4	Congress Hall.....................16 D4	
Cape May Lighthouse.............7 B3	Gingerbread House...............17 E3	
Cape May Point Beach............8 B3	Holly House........................18 E3	
Cape May Whale Watcher.........9 F1	Hotel Clinton......................19 D3	
Concrete Ship....................10 A2	Mainstay Inn......................20 E3	
Emlen Physick Estate.............11 E2	Seventh Sister Guest House......21 E4	
	Virginia Hotel.....................22 E3	

ATLANTIC OCEAN

Cape May Point State Park

Though you can certainly make a day trip here, Cape May is packed with excellent places to rest your weary head. If you come here during the off season many places will have closed their doors, but you'll have your pick of the ones remaining open and at a reasonably cheap price. In high season, many places have a two- to three-night minimum stay during summer weekends. The best budget option remains **Hotel Clinton**. Classy **Virginia Hotel** has gorgeous old-fashioned rooms with costs that vary wildly depending on the season. The sprawling, just-renovated **Congress Hall**, run by the same owners, has a range of quarters to suit various budgets, plus a long, oceanfront porch lined with rocking chairs.

The town is positively overflowing with small B&Bs; try the darling **Gingerbread House**, a six-room B&B where the rates include a Cape May Beach pass, a continental breakfast and a scrumptious afternoon tea. **Holly House** is a cottage built in 1890 and run by a former mayor of Cape May. It's one of the so-called Seven Sisters, a group of seven identical homes; five of them are situated along Jackson St. **Seventh Sister Guest House** is just a few doors down. **Mainstay Inn**, built in 1872 as a men's gambling club, features rooms furnished in opulent dark woods and large beds; all have private bathrooms and rates include breakfast.

Finding good food is not a problem at Cape May. For a beach snack, **Akroteria** is a collection of small fast-food shacks. **Louisa's Café**, a tiny, low-ceilinged dining room, is the town's prize eatery, serving up seasonal eclectic specialties; the casual **Blue Pig Tavern** at Congress Hall is comparable. Diners with more upscale tastes should reserve a table at the award-winning **Ebbitt Room** in the Virginia Hotel or at the **Union Park Dining Room**, at Hotel Macomber.

Sights & Information

Cape May Beach (☎ 609-884-9525; day/week passes $4/10)

Cape May Bird Observatory (☎ 609-861-0700; 701 East Lake Dr; ☼ 9am-4:30pm)

Cape May Jazz Festival (☎ 609-884-7277; www.capemayjazz.com; ☼ Apr & Nov)

Cape May Lighthouse (☎ 609-884-2159; Lighthouse Ave)

Cape May Music Festival (☎ 609-884-5404; www.capemaymac.org; ☼ mid-May–early Jun)

Cape May Point State Park (☎ 609-884-2159; 707 E Lake Dr)

Cape May Whale Watcher (☎ 609-884-5445; www.capemaywhalewatcher.com, Miss Chris Marina, btwn 2nd Ave & Wilson Dr; adult $23-30, child $12-18)

Emlen Physick Estate (☎ 609-884-5404; 1048 Washington St)

Mid-Atlantic Center for the Arts (☎ 609-884-5404, 800-275-4278; www.capemaymac.org; 1048 Washington St)

Nature Center of Cape May (☎ 609-898-8848; 1600 Delaware Ave; admission free; ☼ 9am-4pm summer, 10am-1pm winter, 10am-3pm fall & spring)

Welcome Center (www.capemayfun.com; 405 Lafayette St; ☼ 9am-4pm)

Eating

Akroteria (Beach Ave; entrees $2-6)

Louisa's Café (☎ 609-884-5884; 104 Jackson St; entrees $12-18)

Union Park Dining Room (☎ 609-884-8811; 727 Beach Ave; entrees $18-30)

Sleeping

Congress Hall (☎ 609-884-8422; 251 Beach Ave; r $80-400)

Gingerbread House (☎ 609-884-0211; 28 Gurney St; r $98-260)

Holly House (☎ 609-884-7365; 20 Jackson St; r from $120)

Hotel Clinton (☎ 609-884-3993; 202 Perry St; r $40-50)

Mainstay Inn (☎ 609-884-8690; 635 Columbia Ave; r $115-295)

Seventh Sister Guest House (☎ 609-884-2280; 10 Jackson St; r from $120)

Virginia Hotel (☎ 609-884-8690; 25 Jackson St; r $80-365)

PHILADELPHIA

Only two hours from NYC, Philly provides a great opportunity to get a glimpse of city life beyond New York – especially for history hounds, who will marvel over the abundance of sites that tell the stories of America. It's easy to combine a trip here with one to Atlantic City, Cape May or both.

William Penn made Philadelphia his capital in 1682, basing its plan on a grid with wide streets and public squares – a layout copied by many US cities. For a time the second-largest city in the British Empire (after London), Philadelphia became a center for opposition to British colonial policy. It was the new nation's capital at the start of the Revolutionary War and again after the war until 1790, when Washington, DC, took over. By the 1800s, New York had superseded Philadelphia as the nation's cultural, commercial and industrial center, and Philly never regained its early preeminent status. But in the 1970s, the nation's bicentennial prompted an urban renewal program that continues to this day.

It's an easy city to get around. Most sights and accommodations are within walking distance of each other, or a short bus ride away. East–west streets are named; north–south streets are numbered, except for Broad and Front Sts. Historic Philadelphia includes Independence National Historic Park and Old City, which extend east to the waterfront.

Perhaps the best way to see all the sites and get an idea of the city's layout, especially if you're only here for the day, is to take advantage of one of the many guided tours. The most complete tour is the 90-minute narrated trolley trip by **Philadelphia Trolley Works**, during which you can hop on and off at designated stops to stroll and then reboard when you're ready. For a unique way of getting around, the **76 Carriage Company** will take you around various areas in a horse-drawn carriage. **Phlash** visitor shuttle is a one-hour, do-it-yourself tour that visits about 25 sites. You travel in a bright purple van, which you can hop on and off of whenever you want; there is no tour guide, but you are equipped with a color-coded, easy-to-follow map of the journey. To do it yourself, make your first stop the **Independence Visitors Center**. Run by the knowledgeable folks of the National Park Service, the center distributes the useful 'Philadelphia Official Visitors Guide,' maps and brochures. The nearby **Philadelphia Convention & Visitors Bureau** has information about businesses, tours, hotels and package deals.

The L-shaped 45-acre **Independence National Historic Park** (undergoing a major renovation) along with the Old City area, has been dubbed 'America's most historic square mile,' and can feel like a stroll back through time. Concentrating your sightseeing around this area will make the city easier to tackle, and allow you to visit the most renowned sites in the city. **Carpenters' Hall**, owned by the Carpenter Company, is the USA's oldest trade guild and the site of the First Continental Congress in 1774. Housed in the Second Bank of the US and modeled after the Parthenon, is the **National Portrait Gallery**, which includes several portraits of prominent figures by Charles Willson Peale. **Library Hall** is where you'll find a copy of the Declaration of Independence, handwritten in a letter by Thomas Jefferson, plus first editions of Darwin's *On the Origin of Species*, and Lewis and Clark's field notes.

Liberty Bell Center, Philadelphia's premier tourist attraction, was recently moved to a brand new location (just around the corner from its old pavilion, where it had sat since 1976) as part of the extensive Independence Park makeover. Constructed in London and tolled at the first public reading of the Declaration of Independence, the hefty 2080lb bell became famous when abolitionists decided to adopt it as a symbol of freedom. The bell is inscribed, 'Proclaim liberty through all the land, to all the inhabitants thereof. (Leviticus 25:10).' Extensive cracking along the face eventually made the bell unusable way back in 1846.

The **Franklin Court** complex, a row of restored tenements, pays tribute to Benjamin Franklin with an underground museum displaying his inventions. At the **B Free Franklin Post**

PHILADELPHIA

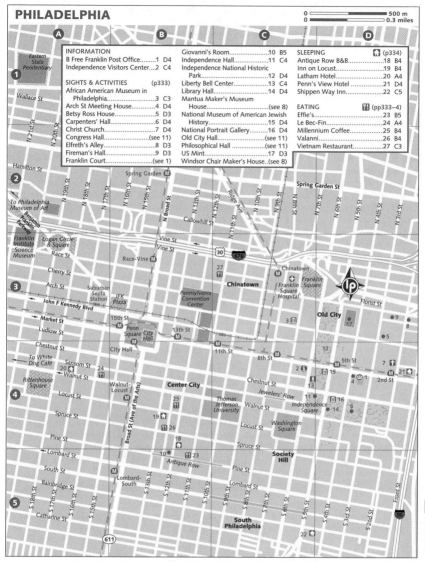

0 — 500 m
0 — 0.3 miles

Office, which has a small US Postal Service Museum, mail receives a special handwritten Franklin postmark. (In addition to being a statesman, author and inventor, the multi-talented Franklin was a postmaster.) **Christ Church**, completed in 1744, is where George Washington and Franklin worshipped.

The **Greek Revival Philadelphia Exchange**, a beautiful Episcopal church designed by William Strickland, is the home of the country's first stock exchange (1834). It's closed to the public, but you can linger at its facade.

Old City – along with Society Hill – comprises the area bounded by Walnut, Vine, Front and 6th Sts. This was early Philadelphia. The 1970s saw its revitalization, when many warehouses were converted into apartments, galleries and small businesses. **Elfreth's Alley** is believed to be the oldest continuously occupied street in the USA; on it, **Mantua Maker's Museum House** has displays of period furniture. **Windsor Chair Maker's House** produced the chairs in Independence Hall. **Fireman's Hall** is where you'll find the nation's oldest fire engine and an exhibit on the rise of organized volunteers, which was led by Ben Franklin. **Betsy Ross House** is where Betsy Griscom Ross (1752–1836), upholsterer and seamstress, is to believed to have sewn the first US flag.

National Museum of American Jewish History features exhibits that examine the historical role of Jews in the USA. At the nearby **US Mint** tours are now only available on a limited basis, mainly to school groups, because of security concerns; call for possible change of status. **Arch St Meeting House** is the USA's largest Quaker meetinghouse, and the **African American Museum in Philadelphia** has excellent collections on black history and culture.

Gay visitors to Philly will be pleased to know that the Philadelphia Convention and Visitors Bureau launched a major ad campaign in 2004 that was specifically aimed at LGBT travelers. 'Get your history straight and your nightlife gay,' the slogan urged. Though the offerings pale in comparison to what's in NYC, there is a pretty hopping nightlife scene for a small city; plus **Millennium Coffee** is a hip java hang, filled with cute boys, while **Giovanni's Room** is a large, well-stocked gay bookstore on Antique Row, and definitely worth a look.

Transportation

Distance from New York City 100 miles

Direction Southwest

Travel Time 2 hours

Car Take the Lincoln Tunnel to the NJ Turnpike (I-95) to Rte 73 toward Philadelphia. Merge onto I-295 and then onto US-30, over the Ben Franklin Bridge and onto I-676, which has exits into Philly.

Bus Greyhound (☎ 800-229-9424) and **Capitol Trailways** (☎ 800-444-2877) all go from Port Authority Bus Terminal to Philly. The trip takes two hours and a one-way ticket costs about $25.

Train Leaving from Penn Station, **Amtrak** (☎ 212-582-6875, 800-872-7245; www.amtrak.com) offers two options for getting to Philly: the high-speed **Acela** (roundtrip $190; one hour), which gets to Philly's 30th St Station; and the regular **coach service** (roundtrip $96; 1½ hours). A great bargain option is **New Jersey Transit** (☎ 973-762-5100; www.njtransit.com; roundtrip $34), which runs a commuter service to Philly from Penn Station, requiring a transfer in Trenton.

If you decide to stay the night here, know that you'll mostly find upscale hotel chains and a sprinkling of quaint B&Bs; the city is sorely lacking in classy boutique-style hotels. **Penn's View Hotel** is an old-fashioned inn that overlooks the water. It offers a range of rooms featuring Chippendale-style furniture, many with exposed-brick walls and working fireplaces. A continental breakfast is included. Similarly, the **Latham Hotel** is a classy, European-style hotel with Victorian rooms. **Shippen Way Inn** is a 1750s colonial house containing nine rooms with quilted beds, plus free wine and cheese in the kitchen and a cozy B&B atmosphere. The **Antique Row B&B** has quirky, period-furnished rooms and good breakfasts on hoppin' Antique Row. **Inn on Locust**, near all the gay nightclubs, gears itself to a business clientele with quarters that convert into board rooms or offices; rooms in the front have great views of one of Philly's huge and colorful outdoor murals.

Eating options are plentiful, with some of the cheapest, most interesting edibles found in the city's compact Chinatown and South Street areas. An always-crowded favorite is

Vietnam Restaurant, serving authentic Vietnamese food like summer rolls, vermicelli and sour fish soup. Two of Philadelphia's most popular spots for a cheese steak (and you can't leave without trying this yummy regional specialty) are Geno's and Pat's King of Steaks.

The indoor Reading Terminal Market is a wonderful indoor marketplace, offering everything from fresh Amish cheeses and Thai desserts to falafel, cheese steaks, salad bars, sushi, Peking duck and great Mexican. At the high end, many gourmets rate Le Bec-Fin as the country's best restaurant for its setting, service and superb French food. Valanni is popular with 50-something theatergoers in the early part of the evening, and later in the evening with sassy gay men, who come for solid Med-Latin cuisine, while Effie's, on Antique Row, has Greek specialties in an intimate setting.

For a full rundown of all of Philly's offerings, pick up a copy of LP's *Philadelphia and the Pennsylvania Dutch Country*.

Sights & Information
The phone number for all Independence National Historic Park (INHP) stops is the same (☎ 215-597-8974). Sites are open 9am to 5pm daily unless otherwise note.

76 Carriage Company (☎ 215-923-8516; www.phillytour.com; cnr 6th & Chestnut Sts; adult $25-70)

African American Museum in Philadelphia (☎ 215-574-0380; www.aampmuseum.org; 701 Arch St; admission $6; ⏱ 10am-5pm Thu-Sun, 10:30am-5pm Tue, 10:30am-7pm Wed)

Arch St Meeting House (320 Arch St; admission by donation; ⏱ closed Sun)

B Free Franklin Post Office (☎ 215-592-1289; 316 Market St)

Betsy Ross House (☎ 215-686-1252; 239 Arch St; admission by donation; ⏱ 9am-5pm)

Carpenters' Hall (INHP, btwn Chestnut & Walnut Sts; ⏱ closed Mon)

Christ Church (☎ 215-922-1695; 2nd St btwn Market & Arch Sts)

Fireman's Hall (☎ 215-923-1438; 147 N 2nd St)

Franklin Court (INHP, Market St btwn S 3rd & S 4th Sts)

Giovanni's Room (☎ 215-923-2960; 345 S 12th St)

Independence Hall/Congress Hall (INHP, Chestnut St btwn S 5th & S 6th Sts)

Independence National Historic Park (☎ 215-597-8974; www.nps.gov/inde)

Independence Visitors Center (☎ 215-965-7676; www.independencevisitorscenter.com; 6th St btwn Market & Arch Sts; ⏱ 8:30am-5pm)

Liberty Bell Center (INHP, 6th St btwn Market & Chestnut Sts)

Library Hall (INHP, S 5th btwn Chestnut & Walnut Sts)

Mantua Maker's Museum House (☎ 215-574-0560; admission $2; ⏱ 10am-4pm Sat, noon-4pm Sun)

National Museum of American Jewish History (☎ 215-923-3811; www.nmajh.org; 55 N 5th St; admission free; ⏱ 10am-5pm Mon-Thu, 10am-3pm Fri, noon-5pm Sun)

National Portrait Gallery (INHP, Chestnut St btwn S 4th & S 5th Sts)

Old City Hall/Philosophical Hall (INHP, Chestnut St btwn S 5th & S 6th Sts)

Philadelphia Trolley Works (☎ 215-925-8687; www.phillytour.com; cnr 6th & Chestnut Sts; adult/child $20/5)

Phlash (☎ 215-474-5274; all-day pass $4)

US Mint (☎ 215-408-0114; INHP, btwn 4th & 5th Sts)

Windsor Chair Maker's House (☎ 215-574-0560; 126 Elfreth's Alley; admission $2; ⏱ 10am-4pm Sat, noon-4pm Sun)

Eating
Effie's (☎ 215-592-8333; 1127 Pine St; entrees $12-15)

Geno's (☎ 215-389-0659; 1219 S 9th St; entrees $3-6)

Le Bec-Fin (☎ 215-567-1000; 1523 Walnut St; dinner prix fixe $38-120)

Millennium Coffee (☎ 731-9798; 212 S 12th St; entrees $2-6)

Pat's King of Steaks (☎ 215-468-1546; 9th St at Wahrton & Passyunk Aves; entrees $3-7; ⏱ 24hr)

Reading Terminal Market (☎ 215-922-2317; www.readingterminalmarket.org; 12th & Arch Sts; entrees $2)

Valanni (☎ 215-790-9494; 1229 Spruce St; entrees $13-18

Vietnam Restaurant (☎ 215-592-1163; 221 N 11th St; entrees $4-11)

Sleeping

Antique Row B&B (☎ 215-592-7802; www.antiquerowbnb.com; 341 S 12th St; r $65-110)

Inn on Locust (☎ 215-985-1905; www.innonlocust.com; 1234 Locust St; r $125-200)

Latham Hotel (☎ 215-563-7474; www.lathamhotel .com; 135 S 17th St; r from $109)

Penn's View Hotel (☎ 215-922-7600; www.pennsview hotel.com; Front & Market Sts; r from $165)

Shippen Way Inn (☎ 215-627-7266; 416-418 Bainbridge St; r $80)

Directory

Directory

TRANSPORTATION

AIR

Three major airports serve New York City. The biggest is John F Kennedy International (JFK), in the borough of Queens, about 15 miles from Midtown Manhattan. Northwest of JFK, but also in Queens, is La Guardia Airport, which is eight miles from Midtown. Newark International Airport (EWR), across the Hudson River in Newark, New Jersey, is about 16 miles from Midtown. There are no baggage-storage facilities at any of the three airports.

There are some rules of thumb for buying cheap tickets: start the hunt early – some of the cheapest tickets and best deals must be purchased months in advance, and popular flights tend to sell out early. Be flexible: play with arrival and departure dates, arrival airports and stopovers. Consider a shorter trip, as ticket prices increase substantially once you surpass the 30-, 60- or 90-day mark.

High season in New York City runs from mid-June to mid-September (summer), and one week before and after Christmas. February and March, and from October to Thanksgiving (the fourth Thursday in November) serve as shoulder seasons, when prices drop slightly. Booking flights is best done online, which will get you the cheapest ticket options and easy e-tickets that will allow you speedy check-in once you reach the airport. Among the best websites for booking flights are: Orbitz (www.orbitz.com), Travelocity (www.travelocity.com), Cheap Tickets (www.cheaptickets.com), Expedia (www.expedia.com), Priceline (www.priceline.com) and Hotwire (www.hotwire.com). Practically every airline in existence has an office in the city, either in Manhattan or at one of the major airports. Though it's rarely necessary to go in person to any one of these offices, you can easily find the office nearest to your hotel by phoning the toll-free directory at ☎ 800-555-1212, or simply by logging onto the airline's website.

If your itinerary is complicated, travel agents can usually find some excellent deals and there is an abundance of agencies in NYC. **Council Travel** (☎ 800-226-8624, reservations ☎ 212-254-2525; www.counciltravel.com) and **STA Travel** (☎ 800-777-0112, reservations ☎ 212-627-3111; www.statravel.com) offer some of the cheapest rates, especially for students. Both agencies have multiple offices in Manhattan. The ubiquitous **Liberty Travel** (☎ 888-271-1584; www.libertytravel.com), an East Coast chain, has more than 30 city locations.

Airlines

The following airlines have offices in New York City:

Aer Lingus (Map pp386-8; ☎ 888-474-7424; www.aerlingus.com; 509 Madison Ave)

Aeromexico (Map pp386-8; ☎ 212-754-2140, 800-237-6639; www.aeromexico.com; 37 W 57th St)

Air Canada (Map pp386-8; ☎ 888-247-2262; www.aircanada.ca; 15 W 50th St)

Air France (Map pp226-7; ☎ 212-830-4000, 800-237-2747; www.airfrance.com; 120 W 56th St)

American Airlines (Map pp386-8; ☎ 800-433-7300; www.aa.com; 18 W 49th St)

British Airways (Map pp386-8; ☎ 800-247-9297; www.british-airways.com; 530 Fifth Ave)

Continental Airlines (Map pp386-8; ☎ 212-319-9494, 800-525-0280; www.continental.com; 100 E 42nd St)

Delta/Delta Song (Map pp386-8; ☎ 800-221-1212; www.delta.com; 100 E 42nd St)

KLM Royal Dutch Airlines (Map pp386-8; ☎ 800-374-7747; www.klm.com; 2nd fl, 100 E 42nd St)

Lufthansa (Map pp386-8; ☎ 800-645-3880; www.lufthansa.com; Suite 1421, 350 Fifth Ave)

Qantas Airways (Map pp386-8; ☎ 800-227-4500; www.qantas.com; 712 Fifth Ave)

Singapore Airlines (Map pp386-8; ☎ 212-644-8801, 800-742-3333; www.singaporeair.com; 55 E 59th St)

United Airlines (Map pp386-8; ☎ 800-241-6522; www.ual.com; 100 E 42nd St)

US Airways (Map pp386-8; ☎ 800-428-4322; www.usairways.com; 101 Park Ave)

Airports

Three major airports serve the New York metropolitan region.

JFK INTERNATIONAL AIRPORT

Map p378 ☎ 718-244-4444; www.panynj.gov

This airport, out in eastern Queens, serves 35 million passengers a year and hosts flights to and from all corners of the globe. It's sprawling and crowded, as airlines used to build showcase terminals at JFK, and thus the airport grew to its uncoordinated state with no coherent plan (it's currently undergoing a major renovation, due to be completed in 2005). While some of the original airlines (eg Eastern and Pan Am) have disappeared, the terminals remain, linked by the JFK Expressway and a free shuttle bus.

It also takes a long time to travel to and from JFK, despite several options for getting there and away. Those who can afford it take a taxi or car service, shelling out the $45 taxi flat rate to sit in traffic, rather than deal with the crawling Rockaway Beach A train – a ride that has the upside of costing only $2, but the downside of taking at least an hour from Midtown. From the end of the line, you can now switch to the much-touted AirTrain, which makes connections to all terminals and costs an additional $5. Another option is to take a shuttle bus service to/from Manhattan: the **New York Airport Service Express Bus** (☎ 718-875-8200; one way $13, every 15 minutes) travels between JFK and the Port Authority Bus Terminal, Penn Station and Grand Central Terminal; **Super Shuttle Manhattan** (☎ 800-258-3826; one way $17-19) is kind of like a shared-taxi ride. The shuttle requires you to make a reservation and will then pick you up, on schedule, along with several others who are traveling at the same time as you.

LA GUARDIA AIRPORT

Map p397 LGA; ☎ 718-533-3400; www.panynj.gov

La Guardia Airport is more convenient than JFK if you're driving or taking a taxi, as it's smaller and closer to Manhattan. Getting there by public transportation, however, is just as taxing. The only option is to take the subway (E, F, R, V, G) to Jackson Heights, Queens, and then connect to the Q33 public bus, which stops at each terminal (it takes around 30 minutes for local neighborhood stops en route). You can also catch the same privately run shuttle services that go to/from JFK – the trip costs about $5 less for the shorter ride.

NEWARK LIBERTY INTERNATIONAL AIRPORT

EWR; ☎ 973-961-6000; www.panynj.gov

This is a well-organized international arrival terminal and a good choice for foreign visitors. Advantages include a large immigration hall (with fast passport checks) and a monorail system that links the terminals.

Moreover, flights to Newark are usually a bit cheaper because of the misplaced perception that the airport is less accessible than JFK – it is in *New Jersey* after all. One of the beauties of Newark, however, is that you can get into Manhattan quickly by bus (see the shuttle options under JFK and La Guardia above) and **New Jersey Transit** (p342), which has trains that stop directly at the airport, linking you to the monorail.

BICYCLE

It's not the most bike-friendly city, but New Yorkers are getting better at tolerating cyclists, thanks in part to improved road conditions, new bike paths (such as the one that's part of Hudson Park, running the length of Manhattan's west side), and awareness campaigns from environmental groups. Transportation Alternatives (Map pp386-8; ☎ 212-629-8080; www.transalt.org; 115 W 30th St) has cycling maps available for downloading, sponsors Bike Week NYC every May and acts as a clearinghouse for loads of cycling-related resources, including your legal rights as a cyclist, antitheft tips and how to take your bike on public transportation.

Still, a great many locals are terrified of vying for road space with the oft-oblivious taxis, trucks, cars and buses that fly up and down the avenues – though some cyclists thrive on the adrenaline, especially the city's fleet of bike messengers who zoom around without helmets or fear, sometimes even removing brakes from their bikes altogether! But if you do ride around the city, be smart: always wear a helmet, choose a bike with wide tires to help you handle potholes and other bits of street debris and be alert so you don't get 'doored' by a passenger exiting a taxi. Unless your urban skills are well honed, stick to the pastoral paths in Central and Prospect Parks and along the Hudson River. And don't even think of peddling on the sidewalks – it's illegal. If you must lock a bike up somewhere in the city, forgo anything that's not the most top-of-the-line U-lock you can find – or, better yet, stick to the $100 coated chains that weigh a ton. Stealthy bike thieves will easily slice through anything else.

Five Borough Bicycle Club (p249) sponsors free or low-cost weekend trips to the outskirts of the city; for more information, visit the club's office at **Hostelling International–New York** (Map pp389-91). The **New York Cycle Club** (p249) sponsors day trips and longer rides and also offers printed guides to 65 of its members' favorite routes, while **Fast & Fabulous** (☎ 212-567-7160; www.fastnfab.org) serves as the city's only bicycling club for gays and lesbians, hosting frequent rides both in and around the city.

You're allowed to bring your bike onto the subway, which is helpful in case you get caught in the rain. But to bring it on a commuter train, which you can only do during nonrush-hour times, you'll need to have first obtained a bike pass at the ticket window. You can get your pass, which is free, during weekday afternoon hours.

Hire

Many places hire bicycles for about $30 per day. Companies include: **Sixth Ave Bicycles** (Map pp382-5; ☎ 212-255-5100; 545 Sixth Ave); **Manhattan Bicycle** (Map pp386-8; ☎ 212-262-0111; 791 Ninth Ave btwn 52nd & 53rd Sts), among other locations; **Central Park Bicycle Tours & Rentals** (Map pp226-7; ☎ 212-541-8759; 2 Columbus Circle at 59th & Broadway); and **Frank's Bike Shop** (Map pp382-5; ☎ 212-533-6332; 533 Grand St), which is a neighborhood shop in the Lower East Side with helpful staff and very low prices.

BOAT

It's highly unusual for anyone to yacht their way into town, and those who do will find few ports ready to receive them – just an exclusive boat slip at the World Financial Center and a long-term slip at the 79th St Boathouse on the Upper West Side.

The zippy yellow boats that make up the fleet of **New York Water Taxi** (☎ 212-742-1969; www.nywatertaxi.com) stop and start at 11 landings around the city, from north Brooklyn and Lower Manhattan to Chelsea and the Upper East Side. One-way trips cost between $4 to $6, and 24-hour passes, which can be used as many times as you'd like in one day, are $15. Note that partial service interruptions have been the norm as the

New York Water Taxi system, relatively new in the city, works out its kinks; be sure to check schedules through its phone service or website. Another bigger, brighter ferry (this one's orange) is the **Staten Island Ferry** (p149), which makes constant free journeys to and from its Lower Manhattan and St George, Staten Island, terminals. It serves mostly commuters, but it's also a popular way to get gorgeous harbor glimpses for free.

For information on boat tours, see p72.

BUS

Many New Yorkers don't ever consider the bus as a viable transportation option. These folks consider buses to be quaint, slow, unreliable hulking objects, their chief purpose being to shuttle senior citizens to and from the grocery store or doctor. But NYC buses are not what they used to be. They run 24 hours a day and the routes are easily navigable, going crosstown at all the major street byways – 14th, 23rd, 34th, 42nd and 72nd Sts, and all the others that are two-way roads – and Uptown and Downtown, depending on which avenue they serve. Stops, many with shelters, are every few blocks and all have maps and clearly marked schedules, which are rough guides as to how often you can expect a bus to pass. The frequency on most routes is remarkably often and, best of all, when you ride a bus instead of a subway, you can look out at the world, often turning a simple ride into a people-watching adventure. That said, buses do get overcrowded at rush hour, as most are smaller than even one subway car, and slow to a crawl in heavy traffic. So when you're in a hurry, stay underground.

The cost of a bus ride is the same as the subway, $2; and you can pay with a Metrocard or exact change but not dollar bills. Transfers from one line to another are free, as are transfers to or from the subway. Transfers are good for two hours and are automatically encoded on the Metrocard when used.

For all suburban and long-distance bus trips, you'll leave and depart from the **Port Authority Bus Terminal** (Map pp386-8; ☎ 212-564-8484; 41st St at Eighth Ave). Though Port Authority has improved in recent years, and it's not quite as rough as its reputation, it's still likely that you'll be hassled by panhandlers or shady types offering to carry bags for tips. **Greyhound** (☎ 800-231-2222; www.greyhound.com) connects New

York with major cities across the country. **Peter Pan Trailways** (☎ 800-343-9999; www .peterpan-bus.com) operates buses to the nearest major cities, including a daily express service to Boston (one way/roundtrip $32/64), with a seven-day advance purchase. **Short Line** (☎ 212-736-4700; www.shortlinebus .com) operates numerous buses to towns in northern New Jersey and upstate New York, while **New Jersey Transit** (☎ 973-762-5100; www .njtransit.com) buses serve all of NJ, with a direct service to Atlantic City (one way around $20).

Undoubtedly the sweetest deal to Boston, however, is with those reliable folks at **Fung Wah** (Map pp382-5; ☎ 212-925-8889; www.fungwahbus.com; 139 Canal St at Bowery), with 10 departures per day between 7am and 10pm for $10 to $25 one way, depending on the time you want to travel. Be sure to book ahead, as what used to be a little-known service used only by Chinese passengers and college students has turned into a booming business. Many competitors have sprung up as well, and you can find them hovering around the same corner in Chinatown.

CAR & MOTORCYCLE

Driving is not recommended in the city unless it's absolutely necessary. There's always traffic, gas is pricey, car hire is expensive, parking is in short supply and it's a way bigger hassle than it's worth, considering all the excellent mass-transit options.

Driving

If you're in a passenger car in New York that isn't a taxi, you should be armed with the Hagstrom five-borough map (p346) and a radio tuned to 1010 WINS, which broadcasts all the gnarly traffic details.

The worst part about driving in New York is getting in and out of the city – joining the masses as they try to squeeze through tunnels and over bridges to traverse the various waterways that surround Manhattan. Besides that, getting around within the city isn't difficult, as most of Manhattan (with the exception of the Village) is laid out in a neat grid, and traffic congestion prevents you from having to move along too swiftly if you're feeling tentative. Just be aware of local laws, such as the fact that you can't make a right on red (like you can

in the rest of the state) and also the fact that every other street is one way, which can cause inexperienced drivers to drive around in frustrating circles.

Heading away from, or in to, the city is pretty easy: I-95, which runs from Maine to Florida, cuts east to west through the city as the Cross Bronx Expressway (another nightmare, recognized locally as the worst roadway around). Outside New York City, I-95 continues south as the New Jersey Turnpike; north as the Connecticut Turnpike. Via I-95, Boston is 194 miles to the north, Philadelphia 104 miles to the south and Washington, DC 235 miles south.

Highway speed limits in Connecticut and upstate New York are 65mph; in New Jersey, they remain 55mph except on certain interstate roads.

Hire

Hiring a car in the city is mighty expensive and, though agencies advertise bargain rates for weekend or week-long rentals, these deals are almost always blacked out in New York. If you want to rent for a few days, perhaps for a road trip out of town, book through a travel agent or online before leaving home. Without a reservation, a rental car will cost at least $75 for a midsize car – and that's before extra charges like the 13.25% tax, various insurance costs etc – and wind up being at least $100 before all is said and done. One trick is to leave the city altogether – at least

---

Alternative NYC Transportation

Parking's a nightmare and car-rental prices are off the radar. But you won't be confined to subways and taxis. If you want to travel around New York City (and beyond), try these nontraditional forms of transportation:

Airtrain (p337) Getting to JFK and Newark airports has never been easier.

Fung Wah (left) Twenty bucks one-way bus fare to Boston? Believe it.

Pedicab (p340) Rickshaw-style bicycle rides through Times Square and Downtown.

Water Taxi (opposite) Yellow and black, plying the Manhattan and Brooklyn waterfronts.

Zipcar (p340) Need to drive? This car-share service rents by hour or day.

Manhattan – via mass transit and rent 'over the border,' as rates in the outer boroughs and New Jersey tend to be much cheaper.

To rent a car, you need a valid driver's license and a major credit card. The law no longer decrees that you need to be over 25 to rent, but companies are still allowed to charge younger folks a higher rate, making it prohibitively expensive. Among the many rental agencies in the city are the following:

Avis (☎ 800-331-1212; www.avis.com)

Budget (☎ 800-527-0700; www.budget.com)

Dollar (☎ 800-800-4000; www.dollar.com)

Hertz (☎ 800-654-3131; www.hertz.com)

Another interesting and popular option is Zipcar (☎ 212-691-2884; www.zipcar.com) geared mostly to locals who might need a car for errands or a flashy hot date. Zipcar is an on-demand car-sharing service that's available 24 hours a day, and cars can be hired per hour or per day. The price includes gas, insurance, designated parking and access to one of the cute little VW Bugs that are parked all over the city. Rates are $8 to $12 Monday to Thursday and $8 to $16 Friday to Sunday plus 40¢ per mile; daily rates start at $65. Eventually, you must become an approved member and Zipcard holder, but you're entitled to a 60-day trial run.

Parking

Finding space in this cramped city to park your car is a challenge, whether you're willing to pay for it or not. Free parking, or parking on the streets, is in extremely short supply – car owners have mastered the knack of moving their vehicles back and forth to alternate sides of the street to make way for the street cleaners. Meters are strictly enforced and on most streets (which run east to west) and avenues (north to south) there are no-parking strips. If you're lucky enough to find a spot, make sure to read every sign posted, as one may appear to make parking legal while another, a few feet away, cancels it out. Parking in lots and garages is usually what drivers must resort to – prices average $20 a day but some have daily specials, which require early entrances and departures. Because so few city travelers will be driving, restaurant and hotel listings in this book will not list any parking icons – although many city hotels do have deals with local lots and garages, affording minor discounts.

PEDICABS

A fairly new addition to NYC's already-crazed streets is bicycle taxis, similar to rickshaws, which are used mostly for novelty rides by tourists. General trips cost between about $8 to $15, but can vary, depending on the distance and number of passengers. Two companies operating pedicabs include Manhattan Rickshaw (☎ 212-604-4729; www .manhattanrickshaw.com) and PONY (☎ 212-965-9334).

SUBWAY

An important part of subway travel is knowing how to refer to your train. Because the various lines began as separately operated subways rather than one cohesive system, lines were known (and are still known by old-timers) by their antiquated names, which included the BMT and IND systems. Now, though, every subway is named with a letter or number – and most lines carry a collection of two to four trains on its track. For example, the red-colored line in Manhattan is the 1, 2, 3, 9 line; they are four separate trains, and though they follow roughly the same path in Manhattan, the 2 and 3 eventually split off on their own in Brooklyn and the Bronx. Plus, the 2 and 3 make express stops in Manhattan, while the 1 and 9 are local. Still, if you ask someone which train to take to W 72 St, they may say 'take the one-nine,' even though the 1, 9, 2 or 3 could take you there. The same goes for all the other lines, whether they're lettered or numbered. But don't fret! The maps are surprisingly easy to negotiate, especially because of the different-colored lines.

Iconic, cheap ($2), round-the-clock and a full century old, the New York City subway system is a remarkable example of mass transit that works, in spite of itself. The 656-mile system can be intimidating at first, but dive in and you'll soon be a fan of its many virtues.

The New York subway (known colloquially as 'the train'), run by the Metropolitan Transportation Authority (MTA), is the fastest and most reliable way to get around and it's also much safer and cleaner than it used to be. Maps are available for the taking at every stop and huge route maps are displayed on every platform, as well as on every subway car of every line. You can also ask someone who looks like they know where they're going (although they may not). The mistake most visitors make is boarding an express train only to see it pass by the local stop they wanted. But the subway map (p398-0) delineates between local and express stops by representing local stops as black circles and express stops as white circles. Still, there are no guarantees: tourists and locals alike are constantly baffled by a local train switching to an express track without warning and vice versa, but that's usually due to construction (or an emergency), as the system is ancient and constantly under repair.

Another common mistake that visitors make is trying to seem cool, calm and collected by not holding onto anything as the train begins to move. Often, you just get knocked into the lap of a jaded local. So just hold on!

A few recent changes have made the subway experience almost unrecognizable for folks who haven't been here in five or more years. First of all, tokens have been replaced with the yellow-and-blue Metrocard, which you can purchase or add money to on one of the several easy-to-use, automated machines that stand at every station. There are two types of Metrocard – pay per ride (allowing one free transfer from subway to bus, or bus to bus in a two-hour time period), or the unlimited ride. Also, many of the older trains have been replaced by models with sleek, clean cars that have automated announcements at each stop – much to the chagrin of New Yorkers who were in love with the various gruff, accented inflections of individual announcers (which still do exist on many lines). However, perhaps the most sweeping change, has been the recent rerouting of many trains (including the N, R, W, B, D and M lines), restoring full service over the Manhattan Bridge, in and out of Brooklyn, for the first time in many years. Updated subway maps reflect all the changes, which are no doubt still throwing off some New Yorkers – so don't worry, you're not alone if you're confused. For subway updates and information, call ☎ 718-330-1234 or visit www.mta.info.

Though there's been a bit of a buzz lately about the construction of a Second Ave subway line (the east side of Manhattan is notoriously underserved), don't expect to notice anything as a visitor. Plans for such a project have been long awaited and, if the MTA stays on schedule, the first phase will be ready for riders in 2011.

TAXI

Hailing and riding in a cab are rites of passage in New York – especially when you get a hack (local lingo for 'taxi driver') who drives like a neurotic speed demon, which is often. Still, most taxis in NYC are clean and, compared to those in many international cities, pretty cheap.

That said, the Taxi & Limousine Commission (TLC; ☎ 311), the taxis' governing body, raised the fares in May 2004 to $2.50 for the initial charge (first one-fifth mile), 40¢ each additional one-fifth mile as well as per 120 seconds of being stopped in traffic, $1 peak surcharge (weekdays 4pm to 8pm), and a 50¢ night surcharge (8pm to 6am daily). But part of the new deal is that you can now pay with your credit or debit card, which can make the whole experience easier. Tips are expected to be 10% to 15%, but give less if you feel in any way mistreated – and be sure to ask for a receipt and use it to note the driver's license number. You can call the TLC with any complaints and if anything else bothers you about your ride, don't be afraid to speak up, as you're protected by the Passenger's Bill of Rights. This gives you the right to tell the driver which route you'd like to take, or ask your driver to stop smoking or turn off an annoying radio station. Also, the driver does not have the right to refuse you a ride based on where you are going; the best thing you can do is not give him or her a chance to, but rather get in, let the meter start, and then give your destination.

To hail a cab, it must have a lit light on its roof. It's particularly difficult to score a taxi in the rain, at rush hour and around 4pm, when many drivers end their shifts.

And note that something called a car service – which is essentially a taxi, though the car isn't yellow and you must call or stop into a storefront dispatcher for your ride – is a common taxi cab alternative in the outer boroughs. Fares differ depending on the neighborhood and length of ride, and must be determined beforehand, as they have no meters. Though these 'black cars' are quite common in Brooklyn and Queens, you should never get into one if a driver simply stops to offer you a ride – no matter what borough you're in. It could be a scam, and in order to be safe, you should always arrange for these rides through a dispatcher.

TRAIN

Penn Station (33rd St btwn Seventh & Eighth Aves) is the departure point for all **Amtrak** (☎ 800-872-7245; www.amtrak.com) trains, including the *Metroliner* and *Acela Express* service to Princeton, NJ, and Washington, DC. The main advantage of the *Metroliner* is that you'll get a reserved seat, while the *Acela* gets there in just over half the amount of time as a regular train; both will cost twice as much as a normal fare, though. A basic one-way service from New York to Washington, DC, costs $72. All fares vary, based on the day of the week and the time you want to travel. Call Amtrak for information about special discount passes if you plan on traveling throughout the USA by train, which, while romantic, is an expensive proposition. There is no baggage-storage facility at Penn Station.

Long Island Rail Road (☎ 718-217-5477; www.mta.nyc.ny.us/lirr/) serves several hundred thousand commuters each day, with services from Penn Station to points in Brooklyn, Queens and to the suburbs of Long Island, including the North and South Fork resort areas. **New Jersey Transit** (☎ 973-762-5100; www.njtransit.com) also operates trains from Penn Station, with services to the suburbs and the Jersey Shore. Another option for getting into NJ, but strictly northern points such as Hoboken and Newark, is the **New Jersey Path** (Map pp380-1; ☎ 800-234-7284; www.pathrail.com), which runs trains on a separate-fare system ($2) along the length of Sixth Ave, with stops at 34th, 23rd, 14th, 9th and Christopher Sts, as well as at the recently reopened World Trade Center site.

The only train line that still departs from Grand Central Terminal, Park Ave at 42nd St, is the **Metro-North Railroad** (☎ 212-532-4900; www.mnr.org), which serves the northern city suburbs, Connecticut and the Hudson Valley.

PRACTICALITIES

ACCOMMODATIONS

In the Sleeping chapter (p291) of this book you'll find hotels listed alphabetically within their neighborhoods, with mid-range and luxury options listed first, followed by Cheap Sleeps. The average room is $275 a night, with some seasonal fluctuations (lowest in January and February, highest in September and October). And beware of the 13.25% room tax. That said, it's not too hard to find a budget room – that's less than $150 by New York standards – or even space for $50 or less in a youth hostel. It's not uncommon to find frequent special rates no matter what time of year it is, but especially in midwinter or midsummer, when weekend rates often get slashed. Other times, weekends can be a problem, as many smaller hotels have a strict three-night minimum. Check-out times vary, but are usually at 11am, while check-in times are usually 3pm; if you need to vary either, though, just ask, as most places are flexible.

For tips on finding discounts through Internet reservations, see p292.

BUSINESS HOURS

Most offices are open 9am to 5pm Monday to Friday, while most shops are on a later clock, typically opening at 10am or 11am or even noon in the Village, and closing between 7pm and 9pm. Restaurants serve breakfast from about 6am to noon, and then lunch till 3pm or 4pm, with just enough time to start serving dinner by 5pm – although prime dinner hour is more like 8pm. Most stores are open on public holidays (except Christmas day) but banks, schools and offices are usually closed. Though most banks are open 9am to 4pm Monday to Friday, a few in Chinatown have limited Saturday hours, and a new chain, Commerce Bank, with locations all over Manhattan, has daily hours that vary.

CHILDREN

Contrary to popular belief, New York can be a pretty child-friendly city – it just takes a bit of guidance to find all the little creature comforts that you're accustomed to having back home. While visiting during warm weather tends to make things easier, as you can always resort to the many parks and playgrounds and zoos to let your kids expel some pent-up energy, there are plenty of indoor activities as well. Some museums (particularly those geared especially to kids), theaters, movie theaters, book and toy stores, an aquarium and even a slew of restaurants are perfect places for families. Sticking to neighborhoods known for their high stroller factor – the Upper West Side and Park Slope, Brooklyn, in particular – will make it easier to find places where a screaming, tired kid will provoke sympathetic smiles rather than horrified glares.

There are some pitfalls, of course, mainly going up and down subway stairs while lugging a stroller, and being left out in the cold when it comes to fine dining and chi-chi accommodations.

For a list of fun activities for children, see For Children (p72) or pick up Lonely Planet's *Travel With Children*.

Babysitting

Most major hotels (not boutique-style places) offer babysitting services, or can at least provide you with some reliable referrals for some. Or you could turn to a local childcare organization. **Baby Sitters' Guild** (☎ 212-682-0227; www.babysittersguild.com), established back in 1940 specifically to serve travelers staying in hotels with children, has a stable of sitters who speak a range of 16 languages. All are carefully screened, most are CPR-certified and many have nursing backgrounds; they'll come right to your hotel room and even bring games and arts-and-crafts projects.

CLIMATE

Spring in New York is absolutely gorgeous – blossoming trees pop into reds and pinks, sunny days glimmer and even rainy days have a lovely, cleansing feel to them. The temperatures can still dip down to a chilly 40°F in early April evenings, but average temperatures hover at around 60°F, creating days that are perfect for strolling in the city.

Summers can be beastly, though, as temperatures in July and August have been known to climb to the 100°F mark; usually it's between 70°F and 80°F, with occasional thunderstorms that light up the sky and cool everything down until the sun comes out again.

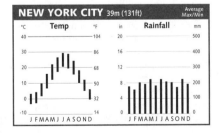

Winters, of course, are cold. It can be grey for days, with sleet and snow showers that quickly turn into a mucky brown film at your feet and temperatures that can easily dip down into the single digits come January. But a good snowstorm is a beautiful thing in these parts, and a cold night inspires cuddling, which can make a damn romantic visit.

COURSES

New York is brimming with universities, colleges and small, focused schools where students reap the benefits of being in an artistic, culinary and cultural hotspot. Why not learn a little something while you're here? As a traveler, it's a great way to gain a different perspective on the city.

Cooking

Peter Kump's **Institute of Culinary Education** (Map pp386–8; ☎ 212-847-0700; www.iceculinary .com; 50 W 23rd St btwn Fifth & Sixth Aves; per class around $75) offers thousands of hands-on and demonstration cooking classes on subjects ranging from cheese making to Asian stir-fry. Many classes are held over one evening and last for around three hours – perfect for a traveler to get a taste of things.

Dancing

Stepping Out Studios (Map pp386–8; ☎ 646-742-9400; www.steppingoutstudios.com; 37 W 26th St at Sixth Ave; open-house free) offers open-house trail classes at the beginning of each new session in swing, salsa and ballroom, plus special events and classes specifically for same-sex partners through its OUTdancing program. For a focus on salsa, head to the music club **SOB's** (p242), where the Monday night La Tropicana series offers one-hour **classes** (per class $5; ⏱7pm), followed by a high-octane dance party at 9pm.

General

The **Learning Annex** (Map pp386–8; ☎ 212-371-0280; www.learningannex.com; 16 W 53rd St btwn Fifth & Sixth Aves; classes $40-200) is infamous for its thick catalogues, available for free in street boxes, offering the wackiest range of classes ever – feng shui, soap making, in-line skating, real estate, screenwriting, chess and how to fall in love. Classes are generally held over the course of one day or an evening.

Language

Get a quick, intensive group lesson in conversational English at the **Language Learning Center** (Map pp386-8; ☎ 212-684-6144; www .speakeasee.com; 21 W 40th St btwn Fifth & Sixth Aves; per hour $6.50). You can stop in just once for two hours, or drop in daily while you're on vacation.

CUSTOMS

US customs allows each person over the age of 21 to bring 1L of liquor (no absinthe!) and 200 cigarettes duty-free into the USA (smokers take note: cigarettes cost around $7 a pack here in the big city, so take advantage of those duty-free shops). US citizens are allowed to import, duty-free, up to $800 worth of gifts from abroad, while non-US citizens are allowed to import $100 worth. If you're carrying more than $10,000 in US and foreign cash, traveler's checks, money orders etc, you need to declare the excess amount. There is no legal restriction on the amount that may be imported, but undeclared sums in excess of $10,000 will probably be subject to investigation. For updates, which happen frequently, check www.customs.ustreas.gov/travel.

DISABLED TRAVELERS

Federal laws guarantee that all government offices and facilities are available to the disabled. Most restaurant listings also note whether the location is accessible by wheelchair. For more information, you can contact the mayor's **Office for People with Disabilities** (☎ 212-788-2830; ⊗ 9am-5pm Mon-Fri). Other excellent resources are the **Society for Accessible Travel & Hospitality** (SATH; Map pp386-8; ☎ 212-447-7284; www.sath.org; 347 Fifth Ave at 34th St; ⊗ 9am-5pm) and the **Hospital Audiences Inc** (☎ 212-575-7660; www.hospaud .org), which publishes an online guide, *Access for All*, revealing how accessible places really are and giving information, including height of telephones, and alternative entrances.

Though things are improving slowly but surely, New York is still hard to navigate: streets are congested, street corners with curb cuts are often overcrowded with pedestrians and the general hustle and bustle is a drawback to anyone not operating at a breakneck pace. What's worse, subways are either on elevated tracks or deep below the ground

and there are few elevators to access them; buses, which all have wheelchair elevation systems and ride space, are definitely the way to go. All movie and Broadway theaters have areas reserved for wheelchairs, and sometimes the newer movie theaters even have those seats near the front, rather than stuck in the back. For detailed information on subway and bus wheelchair accessibility, call the **Accessible Line** (☎ 718-596-8585). Traveling with a companion will make things easier and planning each day's logistics ahead of time should smooth the way.

DISCOUNT PASSES

New York City Pass (http://citypass.net), which you can purchase either online or at any major city attraction (museums, historic sites etc), buys you admission into six major attractions for just $48 ($34 for ages six to 17) – a $96.50 value! **New York Pass** (www.newyorkpass.com), meanwhile, sells online for $49 and gives you day-long access to 40 top attractions (Empire State Building, Statue of Liberty, the Guggenheim etc), as well as discounts at 25 stores and restaurants. Two-, three- and seven-day passes are also available, and you can choose to collect them in NYC or have them sent to you before you leave home.

ELECTRICITY

The electric current in the USA is 110 to 115 volts, 60 Hz AC. Outlets are made for either flat two-prong or three-prong plugs. If your appliance is made for another electrical system, you will need a US converter, which can be bought from hardware stores and drugstores.

EMBASSIES & CONSULATES

The presence of the United Nations in New York City means that nearly every country in the world maintains diplomatic offices in Manhattan. Check the local *Yellow Pages* under 'consulates' for a complete listing. Some foreign consulates, all in Manhattan, include the following:

Australia (Map pp386-8; ☎ 212-351-6500; www .australianyc.org/consulate; 34th fl, 150 E 42nd St; ⊗ 8:30am-5pm Mon-Fri)

Brazil (Map pp226-7; ☎ 917-777-7777; www.brazilny.org; 21st fl, 1185 Sixth Ave; ⊗ 10am-noon & 2:30-4pm Mon-Fri)

Canada (Map pp226-7; ☎ 212-596-1628; ⏲ www.
canada-ny.org; 1251 Sixth Ave; ⏲ 8:45am-5pm Mon-Fri)

France (Map pp389-91; ☎ 212-606-3680; www.consulfrance
-newyork.org; 934 Fifth Ave; ⏲ 9am-1pm Mon-Fri)

Germany (Map pp386-8; ☎ 212-610-9700; www.nyc.com
/government/the_consulate_general_of_germany.aspx;
871 United Nations Plaza; ⏲ 9am-noon Mon-Fri)

Ireland (Map pp386-8; ☎ 212-319-2555, fax 212-980-9475;
17th fl, 345 Park Ave)

Italy (Map pp386-8; ☎ 212-737-9100; www.italconsulnyc
.org; 690 Park Ave; ⏲ 2:30-4:15pm Mon-Fri)

Netherlands (Map pp226-7; ☎ 212-246-1429; www.cgny.
org; 11th fl, 1 Rockefeller Plaza; ⏲ 9am-5:30pm Mon-Fri)

New Zealand (Map pp386-8; ☎ 212-832-4038; www
.nzembassy.com; Suite 2510, 222 E 41st St; ⏲ 9am-noon
Mon-Fri)

Spain (Map pp386-8; ☎ 212-355-4080; www.spainconsul
-ny.org; 150 E 58th St; ⏲ 9am-2pm Mon-Fri)

UK (Map pp386-8; ☎ 212-745-0200; www.britainusa.com
/ny; 845 Third Ave; ⏲ by appointment only)

EMERGENCY

Poison control (☎ 800-222-1222)

Police, fire & ambulance (☎ 911)

GAY & LESBIAN TRAVELERS

It's no big deal to be LGBT in New York
City, the birthplace of the gay rights movement. Since those revolutionary riots back in
1969, at the **Stonewall Bar** (p216) that still exists, New Yorkers' queer tolerance has only
continued to improve by leaps and bounds.
It's acceptable – and by and large ignored
– if same-sex couples hold hands or kiss in
public in practically all of Manhattan and
most outer-borough spots, as well. The gay-
est neighborhoods include Chelsea, Brooklyn's Park Slope, the East Village and the
West Village, which is where you'll find the
city's queer headquarters: the **Lesbian, Gay, Bisexual & Transgender Community Center** (LGBT; Map
pp382-5; ☎ 212-620-7310; www.gaycenter
.org; 208 W 13th St btwn Sixth & Seventh
Aves), which hosts hundreds of meetings and
events weekly, plus offers counseling, traveler
services and loads of local gay publications.
Another great resource to be aware of is the
New York City Gay & Lesbian Anti-Violence Project (Map
pp386-8; 24hr hotline ☎ 212-714-1141; www
.avp.org; 240 W 35th St), which has a hotline for reporting anti-queer bias crimes (in
English or Spanish) and offers advice and
counseling.

HOLIDAYS

Following is a list of major NYC holidays
and special events. These holidays may
force closure of many businesses or attract
crowds, making dining and accommodations reservations difficult. See p9 for a list
of more-specific dates.

If It's Queer, It's Here

New York City has long been one of the centers of gay and lesbian culture in the United States. At least two neighborhoods – Chelsea and Greenwich Village – have become synonymous, in popular consciousness, with gay life, while
lesbians have a strong presence in the East Village and Park Slope, Brooklyn. In truth, though, gay and lesbian visitors
should feel extremely comfortable not just in these areas but practically anywhere else in the city, with the possible
exception of some conservative outer-borough neighborhoods.

The signal moment of the modern gay rights movement occurred in New York on June 27, 1969, when the police
launched a raid on the **Stonewall Bar** (p216), whose patrons were mourning the death of singer Judy Garland, an icon for
the gay community. Many angrily resisted the bust, and three nights of riots followed. The Stonewall rebellion and other
protests led to the introduction in 1971 of the first bill designed to ban discrimination on the basis of sexual orientation.

Today, the **Lesbian, Gay, Bisexual & Transgender parade** (p11), held on Fifth Ave on the last weekend of June,
attracts visitors from around the world, and NYC is famed as a gay and lesbian travel destination.

A great resource is the **LGBT Community Center** (☎ 212-620-7310; www.gaycenter.org; 208 W 13th St), home
base for more than 300 organizations with meeting space, dances and film screenings, drag bingo, and programs on
families, health, gay youth, recovery and much more. It's a good place for a gay visitor to make a first stop and get all
the info on everything else.

For a list of gay and lesbian clubs and bars catering to every taste, pick up the free sheets *HX/Home Xtra*, *Next*, *Met-
rosource* and *Go*, available at many restaurants and bars. Some useful websites include: www.hx.com; www.gaycenter
.org; www.gaycitynews.com.

Easter Mid-April

Memorial Day Late May

Gay Pride Last Sunday in June

Independence Day July 4

Labor Day Early September

Rosh Hashanah and **Yom Kippur** Mid-September to mid-October

Halloween October 31

Thanksgiving Late November

Christmas Day December 25

Boxing Day December 26

New Year's Eve December 31

INTERNET ACCESS

Internet access is easy in NYC – you can even find it on street corners now (and in the area's airports), with the recent additions of nearly 30 payphones equipped with internet portals. The TCC Internet Phones, found mostly in Midtown, but also sprinkled throughout the East Village, Soho, Chinatown and on the Upper East Side, cost $1 for four minutes, although NYC information websites are free. Best of all, the phones have wireless capabilities (within 300 feet), allowing high-speed access to folks who have wireless laptops.

The main branch of the **New York Public Library** (Map pp386-8; ☎ 212-930-0800; E 42nd St at Fifth Ave) offers free half-hour Internet access, though there may be a wait in the afternoons; other branches also have free access and usually with no wait. Free WiFi access hotspots around the city, good for laptop users, include Bryant Park, Tompkins Square Park, Washington Square Park and Columbia University.

At Internet cafés all over the city, you can surf the Net for an hourly fee, which ranges from $1 to $12, or plug in to free WiFi access. Try the following places, all with their own distinct vibe:

Ace Bar (Map pp382-5; ☎ 212-979-8476; 531 E 5th St btwn Ave A & B) Offers plug-ins and free WiFi access.

alt.coffee (Map pp382-5; ☎ 212-529-2233; 139 Ave A; ☒ 8am-late) Computers and free WiFi.

Big Cup (Map pp382-5; ☎ 212-206-0059; 228 Eighth Ave btwn 21st & 22nd Sts) This Chelsea café offers free WiFi access.

Cyberfeld's (Map pp382-5; ☎ 212-647-8830; 20 E 13th St; ☒ 8-3am Mon-Fri, noon-10pm Sat & Sun)

easyEverything (Map pp226-7; ☎ 212-398-0724; 234 W 42nd St; ☒ 24hr) This is the cheapest ($1 per hour), and possibly the biggest, place in town.

LGBT Community Center (Map pp382-5; ☎ 212-620-7310; 208 W 13th St; suggested donation $3) The cyber-center here has 15 computers, open to all.

Net Zone (Map pp386-8; ☎ 212-239-0770; 28 W 32nd St) This Koreatown spot costs $2 per hour from 9am to 1pm.

Time to Compute (Map pp392-3; ☎ 212-722-5700; 2029 Fifth Ave at 125th St)

LEGAL MATTERS

If you're arrested, you have the right to remain silent. There is no legal reason to speak to a police officer if you don't wish to – especially since anything you say 'can and will be used against you' – but never walk away from an officer until given permission. All persons who are arrested have the legal right to make one phone call. If you don't have a lawyer or family member to help you, call your consulate. The police will give you the number upon request.

Gone are the good old days when you could toke a joint and drink in public if you had your beer 'hidden' in a brown paper bag. These became 'quality of life' offenses under Giuliani's New York, and now you party in public at your own risk.

MAPS

Lonely Planet publishes a pocket-size laminated map of New York City, available at most bookstores. You can also pick up free Downtown Manhattan maps in the lobby of any decent hotel and at tourist information booths (p352). If you want to explore the city at large, buy a five-borough street atlas, published by the Long Island City, Queens-based, which also makes great maps of the individual boroughs.

Most subway stations in Manhattan have 'Passenger Information Centers' next to the token booths; these feature a wonderfully large-scale, detailed map of the surrounding neighborhood, with all points of interests clearly marked. Taking a look before heading aboveground may save you from getting lost. You can get free subway and bus maps from the attendant inside the subway booth.

You can buy maps at any bookstore (**Barnes & Noble**, p269, stores usually have the biggest selection), or directly from **Hagstrom Map & Travel Center** (Map pp380-1; ☎ 212-785-5343; 125

Maiden Lane). Hagstrom has another branch in **Lower Manhattan** (Map pp386-8; ☎ 212-398-1222; 57 W 43rd St). **Flight 001** (p267) has a hip and wonderful array of travel bags, books, luggage tags and other jet-setting items.

MEDICAL SERVICES

Healthcare is a major problem in this country, as there is no federal law guaranteeing medical care for all citizens, and health insurance is extremely costly. People living below the poverty line are eligible for Medicaid, which covers many costs, and seniors can apply for Medicare, which works in a similar way. As a visitor, know that all hospital emergency rooms are obliged to receive sick visitors whether they can pay or not. However, showing up without insurance or money will virtually guarantee a long wait unless you are in really bad shape.

New York is practically bursting with 24-hour 'pharmacies,' which are handy all-purpose stores with pharmaceutical counters. The main chains are Duane Reade and Rite Aid, and you'll stumble over them all around Manhattan.

Clinics

If you're sick or injured, but not bad enough for an emergency room, try one of the following options:

Michael Callen-Audre Lorde Community Health Center (Map pp382-5; ☎ 212-271-7200; www.callen-lorde.org; 356 W 18th St btwn Eighth & Ninth Aves) This medical center, dedicated to the LGBT community and people living with HIV/AIDS, serves people regardless of their ability to pay.

New York County Medical Society (☎ 212-684-4670; www.nycms.org) Makes doctor referrals based on type of problem and language spoken.

Planned Parenthood (Map pp382-5; ☎ 212-965-7000; www.plannedparenthood.com; 26 Bleecker St) Make an appointment for birth control, STD screenings and gynecological care.

Emergency Rooms

There are many, many hospitals in the city, both public and private. For a complete listing, consult the local phone directory. Following are some major hospitals with emergency rooms:

Mount Sinai Hospital (Map pp389-91; ☎ 212-241-6500; 1190 Fifth Ave at 100th St)

New York University Medical Center (Map pp386-8; ☎ 212-263-5550; 462 First Ave near 33rd St)

St Vincent's Medical Center (Map pp382-5; ☎ 212-604-7000; 153 W 11th St at Greenwich Ave)

MONEY

The US dollar (familiarly called a 'buck') is divided into 100 cents (¢). Coins come in denominations of 1¢ (penny), 5¢ (nickel), 10¢ (dime), 25¢ (quarter) the practically extinct 50¢ (half-dollar), and the not-oft-seen golden dollar coin, which was introduced in early 2000, featuring a picture of Sacagawea, the Native American guide who led the explorers Lewis and Clark on their expedition through the western United States. While striking, the new coins are prohibitively heavy and jingle conspicuously, alerting panhandlers to your well-heeled presence. These coins are often dispensed as change from ticket and stamp machines. Notes come in $1, $2, $5, $10, $20, $50 and $100 denominations.

In recent years, the US treasury has redesigned the $5, $10, $20, $50 and $100 bills to foil counterfeiters. Yes, they're still that terrible drab green, but the portraits are pretty comical since the presidential heads are all unnaturally huge.

See p21 for information on specific prices of goods and services. To check the exchange rate (though it changes daily), see the Quick Reference guide inside this book's front cover.

ATMs

Automatic teller machines are on practically every corner. You can either use your card at banks – usually a 24-hour-access lobby, filled with up to a dozen monitors – or you can opt for the lone wolves, which sit in delis, restaurants, bars and grocery stores, charging a fierce service fee – as high as $5 for foreign banks in some places. Most New York banks are linked by the New York Cash Exchange (NYCE) system, and you can use local bank cards interchangeably at ATMs – for an extra fee if you're banking outside your system. Getting money this way saves you a step – no changing money from your own currency – and is a safer way to travel, as you only take out what you need, as you go.

Changing Money

Banks and moneychangers, found all over New York City, will give you US currency based on the current exchange rate. Banks are normally open from 9am to 4pm Monday to Friday. Chase Manhattan's Chinatown branch, on the corner of Mott and Canal Sts, is open daily. Several other banks along Canal St also offer weekend opening hours (see p342).

Following are a few of the other myriad options:

American Express (Map pp380-1; ☎ 212-421-8240, for locations ☎ 800-221-7282; World Financial Center, West & Vesey Sts; ☺ 9am-5pm Mon-Fri) American Express has plenty of branches about town. The branch at **Times Square** (Map pp226-7; ☎ 212-687-3700; 1185 Sixth Ave at 47th St) is a reliable currency-exchange service, but there are long lines in the afternoon.

Chase Manhattan Bank (Map pp380-1; ☎ 212-552-2222; 1 Chase Manhattan Plaza at William St btwn Liberty & Pine Sts; foreign exchange ☺ 8am-3:30pm Mon-Fri) Chase offers a commission-free foreign-currency exchange service. It also has a branch at **Midtown** (Map pp386-8; ☎ 800-242-7324; 349 Fifth Ave at 34th St; foreign exchange ☺ 8am-3:30pm Mon-Fri), directly across the street from the Empire State Building.

Chequepoint (Map pp386-8; ☎ 212-750-2400; 22 Central Park South btwn Fifth & Sixth Aves; ☺ 8am-8pm Mon-Sat, 9am-8pm Sun)

Thomas Cook (Map pp226-7; ☎ 212-265-6049; 1590 Broadway at 48th St; ☺ 9am-7pm Mon-Sat, 9am-5pm Sun) Features currency exchange at eight locations in the city, including the Times Square office.

Credit & Debit Cards

Major credit cards are accepted at most hotels, restaurants, shops and car-rental agencies throughout New York City. In fact, you'll find it difficult to perform certain transactions, such as purchasing tickets to performances, without one. Besides, they're handy in emergencies.

Stack your deck with either a Visa or MasterCard, as these are the cards of choice here. Places that accept Visa and MasterCard also accept debit cards, which deduct payments directly from your check or savings account. Be sure to check with your bank to confirm that your debit card will be accepted in other states or countries – debit cards from large commercial banks can often be used worldwide.

If your cards are lost or stolen, contact the company immediately. The following are toll-free numbers for the main credit card companies:

American Express (☎ 800-528-4800)

Diners Club (☎ 800-234-6377)

Discover (☎ 800-347-2683)

MasterCard (☎ 800-826-2181)

Visa (☎ 800-336-8472)

Traveler's Checks

These offer protection from theft or loss. Checks issued by American Express and Thomas Cook are widely accepted, and both offer efficient replacement policies. Keeping a record of the check numbers and the checks you've used is vital when it comes to replacing lost checks. Keep this record in a separate place from the checks themselves.

Bring most of the checks in large denominations. It's toward the end of a trip that you may want to change a small check to make sure you aren't left with too much local currency. Of course, traveler's checks are losing their popularity due to the explosion of ATMs and you may opt not to carry any at all.

NEWSPAPERS & MAGAZINES

There are scads of periodicals to choose from – but what else would you expect from one of the media capitals of the world? Daily newspapers include the definitive *New York Times*, which is especially massive on Sunday (and, at $3, expensive), taking New Yorkers the entire day – and sometimes into the week – to truly read the whole thing. Of the three other major dailies, two are tabloids, the *New York Post* and the *New York Daily News*, and have decidedly sensationalist styles and more conservative perspectives. The third is somewhat of a mixture of styles, the recently relaunched *New York Newsday*. Fighting it out for the younger readership are two free new dailies *amNew York* and *Metro*. Weekly papers include the *Village Voice* and the *New York Press*, both free, offering alternative takes on news and entertainment. Magazines that give a good sense of the local flavor include *New York Magazine* and *Paper*, both monthlies, and *Time Out New York*, a weekly. For more information on newspapers and magazines, see p19.

POST

Rates for sending mail go up every few years, and with increasing frequency it seems. With the latest increase, rates for first-class mail within the USA are 37¢ for letters up to 1oz (23¢ for each additional ounce) and 23¢ for postcards.

International airmail rates for a 1oz letter are 60¢ to Canada and Mexico and 80¢ elsewhere, plus 25¢ and 80¢ for each additional half-ounce. International postcard rates are 50¢ to Canada and Mexico and 70¢ elsewhere. Aerogrammes will cost you 70¢.

The cost for parcels being airmailed anywhere within the USA is $3.95 for up to 2lb, increasing by $1.25 per pound and up to $7.70 for 5lb. For whatever postal questions you may have, call ☎ 800-275-8777 or visit the website at www.usps.com/welcome.htm.

New York City's **General Post Office** (Map pp386-8; ☎ 212-967-8585; James A Foley Bldg, 380 W 33rd St at Eighth St; ⏰ 24hr) can help you with all your postal requirements, as can the **Rockefeller Center** (Map pp386-8; ☎ 212-265-3854; 610 Fifth Ave at 49th St; ⏰ 9:30am-5:30pm Mon-Fri) basement post office. **Cooper Station post office** (Map pp382-5; ☎ 212-254-1389; 93 Fourth Ave at 11th St; ⏰ 8am-6pm Mon-Wed & Fri, 8am-8pm Thu, 9am-4pm Sat) is the place to post in the Village.

Alternatives for mailing include various mail stores, such as the chain **Mailboxes Etc** (www.mbe.com), which has many options around Manhattan; visit the website for a list of locations. The upside is there's always a much shorter wait, and there are more branches to choose from; the downside is that it's much more expensive to ship this way.

RADIO

NYC has some mighty excellent radio options beyond the commercial, pop-music dreck. An excellent programming guide can be found in the *New York Times* entertainment section on Sundays. Below are some of the top station picks, all of which can be heard online:

WBAI 99.5-FM (www.wbai.org) Hear political talk and news with an activist bent, with highlights featuring shows like *Democracy Now!*, on this local Pacifica Radio affiliate.

WFUV 90.7-FM (www.wfuv.org) Fordham University's radio station features excellent indie music – folk, rock and otherwise alternative-type sounds – as well as personable, knowledgeable DJs.

WLIB 1190-AM (www.airamericaradio.com) This is the new Air America station, featuring 24-hour left-leaning talk that's in sharp contrast to the conservative talk shows filling the AM dial.

WNYC 93.9-FM and **820-AM** (www.wnyc.org) NYC's public radio station is the local NPR affiliate, offering a blend of national and local talk and interview shows, with a switch to classical music in the day on the FM station.

WOR 710-AM (www.wor710.com) A talk-show station, it features local mavens Joan Hamburg and Arthur Schwartz, doling out pithy advice on where to eat, shop and travel.

SAFETY

The FBI named New York City the safest big city in America in 2003, and for those who live here, it's not all that surprising. There are few neighborhoods left – in Manhattan, at least – where you can feel scared, no matter what time of night it is. That goes for subway stations, too. That said, there are all sorts of desperate and crazy folks running around here, so it's better to be safe than sorry. Basically, you should use common sense: don't walk around alone at night in unfamiliar, sparsely populated neighborhoods, especially if you're a woman. Don't flash money around on the street. And keep your valuables somewhere safe. Most hotels and hostels provide safekeeping, so you can leave your money there. Unless you must accessorize with the real thing, leave the good jewelry at home (a general rule of thumb for traveling in New York is to not bring anything you can't afford financially, or emotionally, to lose). Carry your daily walking-around money somewhere inside your clothing (in a money belt, bra or sock) rather than in a handbag or an outside pocket. Remember that just using a safety pin or twist tie to hold the zipper tags of a day-pack together can help prevent theft.

TAX

Restaurants and retailers never include the tax in their prices, so beware of ordering the $4.99 lunch special when you only have $5 to your name. New York State imposes a sales tax of 7% on goods, most services and prepared foods. New York City imposes an additional 1.25% tax, bringing the surcharge to 8.25%. Several categories of so-called 'luxury items,' including rental cars and dry-cleaning, carry an additional city surcharge of 5%, so you wind up paying an extra 13.25% in total for these services.

Hotel rooms in New York City are subject to a 13.25% tax, plus a flat $2-per-night occupancy tax. Believe it or not, that reflects a reduction in the previous hotel tax.

Since the US has no nationwide value added tax (VAT), there is no opportunity for foreign visitors to make 'tax-free' purchases.

TELEPHONE

Phone numbers within the USA consist of a three-digit area code followed by a seven-digit local number. If you're calling long distance, dial 1 + the three-digit area code + the seven-digit number.

For local and national directory assistance, dial ☎ 411. To find a number in Manhattan from outside the USA, call ☎ 1 + 212 + 555-1212. (These requests are charged as one-minute long-distance calls.) And, as part of a miraculous new citywide system, you can dial ☎ 311 for anything that's city-related – whether you have a noise complaint, want to get in touch with your local representative, or have a question about parking regulations, recycling or where to find the nearest dog run. Operators are available 24 hours and will quickly connect you to the government office that'll best be able to serve you.

If you're calling New York from abroad, the international country code for the USA is 1. To dial an international number directly, dial ☎ 011, then the country code, followed by the area code and the phone number. (To find the country code, check the phone book or dial ☎ 411 and ask for an international operator.) You may need to wait as long as 45 seconds for the ringing to start. International rates vary depending on the time of day and the destination. For example, the cheapest rates to London are available between 6pm and 7am, but if you're calling Sydney, the cheapest time is 3am to 2pm. Call the operator (☎ 0) for rates.

In New York City, Manhattan phone numbers are in the 212 or 646 area code (although cell phones and some businesses use a 917 area code) and the four outer boroughs are in the 718 zone. No matter where you're calling within New York City, even if it's just across the street in the same area code, you must *always* dial the area code first.

All toll-free numbers are prefixed with an 800, 877 or 888 area code. Some toll-free numbers for local businesses or government offices only work within a limited region. But most toll-free phone numbers can be dialed from abroad – just be aware that you'll be connected at regular long-distance rates, which could become a costly option if the line you're dialing regularly parks customers on hold.

Pay Phones

Though they seem outmoded, pay phones still exist on NYC streets and are almost always available. Just don't expect to find any phone booths, like the kind that Superman changed in, unless you find one of the very few left in existence, such as one on the Upper West Side at West End Ave and 101st St.

To use a pay phone, you can pump in quarters, use a phone credit or debit card or make collect calls. There are thousands of pay telephones on the New York City streets, all with a seemingly different price scheme: many Verizon phones charge 50¢ for unlimited local calls, while others charge 25¢ for three-minute local calls and still others demand $1 for calls anywhere in the USA. On some pay phones in New York City, if you make a long-distance call with a credit card, you could end up with a whopping bill from an unscrupulous long-distance firm. And, although it may seem inconsequential as you read this, it will drive you crazy once you're there: Park Ave has no pay phones whatsoever.

Mobile Phones

Known locally as 'cell phones,' these tiny little accessories are taking over the city. Part communication device and part status symbol, New Yorkers are totally in love with their phones. You really don't need a cell phone in the city, especially with the preponderance of pay phones. Plus, service is less-than-stellar, with frequent silent spots peppered all around town, causing folks to frequently get cut off in mid-sentence.

Phonecards

An excellent long-distance alternative is phone debit cards, which allow you to pay in advance, with access through a toll-free 800 number. In amounts of $5, $10, $20 and $50, these are available from Western Union, machines in airports and train stations, some supermarkets and nearly every corner deli. Certain cards deliver better value depending on where you're calling (eg New York Alliance is better for Brazil, while Payless is better for Ireland) and the purveyors of the cards can usually provide accurate information. The rates are generally unbeatable; for instance, a $10 New York Alliance card allows you 10 hours of chatting to Rio.

TELEVISION

New Yorkers are pop-culture-obsessed creatures by nature, making them natural TV fans. The most popular shows for locals to chatter on and on about include, not surprisingly, those based here: *Queer Eye For the Straight Guy* (Bravo Tuesdays), which has a 'Fab Five' team of gay men giving sorely needed aesthetic makeovers to hetero men, is among the top-watched shows in town. There are also a few local TV stations worth tuning into (note that the channel number varies depending on the source of programming from the TV that you're watching; options range from Cablevision and Time Warner cable providers to Direct TV satellite television). The stations include the ever-popular New York 1, a 24-hour local news channel on Time Warner Cable channel 1; Metro TV (Cablevision 60 and Time Warner 70), an affiliate of *New York Magazine* that has great programming on local fashion, dating, and arts and entertainment; and the local sports channel MSG network, which broadcasts games from Madison Square Garden. Cable also carries dozens of local amateur programs on the Public Access channels. The most (in)famous of them are essentially soft-core porn, carrying strip shows and ads for escort services.

TIME

New York City is in the Eastern Standard Time (EST) zone – five hours behind Greenwich Mean Time, two hours ahead of Mountain Standard Time (including Denver, Colorado) and three hours ahead of Pacific Standard Time (San Francisco and Los Angeles, California). Almost all of the USA observes daylight-saving time: clocks go forward one hour from the first Sunday in April to the last Saturday in October, when the clocks are turned back one hour. (It's easy to remember by the phrase 'spring ahead, fall back.') For the accurate time, call ☎ 212-976-1616.

TIPPING

Tipping is expected in restaurants, bars and better hotels, taxis, and also by hairdressers and baggage carriers. In restaurants, wait staff are paid less than the minimum wage and they rely upon tips to make a living. Tip at least 15% unless the service is terrible, in which case a light tip will get your point across. Most New Yorkers either tip a straight up 20%, or just double the 8.25% sales tax. At bars, bartenders typically expect a $1 tip for every drink they serve (at preferred drinking spots, the old rule of fourth round free stands and decent tips help perpetuate that tradition). Never tip in fast-food, take-out or buffet-style restaurants where you serve yourself.

Taxi drivers expect 10% and hairdressers 15% if their service is satisfactory. Baggage carriers (skycaps in airports, bellhops in hotels) receive $1 for the first bag and 50¢ for each additional bag. In 1st class and luxury hotels, tipping can reach ludicrous proportions – doormen, bellboys and parking attendants all expect to be tipped at least $1 for each service performed – including simply opening a taxi door for you. (Business travelers should tip the cleaning staff $5 a day.)

TOILETS

New York is downright hostile to the weak of bladder or bowels. The explosion in the homeless population in the 1970s led to the closure of subway facilities, and most places turn away nonpatrons from bathrooms. The city has also quietly abandoned its planned program to introduce Paris-style public toilets in the city (the lone soldier in City Hall Park notwithstanding). But there are a few public loos left, including those in Grand Central Terminal, Penn Station and Port Authority Bus Terminal, as well as in Battery Park, Tompkins Square Park, Washington Square Park and Columbus Park in Chinatown, plus many scattered around Central Park. And if you're discreet, the following chainstores, with locations all over town, have easily accessible johns, as well: Starbucks, McDonald's, Barnes & Noble, Kmart and Au Bon Bain.

TOURIST INFORMATION

The most reliable tourist information can be found either online or at official city kiosks and offices.

NYC & Company (Map pp226-7; ☎ 212-484-1200; www .visitnyc.com; 810 Seventh Ave btwn 52nd & 53rd Sts) The city's official tourism arm is the extremely helpful NYC & Company, which offers maps and all sorts of pamphlets at its three information locations, and endless useful stuff online, from upcoming special events and various discounts to historic tidbits and security updates. Other branches include **Lower Manhattan** (Map pp380-1; City Hall Park at Broadway) and **Harlem** (Map pp392-3; 163 W 125th St at Adam Clayton Powell Blvd).

Times Square Visitors Center (Map pp226-7; ☎ 212-768-1569; www.timessquarebid.org; Broadway btwn 46th & 47th Sts) This information center, run by the Times Square Business Improvement District, offers pamphlets, maps and tourism counselors who can advise you in 10 different languages.

VISAS

Due to increasingly strict visa regulations following September 11, foreigners needing visas to travel to the US should plan ahead. However, there is a reciprocal visa-waiver program in which citizens of certain countries may enter the USA for stays of 90 days or less with a passport but without first obtaining a US visa. Currently these countries include Australia, Austria, Denmark, France, Germany, Italy, Japan, the Netherlands, New Zealand, Spain, Sweden, Switzerland and the UK. Under this program you must have a roundtrip ticket that is nonrefundable in the USA, and you will not be allowed to extend your stay beyond 90 days.

Other travelers will need to obtain a visa from a US consulate or embassy. In most countries, the process can be done by mail. Visa applicants may be required to 'demonstrate binding obligations' that will ensure their return home. Because of this requirement, those planning to travel through other countries before arriving in the USA are generally better off applying for their US visa while they are still in their home country – rather than after they're already on the road.

The Non-Immigrant Visitors Visa is the most common visa. It is available in two forms, B1 for business purposes and B2 for tourism or visiting friends and relatives. The validity period for US visitor visas depends on which country you're from. The length of time you'll be allowed to stay in the USA is ultimately determined by US immigration authorities at the port of entry. Non-US citizens with HIV should know that they can be excluded from entry to the USA.

Finally, all visa information is very likely to change, as the federal government is actively making changes all the time due to security situations. For updates on visas and other security issues, you can visit the **government's visa page** (www.unitedstatesvisas .gov), the **US Department of State** (www.travel .state.gov) and the **Travel Security Administration** (www.tsa.gov).

WOMEN TRAVELERS

In general, New York City is a pretty safe place for women travelers, including lesbians who will generally feel welcome. If you are unsure which areas are considered dicey, ask at your hotel or telephone **NYC & Company** (☎ 212-484-1200) for advice; of course, other women are always a great source for the inside scoop. Depending on the neighborhood you're in, you are likely to encounter obnoxious behavior on the street, where men may greet you with whistles and muttered 'compliments.' Any engagement amounts to encouragement – simply walk on. Finally, if you're out late clubbing or at a venue farther afield, consider stashing away money for the cab fare home. If you're ever assaulted, call the **police** (☎ 911). The **Violence Intervention Program** (☎ 212-360-5090) can provide support and assistance in English or Spanish.

WORK

To work legally in the USA you generally need both a work permit and a working visa. To apply for the correct visa at the US embassy you are generally required to obtain a work permit from the Immigration and Naturalization Service (INS) first. Your prospective employer must file a petition with the INS for permission for you to work, so you will first need to find a company that wants to hire you and is willing to file all the necessary paperwork. You can find more detailed information at the website of the **US Department of State** (www .travel.state.gov).

Behind the Scenes

THE LONELY PLANET STORY

The story begins with a classic travel adventure: Tony and Maureen Wheeler's 1972 journey across Europe and Asia to Australia. There was no useful information about the overland trail then, so Tony and Maureen published the first Lonely Planet guidebook to meet a growing need.

From a kitchen table, Lonely Planet has grown to become the largest independent travel publisher in the world, with offices in Melbourne (Australia), Oakland (USA), London (UK) and Paris (France).

Today Lonely Planet guidebooks cover the globe. There is an ever-growing list of books and information in a variety of media. Some things haven't changed. The main aim is still to make it possible for adventurous travelers to get out there – to explore and better understand the world.

At Lonely Planet we believe travelers can make a positive contribution to the countries they visit – if they respect their host communities and spend their money wisely.

THIS BOOK

This edition was written by Beth Greenfield and Robert Reid. The previous (3rd) edition was written by Conner Gorry, and the 1st and 2nd editions were written by David Ellis. The History chapter was written by Kathleen Hulser, and the Architecture chapter was written by Joyce Mendelsohn. Glenn Kenny contributed the NYC Music in the 21st Century boxed text, and Katy McColl contributed the Fashionable NYC boxed text. This edition was commissioned in Lonely Planet's Oakland office and produced by:

Commissioning Editor Jay Cooke
Coordinating Editor Justin Flynn
Coordinating Cartographer Joelene Kowalski
Assisting Editors & Proofreaders John Hinman, Carolyn Bain, Nina Rousseau, Maryanne Netto, Andrea Dobbin & Nancy Ianni
Assisting Cartographer Lachlan Ross
Assisting Layout Designer Adam Bextram
Cover Designer James Hardy
Managing Cartographer Alison Lyall
Managing Editor Kerryn Burgess
Layout Designer Dianne Murdoch
Layout Managers Adriana Mammarella & Kate McDonald
Mapping Development Paul Piaia
Project Managers Rachel Imeson, Kieran Grogan & Celia Wood
Regional Publishing Managers David Zingarelli & Maria Donohoe
Thanks to Brendan Dempsey & Gerilyn Attebery

Cover photographs Taxis, Andrew Shennan/Getty Images (top); Chrysler Building, Kim Grant/Lonely Planet Images (bottom); Baseball at Yankee Stadium, Angus Oborn/Lonely Planet Images (back).

Internal photographs by Angus Oborn/Lonely Planet Images, except for the following: p189 (#1), p282 (#1 & #3) Michelle Bennett/Lonely Planet Images; p56, p192 (#3) Juliet Coombe/Lonely Planet Images; p284 (#1 & #2), p323 Richard Cummins/Lonely Planet Images; p192 (#2) Jon Davison/Lonely Planet Images; p101(#2), p106(#2), p244 Esbin Anderson Photography/Lonely Planet Images; p103(#1) Veronica Garbutt/Lonely Planet Images; p40, p77, p99 (#3), p100 (#4), p104 (#3), p106 (#4), p133, p187 (#3), p188 (#2),p208, p216, p224, p279 (#2 & #3), p280 (#1), p283 (#2) Kim Grant/Lonely Planet Images; p191 (#2) Richard I'Anson/Lonely Planet Images; p188 (#1) James Marshall/Lonely Planet Images;

p100 (#1) Curtis Martin/Lonely Planet Images; p284 (#3) Allan Montaine/Lonely Planet Images; p100 (#3) John Neubauer/Lonely Planet Images; p102 (#1) Robert Reid/Lonely Planet Images; p99 (#1), p188 (#3) Neil Setchfield/Lonely Planet Images; p101 (#4) Tom Smallman/Lonely Planet Images; p99 (#4) Michael Taylore/Lonely Planet Images; p187 (#1), p194 (#1) Bill Wassman/Lonely Planet Images; p103 (#3) Eric Wheater/Lonely Planet Images; p13, p20, p61, p105 (#3), p127, p194 (#1), p277 (#3), p278 (#2 & #3), p281 (#3) Corey Wise/Lonely Planet Images. All images are the copyright of the photographers unless otherwise indicated. Many of the images in this guide are available for licensing from Lonely Planet Images: www.lonelyplanetimages.com.

THANKS
BETH GREENFIELD

Mom and Dad, thank you for being so proud; special thanks to Dad for trekking around town with me and for feeding me, and sorry about the Roosevelt museum! Joe Angio, thanks for giving me the green light. Robert Reid, thank you for sharing your wisdom and your humor. Beatrice, thanks for your apartment. Rod and Meade, thank you for a mid-work vacation. Kiki, my partner in travel and in life, thank you for your encouragement, your healing hands and your love.

ROBERT REID

Large loads of thanks go to Beth G for being great and not yelling at me, Jay C for the job and the energy, and Mai for dealing with my – frequent – 'concerns' over finishing it on time. Also thank you to Diana Dedic for many shopping tips, the kind librarians of Brooklyn Public Library, the delis that sell four fig bars (not three) for $1 (there's one on 42nd St just east of the main library if you're looking), Dmitry Sedgwick, the ever-burgeoning Drinks on Alternating Tuesdays (DOAT) club, Justin Flynn for editing the thing, Joelene Kowalski for mapping the ball game, and just stacks of helpful New Yorkers.

ACKNOWLEDGMENTS

Grateful acknowledgment is made for reproduction permission: New York City Subway Map © 2004 Metropolitan Transportation Authority.

OUR READERS

Many thanks to the travelers who used the last edition and wrote to us with helpful hints, useful advice and interesting anecdotes. Your names follow:

Bas Aldewereld, Emma Allen, Rune Andersen, Kirsten Bayly, Kevin Bruce, John Burnett, John Carey, Angela Carper, Danny Cha, Chungwah Chow, Gavin Costigan, Sandra Costigan, Catriona Crawford, Monique Cremers, Ake Dahllof, Martin de Lange, Anke Dekkers de Wit, Ellen den Braber, Zac Drumsticks, Windy Dryden, Anne Dukelow, Caroline Evans, Roberto Filange, Sarah Florenz, Heiko Gabriel, Ben Godfrey, Helena Golden, Andac Gursoy, Stephanie Hammonds, Eveliina Hihnala, Jackie Hill, Emma Holmbro, Eric Hormell, Darren Jackson, Tony Jonkx, Felicia Kahn, Elizabeth Karpinski, Maxime Lachance, Kerstin Lange, Mikelson Leong, Beverly Leu, Leigh Maclellan, Daniel Mann, Adam Mathews, Michael Matthes, Gareth McFeely, Peter McManus, Neil McRae, Stephanie Monaghan, Will Moore, Meaghan Mulvany, Don Murray, Tim Newton, Eric Nowitzky, Robin O'Donoghue, Kenton Price, Eleanor Priestley, Glen Rajaram, Cathy Ray, John Reeves, M. Rehorst, Geoff Rimmer, Aaron Romero, Nicky Rowe, Rose St John, Jörn Schmidt, Charlotte Seiglow, Mike Shaw, Julia Simeon Foster, Donna Spoerl, Christopher Staake, Frederick Steyn, Vivi Suharto, Charlie Suisman, Daniel Tiede, Scott Toulson, Fredrik Tukk, Colin Turner, Peter Turner, Michiel van Amelsfort, Carlijn van Dehn, Kris van der Meij, Ruud van Leeuwen, Timo-Pekka Viljamaa, Scott Williams, Trevor Wilson, Andrew Young, Jay Zasa

SEND US YOUR FEEDBACK

We love to hear from travelers – your comments keep us on our toes and help make our books better. Our well-traveled team reads every word on what you loved or loathed about this book. Although we cannot reply individually to postal submissions, we always guarantee that your feedback goes straight to the appropriate authors, in time for the next edition. Each person who sends us information is thanked in the next edition – and the most useful submissions are rewarded with a free book.

To send us your updates – and find out about LP events, newsletters and travel news – visit our award-winning website: www.lonelyplanet.com.

Note: We may edit, reproduce and incorporate your comments in Lonely Planet products such as guidebooks, websites and digital products, so let us know if you don't want your comments reproduced or your name acknowledged. For a copy of our privacy policy visit www.lonelyplanet.com/privacy.

Notes

Notes

Notes

Notes

Notes

Index

See also separate indexes for Drinking (p373), Eating (p374), Shopping (p375) and Sleeping (p376).

Index

000 map pages
000 photographs

Index

Index

000 map pages
000 photographs

Index

MAP LEGEND

ROUTES

Tollway
Freeway
Primary Road
Secondary Road
Tertiary Road
Lane
Under Construction
Track
One-Way Street
Unsealed Road
Mall/Steps
Tunnel
Walking Tour
Walking Trail
Walking Path

TRANSPORT

Ferry
Metro
Rail
Rail (Underground)

HYDROGRAPHY

River, Creek
Intermittent River
Swamp
Water

BOUNDARIES

International
State, Provincial
Regional, Suburb

AREA FEATURES

Airport
Area of Interest
Beach, Desert
Building, Featured
Building, Information
Building, Other
Building, Transport
Cemetery, Christian
Forest
Land
Mall
Park
Sports
Urban

POPULATION

☉ CAPITAL (NATIONAL)
● Large City
∘ Small City
⦿ CAPITAL (STATE)
⊙ Medium City
∘ Town, Village

SYMBOLS

Sights/Activities
Beach
Buddhist
Castle, Fortress
Christian
Hindu
Islamic
Jewish
Monument
Museum, Gallery
Ruin
Swimming Pool
Winery, Vineyard
Zoo, Bird Sanctuary

Eating
Eating

Drinking
Drinking

Entertainment
Entertainment

Shopping
Shopping

Sleeping
Sleeping

Transport
Airport, Airfield
Bus Station
General Transport
Parking Area
Taxi Rank
Trail Head

Information
Bank, ATM
Embassy/Consulate
Hospital, Medical
Information
Internet Facilities
Police Station
Post Office, GPO
Telephone
Toilets

Geographic
Lighthouse
Lookout
Mountain, Volcano
National Park
Pass, Canyon
River Flow

Map Section

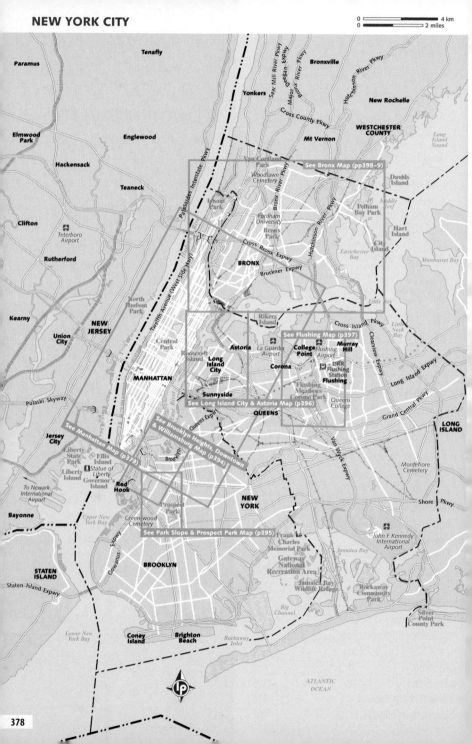

NEW YORK CITY

0 |————| 4 km
0 |————| 2 miles

Paramus

Tenafly

Bronxville

Yonkers

Saw Mill River Expwy

Major Deegan Expwy

Bronx River Pkwy

Cross County Pkwy

Hutchinson River Pkwy

New Rochelle

WESTCHESTER COUNTY

Mt Vernon

Elmwood Park

Englewood

Long Island Sound

Hackensack

Palisades Interstate Pkwy

Van Cortlandt Park

See Bronx Map (pp398–9)

Woodlawn Cemetery

Davids Island

Teaneck

Isham Park

Fordham University

Bronx River Pkwy

Pelham Bay Park

Middle Reef

Clifton

Teterboro Airport

Bronx Park

Hutchinson River Pkwy

Hart Island

City Island

Rutherford

Cross Bronx Expwy

BRONX

Eastchester Bay

Manhasset Bay

Bruckner Expwy

North Hudson Park

Kearny

Twelfth Avenue (West Side Hwy)

Central Park

Rikers Island

See Flushing Map (p397)

Cross Island Pkwy

Little Neck Bay

Little Bay

Union City

NEW JERSEY

Astoria

La Guardia Airport

College Point

Flushing Airport

Murray Hill

Clearview Expwy

Roosevelt Island

Long Island City

Corona

LIRR Flushing Station

Long Island Expwy

MANHATTAN

Sunnyside

Flushing Meadows Corona Park

Flushing

Pulaski Skyway

See Long Island City & Astoria Map (p396)

Queens College

Grand Central Pkwy

LONG ISLAND

Queens Expwy

QUEENS

Jersey City

See Manhattan Map (p379)

See Brooklyn Heights, Downtown & Williamsburg Map (p394)

Broo

Van Wyck Expwy

Liberty State Park

Ellis Island

Statue of Liberty

Red Hook

NEW YORK

Montefiore Cemetery

Liberty Island

Governor's Island

Shore Pkwy

Bayonne

Upper New York Bay

Prospect Park

Green-wood Cemetery

See Park Slope & Prospect Park Map (p395)

Frank Charles Memorial Park

Gateway National Recreation Area

John F Kennedy International Airport

To Newark International Airport

STATEN ISLAND

Gowanus Expwy

BROOKLYN

Jamaica Bay Wildlife Refuge

Jamaica Bay

Rockaway Community Park

Staten Island Expwy

Silver Point County Park

Lower New York Bay

Coney Island

Brighton Beach

Rockaway Inlet

Big Channel

ATLANTIC OCEAN

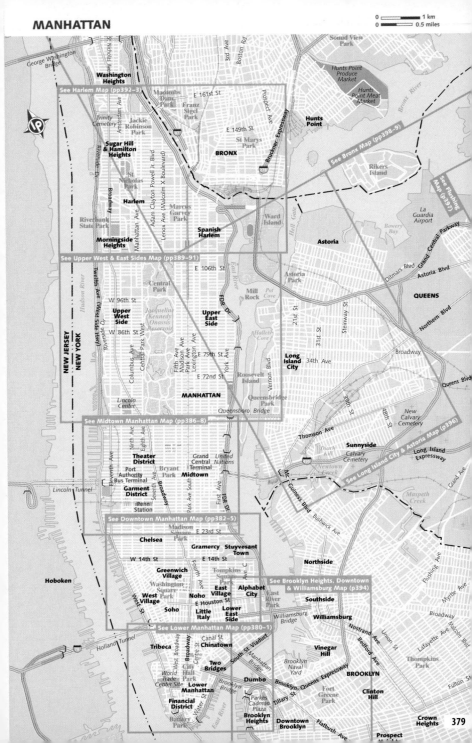

LOWER MANHATTAN

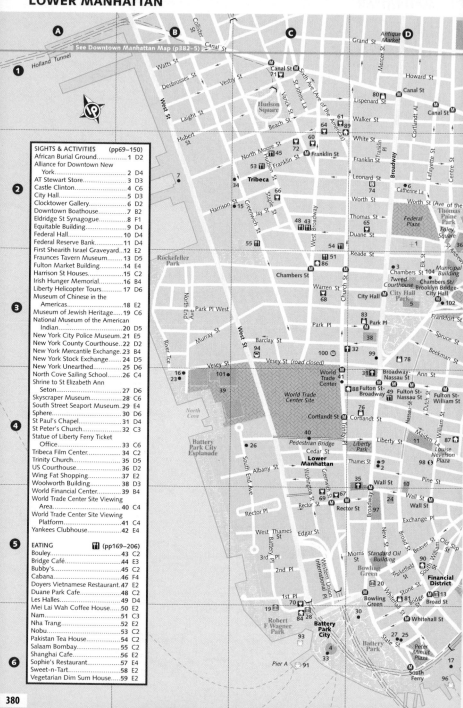

SIGHTS & ACTIVITIES (pp69–150)
African Burial Ground.................1 D2
Alliance for Downtown New
  York.................................2 D4
AT Stewart Store....................3 D3
Castle Clinton.......................4 C6
City Hall.............................5 D3
Clocktower Gallery..................6 D2
Downtown Boathouse................7 B2
Eldridge St Synagogue...............8 F1
Equitable Building...................9 D4
Federal Hall.........................10 D4
Federal Reserve Bank...............11 D4
First Shearith Israel Graveyard....12 E2
Fraunces Tavern Museum............13 D5
Fulton Market Building..............14 E4
Harrison St Houses..................15 C2
Irish Hunger Memorial...............16 B4
Liberty Helicopter Tours............17 D6
Museum of Chinese in the
  Americas...........................18 E2
Museum of Jewish Heritage.....19 C6
National Museum of the American
  Indian..............................20 D5
New York City Police Museum..21 E5
New York County Courthouse...22 D2
New York Mercantile Exchange..23 B4
New York Stock Exchange........24 D5
New York Unearthed.................25 D6
North Cove Sailing School.........26 C4
Shrine to St Elizabeth Ann
  Seton...............................27 D6
Skyscraper Museum.................28 C6
South Street Seaport Museum....29 E4
Sphere..............................30 D6
St Paul's Chapel....................31 D4
St Peter's Church...................32 C3
Statue of Liberty Ferry Ticket
  Office...............................33 C6
Tribeca Film Center.................34 C2
Trinity Church.......................35 D5
US Courthouse......................36 E2
Wing Fat Shopping..................37 E2
Woolworth Building.................38 D3
World Financial Center.............39 B4
World Trade Center Site Viewing
  Area................................40 C4
World Trade Center Site Viewing
  Platform............................41 C4
Yankees Clubhouse.................42 E4

EATING 🍴 (pp169–206)
Bouley..............................43 C2
Bridge Café.........................44 E3
Bubby's.............................45 C2
Cabana.............................46 F4
Doyers Vietnamese Restaurant..47 E2
Duane Park Cafe...................48 C2
Les Halles..........................49 D4
Mei Lai Wah Coffee House........50 E2
Nam................................51 C3
Nha Trang..........................52 E2
Nobu...............................53 C2
Pakistan Tea House................54 C2
Salaam Bombay....................55 C2
Shanghai Cafe......................56 C2
Sophie's Restaurant................57 E4
Sweet-n-Tart.......................58 E2
Vegetarian Dim Sum House.......59 E2

See Downtown Manhattan Map (p382–5)

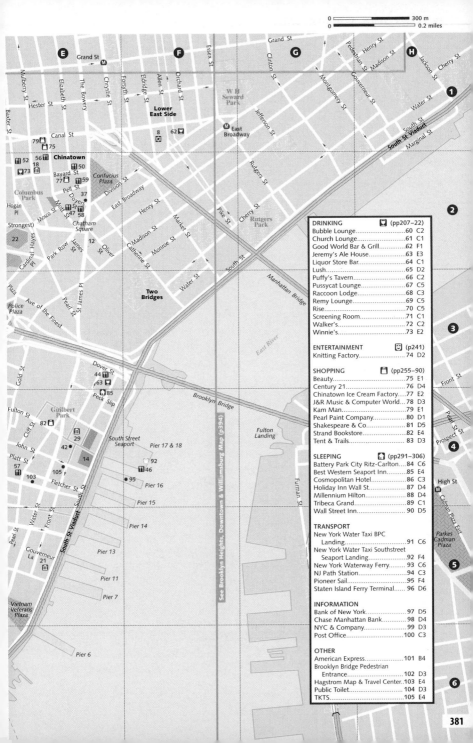

0 | 300 m
0 | 0.2 miles

DRINKING (pp207–22)
Bubble Lounge................................60 C2
Church Lounge................................61 C1
Good World Bar & Grill...............62 F1
Jeremy's Ale House.......................63 E3
Liquor Store Bar............................64 C1
Lush...65 D2
Puffy's Tavern................................66 C2
Pussycat Lounge............................67 C5
Raccoon Lodge..............................68 C3
Remy Lounge..................................69 C5
Rise..70 C5
Screening Room.............................71 C1
Walker's...72 C2
Winnie's...73 E2

ENTERTAINMENT (p241)
Knitting Factory............................74 D2

SHOPPING (pp255–90)
Beauty...75 E1
Century 21.......................................76 D4
Chinatown Ice Cream Factory....77 E2
J&R Music & Computer World...78 D3
Kam Man...79 E1
Pearl Paint Company.....................80 D1
Shakespeare & Co.........................81 D5
Strand Bookstore...........................82 E4
Tent & Trails...................................83 D3

SLEEPING (pp291–306)
Battery Park City Ritz–Carlton....84 C6
Best Western Seaport Inn............85 E4
Cosmopolitan Hotel......................86 C3
Holiday Inn Wall St......................87 D4
Millennium Hilton.........................88 D4
Tribeca Grand.................................89 C1
Wall Street Inn...............................90 D5

TRANSPORT
New York Water Taxi BPC
    Landing..91 C6
New York Water Taxi Southstreet
    Seaport Landing........................92 F4
New York Waterway Ferry..........93 C6
NJ Path Station...............................94 C3
Pioneer Sail.....................................95 F4
Staten Island Ferry Terminal......96 D6

INFORMATION
Bank of New York..........................97 D5
Chase Manhattan Bank................98 D4
NYC & Company.............................99 D3
Post Office....................................100 C3

OTHER
American Express.........................101 B4
Brooklyn Bridge Pedestrian
    Entrance...................................102 D3
Hagstrom Map & Travel Center.103 E4
Public Toilet.................................104 D3
TKTS..105 E4

381

DOWNTOWN MANHATTAN

A

B W 59th St

C

D Central Park South

59th St-Columbus Circle

Columbus Circle

See Upper West & East Sides Map (pp389–91)

W 58th St

1

57th St

W 57th St

Carnegie Hall

48

W 56th St

Tenth Ave

Ninth Ave

Eighth Ave

55th St

W 55th St

W 54th St

Dewitt Clinton Park

W 54th St

W 53rd St

7th Ave

W 52nd St

Twelfth Ave (West Side Hwy)

2

W 51st St

W 51st St

Seventh Ave

W 50th St

50th St

Worldwide Plaza

W 50th St

W 49th St

49th St

W 49th St

W 48th St

W 48th St

Hell's Kitchen

Theater District

W 47th St

47th St

31

W 46th St

3

W 45th St

9

W 44th St

Times Square

129

Eleventh Ave

W 43rd St

123

5

42nd St

Pier 83

125

Port Authority Bus Terminal

W 42nd St

Times Sq-42nd St

Pier 81

W 41st St

W 41st St

Broadway

Lincoln Tunnel

W 40th St

4

W 39th St

W 38th St

Jacob Javits Convention Center

W 37th St

10

Garment District

W 36th St

See Times Square & Theater District Map (p226)

35

W 35th St

153

128

34

W 34th St

57

34th St Penn Station

5

W 33rd St

W 33rd St

Twelfth Ave (West Side Hwy)

General Post Office

145

Madison Square Garden

51

Penn Station

W 32nd St

151

W 31st St

106

Ninth Ave

Eighth Ave

Seventh Ave

91

92

W 30th St

W 29th St

47

W 28th St

28th St

42

37

W 27th St

43

Chelsea Park

54

W 26th St

6

W 25th St

W 24th St

67

12

London Terrace Gardens

45

26

W 23rd St

100

49

West St

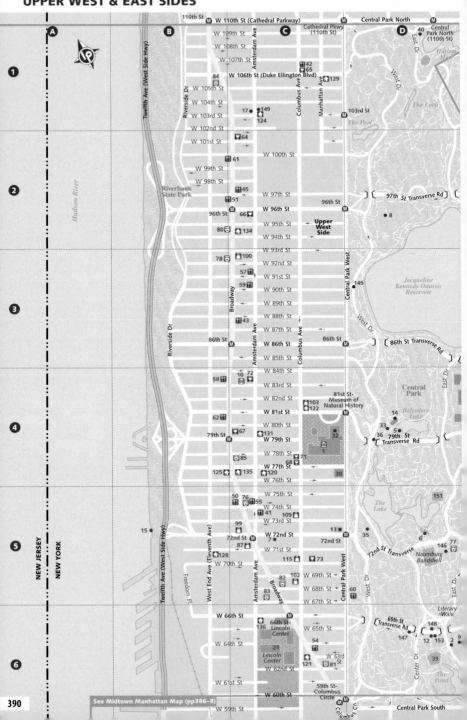

See Midtown Manhattan Map (pp386–8)

0 — 500 m
0 — 0.3 miles

110th St
E 110th St
E 109th St
E 108th St
E 107th St
E 106th St
E 105th St
E 104th St
103rd St
E 103rd St
E 102nd St
E 101st St
E 100th St
E 99th St
E 98th St
E 97th St
96th St
E 96th St
E 95th St
E 94th St
E 93rd St
E 92nd St
E 91st St
E 90th St
E 89th St
E 88th St
E 87th St
86th St
E 86th St
E 85th St
E 84th St
E 83rd St
E 82nd St
E 81st St
E 80th St
E 79th St
E 78th St
77th St
E 77th St
E 76th St
E 75th St
E 74th St
E 73rd St
E 72nd St
E 71st St
E 70th St
E 69th St
68th St–Hunter College
E 68th St
E 67th St
E 66th St
E 65th St
E 64th St
E 63rd St
E 62nd St
E 61st St
E 60th St
59th St
E 59th St

Metropolitan Hospital

Upper East Side

East River

Mill Rock Light Park

Mill Rock

Pot Cove

Triborough Bridge

Carl Schurz Park

East River

Hallets Cove

John Jay Park

Roosevelt Island

Rainey Park

Vernon Blvd

Roosevelt Island Bridge

Conservatory Pond

Rockefeller University

Queensbridge Park

Queensboro Bridge

Roosevelt Island

59th St Bridge

Franklin D. Roosevelt Dr

See Long Island City & Astoria Map (p396)

East End Ave

York Ave

First Ave

Second Ave

Third Ave

Lexington Ave

Park Ave

Madison Ave

Fifth Ave

Main St

East Rd

Vernon Blvd

26th Ave
Second St
Third St
Fourth St
27th Ave
First St
Ninth St
Eighth St

35th Ave
38th Ave
40th Ave
41st Ave

Ninth St
Tenth St
Eleventh St

391

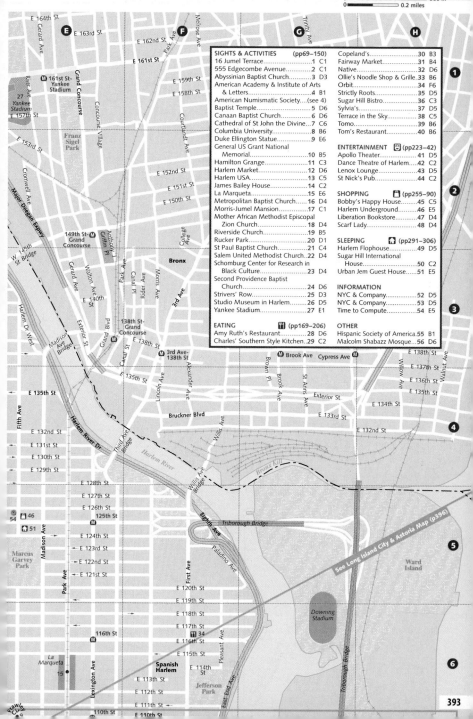

SIGHTS & ACTIVITIES	(pp69–150)
16 Jumel Terrace	1 C1
555 Edgecombe Avenue	2 C1
Abyssinian Baptist Church	3 D3
American Academy & Institute of Arts & Letters	4 B1
American Numismatic Society	(see 4)
Baptist Temple	5 D6
Canaan Baptist Church	6 D6
Cathedral of St John the Divine	7 C6
Columbia University	8 B6
Duke Ellington Statue	9 E6
General US Grant National Memorial	10 B5
Hamilton Grange	11 C3
Harlem Market	12 D6
Harlem USA	13 C5
James Bailey House	14 C2
La Marqueta	15 E6
Metropolitan Baptist Church	16 D4
Morris-Jumel Mansion	17 C1
Mother African Methodist Episcopal Zion Church	18 D4
Riverside Church	19 B5
Rucker Park	20 D1
St Paul Baptist Church	21 C4
Salem United Methodist Church	22 D4
Schomburg Center for Research in Black Culture	23 D4
Second Providence Baptist Church	24 D4
Strivers' Row	25 D3
Studio Museum in Harlem	26 D5
Yankee Stadium	27 E1

EATING	(pp169–206)
Amy Ruth's Restaurant	28 D6
Charles' Southern Style Kitchen	29 C2

Copeland's	30 B3
Fairway Market	31 B4
Native	32 D6
Ollie's Noodle Shop & Grille	33 B6
Orbit	34 F6
Strictly Roots	35 D5
Sugar Hill Bistro	36 C3
Sylvia's	37 D5
Terrace in the Sky	38 C5
Tomo	39 B6
Tom's Restaurant	40 B6

ENTERTAINMENT	(pp223–42)
Apollo Theater	41 D5
Dance Theatre of Harlem	42 C2
Lenox Lounge	43 D5
St Nick's Pub	44 C2

SHOPPING	(pp255–90)
Bobby's Happy House	45 D5
Harlem Underground	46 E5
Liberation Bookstore	47 D4
Scarf Lady	48 D4

SLEEPING	(pp291–306)
Harlem Flophouse	49 D5
Sugar Hill International House	50 C2
Urban Jem Guest House	51 E5

INFORMATION	
NYC & Company	52 D5
NYC & Company	53 D5
Time to Compute	54 E5

OTHER	
Hispanic Society of America	55 B1
Malcolm Shabazz Mosque	56 D6

See Long Island City & Astoria Map (p396)

393

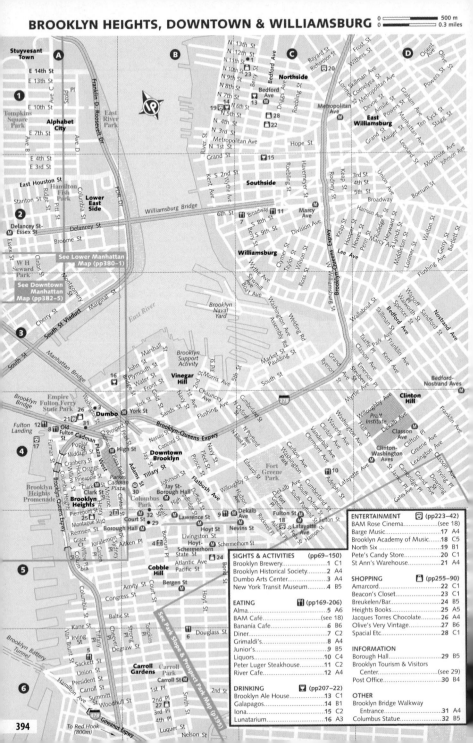

BROOKLYN HEIGHTS, DOWNTOWN & WILLIAMSBURG

Northside

East Williamsburg

Southside

Williamsburg

Brooklyn Naval Yard

Dumbo

Downtown Brooklyn

Brooklyn Heights

Cobble Hill

Carroll Gardens

Clinton Hill

Clinton-Washington Aves

Fort Greene Park

ENTERTAINMENT	☑	(pp223–42)
BAM Rose Cinema		(see 18)
Barge Music	17	A4
Brooklyn Academy of Music	18	C5
North Six	19	B1
Pete's Candy Store	20	C1
St Ann's Warehouse	21	A4

SHOPPING	🛍	(pp255–90)
Amarcord	22	C1
Beacon's Closet	23	C1
Breukelen/Bar	24	B5
Heights Books	25	A5
Jacques Torres Chocolate	26	A4
Olive's Very Vintage	27	B6
Spacial Etc	28	C1

INFORMATION		
Borough Hall	29	B5
Brooklyn Tourism & Visitors Center		(see 29)
Post Office	30	B4

OTHER		
Brooklyn Bridge Walkway Entrance	31	A4
Columbus Statue	32	B5

SIGHTS & ACTIVITIES		(pp69–150)
Brooklyn Brewery	1	C1
Brooklyn Historical Society	2	A4
Dumbo Arts Center	3	A4
New York Transit Museum	4	B5

EATING	🍽	(pp169–206)
Alma	5	A6
BAM Café		(see 18)
Banania Cafe	6	B6
Diner	7	C2
Grimaldi's	8	A4
Junior's	9	B5
Liquors	10	C4
Peter Luger Steakhouse	11	C2
River Cafe	12	A4

DRINKING	☑	(pp207–22)
Brooklyn Ale House	13	C1
Galapagos	14	B1
Iona	15	C2
Lunatarium	16	A3

To Red Hook (800m)

0 — 500 m
0 — 0.3 miles

PARK SLOPE & PROSPECT PARK

0 ____ 500 m
0 ____ 0.3 miles

SIGHTS & ACTIVITIES	(pp69–150)
3rd Street Skate Co.	1 B3
Brooklyn Museum	2 D3
Brooklyn Public Library	3 D3
Carousel	4 D4
Kate Wollman Rink	5 D5
Lefferts Homestead Children's Historic House Museum	6 D4
Soldiers' & Sailors' Monument	7 C2
Zoo	8 D4

EATING	⊓ (pp203–4)
Blue Ribbon Brooklyn	9 B2
Tom's Restaurant	10 D2

DRINKING	⚐ (p221)
Freddy's	11 C1

ENTERTAINMENT	⊡ (pp223–42)
Excelsior	12 B3
Ginger's	13 B3
Southpaw	14 B2
Up Over Jazz Café	15 C2

SHOPPING	⛶ (p289)
Beacon's Closet	16 B2
Eidolon	17 B2

INFORMATION	
Audobon Center Boathouse	18 D4

395

LONG ISLAND CITY & ASTORIA

See The Bronx Map (pp398–9)
See Harlem Map (pp392–3)
See Upper West & East Sides Map (pp389–91)

SIGHTS & ACTIVITIES	(pp69–150)
American Museum of the Moving	
Image	1 C4
Astoria Pool	2 C2
Isamu Noguchi Garden Museum	3 B3
Museum for African Art	4 B5
PS1 Contemporary Art Center	5 A5
Socrates Sculpture Park	6 B3

EATING	(pp169–206)
Uncle George	7 C4
Water's Edge	8 A5

DRINKING	(pp207–22)
Bohemian Hall & Beer Garden	9 C3
Nixterides	10 D3

INFORMATION

Post Office	11 D2
Post Office	12 A5

OTHER

CitiCorp	13 A5
Kaufman Astoria Studios	14 C4
Lighthouse	15 B3

FLUSHING

Map labels:

15th Ave, 18th Ave, 121st St, 20th Ave, 17th Ave, Murray St

22nd Ave, 23rd Ave, 25th Rd, 26th Ave, 28th Ave

College Point

30th Ave, College Point Blvd, 31st Ave, 122nd St

Flushing Bay, Flushing Airport

Murray Hill, 20th Rd, 21st Ave, 22nd Ave, 23rd Ave, 24th Rd, Willets Point Blvd, 24th Dr, 25th Dr, 25th St

Flushing Creek

Worlds Fair Marina, Worlds Fair Marina

Northern Blvd, Bayside Ave, 33rd Ave, 34th Ave, 35th Ave, 38th Ave

Astoria Blvd, Whitestone Expwy, Northern Blvd, Grand Central Pkwy

Shea Stadium, Willets Point-Shea Stadium

Flushing, Flushing Main St, LIRR Flushing Station, 41st Ave, 41st Rd

Roosevelt Ave, Barclay Ave, Sanford Ave, Franklin Ave, Ash Ave

Flushing Meadows Corona Park, Flushing Meadows Park

Queens Botanical Gardens

Kissena Corridor Park

Long Island Expwy, Kissena Blvd

Corona, Long Island Expwy, Horace Harding Expwy

Meadow Lake, Mount Hebron Cemetery

Queens College, Gravett Rd, Melbourne Ave

63rd Dr-Rego Park, Queens Blvd, 67th Ave

SIGHTS & ACTIVITIES (pp69–150)
Arthur Ashe Stadium...................1 B4
Boathouse..................................2 B5
Flushing Council on Culture & the Arts.3 C2
Flushing Meadows Pitch & Putt....4 B3
Flushing Town Hall.................(see 3)
Louis Armstrong House................5 A3
New York Hall of Science.............6 B4
New York State Pavilion Towers.....7 B4
Queens Museum of Art................8 B4
Shea Stadium............................9 B3
Soccer Field.............................10 B4
Soccer Field.............................11 B4
Soccer Field.............................12 B4
Spaghetti Park.........................13 A4
USTA National Tennis Center.....(see 1)

Unisphere................................14 B4
Wildlife Center.........................15 B4
World's Fair Ice Rink...............(see 8)

EATING (p205)
Kum Gang San.........................16 C2
Lemon Ice King of Corona.........17 A4

ENTERTAINMENT (p145)
Queens Theatre in the Park........18 B4

TRANSPORT (p337)
La Guardia Airport....................19 A2

INFORMATION
Police Station...........................20 C3

397

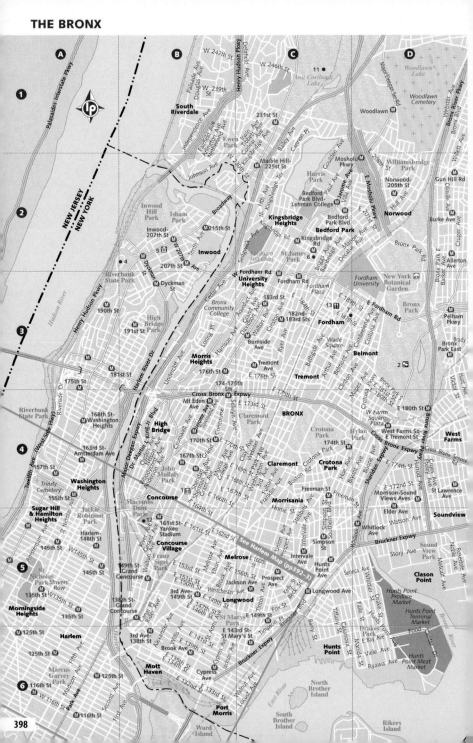

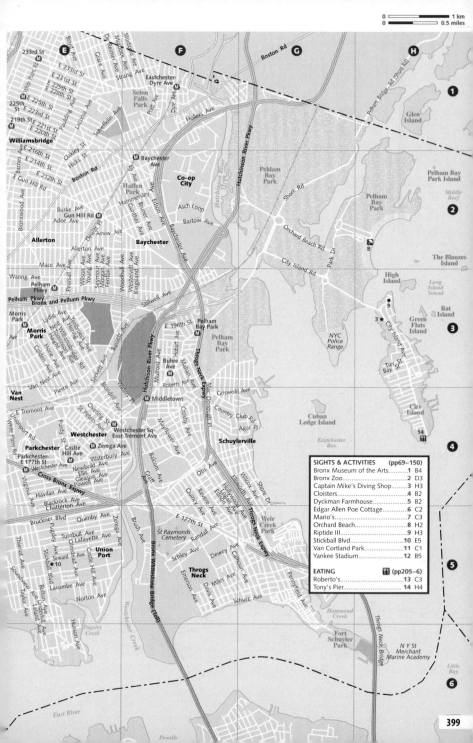

SIGHTS & ACTIVITIES   (pp69–150)
Bronx Museum of the Arts...........1 B4
Bronx Zoo..................................2 D3
Captain Mike's Diving Shop.......3 H3
Cloisters....................................4 B2
Dyckman Farmhouse..................5 B2
Edgar Allen Poe Cottage............6 C2
Mario's......................................7 C3
Orchard Beach...........................8 H2
Riptide III..................................9 H3
Stickball Blvd...........................10 E5
Van Cortland Park....................11 C1
Yankee Stadium........................12 B5

EATING   (pp205–6)
Roberto's..................................13 C3
Tony's Pier...............................14 H4